Physiologic Disposition of Drugs of Abuse

Monographs in Pharmacology and Physiology
Elliot S. Vesell and *Silvio Garattini*, Editors

Volume I
PHYSIOLOGIC DISPOSITION OF DRUGS OF ABUSE
Louis Lemberger and *Alan Rubin*

Physiologic Disposition of Drugs of Abuse

Louis Lemberger, M.D., Ph.D.

and

Alan Rubin, Ph.D.

both of the
Lilly Laboratory for Clinical Research
Wishard Memorial Hospital
and
Indiana University School of Medicine
Indianapolis, Indiana

S P Books Division of
SPECTRUM PUBLICATIONS, INC.
New York

Distributed by Halsted Press
A Division of John Wiley & Sons

New York   Toronto   London   Sydney

SPECTRUM PUBLICATIONS, INC.
86-19 Sancho Street, Holliswood, N.Y. 11423

Distributed solely by the Halsted Press division of John Wiley & Sons, Inc., New York

Library of Congress Cataloging in Publication Data

Lemberger, Louis.
  Physiologic disposition of drugs of abuse.

  (Monographs in pharmacology and physiology ; v. 1)
  Includes index.
  1. Drugs--Physiological effect. 2. Drug metabolism.
I. Rubin, Alan, 1938- joint author. II. Title.
III. Series. [DNLM: 1. Drug abuse. 2. Drugs--Pharma-
codynamics. W1 MO568J / QV38 L549p]
RM300.L443   615'.78   76-13
ISBN 0-470-15021-1

*To Myrna and Karen,
and to Harriet,
Margo, Lori, and Mark
for unselfishly allowing us
the time away from them
to complete this book.*

Preface

We embarked upon writing this book because we felt there was a need to have material concerned with the physiological disposition of drugs of abuse in a single monograph to which investigators and those people interested in drugs of abuse could refer. We hope that this book will be of value and benefit to pharmacologists, psychiatrists, psychologists, and those in the other basic and clinical fields. We would hope that anyone who designs and evaluates data on drugs of abuse could derive benefit from this monograph and we feel that, in general, it would be of value to anyone dealing with the field of drugs of abuse, either directly or indirectly. The physiologic disposition of drugs and the understanding not only of how a drug acts on the body but also how the body acts on the drug is of utmost importance to the scientist. To cite an example, a study was done in an institution whereby investigators administered a cannabinol to squirrel monkeys postpartum and observed the maternal care of the offspring. These investigators reported no effect of the cannabinoid on behavior and concluded, therefore, that this compound did not deleteriously affect rearing behavior. However, these investigators were unaware that at the same institution other investigators had shown that after oral administration of this cannabinoid to squirrel monkeys, a major percentage of the compound was excreted unchanged in the feces, very little being absorbed. However, in the rhesus monkey the compound was adequately absorbed. This exemplifies the necessity for an understanding of the physiological disposition of drugs in designing and evaluating experiments.

Webster's Collegiate Dictionary defines *abuse* as follows: "to put to a wrong or improper use such as to injure or damage." In the case of abuse of drugs, what constitutes "improper use" may change depending upon the observer, the specific social and cultural setting, and the era when the drug is used (e.g., alcohol prohibition). The word "damage" is no less complex since it may refer to harm done to the individual user with respect to organ pathology or aberrant social behavior, or to an ill-defined victim called "society." Clearly then, the term "drug of abuse" involves both subjective and objective considerations by an observer, and these considerations may differ (sometimes illogically) from one time to another and from one place to another. In this book we have concentrated on certain psychoactive drugs that are: 1) used *habitually* (psychological dependence) by individuals in an effort to modify behavior and/or perception and 2) presently considered to be consumed *excessively* in relation to their medically recognized use in the United States, though they may not be uniformly condemned by all members of that society. The abuse of such drugs is frequently, but not always, associated with pharmacological *tolerance, physiological dependence* (resulting in a characteristic withdrawal syndrome), and/or ultimate *detriment* to the user or to society. The qualifying terms in the previous two sentences attest to the complexity of the term "drug of abuse."

Publications dealing with the physiological disposition of drugs of abuse are too numerous to review completely for even a single class of abused drugs. Indeed, it is difficult to know which drugs to classify as "abused." It seems that man, in his blind efforts to change his conception of his environment, will abuse any compound active on the central nervous system. Thus, this book will be restricted to a limited group of drugs with emphasis on the prototype drugs which have been studied more extensively. Drugs were selected for inclusion into this book, for the most part, based on their classification by the drug enforcement agency of the United States Department of Justice. We decided to include those drugs with a high potential for abuse, including, therefore, the Schedule I, II, and III drugs which are commonly abused. Although we realize that some drugs present in Schedule IV, and some not scheduled at all, are, at times, abused, we felt that they were not a major problem since they do have low abuse potential; therefore they were excluded. However, we did feel strongly that we should include a chapter on the recreational drugs of abuse (primarily alcohol and nicotine) because of their wide-spread usage and the potential dire consequences of their habitual abuse as well as the socio-medical problems associated with their use. We also included several drugs which are not commonly abused in the United States but which have been abused in certain other regions of the world. Likewise, for completeness, we included some volatile solvents that are abused. However, we had no intention of covering this heterogeneous group with the same degree that we attempted to cover the other drugs of abuse. In writing this book we were fortunate that our task was made considerably easier by the number of excellent reviews, texts, and monographs on the metabolism of drugs. We regret the inevitable omission of publications by investigators who have made many valuable contributions to the area of research to be discussed. Such omissions are not repudiations of the studies, but rather reflect our personal interests, reliance upon bibliographies of previous publications, and limitations on time and space. We hope that the selected papers are representative to provide readers with an integrated view of advances that have been made and of problems that lie ahead. We have tried to keep this book up to date as we were writing each chapter; however, the literature in this rapidly proliferating field of drug abuse abounds, and this task was not easy. We apologize for those studies which were inadvertently omitted. We specifically would like to express sincere thanks to the Lilly Research Laboratories of Eli Lilly and Company for allowing us the time, materials, and facilities necessary to complete this book. We would also like to thank Dr.

Charles Gruber, Jr. and Dr. William Kirtley for reading portions of the manuscript and for their helpful suggestions. We especially thank Mrs. Patricia Newman, Miss Barbara Hatcher, and Mrs. Beverly Vancil for typing the manuscript and for assisting with the literature search.

Louis Lemberger, Ph.D.,M.D.
Alan Rubin, Ph.D.

Contents

Chapter 1

Fundamental Principles of Drug Disposition

Since the purpose of this monograph is to deal with the metabolism and physiologic disposition of drugs of abuse, a basic understanding of the principles, concepts, and terminology in the field of drug metabolism is essential. Drug metabolism may be considered a subspecialty of the medical sciences of pharmacology, toxicology, and biochemistry. In its broadest sense it is the study of the organism's effect on a drug or foreign chemical and includes the absorption, distribution, biotransformation, and excretion of the drug.

ABSORPTION

Routes of Administration

Drug absorption consists of those processes involved in the passage of a drug from its site of administration into the systemic circulation. There are several commonly used routes of administration for delivering drugs for therapeutic purposes. However, persons with drug-seeking behavior will often use alternative routes to administer their drugs of abuse; sometimes these routes are quite bizarre.

1

The injection of materials (with a needle and syringe) is called parenteral administration. Drugs can be injected directly into the vascular system, most commonly via the intravenous route. In the terminology of the drug abuser, this is known as "mainlining," and it is used extensively for the administration of drugs such as morphine, heroin, and the amphetamines ("speed"). There are indications that any drug which can be abused will, at some time or other, be administered intravenously. Addicted individuals often go to extremes to obtain the euphorigenic effect of a drug. For example, there have been reports that subjects have resorted to preparing a "tea" of marihuana, filtering it through cotton, and injecting the "filtrate" intravenously (King and Cowen, 1969; Gary and Keylon, 1970). Adverse effects result from the deposition of materials such as cotton fibers in the lung capillaries where they form foreign-body reactions and granulomatous lesions secondary to the body's normal defense mechanisms (Louria et al., 1967; Cherubin, 1967). Unfortunately, some individuals do not hesitate to inject intravenously material which is in suspension, nonsterile, or contains impurities.

Abused drugs may commonly be injected via the subcutaneous and intradermal routes ("skin popping"). Among heroin addicts who have had their habit for many years and who have developed scarring and fibrosis of the major accessible veins, "skin popping" becomes a common practice. Due to the lack of consideration for aseptic techniques, and since the instruments used for the injections may be very primitive (e.g., eye droppers and needles), these individuals are plagued with local infections, such as abscesses, that may ultimately result in severe systemic infections and death. It is common in animal experimentation to inject a drug directly into the peritoneal cavity which has a large surface area and from which absorption is quite rapid. This route has not been acceptable to the addict and is rarely used clinically in therapeutics.

Intramuscular administration is another parenteral route. Here the drug is administered deep into the well-perfused muscle tissue, from which it can be readily absorbed into the systemic circulation. This route is also uncommon among addicts.

In addition to parenteral administration, another important route for administration of drugs of abuse is inhalation. Drugs administered by this route are inhaled as gases, enter the tracheo-bronchial tree, and gain access to the alveolar surfaces where they pass through the alveolar capillary membranes into the systemic circulation. Since the lungs are perfused with the entire cardiac output, the absorption of most inhaled drugs is almost as prompt and complete as after intravenous administration. Inhalation was used for centuries for the administration of opium.

The opium was placed on a solid, hot surface, and the volatilized morphine was inhaled. This route of administration is also widely accepted by those using hashish or marihuana and by the large percentage of the population smoking tobacco. In all cases, the drug, whether morphine, Δ 9-tetrahydrocannabinol, or nicotine, is absorbed well into the systemic circulation for subsequent distribution to the tissues.

Recently, the inhalation of organic solvents that are volatile at room temperature has caused great concern because of the severe toxicity of these compounds. This practice has been referred to in lay terminology as "glue sniffing." In this case, materials containing volatile solvents as one or more of their constituents are placed in containers such as plastic bags, and the vapors are inhaled until the subject perceives a euphoriant effect.

In addition to the parenteral and inhalation routes of administration, perhaps the major route of administration of abused drugs is the enteral route, including oral, sublingual (or buccal), and rectal. Most pharmaceutical agents that are used medicinally and that may become candidates for abuse are given orally. Agents such as the barbiturates, amphetamines, hypnotics and sedatives, and synthetic analgesics are administered predominantly in this way. Also, many socially acceptable drugs such as alcohol and caffeine are taken orally. Although most of these agents are ingested by mouth, others are kept in the mouth to facilitate absorption from the mucous membranes. Cocaine is an example of such a drug. It has been used for centuries by natives of Chile and Peru who chew the leaves of the coca plant, *Erythoxylin coca*, which contains the alkaloid cocaine. This drug is rapidly absorbed from the well-perfused mucous membranes and enters the circulation rapidly.

Physicochemical Considerations of Drug Absorption

To be absorbed, a compound must pass through a series of "barriers" composed of biologic membranes of lipoprotein material. A conceptual model of such a membrane modified after Davson and Danielli (1952) is shown in Fig. 1. This membrane is lipoid in nature, and electron microscopic evidence reveals openings or pores in specific areas of the membranes. In general, drugs cross these membranes by various mechanisms: (a) passage through the pores or channels present in the membrane, (b) dissolution in the lipoid membrane and passage through it, i.e., simple passive diffusion, (c) via transport systems which can be either active transport systems (those requiring energy and ATP, examples being the sodium/potassium pump and the neuronal uptake of catecholamines) or facilitated diffusion which involves a carrier substance but no metabolic energy, or (d) by pinocytosis, a process by which the molecule is taken up by an invagination

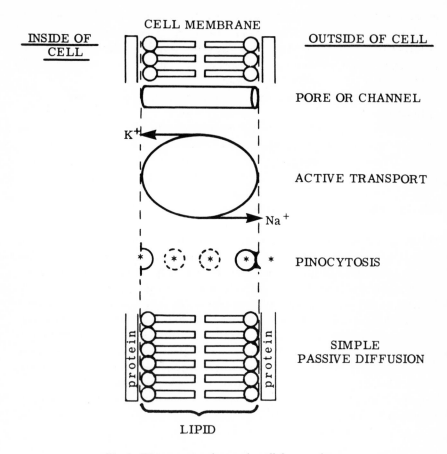

Fig. 1. Diagramatic scheme of a cellular membrane.

of the membrane, transported through the membrane in a vacuolar-type structure, and discharged on the opposite site of the membrane.

Those drugs which have the property of being lipid-soluble can readily traverse biologic membranes by simply dissolving in the membrane. Therefore, an important property of a drug is its lipid solubility. Another consideration is its chemical structure. Most drugs are weak organic acids or bases. This is important when considering absorption from the gastrointestinal tract because absorption depends upon the degree of ionization of the drug molecule. For a drug to be absorbed from the lumen of the gastrointestinal tract into the blood perfusing that region, it should exist in a form capable of readily crossing the lipoid mucosal membranes, i.e., the un-ionized, lipid-soluble form. The principal determinant of the absorption of weak electrolytes depends upon the well-known Henderson-Hasselbach equation:

$$pH = pK_a + \log \frac{(salt)}{(acid)}$$

This equation can be restated simply as:

$$\text{Organic acid: } pH = pK_a + \log \frac{(ionized)}{(unionized)}$$

The degree of ionization of a drug depends upon its pK_a, that pH at which the drug exists in equal concentrations of its ionized and un-ionized forms. Mammalian homeostatic mechanisms regulate the pH of the plasma, maintaining it at approximately 7.4. However, the pH in the gastrointestinal tract varies from one region to another; human gastric juice has a pH of approximately 1, whereas the pH in the intestinal tract varies from approximately pH 5 in the duodenum, where the introduction of acid chyme occurs, to pH 8 in the jejunum and ileum. Thus, acidic compounds exist predominantly in their un-ionized form in acidic gastric juice (e.g., barbiturates), and they are most often absorbed in the stomach. In contrast, organic bases (e.g., morphine and the amphetamines) are essentially ionized in the stomach contents and are not expected to be absorbed there. Instead, basic compounds exist in their un-ionized form in the intestinal tract and, therefore, are absorbed from that region. Examples of the effect of ionization upon the absorption of drugs from the stomach are illustrated in Fig. 2. (For review of this subject, see Schanker, 1971.)

In addition to the physicochemical properties of a drug, such as lipid solubility and electrolyte properties, absorption via the oral route also depends on the pharmaceutical dosage form, especially its solubility and physical characteristics. When a drug is administered in a solid dosage form, i.e., a tablet or capsule, several processes are involved prior to absorption of the drug. These include the physical disintegration of the capsule or tablet to smaller particle size and the subsequent deaggregation and dissolution of the drug in the contents of the stomach or intestinal tract. Another important factor in drug absorption is its concentration, since certain transport systems for absorption can be saturated such that absorption kinetics become dose dependent. Of course, absorption is generally a first-order process, the rate of which, then, is a function of the amount of drug available for absorption.

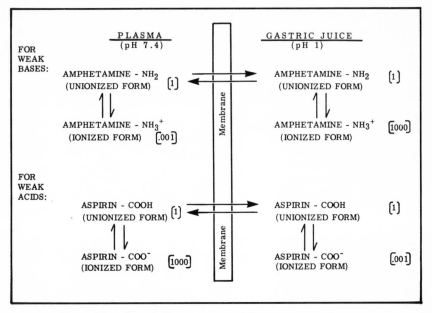

Fig. 2. The effect of pH on transport of drugs across membranes.

DISTRIBUTION

Physiologic Compartments

After a drug is absorbed, it is distributed via the vascular system and it may enter various compartments before gaining access to the molecular site(s) of action (termed receptor sites). Drugs can be distributed in several fluid compartments within the body (Fig. 3). These consist of the intravascular compartment, the extracellular space, and total body water. The intravascular compartment accounts for about 5% of the total body water and, essentially, includes the blood in the cardiovascular system (heart, arteries, and veins). Certain drugs are limited in their distribution to the intravascular compartment, e.g., the dye Evans Blue, which is used to determine plasma volume. This drug is bound avidly to plasma protein and does not leave the circulation.

The extracellular fluid compartment accounts for approximately 20% of the total body water and is composed of the vascular compartment plus the interstitial fluid, which bathes cell surfaces. Many drugs distribute throughout the extracellular space, and an example of such a compound used to estimate the volume of this compartment is thiocyanate.

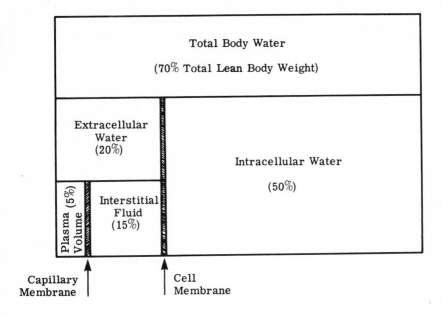

Fig. 3. Distribution of total body water and its compartmentalization.

The third compartment in which a drug can distribute is the total body water, including both the intracellular and extracellular fluid compartments and representing about 70 to 80% of the total body weight. Alcohol exemplifies a drug of abuse that distributes in total body water, and examples of chemicals used to measure the volume of this fluid compartment are antipyrine and deuterated water.

In addition to their distribution in body water, certain drugs are taken up specifically by tissue constituents. Lipid-soluble drugs such as the barbiturate thiopental, Δ⁹-tetrahydrocannabinol (Δ⁹-THC) (the psychoactive principle of marihuana), and the insecticide DDT are examples of agents that concentrate in adipose tissue. After initial distribution throughout the body, these markedly lipid-soluble compounds may be redistributed preferentially to adipose tissue where they are stored and remain in equilibrium with the compound in the plasma compartment. Thus, the distribution of a drug gets it to the site of action; however, distribution of certain drugs to special sites may also function to dissipate the pharmacologic action, as exemplified by thiopental and Δ⁹-THC. In these instances, the redistribution of the drug from active sites to "silent receptors" (adipose tissue storage sites) serves to diminish the overall pharmacologic effects.

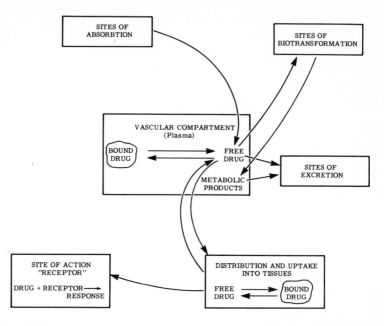

Fig. 4. Schematic representation of the processes associated with the physiologic disposition of drugs.

In addition to the uptake of drugs in adipose tissue, some drugs become bound to tissue protein or nucleic acids. Basic compounds such as amphetamines, tryptamines, and other indoles are avidly sequestered and reach their highest concentrations in lung and liver. Thus, in the case of a drug that acts on the central nervous system, the brain and spinal cord must compete with other tissues for the drug to achieve the concentration required to produce a pharmacologic effect. These other tissues, such as lung and liver, may bind drugs nonspecifically, thereby rendering them pharmacologically "inactive."

Certain drugs and endogenous substances are transported in the body bound to plasma proteins, including albumin, γ-globulin, lipoproteins, etc. In general, those drugs which bind to plasma proteins bind mostly to the albumin fraction, although some drugs such as Δ ^{9}-THC bind to the lipoprotein fraction. It is widely accepted that the unbound or the "free-fraction" of a drug in the plasma is available for transport across membranes to extravascular sites of action. Also, the "free" form is in equilibrium with the "bound" form and is available for biotransformation and excretion. This relationship is illustrated in Fig. 4. Binding of drugs to plasma protein involves several different types of chemical bonding, including ionic bonding, coordinate covalent bonding, and hydrogen bonding (Klotz,

1946). In addition to binding to plasma protein, drugs may also bind to the formed elements of blood.

Transplacental Transfer of Drugs

In addition to the normal distribution of drugs throughout the body, a specialized situation occurs in the pregnant subject where drugs may cross the placental tissue. In this case, the drug passes from one organism to another, that is, from maternal circulation to fetal circulation and vice versa. The placenta is a unique structure in that its membranes are constantly bathed in maternal blood. Drugs cross the placenta by the same mechanisms that are involved when they cross other tissue membranes, i.e. simple diffusion, (the most common type of transport), carrier system (facilitated diffusion), active transport, and/or pinocytosis. Thus the physicochemical principles governing these processes are not unique, and the concept of a placental "barrier" may be a misnomer. Since diffusion of drugs across the placenta is related to molecular weight, most drugs, being of low molecular weight, should readily diffuse through this tissue. However, the rates of diffusion differ for different drugs and are dependent upon their lipid solubility (lipid/water partition coefficient); thus, water-soluble drugs do not diffuse as rapidly as lipid-soluble drugs. The transfer of drugs of abuse across placental membranes is of great clinical importance. For example, children born to heroin-addicted mothers are also addicted to this drug, and cautious withdrawal from heroin during the neonatal period is necessary to avoid precipitation of an abstinence syndrome. Similarly, infants born to women given strong narcotic analgesics during obstetrical delivery may have depressed respiration at the time of delivery and may require the cautious administration of narcotic antagonists to restore normal breathing.

Blood-Brain Barrier

Drug distribution differs in the brain and spinal cord (central nervous system) from that of other tissues. Passage of drugs from the systemic circulation into the central nervous system (CNS) is thought to be limited by a unique capillary organization. In most areas of the brain, the endothelial cells in the capillaries are in juxtaposition without spaces, in contrast to capillaries of other tissues. This lack of intervening space prevents lipid-insoluble materials from diffusing into the brain substance, since it requires that the material pass directly through the endothelial cells of the capillary in order to reach the brain tissue. This system is known as the "blood-brain barrier." An alternative or perhaps adjunctive hypothesis for a morphological explanation of the blood-brain barrier is related to the presence of glial cells surrounding the capillaries of the brain. This lipoidal barrier acts to reduce the entry rate of certain drugs into the CNS. However, certain areas served by the cerebrovasculature are outside the blood-brain barrier (e.g., pineal gland). Again, the passage of a drug into the CNS is dependent upon multiple factors including lipid solubility, binding to plasma proteins, and ionization characteristics at physiologic pH. Since the drugs of abuse are, in general, lipoid in nature, they cross the blood-brain barrier and produce certain of their pharmacologic effects in the brain, resulting in CNS stimulation or depression.

Certain drugs may cross the blood-brain barrier by specialized transport mechanisms that actively transport endogenous agents such as amino acids and sugars. In Parkinsonism, a neurologic disease associated with abnormal muscular activity, Hornykiewicz (1973) has postulated a deficiency of the catecholamine neurotransmitter dopamine in the caudate nucleus. In an attempt to treat this disease, a rational approach seems to be to administer dopamine to increase the levels in the deficient areas. Water-soluble and somewhat ionized at plasma pH, dopamine does not cross the blood-brain barrier. To circumvent this problem and to elevate the levels of dopamine in specific areas, L-dopa, the physiologic precursor of dopamine, is administered systemically. This compound does cross the blood-brain barrier via the amino acid transport system. L-dopa is then decarboxylated in the brain *in situ* to form dopamine which is then thought to ameliorate the symptoms of Parkinson's disease (Cotzias *et al.*, 1969).

Although most drugs of abuse readily cross the blood-brain barrier, their more water-soluble metabolites do not readily do so. Thus, the combination of biotransformation and integrity of the blood-brain barrier is, in part, responsible for terminating the pharmacologic effects of these drugs within the CNS.

BIOTRANSFORMATION

The term biotransformation may be defined as the modification of a drug to another chemical structure by the body. This process may result in either inactivation of the drug or, less commonly, in formation of a compound pharmacologically as active or more active than the parent drug. In general, the body metabolizes drugs which are usually lipid-soluble, nonpolar compounds to more water-soluble, polar compounds, and thus facilitates their elimination from the body. Once the compound is more polar, less lipid soluble, and capable of undergoing ionization, it does not readily pass through membranes, is less prone to protein binding and deposition in fat, and thus is excreted more easily in urine or bile.

In addition to biotransformation of drugs to more polar compounds,

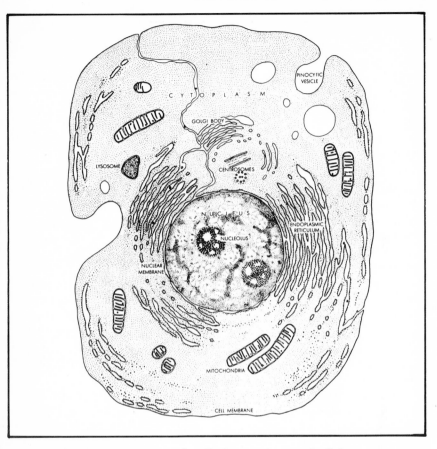

Fig. 5. Schematic representation of a cell, showing the general cellular components as revealed by electron microscopy. (courtesy of Jean Brachet. Prepared with permission from an illustration copyrighted 1961 and 1963 by Scientific American, Inc. All rights reserved).

examples exist whereby polar, highly active drugs are converted to less polar, less active compounds. This is exemplified by the catecholamine norepinephrine which, in the presence of the enzyme catechol-O-methyltransferase (COMT) becomes methylated to normetanepherine, a compound which possesses less pharmacologic activity than the parent compound (Axelrod and Tomchick, 1958).

Microsomal Metabolism of Drugs

The liver is the principal organ for the metabolic conversion of most drugs in mammals. A hepatocyte (liver cell) with its component intra-cellular organelles is illustrated in Fig. 5. These organelles all contain en-

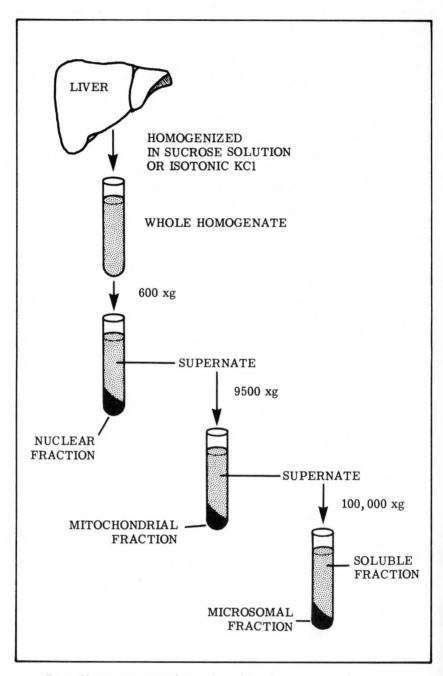

Fig. 6. Homogenization technique for isolating liver microsomal enzymes.

zymes capable of metabolizing drugs or endogenous substances. However, the enzymes predominantly involved in the metabolism of drugs and foreign compounds are localized in the endoplasmic reticulum.

In vitro techniques are frequently used to study the mechanisms of the metabolism of drugs. Such studies utilize liver tissue in various forms, including isolated perfused liver, liver slices, liver homogenates, or subfractions of liver homogenates. To study drug metabolism in broken-cell preparations, liver tissue is homogenized under a variety of conditions and subjected to differential centrifugation according to the method of Schneider and Hogeboom (1951). By this technique, the intracellular organelles can be separated and studied for their individual ability to metabolize drugs. A typical intracellular separation is depicted in Fig. 6. The liver homogenate is centrifuged at 600 x gravity (*g*), and the nuclear and plasma membrane fractions are sedimented. The sedimented fraction contains enzymes such as adenyl cyclase involved in cyclic AMP formation. The supernate is then centrifuged at 9500 *g* with the subsequent sedimentation of the mitochondrial fraction containing many enzymes involved in electron transport as well as monoamine oxidase, an enzyme important in amine metabolism. The resultant supernate is then centrifuged at 100,000 *g*, and a fraction known as the microsomes is sedimented. Localized in this fraction are the so-called microsomal drug-metabolizing enzymes. In addition to their ability to catalyze the metabolism of drugs and foreign chemicals, these enzymes play an important role in the metabolism of endogenous substances, including steroids such as progesterone (Mueller and Rumney, 1957; Kuntzman *et al.*, 1964) and testosterone (Conney and Klutch, 1963), biogenic amines such as tryptamine (Jepson *et al.*, 1962), serotonin (Axelrod, 1962), and tyramine (Axelrod, 1963; Lemberger *et al.*, 1965), vitamins such as vitamin D (Frolik and DeLuca, 1972), bile acids (Trülzsch *et al.*, 1973), and thyroxine (Stanbury *et al.*, 1960). Although the term microsomal enzymes is used widely, this is just an operational definition since there are no intracellular organelles known as microsomes. Microsomes are artifacts created by a homogenization procedure which destroys the tubular structural network of the endoplasmic reticulum with subsequent sealing of the ends of the tubules to form the vesicular "microsome" structures.

Recently, a new method was developed for the preparation of liver microsomes. It utilizes calcium to precipitate the microsomes so that low-speed centrifugation rapidly isolates them. Studies have demonstrated that microsomes prepared by this method are similar to those prepared by conventional ultracentrifugation with respect to histology, enzyme activity, protein content, etc. (Kamath and Rubin, 1972; Cinti *et al.*, 1972).

After the microsomal fraction has been sedimented, the resultant

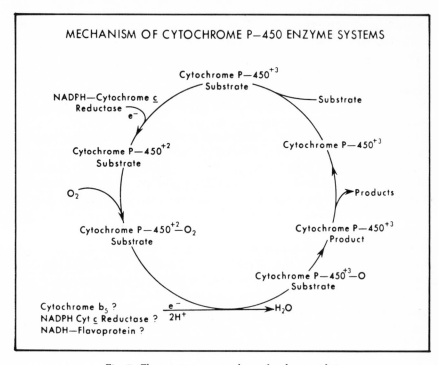

Fig. 7. Electron transport scheme for drug oxidation.

supernate is known as the soluble fraction. Many enzymes involved in the metabolism of drugs and substances of pharmacologic interest are localized in this fraction. These include the enzymes phenylethanolamine-N-methyltransferase (PNMT), catechol-O-methyltransferase (COMT), dopa decarboxylase, etc. Thus, although the liver microsomal enzymes are important in the metabolism of certain drugs, they are by no means the only enzymes involved in drug metabolism. For example, hepatic microsomal enzymes are believed to play only a minor role in the metabolism of alcohol; a non-microsomal enzyme system involving alcohol dehydrogenase is thought to play the more important role (Hawkins and Kalant, 1972). In addition to converting drugs to inactive metabolites, certain enzymes localized in the soluble fraction are capable of converting drugs to potent agents possessing marked psychopharmacologic activity. One such enzyme localized in brain and lung is capable of converting the indole tryptamine to the hallucinogen N,N-dimethyl tryptamine (Axelrod, 1961, 1962; Morgan and Mandell, 1969).

Mueller and Miller (1949, 1953) first demonstrated that a particulate fraction of liver could metabolize the carcinogen 3-methyl monomethyl aminobenzene and demonstrated the requirement of this system for reduced nucleotide. It is of interest that amphetamine was the first drug shown to be metabolized by the liver microsomal enzymes (Axelrod, 1954). Axelrod demonstrated that liver microsomal enzymes, in the presence of molecular oxygen, Mg^{++}, and reduced nicotinamide adenine dinucleotide phosphate (NADPH), can catalyze the conversion of amphetamine *in vitro*. This same enzyme system catalyzes a variety of reactions (Brodie *et al.*, 1958), many of which are oxidations in which cytochrome P-450 serves as the terminal oxidase. The term cytochrome P-450 relates to the fact that the reduced cytochrome absorbs light at 450 nm in the presence of carbon monoxide. This hemoprotein and other enzymes constitute the microsomal electron transport system. The system is responsible for the oxidation of many endogenous substances as well as drugs. A mechanism for the hydroxylation of drugs is shown in Fig. 7 (Gillette *et al.*, 1972). NADPH reacts with an oxidized flavoprotein, NADPH-cytochrome c reductase, with the resultant transfer of its electrons. The reduced flavoprotein then reacts with iron (ferric), which in turn transfers its electrons to cytochrome P-450. It is this later substance which transfers its electrons to the drug (the other substrate) in the presence of oxygen and ultimately results in drug oxidation. (See Estabrook *et al.*, 1973.)

Examples of the major pathways of oxidative metabolism catalyzed by the microsomal drug-metabolizing enzymes are

(1) Aromatic hydroxylation:

AMPHETAMINE   P-HYDROXY AMPHETAMINE

(2) Aliphatic hydroxylation:

PENTOBARBITAL   PENTOBARBITAL ALCOHOL

(3) N-Dealkylation:

METHAMPHETAMINE   AMPHETAMINE

(4) O-Dealkylation:

CODEINE   MORPHINE

(5) Oxidative deamination:

AMPHETAMINE   PHENYLACETONE

In addition to this microsomal oxidative deamination, the enzyme monoamine oxidase (MAO), present in the mitochondrial and to a lesser extent in the microsomal fractions, catalyzes the conversion of biogenic amines of psychopharmacologic interest (discussed later), such as norepinephrine and serotonin, to their acid metabolites (Kopin, 1964).

NOREPINEPHRINE   DIHYDROXYMANDELIC ACID

Hepatic microsomes contain hydrolytic enzymes which cleave esters. These esterases are also localized in blood and other tissues; however, their substrate specificity may vary.

COCAINE   BENZOYLECGONINE

In addition to the oxidative pathways, the hepatic microsomal drug enzyme systems can also catalyze certain reductive reactions.

The aforementioned pathways of drug metabolism represent examples of the conversion of drugs to more water-soluble compounds by the introduction of more polar chemical groups or the degradation of complex molecules to relatively simple polar substances. Other metabolic pathways important in inactivating drugs are the conjugation reactions, also referred to as the synthetic reactions (Williams, 1963). These conjugations also make most drugs more water soluble. Examples of these conjugation reactions are (a) glucuronidation; the liver microsomal enzymes contain the enzyme glucuronyl transferase which catalyzes the reaction of drugs and endogenous compounds (such as steroids containing hydroxyl or acidic groups) with uridine diphosphoglucuronic acid (UDPGA), an endogenous nucleic acid sugar derivative (Dutton and Storey, 1954). (b) Acetylation reaction; various drugs and endogenous amines of psychopharmacologic interest are metabolized by acetylation, including tryptamine, serotonin (its acetylation is of importance in the formation of melatonin), and isoniazid. The enzymes involved in acetylation are localized primarily in the soluble fraction of the liver and transfer the acetate group from acetyl coenzyme A to the substrate (Lipmann, 1945). In addition to its predominant localization in liver, acetyl transferase is present in the pineal gland (Weissbach et al., 1961), the organ in which melatonin is synthesized. (c) Sulfate conjugation; a sulfotransferase catalyzes the reaction of compounds containing aromatic or aliphatic hydroxy groups with an "activated" sulfate (Nose and Lipmann, 1958). The resultant conjugates are referred to as ethereal sulfates. Sulfate formation is important in the metabolism of the biogenic amines of psychopharmacologic interest (norepinephrine, epinephrine, and serotonin), steroids, and certain drugs. (d) Conjugation with amino acids: drugs may be conjugated with amino acids such as glycine. This pathway is important in the metabolism of acidic compounds (i.e., benzoic acid) and is ultimately involved in the metabolism of amphetamine which is excreted by man primarily as hippuric acid, the glycine conjugate of benzoic acid. Another amino acid conjugated with acidic drugs is glutamine. This conjugation reaction, demonstrated in monkeys and man, appears to be specific for higher primates. These species are capable of conjugating a metabolite of mescaline with glutamine to facilitate its excretion.

Although the liver is considered as the primary site for drug metabolism, the ability of other tissues to metabolize drugs is currently receiving greater recognition. Extraheptic tissues, including lung, kidney, skin, placenta, and brain, may also play an important role in the biotransformation of drugs (Wattenberg and Leong, 1970; Gilman and Conney, 1963; Alvares *et al.*, 1973; Welch *et al.*, 1969).

FACTORS INFLUENCING THE METABOLISM OF DRUGS

Species Differences

Of major importance in studying the metabolism of drugs of abuse, and drugs in general, is the recognition of the existence of qualitative and quantitative species differences in drug metabolism. In rats, for example, amphetamine is metabolized *in vivo* predominantly by aromatic hydroxylation; however, in most other species studied the predominant metabolic pathway is oxidative deamination. Obviously, in dealing with drugs of abuse, the animal species with which we are primarily concerned is man. However, to study the mechanisms involved in physical and psychologic dependence and tolerance, appropriate animal models must be found which simulate the physiologic disposition and metabolic pathways occurring in man. Only then can investigators conduct meaningful studies of the effects of these drugs in animal species with hopes of correlating data to man.

Sex Differences

In certain animal species, the metabolism of drugs is markedly affected by the sex of the animal. For example, the hepatic microsomal enzymes from most strains of male rats are capable of metabolizing drugs faster than those of the female rat (Quinn *et al.*, 1958). Treatment of male rats with the female sex hormone estrogen decreases the capacity of the liver microsomal enzymes to metabolize drugs. In contrast, pretreatment of female rats with the male sex hormone testosterone increases the ability of hepatic microsomes from female rats to metabolize drugs. In contrast, sex differences appear to be just the opposite for certain drugs in certain strains of mice. Female mice metabolize many drugs faster than male mice. In man, a few instances of sex differences in the metabolism of drugs have been reported. An example is nortriptyline metabolism which is apparently more rapid in male than in female subjects (Hammer and Sjoqvist, 1967).

Age Differences

In general, very young animals and humans are more susceptible to the actions of drugs than are older subjects. The hepatic microsomal drug-metabolizing enzyme systems do not appear to be as fully developed in neonates as in mature members of the species. Although, in man, these age differences are more marked with respect to conjungation reactions than oxidative pathways, with old age or in certain disease states as increasing organ pathology occurs, again there may be a decrease in the metabolic rate and hence an increased sensitivity to drugs.

Individual Variation

In addition to sex, age, and species differences, another factor affecting the metabolism of drugs involves the individual's genetic make-up or more specifically, pharmacogenetics. The discipline of pharmacogenetics is especially important in clinical pharmacology since man represents a genetically heterogeneous population, as opposed to the inbred strains of rodents commonly used in the laboratory. Therefore, administration of a specific dose of a drug to human subjects usually results in marked intersubject variations in responses, such that the dose of drug necessary to produce response will vary among subjects. An example of pharmacogenetics is the PTC taste test. Phenylthiocarbamide (PTC), when placed on the tongue in low concentrations, tastes bitter to a majority of the population, whereas the minority detect no taste at even markedly higher concentrations (Kitchin et al., 1959). The population is divided into these two groups, and the ability to taste PTC is controlled by a dominant gene and is associated with thyroid disease. There are approximately six well-studied examples of the role of pharmacogenetics in altering human drug metabolism and approximately the same number of pharmacogenetic examples of altered receptor site function (Vesell, 1973).

Isoniazid, a drug used in the treatment of tuberculosis, is metabolized and inactivated by acetylation. The population is divided into two groups: fast acetylators and slow acetylators. The slow rate of inactivation of isoniazid is controlled by an autosomal recessive gene, slow activation being an autosomal recessive trait (Evans et al., 1960) associated with higher blood concentrations of isoniazid, and with consequent pyridoxine deficiency and polyneuritis. No studies have been conducted yet in the field of pharmacogenetics relating to drugs of abuse. Probably certain individuals who misuse drugs metabolize them at differing rates, depending on their genetic constitutions, since it has been demonstrated for several commonly used drugs that large interindividual variations in rates of drug elimination from the body are under genetic control (Vesell, 1973).

Drug-Drug interactions

Enzyme Induction

Almost two decades ago certain drugs and foreign chemicals were shown to influence their own metabolism as well as that of other therapeutic agents. Remmer (1959) and Conney and co-workers (1960) have

Table I. Correlation of Duration of Pharmacologic Effects of Zoxazolamine and
Hexobarbital in Rats with the Activity of the Hepatic Microsomal
Drug-Metabolizing Enzyme System and the Effect of Enzyme Inducers[a]

Pretreatment	Duration of zoxazolamine paralysis (minutes)	Metabolism of zoxazolamine in liver microsomes (enzyme activity μmole/g/hour)	Duration of hexobarbital paralysis (minutes)	Metabolism of hexobarbital in liver microsomes (enzyme activity μmole/g/hour)
Control	730 ± 251	0.53	216 ± 46	0.34
Phenobarbital	102 ± 47	2.02	11 ± 4	1.47
3,4-Benzpyrene	17 ± 7	2.63	302 ± 89	0.33

[a]From Conney et al., (1960).

shown that administration of barbiturates (e.g., phenobarbital) to various
animal species markedly increased that animal's ability to metabolize
barbiturates, certain other drugs, chemical agents, and polycyclic hydrocarbons (e.g., 3-methylcholanthrene and 3,4,benzpyrene). These "enzyme-
inducing" agents can likewise affect the metabolism of certain endogenous
substances such as vitamins, estrogens, androgens, corticosteroids, and
progestogens. Enzyme induction has been extensively studied in animals,
and within the last few years these studies have been extended to clinical
situations. Two classical examples of the effects of inducing agents on drug
metabolism are those correlating the pharmacologic activity of hexobarbital
and zoxazolamine with the rate of metabolism of these drugs, as shown in
Table I (Brodie et al., 1958; Conney et al., 1960). These examples
demonstrate the increased rate of in vitro disappearance of the drugs when
comparing tissue from normal control rats to that obtained from rats pretreated with inducing agents. The in vitro studies correlated with the decreased pharmacologic effects (sleeping or paralysis time) of the drugs in
vivo. Thus, pretreating animals with certain inducing agents markedly
diminishes the pharmacologic effects of the drug due to the correspondingly
enhanced rate of drug metabolism.

The development of tolerance to the pharmacologic effects of barbiturates, such as secobarbital ("red devils"), amobarbital ("blue devils"),
pentobarbital ("yellow jackets"), or certain other CNS hypnotics, whether
taken for therapeutic purposes or not, is well known in chronic users of
these compounds. With long-term use of these agents, the individual requires larger and larger doses to achieve the same pharmacologic effects,
and the tolerance which develops to these drugs is partly related to enzyme
induction (see Chapter 10).

In animals, mechanisms of enzyme induction have been studied extensively. Certain enzyme inducers, specifically those such as phenobarbital, produce a proliferation of the endoplasmic reticulum and increase protein synthesis resulting in increased liver weight, increased microsomal protein content, and increased concentrations of cytochrome P-450, a hemoprotein localized in the microsomal fraction. A degree of specificity exists with regard to the effects of inducing agents, indicating differences in the mechanism of the inductive process. The polycyclic hydrocarbons act more selectively, affecting only certain drug-metabolizing enzyme systems (see Table I), and do not induce proliferation of the endoplasmic reticulum to any great extent. In contrast, the barbiturates appear to be relatively nonspecific, affecting a wide spectrum of enzymes that catalyze the metabolism of drugs.

The different types of enzyme inducers appear to act specifically but differentially on certain of the cytochrome constituents, increasing them in a selective manner. The polycyclic hydrocarbons appear to stimulate formation of a different cytochrome (cytochrome P-448 or cytochrome P_1-450) rather than the common cytochrome P-450 (Sladek and Mannering, 1966; Alvares et al., 1967), whereas phenobarbital increases both cytochromes (Lu et al., 1972). These studies have helped elucidate some reasons for the differences in specificity of phenobarbital-type inducers versus polycyclic hydrocarbon inducers.

Drugs as Inhibitors of the Metabolism of Other Drugs

Many in vitro and in vivo animal studies have demonstrated the inhibitory effects of certain agents on the metabolism of drugs. In addition, studies in man have demonstrated the inhibition of drug metabolism by other drugs given concurrently. One of the earliest examples is that of the inhibition of acetylcholine metabolism by physostigmine. In 1955, shortly after the importance of the liver microsomal enzymes became known, it was found that SKF-525A (2-diethyl aminoethyldiphenyl valerate HCl) could inhibit the metabolism of other drugs by acting on this enzyme system. Subsequently, many other compounds which inhibit the drug-metabolizing enzymes have been discovered. The mechanism whereby SKF-525A produces its inhibitory effects has been extensively studied in vitro. SKF-525A has been postulated to be a competitive substrate for the microsomal enzymes and to compete with other drugs being metabolized (Anders and Mannering, 1966; Gillette, 1966). More recent evidence suggests that SKF-525A is first metabolized to another compound which actually represents the inhibitor of the microsomal enzyme systems (Schenkman et al., 1972). The inhibitors of the drug-metabolizing enzymes may exhibit a biphasic effect. They inhibit initially after acute administration and can induce these enzymes after chronic administration (Serrone and Fjuimoto, 1962). Enzyme inhibitors also potentiate the pharmacologic effects of certain drugs of abuse *in vivo* in animals. The metabolism of amphetamine in rats serves as a model since drugs such as SKF-525A inhibit the parahydroxylation of amphetamine in this species and thus potentiate its pharmacologic effects. In studying interactions of drugs of abuse, or in the use of drugs such as amphetamine as a screening technique for the development of new anti-depressant drugs, it is important to be aware that the investigational agents may interact. The experimental drug may potentiate the amphetamine effect, not because it is an antidepressant in the CNS, but because it inhibits amphetamine metabolism in the liver.

As stated above, there is much evidence from animal studies to substantiate that certain drugs can inhibit the metabolism of other drugs *in vitro* (Rubin *et al.*, 1964a) and *in vivo* (Rubin *et al.*, 1964b). Likewise, clinical studies have shown that this occurs in man and may be of significance in producing untoward and toxic effects. A variety of drugs affect the metabolism of the anticoagulants, warfarin and dicumerol (Carter, 1965; Solomon and Schrogie, 1966; Vessel *et al.*, 1970), the anti-epileptic, diphenylhydantoin (Solomon and Schrogie, 1967; Olesen, 1967; Kutt *et al.*, 1966), and the oral hypoglycemic agent, tolbutamide (Christensen *et al.*, 1963).

EXCRETION

Drugs are excreted by several pathways, including renal excretion into urine, biliary excretion into feces, and expiration via the pulmonary tract. In addition, drugs can also be eliminated in milk, saliva, and sweat, by mammary tissue, salivary glands, or sweat glands, respectively. As previously discussed, the metabolism of drugs usually results in formation of more water-soluble compounds which facilitate their elimination from the body. Theoretically, for many drugs, if they were not metabolized and eliminated from the body, their pharmacologic effects could persist for greatly prolonged periods.

Renal Excretion

The kidney is composed of millions of functional units known as nephrons which are responsible for the excretion of drugs into the urine. The nephron consists of several anatomic subunits and is outlined in Fig. 8. The glomerulus is the bulbous portion of the nephron perfused by the systemic circulation. Blood enters the glomerulus via the afferent arteriole which branches into a capillary network. Here the blood is filtered and

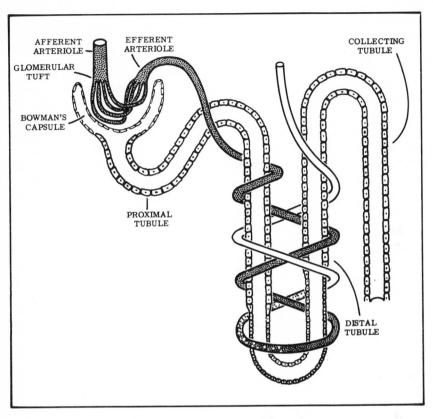

Fig. 8. Schematic representation of the nephron.

drugs diffuse into the glomerular filtrate, essentially an ultrafiltrate of plasma, free of cells and of proteins having a molecular weight greater than 60,000. This ultrafiltration occurs because the intracapillary pressure in the glomerulus is higher than that in the tubular lumen. Thus, in the healthy glomerulus, plasma albumin does not escape into the glomerular filtrate, and drugs bound to albumin are excreted by simple diffusion through the glomerular membrane. This process is accomplished by diffusion of the free form of the drug, which exists in equilibrium with the albumin-bound form. The blood then leaves the glomerulus via the efferent arteriole which then perfuses the remainder of the kidney tubular structure. The filtered fluid flows progressively through the proximal tubule, the loop of Henle, the distal tubule, the collecting duct, and empties into the renal pelvis and eventually into the urinary bladder for storage and subsequent excretion as urine. On this path, drugs can be reabsorbed (along with other solutes such as glucose). This reabsorption occurs in the proximal tubule where specialized cells have the ability to reabsorb these materials by either diffusion or active transport mechanisms. In addition to tubular reabsorption, tubular secretion can occur at the proximal and distal tubules such that drugs can be excreted from the blood directly into the tubular lumen. At this site, certain drugs incompletely filtered through the glomerulus can be actively secreted into the lumen of the tubule. This occurs for compounds such as p-aminohippuric acid (PAH) and penicillin. Other drugs can inhibit the processes of tubular secretion and tubular reabsorption. Probenecid, a drug used in the treatment of gout, competes with other drugs for these tubular processes. Highly polar substances such as morphine glucuronide, which are more soluble in the aqueous glomerular filtrate than in the lipoid membranes of the proximal tubular cells, are poor candidates for reabsorption.

The glomerular filtrate has the same pH as plasma (pH 7.4). The kidney, a major organ for maintaining homeostasis, is capable of regulating the pH of the body by excreting urine ranging from pH 4 to greater than pH 8. The pH of the glomerular filtrate, then, may change as the filtrate progresses down the tubular lumen. Since many drugs are either weak acids or weak bases, renal excretion of such drugs is pH dependent. For example, amphetamine, a lipid-soluble, basic drug having a pK_a of approximately 9.4, exists in alkaline urine predominantly in its un-ionized form. It is no surprise, then, that amphetamine is rapidly reabsorbed from the tubular lumen through the membranes of the proximal and distal tubules, where it can reenter the blood perfusing these areas and be recirculated in the body. Therefore, the plasma half-life and the pharmacologic effects of amphetamines depend upon the pH of the urine. Likewise, weak organic acids, such as the barbiturates which possess the physicochemical properties of lipid-soluble compounds, are also reabsorbed from the tubular lumen when present in their un-ionized form. Thus, pH also markedly affects the duration of their pharmacologic effects. The interrelationship between urinary pH and the excretion of drugs is utilized in treating overdoses of certain psychotropic agents which are abused and used for suicidal purposes. Thus, in the case of barbital or phenobarbital overdoses, the patients are given alkalinizing agents such as an intravenous solution of sodium bicarbonate in attempts to increase the urinary pH. In alkaline urine, the acidic barbiturates are present in their ionized form, are not reabsorbed, and are thus excreted in the urine. In contrast, drugs such as amphetamine (organic bases) are reabsorbed more readily from a basic urine. Therefore the therapeutic regime in amphetamine overdosage is acidification of the urine by administration of agents such as ammonium chloride.

Biliary Excretion

The liver, in addition to having a major role in the biotransformation of drugs, also secretes drugs and their metabolites into the bile. Bile is formed in the liver cell, secreted into the bile canaliculi surrounding these cells, and transported via the hepatic ducts to the gallbladder. Here the bile is concentrated and stored until its release into the duodenum. In some cases, drugs (such as morphine) in the gallbladder bile can be reabsorbed during the concentration processes. Drugs which are excreted into the duodenum with the bile can either pass down the gastrointestinal tract and be eliminated in the feces or can be reabsorbed from the intestinal tract into the circulation. This latter process, known as enterohepatic circulation, plays a role in drug disposition because it can prolong the pharmacologic effects and half-lives of certain drugs which continue to be reabsorbed from the intestines.

In general, the biliary excretion of a drug depends upon its molecular weight. Substances of low molecular weight (usually less than 300) are excreted predominantly in urine and only to a limited extent in bile, whereas compounds with a molecular weight greater than 300 are excreted primarily in bile. However, species differences do exist for determining the relative percentage of a drug which will be excreted in urine or bile (Williams *et al.*, 1965). In addition to molecular weight, the presence of polar, water-soluble substituents on the drug molecule facilitates excretion by the biliary pathway.

Other Sites of Excretion

The lung is the organ responsible for excretion of volatile drugs such as general anesthetics and volatile solvents which are being abused presently. Drugs are excreted by this route in the reverse manner with which they would be absorbed after inhalation; that is, the drug leaves the circulation as it passes through the lung, enters the alveoli, and is eliminated from the body in the expired air.

In addition to the usual methods of excretion, certain drugs are secreted from mammary glands into milk (Knowles, 1965). In general, this secretory process is based upon simple diffusion of the drugs across the alveolar tissue. Drugs are also excreted in sweat (Stowe and Plaa, 1968), and again, the mechanism appears to be that of simple diffusion across the membranes of the sweat glands. Certain drugs can be secreted into the saliva and swallowed, thereby entering the gastrointestinal tract where they may be eliminated from the body or be reabsorbed. Although these extrarenal and extrabiliary routes of excretion account for only small percentages of the excretion of most drugs, in certain instances they may be of relevance in designing a screening program for the detection of drugs (e.g., saliva test) in drug-abuse populations.

REFERENCES

Alvares, A.P., Schilling, G., Levin, W., and Kuntzman, R.: Studies on the induction of CO-binding pigments in liver microsomes by phenobarbital and 3-methylcholanthrene. Biochem. Biophys. Res. Commun. 29:521-526, 1967.

Alvares, A.P., Leigh, S., Kappas, A., Levin, W., and Conney, A.H.: Induction of aryl hydrocarbon hydroxylase in human skin. Drug Disposition and Metabolism 1:386-390, 1973.

Anders, M.W. and Mannering, G.J.: Inhibition of drug metabolism. I. Kinetics of the inhibition of the N-demethylation of ethylmorphine by 2-diethylaminoethyl, 2-diphenylvalerate HCl (SKF 525-A) and related compounds. Mol. Pharmacol. 2:319-327, 1966.

Axelrod, J.: An enzyme for the deamination of sympathomimetic amines: Properties and distribution. J. Pharmacol. Exp. Ther. 110:2, 1954.

Axelrod, J.: Enzymatic formation of psychotomimetic metabolites from normally occurring compounds. Science 134:343, 1961.

Axelrod, J.: The enzymatic N-methylation of serotonin and other amines. J. Pharmacol. Exp. Ther. 138:28-33, 1962.

Axelrod, J.: Enzymatic formation of adrenaline and other catechols from monophenols. Science 140:499-500, 1963.

Axelrod, J. and Tomchick, R.: Enzymatic O-methylation of epinephrine and other catechols. J. Biol. Chem. 233:702-705, 1958.

Brodie, B.B., Gillette, J.R., and LaDu, B.N.: Enzymatic metabolism of drugs and other foreign compounds. Annu. Rev. Biochem. 27:427-454, 1958.

Carter, S.A.: Potentiation of the effect of orally administered anticoagulants by phenyramidol hydrochloride. N. Engl. J. Med. 273:423-426, 1965.

Cherubin, C.E.: The medical sequelae of narcotic addiction. Ann. Int. Med. 67:23-33, 1967.

Christensen, L.K., Hansen, J.M., and Kristensen, M.: Sulphaphenozole-induced hypoglycemic attacks in tolbutamide-treated diabetics. Lancet 2:1298-1301, 1963.

Cinti, D.L., Moldeus, P., and Schenkman, J.B.: Kinetic parameters of drug-metabolizing enzymes in Ca^{++}-sedimented microsomes from rat liver. Biochem. Pharmacol. 21:3249-3256, 1972.

Conney, A.H. and Klutch, A.: Increased activity of androgen hydroxylases in liver microsomes of rats pretreated with phenobarbital and other drugs. J. Biol. Chem. 238:1611-1617, 1963.

Conney, A.H., Davison, C., Gastel, R., and Burns, J.J.: Adaptive increases in drug-metabolizing enzymes induced by phenobarbital and other drugs. J. Pharmacol. Exp. Ther. 130:1-8, 1960.

Cotzias, G.C., Papavasiliou, P.S., and Gellene, R.: Modification of Parkinsonism—chronic treatment with L-dopa. N. Engl. J. Med. 280:337-345, 1969.

Davson, H. and Danielli, J.F.: Permeability of Natural Membranes. New York, Cambridge Univ. Press, 1952.

Dutton, G.J. and Storey, I.D.E.: Uridine compounds in glucuronic acid metabolism. 1. The formation of glucuronides in liver suspensions. Biochem. J. 57:275-283, 1954.

Estabrook, R.W., Gillette, J.R., and Leibman, K.: Microsomes and Drug Oxidations. Baltimore, Williams & Wilkins, 1973.

Evans, D.A.P., Manley, K.A., and McKusick, V.A.: Genetic control of isoniazid metabolism in man. Brit. Med. J. 2:485-491, 1960.

Frolik, C.A. and DeLuca, H.F.: Metabolism of 1,25-dihydroxycholecalciferol in the rat. J. Clin. Invest. 51:2900-2906, 1972.

Gary, N.E. and Keylon, V.: Intravenous administration of marihuana. J.A.M.A. 211:501, 1970.

Gillette, J.R.: Biochemistry of drug oxidation and reduction by enzymes in hepatic endoplasmic reticulum. Advan. Pharmacol. 4:219-261, 1966.

Gillette, J.R., Davis, D.C., and Sasame, H.A.: Cytochrome P-450 and its role in drug metabolism. Annu. Rev. Pharmacol. 12:57-84, 1972.

Gilman, A.G. and Conney, A.H.: The induction of aminoazodye N-demethylase in nonhepatic tissues by 3-methylcholanthrene, Biochem. Pharmacol. 12:591-593, 1963.

Hammer, W. and Sjöqvist, F.: Plasma levels of monomethylated tricyclic antidepressants during treatment with imipramine-like compounds. Life Sci. 6:1895-1903, 1967.

Hawkins, R.D. and Kalant, H.: The metabolism of ethanol and its metabolic effects. Pharmacol. Rev. 24:67-157, 1972.

Hornykiewicz, O.: Parkinson's disease: From brain homogenate to treatment. Fed. Proc. 32:183-190, 1973.

Jepson, J.B., Zaltzman, P., and Udenfriend, S.: Microsomal hydroxylation of tryptamine, indole-acetic acid and related compounds to 6-hydroxy derivatives. Biochem. Biophys. Acta 62:91-102, 1962.

Kamath, S.A. and Rubin, E.: Interaction of calcium with microsomes: A modified method for the rapid isolation of rat liver microsomes. Biochem. Biophys. Res. Commun. 49:52-59, 1972.

King, A.B. and Cowen, D.L.: Effect of intravenous injection of marihuana. J.A.M.A. 210:724-725, 1969.

Kitchin, F.D., Howel-Evans, W., Clark, C.A., McConnell, R.B., and Sheppard, P.M.: PTC taste response and thyroid disease. Brit. Med. J. 1:1069-1074, 1959.

Klotz, I.M.: Spectrophotometric investigations of the interactions of proteins with organic anions. J. Amer. Chem. Soc. 68:2299-2304, 1946.

Knowles, J.A.: Excretion of drugs in milk. A review. J. Pediat. 66:1068-1082, 1965.

Kopin, I.J.: Storage and metabolism of catecholamines: The role of monoamine oxidase. Pharmacol. Rev. 16:179-191, 1964.

Kuntzman, R., Jacobson, M., Schneidman, K., and Conney, A.H.: Similarities between oxidative drug-metabolizing enzymes and steroid hydroxylases in liver microsomes. J. Pharmacol. Exp. Ther. 146:280-285, 1964.

Kutt, H., Winters, W., and McDowell, F.H.: Depression of parahydroxylation of dephenylhydantoin by antituberculosis chemotherapy. Neurology 16:594-602, 1966.

Lemberger, L., Kuntzman, R., Conney, A.H., and Burns, J.J.: Metabolism of tyramine to dopamine by liver microsomes. J. Pharmacol. Exp. Ther. 150:292-297, 1965.

Lipmann, F.: Acetylation of sulfanilamide by liver homogenates and extracts. J. Biol. Chem. 160:173-190, 1945.

Louria, D.B., Hensle, T., and Rose, J.: The major medical complications of heroin addiction. Ann. Int. Med. 67:1-22, 1967.

Lu, A.Y.H., Kuntzman, R., West, S., Jacobson, M., and Conney, A.H.: Reconstituted liver microsomal enzyme system that hydroxylates drugs, other foreign compounds, and endogenous substrates. II. Role of cytochrome P-450 and P-448 fractions in drug and steroid hydroxylations. J. Biol. Chem. 247:1727-1734, 1972.

Morgan, M. and Mandell, A.J.: Indole (ethyl) amine-N-methyl transferase in the brain. Science 165:492-493, 1969.

Mueller, G.C. and Miller, J.A.: The reductive cleavage of 4-dimethylamino azobenzene by rat liver: The intracellular distribution of the enzyme system and its requirement for triphosphopyridine nucleotide. J. Biol. Chem. 180:1125-1136, 1949.

Mueller, G.C. and Miller, J.A.: The metabolism of methylated aminoazo dyes. II. Oxidative demethylation by rat liver homogenates. J. Biol. Chem. 202:579-587, 1953.

Mueller, G.C. and Rumney, G.: Formation of 6β-hydroxy and 6-keto derivatives of estradiol-16C¹⁴ by mouse liver microsomes. J. Amer. Chem. Soc. 79:1004-1005, 1957.

Nose, Y. and Lipmann, F.: Separation of steroid sulfokinases. J. Biol. Chem. 233:1348-1351, 1958.

Olesen, O: The influence of disulfuram and calcium carbimide on the serum diphenyl-hydantoin. Arch. Neurol. 16:642-644, 1967.

Quinn, G.P., Axelrod, J., and Brodie, B.B.: Species, strain and sex differences in metabolism of hexobarbitone, aminopyrine, antipyrine, and aniline. Biochem. Pharmacol. 1:152-159, 1958.

Remmer, H.: Der. Beschleunigte Abbau von Pharmaka in den Lebermikrosomen unter dem Einfluss von Luminal. Arch. Exp. Pathol. Pharmakol. 235:279-290, 1959.

Rubin, A., Tephly, T.R., and Mannering, G.J.: Kinetics of drug metabolism by hepatic microsomes. Biochem. Pharmacol. 13:1007-1016, 1964a.

Rubin, A., Tephly, T.R., and Mannering, G.J.: Inhibition of hexobarbital metabolism by ethylmorphine and codeine in the rat. Biochem. Pharmacol. 13:1053-1057, 1964b.

Schanker, L.S.: Drug absorption. In Fundamentals of Drug Metabolism and Drug Disposition. Eds. LaDu, B.N., Mandel, H.G., and Way, E.L., Baltimore, Waverly Press, Inc., 1971.

Schenkman, J.B., Wilson, B.J., and Cinti, D.L.: Diethylaminoethyl 2,2-diphenylvalerate HCl (SKF 525-A)—in vivo and in vitro effects of metabolism by rat liver microsomes—formation of an oxygenated complex. Biochem. Pharmacol. 21:2373-2383, 1972.

Schneider, W.C. and Hogeboom, G.H.: Cytochemical studies of mammalian tissues: The isolation of cell components by differential centrifugation. Cancer Res. 11:1-22, 1951.

Serrone, D.M. and Fujimoto, J.M.: The effect of certain inhibitors in producing shortening of hexobarbital action. Biochem. Pharmacol. 11:609-615, 1962.

Sladeck, N.E. and Mannering, G.J.: Evidence for a new P-450 hemoprotein in hepatic microsomes from methylcholanthrene-treated rats. Biochem. Biophys. Res. Commun. 24:668-674, 1966.

Solomon, H.M. and Schrogie, J.J.: The effect of phenyramidol on the metabolism of bishydroxycoumarin. J. Pharmacol. Exp. Therap. 154:660-666, 1966.

Solomon, H.M. and Schrogie, J.J.: The effect of phenyramidol on the metabolism of diphenylhydantoin. Clin. Pharmacol. 8:554-556, 1967.

Stanbury, J.B., Morris, M.L., Corrigan, H.J., and Lassiter, W.E.: Thyroxine deiodination by a microsomal preparation requiring ferrous ions, oxygen and cysteine or glutathione. Endocrinology 67:353-362, 1960.

Stowe, C.M. and Plaa, G.L.: Extrarenal excretion of drugs and chemicals. Annu. Rev. Pharmacol. 8:337-356, 1968.

Trülzsch, D., Greim, H., Czygan, P., Hutterer, F., Schaffner, F., Popper, H., Cooper, D.Y., and Rosenthal, O.: Cytochrome P-450 in 7α-hydroxylation of taurodeoxycholic acid. Biochem. 12:76-79, 1973.

Vesell, E.S.: Advances in Pharmacogenetics. Prog. Med. Genet. 9:291-367, 1973.

Vesell, E.S., Passananti, G.T., and Greene, F.E.: Impairment of drug metabolism in man by allopurinol and nortriptyline. N. Engl. J. Med. 283:1484-1488, 1970.

Wattenberg, L.W. and Leong, J.L.: Inhibition of the carcinogenic action of benzo(a)pyrene by flavones. Cancer Res. 30:1922-1925, 1970.

Weissbach, H., Redfield, B.G., and Axelrod, J.: The enzymatic acetylation of serotonin and other naturally occurring amines. Biochem. Biophys. Acta 54:190-192, 1961.

Welch, R.M., Harrison, Y.E., Gommi, B.W., Poppers, P.J., Finster, M., and Conney, A.H.: Stimulatory effect of cigarette smoking on the hydroxylation of 3,4-benzpyrene and the N-demethylation of 3-methyl-4-monomethylaminoazobenzene by enzymes in human placenta. Clin. Pharmacol. Ther. 10:100-109, 1969.

Williams, R.T.: Detoxication mechanisms in man. Clin. Pharmacol. Ther. 4:234-254, 1963.

Williams, R.T., Millburn, P., and Smith, R.L.: The influence of enterohepatic circulation on toxicity of drugs. Ann. N.Y. Acad. Sci. 123:110-124, 1965.

Chapter 2

Amphetamine

Amphetamine is a primary amine first synthesized in 1887; in 1927 the water-soluble sulfate salt was synthesized. The abuse of amphetamine-like drugs may date back to 3000 B.C. when the Chinese became familiar with the stimulant effects of the plant Ma-Huang. This plant was found to contain many pharmacologically active aromatic amines, the one studied most extensively being ephedrine (Chen and Schmidt, 1924, 1930). The CNS effects of amphetamine, a compound related structurally to ephedrine, were soon recognized (Alles, 1933), and shortly thereafter amphetamine was recommended for the treatment of narcolepsy (Prinzmetal and Bloomberg, 1935). About this time, amphetamine (Benzedrine, *dl*-amphetamine) was marketed in inhalers to treat nasal stuffiness, based upon its sympathomimetic vasoconstrictor effects. Being a liquid which is volatile at room temperature, amphetamine was thought to be ideally suited for this purpose. A disadvantage, however, was the CNS stimulant properties which soon became apparent and resulted in some individuals removing the material from the inhalers, dissolving and concentrating the amphetamine, and administering it at large doses by various routes. Thus, with the increased recognition of amphetamine abuse, the Benzedrine inhaler was removed from the consumer market and replaced with another sympathomimetic compound, propylhexedrine, thought to be devoid of CNS effects.

Since amphetamine-like drugs stimulate the CNS, they soon gained a reputation for preventing fatigue and became extensively used by students cramming for examinations, as well as by truck drivers, athletes, etc. These "pep pills" have become a major area of amphetamine abuse. In addition, amphetamine produces euphoria, a sensation of increased physical strength, and an increase in self-confidence. There are many synonyms used for this group of CNS stimulants, including "uppers," "dexies," "bennies," "speed," "eye openers," and "wake-ups."

Sometimes the abuse problem of the amphetamines is related to over-prescription by physicians. When amphetamine was recognized as an appetite suppressant (Nathanson, 1939; Harris et al., 1947), it became widely accepted for treating obesity. Exposure of increasing numbers of persons to amphetamine increased its abuse potential still further. The extensive use and abuse of amphetamine in the treatment of obesity resulted in increased production of amphetamines for medical use. This situation prompted the United States Food and Drug Administration to recommend that the use of amphetamine-like drugs be limited solely to treating obesity, narcolepsy, and hyperkinesis in children. Furthermore, because of the significant potential for amphetamine dependence and abuse, the FDA recommended that the use of amphetamine in obesity be of a short-term nature and only as an adjunct in weight reduction regimens. (See FDA Drug Bulletin, 1972.) Some countries such as Sweden, where these drugs are seriously abused, went a step further. There, prescribing amphetamines is discouraged by the medical community and is considered almost malpractice (Goldberg, 1972). With large-scale production of amphetamines, it was felt that their diversion from legitimate medical uses to illegitimate uses was partly responsible for fostering and supporting drug addiction. Thus, stringent controls have been imposed upon the manufacture of these drugs. Whether this control will have any significant effect on amphetamine abuse is unknown; unfortunately, the drug can be synthesized easily in makeshift or clandestine chemical laboratories.

Soon after the discovery of amphetamine, an extensive search began for agents that would have its beneficial clinical effects, but not its disadvantages. Unfortunately, drugs such as methamphetamine, or "speed," were shown to produce pharmacologic effects similar to amphetamine, and they, too, gained widespread acceptance in the drug subculture. Other chemical modifications of the amphetamine molecule resulted in the discovery of agents possessing marked CNS activity, some of which had substantial hallucinogenic activity (Shulgin et al., 1961). Because communications in the drug subculture are efficient, the introduction of a new drug (for example, into the Haight Ashbury region of San Francisco) resulted within a short time in its spread to other major cities across the United

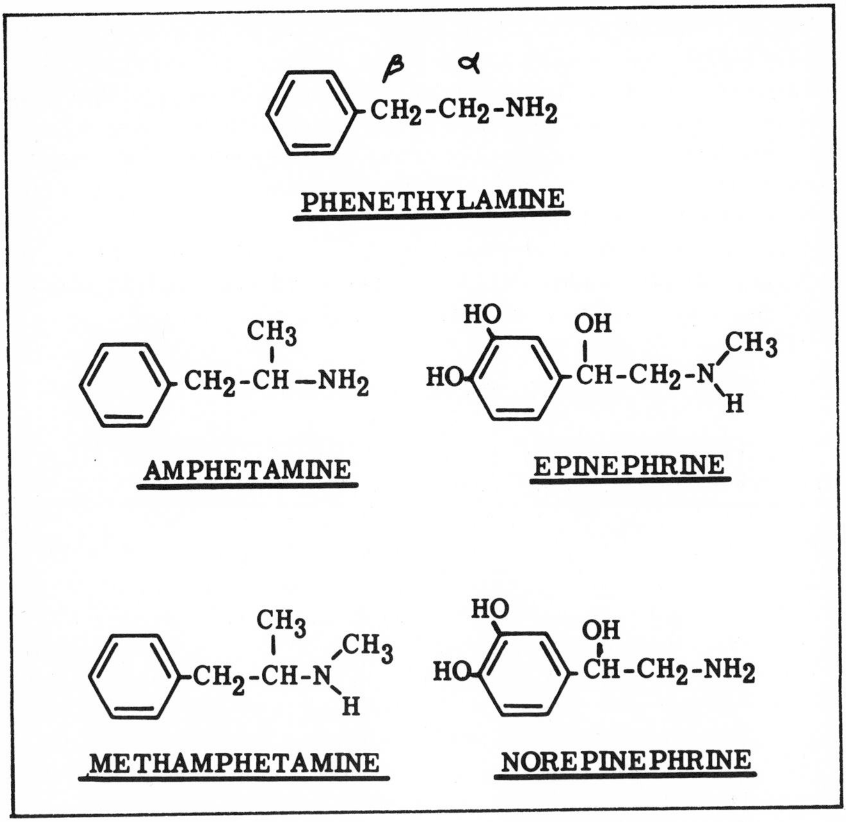

Fig. 1. Structure of phenethylamine and chemically related amines.

States. This rapid dissemination was exemplified by the drug 2,5-dimethoxy-4-methylamphetamine (also known as STP and DOM). This and related drugs of abuse are discussed in chapter 3.

Chemically, amphetamine is a derivative of phenethylamine (Fig. 1), the backbone structure of all of the sympathomimetic amines and the naturally occurring adrenergic substances epinephrine (adrenaline) and norepinephrine (noradrenaline). Amphetamine contains an optical asymmetric center, and thus exists in either the racemic (*dl*), the dextro (*d*), or the levo (*l*) form. It is generally accepted that dextroamphetamine is primarily responsible for the CNS activity of amphetamine, although the levo form also possesses some activity (Taylor and Snyder, 1970).

Several phenethylamine derivatives are rapidly metabolized by the enzyme monoamine oxidase (MAO), which is present in most tissues including liver and intestines, to form pharmacologically inactive products.

However, introduction of a methyl group in the alpha position (Fig. 1) converts phenethylamine to amphetamine, which is an inhibitor of MAO rather than a substrate for this enzyme. As a result of their stability in the presence of MAO, the amphetamines are orally effective and act considerably longer than parenterally administered epinephrine or norepinephrine. (These latter drugs are inactive when given orally because of their rapid metabolism by MAO.)

The metabolism of amphetamine is considered here, whereas the metabolism of structurally related compounds, both synthetic and naturally occurring, is discussed in more detail in the following chapter.

METABOLISM OF AMPHETAMINES *IN VITRO*

Early studies by Axelrod (1954a) demonstrated that amphetamine could be metabolized by homogenates of rabbit liver. He further demonstrated that enzymes in a subcellular fraction (the microsomes) catalyzed the oxidative deamination of amphetamine in the presence of NADPH, Mg^{++}, and molecular oxygen to form phenylacetone and ammonia (Fig. 2). This finding was among the first demonstrations that enzymes localized in liver microsomes could metabolize drugs, and, of course, we now know that many drugs can be metabolized by the microsomal enzymes and by various pathways (see Chapter 1). That Axelrod chose rabbit liver to study amphetamine metabolism was fortuitous because the liver of the rat, the species most extensively used to study drug metabolism, does not readily metabolize amphetamine in an *in vitro*, broken-cell (microsomal) preparation. Interestingly, amphetamine has been shown in many studies to be metabolized by the intact rat and by the isolated perfused rat liver. Under these experimental conditions the metabolic pathway is primarily aromatic hydroxylation leading to the formation of *p*-hydroxyamphetamine (Fig. 3). Many investigators have attempted unsuccessfully to show the metabolism of amphetamine in rat liver homogenates, either via deamination or by hydroxylation. For example, Dingell and Bass (1969) failed to demonstrate the oxidative deamination or aromatic hydroxylation of either *d*- or *l*-amphetamine by a 10,000 *g* microsome-rich supernatant fraction of rat liver homogenate. This fraction did possess drug-metabolizing enzyme activity as evidenced by its capacity to oxidize hexobarbital and aminopyrine. However, these same investigators did demonstrate that amphetamine could be rapidly hydroxylated by the isolated perfused rat liver. Possible explanations for the lack of ability of rat liver microsomes to metabolize amphetamine include: (a) the presence of an unstable and specific amphetamine hydroxylase in the rat preparation; (b) a deficiency in a necessary cofactor in the incubate; (c) the presence of an

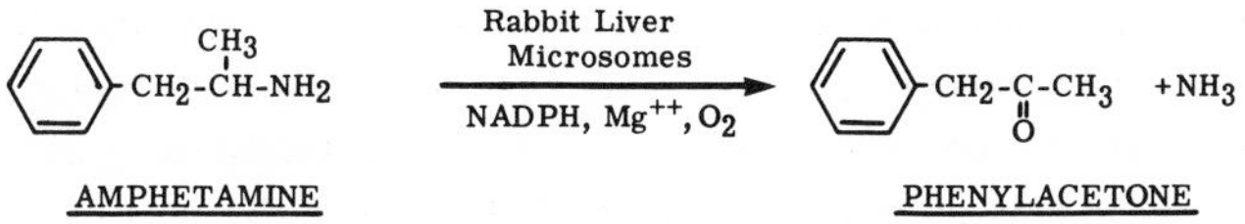

Fig. 2. Conversion of amphetamine to phenylacetone by rabbit liver microsomes.

endogenous inhibitor; and (d) lack of penetration of the amphetamine molecule into the microsomal vesicles. Recently, Billings *et al.* (1976) confirmed the observation that the isolated perfused rat liver could metabolize amphetamine.˙ They also demonstrated that isolated rat hepatocytes could hydroxylate amphetamine and conjugate it at a rate comparable to that of the isolated perfused liver.

In regard to the existence of an endogenous inhibitor, certain findings support this possibility. The oxidative deamination of amphetamine has been shown to occur when amphetamine is incubated with liver microsomes obtained from man (Asatoor *et al.*, 1965), as well as from dog, guinea pig, and rat (Axelrod, 1955). Axelrod (1955) showed that marked species differences existed in the *in vitro* metabolism of amphetamine such that dog, guinea pig, and rat livers possessed only minimal activity for deaminating amphetamine. The addition of microsomes from any of these three species to rabbit liver microsomes resulted in a marked inhibition of the deaminating activity of rabbit liver microsomes, thus suggesting the presence of an endogenous inhibitory substance(s) in the microsomal fractions from dogs, guinea pigs, and rats.

In regard to the lack of penetration of amphetamine into microsomes, Fuller *et al.* (1972a) have recently reported on the metabolism of a series of fluoro-substituted amphetamines. Fluorine is a strongly electronegative atom, and its substitution in the β-carbon of amphetamine reduces the pK_a of the molecule. The pK_a of amphetamine is 9.93, so that at the physiologic pH of 7.4, it exists almost completely in its charged (ionic) form. In contrast, $\beta\beta$-difluoro-amphetamine has a pK_a of 6.97 and exists predominantly in the un-ionized form at pH 7.4. As stated earlier, in rat (*in vivo* and in isolated perfused liver), amphetamine is metabolized by oxidative deamination to only a minimal extent. However, the presence of the fluoro substitutions

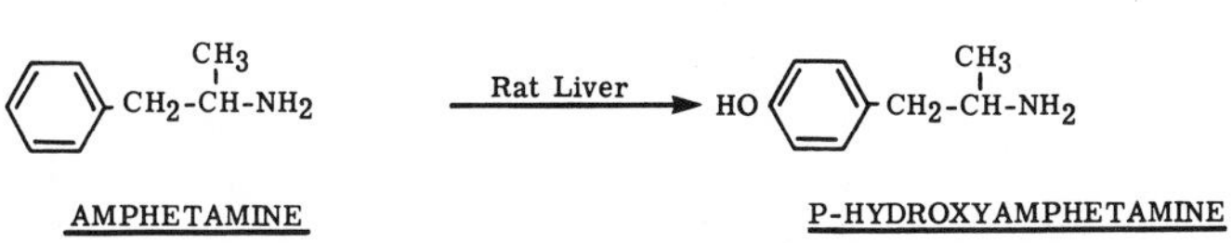

Fig. 3. Conversion of amphetamine to *p*-hydroxyamphetamine.

resulted in a marked increase in the rate of metabolism of the compound and a shift in the metabolic pathway from the normally expected hydroxylation of an amphetamine to that of oxidative deamination forming $\beta\beta$-difluoro-phenylacetone. These data suggest that the difficulty encountered in demonstrating the deamination of amphetamine in the rat may be related to amphetamine's inability to diffuse across the microsomes to the site of transformation.

Recently, several investigators have reported that isolated rat liver microsomes can indeed metabolize amphetamine by p-hydroxylation *in vitro* (Rommelspacher *et al.*, 1974; Cho and Hadshon, 1974). However, this represented far less than 1% conversion, and certainly would not correlate with the *in vivo* findings in rat. Thus, the disparity remains; rat liver microsomes apparently are unable to p-hydroxylate amphetamine *in vitro* to any appreciable extent.

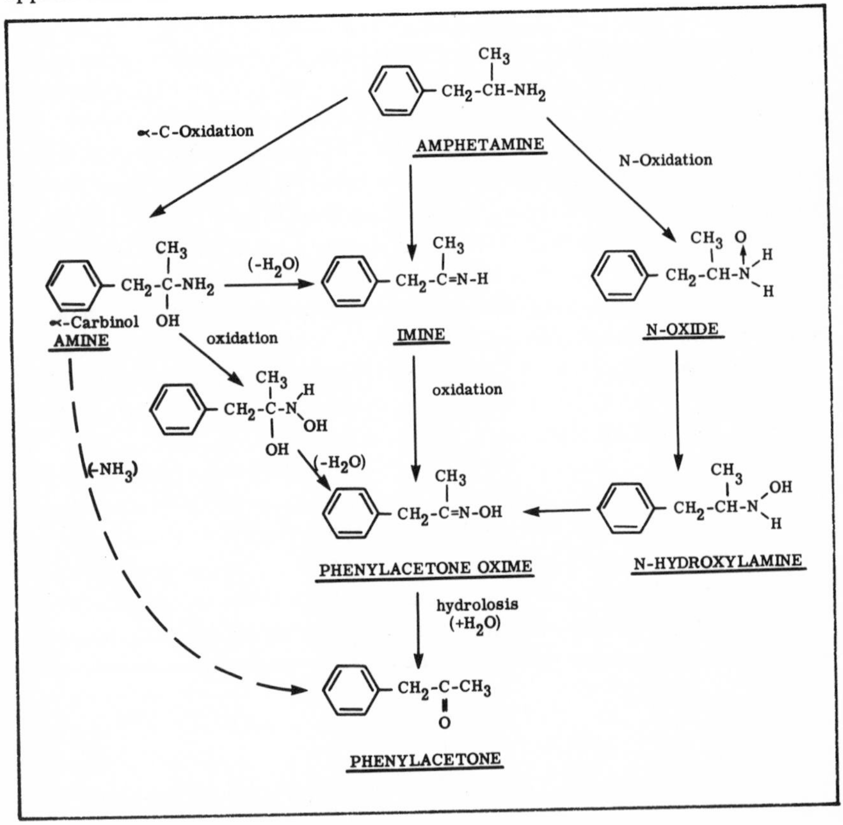

Fig. 4. Scheme for the proposed mechanism of oxidative deamination of amphetamine.

Recently, research has been directed toward the mechanism of the oxidative deamination of amphetamine. After incubating amphetamine with fortified rabbit liver microsomes, Hucker *et al.* (1971) isolated phenylacetone oxime (Fig. 4) and identified it by crystallization to constant specific activity, thin-layer chromatography, gas-liquid chromatography, as well as mass spectroscopy. Prolonging the incubation time and/or using phenylacetone oxime itself as a substrate resulted in formation of phenylacetone (the ketone). One difficulty in demonstrating the presence of the oxime in solution has been its rapid nonenzymatic conversion to the ketone (phenylacetone) during experimental manipulation (e.g., extraction procedures, evaporation) (Hucker *et al.*, 1971; Beckett *et al.*, 1971; Beckett and Al-Sarraj, 1972). Thus, Beckett has referred to phenylacetone oxime and phenylacetone as metabonates (compounds formed nonenzymatically) in contrast to metabolites (compounds formed enzymatically). It is our feeling that this new term for identifying biotransformation products is not appropriate and can only add to additional confusion and misunderstanding in the field of drug metabolism.

Parli *et al.* (1971) studied the oxidation of *d*-amphetamine by rabbit liver microsomes using oxygen-18 and demonstrated the incorporation of molecular oxygen into phenylacetone oxime and phenylacetone. They proposed that the enzymatic reactions producing these two major metabolites were: (1) hydroxylation of amphetamine in the carbon atom a to the amino group, resulting in the formation of a carbinol amine intermediate; (2) dehydration of the carbinol amine and N-oxygenation of the resulting imine to form the oxime; and (3) loss of a molecule of ammonia from the carbinol amine and/or hydrolysis of the oxime to form the phenylacetone (Fig. 4). They believe that hydrolysis of the oxime is a more important pathway, corroborating the results of Hucker *et al.* (1971).

Beckett and Al-Sarraj (1972) isolated an a -methyl- β -phenethyl hydroxylamine from a rabbit liver microsomal preparation incubated with amphetamine. They proposed that, in addition to the formation of the carbinol amine, an N-oxide forms by oxidation of the amino group of amphetamine (Fig. 4). This N-oxide intermediate would then undergo progressive chemical reduction to the N-hydroxylamine, and finally to the oxime. They believe that this conversion is nonenzymatic, the hydroxylamine being spontaneously converted to the oxime and then to phenylacetone with experimental manipulation due to the lability of this compound (Beckett and Al-Sarraj, 1973). Thus, experimental evidence suggests that three possible mechanisms exist whereby the phenylacetone oxime can be formed. These have been listed by Hucker *et al.* (1971) as (1) the formation of an imine which is hydroxylated to form the oxime; (2) the initial hydroxylation of the amino carbon atom (that carbon attached to the

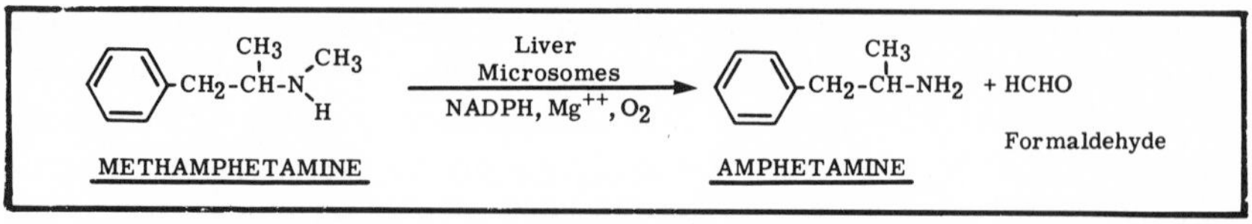

Fig. 5. The demethylation of methamphetamine by liver microsomal enzymes.

amino group) and the amino group itself, followed by the dehydration to the oxime; or (3) hydroxylation of the amino group to form a hydroxylamine followed by dehydrogenation to the oxime (Fig. 4). Perhaps further research into the mechanism of amphetamine oxidation will clarify this issue.

Methamphetamine, a secondary amine containing a methyl substitution in the amphetamine molecule (Fig. 1), can be N-demethylated to amphetamine by liver microsomal enzyme systems of various species (Axelrod, 1954b). This *in vitro* N-demethylation which also requires NADPH, Mg++, and molecular oxygen results in formation of amphetamine and formaldehyde (Fig. 5). The further metabolic pathways for methamphetamine are essentially the same as for amphetamine. Studies of the *in vitro* metabolism of other N-alkyl amphetamines indicate that as the nitrogen substituent is increased from methyl (methamphetamine) to isopropyl, the degree of N-dealkylation is increased (Vree and Van Rossum, 1970; Beckett and Brookes, 1970).

In all species studied, the liver microsomal enzyme system represents the major site of amphetamine metabolism (whether oxidative deamination or aromatic hydroxylation). A relatively minor pathway for amphetamine metabolism, in terms of percentage of administered dose, involves hydroxylation of the β carbon (Goldstein and Anagnoste, 1965; Thoenen

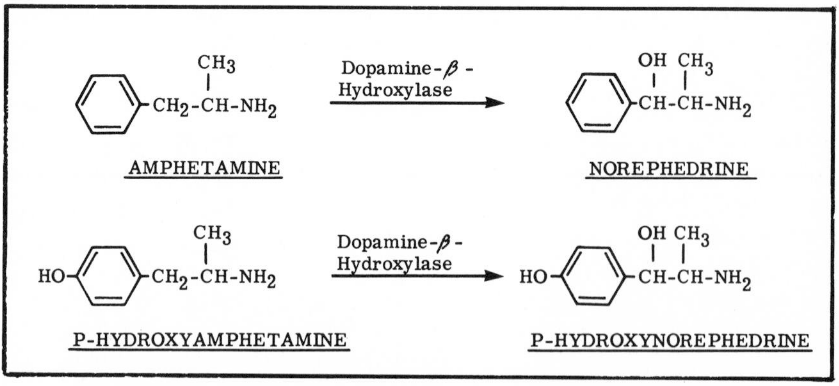

Fig. 6. β-Hydroxylation of amphetamine and p-hydroxyamphetamine.

et al., 1966). The β -hydroxylation of amphetamine and p-hydroxy-amphetamine forms norephedrine and p-hydroxynorephedrine, respectively (Fig. 6). Dopamine- β -hydroxylase, the enzyme which catalyzes this hydroxylation, is localized in synaptic vesicles of sympathetic nerve endings, and thus is distributed throughout the sympathetic portion of the autonomic nervous system (Levin and Kaufman, 1961; Goldstein and Contrea, 1962; Kaufman and Friedman, 1965). This same enzyme catalyzes the final step in the synthesis of the adrenergic neurotransmitter norepinephrine from dopamine (Fig. 7). In addition, it is localized in granules of adrenal medullary cells where it is involved in the synthesis of epinephrine from dopamine.

Although β -hydroxylation represents only a minor metabolic pathway, it may be a most significant pathway in understanding the overall pharmacologic actions of amphetamine. It is allegedly involved in the development of tolerance after long-term amphetamine administration, as well as in the tachyphylaxis produced after repeated acute administration of amphetamine. These studies are discussed in greater detail later in this chapter as well as in Chapter 10 dealing with "tolerance."

Another enzyme involved in the *in vitro* metabolism of amphetamine has been described recently. This enzyme, localized in rat brain, is a dehydrogenase that catalyzes the oxidation of amphetamine, mescaline, and ephedrine (Guha and Mitra, 1971; Mitra and Guha, 1973). This dehydrogenase is localized in the mitochondrial fraction of the brain. Although its activity has been studied *in vitro*, no studies have been done with this enzyme *in vivo*, and its relative pharmacologic importance and the percentage of amphetamine metabolized by this enzyme have not been determined.

In summary, amphetamines can be metabolized *in vitro* by several enzymes, including microsomal enzymes involved in oxidative deamination and N-dealkylation, dopamine- β -hydroxylase localized in sympathetic nerve tissue, and a dehydrogenase localized in brain.

AMPHETAMINE METABOLISM *IN VIVO*

When Axelrod administered d-amphetamine to dogs to study its metabolic fate, he found about 30% of the administered dose excreted in urine as unchanged amphetamine (Axelrod, 1954b). A metabolite, present in urine in large quantities, was isolated and identified as p-hydroxyamphetamine by its paper chromatographic and countercurrent distribution properties. p-Hydroxyamphetamine is itself a potent sympathomimetic agent and has been used clinically for its adrenergic effects. In addition to the presence in urine of free p-hydroxyamphetamine, hydrolysis of urine yielded a larger quantity of this amphetamine metabolite, indicating that it was originally conjugated *in vivo*. The administration of *p*-hydroxy-amphetamine to dog and man resulted in the excretion of 70 and 50% of the administered dose, respectively, as both free and conjugated drug (sulfate and glucuronide) (Axelrod, 1954b; Sjoerdsma and Von Studnitz, 1963.)

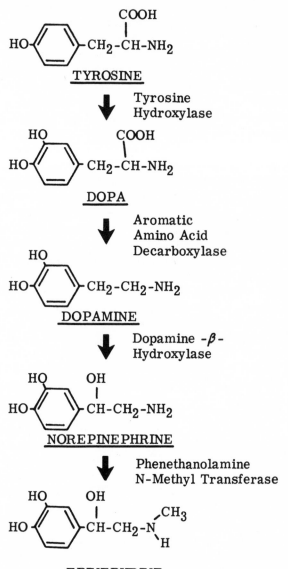

Fig. 7. The biosynthetic pathway for catecholamines.

After his initial studies in dogs, Axelrod (1954b) administered amphetamine to several other species, including rabbits and guinea pigs. In these latter species, amphetamine was completely metabolized; however, to his surprise, only negligible quantities of p-hydroxyamphetamine were found in urine. The finding that major species differences existed for the metabolism of amphetamine was confirmed and further extended by the studies of Dring *et al.* (1966, 1970) and Ellison *et al.* (1966, 1971) using ^{14}C-radiolabeled amphetamine. These investigators examined urinary metabolites of ^{14}C-amphetamine in man, rat, rabbit, squirrel monkey, cat, mouse, guinea pig, and dog (see Table I). In rat, after oral or intraperitoneal administration, approximately 60% of the administered dose of amphetamine was excreted in urine as the p-hydroxy metabolite. In contrast, they found very little of this metabolite excreted in urine of rabbit, guinea pig, monkey, and man, and concluded that aromatic hydroxylation was the major metabolic pathway of amphetamine metabolism in rat, whereas deamination was the major pathway in these other species (Table I). Dog, mouse, and cat appear able to metabolize amphetamine in significant quantities by either pathway (Ellison *et al.*, 1966; Dring *et al.*, 1966; Ellison *et al.*, 1971). In most species, in addition to the urinary excretion of p-hydroxyamphetamine, a considerable portion of the administered dose of ^{14}C-amphetamine was excreted as unchanged drug.

Role of Microsomal Oxidative Deamination

Oxidative deamination of amphetamine has been shown to occur in intact rabbit (Axelrod, 1954b), guinea pig (Beckett and Al-Sarraj, 1972), man (Dring *et al.*, 1966,1970), and mouse (Dring *et al.*, 1970; Fuller *et al.*, 1972b). Intact rats also metabolize amphetamine by oxidative deamination, although much less than the other species (Beckett and Al-Sarraj, 1972).

The aforementioned *in vitro* studies demonstrated that rabbits and guinea pigs oxidatively deaminated amphetamine to phenylacetone. Although this metabolite has been isolated and identified in *in vitro* experiments, it has evaded isolation from urine of animals treated with amphetamine. *In vivo* studies by Williams and co-workers (Smith et al., 1954; El Masry et al., 1956) demonstrated that after amphetamine administration, phenylacetone, itself excreted in urine to only a small extent, was converted to 1-phenylpropan-2-ol (Fig. 8) which was further oxidized to benzoic acid. In addition, small amounts of 1-phenylpropan-2-ol were shown to be conjugated with glucuronic acid. In man, rabbit, and dog, 80% of the benzoic acid formed *in vivo* from amphetamine is excreted primarily as hippuric acid, a conjugate of benzoic acid with the amino acid, glycine. Hippuric acid is normally excreted in urine of mammals because it is the end product of the metabolism of endogenously formed benzoic acid. Thus, the presence

Table Table I. Urinary Excretion Patterns of Metabolites of Amphetamine in Several Species[a]

Urinary Metabolites (% of administered dose)	Rat+[b]	Rabbit+[b]	Man+[b]	Dog+[bc]*	Monkey[c]*	Cat[d]	Horse[d]	Guinea Pig[f]*	Mouse[f]*
Amphetamine (unchanged drug)	13	4	30	38(42)	29	30	9	22	33
p-Hydroxyamphetamine (free and conjugated)	60	7	3	7(17)	2	11	8	0	14
Phenylacetone	0	22	3	ca 3	–	–	28	0	0
1-Phenylpropan-2-ol	0	8	0	2	–	–	12	0	0
Benzoic acid derivatives (hippuric acid and benzoylglucuronide)	3	27	20	32(20)	7	7	29	62	31
Total % dose recovered including unidentified radioactive products	84	81	66	89(83)	44	51	86	83	78

[a] Urinary pH was about 7.5 in rats and dogs, about 8 in rabbit, and 6.5 in man. Urinary pH in cat and monkeys unreported. Drug was given orally to all species.

* = d-amphetamine; + = dl-amphetamine.

[b] Dring, Smith and Williams (1966).

[c] Ellison, Gutzait, and Van Loon (1966).

[d] Ellison, Okun, Silverman, ans Siegel (1971).

[e] Chapman and Marcroft (1973).

[f] Dring, Smith, and Williams (1970).

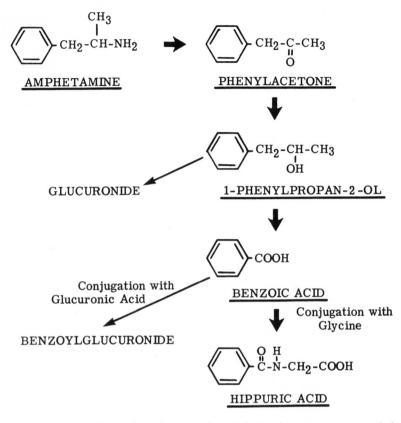

Fig. 8. The metabolism of amphetamine by oxidative deamination to metabolites excreted in urine.

of hippurate in urine is not unexpected *without* drug administration, and this fact may help explain the failure of earlier investigators to recognize this compound as a metabolite of amphetamine. The remaining 20% of benzoic acid is excreted as its glucuronic acid conjugate (benzoylglucuronide).

Humans excrete approximately 3 and 20% of an administered radio-active dose of amphetamine as phenylacetone and conjugates of benzoic acid, respectively (Table I). Comparable values in rabbits are 22% as phenylacetone and 27% as benzoic acid conjugates (Dring *et al.*, 1966). Paper chromatographic studies of urinary extracts from man, dog, and rabbit revealed no radioactive spot corresponding to free benzoic acid after the administration of ^{14}C-amphetamine.

These extensive studies of Dring *et al.* (1966, 1970) clearly demonstrate species differences in the metabolism of amphetamine and corroborate *in vitro* and *in vivo* findings of Axelrod (1954a,b). Thus, quantitative as well as qualitative differences exist between species with regard to amphetamine metabolism.

Role of β-Hydroxylation

In addition to their biotransformation by liver microsomal enzymes, amphetamines are metabolized by the enzyme dopamine- β -hydroxylase as discussed previously. Sjöerdsma and Von Studnitz (1963) demonstrated that in man, *p*-hydroxyamphetamine was a substrate for this enzyme, being hydroxylated in the β position to form *p*-hydroxynorephedrine. They found 4 to 9% of the administered dose excreted as this β -hydroxy metabolite, in both its free and conjugated form, and suggested that measuring urinary *p*-hydroxyamphetamine could be a simple method to estimate dopamine- β -hydroxylase activity in humans.

Recently, Cavanaugh *et al.* (1970) demonstrated that after administration of amphetamine to man, *p*-hydroxynorephedrine was excreted in urine (see Fig. 6) as a result of the combination of aromatic hydroxylation and β -hydroxylation of amphetamine. Norephedrine, another β -hydroxylated metabolite of amphetamine, has also been identified in human urine after amphetamine administration (Davis *et al.*, 1971b; Caldwell *et al.*, 1972c). More recently, Änggård *et al.* (1973) administered large doses of amphetamine to human subjects and reported that norephedrine represented a significant urinary metabolite of amphetamine.

Methamphetamine, a highly abused derivative of amphetamine, is also a substrate for dopamine- β -hydroxylase and for the microsomal aromatic hydroxylase which *p*-hydroxylates amphetamine. In the rat, the major metabolites of methamphetamine are amphetamine, *p*-hydroxymethamphetamine, *p*-hydroxynorephedrine, and *p*-hydroxyamphetamine (Fig. 9). Norephedrine has also been identified as a minor urinary metabolite of methamphetamine in guinea pigs and man. In man, Vree and Van Rossum (1970) and Beckett and Brookes (1970) found that only about 5 to 10% of the administered dose of methamphetamine was excreted in urine as amphetamine, whereas about 40 to 50% was excreted in urine as unchanged methamphetamine. Caldwell *et al.* (1972a) demonstrated that human subjects produced 5 to 10 times more *p*-hydroxynorephedrine after methamphetamine administration than after amphetamine administration. It is not known whether this increased formation of *p*-hydroxynorephedrine is related to the increased potential for methamphetamine abuse as compared to amphetamine.

Because complete studies of tissue distribution of amphetamine and its metabolites cannot be done in man, we must rely on data obtained in infrahuman species to formulate postulates regarding the significance of the

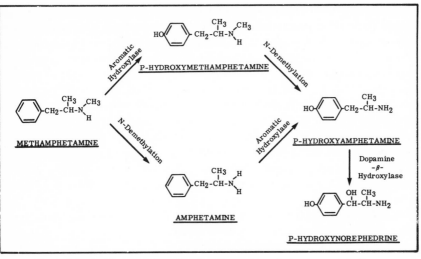

Fig. 9. Metabolic conversions involved in methamphetamine metabolism.

metabolic products of amphetamine. Animal studies reveal that *p*-hydroxy-norephedrine formed after amphetamine administration is stored in sympathetic nerve endings, specifically in the heart (Goldstein and Anagnoste, 1965) and spleen (Thoenen *et al.*, 1966) and could be released from these storage sites upon stimulation of the sympathetic nerves to these organs. *p*-Hydroxynorephedrine is also localized in brain tissue after the administration of amphetamine to rats (Groppetti and Costa, 1969). Kopin and co-workers (Fischer *et al.*, 1965; Breese *et al.*, 1970) postulated that *p*-hydroxynorephedrine was produced *in vivo* in sympathetic nerve endings because the enzyme dopamine-β-hydroxylase is localized there. They found that β-hydroxylation of amphetamine was a prerequisite for the storage of *p*-hydroxynorephedrine in the nerve endings.

The formation of *p*-hydroxynorephedrine from amphetamine has been implicated as a possible mechanism for certain pharmacologic effects produced by amphetamines, such as tolerance and tachyphylaxis. A mechanism proposed for the tachyphylaxis after repeated administration of amphetamine is that *p*-hydroxynorephedrine accumulates in synaptic vesicles of the sympathetic nerve ending and displaces norepinephrine, the natural neurotransmitter from these storage sites. Then *p*-hydroxynor-ephedrine functions as a relatively less potent "false" transmitter. With repeated doses of amphetamine, more norepinephrine is replaced by the weak transmitter and therefore the subsequent responses to amphetamine are diminished since the released norepinephrine is now admixed with a related, but less active substance (Thoenen *et al.*, 1966; Breese *et al.*, 1970; Brodie *et al.*, 1970).

The chronic administration of large doses of amphetamine produces effects directly opposite to those expected after acute amphetamine administration. For example, acute administration increases blood pressure, whereas chronic administration reduces it by diminishing sympathetic nervous system tone (Zalis and Parmley, 1963; Zalis et al., 1967; Vidrio and Pardo, 1967). Paradoxical effects are also seen with the sympathomimetic vasoconstrictor amine, p-hydroxyamphetamine, which produces hypotension on long-term administration to man, presumably due to depletion of norepinephrine from sympathetic nerve endings and its replacement by a false neurotransmitter (Gill et al., 1967). Acutely, amphetamine produces CNS stimulation; however, chronically, it produces a depressive state in subjects when the cumulative dose exceeds 50 mg (Griffith et al., 1970a). This paradox might be analogous to the effects produced by amphetamine in peripheral tissues, i.e., the conversion of a hypertensive effect to a hypotensive action. Recent studies by Sever et al. (in press) have challenged the theory that metabolic conversion of amphetamine to its para-hydroxylated derivative is responsible for amphetamine tolerance. They administered amphetamine chronically to rats and guinea pigs and demonstrated that both species developed tolerance to amphetamine-induced hyperthermia over the same period of time, despite the observation that guinea pigs do not produce the p-hydroxy metabolite of amphetamine to the same extent as the rat. These findings suggest that amphetamine tolerance is not dependent upon the formation of parahydroxylated false transmitters.

Amphetamine metabolites, specifically the β-hydroxylated compounds, have been implicated as the basis for the psychotic manifestations observed after high doses of amphetamine (Griffith et al., 1970a,b; Änggård et al., 1970, 1973).

With increasing doses of amphetamine, a psychosis develops that includes paranoia. Änggård et al. (1973) demonstrated that the intensity of amphetamine psychosis appeared to be positively correlated with the quantity of basic polar metabolites excreted in urine (p-hydroxyamphetamine, p-hydroxynorephedrine, and norephedrine), but was not positively correlated with the plasma levels of amphetamine. The alleviation of the paranoia and its associated symptoms in amphetamine psychosis appeared related to the rate of excretion of amphetamine (Angrist et al., 1969). The duration of the psychosis is prolonged in conditions which interfere with amphetamine excretion (alkaline urine). In contrast, the psychotic symptoms abate rapidly with conditions which facilitate the urinary excretion of amphetamine (acidic urine) (Änggård et al., 1973).

Smythies et al. (1967) demonstrated that administration of p-methoxyamphetamine produced marked abnormal and disruptive behavior in rats, and postulated that in man psychosis after large doses of amphetamine might be due to the formation of p-methoxyamphetamine. Indeed, Shulgin et al. (1969) have reported that this compound does produce psychotic symptoms in humans. More importantly, no p-methoxyamphetamine has been detected in human urine after administering large doses of amphetamine (Angrist et al., 1970; Änggård et al., 1973). Of course, the possibility exists that this compound was present, but at concentrations below the limit of detectability of the analytical method and that in fact this material, or one of its metabolites, might be formed in the central nervous system. That amphetamine might be metabolized to a hallucinogen is intriguing, although at the present time no evidence exists to support such a hypothesis.

In summary, the findings of in vivo metabolic studies with the amphetamines agree with in vitro findings in that: (a) marked species differences exist, and (b) several enzymes are involved in the metabolism of the amphetamines. Several hypotheses have been proposed suggesting that metabolism plays an important role in amphetamine-induced tolerance, tachyphylaxis, and psychosis. The metabolic pathways of amphetamine are summarized in Fig. 10.

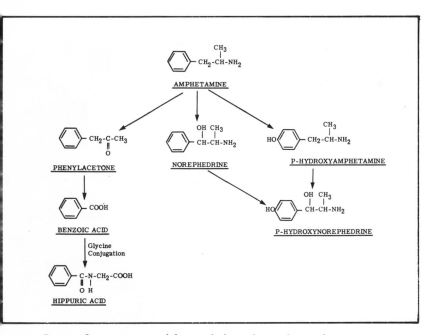

Fig. 10. Summarization of the metabolic pathways for amphetamine.

DRUG INTERACTIONS THAT AFFECT AMPHETAMINE METABOLISM

Much research of interactions of drugs with amphetamine has been conducted, particularly between psychotropic agents and amphetamines. Perhaps this is partly due to the chemical and pharmacologic similarities between amphetamines and the catecholamines and to the role of the latter compounds in the postulated catecholamine theory for affective disorders (Schildkraut et al., 1967). This hypothesis proposes that certain depressions are associated with a deficiency of catecholamines in brain, whereas mania is associated with increased amounts of catecholamines in the CNS. An animal model for screening tricyclic antidepressants in rats was developed in hopes of discovering new antidepressants. This model is dependent on the ability of antidepressants to potentiate amphetamine locomotor activity and to facilitate amphetamine effect in hypothalamic self-stimulation experiments (Morpurgo and Theobald, 1965; Stein, 1964; Carlton, 1961). Extensive investigations of underlying mechanisms involved in interactions of tricyclic antidepressants with amphetamine have been conducted.

Studies by Consolo et al. (1967), Sulser et al. (1966), Valzelli et al. (1967), Lewander (1969), Gropetti and Costa (1969), and Lemberger et al. (1970a) demonstrated that potentiation of amphetamine locomotor activity by the antidepressant desmethylimipramine (DMI) could be explained mainly by the DMI-induced inhibition of amphetamine metabolism. Consolo et al. (1967) showed that, in rats, DMI increased the urinary excretion of amphetamine and decreased p-hydroxyamphetamine excretion. Furthermore, Sulser et al. (1966) and Lemberger et al. (1970a) demonstrated that DMI prolonged amphetamine half-life in brain tissue and in the whole animal. Since aromatic hydroxylation is the major pathway of amphetamine metabolism in the rat, these studies suggest that DMI can inhibit the hydroxylation of amphetamine to p-hydroxyamphetamine. In support of this concept, this interaction between DMI and amphetamine did not occur in mice (Dolfini et al., 1969; Lew et al., 1971), guinea pigs, or rabbits (Lemberger et al., 1970a), all species which do not substantially hydroxylate amphetamine. The finding that DMI inhibits the metabolism of the p-hydroxylation of amphetamine in rats is to be expected from studies showing that DMI is a potent inhibitor of microsomal enzymes systems in rat liver (Lemberger et al., 1965; Sjoqvist et al., 1968).

Other clinically effective tricyclic antidepressant drugs such as protriptyline, nortriptyline (Lewander, 1969) and iprindole (Lemberger et al., 1970a; Freeman and Sulser, 1972) also potentiate amphetamine effects in rats by blocking its metabolic degradation. Whereas DMI was relatively nonspecific in its effects and inhibited the metabolism of amphetamine and several other agents such as hexobarbital and zoxazolamine, iprindole had no effect on the *in vitro* metabolism of hexobarbital or zoxazolamine, nor did it affect the duration of loss of righting reflex (sleep time) induced by these agents (Lemberger *et al.*, 1970a). In rats, pretreatment with iprindole markedly reduced the urinary excretion of *p*-hydroxyamphetamine and reduced the accumulation of *p*-hydroxynorephedrine in tissues after amphetamine administration (Freeman and Sulser, 1972).

At low doses, the widely used tranquilizer chlorpromazine markedly prolongs the stimulant actions of amphetamines. At larger doses of chlorpromazine, its inherent CNS depressant effect masks the amphetamine-induced locomotor stimulation (Sulser and Dingell, 1968; Borella *et al.*, 1969) and stereotype behavior (Lemberger *et al.*, 1970b), even though brain amphetamine concentrations exceed those seen in rats given amphetamine alone (Valzelli *et al.*, 1968; Lemberger *et al.*, 1970b). Borella *et al.* (1969, 1970) showed that the increased locomotor activity after the combination of chlorpromazine and amphetamine administration occurred predominantly by increasing the half-life of amphetamine in rat brain and liver by inhibiting its metabolism, viz., *p*-hydroxylation. Lemberger *et al.* (1970b) reported that chlorpromazine markedly prolonged the disappearance of radiolabeled amphetamine from brain such that the 52-minute half-life in amphetamine-treated animals became 140 minutes in rats receiving the combination treatment. They also demonstrated that pretreating rats with chlorpromazine markedly inhibited whole-body amphetamine metabolism from 93% metabolized in 3 hours in amphetamine-treated control animals to only 29% metabolized in animals treated with the combination.

Another psychotropic drug shown to inhibit the metabolism of amphetamine is ethanol. Pretreating rats with this drug markedly increased the urinary excretion of unchanged amphetamine and greatly reduced the urinary concentration of free and conjugated *p*-hydroxyamphetamine (Creaven and Barbee, 1969). Ethanol also increases amphetamine brain and plasma concentrations when both drugs are administered concurrently (Jonsson and Lewander, 1973).

Monoamine oxidase (MAO) inhibitors have been used as psychotropic agents for some time, and their inhibitory effects on liver microsomal enzymes are well documented (Fouts and Brodie, 1955). Recently, Trinker and Rand (1970) have shown that MAO inhibitors can interfere with the metabolism of amphetamine in isolated perfused liver. Lew *et al.* (1971), investigating the interaction of iproniazid and amphetamine in mice, demonstrated that iproniazid was effective in potentiating amphetamine behavioral responses as well as producing a marked increase in brain amphetamine levels when compared to animals treated only with amphetamine. Possibly, iproniazid, which inhibits a variety of liver microsomal enzymes, inhibits oxidative deamination of amphetamine in the mouse, which is then responsible for the drug-drug interaction that these investigators observed.

Many other psychotropic drugs, including reserpine, phenothiazine tranquilizers, and other tricyclic antidepressants, also have been shown to affect the metabolism of amphetamine in rats (Valzelli *et al.*, 1968; Lewander, 1969; Lal *et al.*, 1971). It is important to note that studies attempting to demonstrate a metabolic interaction between amphetamine and psychotropic drugs in man have been unsuccessful (L. Lemberger and J.M. Davis, unpublished observations; Lemberger, 1972). After intravenous administration of tritiated amphetamine to man, amphetamine disappeared from plasma with a half-life of approximately 30 hours. Pretreatment with therapeutic doses of chlorpromazine or haloperidol had no effect on the plasma half-life of amphetamine, nor on its qualitative or quantitative urinary excretion. This is further evidence that *p*-hydroxylation plays only a minor role in the overall metabolism of amphetamine in humans.

SKF-525A is a prototype inhibitor of microsomal drug-metabolizing enzymes under certain experimental conditions. This compound inhibits amphetamine metabolism in rats. Clay *et al.* (1971) pretreated rats with SKF-525A for the purpose of further investigating the mechanisms of amphetamine pharmacology. They observed a decrease in the amphetamine-induced depletion of cardiac norepinephrine, but no effect of SKF-525A on the amphetamine-induced depletion of catecholamines in brain. After the combination of SKF-525A and amphetamine, increases in amphetamine concentrations in both heart and brain occurred, whereas concentrations of amphetamine metabolites in these tissues were markedly reduced. Based on these results, they concluded that effects of amphetamine on cardiac norepinephrine were dependent on one or more of its metabolites, *vis-à-vis* a direct effect of amphetamine itself. The failure of the combination to affect brain catecholamines is puzzling, except that it suggests that perhaps both the parent drug and its metabolites are equally active in altering these amines. Studies concerned with the effects of enzyme-inducing (or metabolism-stimulating) agents on the metabolism of amphetamine have been relatively meager. Lewander (1969) showed that after the administration of a single dose of amphetamine to rats who had been pretreated with phenobarbital for 5 days, the urinary excretion of unchanged amphetamine decreased, whereas the concentration of *p*-hydroxyamphetamine in urine increased. These results suggest that in rat, *p*-hydroxylation of amphetamine is an inducible pathway. Although this increase in *p*-hydroxyamphetamine excretion is statistically significant, it probably is not of much pharmacologic significance. Because the increased excretion of *p*-hydroxyamphetamine accounted for only less than a 10% reduction in unchanged amphetamine excreted in urine, it appears that enzyme stimulation has a much less significant effect on reducing the pharmacologic effects of amphetamine in rats than that seen with agents which inhibit amphetamine metabolism and thereby potentiate its pharmacologic effects.

TISSUE DISTRIBUTION

The tissue distribution of amphetamine, its metabolism, and its pharmacologic actions are all interrelated. Amphetamine conversion to pharmacologically active metabolites such as p-hydroxyamphetamine and p-hydroxynorephedrine is, in part, responsible for its unique tissue distribution. Axelrod et al. (1954b), studying the distribution of amphetamine in dog, found amphetamine to be present in essentially all tissues, its highest concentration being in lung, liver, brain, spleen, and kidney. The presence of large concentrations of amphetamine in lung would be expected since it is an amine and, in general, basic compounds tend to localize there. In rats, after the intraperitoneal administration of tritiated amphetamine, disposition studies indicate a high degree of localization of amphetamine in all tissues except fat (Maickel et al., 1969). Tissue amphetamine concentrations were greater than plasma amphetamine concentrations for more than 8 hours.

Concentrations of amphetamine are similar in plasma and cerebrospinal fluid, showing that amphetamine can rapidly cross the blood-brain barrier (a finding which is supported by the marked and immediate onset of CNS effects produced after intravenous administration of amphetamine). This is further substantiated by the high level of amphetamine present in brain tissue after its systemic administration.

Recently, Pardridge and Connor (1973) questioned the role of simple diffusion in the ability of amphetamine to cross the blood-brain barrier, stating that at physiologic pH, amphetamine existed predominantly in its ionized form. Indeed, they demonstrated that a carrier-mediated transport system was responsible for permitting amphetamine to rapidly enter the brain. This system was saturable and was competitively inhibited by drugs of similar structure.

Subcellular distribution studies of amphetamine in rat brain demonstrate that amphetamine occurs in highest concentrations in the soluble fraction of the whole brain homogenate, as well as in the soluble fraction associated with the axoplasm of the vesicles (Pfeifer et al., 1969).

Groppetti and Costa (1969) demonstrated that p-hydroxynorephedrine was present in the brain and heart of rats treated with amphetamine and that it persisted in these tissues for over 24 hours. Pretreatment with DMI, which inhibits p-hydroxylation, prevented this accumulation of p-hydroxynorephedrine. They found amphetamine disappearing from plasma and various tissues with a half-life of about 1 hour, whereas the concentration of p-hydroxynorephedrine remained virtually unchanged in brain and heart for 8-24 hours after a single injection of amphetamine. In addition, p-hydroxynorephedrine appeared to be more potent than amphetamine in depleting cardiac norepinephrine with regard to its onset of action and rate of norepinephrine depletion. These investigators also found p-hydroxynorephedrine persisting in tissues longer than p-hydroxyamphetamine, and concluded that the cardiac concentration of p-hydroxynorephedrine correlated positively with the degree of norepinephrine depletion. Since species differences exist for amphetamine metabolism, they studied the formation and distribution of p-hydroxynorephedrine in rat and guinea pig. In contrast to rat, the guinea pig failed to accumulate p-hydroxynorephedrine in heart, brain, or plasma after amphetamine administration, indicating again that this species does not p-hydroxylate amphetamine to any significant degree. The positive correlation between tissue levels of p-hydroxynorephedrine and norepinephrine depletion has since been confirmed by Lewander (1971a,b).

Thoenen *et al.* (1966), utilizing a splenic preparation which was perfused *in situ*, demonstrated that p-hydroxynorephedrine was formed *in vivo* from amphetamine, was stored in the splenic tissue, and could be liberated into the perfusion fluid after stimulation of the splenic nerve. This was the first evidence that metabolites of amphetamine could be stored and released on nerve stimulation and is the basis for later studies which showed that they could serve as "false transmitters." In addition to finding p-hydroxynorephedrine in splenic homogenates, small amounts of norephedrine and p-hydroxyamphetamine were found. However, neither p-hydroxynorephedrine nor norephedrine were detected when the spleen was sympathetically denervated. Thus, the presence of these amphetamine metabolites was dependent on a functionally intact sympathetic nervous system. This further indicates that the enzyme responsible for the β-hydroxylation of amphetamine and p-hydroxyamphetamine is localized in sympathetic nerve endings.

Studies by Goldstein and Anagnoste (1965), utilizing the same experimental approach, demonstrated the accumulation of p-hydroxynorephedrine in rat cardiac tissue after amphetamine administration. Similarly, Brodie *et al.* (1970) showed that maximum levels of p-hydroxynorephedrine accumulated in rat heart in 4 hours and declined only slightly over a period of 24 hours after the administration of 5 mg/kg of amphetamine. In contrast, no amphetamine was detectable in the tissue at 24 hours after administration. Maximal levels of p-hydroxyamphetamine were reached in 2 hours and declined at a slow rate. However, levels of this compound in heart were only about 20% of p-hydroxynorephedrine 24 hours after amphetamine administration. The postulate that the p-hydroxynorephedrine localized in sympathetic nerve endings is of major importance in explaining some of the pharmacology of amphetamine is further supported by the finding that, in contrast to this metabolite, amphetamine itself is localized extraneuronally and does not accumulate in nerve endings (Thoenen et al., 1968).

Studies have been concerned with the disposition of amphetamine in brain in a variety of experimental conditions. Although it has been known for many years that amphetamine toxicity is greater in animals housed in groups as opposed to those housed individually (Chance, 1946; Lasagna and McCann, 1957), little is known about the mechanisms involved. Several investigators have studied the disposition of amphetamine in animals housed under various conditions to determine whether the increased toxicity is positively correlated to increased brain levels of amphetamine. Consolo et al. (1965a,b) demonstrated that, indeed, grouped animals have higher brain levels of amphetamine than animals which are isolated, and thus postulated that differences in the metabolism of amphetamine between animals housed under these two conditions could be a contributing factor in explaining the toxicity of amphetamine. The effect of other models of stress on toxicity of amphetamine and its brain levels has also been studied (Salama and Goldberg, 1969). Salama and Goldberg found varying levels of amphetamine in the brain after certain stresses. When electric shock preceded the injection of amphetamine by 15 minutes to 1 hour, slightly higher brain levels of amphetamine were present. However, they believed this probably could not account for the increased toxicity of amphetamine observed under these conditions because the increase in levels were not of a sufficient magnitude.

In addition to studies concerned with the disposition of amphetamine in brain and other tissues, several investigators have studied the rate of amphetamine disappearance from plasma. In dogs, Axelrod (1954b) showed that amphetamine disappeared from plasma with a half-life of about 7 hours, whereas one of its metabolites, p-hydroxyamphetamine, disappeared with a half-life of about 1 hour. Baggot and Davis (1972), studying the pharmacokinetics of amphetamine in dogs and swine, found its half-life to be approximately 4½ hours and 1 hour, respectively. In horses, amphetamine plasma half-life was about 2 hours (Baggot et al., 1972a; Chapman and Marcroft, 1973).

Beckett and Rowland (1964) first demonstrated that plasma amphetamine levels were dependent upon urinary pH. After the administration of ^{14}C-labeled amphetamine, they observed a more rapid decline in plasma amphetamine levels during an ammonium chloride treatment regimen (designed to produce acidification of the urine) than when a more fluctuating urinary pH was present, indicating that amphetamine's plasma half-life is much shorter when associated with an acid urinary pH. This appears to be related to a shift to the drug's ionic state in the renal tubular lumen. Renal tubular reabsorption of amphetamine is prevented, thus allowing the drug to be excreted faster, resulting in a more rapid clearance of amphetamine from plasma. Davis et al. (1971a) confirmed the early observations of Beckett et al. (1969) that subjects maintained on acidifying agents (ammonium chloride) exhibited a much shorter plasma amphetamine half-life (about 8-10 hours) than when they were maintained on alkalinizing agents (sodium bicarbonate), a procedure which markedly prolonged amphetamine plasma half-life (16-30 hours). In addition to an increase in its half-life during alkalinization, studies revealed that amphetamine was metabolized to a greater extent during alkalinization than during acidification or in the presence of a fluctuating urinary pH, probably because the drug had more time to be metabolized by the liver enzymes.

After treatment of subjects with large doses of amphetamine sulfate (up to 200 mg i.v.) a dose-related euphoria is produced (Änggård et al., 1970). There appeared to be a positive correlation between the plasma levels of amphetamine and the time course of the euphoria produced in those subjects whose urine was maintained at an acid pH. The amphetamine half-life in plasma was about 5 hours, while the "euphoria half-life" was about 6 hours (Jonsson et al., 1971).

In contrast to this euphoria study, Änggård et al. (1973), studying the effect of urinary pH on amphetamine psychosis, demonstrated that although the psychotic symptoms cleared more rapidly in subjects with acidic urine (plasma half-life of amphetamine 7-14 hours) than in those with alkaline urine (plasma amphetamine half-life 18-34 hours), the intensity of the psychosis was positively correlated to the quantity of basic polar metabolites of amphetamine excreted in urine rather than to the concentration of amphetamine in plasma.

For some drugs, the ability to bind to plasma proteins has pharmacologic significance and may even be responsible for interactions with other drugs which are bound. However, based on in vitro studies with amphetamine, plasma protein binding appears to be of no major significance in this drug's overall pharmacology. Baggot et al. (1972b), studying the in vitro binding of amphetamine to the plasma proteins of many animal species, showed that amphetamine was bound primarily to the plasma albumin fraction and binding was independent of drug concentration within the range studied. The extent of binding was less than 45% in all species studied, and a considerable variation was seen among species, goat exhibiting the highest percent bound amphetamine (40.7%), whereas in man binding was only about 16.2%. No difference in the plasma protein binding of amphetamine was found between plasma from untreated subjects and plasma from tolerant amphetamine-dependent subjects (Franksson and Änggård, 1970).

EXCRETION

Early published studies investigating the urinary excretion of amphetamine were by Richter (1938), Jacobson and Gad (1940), and Beyer and Skinner (1940). These investigators measured urinary amphetamine concentrations after the administration of doses of 5-30 mg of either *dl*- or *d*-amphetamine. In all these studies, urinary amphetamine was assayed colorimetrically by a procedure involving a coupling reaction, either by formation of a diazoamino compound or by amphetamine interaction with picric acid. These investigators showed that wide intersubject variations existed for the urinary excretion of amphetamine, ranging in some studies from 15 to 60%. The mean excretion of unchanged amphetamine in urine was about 40% of the administered dose. Alles and Wisegarver (1961) administered large doses of *dl*-amphetamine sulfate (up to 600 mg) and studied its excretion pattern. Even at these very large doses, they found that the proportion of amphetamine excreted as either metabolites or unchanged compound was similar to that seen after the administration of therapeutic doses of amphetamine.

In all these early studies, no attempt was made to control urinary pH since its importance in amphetamine disposition was not yet recognized. Not until the studies of Beckett and Rowland (1964, 1965) did it become apparent that the urinary excretory pattern of amphetamine depended on the urinary pH. These same investigators observed a marked intersubject variation in the excretion of unchanged amphetamine, ranging from 30 to 66%, values consistent with the earlier reports. Seeking an explanation for this variability, they pretreated a group of subjects with ammonium chloride to acidify their urine prior to amphetamine administration. In this experimental situation, they found about 60% of the amphetamine excreted unchanged over a 48-hour period with a very small variation among subjects. Subjects pretreated with sodium bicarbonate to alkalinize the urine, excreted only about 5% of the administered dose excreted as unchanged amphetamine during the 48-hour collection period. Thus a low urinary pH increased the amphetamine excretion rate, whereas a high urinary pH decreased it.

The results of these studies agree with the theory of nonionic diffusion of bases in the renal tubules (Milne *et al.*, 1958; Weiner and Mudge, 1964).

Thus, for organic bases, the higher the urinary pH, the greater percentage of drug existing in un-ionized form. Therefore, amphetamine, when present in alkaline tubular luminal fluid, is reabsorbed by the kidney tubules and returned to the plasma to be excreted later and/or to be further metabolized.

Milne et al. (1958) demonstrated that amphetamine exhibited a high lipid-water partition ratio when present in its un-ionized form and postulated that its excretion should be expected to be influenced by changes in urinary pH. Asatoor et al. (1965) found that 50 to 70% of an administered dose of amphetamine was excreted in acid urine, whereas only 7% was excreted in alkaline urine. Davis et al. (1971a) extended these studies and demonstrated an increased total urinary excretion of hippuric acid (the major metabolite of amphetamine in man) in an alkaline urine as opposed to an acid urine. Thus, the alkaline urine favored an increase in tubular reabsorption of amphetamine and a greater percentage of the amphetamine became available for further metabolism. Similar findings were reported by Änggård et al. (1973).

Although many studies have dealt with the urinary excretion of amphetamine, until recently studies of other excretory routes have been scarce. Caldwell et al. (1971, 1972a,b) investigated the biliary excretion of amphetamine and methamphetamine in the rat and found about 16% of a radiolabeled dose of amphetamine excreted in the bile, predominantly as the glucuronide conjugate of p-hydroxyamphetamine (12%), plus about 1 to 2% as unchanged amphetamine. After methamphetamine administration, biliary excretion accounted for about 18% of the dose of radioactivity, approximately 2% being present as amphetamine and 11% as p-hydroxynorephedrine glucuronide. Previously they had postulated that compounds excreted in bile must be polar and possess a molecular weight greater than 325 (in the rat). Their experimental results support this hypothesis, since they demonstrated that after amphetamine administration, only p-hydroxyamphetamine glucuronide (molecular weight 327) met these criteria and was excreted in bile. However, after methamphetamine administration, p-hydroxynorephedrine glucuronide (molecular weight 343) best met these criteria. In contrast to the rat studies, neither amphetamine nor its metabolites was detected in human bile after ingestion of the drug (Beckett and Rowland, 1965). It is possible that these compounds are not excreted in human bile because oxidative deamination to form hippuric acid is the major pathway for amphetamine metabolism in man, and hippuric acid is excreted primarily in urine. An alternative hypothesis is that in man the molecular weight requirements for significant biliary excretion exceed those necessary for the rat (and exceed those molecular weights which would be characteristic of the metabolites of amphetamine in man). In support of this, Millburn (1970) stated that in man the molecular weight requirement for significant biliary excretion is probably about 500. Thus, although a small amount of p-hydroxyamphetamine is formed in humans, it might escape biliary excretion because its molecular weight (327 as the glucuronide) does not satisfy the alleged requirements.

In addition to excretion in urine and bile, amphetamine is also excreted to a small extent in the saliva, and it has been shown that salivary excretion parallels the blood concentration decay curves (Rowland, 1969; Van Rossum et al., 1971). Recent studies by Vree et al. (1972) have shown that after administration of dimethylamphetamine to man, this compound and its metabolite methamphetamine are excreted in sweat. The rate of excretion into sweat parallels that observed in urine, and the concentrations are similar in these two body fluids. Thus, they propose that sweat can be used to detect drugs in body fluids for forensic purposes. Although these investigators state that excretion of amphetamines in sweat is probably independent of pH, the difference between the pH of sweat in their subjects (4.6 to 7.8) and that of plasma (7.4) is of little significance when one considers the high pK_a (about 9.9) of amphetamine and methamphetamine.

REFERENCES

Alles, G.A.: The comparative physiological actions of dl- β -phenylisopropylamines. I. Pressor effect and toxicity. J. Pharmacol. Exp. Ther. 47:339-354, 1933.

Alles, G.A. and Wisegarver, B.B.: Amphetamine excretion studies in man. Toxicol. Appl. Pharmacol. 3:678-688, 1961.

Änggård, E., Gunne, L.M., Jonsson, L.E., and Niklasson, F.: Pharmacokinetic and clinical studies on amphetamine-dependent subjects. Eur. J. Clin. Pharmacol. 3:3-11, 1970.

Änggård, E., Jonsson, L., Hogmark, A., and Gunne, L.: Amphetamine metabolism in amphetamine psychosis. Clin. Pharmacol. Ther. 14:870, 1973.

Angrist, B.M., Schweitzer, J., Friedhoff, A.J., Gershon, S., Hekimian, L.J., and Floyd, A.: The clinical symptomatology of amphetamine psychosis and its relationship to amphetamine levels in urine. Int. Pharmacopsychiat. 2:125-139, 1969.

Angrist, B.M., Schweitzer, J.W., Friedhoff, A.J., and Gershon, S.: Investigation of p-methoxyamphetamine excretion in amphetamine-induced psychosis. Nature (London) 225:651-652, 1970.

Asatoor, A.M., Galman, B.R., Johnson, J.R., and Milne, M.D.: The excretion of dex-amphetamine and its derivatives. Pharmacology. 24:293-300, 1965.

Axelrod, J.: An enzyme for the deamination of sympathomimetic amines: Properties and distribution. J. Pharmacol. Exp. Ther. 110:2, 1954a.

Axelrod, J.: Studies on sympathomimetic amines. II. The biotransformation and physiological disposition of d-amphetamine, d-p-hydroxyamphetamine and d-methamphetamine. J. Pharmacol. Exp. Ther. 110:315-326, 1954b.

Axelrod, J.: The enzymatic deamination of amphetamine (Benzedrine). J. Biol. Chem. 214:753, 1955.

Baggot, J.D. and Davis, L.E.: Pharmacokinetic study of amphetamine elimination in dogs and swine. Biochem. Pharmacol. 21:1967-1976, 1972.

Baggot, J.D., Davis, L.E., Murdick, P.W., Ray, R.S., and Noonan, J.S.: Certain aspects of amphetamine elimination in the horse. Amer. J. Vet. Res. 33:1161-1164, 1972a.

Baggot, J.D., Davis, L.E., and Neff, C.A.: Extent of plasma-protein binding of amphetamine in different species. Biochem. Pharmacol. 21:1813-1816, 1972b.

Beckett, A.H. and Al-Sarraj, S.: The mechanism of oxidation of amphetamine enantiomorphs by liver microsomal preparations from different species. J. Pharm. Pharmacol. 24:174-176, 1972.

Beckett, A.H. and Al-Sarraj, S.: Identification, properties and analysis of n-hydroxyamphetamine—a metabolite of amphetamine. J. Pharm. Pharmacol. 25:328-334, 1973.

Beckett, A.H. and Brookes, L.G.: The effect of chain and ring substitution on the metabolism, distribution and biological action of amphetamines. In International Symposium on Amphetamines and Related Compounds. Eds. Costa, E. and Garattini, S., New York, Raven Press, 1970.

Beckett, A.H. and Rowland, M.: Rhythmic urinary excretion of amphetamine in man. Nature (London) 204:1203-1204, 1964.

Beckett, A.H. and Rowland, M.: Urinary excretion kinetics of amphetamine in man. J. Pharm. Pharmacol. 17:628-639, 1965.

Beckett, A.H., Salmon, J.A., and Mitchard, M.: The relation between blood levels and urinary excretion of amphetamine under controlled acidic and under fluctuating urinary pH values using (^{14}C)amphetamine. J. Pharm. Pharmacol. 21:251-258, 1969.

Beckett, A.H., Van Dyk, J.M., Chissick, H.M., and Gorrod, J.W.: 'Metabolism' of 'amphetamines' to oximes as a route to deamination. J. Pharm. Pharmacol. 23:560, 1971.

Beyer, K.H. and Skinner, J.I.: The detoxication and excretion of beta-phenylisopropylamine (benzedrine). J. Pharmacol. Exp. Ther. 68:419-432, 1940.

Billings, R.E., Murphy, P.J., Bellamy, G., McMahon, R.E., and Ashmore, J.: The aromatic hydroxylation of amphetamine with rat liver microsomes, perfused liver and isolated hepatocytes. Fed. Proc. 36, 243, 1976.

Borella, L., Herr, F., and Woidon, A.: Prolongation of certain effects of amphetamine by chlorpromazine. Can. J. Physiol. Pharmacol. 47:7-13, 1969.

Borella, L.E., Pinski, J. and Herr, F.: Effect of chlorpromazine on the disposition of amphetamine in the rat. Res. Commun. Chem. Pathol. Pharmacol. 1:667-676, 1970.

Breese, G.R., Kopin, I.J., and Weise, V.K.: Effects of amphetamine derivatives on brain dopamine and noradrenaline. Brit. J. Pharmacol. 38:537-545, 1970.

Brodie, B.B., Cho, A.K., and Gessa, G.L.: Possible role of p-hydroxynorephedrine in the depletion of norepinephrine induced by d-amphetamine and in tolerance to this drug. In International Symposium on Amphetamines and Related Compounds. Eds. Costa, E. and Garattini, S., New York, Raven Press, 1970.

Caldwell, J., Dring, L.G., and Williams, R.T.: Biliary excretion of amphetamine and methamphetamine in rat. Biochem. J. 124:16-17, 1971.

Caldwell, J., Dring, L.G., and Williams, R.T.: Metabolism of (^{14}C)methamphetamine in man, the guinea pig and the rat. Biochem. J. 129:11-22, 1972a.

Caldwell, J., Dring, L.G., and Williams, R.T.: Biliary excretion of amphetamine and methamphetamine in the rat. Biochem. J., 129:25-29, 1972b.

Caldwell, J., Dring, L.G., and Williams, R.T.: Norephedrines as metabolites of (^{14}C)amphetamine in urine in man. Biochem. J. 129:23-24, 1972c.

Carlton, P.L.: Potentiation of the behavioral effects of amphetamine by imipramine. Psychopharmacologia 2:364-369, 1961.

Cavanaugh, J.H., Griffith, J.D., and Oates, J.A.: Effect of amphetamine on the pressor response to tyramine: Formation of p-hydroxynorephedrine from amphetamine in man. Clin. Pharmacol. Ther. 11:656-664, 1970.

Chance, M.R.A.: Aggregation as a factor influencing the toxicity of sympathomimetic amines in mice. J. Pharmacol. Exp. Ther. 87:214-219, 1946.

Chapman, D.I. and Marcroft, J.: Studies on the metabolism of sympathomimetic amines. The metabolism of (±)-[^{14} C]amphetamine in the horse. Xenobiotica 3:49-61, 1973.

Chen, K.K. and Schmidt, C.F.: The action of ephedrine, an alkaloid from Ma Huang. Proc. Soc. Exp. Biol. Med. 21:351, 1924.

Chen, K.K. and Schmidt, C.F.: Ephedrine and related substances. Medicine 9:1-117, 1930.

Cho, A.K. and Hodshon, B.J.: The 4-hydroxylation of amphetamine and phentermine by rat liver microsomes. Pharmacologist 16:218, 1974.

Clay, G.A., Cho, A.K., and Roberfroid, M.: Effect of diethylaminoethyl diphenyl-propylacetate hydrochloride (SKF-525A) on the norepinephrine-depleting actions of d-amphetamine. Biochem. Pharmacol. 20:1821-1831, 1971.

Consolo, S., Garattini, S., and Valzelli, L.: Amphetamine toxicity in aggressive mice. J. Pharm. Pharmacol. 17:53 1965a.

Consolo, S., Garattini, S., Ghielmetti, R., and Valzelli, L.: Concentrations of amphet-amine in the brain in normal or aggressive mice. J. Pharm. Pharmacol. 17:666, 1965b.

Consolo, S., Dolfini, E., Garrattini, S., and Valzelli, L.: Desipramine and amphetamine metabolism. J. Pharm. Pharmacol. 19:253-256, 1967.

Creaven, P.J. and Barbee, T.: The effect of ethanol on the metabolism of amphetamine by the rat. J. Pharm. Pharmacol. 21:859, 1969.

Davis, J.M., Kopin, I.J., Lemberger, L., and Axelrod, J.: Effects of urinary pH on am-phetamine metabolism. Ann. N.Y. Acad. Sci. 179:493-501, 1971a.

Davis, J.M., Fann, E., Griffith, J., and Lemberger, L.: Pharmacological aspects of the treatment of amphetamine abuse: The effects of urinary pH. In Advances in Neuro-psychopharmacology. Proc. of the Symposia held at the VII Congress of the Collegium Internationale Neuro-Psychopharmacologicum, Prague, August 11-15, 1970, Eds. O. Vinar, Z. Votava, and P.B. Bradley, 1971b.

Dingell, J.V. and Bass, A.: Inhibition of the hepatic metabolism of amphetamine by desipramine. Biochem. Pharmacol. 18:1535-1538, 1969.

Dolfini, E., Tansella, M., Valzelli, L., and Garattini, S.: Further studies on the inter-action between desipramine and amphetamine. Eur. J. Pharmacol. 5:185-190, 1969.

Dring, L.G., Smith, R.L., and Williams, R.T.: The fate of amphetamine in man and other mammals. J. Pharm. Pharmacol. 18:402-405, 1966.

Dring, L.G., Smith, R.L., and Williams, R.T.: The metabolic fate of amphetamine in man and other species. Biochem. J. 116:425-435, 1970.

Ellison, T., Gutzait, L., and Van Loon, E.J.: The comparative metabolism of d-amphetamine-C^{14} in the rat, dog and monkey. J. Pharmacol. Exp. Ther. 152:383-387, 1966.

Ellison, T., Okun, T., Silverman, A., and Siegel, M.: Metabolic fate of amphetamine in the cat during development of tolerance. Arch. Int. Pharmacodyn. 190:135-149, 1971.

El Masry, A.M., Smith, J.N., and Williams, R.T.: Studies in detoxication. 69. The metabolism of alkylbenzenes: n-Propylbenzene and n-butylbenzene with further ob-servations on ethylbenzene. Biochem. J. 64:50-56, 1956.

FDA Drug Bulletin. Anorectics have limited use in treatment of obesity. FDA requires new labeling. Dec. 1972.

Fischer, J.E., Horst, W.D., and Kopin, I.J.: β-Hydroxylated sympathomimetic amines as false neurotransmitters. Brit. J. Pharmacol. Chemother. 24:477-484, 1965.

Fouts, J.R. and Brodie, B.B.: Inhibition of metabolic pathways. J. Pharmacol. Exp. Ther. 115:68-73, 1955.

Franksson, G. and Anggard, E.: The plasma protein binding of amphetamine, catecholamines and related compounds. Acta Pharmacol. Toxicol. 28:209-214, 1970.

Freeman, J.J. and Sulser, F.: Iprindole-amphetamine interactions in the rat: The role of aromatic hydroxylation of amphetamine in its mode of action. J. Pharmacol. Exp. Ther. 183:307-315, 1972.

Fuller, R.W., Molloy, B.B., Roush, B.W., and Hauser, K.L.: Disposition and behavioral effects of amphetamine and β,β-difluoroamphetamine in mice. Biochem. Pharmacol. 21:1299, 1972a.

Fuller, R.W., Shaw, W.N., and Molloy, B.B.: Dissociation of the lipid mobilizing and hyperthermic effects of amphetamine by β-fluoro substitution. Arch. Int. Pharmacodyn. 199:194, 1972b.

Gill, J.R., Mason, D.T., and Bartter, F.C.: Effects of hydroxyamphetamine (Paredrine) on the function of the sympathetic nervous system in normotensive subjects. J. Pharmacol. Exp. Ther. 155:288-295, 1967.

Goldberg, L.: Epidemiology of drug abuse in Sweden. In Drug Abuse. Proceedings of the International Conference. Ed. Zarafonetis, C.J.D., Philadelphia, Lea & Febiger, 1972.

Goldstein, M., and Anagnoste, B.: The conversion in vivo of d-amphetamine to (+)-p-hydroxynorephedrine. Biochim. Biophys. Acta 107:166-168, 1965.

Goldstein, M., and Contrea, J.F.: The substrate specificity of phenylamine-β-hydroxylase. J. Biol. Chem. 237:1898, 1962.

Griffith, J.D., Cavanaugh, J.H., Held, J. and Oates, J.A.: Experimental psychosis induced by the administration of d-amphetamine. In International Symposium on Amphetamines and Related Compounds, Eds. Costa, E. and Garattini, S., New York, Raven Press, 1970, pp. 897-904. 1970a.

Griffith, J.D., Cavanaugh, J.H., and Oates, J.A.: Psychosis induced by the administration of d-amphetamine to human volunteers. In Psychotomimetic Drugs. Ed. Efron, D.H., New York, Raven Press, 1970, p. 287, 1970b.

Groppetti, A., and Costa, E.: Tissue concentrations of p-hydroxynorephedrine in rats injected with d-amphetamine: Effect of pretreatment with desipramine. Life Sci. 8:653-665, 1969.

Guha, S.R. and Mitra, C.: Amphetamine-tetrazolium reductase activity in brain. Biochem. Pharmacol. 20:3539-3542, 1971.

Harris, S.C., Ivy, A.C., and Searle, L.M.: The mechanism of amphetamine-induced loss of weight: A consideration of the theory of hunger and appetite. J.A.M.A. 134:1468-1475, 1947.

Hucker, H.B., Michniewicz, B.M., and Rhodes, R.E.: Phenylacetone oxime—an intermediate in the oxidative deamination of amphetamine. Biochem. Pharmacol. 20:2123-2128, 1971.

Jacobson, E. and Gad, I.: Die Aussiheidung des β-phenylisopropylamine bei Menschem. Arch. Exp. Pathol. Pharmacol. Naunyn-Schmiedeberg's 196:280-289, 1940.

Jonsson, J. and Lewander, T.: Effects of diethyldithiocarbamate and ethanol on the in vivo metabolism and pharmacokinetics of amphetamine in the rat. J. Pharm. Pharmacol. 25:589-591, 1973.

Jonsson, L.E., Anggard, E., and Gunne, L.-M.: Blockade of euphoria induced by intravenous amphetamine in humans. Clin. Pharmacol. Ther. 12:889, 1971.

Kaufman, S. and Friedman, S.: Dopamine β-hydroxylase. Pharmacol. Rev. 17:71-100, 1965.

Lal, S., Missala, K., and Sourkes, T.L.: Effect of neuroleptics on brain amphetamine concentrations in the rat. J. Pharm. Pharmacol. 23:967, 1971.

Lasagna, L. and McCann, W.P.: Effect of "tranquilizing" drugs on amphetamine toxicity in aggregated mice. Science 125:1241-1242, 1957.

Lemberger, L.: Role of drug metabolism in drug research and development: Importance of drug metabolism in clinical pharmacological evaluation of new drugs. J. Pharm. Sci. 61:1690-1694, 1972.

Lemberger, L., Kuntzman, R., Conney, A.H., and Burns, J.J.: Metabolism of tyramine to dopamine by liver microsomes. J. Pharmacol. Exp. Ther. 150:292-297, 1965.

Lemberger, L., Sernatinger, E., and Kuntzman, R.: Effect of desmethylimipramine, iprindole and dl-erythro-a-(3,4-dichlorophenyl)-β-(t-butyl amino) propanol HCL on the metabolism of amphetamine. Biochem. Pharmacol. 19:3021-3028, 1970a.

Lemberger, L., Witt, E.D., Davis, J.M., and Kopin, I.J.: The effects of haloperidol and chlorpromazine on amphetamine metabolism and amphetamine stereotype behavior in the rat. J. Pharmacol. Exp. Ther. 174:428-433, 1970b.

Levin, E.Y. and Kaufman, S.: Studies on the enzyme catalyzing the conversion of 3,4-dihydroxyphenylethylamine to norepinephrine. J. Biol. Chem. 236:2043-2049, 1961.

Lew, C., Iversen, S.D., and Iversen, L.L.: Effects of imipramine, desipramine and monoamine oxidase inhibitors on the metabolism and psychomotor stimulant actions of d-amphetamine in mice. Eur. J. Pharmacol. 14:351-359, 1971.

Lewander, T.: Influence of various psychoactive drugs on the in vivo metabolism of d-amphetamine in the rat. Eur. J. Pharmacol. 6:38-44, 1969.

Lewander, T.: On the presence of p-hydroxynorephedrine in the rat brain and heart in relation to changes in catecholamine levels after administration of amphetamine. Acta Pharmacol. Toxicol. 29:33-48, 1971a.

Lewander, T.: Displacement of brain and heart noradrenaline by p-hydroxynorephedrine after administration of p-hydroxyamphetamine. Acta Pharmacol. Toxicol. 29:20-32, 1971b.

Maickel, R.P., Cox, R.H., Miller, F.P., Segal, D.S., and Russell, R.W.: Correlation of brain levels of drugs with behavioral effects. J. Pharmacol. Exp. Ther. 165:216-224, 1969.

Millburn, P.: In Metabolic Conjugation and Metabolic Hydrolysis. Ed. Fishman, W.H., New York and London, Academic Press, 1970, Vol. 2, pp. 1-74.

Milne, M.D., Scribner, B.H., and Crawford, M.A.: Non-ionic diffusion and the excretion of weak acids and bases. Amer. J. Med. 24:709-729, 1958.

Mitra, C. and Guha, S.R.: Amphetamine oxidation in rat brain. Biochem. Pharmacol. 22:651-657, 1973.

Morpurgo, C. and Theobald, W.: Influence of imipramine-like compounds and chlorpromazine on the reserpine-hypothermia in mice and the amphetamine-hyperthermia in rats. Med. Pharmacol. Exp. 12:226-232, 1965.

Nathanson, M.H.: The central action of beta-amino-aminopropylbenzene (BENZEDRINE): Clinical observations. J.A.M.A. 108:528-531, 1939.

Pardridge, W.M. and Connor, J.D.: Saturable transport of amphetamine across blood-brain barrier. Experientia 29:302-304, 1973.

Parli, C.J., Wang, N., and McMahon, R.E.: The mechanism of the oxidation of d-amphetamine by rabbit liver oxygenase. Oxygen-18 studies. Biochem. Biophys. Res. Commun. 43:1204-1209, 1971.

Pfeifer, A.K., Csaki, L., Fodor, M., Gyorgy, L., and Okros, I.: The subcellular distribution of (+)-amphetamine and (+)-p-chloroamphetamine in the rat brain as influenced by reserpine. J. Pharm. Pharmacol. 21:687-689, 1969.

Prinzmetal, M. and Bloomberg, W.: Use of benzedrine for treatment of narcolepsy. J.A.M.A. 105:2051-2054, 1935.

Richter, D.: Elimination of amines in man. Biochem. J. 32:1763-1769, 1938.

Rommelspacher, H., Honecker, H., Schulze, G., and Strauss, S.M.: The hydroxylation of D-amphetamine by liver microsomes of the male rat. Biochem. Pharmacol. 23:1065-1071, 1974.

Rowland, M.: Amphetamine blood and urine levels in man. J. Pharm. Sci. 58:508-509, 1969.

Salama, A.I. and Goldberg, M.E.: Effect of several models of stress and amphetamine on brain levels of amphetamine and certain monoamines. Arch. Int. Pharmacodyn. 181:474-483, 1969.

Schildkraut, J.J., Schanberg, S.M., Breese, G.R., and Kopin, I.J.: Norepinephrine metabolism and drugs used in the affective disorders: A possible mechanism of action. Amer. J. Psychiat. 124:600-608, 1967.

Sever, P.S., Caldwell, J., and Williams, R.T.: Tolerance to amphetamine in two species (rat and guinea pig) that metabolize it differently. Psychological Med., 1976 (in press).

Shulgin, A.T., Bunnell, S., and Sargent, T.: The psychotomimetic properties of 3,4,5,-trimethoxyamphetamine. Nature (London) 189:1011, 1961.

Shulgin, A.T., Sargent, T., and Naranto, C.: Structure-activity relationships of one-ring psychotomimetics. Nature (London) 221:537-541, 1969.

Sjoerdsma, A., and Von Studnitz, W.: Dopamine-β oxidase activity in man, using hydroxyamphetamine as substrate. Brit. J. Pharmacol. 20:278-284, 1963.

Sjöqvist, F., Hammer, W., Schumacher, H., and Gillette, J.R.: The effect of desmethylimipramine and other "anti-tremorine" drugs on the metabolism of tremorine and oxotremorine in rats and mice. Biochem. Pharmacol. 17:915-934, 1968.

Smith, J.N., Smithies, R.H., and Williams, R.T.: Studies in detoxication. 59. The metabolism of alkylbenzenes. The biological reduction of ketones derived from alkylbenzenes. Biochem. J. 57:74-76, 1954.

Smythies, J.R., Johnston, V.S., Bradley, R.J., Benington, F., Morin, R.D., and Clark, L.C., Jr.: Some new behavior-disrupting amphetamines and their significance. Nature (London) 216:128-129, 1967.

Stein, L.: Self-stimulation of the brain and the central stimulant action of amphetamine. Fed. Proc. 23:836-850, 1964.

Sulser, F. and Dingell, J.V.: The potentiation and blockade of the central action of amphetamine by chlorpromazine. Biochem. Pharmacol. 17:634-636, 1968.

Sulser, F., Owens, M.L., and Dingell, J.V.: On the mechanism of amphetamine potentiation by desipramine (DMI). Life Sci. 5:2005-2010, 1966.

Taylor, K.M. and Snyder, S.H.: Amphetamine: Differentiation by d and l isomers of behavior involving brain norepinephrine or dopamine. Science 168:1487-1489, 1970.

Thoenen, H., Hurlimann, A., Gey, K.F., and Haefely, W.: Liberation of p-hydroxynorephedrine from cat spleen by sympathetic nerve stimulation after pretreatment with amphetamine. Life Sci. 5:1715-1722, 1966.

Thoenen, H., Hurlimann, A., and Haefely, W.: Mechanism of amphetamine accumulation in the isolated perfused heart of the rat. J. Pharm. Pharmacol. 20:1-11, 1968.

Trinker, F.R. and Rand, M.J.: The effect of nialamide, pargyline and tranylcypromine on the removal of amphetamine by the perfused liver. J. Pharm. Pharmacol. 22:469-499, 1970.

Valzelli, L., Consolo, S., and Morpurgo, C.: Influence of imipramine-like drugs on the metabolism of amphetamine. In: Antidepressant Drugs, Proc. Int. Symp., Milan, 1966, pp. 61-69, Excerpta Medica Foundation, Amsterdam, 1967.

Valzelli, L., Dolfini, E., Tansella, M., and Garattini, S.: Activity of centrally acting drugs on amphetamine metabolism. J. Pharm. Pharmacol. 20:595-599, 1968.

Van Rossum, J.M., Breimer, D.D., Van Ginneken, C.A.M., Van Kordelaar, J.M.G., and Vree, T.B.: Gas-liquid chromatography in pharmacology and toxicology. Pharmacokinetic analysis limited by the sensitivity of the analytical technique. Clin. Chim. Acta 34:311, 1971.

Vidrio, H. and Pardo, E.G.: Antihypertensive actions of a group of sympathomimetic amines. Fed. Proc. 26:459, 1967.

Vree, T.B. and Van Rossum, J.M.: Kinetics of metabolism and excretion of amphetamines in man. In: International Symposium on Amphetamines and Related Compounds. Eds. Costa, E., and Garattini, S., New York, Raven Press, 1970.

Vree, T.B., Muskens, A.T.J.M., and Van Rossum, J.M.: Excretion of amphetamines in human sweat. Arch. Int. Pharmacodyn. 199:311-317, 1972.

Weiner, I.M. and Mudge, G.H.: Renal tubular mechanisms for excretion of organic acids and bases. Amer. J. Med. 36:743-762, 1964.

Zalis, E.G. and Parmley, L.F.: Fatal amphetamine poisoning. Arch. Intern. Med. 112:60-64, 1963.

Zalis, E.G., Lundberg, G.D., and Knutson, R.A.: The pathophysiology of acute amphetamine poisoning with pathologic correlation. J. Pharmacol. Exp. Ther. 158:115-127, 1967.

Chapter 3

Mescaline and Chemically Related Phenylalkylamines

Amphetamine and several other phenethylamine derivatives have been classified as drugs of abuse and psychotomimetic agents. Certain of these, for example, peyote and nutmeg, occur naturally as constituents of plants and have been utilized in certain religious ceremonies in portions of North and South America. This chapter is concerned primarily with the physiologic disposition of the phenethylamines mescaline and 3,4-dimethoxyphenethylamine (DMPEA), the methoxy-substituted phenylalkylamine derivatives of amphetamines such as trimethoxy-amphetamine, and the chemically related nonnitrogenous analogs of the methoxy-substituted amphetamines, such as myristicin.

MESCALINE

For centuries, the peyote cactus *Lophophora willionsii* (also known as *Anhalonium lewinii*) has constituted an integral part of religious ceremonies and rituals of the Indians of the Southwestern United States and Northern Mexico. In fact, peyote is a religion, and a church has been organized by certain North American Indians who utilize this plant as a sacrament during ritual dances and prayers.

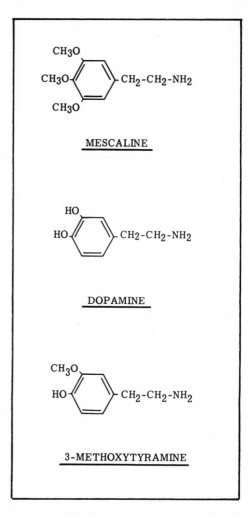

Fig. 1.

Structure of mescaline and
related biogenic amines.

In 1888 Lewin recognized the hallucinogenic properties of peyote, and
in 1896 Heffter systematically studied the constituents of this cactus and
demonstrated that mescaline was the psychoactive principle responsible for
its pharmacologic and toxicologic effects in man (Holmstedt, 1967). In
1918, Spath synthesized mescaline and characterized it as 3,4,5-trimethoxy-
phenylethylamine (Fig. 1). Peyote is not the sole source of mescaline; it is
also present in other species of cacti and is thought to be responsible for
their hallucinatory effects (Gutierrez-Noriega, 1950).

Mescaline is structurally similar to the catecholamine dopamine and to
its metabolite 3-methoxytyramine (Fig. 1). Certain pharmacologic effects of
mescaline which are similar to those produced by sympathomimetic amines

include anxiety, pupillary dilatation, and tachycardia. However, its most notable pharmacologic actions are related to its CNS effects, which include visual hallucinations consisting of the appearance of geometric designs, brightly colored spots and lights, and altered color and space perception.

The close similarity between mescaline and the metabolic products of the catecholamines has stimulated research into the use of mescaline as an experimental tool in attempts to understand schizophrenia and other mental diseases. Mescaline has been used to test the hypothesis of a biochemical basis of schizophrenia. It is not difficult to imagine that the formation of a mescaline-like substance could be produced aberrantly during catecholamine metabolism and could theoretically account for this mental disease.

In Vitro Metabolism of Mescaline

By simply studying mescaline's chemical structure, one would expect it to be oxidatively deaminated like other phenethylamines. Indeed, results of *in vivo* and *in vitro* studies indicate that mescaline is oxidatively deaminated by an amine oxidase to form 3,4,5-trimethoxyphenylacetic acid (TMPA) (Fig. 2). However, this reaction is a source of much controversy because several enzymes can catalyze it. These enzymes are classified by their differential susceptibility to inhibitors and by their relative affinities for certain substrates. One amine oxidase, amphetamine oxidase, catalyzes the metabolism of *a*-methylated phenethylamines such as amphetamine (Axelrod, 1954). The other amine oxidases are incapable of metabolizing such compounds. The most extensively studied amine oxidase is monoamine oxidase (MAO) which is differentiated from the others by its resistance to the inhibitory effect of semicarbazides. MAO oxidatively deaminates monoamines such as epinephrine, norepinephrine, dopamine, serotonin, and phenethylamine. Zeller (1963) states that it is a "well-known fact that mescaline is not attacked by MAO, although this biogenic amine appears to fulfill all the necessary structural requirements for being an excellent substrate of this enzyme."

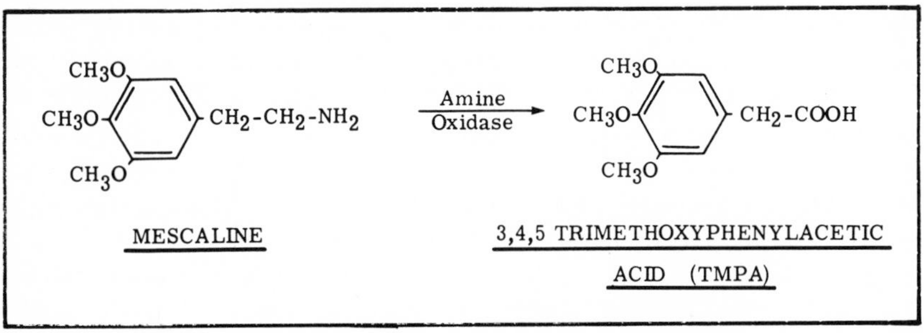

Fig. 2. Metabolism of mescaline by monoamine oxidase.

In 1938, Bernheim and Bernheim, utilizing a rabbit liver preparation, studied the metabolism of mescaline *in vitro* and isolated TMPA as a biotransformation product. They called the enzyme responsible for this conversion mescaline oxidase, assuming that it was a monoamine oxidase, which differed from the typical MAO since it was inhibited by cyanide (MAO is not inhibited by cyanide). In contrast to rabbit liver, when liver from other species (dog, rat, guinea pig, and cat) was used as the enzyme source, little or no TMPA was formed from mescaline (Blaschko, *et al.*, 1937).

Studies by Blaschko (1944) and Steensholt (1947) revealed that the effects of inhibitors and heavy metal salts on this enzyme in rabbit liver differed from those expected with MAO. They therefore cast doubt that the mescaline oxidase in rabbit liver was simply monoamine oxidase and suggested that some other amine oxidase was involved in the metabolism of mescaline.

Zeller and co-workers (Zeller *et al.*, 1958; Zeller, 1963), investigating the effects of inhibitors on the mescaline oxidase derived from rabbit liver, found it to be affected by those inhibitors which would categorize the enzyme as a diamine oxidase (DAO), a group of amine oxidases which is sensitive to the inhibitory effects of semicarbazide and whose substrates include histamine (although the latter is also a weak substrate for MAO). They found that partially purified hog DAO deaminated mescaline and that the rabbit liver enzyme was blocked by all typical DAO inhibitors but not by the classical MAO inhibitors, such as iproniazid and pargyline. Thus, Zeller (1963) stated that the rabbit liver mescaline oxidase described by Bernheim and Bernheim displayed the characteristics of a diamine oxidase. Just as histamine is a weak substrate for MAO, Zeller *et al.* (1958) reported that mescaline is also a weak substrate for MAO isolated from mouse and hog liver mitochondria. In contrast, the MAO derived from rabbit liver mitochondria was incapable of oxidatively deaminating mescaline.

In an attempt to clarify this enigma (i.e., the failure of mescaline to serve as a substrate for MAO), Zeller (1963) synthesized a series of amines, including their trimethoxy derivatives, in order to develop a hypothetical model for the active site and to determine the substrate requirements for MAO derived from beef and rabbit liver mitochondria. The model of the active site of MAO was shown to have no space for three consecutive large residues such as the three methoxy residues of mescaline, and thus did not permit mescaline to react with the active site of MAO. These data appear to explain why mescaline is a poor substrate for MAO in liver.

Most *in vitro* studies of mescaline metabolism have been conducted with liver tissue. However, recently Seiler and Demisch (1971) investigated mescaline metabolism by homogenates of mouse brain. They found that the

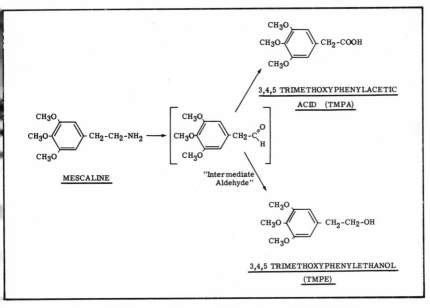

Fig. 3. Mechanism of the metabolism of mescaline by MAO.

deamination of mescaline in brain proceeded slowly and that it was inhibited by the classical MAO inhibitors (iproniazid, tranylcypromine, and pargyline) but not by an inhibitor of DAO (semicarbazide). Another enzyme present in rat brain can also oxidize mescaline (Mitra and Guha, 1973), as well as amphetamine. Additional evidence for a possible role of MAO in the oxidative deamination of mescaline will be discussed in the section describing metabolism *in vivo*.

The pathway for the oxidative deamination of mescaline *in vitro* in all likelihood is similar to that for other phenylethylamines, proceeding either in the direction of the alcohol 3,4,5-trimethoxyphenylethanol (TMPE) or the acid (TMPA) with the aldehyde serving as the intermediate (Fig. 3). Indeed, Goldstein *et al.* (1961) identified TMPE as a metabolite of mescaline *in vivo*.

Although oxidative deamination is the major metabolic pathway for mescaline, studies *in vitro* have demonstrated the existence of several minor metabolic pathways. Mescaline can be O-demethylated by a liver microsomal enzyme system to form 3,4-dimethoxy-5-hydroxy-phenethylamine and 3,5-dimethoxy-4-hydroxyphenethylamine (Axelrod, 1956; Daly *et al.*, 1962) (Fig. 4). This enzyme reaction requires NADPH and molecular oxygen and is a dealkylation reaction.

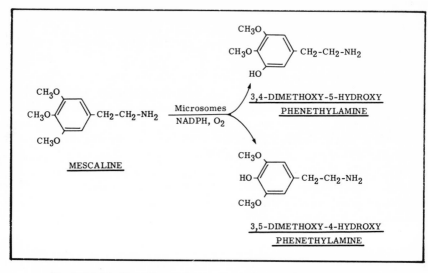

Fig. 4. Metabolism of mescaline by liver microsomal enzyme systems.

Another minor pathway of mescaline metabolism *in vitro* is N-methylation. Axelrod (1961) isolated an enzyme from rabbit lung which was capable of catalyzing the N-methylation of indolealkylamines, including serotonin and tryptamine. This enzyme is associated with the soluble fraction of lung and requires Mg^{++} and S-adenosylmethionine as the methyl donor. This enzyme was also found to catalyze the N-methylation of several phenethylamines, including mescaline; however, the rate of metabolism of the phenethylamines is only about one-fifth that of the indolealkylamines and probably is not significant in the overall peripheral metabolism of mescaline (Axelrod, 1962).

Goldstein and Contrera (1962) have demonstrated that *in vitro* mescaline is a poor substrate for the enzyme dopamine-β-hydroxylase. The product of this enzymic reaction is β-hydroxymescaline. However, although this reaction has been demonstrated to occur *in vitro*, Musacchio and Goldstein (1967) failed to detect any β-hydroxymescaline in rat urine after ^{14}C-mescaline administration. If this compound were formed *in vivo*, it would represent an inactivation of mescaline, since psychopharmacologic evaluation of this compound revealed that it produced no bizarre behavioral effects in animals at doses four times the dose of mescaline that produces bizarre behavior. Thus it is unlikely that the behavioral effects of mescaline are mediated by this β-hydroxylated metabolite (Musacchio and Goldstein, 1967).

Studies with Mescaline *In Vivo*

Tissue Distribution

It was not until the early 1950's when Cochin *et al.* (1951), using non-radioactive methodology designed to measure organic amines, and Block *et al.* (1952a), using ^{14}C-mescaline, studied the tissue distribution of the compound in dog and mouse. These investigators found the highest concentration of mescaline in kidney, liver, and spleen and showed that these organs contained several times the level of radioactivity found in brain and plasma. Block *et al.* (1952b) found that after liver homogenates from mice injected with ^{14}C-mescaline were hydrolyzed and subjected to paper chromatography, the radioactivity was bound to a constituent of the liver protein fraction and was primarily in the form of the parent compound.

Recently, Shah *et al.* (1973b), studying the tissue distribution of mescaline in the mouse, confirmed the earlier studies of Block and his co-workers and demonstrated that 15 minutes after the i.p. injection of ^{14}C-mescaline to pregnant rats, mescaline was present in the following tissues in descending order of activity: kidney, liver, lung, spleen, heart, and brain. Brain contained about 10-30 times less mescaline than any of these other organs. One hour after injection, the activity in other tissues had decreased by as much as 50%, whereas the activity in the brain had increased by approximately one-third. According to Block *et al.* (1952b), it is not until 2 to 3 hours after mescaline administration that hallucinogenic activity occurs in the mouse. This occurs at a time when the brain levels had already begun to decline (although not to the same extent as was evidenced in other tissues). In brain, the ratio of mescaline to its major metabolite, TMPA, is about 10:1 at 15 minutes and 4 hours after mescaline administration. In monkey, mescaline's tissue distribution is similar to that found in other species. However, very high concentrations of radioactivity (not necessarily mescaline) were present in bone marrow and glandular tissue such as adrenal gland, pancreas, and submandibular gland (Taska and Schoolar, 1973). Fat was one of the few tissues examined which had less radioactivity than blood.

Neff *et al.* (1964) studied the distribution of ^{14}C-mescaline in the cat brain. They found maximum concentrations of mescaline in brain between ½ and 2 hours after injection, and the drug levels gradually declined thereafter. They found that mescaline was preferentially concentrated in the cortical and subcortical gray matter (cell bodies), whereas white matter (primarily myelinated nerve fibers) accumulated only low levels of mescaline. After 1 hour, the levels of mescaline were highest in the pituitary (which lies outside of the blood-brain barrier), followed in descending order by cortex, thalamus, hypothalamus; then by cerebellum, caudate, midbrain, and pons (all containing similar concentrations); and finally by medulla and spinal cord which contained the lowest concentrations of mescaline. Similar results were reported in monkey brain using autoradiography (Taska and Schoolar, 1973). These latter investigators attributed the poor distribution of mescaline across the blood-brain barrier to the high degree of ionization (99.3%) of mescaline at physiologic pH and to the low lipid solubility of the un-ionized form of mescaline.

Sethy and Winter (1973) studied the effect of chronic treatment of rats with mescaline on the concentrations of drug in brain and liver. They found the level of drug in these tissues to be lower in chronically treated rats (40 mg/kg i.p. for 3 days) at all time periods studied (20, 30, and 60 minutes) than in those given only a single injection of mescaline. The reason for this difference is obscure. One possible explanation might be more rapid metabolism.

Recently, Shah and Gibson (1973) studied the effect of the antipsychotic drug chlorpromazine on the concentration of mescaline in mouse brain and liver. A single injection of chlorpromazine 30 minutes or 4 hours prior to ^{14}C-mescaline resulted in markedly higher concentrations (3 to 5 times) of the latter drug in brain and liver of animals sacrificed 3 hours after mescaline administration. After chronic pretreatment with chlorpromazine for 5 days, the concentrations of ^{14}C-mescaline were 4 to 10 times higher in the brain and liver than in saline pretreated controls. The mechanism for this is not known. However, other studies have shown that chlorpromazine does not block the oxidative deamination of mescaline (Shah et al., 1972), nor does it influence the initial accumulation of mescaline in the brain. (Shah and Green, 1973). Its effect on tissue distribution was probably not related to tranquilization since reserpine, another tranquilizer, did not produce a similar accumulation of mescaline in tissue (Shah et al., 1973a).

It is thought, and has been dramatized in the lay literature, that hallucinogens and psychotomimetics might adversely affect the fetus. Indeed, Geber (1967) has demonstrated that mescaline can induce congenital malformations in hamsters. Studies to determine the ability of ^{14}C-mescaline to enter the fetus have been conducted in pregnant mice (Shah et al., 1973b). This drug is distributed similarly in fetal and maternal tissues, except that in brain the concentrations of mescaline are 2 to 4 times higher in the fetus than in the mother. Perhaps this is related to an incompletely developed blood-brain barrier in the fetus rather than to any preferential uptake into the fetal brain. In pregnant monkey, ^{14}C-mescaline also crosses the placental barrier and distributes similarly in fetal and maternal tissues, with high concentrations in lung, liver, and kidney, and low concentrations in blood and brain (Taska and Schoolar, 1973).

Plasma Levels

Studies of several animal species have demonstrated that mescaline is present in whole blood after the administration of ^{14}C-mescaline by various routes. The mescaline in whole blood appears to be distributed between both plasma and erythrocytes so that at certain times after its administration the concentration of mescaline may be higher in whole blood than in plasma (Block *et al.*, 1952c; Cochin *et al.*, 1951; Neff *et al.*, 1964; Taska and Schoolar, 1973). In contrast, studies in humans given ^{14}C-mescaline showed that the levels of radioactivity in whole blood were approximately half those found in plasma, indicating that virtually all the radioactivity in the blood was in the plasma (Charalampous *et al.*, 1966).

After intravenous administration of ^{14}C-mescaline to cats, Neff *et al.* (1964) determined its rate of disappearance from plasma and blood by measuring concentrations between ½ and 6 hours. Over this time interval, mescaline disappeared from whole blood and plasma at a first-order rate; the $t_{1/2}$ was about 2 hours. A similar $t_{1/2}$ was seen for the disappearance of mescaline from cerebrospinal fluid. In plasma and CSF, the concentrations of mescaline were about twice those of its metabolite TMPA.

After the intraperitoneal administration of mescaline to pregnant mice, peak plasma concentrations of mescaline were reached in 15 minutes and declined in a multiphasic fashion during the next 24 hours to barely detectable levels (Shah *et al.*, 1973b).

Mokrasch and Stevenson (1959), using a nonradioactive analytical procedure, measured plasma mescaline levels for up to 8 hours in human volunteers given 350-400 mg of mescaline intravenously. Mescaline concentrations in plasma disappeared in a multiphasic manner, rapidly declining over the first 2 hours, gradually decreasing over the next 6 hours with the suggestion of an increase in plasma drug concentrations 5 hours after drug administration. Charalampous *et al.* (1966) administered ^{14}C-mescaline orally to human volunteers and measured the plasma concentration of total radioactivity (mescaline plus its metabolites) over the next 12 hours. Peak plasma concentrations were reached at 2 hours and declined over the next 10 hours. It is unfortunate that these authors did not differentiate the parent compound from its metabolites, since more meaningful information could have been obtained from this study, such as the kinetics of mescaline absorption and disappearance.

Excretion and *In Vivo* Metabolism

Studies on the excretion of mescaline and its metabolites have been possible primarily as a result of the availability of radiolabeled mescaline.

In various species of animals, mescaline and mescaline metabolites are excreted predominantly in urine. In dogs, Slotta and Muller (1936) found 38% of a dose of mescaline excreted as TMPA and none excreted as the parent compound. In contrast, Cochin *et al.* (1951) reported in dogs only trace quantities of TMPA excreted in urine and 28-46% of the administered dose excreted as parent drug. However, Spector (1961) did isolate TMPA from dog urine and found it to be the major metabolite present; he also found a significant amount of unchanged mescaline excreted in the urine.

In man, the percentage of administered dose of mescaline recovered unchanged in urine from study to study ranges from 12 to 67% (mean = 31%) of the dose in 6 hours (Mokrasch and Stevenson, 1959); 35% in 24 hours (Harley-Mason *et al.*, 1958); 30% in 8 hours (Salomon *et al.*, 1949); and up to 58% in 24 hours (Richter, 1938). In addition to excretion of the mescaline in urine, Mokrasch and Stevenson (1959) could account for about 8% of the administered dose of mescaline as its acidic metabolite TMPA. In contrast, others (Slotta and Muller, 1936; Harley-Mason *et al.*, 1958) were unable to detect TMPA in human urine.

After oral administration of ^{14}C-mescaline to human volunteers, Charalampous *et al.* (1966) recovered from urine essentially all the radiolabel within 30 hours—about 60% as unchanged mescaline and 30% as TMPA. The discrepancies between different studies with respect to the percentages of mescaline and its metabolites excreted in urine may be related to multiple factors. For example, one which apparently has not been considered in man is the possibility of an alternate route of excretion, i.e., feces. Within 10 minutes after administration of ^{14}C-mescaline to monkeys, radioactivity was present in bile at about the same concentration as found in plasma (Taska and Schoolar, 1973). However, from 1 to 16 hours after mescaline administration, the concentration of radioactivity in bile was 600 times that present in plasma! Since previously reported studies made no mention of any attempt to study fecal excretion of mescaline and its metabolites, the possibility exists that in some cases the drug may be excreted to an appreciable extent via this route. Of course, the presence of radioactivity in bile does not necessarily mean that mescaline is excreted in feces since the drug could be reabsorbed further down the intestinal tract and subsequently be excreted in urine.

The oxidative deamination of mescaline to form TMPA *in vitro* has been described earlier (Fig. 3). This is the major metabolic pathway for mescaline *in vivo*, and the acidic metabolite, TMPA, accounts for between 8 and 30% of an administered dose of mescaline, depending upon the studies cited. TMPA has been isolated from urine and tissue of many animal species, including cat (Neff *et al.*, 1964), rabbit (Slotta and Muller, 1936), dog (Slotta and Muller, 1936; Spector, 1961), rat (Goldstein *et al.*, 1961;

Musacchio and Goldstein, 1967), monkey (Taska and Schoolar, 1973), and man (Mokrasch and Stevenson, 1959). Its identification has been proved by several physicochemical criteria, including elemental analysis, co-crystalization to constant specific activity with authentic TMPA, infrared spectroscopy, mixed melting points, and paper chromatography (Spector, 1961; Charalampous et al., 1964).

TMPA is usually excreted unchanged in urine. However, in man and the chimpanzee, phenylacetic acid derivatives can be excreted as glutamine conjugates (Williams, 1963). In this respect, TMPA and its O-demethylated metabolite 3,4-dihydroxy-5-methoxyphenylacetic acid are indeed excreted, in part, as glutamine conjugates (Fig. 5).

Although an aldehyde intermediate in the oxidative deamination of mescaline has not yet been isolated, indirect evidence for its existence is the isolation and identification of TMPE, the alcoholic counterpart of TMPA. (See Fig. 3.) Goldstein et al. (1961) isolated TMPE from urine after the administration of ^{14}C-mescaline to rats. In control rats, the ratio of acid (TMPA) to alcohol (TMPE) was 10:1. However, pretreatment of rats with various inhibitors of oxidative deamination resulted in an increased production of the alcohol at the expense of the acid. The maximum effect

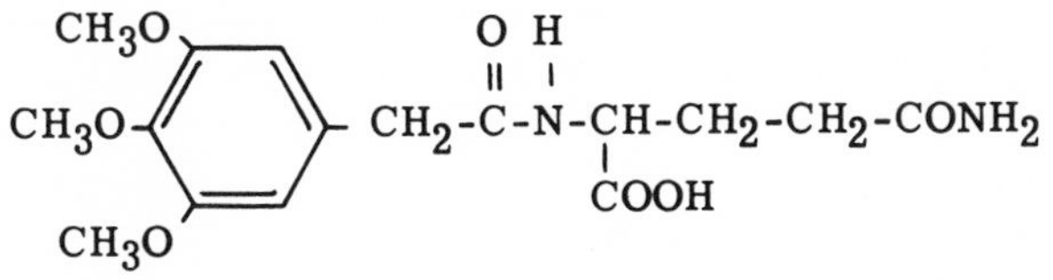

3,4,5-TRIMETHOXYPHENACETYL GLUTAMINE

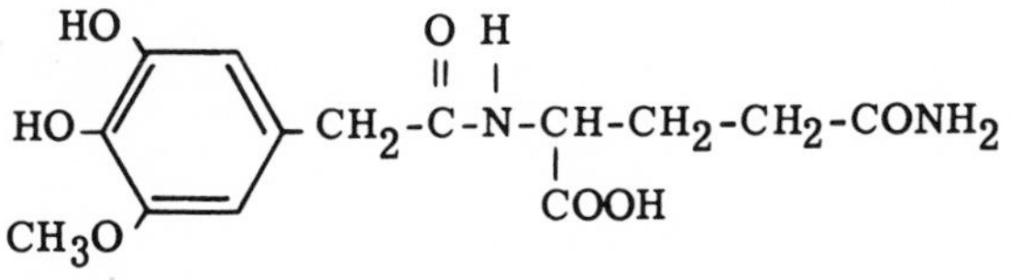

3,4-DIHYDROXY-5-METHOXYPHENACETYL GLUTAMINE

Fig. 5. Structures of several glutamine conjugates of mescaline metabolites.

occurred in rats pretreated with calcium carbimide, an aldehyde oxidase inhibitor. Under these experimental conditions, equal quantities of alcohol and acid were excreted in urine. TMPE has also been isolated from the livers of monkeys treated with ^{14}C-mescaline (Taska and Schoolar, 1973).

In vivo, mescaline is also N-acetylated. Certain other amines, such as tyramine, tryptamine, and serotonin, are substrates for an N-acetylase system localized in liver (Weissbach et al., 1962). Mescaline could also be a substrate for this enzyme system in vivo since N-acetylmescaline and metabolites thereof have been isolated from tissue and urine of animals and man given mescaline (Fig. 6). In monkeys, N-acetylmescaline has been identified as the major metabolite present in liver tissue (Taska and Schoolar, 1972, 1973) although it represents only about 10 to 15% of the hepatic concentration of total mescaline. In rats, N-acetylmescaline (and its metabolic products) accounted for about 30% of the administered dose of mescaline recovered in the urine (Musacchio and Golstein, 1967). In man, it is excreted only in trace quantities. However, one of its metabolites, N-acetyl-3,4-dimethoxy-5-hydroxyphenethylamine (Fig. 6) is excreted in human urine, accounting for 5% of the administered dose of mescaline

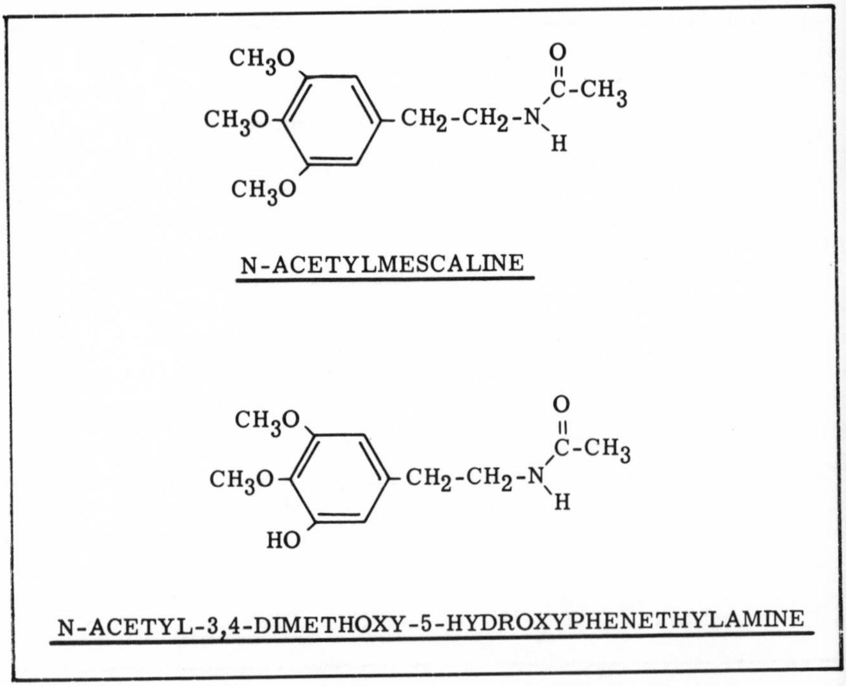

Fig. 6. Structures of N-acetylated mescaline and a further metabolite.

Charalampous *et al.*, 1966). Charalampous and co-workers (1966) reported that, in human urine, TMPA and N-acetylated derivatives of mescaline represented about 30 and 5% of the administered dose of mescaline, respectively. However, in cerebrospinal fluid, concentrations of N-acetylated derivatives of mescaline were greater than concentrations of TMPA. They suggested that in the CNS, N-acetylation may be more important than oxidative deamination as a detoxification mechanism for mescaline. Although this finding is of interest, much more research is required to establish its significance.

As stated earlier, mescaline is O-demethylated *in vitro*. Therefore, as expected, O-demethylated metabolites have been isolated from urine after the administration of ^{14}C-mescaline to man (Charalampous *et al.*, 1966). These metabolites included N-acetyl-3,4-dimethoxy-5-hydroxy-phenethylamine (as an unidentified conjugate) and an unidentified O-demethylated derivative of TMPA. Earlier human studies by Harley-Mason *et al.* (1958) demonstrated the presence of 3,4-dihydroxy-5-methoxyphenyl-acetylglutamine. (See Fig. 5.) This obviously represents a partial O-demethylation of TMPA, and subsequent conjugation with glutamine Williams, 1963). Likewise, in rats treated with ^{14}C-mescaline, several O-dealkylated compounds were detected in urine (Musacchio and Goldstein, 1967), and include N-acetyl-3,5-dimethoxy-4-hydroxyphenethylamine and its isomer N-acetyl-3,4-dimethoxy-5-hydroxyphenethylamine (Fig. 7).

Based upon the small percentage of O-demethylated metabolites of mescaline found relative to other metabolites, O-demethylation probably represents a secondary pathway. In this connection, studies in rats Musacchio and Goldstein, 1967) and in man (Charalampous *et al.*, 1966) demonstrated that after the administration of N-acetylmescaline-^{14}C, greater percentages of O-demethylated metabolites were found in urine than after the administration of ^{14}C-mescaline, suggesting that N-acetylation preceded O-demethylation. Since N-acetylmescaline undergoes more extensive O-dealkylation than either mescaline or TMPA, Musacchio and Goldstein (1967) postulated that this "might be explained on the basis of the greater penetration of N-acetyl derivatives into the microsomes where the demethylating enzymes are localized." These investigators found that N-acetylmescaline was not oxidatively deaminated and stated that O-demethylation represented the only process by which this compound became hydrophilic before its excretion in either free or conjugated form.

As stated earlier, mescaline is a substrate for dopamine-β-hydroxylase *in vitro*; however, Goldstein and co-workers (Musacchio and Goldstein, 1967) were unable to detect evidence of β-hydroxylation of mescaline *in vivo* in rats.

In addition to the more conventional pathways for mescaline

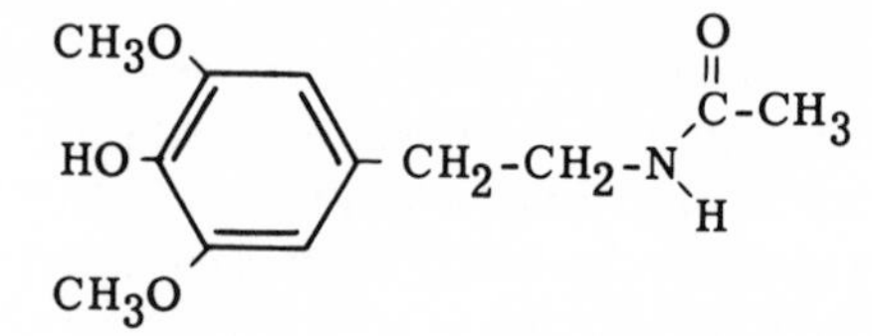

N-ACETYL-3,5-DIMETHOXY-4-HYDROXYPHENETHYLAMINE

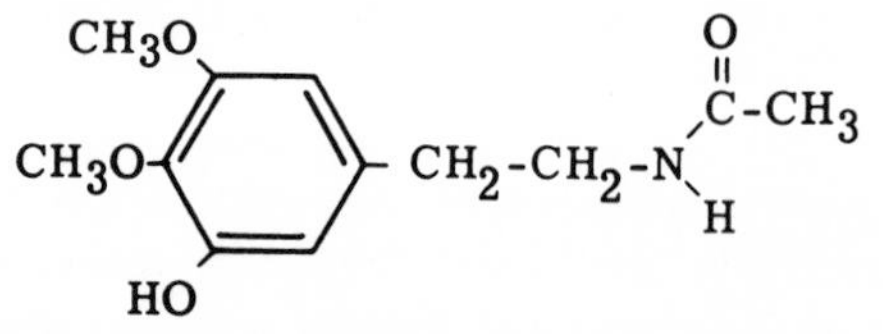

N-ACETYL-3,4-DIMETHOXY-5-HYDROXYPHENETHYLAMINE

Fig. 7. Structures of additional N-acetylated mescaline metabolites.

metabolism, Fischer (1955) proposed that mescaline can be cyclized *in vivo* to an indolic compound resembling lysergic acid diethylamide (LSD) and that this latter compound may be responsible for the psychotomimetic effects of mescaline. Although this is an interesting hypothesis, it would be necessary to demonstrate the occurrence of such a compound in man after mescaline administration using rigorous techniques to rule out the possibilities of its being artifactual.

In summary, mescaline is metabolized *in vivo* by several pathways; the primary metabolic route being oxidative deamination to TMPA. Other metabolic routes for mescaline include N-acetylation and O-demethylation. Metabolic products representing combinations of several of these metabolic pathways can occur.

Factors Affecting Mescaline Metabolism

The metabolism and disposition of mescaline can be affected by prior treatment with other pharmacologic agents. For example, pretreatment of mice with chlorpromazine can markedly prolong the disappearance of nescaline from the brain and other tissues (Shah and Gibson, 1973) as has een discussed previously.

Rats treated with aldehyde dehydrogenase inhibitors (disulfuram or alcium carbimide) prior to mescaline administration excreted less TMPA in neir urine and more TMPE (Goldstein et al., 1961). Goldstein and co-workers (1961) have demonstrated that treating rats with the amine oxidase nhibitor iproniazid prior to the administration of ^{14}C-mescaline markedly lters the metabolic route of mescaline. The iproniazid-treated rats excreted bout three times the quantity of unchanged mescaline in urine as did ntreated rats. Urine from the group treated with iproniazid had con-iderably less TMPA than urine from the control group.

Musacchio and Goldstein (1967) demonstrated that the urinary ex-retion of N-acetylmescaline and its metabolites was increased in rats pre-reated with the MAO inhibitor iproniazid before the administration of ^{14}C-nescaline. As in their earlier studies, they showed that in vivo, iproniazid nhibited the metabolism of mescaline. Their results were consistent with arlier findings in vitro of Zeller et al. (1958), who showed that in an en-yme system utilizing liver homogenates, mescaline was a substrate for)AO and that iproniazid inhibited this enzyme system. Thus, iproniazid ppears to inhibit both MAO and DAO.

Seiler and Demisch (1971), studying the effects of inhibitors of nescaline deamination in brain, found that iproniazid and other MAO nhibitors inhibited the conversion of mescaline to TMPA. However, in neir study, semicarbazide, an inhibitor of DAO, was found to be a very oor inhibitor of the oxidative deamination of mescaline, suggesting that in rain, unlike liver, MAO is the enzyme responsible for oxidative eamination of mescaline. In all probability the major urinary metabolites f mescaline are mostly a reflection of its hepatic metabolism which are atalyzed by DAO. However, the metabolism of mescaline occurring in the rain may be of greater significance with respect to its duration of phar-nacologic action.

harmacologic Activity: Mescaline vs. an Active Metabolite

That mescaline's pharmacologic activity was possibly due to the ormation of metabolic products was first proposed by Block et al. 1952a,b,c), who observed in animals that the apparent hallucinogenic ffects did not correlate temporally with peak concentrations of unchanged nescaline in liver. In man, Mokrasch and Stevenson (1959) found a lack of orrelation between the behavioral activity produced by mescaline and its oncentration in blood. Generally, the peak psychologic effects occurred 1-hours after the peak blood levels and after the peak urinary excretion of nescaline and its metabolites. Again, this suggested that mescaline's psychotomimetic effects depended upon its biotransformation to an active metabolite. Indeed, in their studies in man the peak psychologic effects produced after mescaline adminstration were positively correlated to the peak blood concentration of mescaline's major metabolite, TMPA. This, however, does not provide any clue to the possible identification of TMPA as an active metabolite in man, if in fact, one exists, especially since no physiologic or psychologic effects could be elicited in human subjects after administering TMPA at dosages as high as 750 mg (Slotta and Muller, 1936; Charalampous *et al.*, 1964). In contrast, oral dosages of 350-500 mg of mescaline produce definite physiologic and psychologic effects.

Attempting to determine whether *N*-acetylmescaline, another metabolite of mescaline, was in part responsible for mescaline's behavioral activity, Charalampous *et al.* (1966) administered this metabolite orally to man. At dosages of 300 to 750 mg, *N*-acetylmescaline produced no behavioral or physiological effects, thus discounting the possibility that this compound or any of its metabolic products were responsible for the hallucinogenic effects of mescaline. Similarly, failure to detect the β-hydroxylated product of mescaline (β-hydroxymescaline) in rat urine after administration of mescaline suggests it, too, is not a candidate for the active metabolite of mescaline (Musacchio and Goldstein, 1967).

Attempts to attribute the pharmacologic activity of mescaline to metabolite have been unsuccessful. Of course, the possibility remains that mescaline itself "triggers" some endogenous transducer or transmitter in the CNS which slowly produces mental abberations at a time when mescaline levels in brain and blood are already declining.

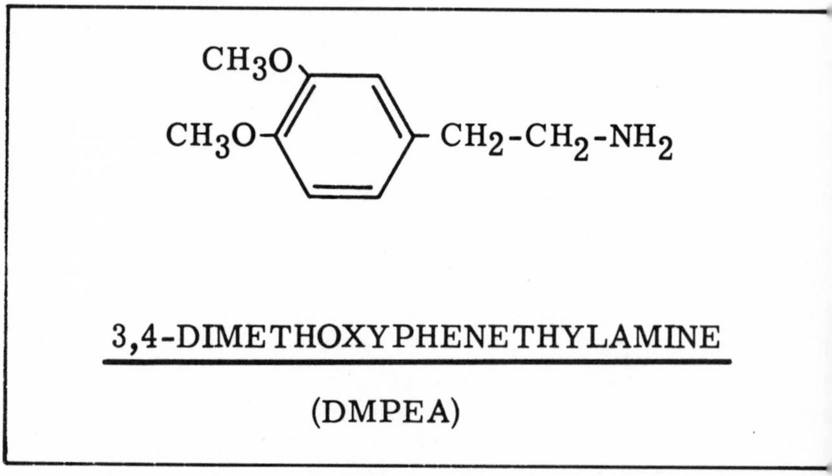

CH_3O

CH_3O — ⟨ ⟩ — CH_2-CH_2-NH_2

3,4-DIMETHOXYPHENETHYLAMINE

(DMPEA)

Fig. 8. Structure of 3,4-dimethoxyphenethylamine (DMPEA).

4-DIMETHOXYPHENETHYLAMINE (DMPEA)

Although DMPEA (Fig. 8) is not a drug of abuse, it will be considered here since it is a phenethylamine derivative structurally related to mescaline and because it and/or its metabolites have been implicated as possible endogenous psychotomimetics.

In 1952 Osmond and Symthies proposed that schizophrenia and other mental disturbances might be the result of a dysfunction in normal metabolic pathways which could give rise to the endogenous production of psychotomimetic compounds. This theory stimulated much research to find compounds which could be isolated from human blood or urine and which were both unique to schizophrenics and might themselves produce psychologic effects. In 1962, Friedhoff and Van Winkle first reported on the isolation and characterization of DMPEA from urine of schizophrenic patients. Since then a great deal of controversy has occurred regarding the clinical significance of this finding since some investigators have shown that DMPEA is also excreted in urines from normal subjects (Kuehl et al., 1966) while other investigators have failed to detect DMPEA in urine from schizophrenics (Perry et al., 1964).

DMPEA is chemically the dimethoxylated product of dopamine. It is known that dopamine is metabolized normally to the O-methoxylated compounds 3-methoxytyramine and to homovanillic acid (Fig. 9), compounds closely related to DMPEA. In vitro studies show that dopamine can be O-methylated in both the 3 and 4 position by specific O-methyltransferases localized in liver and brain (Senoh et al., 1959; Goldstein et al.,

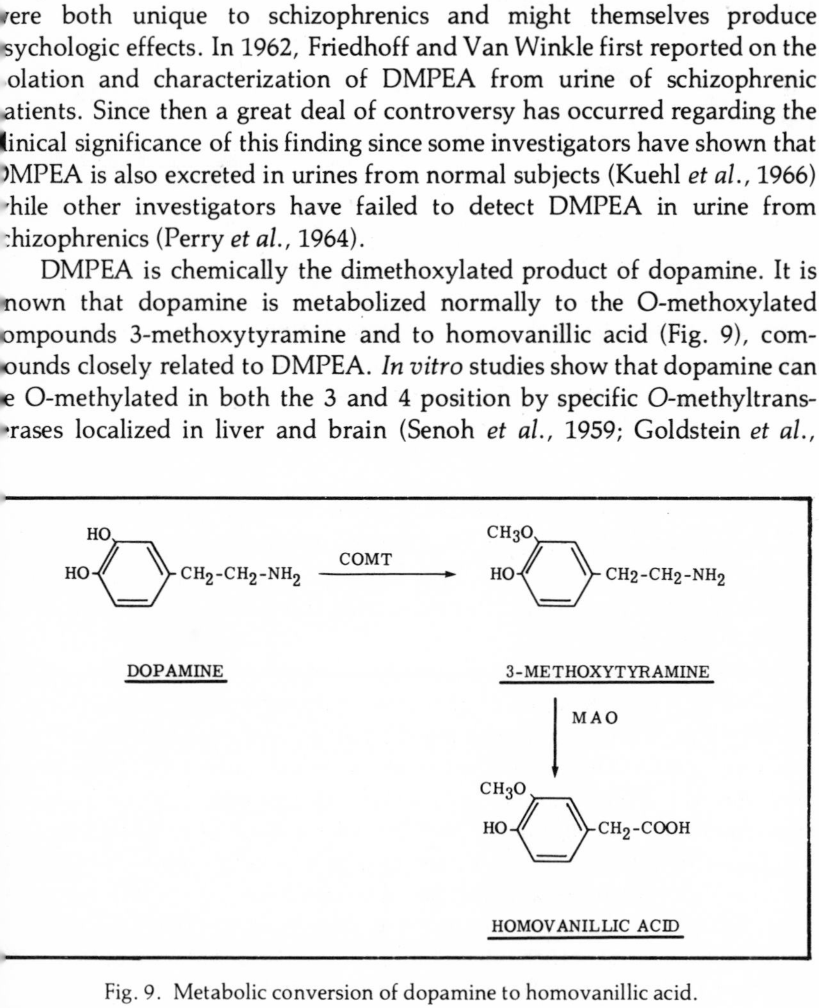

HO—⟨ ⟩—CH₂-CH₂-NH₂ —COMT→ HO—⟨ ⟩—CH₂-CH₂-NH₂

DOPAMINE   3-METHOXYTYRAMINE

| MAO

CH₃O—⟨ ⟩—CH₂-COOH

HOMOVANILLIC ACID

Fig. 9. Metabolic conversion of dopamine to homovanillic acid.

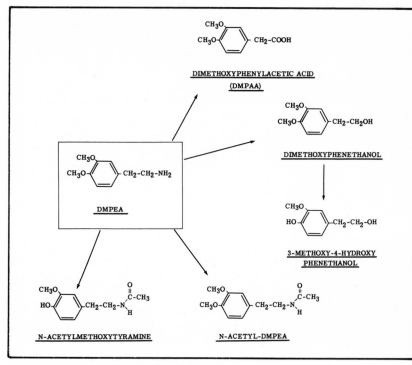

Fig. 10. Metabolic pathways of DMPEA.

1959). Recently, a mammalian enzyme termed guaiacol-O-methy. transferase (GOMT) was described which converts 4-methoxytryamine t DMPEA (Friedhoff et al., 1972; Friedhoff, 1973). Although these enzymati pathways can occur in vitro, no indisputable evidence exists that they ar significant in vivo.

Schweitzer and Freidhoff (1966) isolated and identified sever metabolites from the urine of rats after intraperitoneal administration c ^{14}C-DMPEA. They found unchanged DMPEA representing about 16% the total urinary radioactivity. The major metabolite of DMPEA in viv was dimethoxyphenylacetic acid (DMPA) (the product of oxidativ deamination) which accounted for 77% of the dose of radioactivity (Fig 10). Demethylation of DMPEA must also be a metabolic pathway since, N acetylmethoxytyramine glucuronide accounted for 6% of the recovere dose. Similar conclusions were drawn by Sargent et al. (1967). In additior trace quantities of other metabolites were tentatively identified. Th metabolic pathways for DMPEA are illustrated in Fig. 10.

In the rat, DMPEA and mescaline appear to be metabolized pre-dominantly by oxidative deamination to the corresponding acids. In contrast, in man, Friedhoff and Hollister (1966) demonstrated that DMPEA was almost completely metabolized to its acid (DMPA) since less than 1% of the administered dose was recovered in urine as unchanged DMPEA. In contrast, in these same subjects, about 23% of the administered mescaline was excreted as unchanged drug while only about 18% was excreted as the acid (TMPA) during the same time period.

Thus, although DMPEA is not a drug of abuse, and when given exogenously is not hallucinogenic, its metabolism is of interest since it may serve as a precursor for an endogenous hallucinogen, and because of the differences which exist between its metabolism and that of mescaline, a compound which contains only one additional methoxy group.

SUBSTITUTED METHOXYAMPHETAMINES

The methoxy-substituted derivatives of amphetamines comprise a group of compounds which have reputations as potent psychotomimetics among drug abusers as well as among investigators of drugs of abuse. These compounds are structurally related both to amphetamine and mescaline. Their chemical names are rarely cited and they are usually designated by abbreviations and initials as if someone spilled a plate of "alphabet" soup. They are fondly known, for example, as DOM(STP), DOET, MDA, TMA, TMA-2, TMA-3, DMA, MMDA, and DMMDA. The structures of these compounds and their relative activities are shown in Fig. 11.

The first of these drugs to be studied was 3,4,5-trimethoxy-amphetamine (TMA). Peretz et al. (1955) reported that it produced psychologic effects in man similar to those produced after mescaline ad-ministration. Subsequently, Shulgin and co-workers (Shulgin et al., 1961; Shulgin, 1963, 1964a,b) synthesized and studied the pharmacologic profiles of a large series of methoxy and methylenedioxyamphetamine derivatives. For comparative purposes, they have used "mescaline units" to express their relative potencies in man. Smythies and co-workers (Peretz et al., 1955; Smythies et al., 1967) and Shulgin (1963, 1964a,b) found that not all the studied derivatives of amphetamine were psychotomimetic. In fact, many compounds in this series were without any psychologic activity. Structure-activity studies led them to conclude that methoxy substituents in the 2,4,5 and 3,4,5 positions of the aromatic ring led to the most potent hallucinogens.

From these chemical syntheses, a compound structurally related to 2,4,5-TMA emerged which was found to be 50 to 100 times more potent

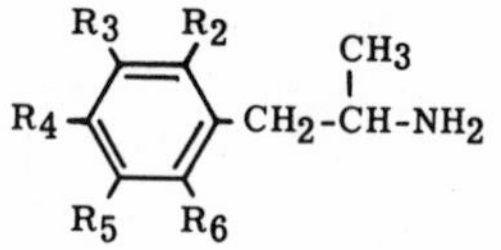

COMPOUND	R_2	R_3	R_4	R_5	R_6	Activity in Mescaline Units
DOM	CH_3O	H	CH_3	CH_3O	H	50-100
DOET	CH_3O	H	C_2H_5	CH_3O	H	50-100
MDA	H	$O-CH_2-O$		H	H	2
TMA	H	CH_3O	CH_3O	CH_3O	H	2
TMA-2	CH_3O	H	CH_3O	CH_3O	H	17
TMA-3	CH_3O	CH_3O	CH_3O	H	H	<2
DMA	CH_3O	H	H	CH_3O	H	8
MMDA	H	$O-CH_2-O$		CH_3O	H	10
DMMDA	CH_3O	$O-CH_2-O$		CH_3O	H	12

Fig. 11. Structures of substituted methoxyamphetamines and their relative potency in mescaline units.

than mescaline (Snyder *et al.*, 1967). It was not long before the potent hallucinogenic properties of this compound, 2,5-methoxy-4-methyl-amphetamine (DOM) were discovered by the "hippie" community in the San Francisco Bay area. The marked "high" and the other psycho-pharmacologic properties of this compound prompted its designation as STP, alluding to the gasoline additive which is widely advertised to energize automobile engines. This drug is reported to produce hallucinations at dosages of 5 to 10 mg (Snyder *et al.*, 1968).

Not much scientific information exists on the physiologic disposition of DOM. When first synthesized by Shulgin, the rationale was to produce an agent that would resist metabolic degradation by O-demethylation of the methoxy group in the para position of the benzene ring of TMA (Snyder *et al.*, 1970). If one prevented this by replacing the methoxy group of TMA with a methyl (as in DOM), then the *p*-hydroxy derivative might not become available for conjugation and subsequent excretion and therefore one might expect a compound with a longer duration of action. In contrast to reports that DOM had prolonged activity, with hallucinations lasting up to 3 days, studies conducted under controlled conditions revealed that its effects dissipated within 8 hours (Snyder *et al.*, 1967; Hollister *et al.*, 1969).

Although no studies have been conducted with DOM *in vitro*, some predictions can be made regarding its metabolism in several *in vitro* enzyme systems. Since these substituted methoxyamphetamines are phenylisopropylamine derivatives (like amphetamine) rather than phenethylamine derivatives (like mescaline), they should not be substrates for monoamine oxidase, and would be expected to inhibit this enzyme. (See Chapter 2). Indeed, in rats, trace quantities of the ketone derived from oxidative deamination of the side chain of DOM were excreted in urine (Ho *et al.*, 1971a) suggesting that, like amphetamine, DOM is a substrate for the microsomal oxidative deamination system in microsomes (although a weak substrate in this species).

Ho and co-workers (1971a) administered DOM to rats and isolated several metabolites from urine and feces. The major urinary metabolite of DOM was 4-hydroxymethyl-DOM (Fig. 12). This compound accounted for 50% of the metabolites isolated in 24-hour urine samples. The alcoholic hydroxy group was further oxidized to a 4-carboxy metabolite, an oxidation reaction known to occur for other drugs, such as ethyl alcohol and Δ⁹-tetrahydrocannabinol. In addition to these metabolites, only small quantities of DOM were excreted unchanged in urine. In feces, DOM is excreted predominantly as the 4-carboxy metabolite, and to a lesser extent as the 4-hydroxymethyl metabolite.

In man, Snyder *et al.* (1967) found that 20% of an ingested dose of DOM was excreted unchanged in urine. They noted a peak excretion of

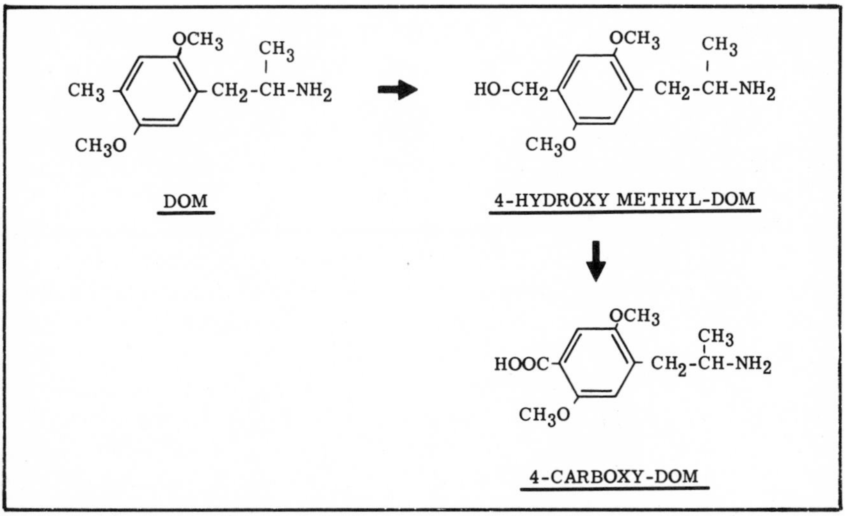

Fig. 12. Metabolic pathway for DOM.

drug between 3 and 6 hours after administration of the drug. This period corresponded to the peak psychologic effects seen in their volunteers. The significance of this is not known.

Ho and co-workers (1971b) administered tritium-labeled DOM to rats and squirrel monkeys and studied the regional distribution of this drug and its metabolites in brain, as well as its rate of appearance into and disappearance from brain. In rats, after intravenous administration of DOM, about 1% of the dose was localized in the brain at 30 to 60 minutes. The disappearance from brain was rapid, and at 4 hours, less than 0.1% of the radioactive dose of DOM was still present in rat brain. In contrast, in monkeys, 8% of the dose was present in brain within 30 to 60 minutes and persisted for a longer time, so that after 4 hours 2% of the total administered dose remained in brain. The explanation for the longer retention of DOM in monkey brain is not known, although their data suggest that the plasma and tissue levels of radioactivity are less overall in rat than in monkey. Although these investigators studied numerous brain regions, they could demonstrate no selective uptake or storage of radioactivity, the distribution appearing homogenous throughout the brain.

Examination by extraction and thin-layer chromatography of the radioactive compounds present in monkey brain revealed that most of the radioactivity present in the tissue was unchanged DOM. About 0.5% was present as the 4-hydroxy metabolite, and a trace quantity as the ketone. In rat brain, the radioactivity was exclusively DOM. These findings strongly suggest that the psychopharmacologic effects of DOM are due to DOM itself rather than to one of its metabolites.

The psychopharmacologic effects of p-methoxyamphetamine (PMA), another methoxy derivative of amphetamine, have been studied in animals and man. In animals. Smythies et al. (1967) reported it to be a potent and long-acting disrupter of normal behavioral patterns. Based upon its structural similarity to an amphetamine metabolite (p-hydroxyamphetamine), they postulated that PMA might be responsible for the psychosis found in conjunction with amphetamine addiction. In man, Shulgin et al. (1969) demonstrated that PMA was hallucinogenic and that its potency relative to mescaline was five times greater (5 MU). Schweitzer et al. (1971) were able to recover from 0.3 to 15% (mean 6.7%) of unchanged PMA from urine of five normal volunteers to whom 10 to 65 mg of PMA were orally administered. Since no attempt was made to control urinary pH, the wide variation may be related to this factor. When these investigators administered large quantities of amphetamine (600 mg) to volunteers, they were unable to detect any PMA in urine, indicating that the PMA-amphetamine psychosis hypothesis is not valid (Angrist et al., 1970).

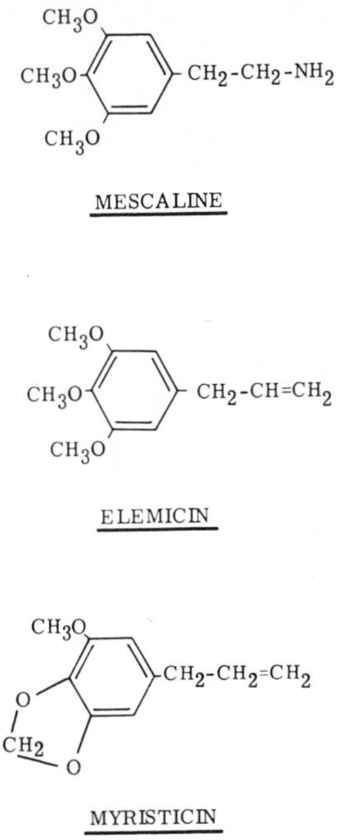

Fig. 13.

Structural relationships between mescaline, elemicin, and myristicin.

NON-NITROGENOUS ANALOGS OF SUBSTITUTED METHOXYAMPHETAMINES

Certain substances, which are non-nitrogenous analogs of the ring-substituted methoxyamphetamines, exist naturally as plant constituents. The most commonly known are myristicin (3-methoxy-4,5-methyl-enedioxyallylbenzene) and elemicin (3,4,5-trimethoxyallylbenzene), chemicals which are thought to be the psychoactive constituents of nutmeg. Their structural resemblance to mescaline, TMA, and MMDA is obvious (Fig. 13). Nutmeg is the common name for the fruit of the nutmeg tree, *Myristica fragrans*. The active pharmacologic ingredients, myristicin and elemicin comprise the major portion of the volatile oil which can be distilled from the remainder of the spice (Shulgin et al., 1967). For centuries it has been known that high doses of nutmeg could produce intoxicating effects in man. However, only in the past 20 years was it recognized that nutmeg was a drug of abuse. Payne (1963) described two cases of deliberate ingestion of powdered nutmeg for its psychotomimetic effects. The users experienced tachycardia, palpitations, and a dreamlike, unreal, detached mental state followed by drowsiness.

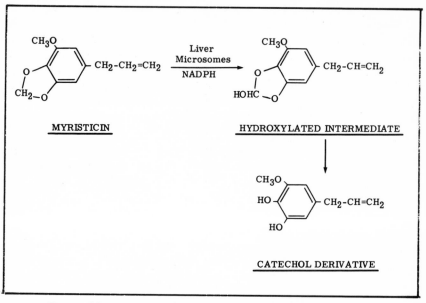

Fig. 14. Myristicin metabolism by liver microsomal enzyme systems.

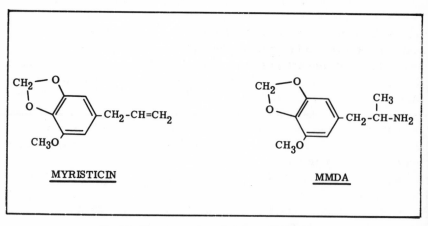

Fig. 15. Structures of myristicin and MMDA.

Again, as in the case of the methoxy-substituted amphetamines, little is known about the physiologic disposition of myristicin and the other non-nitrogenous analogs of amphetamine. Studies *in vitro* with myristicin indicate that an NADPH-dependent microsomal enzyme system from mouse liver can convert myristicin to a catechol by attack at the methylenedioxy bridge (Fig. 14) (Casida *et al.*, 1966). The proposed mechanism of this metabolic conversion was by the elimination of carbon dioxide.

Shulgin and co-workers (Shulgin, 1966; Shulgin *et al.*, 1967) theorized that myristicin could be converted to 3-methoxy-4,5-methylenedioxy-amphetamine (MMDA) in mammalian tissue by an enzymatic process analoguous to transamination (Fig. 15). He also postulated that an oxidative reaction preceded this theoretical transmaination. Braun and Kalbhen (1973), utilizing isolated perfused liver preparations and whole liver homogenates, demonstrated that MMDA could be formed from myristicin in the perfusion fluid and/or in extracts of the incubate from liver homogenate. These findings suggest that indeed the intoxicating effects of nutmeg could be due to the conversion of its major ingredients, myristicin and elemicin, to methoxylated amphetamines.

REFERENCES

Angrist, B.M., Schweitzer, J.W., Friedhoff, A.J., and Gershon, S.: Investigation of *p*-methoxyamphetamine excretion in amphetamine-induced psychosis. Nature (London) *225*:651-652, 1970.

Axelrod, J.: An enzyme for the deamination of sympathomimetic amines: Properties and distribution. J. Pharmacol. Exp. Ther. *110*:2, 1954.

Axelrod, J.: The enzymic cleavage of aromatic ethers. Biochem. J. *63*:634-639, 1956.

Axelrod, J.: Enzymatic formation of psychotomimetic metabolites from normally occurring compounds. Science *134*:343-344, 1961.

Axelrod, J.: The enzymatic N-methylation of serotonin and other amines. J. Pharmacol. Exp. Ther. *138*:28-33, 1962.

Bernheim, F. and Bernheim, M.L.C.: The oxidation of mescaline and certain other amines. J. Biol. Chem. *123*:317-326, 1938.

Blaschko, H.: Enzymic oxidation of mescaline in the rabbit's liver. J. Physiol. (London) *103*:13P, 1944.

Blaschko, H., Richter, D., and Schlossmann, H.: The oxidation of adrenaline and other amines. Biochem. J. *31*:2187-2196, 1937.

Block, W., Block, K., and Patzig, B.: Zur Physiologie des 14C-radioaktiven Mescalins im Tierversuch. Z. Physiol. Chem. *290*:160-168, 1952a.

Block, W., Block, K., u Patzig, B.: Zur Physiologie des 14-C-radioaktiven Mescalins im Tierversuch. III. Mitteilung. Mescalineinbau in Leberprotein. Hoppe-Seylers Z. Physiol. Chem. *291*:119-128, 1952b.

Block, W., Block, K., and Patzig, B.: Zur Physiologie des ¹⁴C-radioaktiven Mescaline im Tierversuch. II. Mitteilung Verteilung der Radioaktivitat in den Organen in Abhangigkeit von der Zeit. Hoppe-Seylers Z. Physiol. Chem. 290:230-236, 1952c.

Braun, U. and Kalbhen, D.A.: Evidence for biogenic formation of amphetamine derivatives from components of nutmeg. Pharmacology 9:312-316, 1973.

Casida, J.E., Engel, J.L., Esaac, F.G., Kamieuski, F.X., and Kuwatsuda, A.: Methylene-C¹⁴-dioxyphenyl compounds: Metabolism in relation to their synergistic action. Science 153:1130-1133, 1966.

Charalampous, K.D., Orengo, A., Walker, K.E., and Kinross-Wright, J.: Metabolic fate of -(3,4,5-trimethoxyphenyl)-ethylamine (mescaline) in humans: Isolation and identification of 3,4,5-trimethoxyphenylacetic acid. J. Pharmacol. Exp. Ther. 145:242-246, 1964.

Charalampous, K.D., Walker, K.E., and Kinross-Wright, V.: Metabolic fate of mescaline in man. Psychopharmacologia 9:48-63, 1966.

Cochin, J., Woods, L.A., and Seevers, M.H.: The absorption, distribution and urinary excretion of mescaline in the dog. J. Pharmacol. Exp. Ther. 101:205-209, 1951.

Daly, J., Axelrod, J., and Witkop, B.: Methylation and demethylation in relation to the in vitro metabolism of mescaline. Ann. N.Y. Acad. Sci. 96:37, 1962.

Fischer, R.: Possible biosynthesis of d-lysergic acid diethylamide-like compounds from mescaline. Experientia 11:162-163, 1955.

Friedhoff, A.J.: Biosynthesis of DMPEA and its metabolites in mammalian tissues. Biol. Psychiat. 6:187-191, 1973.

Friedhoff, A.J. and Hollister, L.E.: Comparison of the metabolism of 3,4-dimethoxyphenylethylamine and mescaline in humans. Biochem. Pharmacol. 15:269-273, 1966.

Friedhoff, A.J. and Van Winkle, E.: Isolation and characterization of a compound from the urine of schizophrenics. Nature (London) 194:867-868, 1962.

Friedhoff, A.J., Schweitzer, J.W., Miller, J., and Van Winkle, E.: Guaiacol-O-methyltransferase, A mammalian enzyme capable of forming di-O-methyl catecholamine derivatives. Experientia 28:517, 1972.

Geber, W.F.: Congenital malformations induced by mescaline, lysergic acid diethylamide, and bromolysergic acid in the hamster. Science 157:265-266, 1967.

Hollister, L.E., MacNicol, M.F., and Gilespie, H.K.: An hallucinogenic amphetamine analog (DOM) in man. Psychopharmacologia 14:62-73, 1969.

Kuehl, F.A., Ormond, R.E., and Vanderheuval, W.J.A.: Occurrence of 3,4-dimethoxyphenylacetic acid in urines of normal and schizophrenic individuals. Nature (London) 211:606-608, 1966.

Mitra, C. and Guha, S.R.: Amphetamine oxidation in rat brain. Biochem. Pharmacol. 22:651-657, 1973.

Mokrasch, L.C. and Stevenson, I.: The metabolism of mescaline with a note on correlations between metabolism and psychological effects. J. Nerv. Ment. Dis. 129:177-183, 1959.

Musacchio, J.M. and Goldstein, M.: The metabolism of mescaline-¹⁴C in rats. Biochem. Pharmacol. 16:963-970, 1967.

Neff, N., Rossi, G.V., Chase, G.D., and Rabinowitz, J.L.: Distribution and metabolism of mescaline-C¹⁴ in the cat brain. J. Pharmacol. Exp. Ther. 144:1-7, 1964.

Osmond, H. and Smythies, J.: Schizophrenia: A new approach. J. Ment. Sci. 98:309-315, 1952.

Payne, R.B.: Nutmeg intoxication. New Engl. J. Med. 269:36-38, 1963.

Peretz, D.I., Smythies, J.R., and Gibson, W.C.: A new hallucinogen: 3,4,5-Trimethoxyphenyl- β -aminopropane. J. Ment. Sci. *101*:317, 1955.

Perry, T.L., Hansen, S., and Macintyre, L.: Failure to detect 3,4-dimethoxyphenylethylamine in the urine of schizophrenics. Nature (London) *202*:519-520, 1964.

Richter, D.: Elimination of amines in man. Biochem. J. *32*:1763-1769, 1938.

Salomon, K., Gabric, B.W., and Thale, T.A.: A study on mescaline in human subjects. J. Pharmacol. Exp. Ther. *95*:455-459, 1949.

Sargent, T.W., Israelstam, D.M., Shulgin, A.T., Landaw, S.A., and Finley, N.N.: A note concerning the fate of the 4-methoxyl group in 3,4-dimethoxyphenethylamine (DMPEA). Biochem. Biophys. Res. Commun. *29*:126-130, 1967.

Schweitzer, J.W. and Friedhoff, A.J.: The metabolism of a-^{14}C-3,4-dimethoxyphenethylamine. Biochem. Pharmacol. *15*:2097-2103, 1966.

Schweitzer, J.W., Friedhoff, A.J., Angrist, B.M., and Gershon, S.: Excretion of p-methoxyamphetamine administered to humans. Nature (London) *229*:133-134, 1971.

Seiler, N. and Demisch, L.: Oxidative metabolism of mescaline in the central nervous system-II. Biochem. Pharmacol. *20*:2485-2493, 1971.

Senoh, S., Daly, J., Axelrod, J., and Witkop, B.: Enzymatic p-O-methylation by catechol O-methyltransferase. J. Amer. Chem. Soc. *81*:6240, 1959.

Sethy, V.H. and Winter, J.C.: Effect of chronic treatment with mescaline upon tissue levels of the drug. Experientia *29*:571-572, 1973.

Shah, N.S. and Gibson, B.R.: Effect of single or repeated administration of chlorpromazine on the disappearance of mescaline in mouse. Res. Commun. Chem. Pathol. Pharmacol. *6*:321-324, 1973.

Shah, N.S. and Green, C.: Tissue levels of mescaline in mice: Influence of chlorpromazine on repeated administration of mescaline. Eur. J. Pharmacol. *24*:334-340, 1973.

Shah, N.S., Lawrence, S., Shah, K.R., and Neely, A.: Effects of chlorpromazine and haloperidol on the disposition of ^{14}C-mescaline in mice. 5th Int. Cong. Pharmacol., p. 209, 1972.

Shah, N.S., Gibson, B., and Neely, A.: Effect of chlorpromazine and reserpine on physiological disposition of mescaline in pregnant mouse. Fed. Proc. *32*:748, 1973a.

Shah, N.S., Neely, A.E., Shah, K.R., and Lawrence, R.S.: Placental transrer and tissue distribution of mescaline-^{14}C in the mouse. J. Pharmacol. Exp. Ther. *184*:489-493, 1973b.

Shulgin, A.T.: Psychotomimetic agents related to mescaline. Experientia *19*:127, 1963.

Shulgin, A.T.: Psychotomimetic amphetamines: Methoxy-3,4-dialkoxyamphetamines. Experientia *20*:366-367, 1964a.

Shulgin, A.T.: 3-Methoxy-4,5-methylenedioxyamphetamine, a new psychotomimetic agent. Nature (London) *201*:1120, 1964b.

Shulgin, A.T.: Possible implication of myristicin as a psychotropic substance. Nature (London) *210*:380, 1966.

Shulgin, A.T., Bunnel, S., and Sargent, T.: The psychotomimetic properties of 3,4,5-trimethoxyamphetamine. Nature (London) *189*:1011, 1961.

Shulgin, A.T., Sargent, T., and Naranjo, C.: The chemistry and psychopharmacology of nutmeg and of several related phenylisopropylamines. In Ethnopharmacologic Search for Psychoactive Drugs. Ed. D.H. Efron, Washington, D.C., Publ. Health Ser. Publ. No. 1645, 1967, pp. 202-214.

Shulgin, A.T., Sargent, T., and Naranjo, C.: Structure-activity relationships of one-ring psychotomimetics. Nature (London) 221:537-541, 1969.

Slotta, K.H. and Muller, J.: On the catabolism of mescaline and mescaline-like substances in the organism. Hoppe-Seyler's Z. Physiol. Chem. 238:14-22, 1936.

Smythies, J.R., Johnston, V.S., Bradley, R.J., Benington, F., Morin, R.D., and Clark, L.D.: Some new behavior-disrupting amphetamines and their significance. Nature (London) 216:128-129, 1967.

Snyder, S.H. and Richelson, E.: Steric models of drugs predicting psychedelic activity. In Psychotomimetic Drugs, Ed. Effron, Daniel H. New York 1970, pp. 43-58.

Snyder, S.H., Faillace, L., and Hollister, L.: 2,5-Dimethoxy-4-methyl-amphetamine (STP): A new hallucinogenic drug. Science 158:669-670, 1967.

Snyder, S.H., Faillace, L.A., and Weingartner, H.: DOM (STP), a new hallucinogenic drug, and DOET: Effects in normal subjects. Amer. J. Psychiat. 125:356-364, 1968.

Snyder, S.H., Richelson, E., Weingartner, H. and Faillace, L.A.: Psychotropic methoxyamphetamines: structure and activity in man In Amphetamines and Related Compounds, Eds. Costa, E. and Garattini, S., New York, 1970, pp. 905-928.

Spector, E.: Identification of 3,4,5-trimethoxy phenylacetic acid as the major metabolite of mescaline in the dog. Nature (London) 189:751-752, 1961.

Steensholt, G.: On an amine oxidase in rabbit's liver. Acta Physiol. Scand. 14:356-362, 1947.

Taska, R.J. and Schoolar, J.C.: Placental transfer and fetal distribution of mescaline-^{14}C in monkeys. J. Pharmacol. Exp. Ther. 183:427-432, 1972.

Taska, R.J. and Schoolar, J.C.: Peripheral tissue distribution, brain distribution and metabolism of mescaline-^{14}C in monkeys. Arch. Int. Pharmacodyn. 202:66-78, 1973.

Weil, A.T.: Nutmeg as a narcotic. Econ. Bot. 19:194, 1965.

Weissbach, H. Redfield, B.G., and Axelrod, J.: The enzymic acetylation of serotonin and other naturally occurring amines. Biochim. Biophys. Acta 54:190-192, 1962.

Williams, R.T.: Detoxication mechanisms in man. Clin. Pharmacol. Ther. 4:234-254, 1963.

Zeller, E.A.: A new approach to the analysis of the interaction between monoamine oxidase and its substrates and inhibitors. Ann. N.Y. Acad. Sci. 107:811-821, 1963.

Zeller, E.A., Barsky, J., Berman, E.R., Cherkas, M.S., and Fouts, J.R.: Degradation of mescaline by amine oxidases. J. Pharmacol. Exp. Ther., 124:282-289, 1958.

Chapter 4

LSD and Related
Indolealkylamines

The most potent psychotomimetic drugs known to man are indolic compounds that are derivatives of tryptamine. These agents are widely abused; the most commonly used and notorious member of this group is lysergic acid diethylamide (LSD). The indolealkylamine psychotomimetics frequently occur in nature as plant alkaloids, having been found in certain mushrooms, morning glory seeds, and various plant snuffs. Others of this group of psychotomimetics are chemically synthesized derivatives of the naturally occurring alkaloids. Some are similar in structure to the ergot alkaloids, a class of drugs having many and varied uses in medicine, e.g., treating migraine headaches, gynecologic dysfunctions, and hypertension.

The indolealkylamine drugs are also chemically related to constituents normally present in mammalian central nervous systems such as serotonin (5-hydroxytryptamine) and are thought to produce their effects by altering the functions of this and other neurotransmitters in the CNS.

The present chapter deals with the physiologic disposition of the indolealkylamines. LSD, the most commonly abused drug of this class, is the agent about which most information has been gathered, and therefore will serve as the prototype.

LYSERGIC ACID DIETHYLAMIDE

Lysergic acid diethylamide (Fig. 1), more commonly known as LSD, is a widely abused drug. It has several synonyms such as LSD-25 and lysergide, and is fondly known in street lore as "acid." This latter appellation is based upon the fact that LSD is synthesized chemically from lysergic acid (Fig. 1), a substance produced by *Claviceps purpurea*, a fungus which can inhabit the rye plant and that is involved in the synthesis of the ergot alkaloids.

The discovery of the pharmacologic properties of LSD is one of the classical serendipitous findings in pharmacology. Hofmann first synthesized LSD in 1938. However, not until 1943 did he discover the marked potency and unusual properties of this drug. One could paraphrase his report, however, this detracts from the personalization. Thus we have included a few passages from his memoirs about this discovery (Hofmann, 1959).

> "Among many other derivatives, I prepared *d*-lysergic acid with the hope of getting an analeptic. This could be expected because lysergic acid diethylamide has many structural features in common with coramine, which is nicotinic acid diethylamide, the well known analeptic (see Fig. 1).
>
> The afternoon of 16 April 1943, when I was working on this problem, I was seized by a peculiar sensation of vertigo and restlessness. Objects, as well as the shape of my associates in the laboratory, appeared to undergo optical changes. I was unable to concentrate on my work. In a dreamlike state I left for home, where an irresistible urge to lie down overcame me. I drew the curtains and immediately fell into a peculiar state similar to drunkeness, characterized by an exaggerated imagination. With my eyes closed. fantastic pictures of extraordinary plasticity and intensive colour seemed to surge toward me. After two hours this state gradually wore off.
>
> The nature and course of this extraordinary disturbance immediately raised my suspicions . . . that the lysergic acid diethylamide, with which I had been working that afternoon, was responsible. . . . I decided to get to the root of the matter by taking a definite quantity of the compound in question. Being a cautious man, I started my experiment by taking 0.25 mg of *d*-lysergic acid diethylamide tartrate, thinking that such an extremely small dose would surely be harmless. . . . After 40 minutes I noted the following symptoms in my laboratory journal: slight giddiness, restlessness, difficulty in concentration, visual disturbances, laughing. At this point the laboratory protocol ends. The last words are hardly legible and were written only with greatest difficulty. It was now obvious that LSD was responsible for the earlier intoxication."

The active form of LSD is *d*-LSD; *l*-LSD, the *l*-isomer, and another similar agent, *d*-iso-LSD, are devoid of psychotomimetic activity (Fig. 1). Likewise, a bromine-substituted derivative, 2-brom-LSD (BOL), is non-hallucinogenic. Therefore, a specific chemical structure and spatial orientation are essential for LSD's hallucinogenic activity. Compounds chemically related to LSD and having comparatively weak hallucinogenic properties have been isolated from the seeds of some species of the American Tropical Morning Glory. Known collectively by their Aztec name, Ololiuqui, these compounds have been used in religious ceremonies in remote mountains of southern Mexico; the active principles are thought to be lysergic acid amide and isolysergic acid amide (Fig.1) (Hofmann and Tscherter, 1960; Hofmann, 1961; Hofmann and Cerletti, 1961).

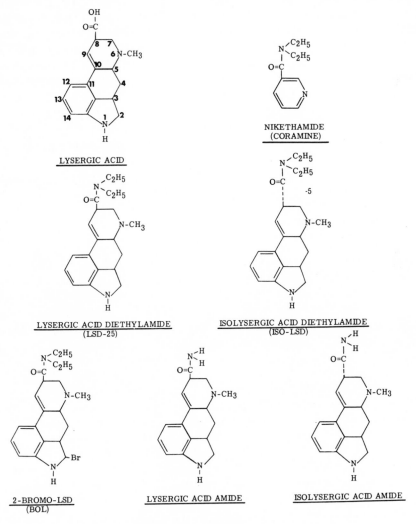

Fig. 1. Structure of lysergic acid and chemically related compounds.

LSD's usage was most prominent during the late 1950's and early 1960's when it was commonly used on many college campuses. Cults and communes were developed around the use of this agent. Fortunately, its use has declined within the past decade, perhaps due to an increased awareness of its adverse effects. Like mescaline and other psychotomimetics described in earlier chapters, LSD and the related indolealkylamines have both physiologic and psychologic effects. The peripheral effects of LSD involve activation of the autonomic nervous system and include: salivation, lacrimation, pupillary dilation, and an increased heart rate. Its psychic effects are in part related to (1) the dose, (2) the subject's underlying personality, (3) the environment in which the drug is taken (the setting), and (4) what experiences the subject anticipates from the drug (the set). LSD's psychic effects include mood changes, hallucinations, illusions, disordered thinking processes with loose associations, perceptual disturbances, and sensory interactions (synesthesia) where one sensory modality is perceived as another; e.g., colors are heard and sounds are visualized or felt. In susceptible individuals, LSD has precipitated adverse side effects such as acute paranoid reactions, acute panic reactions, schizophrenic-like reactions, and depersonalization and depression which may lead to suicide.

LSD is remarkedly potent*; about 20-100 μg of LSD are usually taken orally, frequently adsorbed onto a sugar cube.

In Vitro Metabolism

The most important requisite for studying the metabolism of any drug is the development of a satisfactory assay method. In the case of LSD, it was not until Axelrod et al. (1956) developed a specific and sensitive method for the determination of LSD that its in vitro and in vivo metabolism was subject to investigation. By using an extraction procedure coupled with either fluorometry or spectrophotometry, they were able to measure as little as 0.001 μg of LSD (1 ng) in biological specimens.

Axelrod et al. (1956, 1957) incubated LSD with slices of guinea pig liver, brain, kidney, spleen, and muscle for 2 hours and measured the LSD remaining in the incubation mixture. The concentration of LSD decreased only in the preparation of liver slices, a finding that indicated that hepatic tissue was capable of metabolizing the drug. Then they incubated LSD in the presence of guinea pig liver microsomes and soluble fraction and again demonstrated that LSD could be metabolized. They also showed that this system was inactive if NADP and oxygen were omitted, and that an NADPH-generating system could be substituted for the soluble fraction.

---

*A dose of LSD necessary to produce psychic effects in man is equivalent to about 3000 mescaline units.

Having determined that LSD could be metabolized by liver microsomes in the presence of NADPH and oxygen, they proceeded to investigate the nature of the metabolites produced. The chemical structure of LSD suggested that a likely route of metabolism would be hydrolysis of the amide to form free lysergic acid. They attempted to isolate the free acid, but were unable to find any in the incubation mixture. Another possible route of LSD biotransformation was N-demethylation to form nor-LSD. Using sensitive methods capable of detecting formaldehyde (the end product of N-demethylation), they were unable to isolate any formaldehyde, indicating that N-demethylation was not a metabolic pathway for LSD. They did not attempt to determine if N-deethylation of LSD occurred in the diethylamide moiety of the molecule; however, evidence from *in vivo* studies of Boyd *et at.* (1955b) suggests that this may occur since in their studies, using ^{14}C labeled LSD (with the ^{14}C in the ethyl position of the N,N-diethyl), they found approximately 4% of the administered dose in expired air as $^{14}CO_2$.

The possibility that LSD underwent oxidation in their guinea pig liver microsomal preparation prompted Axelrod and co-workers (1957) to search for an oxidized metabolite. They extracted the incubation mixture free of residual LSD using organic solvents, and then subjected aliquots of the LSD-free incubation mixture to several color tests. Their results indicated the presence of a reducing indole which had a substitution on the 2-position of the indole ring. The metabolite was tentatively identified as 2-oxy-LSD (Fig. 2). Chemical synthesis of this compound (Freter *et al.*, 1957) showed

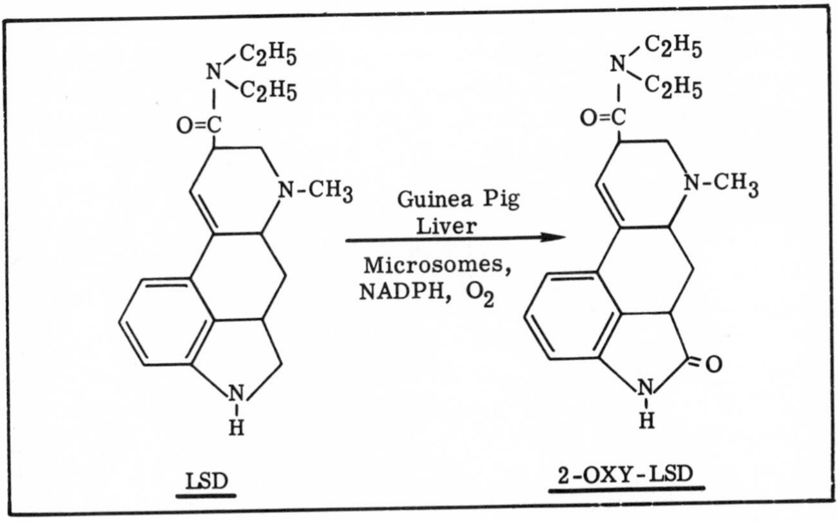

Fig. 2. Conversion of LSD to 2-oxy-LSD by guinea pig liver microsomes.

that it had the same properties and was identical to enzymatically synthesized 2-oxy-LSD. LSD is stoichiometrically converted to 2-oxy-LSD in this system, 1 mole of the former being metabolized to 1 mole of the latter. Axelrod and his associates (1957) investigated the biologic activity of this 2-oxy metabolite in animal models *in vivo* and in man. This oxindole metabolite had no measurable activity in neuropharmacologic studies in cats. Likewise, 300 μg of 2-oxy-LSD administered orally produced no psychologic effects in an individual who previously exhibited behavioral effects from 30 μg of LSD.

The marked species differences in the hydroxylation of tryptamine derivatives prompted Szara (1963) to compare the metabolism of LSD in guinea pig and rat liver microsomes. Using the same experimental conditions as Axelrod *et al.* (1957), he confirmed their findings with guinea pig microsomes. However, when rat liver microsomes were incubated with LSD under identical conditions, Szara found a different metabolite formed. This compound gave a positive reaction to Ehrlichs reagent (*p*-dimethylaminobenzaldehyde), indicating that the hydroxylation was not occurring in the 2-position of the indole ring. Rather, the compound exhibited properties consistent with a phenolic hydroxyl group on a benzene ring. On the basis of previous studies indicating that rat liver microsomes hydroxylate indoles in the 6-position, Szara proposed that the hydroxylation of LSD occurred in the 13-position (which corresponds to the 6-position of the indole structure (Fig. 3).

Although rat liver microsomes can hydroxylate LSD, it is a poor substrate when compared with *N,N*-diethyltryptamine (DET). The latter compound is converted to its 6-hydroxylated metabolite six times faster than the rate of conversion of LSD to 13-hydroxy-LSD (Szara, 1963).

Inhibitors of the *in vitro* hydroxylation of LSD have been found. Chlorpromazine (10^{-4} M) and SKF-525A (10^{-4} M) inhibit the conversion of LSD to 2-oxy-LSD by a guinea pig liver microsomal enzyme system by 70 and 90%, respectively (Axelrod *et al.*, 1957). Szara (1963) has shown that DET can inhibit the conversion of LSD to 13-hydroxy-LSD in a rat liver microsomal enzyme system. This inhibition appears to be competitive, indicating that both LSD and DET share a common enzyme system for microsomal hydroxylation.

Other *in vitro* experiments investigating LSD metabolism have been reported by Rothlin (1956). He incubated LSD for 6 hours at 30°C in rat blood and provided evidence that LSD was neither bound nor metabolized in blood. In contrast, when LSD was incubated with homogenates from rat organs (liver, brain, and skeletal muscle), there was a greater than 50% decrease in LSD concentration (as determined by *bioassay*) within only a few minutes of incubation. This probably did not represent metabolism of

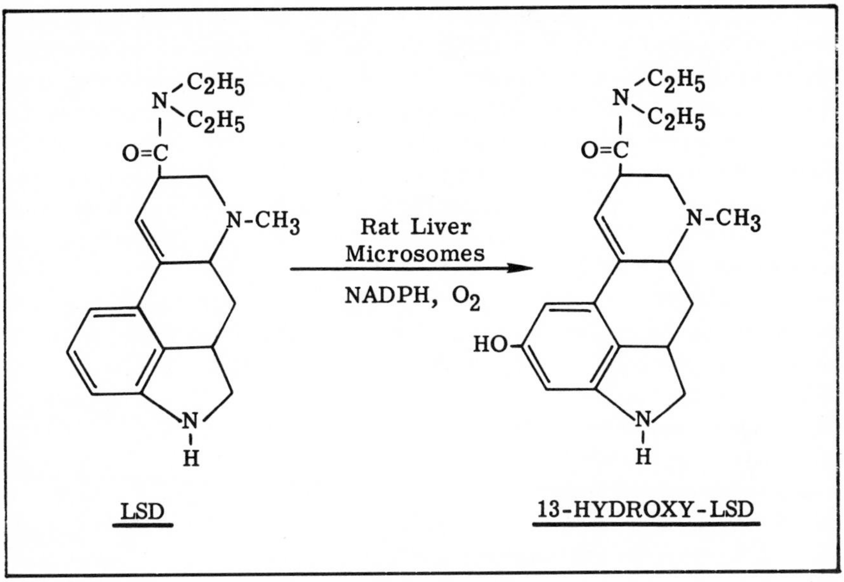

Fig. 3. Conversion of LSD to 13-hydroxy-LSD by rat liver microsomes.

the LSD to inactive metabolites since it occurred at 38°C as well as at 3°C. This decrease in LSD activity might be due to nonspecific binding to the tissue protein in the homogenates rather than to metabolic conversion.

In Vivo Metabolism and Disposition

Absorption

LSD is rapidly absorbed after the usual routes of administration. After oral ingestion by man, behavioral changes occur within 30 to 120 minutes; they occur more rapidly after parenteral administration. In mice, changes in behavior begin immediately after intracerebral injection and within 3 minutes after intravenous administration (Haley and Rutschmann, 1957). Studies of Upshall and Wailling (1972) suggest that LSD absorption (as determined by LSD plasma concentrations) was decreased when the drug was ingested shortly after a meal compared to absorption in the fasted state.

Distribution

The distribution of LSD in blood and tissues has been investigated by several research groups using sensitive techniques, including spectrofluorometry, radioactivity, and bioassay techniques based upon the highly sensitive antagonistic action of LSD to serotonin-induced contraction of smooth muscle. The first studies utilizing the bioassay technique were those of Lanz et al. (1955). Studying the disposition of LSD in mice, they found this drug to be rapidly removed from blood and concentrated in tissues. The tissue concentrations of LSD increased for 15 to 30 minutes after injection and then gradually decreased during the next few hours. The highest concentrations of LSD were present in liver, followed in decreasing order by kidney, adrenal, lung, spleen, heart, and brain. The concentrations in brain were less than those in blood at all time periods. They estimated that LSD disappeared from mouse blood with a half-life of 37 minutes. These results, obtained by the aforementioned bioassay procedure, are probably quite reliable because studies have shown that the activity in this assay is much less responsive to the presence of some metabolites of LSD than to LSD itself (Slaytor and Wright, 1962).

These early studies were repeated using LSD labeled with ^{14}C in the side chain (Stoll et al., 1954, 1955). After the intravenous administration of ^{14}C-LSD to mice, the distribution of radioactivity was similar to that of LSD found by the earlier bioassay studies.

Of considerable interest was the finding that the appearance of radioactivity in the small intestine increased with time, and after 2 hours represented about 50% of the intravenous dose. This radioactivity moved down the gastrointestinal tract with the intestinal contents, and by 4 to 5 hours after i.v. administration was present in the colon. These findings indicate that LSD or its metabolites had been excreted into bile.

In an attempt to determine the quantity of radioactivity present as unchanged LSD, the tissues were extracted, and aliquots of the extracts were purified by paper chromatography. Using this technique, only 10% of the radioactivity present in brain and liver was present as unchanged LSD. Although LSD disappears more slowly from blood of most species with a half-life of 1 or 2 hours, it has been stated by Rothlin (1956, 1957) that the half-life of LSD in mouse blood is 7 minutes. While this value appears to disagree with data reported in other species, additional evidence supports the short $t_{1/2}$ in mice. Mice given LSD intraperitoneally and killed 20 minutes later also displayed a biologic half-life of 7 minutes for LSD when body concentrations of this drug were determined by homogenization of the whole animal (Axelrod et al., 1957).

Boyd et al. (1955a,b; Boyd, 1959) administered ^{14}C-LSD intraperitoneally and intravenously to rats and reported a distribution similar to that of previously mentioned studies in mice. In addition, they showed that adipose tissue had the lowest concentration of LSD of any tissues examined and thus would not serve as a repository site for the drug.

Axelrod *et al.* (1956, 1957), utilizing a spectrofluorometric assay specific for LSD, studied LSD distribution in tissues of the cat. Ninety minutes after intravenous administration, plasma and bile contained the highest LSD concentrations; all tissues examined had at least half the concentration of LSD as did plasma. Except for relatively high concentrations in plasma, the distribution of LSD was again similar to that determined by other methods. These investigators found LSD to disappear from cat plasma; the half-life was 130 minutes. Significant quantities of LSD appeared in the cerebrospinal fluid 90 minutes after injection. The relationship between plasma and CSF concentrations of LSD was then studied in monkey. After i.v. administration to this species, LSD concentrations in plasma declined in a biphasic fashion. The rapid phase is probably due to the distribution of LSD from plasma to tissues, and the latter phase is a reflection of the rate of metabolism. Based upon this latter phase, the half-life was determined to be 100 minutes. The LSD level in CSF was one-sixth of that seen in plasma when the levels of LSD in the CSF was at its maximum concentration (10 minutes after administration) and then declined slowly. The amount of LSD in CSF was estimated to be the same as that present as the unbound form in plasma; the unbound form of LSD probably traverses the blood-brain barrier readily.

Passage through the blood-brain barrier is of interest in light of the studies of Diab *et al.* (1971) who demonstrated by autoradiographic techniques in rats that LSD accumulated in highest concentration in epithelial layers of the choroid plexus. This tissue is known to be associated with the active transport of chemicals from blood to brain and is also known to play an important role in the production of cerebrospinal fluid. Haley and Rutschmann (1957) demonstrated that after intracerebral injection of LSD to mice, the drug leaves the brain rapidly, suggesting that some mechanism such as active transport by the choroid plexus facilitates passage of the drug into the systemic circulation.

In man, Aghajanian and Bing (1964) reported that LSD persisted in plasma in relatively high concentrations for several hours after its intravenous administration. A biphasic plasma decay curve was found; a half-life of 175 minutes was estimated from the β-elimination phase. These investigators found that the subjects were unable to perform simple arithmetic tasks; this inability was positively correlated with the presence of LSD in the plasma of the volunteers, in contrast to impressions from some animal studies that LSD disappears from the organism before its psychic effects are manifest. In an attempt to estimate the tissue levels of LSD in humans, Wagner *et al.* (1968) subjected the human data of Aghajanian and Bing (1964) to a computerized analysis. Assuming a two-compartment model, he calculated the plasma volume (inner compartment) and the tissue volume (outer compartment) and concluded that the volume of distribution for LSD in man was 27.8% of body weight and that the drug was essentially distributed in extracellular water. He also found an excellent negative correlation between the performance scores and the estimated "tissue" concentrations such that higher "brain" concentrations were associated with lower performance.

Because LSD does produce aberrant behavior in such small doses, emphasis has been placed on determining if it selectively accumulates in specific brain areas which could be correlated with its behavioral effects, e.g., does it concentrate in areas affecting vision such as the visual cortex or geniculate body?

Based on the dose administered to man and the quantity of LSD found in brain tissue, Axelrod et al. (1957) calculated that the drug could exert its psychologic effect at a concentration of 0.5 ng/gm of brain tissue. These authors studied the distribution of LSD in cat brain and found no differences in the concentrations of this drug in cortex, midbrain, spinal cord, or hypothalamus. Several years later, Snyder and Reivich (1966) conducted similar studies in conscious squirrel monkey to whom LSD was given by slow i.v. injection. They found LSD to be unequally distributed in different brain areas. High concentrations were present in pituitary and pineal glands (both outside the "blood-brain barrier") 20 minutes after injection. At this time, frontal cortex, cerebellum, midbrain pons, and medulla all had one-half to one-third the level of activity when compared with visual and auditory reflex areas, hypothalamus, and the limbic system. There was no preferential accumulation of LSD in lipid-rich white matter (which is consistent with its failure to concentrate in adipose tissue). Snyder and Reivich (1966) also studied the subcellular localization of LSD in monkey brain and concluded that LSD did not localize in a specific subcellular brain particle, being present predominantly in the soluble supernatant fluid (about 75-79%); the microsomal-myelin fraction contained less (15-20%), and the synaptosomal-mitochondrial fraction contained the least (3-8%).

Arnold et al. (1958), studying the distribution of ^{14}C-LSD in mouse brain by radioautography, found a similar distribution of radioactivity to that seen in the monkey by Snyder and Reivich (1966). Also using autoradiographic techniques, Diab et al. (1971) attempted to distinguish between LSD in its free and bound forms in various brain regions of the rat. Their results indicated that LSD was present in pituitary, pineal, and hippocampus in its free form, and that in certain specific neurons in caudate, midbrain, and cortex the drug was bound to the neuronal membranes rather than to the cell nucleus.

Recently, Farrow and Van Vunakis (1972, 1973) conducted an extensive study of the binding properties of LSD to subcellular fractions of rat brain. They found brain subfractions to possess high, medium, and low affinity binding sites for LSD. All brain regions possessed low affinity binding sites; however, certain particles such as those obtained from cerebrocortical synaptic membranes contained twice as many high affinity sites per milligram of protein as synaptosomes from this same region. These synaptosomes, however, had about five times more medium affinity sites than did the synaptic membranes. These medium affinity sites were absent from myelin or mitochondria. *In vitro* and *in vivo* studies with LSD demonstrated that about 25% of the LSD was irreversibly bound to cortex of brain (by extraction criteria). The binding of LSD to synaptosomes could be inhibited by hallucinogenic compounds, but not by their nonhallucinogenic congeners. This suggests that many structurally unrelated hallucinogens may in fact be acting at the same site, a finding supported by the demonstrations of cross tolerance between some of these drugs. (See Chapter 10.)

The specific chemical entity to which LSD binds has been investigated by Yielding and Sterglanz (1968). They reported that *d*-LSD (the active isomer) became bound to purified DNA but not to RNA. One cautionary note in interpreting this data is that *l*-LSD (the inactive isomer) also became bound to DNA with a similar affinity. The significance of this LSD binding to DNA, the chemical basis of inheritance, must await further research.

Voss *et al.* (1973a,b), studying the effect of LSD on the immune system, reported that LSD inhibits formation of the 7 S form of immunoglobin *in vitro*. After incubating ^{3}H-LSD with antibody-producing lymphoid cells, they isolated labeled protein from the incubate and concluded that LSD or a metabolite was incorporated. This incorporation was inhibited by the presence of puromycin in the media.

In addition to its binding to brain and other tissues, the early studies of Axelrod *et al.* (1957) revealed that LSD was present in plasma in considerable quantities. In studying the binding of this drug to plasma proteins (using equilibrium dialysis), they found that at concentrations of LSD expected to be present in blood after a usual dose, 90% of the drug was bound to plasma proteins. Even at large concentrations (20 mg/liter, a concentration which could not possibly be achieved *in vivo*) 65% of the LSD was bound. Boyd (1959) confirmed the binding of LSD to plasma proteins and showed that 10 to 30% of the radioactivity in blood was present in the cellular fraction. As stated previously, the concentration of LSD in the CNS is equal to that of the free form of the drug present in plasma. Thus, it does not appear that a "blood-brain barrier" is responsible for the low concentrations of LSD in brain; rather the low concentration seems to be related to the binding of LSD to plasma proteins, which prevents it from entering the brain in substantial amounts. Freedman *et al.* (1964) studied the effect of reserpine pretreatment on the binding properties of LSD administered intravenously to the rat. To their surprise, they found that with reserpine pretreatment the brain concentrations of LSD were lowered. This was associated with an increase in plasma concentration of LSD. Further studies revealed that reserpine caused an increased binding of LSD in plasma. The mechanism for this remains to be elucidated.

Because of the concern about LSD and teratogenicity, and the reports of these effects in the scientific and lay press, Idanpaan-Heikkila and Schoolar (1969a,b) studied the tissue distribution of ^{14}C-LSD in pregnant hamsters and mice. Autoradiographic studies showed that after i.v. administration of ^{14}C-LSD to pregnant mice, some radioactivity crossed the placenta and was present in the fetus within 5 minutes after injection. The percentage of the radioactivity present in the fetus depended upon the stage of pregnancy; 2.5% and 0.5% of the dose was found in the fetus during the early and late stages, respectively. The major portion of the radioactivity present in the fetus was unchanged LSD. Studies in the pregnant hamster revealed similar results with less radioactivity present in the fetus during later stages of pregnancy, presumably due to the placenta impeding the transfer of LSD to the fetus.

Metabolism

As discussed earlier, major progress in studying the metabolism of LSD involved the use of liver slices and liver microsomal preparations. Unfortunately, the problem is more complex when one investigates the metabolism of this drug *in vivo*, and, therefore, the available data are only fragmentary.

Stoll *et al.* (1955), using rats with biliary fistulae, found 70% of a radioactive dose of ^{14}C-LSD excreted in the bile in 6 hours. When this bile was subjected to paper chromatography, less than 1% of the total radioactivity coincided with unchanged LSD. Three other radioactive compounds were present which were more polar than LSD and, in contrast to LSD, were water soluble. Two of these metabolites gave a positive color reaction with Ehrlichs reagent (a typical reaction for indoles with no substitution in the 2-position) and had a blue fluorescence in ultraviolet light (a characteristic of LSD derivatives). These investigators concluded that neither of these two metabolites was the 2-oxy-LSD (Fig. 2) found *in vitro* by Axelrod, since they did not share similar chemical properties (Rothlin, 1956); however, they could not rule out the possibility that the third metabolite was indeed a derivative of 2-oxy-LSD.

Biliary metabolites of LSD were studied using rats with biliary fistulae (Boyd, 1959; Boyd *et al.*, 1955b). Two polar compounds were found that reacted similarly to those found by Stoll and co-workers; one yielded a blue color with Ehrlichs reagent, in contrast to the violet color produced by the parent LSD. This is interesting since Jepson *et al.* (1962) found that 6-hydroxylated *indoles* produce a blue color with this reagent (hydroxylation in other positions or the lack of any hydroxylation produces different color reactions). If such a color reaction can be extrapolated to the LSD structure, it suggests that LSD was hydroxylated in the 13-position (Fig. 3) (analogous to the 6-position of the indoles). In addition, two other LSD metabolites were isolated. Incubation of these metabolites with β-glucuronidase yielded less polar compounds that retained the activity of the LSD moiety with regard to color reactions and fluorescence. These metabolites appear to be phenolic compounds conjugated with glucuronic acid.

Slaytor and Wright (1962) repeated and confirmed the earlier findings of Stoll and Boyd with respect to LSD metabolites in bile. In addition, they isolated the glucuronides of hydroxy-LSD and hydroxy-iso-LSD in pure crystalline form and determined their melting points and other physical characteristics. They were able to interconvert these metabolites by various treatments and thus suggested that these two metabolites represented derivatives of *d*-lysergic and *d*-isolysergic acids. One of the metabolites was more active than the other in inhibiting serotonin-induced contractions of rat uterus, and they concluded that it was a derivative of *d*-isolysergic acid. Although active in this bioassay, this metabolite of LSD possessed only 5% of the activity of the parent compound, while the "inactive" metabolite possessed less than 0.5% of the activity (Slaytor *et al.*, 1959).

Dring *et al.* (1975) administered intravenously to rabbits purified LSD metabolites obtained from rats. Most of the metabolites had no effect on the rabbit electroencephalogram. However, desethyl-LSD, a minor metabolite found in rat urine, (0.5%) did alter the EEG pattern similarly to LSD. Boyd *et al.* (1955b) recovered $^{14}CO_2$ in expired air after administering ^{14}C-LSD (labeled in the ethyl position of the N,N-diethyl) to rats. This accounted for 4% of the administered dose and indicates that LSD must be dealkylated to desethyl-LSD.

The major portion of a dose of LSD is metabolized to more water-soluble compounds containing a phenolic hydroxyl group. Recently, Siddik *et al.* (1975) extensively studied the metabolism of C^{14}-LSD *in vivo*, using mass spectroscopy. They isolated several LSD metabolites from the urine and feces of intact rats as well as from the bile of cannulated rats. They identified the glucuronides of 13- and 14-hydroxy LSD in bile (accounting for a total of 51% of the administered radioactivity). They also identified the free phenolic compounds, 13- and 14-hydroxy LSD, in the feces of intact rats which suggests that deconjugation of the glucuronides may have occurred in the intestinal tract.

Excretion

The excretion of LSD has been studied in several animal species. The most complete study to date was performed in rats by Boyd and co-workers (1955a,b; Boyd, 1959). After the intravenous or intraperitoneal administration of ^{14}C-LSD (side-chain labeled), they found about 70% of the radioactive dose present in the gastrointestinal contents; as much as 20% was present after only 30 minutes. This suggested that excretion was occurring primarily via the biliary route. In biliary cannulated rats, excretion of radioactivity in bile increased in a linear fashion for 2 to 3 hours after an intravenous injection, and by 4 hours, 70% of the dose was present in bile. In rats Boyd (1959) demonstrated that 80% of a radioactive dose of LSD was excreted in feces, 8% in urine, and about 4% as CO_2 in expired air. Studies concerning the chemical structure of the excretory products indicated they were metabolites of LSD rather than the drug itself.

Monkeys, given LSD intravenously, excreted less than 1% of the dose unchanged in urine and feces during a 24-hour period (Axelrod et al., 1957); LSD undergoes a virtually complete metabolic change in this species.

Taunton-Rigby et al. (1973), using a highly specific radioimmunoassay, have detected LSD in human urine. Their data indicate that only small quantities of LSD are excreted in human urine. However, the possibility exists that metabolites of LSD may be excreted in human urine, since their method was reported to be specific for only unchanged LSD.

Faed and McLeod (1973), using a spectrofluorometric assay, reportedly recovered at least 80% of a dose of LSD as LSD-like material in the urine of an individual to whom 200 μg of the drug was administered. Since this study was not carefully controlled, and since the specificity of the assay in urine can be questioned, these findings must await confirmation. It is obvious from the paucity of data available on the excretion of LSD in man that carefully controlled clinical studies are needed.

Biochemical Correlates of Clinical Findings

The presence of high concentrations of LSD in regions of brain which are involved in altering behavior must be more than coincidental. For example, LSD-induced visual and auditory hallucinations and distortions are positively correlated with the presence of drug in these sensory regions of the cortex.

The rapid onset of action of LSD in animals, and the positive correlation between theoretical brain concentrations of LSD and its effects in man suggest that the effects are due, at least in part, to the parent compound rather than a metabolite. In addition, the failure to detect any significant psychoactive activity in any of its suspect metabolites further supports this contention. It is well known that spontaneous recurrent episodes of LSD-like effects, including feelings of depersonalization and distortion of perceptual stimuli, may occur a year or more after ingesting the drug. These so-called "flash-backs" have been reported to occur in approximately 20% of LSD users (Horowitz, 1969). These effects can be precipitated at times of increased anxiety and by the administration of other psychotropic agents. Based upon the data available on the disposition and biologic half-life of LSD in mammals, these flashbacks would not appear to be due to the presence of residual LSD in the body. It is possible, however, that after its administration, LSD interacts with some neural components such as may be involved in memory and produces an effect that persists long after the drug has been eliminated from the body.

METHYLTRYPTAMINE DERIVATIVES

As stated in the introduction to this chapter, the tryptamine derivatives (Fig. 4) are potent psychoactive agents. Plant materials containing these drugs have been used since pre-Columbian times for their CNS effects in the West Indies, and Central and South America. They are employed as a snuff (solid particles inhaled via the nasal passages) in mystical religious ceremonies, using exotic tubes and trays to deliver the material to the body.

Fish *et al.* (1955) first isolated and identified *N, N*-dimethyltryptamine (DMT) (Fig. 4) as a constituent of seeds and pods of *Piptadenia peregrina,* a plant made into a snuff known as cohoha and utilized for its psychotomimetic effects. They used paper chromatography, infrared spectrometry, color reactions, and fluorescence to identify this substance. Stromberg (1954) isolated from this plant 5-hydroxydimethyltryptamine (bufotenine*) (Fig. 4), a drug also thought to have psychoactivity. Since a variety of snuffs of different botanical origins have been used for their psychotomimetic effects, Holmstedt and Lindgren (1967) studied the chemical constituents of snuffs from five different plants obtained from South America, including Epena and Yopo snuffs. Using gas chromatography coupled with mass spectroscopy, they identified the following tryptamine derivatives in these plant specimens: DMT, *N*-monomethyltryptamine (MMT), bufotenine, 5-methoxy DMT, and 5-methoxy-MMT (Fig. 4).

In addition to the chemical synthesis of *N*-methyltryptamine derivatives and their isolation from plant materials, bufotenine and DMT

---

*Bufotenine was originally isolated from secretion of the skin glands present in the back of poisonous toads, *Bufo vulgaris,* and hence its name (Weiland *et al.,* 1934).

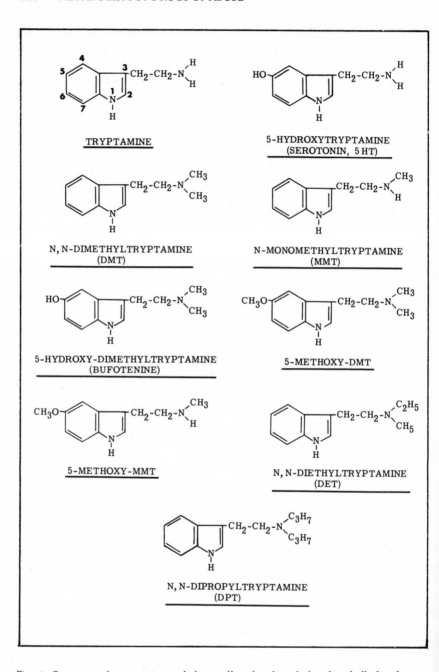

Fig. 4. Structure of tryptamine and chemically related methylated and alkylated tryptamines.

can be synthesized by mammalian tissue *in vitro* by an enzyme in lung which is capable of methylating serotonin and tryptamine, respectively (Axelrod, 1961, 1962). Morgan and Mandell (1969) and Saavedra and Axelrod (1972) found a mammalian enzyme in brain which was also capable of catalizing this reaction. Since the discovery of these psychotomimetic chemicals in plants, investigators have been searching for these or similar chemicals in the blood and urine of schizophrenic patients in an attempt to substantiate a biochemical basis for this mental disorder (Fisher, 1968; Saavedra and Udabe, 1970; Heller *et al.*, 1970, Narasimhachari *et al.*, 1971; Narasimhachari and Himwich, 1973). To date, this hypothesis (the transmethylation/psychotomimetic hypothesis for the pathogenesis of schizophrenia) is still controversial since these methylated tryptamines have not been found in blood or urine of schizophrenics, or they have been found in only a small percentage of the subjects and in very low concentrations (Axelson and Nordgren, 1974; Wyatt *et al.*, 1973a,b; Bidder *et al.*, 1974).

N,N-Dimethyltryptamine (DMT)

The knowledge that tryptamine derivatives were present in psychoactive snuffs was soon followed by chemical synthesis of these drugs and their subsequent clinical investigation. Szara (1957, 1961) and Boszormenyi and Brunecker (1957) administered DMT to humans and reported that its effects were similar to those produced by LSD, including perceptual distortions (primarily visual), a sense of loss of contact with reality, and autonomic symptoms, including tachycardia and mydriasis.

As is obvious from its use pattern, DMT is rapidly absorbed and is quite active after inhalation as a snuff or smoke. In contrast, DMT is inactive after oral administration because it is rapidly metabolized by the intestinal mucosa and liver. After intramuscular injection, the pharmacologic effects are of rapid onset (2-5 minutes after injection). The effects last only 40-50 minutes, in contrast to LSD, whose effects last 4-10 hours. (Szara, 1961). This short duration is due to its rapid rate of metabolism. DMT, being a simple monoamine, is an excellent substrate for MAO, and Szara (1956) has shown that after its administration to man, about 33% is excreted as its deaminated product, 3-indoleacetic acid, in both the free and conjugated form (Fig. 5). Szara (1961) reported that the variation in intensity of the psychotomimetic effects among individuals appeared to be, in part, closely related to the individual variation in the metabolism of DMT.

Szara and Axelrod (1959) incubated DMT with a rabbit liver microsomal drug-metabolizing system fortified with NADPH and demonstrated that DMT could be N-demethylated to *N*-methyltryptamine (Fig. 5). They

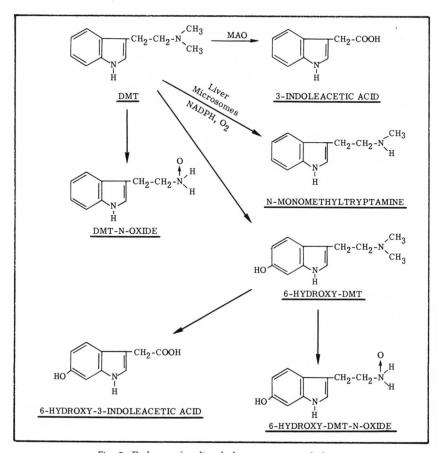

Fig. 5. Pathways for dimethyltryptamine metabolism.

found no evidence for tryptamine formation, indicating that only one methyl group of DMT can be removed. It should be stated that in their studies the animals were first pretreated with iproniazid, a potent MAO inhibitor, prior to isolating the microsomes; otherwise, the DMT was rapidly deaminated and the N-demethylation reaction could not be demonstrated. In addition to identifying the N-demethylated metabolite of DMT (by chromatography of the compound and by the formation of formaldehyde), these investigators found additional metabolites, including DMT-N-oxide, 6-hydroxy-DMT, and 6-hydroxy-DMT-N-oxide (Fig. 5). They found no evidence that DMT was converted to bufotenine (which would have been formed had DMT been hydroxylated in the 5-position).

After the intraperitoneal administration of DMT to rats, DMT, 6-OH-DMT, and N-methyltryptamine were isolated from urine; also isolated were the acidic metabolites, 6-OH-3-indoleacetic acid and 3-indoleacetic acid (Fig. 5) (Szara and Axelrod, 1959).

Several analogs of DMT have been synthesized, including N,N-diethyltryptamine (DET) (Fig. 4) and N,N-dipropyltryptamine (DPT) (Fig. 4). These compounds also produce psychotomimetic effects after injection into man (Faillace et al., 1967; Szara, 1961; Szara et al., 1966). Szara (1963) has studied the metabolism of DET by a rat liver microsomal system. It was hydroxylated in the 6-position about 6 times faster than the hydroxylation of LSD. In addition, studies of its metabolism in vivo have been conducted. In rats and mice, 40-50% of an administered dose of DET is found in the urine as hydroxylated derivatives, whereas in guinea pig less than 2% of the 6-hydroxylated derivative is found in urine. Man excretes 4-20% of an administered dose of DET as hydroxylated metabolites. Szara (1961) investigated the relationship between the variation in the psychologic effects of individuals to DET and its conversion to 6-hydroxy-DET. Subjects excreting more 6-OH-DET in the urine had a much more intense reaction to the drug than those excreting less. This, in addition to other evidence,* led Szara to hypothesize that DMT, DET, and other N-alkylated tryptamines are converted to psychoactive compounds by hydroxylation in the 6-position (Szara and Hearst, 1962). Evidence against this hypothesis came from the studies of Rosenberg et al. (1963) that indicated that 6-OH-DMT was not the active form of DMT in man. They administered placebo, DMT, and 6-OH-DMT to volunteers and reported that 6-OH-DMT was without activity or was definitely less active than DMT.

Although the tissue distribution of the N-methylated tryptamines has not been investigated, it is probably similar to that of the parent compound tryptamine, which has its highest concentrations in lung, liver, and spleen, and its lowest concentrations in brain and blood (Lemberger et al., 1971; Pletscher et al., 1963).

Bufotenine

Bufotenine, the 5-hydroxylated derivative of DMT, is also an analog of serotonin (5-HT) (Fig. 4). After its intravenous administration to volunteers, bufotenine produces psychotomimetic effects of short duration (less than 1 hour) (Fabing and Hawkins, 1956; Turner and Merlis, 1959). The effects are similar to those produced by other psychotomimetic agents. Bufotenine is oxidatively deaminated by liver MAO at about 20% the rate as

---

*After the substitution of a fluorine group in the 6-position of DET, there is no chance for 6-hydroxylation to occur. The administration of 6-fluoro-DET to man produced no psychologic effects (Kalir and Szara, 1963), and no 6-hydroxylated tryptamines were present in urine.

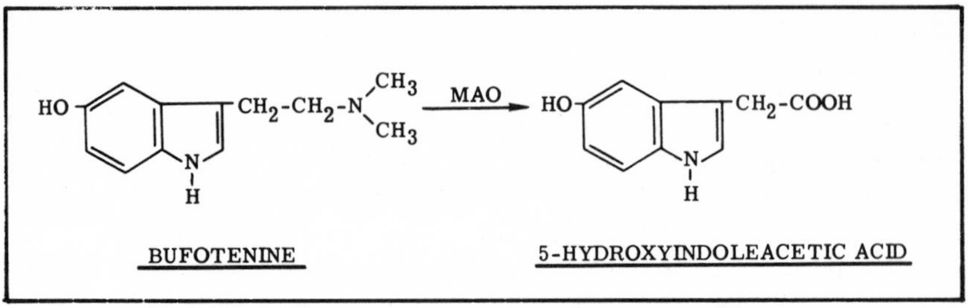

Fig. 6. Metabolism of bufotenine by monoamine oxidase.

serotonin (Govier et al., 1953; Blaschko and Philpot, 1953). Both of these compounds are metabolized to 5-hydroxyindoleacetic acid (5-HIAA) (Fig. 6).

After subcutaneous administration of bufotenine to rats, about 22% of the dose was excreted unchanged, and about 7% as 5-HIAA, including its free form and glucuronide conjugate (Gessner et al., 1960). In contrast, when 5-HT was administered to rats, more than 39% of the dose was excreted in urine as 5-HIAA. These findings confirm the earlier observation that bufotenine is not as good a substrate for MAO as is serotonin.

Sanders and Bush (1967) have investigated the distribution, metabolism, and excretion of ^{14}C-bufotenine in rats. After the intravenous administration of this drug, the concentrations of bufotenine and its metabolites were lower in brain relative to their concentrations in blood. The half-life of bufotenine in rat blood was about 40 minutes. Five minutes after its administration, bufotenine was present at highest concentrations in the lung, heart, and blood. However, at this time period the concentrations of bufotenine metabolites were 2-3 times greater in liver and kidney. In fact, the concentrations of metabolites in liver were 35 times that of the parent compound. Greater than 90% of bufotenine and its metabolites was excreted in rat urine within 3 days after its i.v. administration. Less than 2% of the dose was eliminated via the feces. Bufotenine was extensively metabolized, 4-6% of the administered dose being excreted in the urine as parent drug. About 15% of the administered dose was excreted as 5-HIAA and 35% as the glucuronide conjugate of bufotenine. The fate of the remainder of bufotenine in rats in unknown.

After the intravenous administration of bufotenine to two human subjects, Sanders-Bush et al. (1975) found the 90-100% of the dose was excreted in urine. Only 1-6% of the administered dose was excreted as parent drug, whereas 66-75% of the dose was present in urine as 5-HIAA. A small amount of 5-hydroxytryptophol was identified tentatively in one subject.

Psilocybin and Psilocin

The Mexican mushroom, *Psilocybe mexicanna* Heim, is a plant that possesses hallucinogenic properties. It has been prepared as a liquid potion and used in ceremonial rituals by Central American and Mexican Indians for centuries. In 1953, an American banker and ethnologist and a French botanist obtained samples of the active plant, identified it botanically, and supplied material to Hofmann and co-workers who subsequently isolated and identified the active hallucinogenic principles as tryptamine derivatives. Psilocybin and psilocin (Fig. 7) are the two indolealkylamines which were isolated from this Mexican mushroom (Hofmann *et al.*, 1958a). Psilocybin was isolated in major quantity in crystalline form, whereas only traces of psilocin were found.

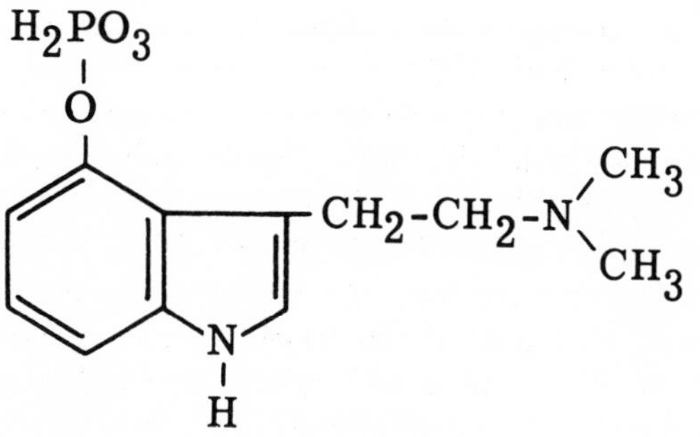

$$H_2PO_3$$

PSILOCYBIN

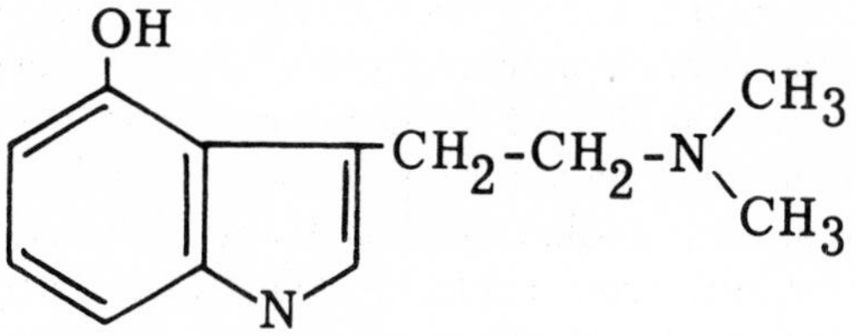

PSILOCIN
(4-HYDROXY-N, N-DIMETHYLTRYPTAMINE)

Fig. 7. Chemical structures of psilocybin and psilocin.

Hofmann *et al.* (1958b) elucidated the structure of psilocybin as the phosphoric acid ester of 4-hydroxy-*N,N*-dimethyltryptamine and confirmed this by total synthesis. Psilocin is the dephosphorylated product, 4-hydroxy-*N,N*-dimethyltryptamine. Psilocin differs structurally from bufotenine only by the presence of a hydroxyl group in the 4- rather than the 5-position.

Psilocybin and psilocin both possess similar pharmacologic actions in man and animals, resembling those produced by the other indole psychotomimetic drugs. The pharmacologic effects of these drugs are of shorter duration than LSD (3 to 4 hours compared to 8 to 10 hours for the latter) (Cohen, 1971), but are of longer duration than those produced by DMT and bufotenine (30 to 60 minutes) (Hollister, 1972). Psilocybin and psilocin are about 1/150th as potent as LSD since in man a dose of LSD of 1.5 μg/kg produces a clinical syndrome comparable to that of a dose of 225 μg/kg of psilocybin. Its psychotomimetic potency is about 25 mescaline units.

Since Hofmann *et al.* (1959) reported that the pharmacologic actions and psychotic properties of psilocybin and psilocin were quantitatively and qualitatively similar, psilocybin was assumed to be rapidly dephosphorylated *in vivo* to form psilocin, the active compound. Additional evidence suggesting that psilocybin is not the pharmacologically active agent, but acts solely as a precursor, comes from the physicochemical data of Horita (1963). He found that psilocin possessed a much greater oil/water distribution ratio at pH 7.4 than psilocybin. This indicates a greater lipid solubility and therefore a potentially greater degree of transferance across biologic membranes, notably the blood-brain barrier. Psilocybin, being a charged ion at physiologic pH, would have more difficulty than psilocin in penetrating biologic membranes.

Indeed, Horita and co-workers (Horita and Weber, 1962; Horita, 1963) have demonstrated that calf intestinal phosphatase catalyzes the hydrolysis of the phosphate group of psilocybin (O-dephosphorylation) to psilocin *in vitro*, with the liberation of inorganic phosphate. This dephosphorylation proceeds rapidly for the first 15 to 30 minutes, and then proceeds more slowly. The dephosphorylation of psilocybin could also occur in the presence of human serum alkaline phosphatase. These investigators also demonstrated that psilocybin could be dephosphorylated *in vivo*. They administered the phosphorylated compound to mice, sacrificed them at periodic intervals, and analyzed the liver, kidneys, and brain for psilocin. Psilocin appeared rapidly in liver and kidney and slowly in brain. Conducting studies employing another substrate (sodium β-glycerophosphate) of the phosphatase, they attempted to saturate the enzyme in order to competitively inhibit the conversion of psilocybin to psilocin. Using this technique, they demonstrated that psilocin was indeed the active form of psilocybin because the psilocybin now produced less pharmacologic effects.

Kalberer *et al.* (1962) synthesized ^{14}C-psilocin with the radiolabel in either a stable position in the side chain or in the N-methyl group. The latter compound was designed to determine the extent of demethylation or oxidative deamination. They proceeded to study the absorption, distribution, excretion, and metabolism of these compounds in rats. Their studies suggest that slightly more than 50% of an oral dose of psilocin was absorbed. The drug was distributed throughout the body, with highest concentrations in liver, kidney, adrenals, and brain at 30 minutes after administration. The tissue concentrations declined during the next 8 to 24 hours. Oddly enough, the rate of decline was inexplicably much slower from adrenal gland than from other tissues. After ^{14}C-psilocin administration, 62% of the radioactivity was excreted in the urine and 21% in the feces during the first 24 hours. Total excretion of radiolabel after 1 week was 89% of the dose. In biliary cannulated rats, similar results were seen, i.e., 64% excreted in urine and 15% excreted in bile. Using the N-[14]CH$_3$-psilocin, they found only 4% of the label expired as [14]CO$_2$ during a 48-hour collection period. From these studies, they concluded that less than 4% of psilocin can be either N-demethylated or oxidatively deaminated to 4-hydroxy-3-indoleacetic acid (4-HIAA) (Fig. 8).

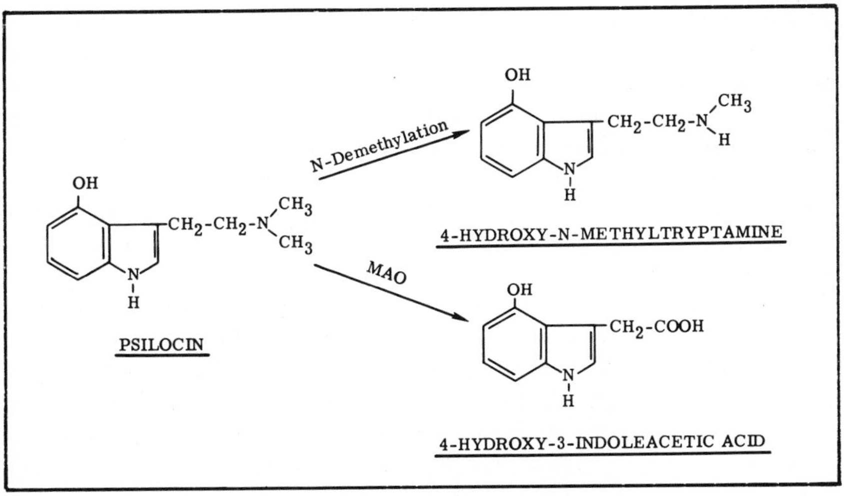

Fig. 8. The metabolism of psilocin.

They were able to identify unchanged psilocin and 4-HIAA in urine of rats treated with psilocin. Both compounds represented about 40% of the urinary radioactivity, about 25% of the administered dose being excreted as parent drug. The other metabolites were more polar and presumably conjugated; they have not yet been identified.

In another series of experiments, Gessner et al. (1960) administered psilocybin to rats intraperitoneally. They found 11% of the dose of psilocybin excreted unchanged in the urine. In addition, they found another metabolite conjugated to glucuronic acid and a trace metabolite which appeared to have properties like 4-HIAA.

The finding that psilocin is oxidatively deaminated to only a small degree in vivo is consistent with in vitro studies of Gessner et al. (1960) who demonstrated that psilocybin was such a poor substrate for MAO that it was relatively resistant to degradation by this enzyme. In contrast, 5-HT was an excellent substrate for MAO. Thus, oxidative metabolism plays only a minor role in the metabolism of psilocin and psilocybin.

HARMINE AND RELATED COMPOUNDS

Plants containing hallucinogenic alkaloids grow in numerous regions. *Peganum harmala*, a plant that is indigenous to the Russian Steppes, Syria, and India, has been used as an intoxicant for centuries (Naranjo, 1967; Deulofeu, 1967). The harmala alkaloids, harmine, harmaline, and harmalol (Fig. 9), were isolated from this plant in 1841 and were found to be responsible for its intoxicating effects. Years later another family of plants growing in the western hemisphere was found to be used as intoxicants. The vines of the plant *Banisteriopsis caapi*, which are indigenous to South America, specifically around Columbia and Amazonian Brazil, were used in native rituals as snuffs and intoxicating drinks. The plant was locally called by different names such as caapi and yage. In 1905 an alkaloid was isolated from these plants and given the name telephatine, suggesting a mystical quality. Several years later it was recognized that this material was identical to harmine, the chemical isolated more than a century earlier from *Peganum harmala*.

All harmala alkaloids isolated from these plants possess a β-carboline skeleton with varying degrees of dehydrogenation in the pyridine ring (Fig. 9). Interestingly, this β-carboline structure is chemically related to tryptamine and can be considered a fused N-methyltryptamine derivative. In fact, either tryptamine itself or tryptophan can serve as a precursor to harmine in its biosynthesis by *Peganum harmala* (Stolle and Groeger, 1968). Thus, it is not surprising that the harmala alkaloids and N-methylated tryptamines produce similar pharmacologic and psychologic effects,

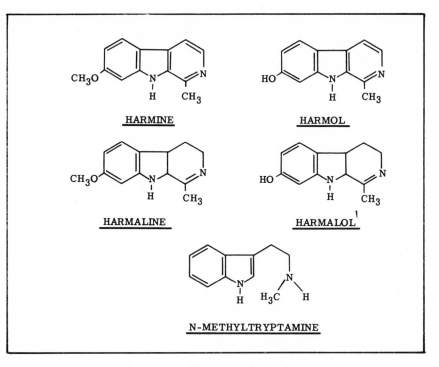

Fig. 9. The structure of harmine and related compounds.

including parasthesias followed by numbness, distortions of body images, visual imagery, etc. In animals these alkaloids produce tremors and convulsions and have been shown to be monoamine oxidase inhibitors (Pletscher *et al.*, 1959, 1960). In man, harmaline produces hallucinations at doses of 1 mg/kg i.v. and 4 mg/kg p.o. (Naranjo, 1967). When harmine is administered, doses twice as large as those of harmaline are necessary to produce hallucinations (Pennes and Hoch, 1957). The onset of effects occurs about 1 hour after oral administration of harmaline, whereas the onset is almost instantaneous after i.v. administration.

Ho and associates (1970, 1971) synthesized radiolabeled harmaline and studied its tissue distribution in rats and monkeys using autoradiography and other methods. Thirty minutes after subcutaneous injection of ^{3}H-harmaline to rats, high concentrations of radioactivity were found in small intestine, liver, kidney, adrenal, lung, and brain. A 50% decline in radioactivity was observed in most tissues during the second hour after injection. In brain, the concentration of radioactivity peaked at 30-60 minutes and accounted for about 1.5% of the injected dose; 75% of the radioactivity was due to the presence of unchanged harmaline. In monkeys, 15 minutes after intravenous administration of ^{3}H-harmaline, radioactivity was distributed unevenly throughout the brain, with highest concentrations of radioactivity present primarily in the cortical gray matter. However, 1 hour after injection, the radioactivity was evenly distributed throughout the brain. Similar to the results in rats, the majority of this radioactivity was unchanged ^{3}H-harmaline (Ho et al., 1970).

In the rat, Ho et al. (1971) found that after ^{3}H-harmaline administration, 62% of the injected radioactivity was excreted in the urine and about 12% in the feces during a 4-day collection period. The urinary radioactivity was composed of harmaline, accounting for less than 20% of the urinary radioactivity, and several of its metabolic products, including harmalol (the O-demethylated analog), harmol (resulting from O-demethylation and dehydrogenation of the pyridine ring), and the glucuronide conjugates of harmol and harmalol (Fig. 9). The latter compound accounted for most of the urinary radioactivity. The isolation of harmalol confirms and substantiates the earlier findings of Pletscher et al. (1960) and Villeneuve and Sourkes (1966), who found harmalol as a urinary metabolite of harmaline. Ho and co-workers were unable to find either harmine or harminic acid in rat urine after harmaline administration. In contrast, these two compounds had been reported earlier by Flury (1911) as being metabolic products of harmaline.

After intravenous administration of ^{3}H-harmine to rats or humans, the concentration of tritium rapidly declined from plasma as the drug and its metabolites were distributed into tissues (Slotkin et al., 1970). The tissue distribution of harmine appeared to be similar to that of harmaline; i.e., the tissue levels were high initially and then declined rapidly within 2 hours (Villeneuve and Sourkes, 1966; Slotkin and Distefano, 1970b). In the rat, 99% of a radioactive dose of ^{3}H-harmine was excreted within 48 hours: 73% in bile and 26% in urine (Slotkin and Distefano, 1970b). There did not appear to be any enterohepatic circulation for harmine or its metabolites since the urinary excretion of harmine and its metabolites in rats with cannulated bile ducts was identical to that in rats with intact bile ducts (Slotkin et al., 1970). The urinary excretion of harmine and its metabolites is rapid; about 40% of the dose is excreted within the first hour after injection and 70% within 4 hours. Urinary radioactivity was composed of unchanged harmine (1-2%), harmol (11%), harmol sulfate (69-77%), and harmol glucuronide (18-21%) (Slotkin and Distefano, 1970a,b). These same four compounds were found in bile of rats treated with harmine (Slotkin and Distefano, 1970a). In man, these metabolites are also present in urine after intravenous administration of ^{3}H-harmine. However, in contrast to the rat, man excretes harmol glucuronide and harmol sulfate in the same proportions (about 45% of each). It is of interest that a harmine metabolite i.e. harmol is produced and excreted after harmaline administration, indicating that dehydrogenation of harmaline occurs *in vivo*. However, available data indicate that the reverse reaction, i.e., the hydrogenation of harmine to form harmaline, does not occur *in vivo* since no harmaline derivatives were found after harmine administration

REFERENCES

Aghajanian, G.K. and Bing, O.H.L.: Persistence of lysergic acid diethylamide in the plasma of human subjects. Clin. Pharm. Ther. *5*:611-614, 1964.

Arnold, O.H., Hofmann, G., and Leupold-Lowenthal, H.: Untersuchungen zum Schizophrenieproblem. IV. Mittelung: Die Verteilung des C-14-radioaktiven Lysergsaurediathylamids im tierichen Organismus. Wein. Z. Nervenh. *15*:15-17, 1958.

Axelrod, J.: Enzymatic formation of psychotomimetic metabolites from normally occurring compounds. Science *134*:343, 1961.

Axelrod, J.: The enzymatic N-methylation of serotonin and other amines. J. Pharmacol. Exp. Ther. *138*:28-33, 1962.

Axelrod, J., Brady, R.O., Witkop, B., and Evarts, E.V.: Metabolism of lysergic acid diethylamide. Nature (London) *178*:143-144, 1956.

Axelrod, J., Brady, R.O., Witkop, B., and Evarts, E.V.: The distribution and metabolism of lysergic acid diethylamide. Ann. N.Y. Acad. Sci. *66*:435, 1957.

Axelson, S. and Nordgren, L.: Indoleamines in blood plasma of schizophrenics. A critical study with sensitive and selective methods. Life Sci. *14*:1261-1270, 1974.

Bidder, T.G., Mandel, L.R., Ahn, H.S., VandenHeuvel, W.J.A., and Walker, R.W.: Blood and urinary dimethyltryptamine in acute psychotic disorders. Lancet *1*:165, 1974.

Blaschko, H. and Philpot, F.J.: Enzymic oxidation of tryptamine derivatives. J. Physiol. (London) *122*:403-408, 1953.

Boszormenyi, Z. and Brunecker, G.: Dimethyltryptamine (DMT) experiments with psychotics. In Psychotropic Drugs. Garattini and Ghetti (Eds.), Amsterdam, Elsevier Publ. Co., 1957. pp. 580-581.

Boyd, E.S.: The metabolism of lysergic acid diethylamide. Arch. Int. Pharmacodyn. *CXX*:292-311, 1959.

Boyd, E.S., Rothlin, E., Bonner, J.F., Slater, I.H., and Hodge, H.C.: Preliminary studies of the metabolism of lysergic acid diethylamide using radioactive carbon-marked molecules. J. Nerv. Mental Dis. *122*:470-471, 1955a.

Boyd, E.S., Rothlin, E., Bonner, J.F., Slater, I.H., and Hodge, H.C.: Preliminary studies on the metabolism of lysergic acid diethylamide. J. Pharmacol. Exp. Ther. *13*:6-7, 1955b.

Cohen, S.: The psychotomimetic agents. In Progress in Drug Research *15*:68-102, 1971.

Deulofeu, V.: Chemical compounds isolated from *banisteriopsis* and related species. In Ethnopharmacologic Search for Psychoactive Drugs. Public Health Service Pub. No. 1645, 1967.

Diab, I.M., Freedman, D.X., Roth, L.J.: (^{3}H)-Lysergic acid diethylamide: Cellular autoradiographic localization in rat brain. Science *173*:1022-1024, 1971.

Dring, L.G., Baines, R.D., Siddik, Z.H., Smith, R.L., and Williams, R.T.: The metabolism of ¹⁴C-LSD in the rat. Abstracts, Sixth Internat. Cong. Pharmacol. 1975, p. 645.

Fabing, H.D. and Hawkins, J.R.: Intravenous bufotenine injection in the human being. Science 123:886-887, 1956.

Faed, E.M. and McLeod, W.R.: A urine screening test for lysergide (LSD-25). J. Chromatographic Sci. 11:4-6, 1973.

Faillace, L.A., Vourlekis, A., and Szara, S.: Clinical evaluation of some hallucinogenic tryptamine derivatives. J. Nerv. Ment. Dis. 145:306-313, 1967.

Farrow, J.T. and Van Vunakis, H.: Binding of d-lysergic acid diethylamide to subcellular fractions from rat brain. Nature (London) 237:164-166, 1972.

Farrow, J.T. and Van Vunakis, H.: Characteristics of d-lysergic acid diethylamide binding to subcellular fractions derived from rat brain. Biochem. Pharmacol. 22:1103-1113, 1973.

Fish, M.S., Johnson, N.M., and Horning, E.C.: Piptadenia alkaloids—indole bases of P. peregrina (L.) benth. and related species. J. Amer. Chem. Soc. 77:5892-5895, 1955.

Fisher, R.: Chemistry of the brain. Nature (London) 220:411-412, 1968.

Flury, F.: Beitrage zur Pharmakologie der Steppenraute (Peganum harmala). Naunyn-Schmiedebergs Arch. Pharmakol. 64:105-125, 1911.

Freedman, D.X., Aghajanian, G.K., and Coquet, C.A.: Effect of reserpine on plasma binding and brain uptake of LSD-25. Fed. Proc. 23:147, 1964.

Freter, K., Axelrod, J., and Witkop, B.: Studies on the chemical and enzymatic oxidation of lysergic acid diethylamide. J. Amer. Chem. Soc. 79:3191, 1957.

Gessner, P.K., Khairallah, P.A., McIsaac, W.M., and Page, I.H.: The relationship between the metabolic fate and pharmacological actions of serotonin, bufotenine and psilocybin. J. Pharmacol. 130:126-133, 1960.

Govier, W.M., Howes, B.G., and Gibbons, A.J.: The oxidative deamination of serotonin and other 3-(beta-aminoethyl)-indoles by monamine oxidase and the effect of these compounds on the deamination of tyramine. Science 118:596-597, 1953.

Haley, T.J. and Rutschmann, J.: Brain concentrations of LSD-25 (Delysid) after intracerebral or intravenous administration in conscious animals. Experientia 13:199-202, 1957.

Heller, B., Narasimhachari, N., Spaide, J., Hascovec, L., and Himwich, H.E.: N-Di-methylated indoleamines in blood of acute schizophrenics. Experientia 26:503-504, 1970.

Ho, B.T., Fritchie, G.E., Idanpaan-Heikkila, J.E., Tansey, L.W., and McIsaac, W.M.: (³H)Harmaline distribution in monkey brain; pharmacological and autoradiographic study. Brain Res. 22:397-401, 1970.

Ho, B.T., Estevez, V., Fritchie, G.E., Tansey, L.W., Idanpaan-Heikkila, J., and McIsaac, W.M.: Metabolism of harmaline in rats. Biochem. Pharmacol. 20:1313-1319, 1971.

Hofmann, A.: Psychotomimetic drugs. Chemical and pharmacological aspects. Acta. Physiol. Pharmacol. Neerl. 8:240-258, 1959.

Hofmann, A.: Chemical, pharmacological and medical aspects of psychotomimetics. J. Exp. Med. Sci. 5:31-51, 1961.

Hofmann, A. and Cerletti: Die Wirkstoffe der dritten aztekischen Zauberdroge. Deut. Med. Wochenschr. 86:885-888, 1961.

Hofmann, A. and Tscherter, H.: Isolierung von Lysergaaure Alkaloiden aus der mexikanischen Zauberdroge Ololiuqui. Experientia 16:414, 1960.

Hofmann, A., Heim, R., Braek, A., and Kobel, H.: Psilocybin, ein psychotroper Wirkstoff aus dem mexikanischen Rauschpilz Psilocybe mexicana Heim. Experientia 14:107-109, 1958a.

Hofmann, A., Frey, A., Ott, H., Petrzilka, T.H., und Troxler, F.: Konstitution-saufklarung und Synthese von Psilocybin. Experientia *14*:397-398, 1958b.

Hollister, L.E.: Clinical pharmacology of hallucinogens and marihuana. In Drug Abuse. Proceedings of the International Conference. C.J.D. Zarafonetis, (Ed.) Lea & Febiger, 1972. pp. 321-332.

Holmstedt, B. and Lindgren, J.E.: Chemical constituents and pharmacology of South American snuffs in Ethnopharmacologic Search for Psychoactive Drugs, pp. 339-373. Public Health Service Pub. No. 1645, 1967.

Horita, A.: Some biochemical studies on psilocybin and psilocin. J. Neuropsychiat. *4*:270-273, 1963.

Horita, A., and Weber, L.J.: Dephosphorylation of psilocybin to psilocin by alkaline phosphatase. Proc. Soc. Exp. Biol. Med. *106*:32-34, 1962.

Horowitz, M.J.: Flashbacks: Recurrent intrusive images after the use of LSD. Amer. J. Psychiat. *126*:565, 1969.

Idanpaan-Heikkila, J.E. and Schoolar, J.C.: LSD: Autoradiographic study on the placental transfer and tissue distribution in mice. Science *164*:1295-1296, 1969a.

Idanpaan-Heikkila, J.E. and Schoolar, J.C.: ^{14}C-Lysergide in early pregnancy. Lancet *2*:221, 1969b.

Jepson, J.B., Zaltzman, P., and Udenfriend, S.: Microsomal hydroxylation of trypt-amine, indoleaceticacid, and related compounds to 6-hydroxy derivatives. Biochim. Biophys. Acta *66*:91-102, 1962.

Kalberer, F., Kreis, W., and Rutschmann, J.: The fate of psilocin in the rat. Biochem. Pharmacol. *11*:261-269, 1962.

Kalir, A. and Szara, S.: Synthesis and pharmacological activity of fluorinated trypt-amine derivatives. J. Med. Chem. *6*:716-719, 1963.

Lanz, U., Cerletti, A., and Rothlin, E.: Uber die Verteilung des Lysergsaure-diathylamids im Organismus. Helv. Physiol. Pharmacol. Acta *13*:207, 1955.

Lemberger, L., Axelrod, J., and Kopin, I.J.: The disposition and metabolism of trypt-amine and the *in vivo* formation of 6-hydroxytryptamine in the rabbit. J. Pharmacol. Exp. Ther. *177*:169-176, 1971.

Morgan, M. and Mandell, M.: Indole(ethyl)amine N-methyltransferase in the brain. Science, *165*:492-493, 1969.

Naranjo, C.: Psychotropic properties of the harmala alkaloids in Ethnopharmacologic Search for Psychoactive Drugs, pp. 385-391. Public Health Service Pub. No. 1645, 1967.

Narasimhachari, N. and Himwich, H.E.: GC-MS identification of bufotenin in urine samples from patients with schizophrenia or infantile autism. Life Sci. *12*:475-478, 1973.

Narasimhachari, N., Heller, B., Spaide, J., Haskovec, L., Meltzer, H., Strahilevitz, M., and Himwich, H.E.: N,N-Dimethylated indoleamines in blood. Biol. Psychiat. *3*:21-23, 1971.

Pennes, H.H. and Hoch, P.H.: Psychotomimetics, clinical and theoretical con-siderations: Harmine, WIN-2299 and Nalline. Amer. J. Psychiat. *113*:887-892, 1957.

Pletscher, A., Besendorf, H., Bachtold, H.P., and Gey, K.F.: Uber pharmakologische Beeinflussung des Zentralnervensystems durch kurzwirkende Mono-aminoxydasehemmer aus der Gruppe der Harmala-Alkaloide. Helv. Physiol. Pharmacol. Acta *17*:202-214, 1959.

Pletscher, A., Gey, K.F., and Zeller, P.: Monoamine oxidase inhibitors. Prog. Drug Res. *2*:417-590, 1960.

Pletscher, A., Kunz, E., Staebler, H., and Gey, K.F.: The uptake of tryptamine by brain *in vivo* and its alteration by drugs. Biochem. Pharmacol. *12*:1065-1070, 1963.

Rosenberg, D.E., Isbell, H., and Miner, E.J.: Comparison of a placebo, N-dimethyltryptamine, and 6-hydroxy-N-dimethyltryptamine in man. Psychopharmacologia 4:39-42, 1963.

Rothlin, E.: Metabolism of lysergic acid diethylamide. Nature (London) 178:1400-1401, 1956.

Rothlin, E.: Pharmacology of lysergic acid diethylamide and some of its related compounds. J. Pharm. Pharmacol. 9:569-587, 1957.

Saavedra, J.M. and Axelrod, J.: Psychotomimetic N-methylated tryptamines: Formation in brain in vivo and in vitro. Science 175:1365-1366, 1972.

Saavedra, J.M. and Udabe, U.: Quantitative assay of bufotenine in psychosomatics. Psychosomatics 11:90-94, 1970.

Sanders, E. and Bush, M.T.: Distribution, metabolism and excretion of bufotenine in the rat with preliminary studies of its O-methyl derivative. J. Pharmacol. Exp. Ther. 158:340-352, 1967.

Sanders-Bush, E., Oates, J.A., and Bush, M.T.: Metabolic fate of bufotenine-2^{14}C in man. Fed. Proc. 34:809, 1975.

Siddik, Z.H., Barnes, R.D., Dring, L.G., Smith, R.L., and Williams, R.T.: The fate of lysergic acid di(^{14}C)-ethylamide (LSD) in the rat. Biochem. Soc. Transac. 3:290-292, 1975.

Slaytor, M., Pennefather, J.N., and Wright, S.E.: Metabolites of LSD and ergometrine. Metabolism 15:111, 1959.

Slaytor, M.B. and Wright, S.E.: The metabolites of ergometrine and lysergic acid diethylamide in rat bile. J. Med. Pharm. Chem. 5:483-490, 1962.

Slotkin, T. and Distefano, V.: Urinary metabolites of harmine in the rat and their inhibition of monoamine oxidase. Biochem. Pharmacol. 19:125-131, 1970a.

Slotkin, T.A. and Distefano, V.: A model of harmine metabolism in the rat. J. Pharmacol. Exp. Ther. 174:456-462, 1970b.

Slotkin, T.A., Distefano, V., and Au, W.Y.W.: Blood levels and urinary excretion of harmine and its metabolites in man and rats. J. Pharmacol. Exp. Ther. 173:26-30, 1970.

Snyder, S.H. and Reivich, M.: Regional localization of lysergic acid diethylamide in monkey brain. Nature (London) 209:1093-1095, 1966.

Stoll, A., Rutschmann, J., and Hofmann, A.: Ergot alkaloids XXXIII. Alkylation of dl-dihydro-nor-lysergic acid and correction of communication XXXII of this series. Helv. Chim. Acta 37:814-820, 1954.

Stoll, A., Rothlin, E., Rutschmann, J., and Schalch, W.R.: Distribution and fate of ^{14}C-labeled lysergic acid diethylamide (LSD 25) in the animal body. Experientia 11:396-397, 1955.

Stolle, K. and Groeger, D.: Untersuchungen zur Biosynthese des Harmins. Arch. Pharm. (Weinheim, Ger.) 301:561-571, 1968.

Stromberg, V.L.: The isolation of bufotenine from Piptadenia peregrina. J. Amer. Chem. Soc. 76:1707, 1954.

Szara, S.: Dimethyltryptamine: Its metabolism in man; the relation of its psychotic effect to the serotonin metabolism. Experientia 12:441-442, 1956.

Szara, S.: The comparison of psychotic effect of tryptamine derivatives with the effects of mescaline and LSD-25 in self-experiments. In Psychotropic Drugs, Garattini and Ghetti, Eds. Amsterdam, Elsevier Pub. Co., 1957. pp. 460-466.

Szara, S.: Hallucinogenic effects and metabolism of tryptamine derivatives in man. Fed. Proc. 20:885-888, 1961.

Szara, S.: Enzymatic formation of a phenolic metabolite from lysergic acid diethylamide by rat liver microsomes. Life Sci. 9:662-670, 1963.

Szara, S. and Axelrod, J.: Hydroxylation and N-demethylation of N,N-dimethyltrypt-amine. Experientia 15:216-220, 1959.

Szara, S. and Hearst, E.: The 6-hydroxylation of tryptamine derivatives: A way of producing psychoactive metabolites. Ann. N.Y. Acad. Sci. 96:134, 1962.

Szara, S., Rockland, L.H., and Rosenthal, D.: Psychological effects and metabolism of N,N-diethyltryptamine in man. Arch. Gen. Psychiat. 15:320-329, 1966.

Taunton-Rigby, A., Sher, S.E., and Kelley, P.R.: Lysergic acid diethylamide: Radioim-munoassay. Science 181:165-166, 1973.

Turner, W.J. and Merles, S.: Effects of some indolealkylamines on man. Arch. Neurol. Psychiat. 81:121, 1959.

Upshall, D.G. and Wailling, D.G.: The determination of LSD in human plasma fol-lowing oral administration. Clin. Chim. Acta 36:67-73, 1972.

Villeneuve, A. and Sourkes, T.L.: Metabolism of harmaline and harmine in the rat. Rev. Can. Biol. 25:231-239, 1966.

Voss, E.W., Jr., Babb, J.E., Metzel, P., and Winkelhake, J.L.: In vitro effect of d-lysergic acid diethylamide on immunoglobulin synthesis. Biochem. Biophys. Res. Commun. 50:950-956, 1973a.

Voss, E.W., Jr., Metzel, P., and Winkelhake, J.L.: Incorporation of a lysergic acid di-ethylamide intermediate into antibody protein in vitro. Mol. Pharmacol. 9:421-425, 1973b.

Wagner, J.G., Aghajanian, G.K., and Bing, O.H.L.: Correlation of performance test scores with "tissue concentration" of lysergic acid diethylamide in human subjects. Clin. Pharm. Ther. 9:635-638, 1968.

Weiland, H., Konz, W., and Mittasch, H.: Die Konstitution von Bufotenin und Bufotenidin. Uber Kroten-Giftstoffe. VII; Justus Liebigs. Ann. Chem. 513:1-25, 1934.

Wyatt, R.J., Saavedra, J.M., and Axelrod, J.: A dimethyltryptamine-forming enzyme in human blood. Amer. J. Psychiat. 130:754-760, 1973a.

Wyatt, R.J., Mandel, L.R., Ahn, H.S., Walker, R.W., and Van Den Heuvel, W.J.A.: Gas chromatographic mass spectrometric isotope dilution concentrations in normal and psychiatric patients. Psychopharmacologia 31:265-270, 1973b.

Yielding, K.L. and Sterglanz, H.: Lysergic acid diethylamide (LSD) binding to deoxyribonucleic acid DNA) (33203). Proc. Soc. Exp. Biol. Med. 128:1096-1098, 1968.

Chapter 5
Morphine and Morphine Substitutes

Preparation of this chapter on the physiologic disposition of the narcotic alkaloids and their substitutes has been aided by the numerous outstanding reviews predating this monograph, particularly those by Way and Adler (1960, 1962) and the book by Reynolds and Randall (1957). For the sake of brevity, we focus on morphine, its O-methylated analogue, codeine, and its diacetyl ester analogue, heroin. In addition, we have included methadone and meperidine (Demerol).* In many ways, these drugs exert similar effects and reflect abuse patterns of opiates in general, many of the alkaloids having been used and abused by man for ages. We believe that it is particularly appropriate to include methadone in this chapter because it is so closely involved in drug abuse problems, and as such is being actively studied by investigators representing many diversified sociomedical disciplines.

Opium comes from the milky juice obtained from the seed capsules of the poppy *Papaver somniferum*, which is grown largely in Turkey, India, and China. As long ago as the third century B.C., the medicinal properties of opium were recognized. As efforts were made to purify the active alkaloids present in opium, various crude drugs were prepared, such as tincture of opium and paregoric. Of the 25 or so alkaloids present in opium, about 10% is morphine and 0.5% is codeine. Continual efforts to obtain an

---

*The chemical structures of the compounds discussed in this chapter appear on Figs. 1-3.

analgesic devoid of the abuse liabilities of opium prompted early efforts to isolate the active principles of opium in pure form. When morphine was identified as the major active constituent of opium, it soon became evident that the ideal analgesic had not been found. Efforts to modify the morphine structure and thus to preserve its beneficial effects but eliminate its adverse effects led to the development of heroin or diacetylmorphine. Originally touted as the miracle analgesic of the day, it soon fell in wide disrepute in the practice of medicine, although it still is preferred in some countries as the analgesic of choice for the alleviation of deep visceral pain.

As organic chemistry became increasingly sophisticated, new synthetic compounds became available for testing as morphine substitutes. Among those gaining the most stature were meperidine in 1939 and methadone in 1945. These compounds and others have largely replaced morphine in many parts of the world, but they have been sources of continued disappointment to those who had hoped that their arrivals on the medical scene heralded the elimination of the more serious side effects of morphine (e.g., respiratory depression, euphoria, habituation, and tolerance). In this chapter we have tried to provide to the reader not only a descriptive account of the disposition of this class of psychoactive drugs, but also to provide a basis (where one exists) for correlating drug disposition and pharmacologic activity. We hope that through such analyses of pharmacodynamic findings, a more fundamental understanding of the actions of these drugs may be provided, which in turn could contribute to the future development of more effective and safer analgesics.

ABSORPTION OF OPIATES

Opiate addicts usually administer their drugs intravenously ("mainlining") and subcutaneously ("skin popping"), and much less frequently intramuscularly. As is the case with organic bases in general, the opiates are rather well absorbed from parenteral sites of administration and absorption is determined mainly by passive physical processes rather than energy-dependent mechanisms (Way and Adler, 1962; Reynolds and Randall, 1957).

Absorption from the buccal mucosa is generally rather slow for this class of drugs. Absorption of the narcotic alkaloids from the gastrointestinal tract also depends upon passive diffusion rather than active transport processes. Although their absorption from the gastrointestinal tract is generally erratic and unpredictable, evidence is available to suggest that this is due not only to the absorptive process *per se*, but also to a significant "first pass effect," whereby vastly different amounts of the opiates are metabolized by the liver immediately after absorption (Brunk and Delle, 1972). Meperidine is absorbed rapidly and extensively from the gastrointestinal tract (Way *et al.,* 1949b).

DISTRIBUTION OF OPIATES

General

As might be predicted, the distribution of morphine and related compounds is akin to that of organic bases in general. A basic principle of drug distribution, discussed earlier in Chapter 1, is that drugs pass through membranes in their undissociated forms. Acidic compounds, mostly ionized at blood pH, tend to be distributed extracellularly and to be excreted rapidly in urine. In contrast, basic compounds exist in sufficient quantity in the undissociated form at pH 7.4 to favor penetration into cells and, thus, be less available for excretory mechanisms. Therefore, it would be expected that the morphine bases would occur in very low concentrations in blood and in much higher concentrations in tissues, other factors (e.g., active transport) aside. Indeed, shortly after their absorption, these alkaloids become concentrated in tissues, especially kidney, liver, skeletal muscle, lung, and spleen; the concentrations therein quickly exceed those in blood. In one study, wherein rats were injected intravenously with morphine, only 0.1% of the administered dose was measurable in serum within 5 minutes after injection (Spector, 1971). The long half-life of morphine in rat and man is largely due to its slow redistribution out of "silent receptor" tissues (Way and Adler, 1962) as well as to an enterohepatic recirculation (March and Elliott, 1964).

We are becoming increasingly accustomed to the fact that many drugs can become bound to proteins in blood; we may even expect this to be the case. We equally well may expect that albumin would be the most likely protein involved in the binding process. For morphine, however, this does not appear to be the situation and its binding is somewhat unique. In 1972, Ringle and Herndon indicated that the prolonged exposure of rabbits to morphine was associated with an increase in the serum binding of morphine. The occurrence and timing of increased binding coincided with the appearance in serum of a factor that was responsive to morphine and had antibody characteristics. This serum morphine binding activity appeared to be localized primarily in the globulin fraction of serum, which supported the concept that the binding factor was an immunoglobulin. This is consistent with the findings of Ryan *et al.* (1971, 1972) who recently reported on the apparent presence of antibodies against morphine in the sera of approximately 40% of heroin addicts. They also reported that opiates were bound to γ-globulin in the sera of a fair percentage of both normal and addicted individuals. However, the nature of this binding was apparently different because it was reversible after dialyzing the γ-globulin of normal sera, but not after dialyzing the γ-globulin of addict sera. The exact role that this binding may play in explaining some of the effects of morphine (viz., tolerance development) is not presently understood. Future studies of this binding phenomenon deserve the careful attention of those who might be interested in the mechanisms of opiate action.

The birth of opiate-dependent babies born to addicted mothers serves as dramatic and tragic testimony to the passage of opiates through the placenta. The fact that only about 1% of an administered dose of morphine passes the placenta is probably of little consequence. The CNS of an adult appears to be highly sensitive to the effects of these compounds, and it is not difficult to imagine that a neonate would be even more sensitive in view of the incomplete development of the blood-brain barrier to opiates and a generally lower level of drug metabolism occurring in the fetus.

Yeh and Woods (1970a) injected ^{3}H-dihydromorphine* into nonpregnant and pregnant rats that were opiate tolerant and nontolerant. The plasma concentrations of ^{3}H-dihydromorphine 1 hour after injection were lower in tolerant maternal rats than in nontolerant rats. Conversely, fetal plasma levels were higher in the tolerant animal group. Thus, the passage of ^{3}H-dihydromorphine across the placental barrier appears to differ somehow in tolerant and in nontolerant rats.

Central Nervous System

A barrier exists to the passage of morphine from the blood into the CNS such that the concentrations found in brain are generally quite low. In contrast, when ^{14}C-codeine was injected into rats, the radiocarbon levels in the brain were almost identical to those in plasma and muscle (Elliott and Adler, 1956).

Despite the very low concentrations of morphine in brain, its central effects probably reflect an extraordinary receptor sensitivity (Adler et al., 1957). In general, the levels of morphine, codeine, and methadone in the CNS have been reported to correlate quite well with the onsets, intensities, and durations of their analgesic effects (Misra et al., 1974; Miller and Elliott, 1955).

---

*Dihydromorphine (DHM) appears to be similar to morphine in its physicochemical characteristics and pharmacologic properties. These characteristics coupled with the availability of its tritiated form make DHM-^{3}H uniquely suited to studies of morphine distribution. There are minimal quantitative differences in the metabolism and excretion of DHM-^{3}H and morphine; qualitatively the physiologic disposition of the two compounds is virtually identical (Hug and Mellett, 1965).

Although studies of opiate distribution have contributed to some understanding of the temporal relation between dose and effect, these studies have, for the most part, contributed little to our understanding of the mechanisms of actions of these compounds. Early studies of their distribution in the CNS were concerned primarily with distribution into whole brain and/or into relatively large regions thereof. As will be discussed in a subsequent chapter, the overwhelming majority of findings indicates that the development of tolerance to narcotic alkaloids is not related to an altered distribution of the narcotics to major anatomic subdivisions of brain. However, the CNS distribution of these drugs among various species and between different laboratories is not always consistent or predictable. More recently, investigators have undertaken the considerable task of estimating the concentrations of these drugs within discrete areas of brain in the hope of providing a more basic understanding of the nature of the interactions between receptor site and narcotic alkaloid. However, it seems ill-advised at this time to consider the preferential accumulation of opiates into specific anatomic areas of brain as *a priori* evidence for binding of these drugs to specific narcotic receptor sites. For example, the narcotic antagonist nalorphine, though it has been shown to reduce the uptake of opiates into brain, did so at inordinately high concentrations, and even then the reduction in uptake was only slight. Thus, Ingoglia (1970), utilizing tritiated morphine in experiments with mice and rats, showed an accumulation of morphine in the lateral cerebral ventricle as well as in the ventromedial portion of the hypothalamus. He demonstrated that a dose as high as 100 mg/kg of nalorphine, injected 30 minutes prior to the intraventricular injection of morphine, did not abolish this morphine accumulation. Based on this finding, he suggested that the accumulation of morphine was probably not receptor specific. As further evidence of a lack of receptor specificity, he injected morphine chronically until the experimental animals developed tolerance. In these experiments, the animal brains exhibited a reduced size of the cell nuclear area of the ventromedial nucleus; however, the reduced size was apparently due more to morphine-induced starvation than to a direct effect of morphine on these cells.

When morphine was administered to rats of increasing age, Kupferberg and Way (1963) found increasing blood:brain ratios of morphine. This suggested that as the animal aged, a blood-brain barrier to morphine developed and that this might account for the greater tolerance of older animals exposed repeatedly to morphine. In a preliminary report, Kerr (1974) provided evidence for a change in the permeability of the blood-brain barrier during the development of tolerance to opiates in rats. He first established a lethal dose of morphine by direct intraventricular injection into naive rats. The rats were then made tolerant to increasing doses of morphine administered intraperitoneally. Twenty-four hours later the rats received the predetermined lethal dose of morphine directly into the left lateral cerebral ventricle. This dose of drug was still lethal, i.e., the animals made tolerant to peripherally administered morphine did not appear to be tolerant to centrally administered morphine. These results suggested that tolerance might be associated with a decreased permeability across the blood-brain barrier rather than to lesser responsiveness of specific neurons in the CNS. On the other hand, Johannesson and Woods (1964) demonstrated that the brain:plasma ratios of free morphine in tolerant rats showed a trend toward *higher* values than those in nontolerant animals. These data, of course, imply that the permeability of the blood-brain barrier to morphine is increased during tolerance, rather than decreased.

Narcotic analgesics have been shown to be taken up by the kidney (Hug *et al.*, 1965; Hug, 1967; May *et al.*, 1967) as well as by the choroid plexus (Takemori and Stenwick, 1966; Hug, 1967), both uptakes involving active transport processes. It has been suggested that the transport of these drugs by the choroid plexus may facilitate their removal from cerebrospinal fluid, just as their transport by the kidney promotes their elimination from blood. The narcotic analgesics have also been shown to be taken up by brain slices of the rat by a process having the characteristics of active transport, including uptake against an apparent concentration gradient, saturability, energy dependence, structural specificity, and substrate competition. Certain differences between the uptake into brain slices and transport in both the kidney and choroid plexus suggest different transport mechanisms are operative. For example, quaternary organic bases can compete with opiates for transport in both kidney and choroid plexus, but they reportedly do not affect the uptake of dihydromorphine into brain slices (Scrafani and Hug, 1968).

Craig, O'Dea, and Takemori (1971), addressing themselves to the question of distribution of morphine within the CNS and its possible relation to opiate tolerance, showed that uptake of morphine from the systemic circulation by the plexus of tolerant rabbits did not differ from that of nontolerant rabbits, nor was there a difference *in vitro* in the active transport of morphine in cerebrocortical slices from tolerant and nontolerant rats. They concluded that it was unlikely that the carrier-mediated transport systems for morphine uptake in the choroid plexus or cortical slices played a role in the development of tolerance to effects of morphine-type drugs.

In rabbits, morphine was reported to be removed from the fluid perfusing the cerebral ventricles by a system exhibiting many characteristics of active transport (Asghar and Way, 1970). Others have reported that this transport is a simple diffusion process (Wang and Takemori, 1972a). Perhaps more importantly, no differences were observed between nontolerant and tolerant rabbits with respect to their ability to transport morphine from blood into the cerebrospinal fluid (Wang and Takemori, 1972b). Similarly, Siminoff and Saunders (1958) reported no differences in the concentrations of free and conjugated morphine in the brains and tissues of tolerant and nontolerant rabbits. Similar findings also were reported in dogs (Mulé and Woods, 1962), monkeys (Mellet and Woods, 1965), and rats (Woods, 1954). These data, considered collectively, strongly suggest that the phenomenon of opiate tolerance is not explainable by differences in the transport or distribution of morphine into the brain or cerebrospinal fluid. It is possible, however, that future studies may reveal that the *micro*distribution of opiates in the CNS may be closely involved in the development of tolerance.

As has been previously pointed out (Way and Adler, 1960), those factors that alter the physiologic disposition of opiates, or more specifically their availability to the CNS receptors, should be separated from events that occur at the target organ itself. In Chapter 10 dealing with drug tolerance, we discuss studies involving the use of inhibitors of protein synthesis to block the development of tolerance to morphine and allied drugs. Studies by Loh et al. (1969, 1971) emphasize some of the potential pitfalls of such studies. Actinomycin-D is a compound which is widely accepted as an inhibitor of protein synthesis by inhibition of DNA-directed RNA synthesis (Goldberg and Reich, 1964). This compound had been shown to attenuate the development of tolerance to morphine (Cohen et al., 1965; Smith, 1968; Cox et al., 1968) by virtue of its inhibition of protein synthesis. However, Loh and his associates demonstrated that actinomycin-D can inhibit tolerance development to morphine by at least two mechanisms. In addition to inhibiting protein synthesis, actinomycin-D appears to facilitate the entrance of morphine into the CNS by increasing the permeability of the blood-brain barrier. Thus, after treatment of mice with actinomycin-D, a higher brain:blood ratio of morphine was obtained (without any alteration in the plasma binding of morphine). They concluded that the initial effect of actinomycin-D was on the blood-brain barrier so as to facilitate morphine entry into the CNS. Thus, the early phase of tolerance inhibition by actinomycin-D, according to the authors, might more appropriately be interpreted as an enhancement of morphine toxicity rather than as an inhibition of tolerance development *per se*. The delayed effect of actinomycin-D, which becomes increasingly significant in preventing tolerance with continued opiate administration, is presumably related to inhibition of protein synthesis.

Narcotic analgesics have been shown to be localized in the synaptosomal fraction of rat brain after incubation of brain homogenates with drug *in vitro*. This brain fraction also localizes these drugs after *in vivo* injection in analgesic doses to rats (Hug and Oka, 1969; Scrafani *et al.*, 1970; Hug and Oka, 1971; Clouet and Williams, 1971). This preferential accumulation appears to be mediated by both passive and active transport systems. In contrast, Mulé *et al.* (1967) observed no such preferential localization in guinea pigs injected with tritiated morphine. Indeed, the radioactivity was distributed mostly in the soluble fraction and the remainder was distributed rather evenly in various particulate fractions of brain. The myriad of factors affecting tissue distribution *in vivo* (e.g., blood flow, plasma protein binding) and *in vitro* (e.g., pH, buffer systems, concentrations of various constituents, cell washing and redistribution) probably contributes largely to different findings between various investigators. Therefore, the significance of this binding remains to be explained; for example, the localization of dihydromorphine in the synaptosomal fraction is reportedly not reversed by the administration of opiate antagonists and/or by tolerance (Clouet and Williams, 1971). The binding of narcotics to nerve endings continues to be of interest to investigators in this field, especially in view of the reports wherein the effects of the narcotic alkaloids appear to be related to their actions on synaptic function, or at least to influences on various central neurotransmitters (see Chapter 10).

METABOLISM OF OPIATES

General

In addition to distribution to extraneural tissues and the existence of a blood-brain barrier (particularly to the passage of morphine), biotransformation of morphine and its surrogates is another prime factor limiting the onsets, durations, and magnitudes of their pharmacologic effects. The predominant metabolic changes to be considered include N-dealkylation, O-dealkylation, and hydrolysis; the resulting products of these reactions are frequently conjugated prior to excretion in urine, and to a lesser extent in feces.

N-Dealkylation

The N-dealkylation of morphine-type compounds (Fig. 1) has been demonstrated in many animal species and in man both *in vitro* and *in vivo*. The reaction is catalyzed by enzyme systems largely localized in the endoplasmic reticulum (microsomes) of liver. The enzymatic N-demethylation of narcotic drugs was originally investigated *in vitro* by Axelrod (1956a) who demonstrated that the cofactor requirements for this enzymatic reaction were NADPH and molecular oxygen.

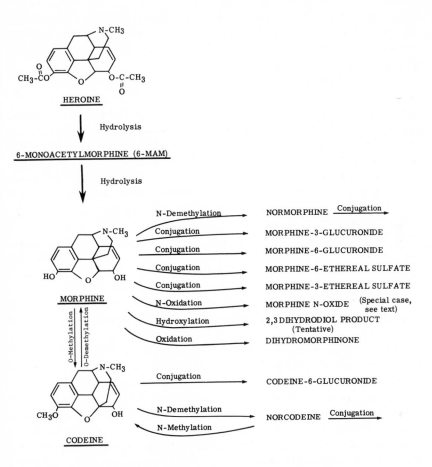

Fig. 1. Metabolism of morphine, heroine, and codeine.

It is not surprising that those factors which affect the activities of enzymes localized in the microsomes will also affect the rates of N-dealkylation of morphine and morphine surrogates. It is also not surprising that based upon wide species variations in the activities of the microsomal enzymes, the rates and amounts of N-demethylation of morphine surrogates vary markedly in various species. In fact, strain and sex differences in the metabolism of opiates are well known. For example, in many strains of rats used experimentally, the N-demethylation of morphine to normorphine has been found to be sex related, such that males N-demethylate more readily than females. These findings were consistent with the higher N-demethylating activity in hepatic microsomes from male rats as compared to those from females (Axelrod, 1956a; March and Elliott, 1964; Yeh and Woods, 1969b). However, such sex differences have not been reported *in vivo* in man (Elliott *et al.*, 1954) or *in vitro* in the rabbit, mouse, or guinea pig (Kato and Onoda, 1966).

Normorphine has been identified as a minor metabolite after morphine administration in several species, including man (Oguri *et al.*, 1970; Spector, 1971; Yeh *et al.*, 1971; Yeh, 1973, 1975; Misra *et al.*, 1961a, b; Milthers, 1962c). Early evidence for the formation of normorphine *in vivo* was indirect, based upon the observation that $^{14}CO_2$ appeared in the expired air shortly after injection of N-$^{14}CH_3$-morphine into rats (March and Elliott, 1964) and man (Elliott *et al.*, 1954). In these species about 0.5 to 6% of the administered dose of morphine may be excreted via the pulmonary route as $^{14}CO_2$. Normorphine formation was further inferred from studies *in vitro* showing release of $^{14}CO_2$ from N-$^{14}CH_3$-morphine by rat liver slices (March and Elliott, 1964), or showing formaldehyde formation in direct stoichiometric relation to normorphine production from morphine by liver microsomes (Axelrod, 1956a). (Trapping of formaldehyde is an indirect means of quantitating the degree of N-demethylation *in vitro*.)

Yeh (1973, 1975) has reportedly isolated normorphine and an unspecified, acid-labile normorphine conjugate as metabolites of morphine in man. The normorphine conjugate was estimated to represent about 1-5% of the administered dose; free normorphine represented about 0.5%. Conjugates of normorphine have also been found in the urine of dogs and monkeys after administration of normorphine (Misra *et al.*, 1960).

Other opiate-like drugs are also N-demethylated. In man, significant amounts of meperidine (Fig. 2) have been shown to be N-demethylated, about one-third of the dose appearing in urine as normeperidine and its derivatives (Plotnikoff *et al.*, 1952). Only 5% of the dose of meperidine was excreted unchanged. The rate of biotransformation of meperidine in man is the same in both tolerant and nontolerant subjects. Similarly, in man about 10% of a dose of codeine (Fig. 1) is excreted in urine as norcodeine conjugates and lesser amounts as free norcodeine (Adler *et al.*, 1955).

The formation of N-dealkylated metabolites of opiates *in vivo* cannot be viewed simply as a "detoxication" mechanism because these metabolites have been shown to possess significant pharmacologic activities. For example, Miller and Anderson (1954) found that in mice normorphine and normeperidine were less analgetic, but were more toxic than were morphine and meperidine, respectively. Norcodeine, on the other hand, was found to be both less analgetic and less toxic than codeine. In man, norcodeine appears to be as potent as codeine (sedative properties) in normal subjects, and about three times more potent than codeine in individuals addicted to either norcodeine or codeine (Fraser *et al.*, 1958). Thus, whether N-de-

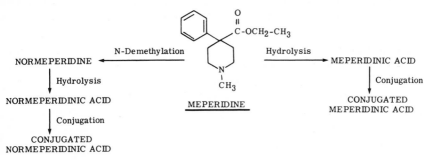

Fig. 2. Metabolism of meperidine.

methylation (or any drug biotransformation for that matter) is viewed as a detoxication process depends upon, among other things, the specific compound, the specific pharmacologic effect, and the species being studied; the simplistic acceptance of biotransformation as a general detoxication mechanism is ill-advised.

A possible relationship between the N-demethylation of narcotic alkaloids and their pharmacologic activities was proposed by Beckett, Casy, and Harper (1956). Based upon their studies of the structures and activities of various opiates, they postulated that the combination of an opiate with its receptor did not itself produce analgesia, but that following attachment of the drug to the receptor surface there occurred an oxidative N-dealkylation. The resultant metabolite-receptor complex was considered to be responsible for initiating the analgesic response. At about this same period, Axelrod (1956c) hypothesized that the liver N-demethylating enzyme system might serve as a useful model to study opiate receptors within the CNS. This hypothesis was based upon certain similarities between the analgesic responses of rats to the opiates and upon certain characteristics of the opiate N-demethylating system of the liver microsomes *in vitro*, which included the following: (a) stereoisomers of certain narcotic compounds varied in their analgesic potencies and varied correspondingly in their capacity to serve as substrates for the N-demethylating system; (b) nalorphine antagonized both the analgesic activity and the N-demethylation of several opiates; (c) the development of analgetic tolerance was accompanied by reduced N-demethylating activity after chronic morphinization; and (d) the recovery of analgesic activity paralleled the recovery of N-demethylating activity upon withdrawal of opiate. The hypotheses were further supported by reports that N-demethylation occurred not only in liver tissue, but also in the CNS, the "target organ" of the opiates (Milthers, 1961, 1962 a, b; Elison and Elliott, (1963).

With time, however, the similarities between the microsomal N-demethylating enzymes and the CNS receptors for opiates were overshadowed by the dissimilarities which researchers had demonstrated. For example, the less potent morphine surrogates, meperidine and codeine, were found to be N-demethylated by microsomes more readily than the more potent analgesic morphine (Axelrod, 1956a,c; Elliott et al., 1961; Elison et al., 1963). Also Takemori and Mannering (1958) reported that in rabbit and mouse liver microsomes, the d- and l-stereoisomers of 3-hydroxy-N-methyl morphinan were N-demethylated with equal facility, although only the l-forms exhibited the pharmacologic activity typical of opiates. Similarly, in the morphinan series, the pharmacologically inactive d-3-hydroxy-N-allyl morphinan inhibited N-demethylation by mouse liver microsomes as effectively as its pharmacologically active l-isomer. Other N-substituted morphinans showed an inverse relationship between their capacities to antagonize analgesia and to inhibit N-demethylation (Chernov et al., 1959). Furthermore, in tolerant animals, the degree to which the analgesic response was diminished did not parallel the degree to which N-demethylation was depressed (Cochin and Axelrod, 1959). During withdrawal the recovery of analgesic response and recovery of microsomal N-demethylating activity did not always correspond temporally. Indeed, in at least one instance, the development of tolerance was not accompanied at all by an observable effect on the N-demethylating activity of the liver in vitro (Herken et al., 1959). Furthermore, when the amount of $^{14}CO_2$ in the expired air was used as a measure of narcotic N-demethylation in vivo, no evidence of inactivation of the N-demethylating system was observed to accompany the development of tolerance in man or experimental animals (Elliott et al., 1954; March and Elliott, 1964).

Although liver tissues obtained from tolerant animals may have been less able to N-demethylate narcotics in vitro than those from nontolerant animals, brain slices were shown to N-demethylate morphine to the same degree in tolerant animals as in nontolerant animals (Elison and Elliott, 1963).

As mentioned above nalorphine was reported to be an inhibitor of the enzymatic N-demethylation of morphine and other narcotic drugs in vitro (Axelrod and Cochin, 1957; Minegishi et al., 1968). However, the significance of these findings is in question. For example, it has been reported that treating rats with nalorphine increases the proportion of normorphine found in brain and liver (Johannesson and Milthers, 1963). Tampier and his associates (1970) observed that nalorphine treatment increased significantly the glucuronidation and the N-demethylation of morphine both in vivo and in vitro by stimulating the activities of glucuronyl transferase and N-demethylase. It was their feeling that the antagonistic effects of nalorphine on morphine actions could be partly explained through an *enhancement* of morphine metabolism, in addition to the more conventionally accepted competitive antagonism at phamacologic receptors.*

Other findings suggested that N-dealkylation of opiates in the CNS was not a prerequisite for narcotic analgesic activity. For example, concentrations of normorphine in the brains of animals receiving normorphine were shown to be 4-5 times higher than the concentrations observed in animals rendered "equally analgesic" by administration of morphine (Johanneson and Schau, 1963).

Thus, the liver microsomal N-demethylating enzymes did not necessarily reflect events occurring at opiate receptor sites in the CNS; and the hypothesis suggesting that these enzymes might be a model for the opiate receptors in the CNS is presently untenable (Jenner and Testa, 1973). The theory that the development of tolerance to narcotics might be related to an impairment in the ability of an organism to N-demethylate morphine centrally has likewise been abandoned. It has been suggested that Beckett's earlier concept of a single rigid receptor for opiates might better be modified to accommodate data which have accumulated in recent years (Portoghese, 1966; Goldstein, 1974). A more flexible receptor is envisioned which incorporates some contemporary concepts of conformational changes in protein structures.

Notwithstanding the aforementioned discrepancies between experimental findings and the hypothesis of a relation between N-dealkylation and opiate receptors in the CNS, Axelrod, Beckett, and their associates have presented significant and imaginative contributions to further the understanding of opiate action. They provided a stimulus for new approaches to the study of the metabolism of these compounds, and to the study of the structural configurations and the functional nature of the CNS receptor site(s) for opiates. All too frequently investigators who make the most significant contributions to a field of research have, at one time or another, proposed theories which have been subsequently abandoned. In any case, considering that some of the nor metabolites of opiates can exert pharmacologic effects of their own, N-dealkylation of these drugs cannot be viewed simply as a detoxication process.

O-Dealkylation

As discussed above, several species can N-demethylate drugs such as morphine and codeine to form normorphine and norcodeine, respectively.

---

*This explanation probably has little or no clinical significance since the reversal of opiate effects by nalorphine is so rapid that metabolic effects are unlikely to be involved.

In addition, narcotic alkaloids having an O-methyl substituent (typically, codeine) can undergo O-dealkylation (Adler and Latham, 1950). Accordingly, investigators have shown the formation of morphine from codeine in a variety of experimental animals both *in vivo* and *in vitro* (Way and Adler, 1960; Yeh and Woods, 1969a).

The liver is by and large the main site of O-dealkylation of narcotic alkaloids; once again the microsomal enzyme system is involved, and the reaction requires the presence of NADPH and O_2, as is customarily encountered for the microsomal oxidation of drugs. Early evidence was obtained to suggest that more than one demethylating enzyme existed (Axelrod, 1955, 1956b). Takemori and Mannering (1958) showed that large differences existed between the amounts of formaldehyde formed *in vitro* from the N-methyl and from the O-methyl groups of codeine, thus offering evidence that the O- and N-demethylating enzyme systems probably differed. Later, Elison and Elliott (1964) demonstrated that there were certain kinetic differences in the behavior of N- and O-demethylases which act on codeine and dextromethorphan in rat liver microsomes. Data obtained *in vitro* involving the N-dealkylation of ethyl morphine and the O-dealkylation of norcodeine indicate that though there is a mutual dependency of both reactions on cytochrome P-450 activity, there are different rate-controlling events in the two oxidative reactions (George and Tephly, 1968).

Over 30 years ago, it was proposed that the CNS depressant actions of codeine were dependent upon release of the O-methyl group and the resultant formation of morphine; accordingly, then, morphine would account for the pharmacologic activity observed after a dose of codeine. In man, three pathways are primarily involved in codeine metabolism. These are N-demethylation to form norcodeine, O-demethylation to morphine, and glucuronide formation. In general, N-demethylation occurs to a greater extent than does O-demethylation. Within 24 hours after administration of codeine to man, urine contains morphine, conjugated norcodeine, and free and conjugated codeine (Adler, 1952; Mannering et al., 1954; Adler et al., 1955).

In man and rat, about 10% of an administered dose of codeine is converted to morphine, and several studies have demonstrated that this amount of morphine and the rate of its formation could not account for the onset, magnitude, and duration of analgesic effect after codeine administration. Furthermore, in the dog only 2% of a dose of codeine is converted to morphine. This small amount is reportedly conjugated about 10 times more rapidly than an equivalent amount of morphine injected into the animal (Paerregaard, 1958; Paerregaard and Poulsen, 1958). Therefore, if the actions of codeine in the dog were due to morphine formation, it has been calculated that about 500 times more codeine than morphine would be required to produce equivalent pharmacologic effects; the actual ratio of codeine to morphine required for such equivalence is less than 20. For these reasons (and others discussed in the 1960 and 1962 reviews of Way and Adler), it is difficult to accept the hypothesis that codeine has to be O-dealkylated to morphine in order to produce its pharmacologic effects.

Methylation

Interestingly, the reverse of N-demethylation, namely, N-methylation of opiates has been shown to occur *in vivo* (Clouet, 1962a, b), and *in vitro* in both brain and liver tissue (Clouet, 1962b; Axelrod, 1962; Clouet, 1963; Clouet et al., 1963). Thus, after administration of normorphine, morphine can be detected in tissues. Methylation of the nor derivatives of meperidine and codeine has also been reported.

In addition to N-methylation, O-methylation of opiates can also occur (Elison and Elliott, 1964). Thus, in experimental animals the phenolic hydroxyl group of morphine has been shown to be susceptible to methylation both *in vivo* and *in vitro*, with the resultant formation of codeine. In man as well, codeine is formed from O-methylation of morphine (Borner and Abbott, 1973). However, in at least one instance, the formation of codeine as a urinary metabolite of morphine in the rat was not confirmed (Abrams and Elliott, 1974). It is interesting that the methyl donor for this reaction does not seem to be methionine of S-adenosylmethionine as is typical for most reported O-methylation reactions.

Hydrolysis

Hydrolysis is a major metabolic pathway for esterified narcotic analgesics, notably heroin (Fig. 1) and meperidine (Fig. 2). In the latter case, a portion of meperidine and its N-demethylated metabolite, normeperidine, are hydrolyzed to meperidinic and normeperidinic acids, respectively (Fig. 2).

It has been shown that normeperidine can penetrate the CNS and that it is more toxic than meperidine, but has less analgesic potency (Miller and Anderson, 1954). The non-analgetic meperidinic and normeperidinic acids are readily conjugated and excreted in urine and these biotransformations can confidently be considered as "detoxication" mechanisms (MacDonald et al., 1946; Burns et al., 1955; Gaudette and Brodie, 1959; Way and Adler, 1962). In the case of heroin, however, its hydrolysis results in formation of pharmacologically active compounds (Way et al., 1960).

The metabolism of heroin has been studied extensively in animals (Way and Adler, 1960) and in man (Oberst, 1943; Elliott et al., 1971). Although studies from laboratory to laboratory frequently exhibit quantitative differences in the disposition of a dose of heroin, they can often be attributed to differences in dosages, routes of administration, species, etc. Extensive evidence indicates that heroin is deacetylated (hydrolyzed) at the 3-position to form 6-monoacetylmorphine (6-MAM) (Fig. 1). The 6-MAM can then be further deacetylated to morphine, which can be conjugated and subsequently excreted in urine as morphine-3-glucuronide. The initial deacetylation occurs rapidly and extensively and results in the rapid disappearance of free heroin from blood. The hydrolysis of heroin is so complete that only small amounts of unchanged drug are excreted in urine. In one study, heroin was infused intravenously into volunteers at a constant rate and blood was drawn when the subjects were experiencing the drug's subjective and depressant effects (Elliott et al., 1971). At such times, the blood contained no detectable amounts of free heroin, free or conjugated morphine, or free 6- or 3-MAM. About half the administered dose was ultimately excreted in urine, mostly as conjugated morphine.

Hydrolysis of heroin is catalyzed by enzymes present in many mammalian tissues. Of those examined, liver generally exhibited the highest esterase activity, followed in order by kidney, brain, and serum (Wright, 1941, 1942). Because this ranking of tissue enzyme activity differed for choline esterase activity, it was concluded that that enzyme did not hydrolyze heroin. Similarly, sera from rabbits with almost identical abilities to hydrolyze acetylcholine differed in their ability to hydrolyze heroin and 6-MAM. Ellis (1948) confirmed that the enzyme which hydrolyzed heroin could not be acetylcholine esterase, nor did it appear to be pseudocholine esterase. He also reported that heroin was not hydrolyzed by the plasma esterase which hydrolyzes acetylsalicyclic acid, a compound hydrolyzed rapidly by guinea pig plasma and only slowly by the plasma of man, dog, and rabbit. Heroin, on the other hand, was hydrolyzed rapidly by both rabbit and guinea pig plasma, slowly by human, and not at all by dog plasma.*

An obvious question is "To what extent do the products of heroin hydrolysis contribute to its pharmacologic effects?" Heroin differs structurally from morphine only in the presence of the acetyl groups in the 3- and 6-positions. Almost 40 years ago, it was suggested that heroin acted principally by virtue of its conversion to 6-MAM. Heroin and 6-MAM were found to be virtually equipotent in pharmacologic activity (Eddy and Howes, 1935; Wright and Barbour, 1935). Various studies have been

---

*The hydrolysis of meperidine in liver also appears to be catalyzed by an enzyme system that differs from known tropine esterases, choline esterase, and esterases which hydrolyze aliphatic esters (Bernheim and Bernheim, 1945).

conducted to elucidate a possible role of morphine and 6-MAM in the overall pharmacologic effects produced after heroin administration. It should be noted at the outset that the apparent half-life of heroin in plasma is quite short (for example, about 2½ minutes in the mouse). As heroin disappears from blood, 6-MAM appears in brain and soon thereafter morphine appears (Way et al., 1960). In regard to the distribution into the CNS of the three compounds heroin, 6-MAM, and morphine, morphine appears to have the most limited access (although, as mentioned earlier, only very little morphine needs to enter the CNS in order to produce opiate effects).

Most likely, heroin is deacetylated rapidly to 6-MAM in blood. The liberated 6-MAM gains ready access to the CNS. Probably 6-MAM exerts pharmacologic effects under these conditions, but also small amounts of morphine may be furnished to brain tissue by penetration as 6-MAM and subsequent deacetylation to morphine, a reaction which has been reported to occur in vitro (Kemp and Way, 1959). Pharmacologic effects after heroin administration are still apparent after both heroin and 6-MAM have disappeared from the animal, but when brain morphine levels are detectable. Thus, the pharmacologic effects of heroin present a rather interesting picture from a pharmacodynamic viewpoint: the immediate effects (after intravenous administration) are probably due to heroin itself (Oldendorf et al., 1972); the rapid conversion of heroin to 6-MAM and the rapid transfer of the latter compound to the CNS probably account for maintenance of the effects as the heroin concentration in brain declines; the persistent effects are likely due to the presence of morphine in the CNS (from peripheral sources and possibly from local formation via 6-MAM hydrolysis) after both heroin and 6-MAM have disappeared from the animal.

Conjugation

Conjugation is an important final common pathway for the metabolic elimination of morphine and its surrogates. Although varying amounts of morphine glucuronide are reportedly formed in man after morphine administration, there is little doubt that it is the major morphine metabolite. Recent reports indicate that about 65% of an administered dose of morphine is excreted as morphine glucuronide in human urine (Yeh, 1975; Brunk and Delle, 1974). It has been claimed that because the conjugation of morphine with glucuronic acid occurs so rapidly in the cells of the intestinal mucosa and liver, the levels of free morphine are very low in the plasma and urine of man after oral administration (Brunk and Delle, 1974). Morphine surrogates which are metabolized to morphine can be excreted ultimately as glucuronides of morphine. Thus, heroin is excreted in urine largely as morphine-3-glucuronide. In the case of codeine, an administered dose is accounted for in urine largely as glucuronide conjugates of codeine, nor-codeine, and morphine.

As previously mentioned, in man, meperidine and its N-dealkylated metabolite normeperidine can be hydrolyzed to meperidinic and nor-meperidinic acids, respectively. These latter two compounds are excreted in human urine as conjugates (Burns et al., 1955; Plotnikoff et al., 1952, 1956).

It has been established that the major urinary and biliary metabolite of morphine is morphine-3-glucuronide. This conjugate was identified in the urine of dogs by Woods (1954) and later in the urine of human addicts by Fujimoto and Way (1957). Morphine-6-glucuronide has also been demonstrated as a minor urinary metabolite of morphine in rabbits, guinea pig, rat, mouse, and human (Yoshimura et al., 1969b; Oguri et al., 1970). In chapter 1 of this monograph, the biochemical mechanisms involved in the formation of glucuronides by liver tissue are discussed. It may be recalled that glucuronide pathways utilize the uridine disphosphoglucuronic acid (UDPGA)/glucuronyltransferase pathways described by Dutton and Storey (1954). No consistent evidence exists for a causal relationship between the development of tolerance to the pharmacologic effects of the opiates and effects they might exert on the UDPGA system to accelerate their own rates of conjugation.

Abrams and Elliott (1974) have recently reported on the excretion of morphine by the Gunn rat, a mutant strain of Wistar rat in which certain uridine diphosphoglucuronyltranserases are virtually absent. In the Gunn rat, glucuronide formation is, however, not always absent and varies with the substrate studied and the age of the animal. These and other findings support the concept that UDPGA-transferase is a family of enzymes, each with its own characteristics. This concept was supported by the lack of any difference in the urinary excretion of conjugated morphine or in the con-jugation of morphine in vitro between Gunn and (control) Wistar rats.

In general, drug conjugates are believed to be pharmacologically in-active and, indeed, morphine and its surrogates are primarily "detoxified" by conjugation, particularly to the glucuronides. Early studies of morphine-3-glucuronide indicated it had less analgesic activity than morphine (Woods, 1954). Morphine-3-glucuronide and morphine-3-ethereal sulfate have been shown to be ineffective after subcutaneous administration at doses exceeding 20 mg/kg. More recent evidence involving the intracerebral injection of morphine-3-glucuronide into mice demonstrated a resultant analgesic effect (Sasajimia, 1970; Hosoya and Oka, 1970; Schulz and Goldstein, 1972). The lack of an analgesic effect when it is administered parenterally is probably not due to exclusion of the compound from the CNS by an active process; it is more likely that this conjugate is so polar that it simply does not enter the CNS where it can exert its analgesic effects (Muraki, 1971). Also, the demonstration of analgesic activity upon intra-cerebral administration does not necessarily mean that the conjugated form of the opiate is active *per se*. Indeed, the studies of Schulz and Goldstein (1972) would indicate that glucuronides of opiates can be hydrolyzed to the parent opiate in brain tissue *in vivo* to an extent sufficient to account for the analgesia observed after their intracerebral administration.

In contrast to findings with the 3-position phenolic conjugates, analgesic effects (hot plate) have been observed in mice injected sub-cutaneously with the 6-position alcoholic conjugates of morphine, i.e., morphine 6-glucuronide, and morphine-6-ethereal sulfate. The analgesic effects were much *higher* in intensity and *longer* in duration than those observed after morphine administration (Kamata *et al.*, 1969; Mori *et al.*, 1972). As if that were not indicative of an intrinsic pharmacologic activity of these conjugates, it has also been reported that morphine-6-glucuronide, but not free morphine, was present in the brains of rats 45 minutes after i.p. injection of morphine-6-glucuronide (Yoshimura *et al.*, 1969a; Shimomura *et al.*, 1971). The ratio of morphine-6-glucuronide to the 3-isomer present in 24-hour urine specimens is about 1:100 in rabbits, guinea pigs, and man (slightly less in rats and mice). Thus, despite a probable intrinsic analgesic activity, it has been suggested that morphine-6-glucuronide does not con-tribute to any significant extent to the analgetic action of morphine *in vivo*, considering the small amounts of the conjugate excreted into the urine of the species studied. On the other hand, it is worth recalling that only a very small fraction of a dose of morphine is present in the CNS at the time of peak pharmacologic effect. Therefore, it may be unjustified to ignore any potential contribution to morphine's pharmacologic activity from a metabolite simply because that metabolite is formed in small quantities.

Morphine-3-ethereal sulfate has been reported in the urine of the chicken, dog, rat, and cat (Woods and Chernov, 1966; Fujimoto and Haarstad, 1969; Misra *et al.*, 1970; Yeh *et al.*, 1971; Mori *et al.*, 1972; Peterson and Fjuimoto, 1973). It appears that, in the chicken at least, morphine is actively secreted by the renal tubular cells and is metabolized therein to morphine-3-ethereal sulfate (Watrous and Fujimoto, 1971).

Other Metabolites of Opiates

From the foregoing discussion, it is evident that N- and O-dealkylation, hydrolysis, and conjugation are the major metabolic path-ways for the biotransformation of morphine and its surrogates. As im-proved techniques for separations of drugs and metabolites are coupled with highly sensitive and uniquely specific techniques for detection and identification of compounds (viz., gas chromatography/mass spectroscopy; radioimmunoassay), minor metabolites of morphine continue to be reported, the importance of which should not be minimized. For example, dihydromorphinone (Dilaudid) was identified as a minor metabolite of morphine present in the urine of morphine-treated rats (Klutch, 1974). About 4% of the dose was excreted as this metabolite, comparable to the amounts of normorphine excreted by the rat after morphine administration.

Studies have shown that drugs can undergo N-oxidation *in vitro*, and that NADPH and O_2-dependent liver microsomal enzymes are capable of catalyzing this reaction (McMahon, 1966). Fish *et al.* (1955) have suggested that N-oxides may be formed as intermediates in the oxidative N-demethylation of drugs. In man, several drugs have been shown to be excreted as *N*-oxides. Under unique circumstances morphine may be metabolized to morphine *N*-oxide in man (Woo *et al.*, 1968). That is to say, a substance which met various criteria for morphine *N*-oxide was present in urine of cancer patients to whom morphine was administered, in addition to their regular antitumor medication consisting of 1,2,3,4-tetrahydro-9-amino-acridine (THA) or amiphenazole. This metabolite was not detected when morphine was given alone to these patients. This suggests that THA and amiphenazole may influence the excretion of morphine *N*-oxide either by inhibiting its degradation to other metabolites or by inhibiting an alternative pathway for the metabolism of morphine. Of course, it is possible that THA and amiphenazole can stimulate the formation of morphine *N*-oxide directly, but this appears unlikely since morphine *N*-oxide has not been found previously in human urine, even in trace quantities. However, small amounts of morphine N-oxide do appear to be formed from morphine by liver homogenates of experimental animals.

Recently, evidence has been presented for the excretion in the rat of yet another urinary metabolite of morphine, to which the 2,3-dihydrodiol structure has been tentatively assigned (Misra *et al.*, 1973b). Both brain and liver homogenates of the rat were capable of producing the 2,3-catechol type of metabolite by aromatic hydroxylation of morphine.

Role of Metabolism in Opiate Tolerance

The use of morphine as one of the most potent analgesics has a lengthy history. In recent years, extensive metabolic studies have been performed by many workers using various animal species in a variety of experimental conditions. As will be discussed here and in Chapter 10, the rate, route, and extent of metabolism and the excretory pattern of the narcotics do not appear to be consistently altered by their chronic intake in such a way as to account for tolerance development to and/or physical dependence upon these drugs.

In this connection, Jansen and Greene (1970) demonstrated that morphine was taken up by goldfish but was not metabolized. Nevertheless, development of tolerance to the "analgesic" (electric prod stimulus) effects of morphine could be demonstrated in the goldfish. Such findings add to the already impressive evidence that tolerance to the "analgesic" actions of the narcotics is not the result of altered metabolism (Way and Adler, 1962). Despite the failure to demonstrate a *causal* relationship, however, there have been some reports indicating that animals tolerant to the narcotic alkaloids are unable to dispose of these drugs at normal rates and/or by normal pathways. In nontolerant dogs, for example, 80-92% of a dose of administered morphine was recovered in the urine, while in tolerant dogs only 33-66% was recovered (Gross and Thomson, 1940). Also, liver slices from tolerant rats have been shown to conjugate morphine more rapidly than liver slices from nontolerant animals (Zauder, 1952). Others report no such increase *in vitro*, or a decrease *in vivo* (Fawaz, 1948; Way *et al.*, 1954; Way and Adler, 1962). Szerb and McCurdy (1956) have reported that morphine-tolerant rats conjugate morphine less readily than nontolerant rats and that this impaired metabolism may have contributed to a slower disappearance of morphine from the blood of tolerant animals. Chronic administration of morphine to rats is reported to decrease the activity of hepatic microsomal enzymes responsible for the N-demethylation of morphine (Axelrod, 1956c; Cochin and Axelrod, 1959). As predicted, then, when rats are chronically treated with morphine, the N-demethylation by liver tissue is reported to decrease from about 4% of the dose to about 0.8% as tolerance develops; N-demethylation increases again after withdrawal of the drug (Axelrod, 1956a, b, c; Cochin and Economon, 1959). Similarly, rats made tolerant to the CNS-depressant effects of dihydromorphine have a marked impairment in their ability to N-demethylate this compound (Yeh and Woods, 1969b). In nontolerant rats, 3.7% of injected $^{14}CH_3$-dihydromorphine has been recovered in expired air as $^{14}CO_2$, while in animals which had received daily injections of the drug for 3 weeks, only 0.5% of injected radioactivity was recovered as $^{14}CO_2$. Furthermore, when the drug treatment was stopped after 7 weeks of treatment, $^{14}CO_2$ production returned to normal (nontolerant) levels within 9 days.

EXCRETION OF OPIATES

The narcotic alkaloids and meperidine are eliminated from the body largely via the kidney into the urine. As we have seen, this excretion process is preceded by extensive biotransformation of these compounds to readily excretable, water-soluble polar metabolites. If this did not occur, the widespread distribution of the parent drugs into tissues would tend to greatly reduce their rates of elimination from the body.

Depending upon such factors as dose, frequency of administration, and the species studied, 80-90% of administered morphine may be excreted in urine; only about 1-10% is excreted as unchanged morphine. Some morphine can be reabsorbed from the renal tubules by a pH-dependent process. Evidence has been obtained to indicate that the major metabolite of morphine, morphine-3-glucuronide, is excreted in urine by glomerular filtration rather than by tubular secretion (Brunk and Delle, 1974); it is also excreted in bile.

Morphine itself can be secreted by the active renal tubular system that secretes organic cations (May et al., 1967; Watrous et al., 1970). It is not unexpected then that certain organic bases block the transport process for morphine excretion in the kidney. Among those organic bases which have been shown to block morphine transport in the kidney are SKF-525A and Lilly 18947 (Fujimoto et al., 1972). These compounds are of particular interest in regard to inhibition of renal transport because they typify the classic microsomal enzyme inhibitors, and as such are frequently used to assess the role of metabolism in drug elimination studies. Therefore, studies conducted in vivo in which these "microsomal inhibitors" are utilized should be interpreted conservatively and with appropriate regard for their potential effects on organic base excretion.

Morphine-3-glucuronide has been isolated from the urine and bile of rats injected with codeine (Yeh and Woods, 1970b). Nonconjugated codeine, morphine, norcodeine, and normorphine were likewise identified in the free alkaloid fraction of urine and bile extracts. About 75% of a dose of codeine appears in the urine within 24-30 hours; about 10% of the dose is unchanged; the remainder is in the form of metabolites. An additional 7% appears in expired air and only 0.5% appears in feces (Greene, 1968).

The urinary excretion of morphine and morphine-3-ethereal sulfate in the chicken was examined by Watrous and his associates (1970). It had already been well defined that morphine was secreted by the organic base transport system of the renal tubular cells of the chicken. Their prime concern was to determine the nature of the renal excretion of the morphine-3-ethereal sulfate metabolite, an organic acid. Probenecid, the classic inhibitor of the organic acid renal transport system, blocked the excretion of infused morphine-3-ethereal sulfate; however, when this sulfate was formed in vivo in renal tubular cells its excretion was not blocked by probenecid. This finding supports the concept that probenecid inhibits organic acid excretion by its effects at the peritubular border of the renal cell.

Free morphine appears in feces, probably due to intestinal hydrolysis of the glucuronide conjugate, significant amounts of which are excreted into the intestinal lumen via the bile (Yeh and Woods, 1969b). The morphine liberated in the gastrointestinal tract can become available again for absorption and this enterohepatic circulation can contribute substantially to the persistent appearance of free morphine in urine for several days after its administration.

Although, rats, in general, excrete more free than conjugated morphine in urine, they excrete generally less of an administered dose in urine than do other species. This is probably due to the efficiency of biliary excretion in the rat (Abou-El-Makarem et al., 1967).

Both morphine-3-glucuronide and morphine-3-ethereal sulfate are excreted in rat bile; evidence indicates different mechanisms for the biliary excretion of these two compounds in the rat (Peterson and Fujimoto, 1973). Thus, phenobarbital pretreatment, which increases bile flow and hepatic blood flow (Branch et al., 1974), enhanced the biliary excretion of morphine-3-ethereal sulfate, but not of morphine-3-glucuronide; predictably, then, morphine-3-ethereal sulfate excretion was positively correlated with bile flow, but excretion of morphine-3-glucuronide was not.* In another study (Smith et al., 1973), urinary excretion was blocked by ligating the cystic duct of the cat and the renal pedicles of the cat and rat. When administered to both species, morphine-3-glucuronide and morphine-3-ethereal sulfate were excreted into the bile unchanged. Both species excreted less than 30% of the sulfate in the bile during the first 3 hours after administration. In contrast, the rat excreted over 60% of the dose of the glucuronide in bile, and the cat excreted less than 30% during the same time period. These data offer further evidence that the two conjugates may not be excreted in bile by the same pathways (Smith et al., 1973).

Although morphine and other narcotic alkaloids have, at various times, been reported to be excreted in saliva, tears, sweat, and milk, the amounts excreted by such routes are generally very low (Krueger et al., 1941; Way and Adler, 1962); the important routes of elimination are via the kidney and intestinal tract.

METHADONE

Methadone is a synthetic substitute for morphine. The compound was synthesized as a racemate; the pharmacologic activity has been attributed almost exclusively to the l-isomer (Scott, Robbins and Chen, 1948).

---

*The effects of phenobarbital on hepatic blood flow and bile flow should be considered when that drug is being used as a tool in studies involving its use as an "enzyme inducer." The caveat here is no less important than the one mentioned earlier for studies involving the microsomal "inhibitors" SKF-525A and Lilly 18947.

Absorption

Studies *in vivo* have demonstrated that methadone is rather well absorbed after both subcutaneous and oral administration (Adler and Eisenbrandt, 1949; Way et al., 1949a). About 40% of methadone in plasma is bound to albumin (Olsen, 1972). The plasma level declines slowly with a rather lengthy half-life of about 25 hours which surely relates to the long duration of action of methadone (Inturrisi and Verebely, 1972).* This persistence of methadone in plasma is also consistent with the slow onset and long duration of the abstinence syndrome seen in subjects withdrawn from methadone. (Isbell and Vogel, 1949). To be sure, reports of large individual differences in methadone disposition could be quite significant when evaluating the effectiveness of methadone maintenance therapy on a rational basis.

Distribution

Methadone is distributed in general accord with prediction for organic bases. Thus, the drug leaves the blood rapidly and appears in highest concentrations in lung, liver, kidney, and spleen. Lesser amounts are found in brain, heart, and skeletal muscle (Way and Adler, 1962).

In studying the distribution of methadone in human autopsy specimens, it was learned that lung contained more than the other organs; the liver and kidney concentrations were about equal (Garriott and Mason, 1973).

Although there is evidence for selective uptake of methadone by specific areas of rat brain, for example, the diencephalon, the pharmacologic significance of such accumulation is unknown (Ingoglia, 1970).

Metabolism

Very little methadone is excreted unchanged (Way et al., 1951). A major route of its metabolism in man appears to be N-demethylation involving the hepatic microsomal enzyme system (Axelrod, 1956a; Beckett et al., 1968; Pohland et al., 1971; Baselt and Casarett, 1972) (Fig. 3). The nor compound can also be further demethylated to the di-nor compound (i.e., removal of both methyl groups).**

*In the study cited, the last blood sample drawn for analysis of methadone was at 24 hours after methadone administration. Therefore, the estimated mean half-life of 25 hours was based upon data when about half the drug was theoretically still in the body.

**Attempts to isolate normethadone have failed due to instability of the compound, whereby it spontaneously cyclizes to 2-ethylidene-1,5-dimethyl-3,3-diphenylpyrrolidine (Sullivan and Due, 1973). The di-nor compound cyclizes similarly.

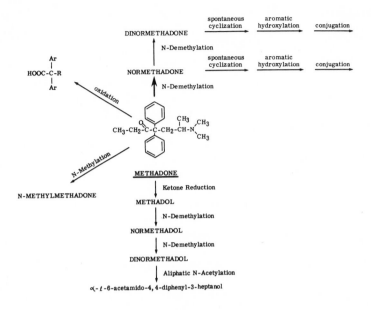

Fig. 3. Metabolism of methadone.

Data from Alvares and Kappas (1972) suggest that the N-demethylation of methadone is a detoxication reaction. In their studies, pretreatment of rats with the microsomal enzyme inducer phenobarbital resulted in a three- to fourfold increase in the N-demethylation of methadone by hepatic microsomes. At the same time this pretreatment caused a marked decrease in the duration of the analgesic effect of methadone (hot plate method).

In contrast, Sullivan and his associates (1972) demonstrated formation of analgesically active metabolites from d-methadone, a compound which was shown to be active as an analgesic at high doses. Until 1972 when their studies were reported, none of the known metabolites of methadone had been shown to possess specific analgesic activity to suggest their role as active metabolites. Not yet investigated were those potential metabolites in which the ketone group of methadone might have been reduced to an alcohol. Reduction of methadone *in vitro* to methadol was accomplished by use of the 15,000 g fraction of rat liver homogenates (Sullivan *et al.*, 1972). The overall reductive pathway for d-methadone metabolism as proposed by Sullivan *et al.* (1973a) is illustrated in Fig. 3: Methadone → a-l-methadol (reduction) → a-l-normethadol (N-demethylation) → a-l-dinormethadol (N-demethylation). Each of these steps occurs *in vitro* in rat liver homogenates, and it has been suggested that these metabolites contribute significantly to the pharmacologic responses observed after administration of methadone (Sullivan *et al.*, 1972; Smits and Booher, 1973; Smits and Myers, 1974). In the mouse (writhing) and rat (tail jerk) the relative analgesic potencies were: *a-l*-normethadol > *a-l*-methadol > *a-l*-dinormethadol *d*-methadone. When *a-l*-methadol is given to rats, this compound is demethylated progressively to form *a-l*-dinormethadol. This primary amine can then undergo aliphatic N-acetylation to the pharmacologically inactive *a-l*-6-acetamido-4,4-diphenyl-3-heptanol as a major urinary and biliary metabolite (Sullivan *et al.*, 1973b). This pathway is less common than acetylation of aromatic amines, though it does occur in the conversion of mescaline to N-acetylmescaline or histamine to N-acetylhistamine.

Unaltered *dl*-methadone can be eliminated in the urine of human subjects given dl-methadone (Pohland *et al.*, 1971). The major route of bio-transformation of the drug is N-demethylation to the secondary amine. Further N-demethylation occurs to a lesser extent and the demethylated metabolites can undergo aromatic hydroxylation (Sullivan and Due, 1973). Also *a-l*-normethadol, which in the rat exhibits pharmacologic activity comparable to *l*-methadone, was reported to be a urinary metabolite of *dl*-methadone in man (Pohland *et al.*, 1971; Sullivan *et al.*, 1972; Sullivan and Due, 1973). In addition to N-demethylation, reduction, and aromatic hydroxylation, small amounts of methadone reportedly undergo oxidation to 4-dimethylamino-2,2-diphenylvaleric acid in man.

When methadone was incubated with liver slices of guinea pigs, methylation of methadone was reported (Schaumann, 1960). Formation *in vivo* of the quaternary base, N-methylmethadone, has not yet been established, but Schaumann suggested that an unknown metabolite excreted in the urine of methadone addicts was probably N-methylmethadone (Vidic, 1957).

It is generally believed that tolerance to the effects of narcotics is adaptive rather than dispositional, and that the narcotics do not stimulate their own rates of metabolism after repeated administration. Indeed, we have cited studies in which N-demethylation of opiates decreases after their chronic administration. In the case of methadone, some studies suggest that tolerance is not related to an increased rate of methadone metabolism (Sung *et al.*, 1953; Alvares and Kappas, 1972; Peters, 1973; Inturrisi and Verebely, 1972) whereas others suggest that an increased metabolism may be at least partially involved (Baselt and Casarett, 1972; Misra *et al.*, 1973a,b; Masten *et al.*, 1974; Spaulding and Takemori, 1974; Verebely *et al.*, 1975).

Excretion

In the rat, biliary excretion is the major route of elimination of methadone and its metabolites (Way *et al.*, 1951; Pohland *et al.*, 1971).

Way and his associates found that only a minor portion of the organic bases in bile was unaltered methadone; the major portion contained biotransformation products.

In man, early studies of the excretion of methadone were carried out using relatively low doses and they did not distinguish between methadone and its metabolites. Accordingly, the urine was considered as a minor pathway for the elimination of methadone and fecal excretion was believed to account for the greater part of the dose. A recent study suggests that after daily doses of methadone exceeding 55 mg, urinary excretion becomes the major elimination pathway (Baselt and Casarett, 1972). About 60% of a daily oral dose of 160 mg may be excreted in urine as unchanged methadone, the remainder of the dose being excreted largely as the aforementioned N-demethylated metabolites. As might be expected from the pH dependency of the urinary excretion of weakly basic drugs, the excretion of methadone in both tolerant and nontolerant individuals may be influenced by changes in urinary pH. Accordingly, acidification of the urine promotes the excretion of unchanged methadone. Urinary excretion of the more polar N-demethylated metabolite, however, is not significantly affected by changes in urinary pH. Baselt and Casarett (1972) observed considerable variations between individuals in the urinary excretion of methadone and demethylated metabolites. They speculated that these differences were dependent upon fluctuations in urinary pH as well as upon the sex of the patient.

Women may N-demethylate methadone to a greater extent than men, based upon the observation that women excrete a significantly higher concentration of the N-demethylated metabolite than do men (Baselt and Casarett, 1972).

March and associates (1950) reported a sex difference in the excretion of methadone in rats. They found that kidneys of female rats contained 2.7 times higher concentrations of methadone than those of male rats. Although they did not differentiate between methadone and its metabolites, the authors did report identical kidney concentrations of the drug in female and castrated male rats, and lower levels in castrated males receiving testosterone.

Henderson and Wilson (1973), prompted by their observation that some patients in their methadone maintenance program experienced withdrawal symptoms following periods of vigorous physical exercise or elevated environmental temperatures, undertook a study of the excretion of methadone and its metabolites in the sweat of their patients. The concentrations of these compounds found in the sweat of the methadone maintenance patients was surprisingly high. Indeed, the concentrations of methadone were higher in sweat than in urine of three of the five patients! These findings indicated that sweat was a significant route of methadone excretion. Furthermore, the results correlated with the clinical impression of a more rapid onset of opiate withdrawal symptoms in those patients who sweated excessively. With the number of problems remaining to be solved in pharmacology, it is not surprising that more sweat is produced than is studied. The fact is that sweat secretion is not routinely considered as an important route of elimination of drugs. It is true that normal daily sweat excretion is only 500 ml, compared to a urinary output of about 1200 ml. However, sweat excretion can reach as much as 2400 ml per day during periods of strenuous exercise or when environmental temperatures approach 100° F (Adolph, 1947). Surely fevered patients would be expected to dispose of methadone differently than those without fever. Since elimination of drugs in sweat is generally viewed as a nonionic passive diffusion process, it should not be surprising that organic bases (such as methadone) which are relatively nonionized at pH 7.4 are excreted into sweat. It becomes increasingly evident that the extensive variations in the physiologic disposition of methadone from one individual to another could be of the utmost significance since maintenance of steady-state plasma levels of methadone are desirable for optimal management of the methadone maintenance patient.

CONCLUSIONS

Since we devoted a significant portion of this chapter and a subsequent chapter to a discussion of the disposition of opiates as it relates to tolerance, it seems to belabor the point to discuss this matter further. We cannot, however, resist the temptation to quote from the review of Way and Adler (1960):

> Numerous studies have been directed toward an attempt to delineate differences between the biological disposition of morphine or its surrogates in tolerant and nontolerant animals. . . . Certain differences were undeniably found on occasion to exist between tolerant and nontolerant animals with respect to the distribution and excretory pattern of morphine or its surrogates. . . . A more relevant approach is found in recent disposition studies seeking differences in the distribution of the agent within the central nervous system. . . . At the present time, despite many interesting findings, no experimentally verifiable concept has emerged clarifying the mechanism of tolerance, or relating this to physical dependence or addiction.

One might naively state that it is a sad commentary that since their 1960 review, no "experimentally verifiable concept" has emerged to explain opiate action and tolerance. The realist will recognize and appreciate that the lack of an explanation is due more to the complexity of the problem rather than to an overall inadequacy of imaginative experimentation or to scientific myopia.

ADDENDUM

A pentapeptide that exhibits morphine-like pharmacologic actions has been identified in brain as H-Tyr-Gly-Gly-Phe-Met-OH (or methionine enkephalin). Endogenous substances having opioid activity have been designated as "endorphins." Recently a heptapeptide, H-Tyr-Gly-Gly-Gly-Lys-Met-Gly-OH, was designed and synthesized; it also was shown to exhibit certain opioid actions. It will be interesting to see to what extent this line of research will help to explain opiate actions and tolerance. The potential therapeutic utility of such compounds is also to be considered. (Goldstein et al., Life Sci. 17:1643-1654, 1975; Hughes et al., Nature 258:577-579, 1975)

REFERENCES

Abou-El-Makarem, M.M., Milburn, P., Smith, R.L., and Williams, R.T.: Biliary excretion of foreign compounds. Biochem. J. 105:1289-1293, 1967.

Abrams, L.S. and Elliott, H.W.: Morphine metabolism in vivo and in vitro by homozygous Gunn rats. J. Pharmacol. Exp. Ther. 189:285-292, 1974.

Adler, T.K.: A newly identified metabolic product of codeine: N-Demethylated codeine. J. Pharmacol. 106:371, 1952 (abstract).

Adler, T.K. and Eisenbrandt, L.L.: The initial uptake of C^{14}-labelled methadone by rat tissues. Proc. Soc. Exp. Biol. Med. 72:347-349, 1949.

Adler, T.K. and Latham, M.E.: Demethylation of C^{14}-labelled codeine in the rat. Proc. Soc. Exp. Biol. Med. 73:401-404, 1950.

Adler, T.K., Fujimoto, J.M., Way, E.L., and Baker, E.M.: The metabolic fate of codeine in man. J. Pharmacol. Exp. Ther. 114:251-262, 1955.

Adler, T.K., Elliott, H.W., and George, R.: Some factors affecting the biological disposition of small doses of morphine in rats. J. Pharmacol. Exp. Ther. 120:485-487, 1957.

Adolph, E.F.: Physiology of Man in the Desert. New York, Hafner, 1947, pp. 59-60.

Alvares, A.P. and Kappas, A.: Influence of phenobarbital on the metabolism and analgesic effect of methadone in rats. J. Lab. Clin. Med. 79:439-451, 1972.

Asghar, K. and Way, E.L.: Active removal of morphine from the cerebral ventricles. J. Pharmacol. Exp. Ther. 175:75-83, 1970.

Axelrod, J.: The enzymatic conversion of codeine to morphine. J. Pharmacol. 115:259-267, 1955.

Axelrod, J.: The enzymatic N-demethylation of narcotic drugs. J. Pharmacol. Exp. Ther. 117:322-350, 1956a.

Axelrod, J.: The enzymic cleavage of aromatic ethers. Biochem. J. 63:634-639, 1956b.

Axelrod, J.: Possible mechanisms of tolerance to narcotic drugs. Science 124:263-264, 1956c.

Axelrod, J.: Enzymatic formation of morphine and nicotine in a mammal. Life Sci. 1:29-30, 1962.

Axelrod, J. and Cochin, J.: The inhibitory action of nalorphine on the enzymatic N-demethylation of narcotic drugs. J. Pharmacol. Exp. Ther. 121:107-112, 1957.

Baselt, R.C. and Casarett, L.J.: Urinary excretion of methadone in man. Clin. Pharm. Ther. 13:64-70, 1972.

Beckett, A.H., Casy, A.F., and Harper, N.J.: Analgesics and their antagonists: Some steric and chemical considerations, Part III. The influence of the basic group on the biological response. J. Pharm. Pharmacol. 8:874-884, 1956.

Beckett, A.H., Taylor, J.F., Casy, A.F., and Hassan, M.M.A.: The biotransformation of methadone in man: Synthesis and identification of a major metabolite. J. Pharm. Pharmacol. 20:754-762, 1968.

Bernheim, F. and Bernheim, M.L.C.: The hydrolysis of Demerol by liver in vitro. J. Pharmacol. 85:74-77, 1945.

Borner, U. and Abbott, S.: New observations in metabolism of morphine—formation of codeine from morphine in man. Experientia 29:180, 1973.

Branch, R.A., Shand, D.G., Wilkinson, G.R., and Nies, A.S.: Increased clearance of antipyrine and d-propranolol after phenobarbital treatment in the monkey. J. Clin. Invest. 53:1101-1107, 1974.

Brunk, S.F. and Delle, M.: Effect of route of administration on morphine metabolism in man. Clin. Res. 20:721, 1972.

Brunk, S.F., and Delle, M.: Morphine metabolism in man. Clin. Pharmacol. Ther. 16:51-57, 1974.

Burns, J.J., Berger, B.L., Leif, P.A., Wollack, A., Papper, E.M., and Brodie, B.B.: The physiological disposition and fate of meperidine (Demerol) in man and a method for its estimation in plasma. J. Pharmacol. 114:289-297, 1955.

Chernov, H.I., Miller, J.W., and Mannering, G.J.: Possible relationships between the antagonism of morphine-induced respiratory depression and analgesia and in vitro demethylation of 3-methoxy-N-methylmorphinan by N-substituted analogues of 1-3-OH-morphinan. Fed. Proc. 18:376, 1959.

Clouet, D.H.: The methylation of normorphine in rat liver and brain. Fed. Proc. 21:326, 1962a (abstract).

Clouet, D.H.: The methylation of normorphine in rat brain and liver. Life Sci. 1:31-34, 1962b.

Clouet, D.H.: The methylation of normorphine in rat brain in vivo. Biochem. Pharmacol. 12:967-972, 1963.

Clouet, D.H. and Williams, N.: The binding of narcotic analgesics in synaptosomal and other particulate fractions of rat brain. Pharmacologist 13:313, 1971 (abstract).

Clouet, D.H., Ratner, M., and Kurzman, M.: N-Methylation of normorphine by tissues in vitro. Biochem. Pharmacol. 12:957-966, 1963.

Cochin, J. and Axelrod, J.: Biochemical and pharmacological changes in the rat following chronic administration of morphine, nalorphine and normorphine. J. Pharmacol. Exp. Ther. 125:105-110, 1959.

Cochin, J. and Economon, S.: Recovery of N-demethylating activity and analgesic sensitivity in the rat following abrupt withdrawal of morphine. Fed. Proc. 18:377, 1959.

Cohen, M., Keats, A.S., Krivoy, W., and Ungar, G.: Effect of actinomycin-D on morphine tolerance. Proc. Soc. Exp. Biol. Med. 119:381-384, 1965.

Cox, B.M., Ginsburg, M., and Osman, O.H.: Acute tolerance to narcotic analgesic drugs in rat. Brit. J. Pharmacol. 33:245-256, 1968.

Craig, A.L., O'Dea, R.F., and Takemori, A.E.: The uptake of morphine by the choroid plexus and cerebral cortical slices of animals chronically treated with morphine. Neuropharmacology 10:709-714, 1971.

Dutton, G.J. and Storey, I.D.E.: Uridine compounds in glucuronic acid metabolism. Biochem. J. 57:275-283, 1954.

Eddy, N.B. and Howes, H.A.: Studies of morphine, codeine and their derivatives. VIII. Monoacetyl and diacetylmorphine and their hydrogenated derivatives. J. Pharmacol. 53:430-439, 1935.

Elison, C. and Elliott, H.W.: N- and O-demethylation of some narcotic analgesics by brain slices from male and female Long-Evans rats. Biochem. Pharmacol. 12:1363-1366, 1963.

Elison, C. and Elliott, H.W.: Studies on the enzymatic N- and O-demethylation of narcotic analgesics and evidence for the formation of codeine from morphine in rats and dogs. J. Pharmacol. Exp. Ther. 144:265-275, 1964.

Elison, C., Elliott, H.W., Look, M., and Rapoport, H.: Some aspects of the fate and relationship of the N-methyl group of morphine to its pharmacological activity. J. Med. Pharmacol. Chem. 6:237-246, 1963.

Elliott, H.W. and Adler, T.K.: Some factors affecting rat tissue levels of carbon-14 labeled codeine. J. Pharmacol. 116:1, 1956.

Elliott, H.W., Tolbert, B.M., Adler, T.K., and Anderson, H.H.: Excretion of carbon-14 by man after administration of morphine-N-methyl-C[14]. Proc. Soc. Exp. Biol. Med. 85:77-81, 1954.

Elliott, H.W., Tolbert, B.M., Adler, T.K., and Anderson, H.H.: Effect of deuteration of N-CH$_3$ group on potency and enzymatic N-demethylation of morphine. Science 134:1078-1079, 1961.

Elliott, H.W., Parker, K.D., Crim, M., Wright, J.A., and Nomof, N.: Actions and metabolism of heroine administered by continuous intravenous infusion to man. Clin. Pharm. Ther. 12:806-814, 1971.

Ellis, S.: Enzymic hydrolysis of morphine esters. J. Pharmacol. 94:130-135, 1948.

Fawaz, G.: Role of the liver in tolerance to morphine in the rat. Proc. Soc. Exp. Biol. N.Y. 68:262-263, 1948.

Fish, M.S., Johnson, N.M., Lawrence, E.D., and Horning, E.C.: Oxidative N-dealkylation. Biochem. Biophys. Acta 18:564-565, 1955.

Fraser, H.F., Isbell, H., and Van Horn, G.D.: Norcodeine in man. Fed. Proc. 17:367, 1958.

Fujimoto, J.M. and Haarstad, V.B.: The isolation of morphine ethereal sulfate from urine of the chicken and cat. J. Pharmacol. Exp. Ther. 165:45-51, 1969.

Fujimoto, J. M. and Way, E.L.: Isolation and crystallization of "bound" morphine from urine of human addicts. J. Pharmacol. Exp. Ther. 121:340-346, 1957.

Fujimoto, J.M., Hakim, R., and Zamiatowski, R.: Inhibition of renal tubular transport of morphine by diethylaminoethanol in the chicken. Biochem. Pharmacol. 21:2877-2886, 1972.

Garriott, J.C. and Mason, M.F.: Distribution of methadone in autopsy specimens after overdose. Clin. Tox. 6:289-290, 1973.

Gaudette, L.E. and Brodie, B.B.: Relationship between the lipid solubility of drugs and their oxidation by liver microsomes. Biochem. Pharmacol. 2:89-96, 1959.

George, W.J. and Tephly, T.R.: Studies on hepatic microsomal N- and O-dealkylation of morphine analogues. Mol. Pharmacol. 4:502-509, 1968.

Goldberg, I.H. and Reich, E.: Actinomycin inhibition of RNA synthesis directed by DNA. Fed. Proc. 23:958-964, 1964.

Goldstein, A.: Opiate receptors, Minireview. Life Sci. 14:615-623, 1974.

Greene, N.M.: The metabolism of drugs employed in anesthesia Part II. Anesthesiology 29:327-360, 1968.

Gross, E.G. and Thomson, V.: Excretion of a combined form of morphine in tolerant and non-tolerant dogs. J. Pharmacol. Exp. Ther. 68:413-418, 1940.

Henderson, G.L. and Wilson, B.K.: Excretion of methadone and metabolites in human sweat. Res. Commun. Chem. Pathol. Pharmacol. 5:3-8, 1973.

Herken, H., Neubert, D., and Timmler, R.: Die enzymatische N-demethylierung durch Leber-Mikrosomen bie der Morphin-Gewöhnung. Arch. Exp. Pathol. Pharmakol. 237:319-333, 1959.

Hosoya, E. and Oka, T.: Studies on morphine glucuronide. Med. Center J. Univ. Mich. 36:241, 1970.

Hug, C.C., Jr.: Transport of narcotic analgesics by choroid plexus and kidney tissue in vitro. Biochem. Pharmacol. 16:345-359, 1967.

Hug, C.C., Jr. and Mellett, L.B.: Tritium labeled dihydromorphine: Its metabolic fate and excretion in the rat. J. Pharmacol. Exp. Ther. 149:446-453, 1965.

Hug, C.C., Jr. and Oka, T.: Uptake of dihydromorphine-³H (DHM) by synaptosomes of brain. Pharmacologist 11:293, 1969 (abstract).

Hug, C.C., Jr. and Oka, T.: Uptake of dihydromorphine-³H by synaptosomes. Life Sci. 10:201-213, 1971.

Hug, C.C., Jr., Mellett, L.B., and Cafruny, E.J.: Stopflow analysis of the renal excretion of tritium-labeled dihydromorphine. J. Pharmacol. Exp. Ther. 150:259-269, 1965.

Ingoglia, N.A.: Localization and the effects of chronic administration of methadone and morphine in mice and rats. Dissertation Abst. Intern. 31:1437b-1438b, 1970.

Inturrisi, C.E. and Verebely, K.: The levels of methadone in the plasma in methadone maintenance. Clin. Pharm. Ther. 13:633-637, 1972.

Isbell, H. and Vogel, V.H.: The addiction liability of methadone and its use in the treatment of the morphine abstinence syndrome. Amer. J. Psychiat. 105:909-914, 1949.

Jansen, G.A. and Greene, N.M.: Morphine metabolism and morphine tolerance in goldfish. Anesthesiology 32:231-235, 1970.

Jenner, P. and Testa, B.: Influence of stereochemical factors on drug disposition. Drug. Metab. Rev. 2:117-184, 1973.

Johannesson, T. and Milthers, K.: The lethal action of morphine and nalorphine given jointly to morphine tolerant and nontolerant rats. Acta Pharmacol. Toxicol. 20:80-89, 1963.

Johannesson, T. and Schou, J.: Morphine and normorphine in the brains of rats given identically analgesic doses of morphine, codeine or normorphine. Acta Pharmacol. Toxicol. 20:165-173, 1963.

Johannesson, T. and Woods, L.A.: Analgesic action and brain and plasma levels of morphine and codeine in morphine tolerant, codeine tolerant and non-tolerant rats. Acta Pharmacol. Toxicol. 21:381-396, 1964.

Kamata, O., Watanabe, S., Ishii, S., Ueki, S., Oguri, K., Ida, S., Yoshimura, H., and Tsukamoto, H.: Abstract, 89th Annual Meeting of Pharmaceutical Society of Japan. Nagoya, April 1969, p. 443.

Kato, R. and Onoda, K.: Effect of morphine administration on the activities of microsomal drug-metabolizing enzyme systems in liver of different species. Jap. J. Pharmacol. 16:217-219, 1966.

Kemp, J. and Way, E.L.: *In vitro* studies of the metabolism of heroin. Fed. Proc. *18*:409, 1959 (abstract).

Kerr, F.W.L.: Tolerance to morphine and the blood brain/CSF barrier. Fed. Proc. *33*(3):528, 1974 (abstract).

Klutch, A.: A chromatographic investigation of morphine metabolism in rats, confirmation of N-demethylation of morphine and isolation of a new metabolite. Drug Metab. Disp. *2*:23-30, 1974.

Krueger, H., Eddy, N.B., and Sumwalt, M.: The pharmacology of the opium alkaloids, Part I. Washington, D.C., U.S. Government Printing Office (U.S. Public Health Reports, Suppl. 65), 1941.

Kupferberg, H.J. and Way, E.L.: Pharmacologic basis for the increased sensitivity of the newborn rat to morphine. J. Pharmacol. Exp. Ther. *141*:105-112, 1963.

Loh, H.H., Shen, F., and Way, E.L.: Enhancement of brain permeability to morphine by dactinomycin. Pharmacologist *11*:269, 1969 (abstract).

Loh, H.H., Shen, F., and Way, E.L.: Effect of dactinomycin on the acute toxicity and brain uptake of morphine. J. Pharmacol. Exp. Ther. *177*:326-331, 1971.

MacDonald, A.D., Woolfe, G., Bergel, F., Morrison, A.L., and Rinderknecht, H.: Analgesic actions of pethidine derivatives and related compounds. Brit. J. Pharmacol. *1*:4-14, 1946.

Mannering, G.J. and Takemori, A.E.: The effect of repeated administration of levorphan, dextrophan and morphine on the capacity of rat liver preparations to demethylate morphine and morphinan-type analgesics. J. Pharmacol. Exp. Ther. *127*:187-190, 1959.

Mannering, G.J., Dixon, A.C., Baker, E.M. III, and Asami, T.: The *in vivo* liberation of morphine from codeine in man. J. Pharmacol. Exp. Ther. *111*:142-146, 1954.

March, C.H. and Elliott, H.W.: Distribution and excretion of radioactivity after administration of morphine-N-methyl-^{14}C to rats. Proc. Soc. Exp. Biol. *86*:494-497, 1964.

March, C.H., Gordan, G.S., and Way, E.L.: The effect of castration and of testosterone on the action and distribution of *dl*-methadone in the rat. Arch. Int. Pharmacodyn. Ther. *83*:270-276, 1950.

Masten, L.W., Peterson, G.R., Burkhalter, A., and Way, E.L.: Effect of oral administration of methadone on hepatic microsomal mixed function oxidase activity in mice. Life Sci. *14*:1635-1640, 1974.

May, D.G., Fujimoto, J.M., and Inturrisi, C.E.: The tubular transport and metabolism of morphine-N-methyl-C^{14} by the chicken kidney. J. Pharmacol. Exp. Ther. *157*:626-635, 1967.

McMahon, R.E.: Microsomal dealkylation of drugs: Substrate specificity and mechanism. J. Pharm. Sci. *55*:457-466, 1966.

Mellet, L.B. and Woods, L.A.: The distribution and fate of morphine in the non-tolerant and tolerant monkey. J. Pharmacol. Exp. Ther. *116*:77-83, 1965.

Miller, J.W. and Anderson, H.H.: The effect of N-demethylation on certain pharmacologic actions of morphine, codeine and meperidine in the mouse. J. Pharmacol. *112*:191-196, 1954.

Miller, J.W. and Elliott, H.W.: Rat tissue levels of carbon-14 labeled anagetics as related to pharmacological activity. J. Pharmacol. Exp. Ther. *113*:283-291, 1955.

Milthers, K.: Normorphine, nalorphine and morphine. Quantitative separation and determination of small amounts in blood and tissue. Acta Pharmacol. Toxicol. *18*:199-206, 1961.

Milthers, K.: N-Dealkylation of morphine and nalorphine in the brain of living rats. Nature (London) *195*:607, 1962a.

Milthers, K.: The *in vivo* transformation of morphine and nalorphine into normorphine in the brain of rats. Acta Pharmacol. Toxicol. *19*:235-240, 1962b.

Milthers, K.: The N-demethylation of morphine in rats. Quantitative determination of normorphine and morphine in the urine and feces of rats given subcutaneous morphine. Acta Pharmacol. Toxicol. *19*:149-155, 1962c.

Minegishi, K., Kuroiwa, Y., and Okui, S.: Studies on the metabolic N-demethylation. VI. Effect of morphine and nalorphine on the oxidative demethylation *in vitro* in the liver from intact and adrenalectomized rats. Chem. Pharm. Bull. (Tokyo) *16*:1649-1954, 1968.

Misra, A.L., Jacoby, H.I., and Woods, L.A.: The preparation of tritium-labeled normorphine and its physiological disposition in dog and monkey. J. Pharmacol. Exp. Ther. *132*:311-316, 1960.

Misra, A.L., Mulé, S.J., and Woods, L.A.: *In vivo* formation of normorphine in the rat as a metabolite of tritium-nuclear labelled morphine. Nature (London) *190*:82-83, 1961a.

Misra, A.L., Mulé, S.J., and Woods, L.A.: The preparation of tritium nuclear-labelled morphine and evidence for its *in vivo* biotransformation to normorphine in the rat. J. Pharmacol. Exp. Ther. *132*:317-322, 1961b.

Misra, A.L., Yeh, S.Y., and Woods, L.A.: Morphine conjugates in the dog. Biochem. Pharmacol. *19*:1536-1539, 1970.

Misra, A.L., Mulé, S.J., Bloch, R. and Vadlamani, N.L.: Physiological disposition and metabolism of *lewo*-methadone-1-3H in nontolerant and tolerant rats. J. Pharmacol. Exp. Ther. *185*:287-299, 1973a.

Misra, A.L., Vadlamani, N.L., Pontani, R.B., and Mulé, S.J.: Evidence for a new metabolite of morphine-*N*-methyl- C in the rat. Biochem. Pharmacol. *22*:2129-2139, 1973b.

Misra, A.L., Vadlamani, N.L., Bloch, R., and Mulé, S.J.: Differential pharmacokinetic and metabolic profiles of the stereoisomers of 3-hydroxy-*N*-methyl morphinan. Res. Commun. Chem. Pathol. Pharmacol. 7:1-16, 1974.

Mori, M., Oguri, K., Yoshimura, H., Shimomura, K., Kamata, O., and Ueki, S.: Chemical synthesis and analgesic effect of morphine ethereal sulfates. Life Sci. *11*:525-533, 1972.

Mulé, S.J. and Woods, L.A.: Distribution of N-^{14}C-labelled morphine. I. In the central nervous system of non-tolerant and tolerant dog. J. Pharmacol. Exp. Ther. *136*:232-241, 1962.

Mulé, S.J., Redman, C.M., and Flesher, J.W.: Intracellular disposition of H^3-morphine in the brain and liver of nontolerant and tolerant guinea pigs. J. Pharmacol. Exp. Ther. *157*:459-471, 1967.

Muraki, T.: Uptake of morphine-3-glucuronide by choroid plexus *in vitro*. Eur. J. Pharmacol. *15*:393-395, 1971.

Oberst, F.W.: Studies on the fate of heroin. J. Pharmacol. Exp. Ther. *79*:266-270, 1943.

Oguri, K., Ida, S., Yoshimura, H., and Tsukamoto, H.: Metabolism of drugs. LXIX. Studies on the urinary metabolism of morphine in several mammalian species. Chem. Pharm. Bull. (Tokyo) *18*:2414-2419, 1970.

Oldendorf, W.H., Hyman, S., Braun, L., and Oldendorf, S.Z.: Blood-brain barrier: Penetration of morphine, codeine, heroin, and methadone after carotid injection. Science *178*:984-986, 1972.

Olsen, G.D.: Methadone binding to human plasma albumin. Fed. Proc. *31*:537, 1972.

Paerregaard, P.: The liberation of morphine from codeine in man and dog. Acta Pharmacol. Toxicol. *14*:394-399, 1958.

Paerregaard, P. and Poulsen, E.: Excretion of morphine in the urine of non-tolerant dogs. Acta Pharmacol. Toxicol. *14*:390-393, 1958.

Peters, M.A.: The effect of acute and chronic methadone treatment on the *in vitro* N-demethylation of methadone by microsomal enzymes of male and pregnant and nonpregnant female rats. Arch. Int. Pharmacodyn. *205*:259-266, 1973.

Peterson, R.E. and Fujimoto, J.M.: Biliary excretion of morphine-3-glucuronide and morphine-3-ethereal sulfate by different pathways in rat. J. Pharmacol. Exp. Ther. *184*:409-418, 1973.

Plotnikoff, N.P., Elliott, H.W., and Way, E.L.: The metabolism of N-C^{14}H$_3$-labeled meperidine. J. Pharmacol. *104*:377-386, 1952.

Plotnikoff, N.P., Way, E.L., and Elliott, H.W.: Biotransformation products of meperidine excreted in the urine of man. J. Pharmacol. *117*:414-419, 1956.

Pohland, A., Boaz, H.E., and Sullivan, H.R.: Synthesis and identification of metabolites resulting from the biotransformation of *dl*-methadone in man and in the rat. J. Med. Chem. *14*:194-197, 1971.

Portoghese, P.S.: Stereochemical factors and receptor interactions associated with narcotic analgesics. J. Pharmaceut. Sci. *55*:865-887, 1966.

Reynolds, A.K. and Randall, L.O., Morphine and Allied Drugs. Canada, Univ. of Toronto Press, 1957.

Ringle, D.A. and Herndon, B.L.: *In vitro* morphine binding by sera from morphine-treated rabbits. J. Immunol. *109*:174-175, 1972.

Ryan, J., Parker, C.W., and Williams, R.C.: Serum binding of morphine in heroine addicts. Clin. Res. *19*:182, 1971 (abstract).

Ryan, J.J., Parker, C.W., and Williams, R.C., Jr.: Gammaglobulin binding of morphine in heroin addicts. J. Lab. Clin. Med. *80*:155-164, 1972.

Sasajima, M.: Analgesic effect of morphine-3-monoglucuronide. Keio Igaku *47*:421-426, 1970 (in Japanese).

Schaumann, O., Methylierung des Methadon am Stickstoff zur Quartaren Ammonium Base. Arch Exp. Pathol. Pharmakol. *239*:311-320, 1960.

Schulz, R. and Goldstein, A.: Inactivity of narcotic glucuronides as analgesics and on guinea-pig ileum. J. Pharmacol. Exp. Ther. *183*:404-410, 1972.

Scott, C.C., Robbins, E.B., and Chen, K.K.: Pharmacologic comparison of the optical isomers of methadone. J. Pharmacol. Exp. Ther. *93*:282-286, 1948.

Scrafani, J.T. and Hug, C.C., Jr.: Active uptake of dihydromorphine and other narcotic analgesics by cerebral cortical slices. Biochem. Pharmacol. *17*:1557-1566, 1968.

Scrafani, J.T., Williams, N., and Clouet, D.H.: Binding to rat brain synaptosomes of narcotic analgesics administered *in vivo*. The Pharmacologist *12*:230, 1970 (abstract).

Shimomura, K., Kamata, O., Ueki, S., Ida, S., Oguri, K., Yoshimura, H., and Tsukamoto, H.: Analgesic effect of morphine glucuronides. Tohoku J. Exp. Med. *105*:45-52, 1971.

Siminoff, R. and Saunders, P.R.: Concentration of free and conjugated morphine in brain and other tissues of tolerant and non-tolerant rabbits. J. Pharmacol. Exp. Ther. *124*:252-254, 1958.

Smith, A.A.: Adrenergic regulation of the lenticular response to opioids in mice. In The Addictive States. Ed. A. Wilker, Baltimore, Williams Wilkins Co., 1968, pp. 74-88.

Smith, D.S., Peterson, R.E., and Fujimoto, J.M.: Species differences in biliary-excretion of morphine, morphine-3-glucuronide and morphine-3-ethereal sulfate in cat and rat. Biochem. Pharmacol. *22*:485-492, 1973.

Smits, S.E. and Booher, R.: Analgesic activity of some of the metabolites of *d*-methadone and of alpha-acetylmethadol in mice and rats. Fed. Proc. *32*:3103, 1973 (abstract).

Smits, S.E. and Myers, M.B.: Some comparative effects of racemic methadone and its optical isomers in rodents. Res. Commun. Chem. Pathol. Pharmacol. *7*:651-662, 1974.

Spaulding, T.C. and Takemori, A.E.: Studies on N-demethylation of methadone in methadone-dependent rats. The Pharmacologist *16*:194, 1974.

Spector, S.: Quantitative determination of morphine in serum by radioimmunoassay. J. Pharmacol. Exp. Ther. *178*:253-258, 1971.

Sullivan, H.R. and Due, S.L.: Urinary metabolites of *dl*-methadone in maintenance subjects. J. Med. Chem. *16*:909-913, 1973.

Sullivan, H.R., Smits, S.E., Due, S.L., Booher, R.E., and McMahon, R.E.: Metabolism of *d*-methadone: Isolation and identification of analgesically active metabolites. Life Sci. *11*:1093-1104, 1972.

Sullivan, H.R., Due, S.L., and McMahon, R.E.: Enzymatic reduction. An important pathway in the biotransformation of methadone in man and rat. Fed. Proc. *32*:3104, 1973a (abstract).

Sullivan, H.R., Due, S.L., and McMahon, R.E.: Metabolism of *α*-l-methadol: N-Acetylation, a new metabolic pathway. Res. Commun. Chem. Pathol. Pharmacol. *6*:1072-1078, 1973b.

Sung, C-Y., Way, E.L., and Scott, K.G.: Studies on the relationship of metabolic fate and hormonal effects of *d,l*-methadone to the development of drug tolerance. J. Pharmacol. Exp. Ther. *107*:12-23, 1953.

Szerb, J.C. and McCurdy, D.H.: Concentration of morphine in blood and brain after intravenous injection of morphine in non-tolerant, tolerant and neostigmine-treated rats. J. Pharmacol. Exp. Ther. *118*:446-450, 1956.

Takemori, A.E. and Mannering, G.J.: Metabolic N- and O-demethylation of morphine and morphinan-type analgesics. J. Pharmacol. Exp. Ther. *123*:171-179, 1958.

Takemori, A.E. and Stenwick, M.W.: Studies on the uptake of morphine by the choroid plexus *in vitro*. J. Pharmacol. Exp. Ther. *154*:586-594, 1966.

Tampier, L., Sanchez, E., and Mardones, J.: Effects of nalorphine in the *in vitro* morphine metabolism and on the *p*-nitrophenol conjugation in rat liver. Arch Int. Pharmacodyn. *188*:290-297, 1970.

Verebely, K., Volavka, J., Mulé, S., and Resnick, R.: Methadone in man: Pharmacokinetic and excretion studies in acute and chronic treatment. Clin. Pharmacol. Ther. *18*:180-190, 1975.

Vidic, E.: Nachweis der renalen Ausscheidungsprodukte toxicologisch wichtiger Arzneistoffe mit Hilfe der Papierchromatogrophie. Arzneimittel Forsch. *7*:314-319, 1957.

Wang, J.H. and Takemori, A.E.: Studies on the transport of morphine out of the perfused cerebral ventricles of rabbits. J. Pharmacol. Exp. Ther. *181*:46-52, 1972a.

Wang, J.H. and Takemori, A.E.: Studies on the transport of morphine into the cerebrospinal fluid of rabbits. J. Pharmacol. Exp. Ther. *183*:41-48, 1972b.

Watrous, W.M. and Fujimoto, J. M.: Inhibition of morphine metabolism by catechol in the chicken kidney. Biochem. Pharmacol. *20*:1479-1491, 1971.

Watrous, W.M., May, D.G., and Fujimoto, J.M.: Mechanism of the renal tubular transport of morphine and morphine ethereal sulfate in the chicken. J. Pharmacol. Exp. Ther. *172*:224-229, 1970.

Way, E.L. and Adler, T.K.: The pharmacologic implications of the fate of morphine and its surrogates. Pharmacol. Rev. *12*:383-446, 1960.

Way, E.L. and Adler, T.K.: The biological disposition of morphine and its surrogates (monograph). Geneva, World Health Organization, 1962, pp. 3-117.

Way, E.L., Sung, C-Y., and McKelway, W.P.: The absorption, distribution and excretion of d,l-methadone. J. Pharmacol. Exp. Ther. 97:222-228, 1949a.

Way, E.L., Gimble, A.I., McKelway, W.P., Ross, H., Sung, C-Y., and Ellsworth, H.: The absorption, distribution and excretion of isonipecaine (Demerol). J. Pharmacol. 96:477-484, 1949b.

Way, E.L., Signorotti, B.T., March, C.H., and Peng, C.T.: Studies on the urinary, fecal and biliary excretion of dl-methadone by countercurrent distribution. J. Pharmacol. Exp. Ther. 101:249-258, 1951.

Way, E.L., Sung, C-Y., and Fujimoto, J.M.: The effect of adrenalectomy on the development of tolerance to morphine and methadone. J. Pharmacol. 110:51, 1954.

Way, E.L., Kemp, J.W., Young, J.M., and Grassetti, D.R.: The pharmacologic effects of heroin in relationship to its rate of biotransformation. J. Pharmacol. Exp. Ther. 129:144-154, 1960.

Woo, J.T.C., Gaff, G.A., and Fennessy, M.R.: A note on the effects of 2,4-diamino-5-phenylthiazole and 1,2,3,4-tetrahydro-9-aminoacridine on morphine metabolism. J. Pharm. Pharmacol. 20:763-767, 1968.

Woods, L.A.: Distribution and fate of morphine in non-tolerant and tolerant dogs and rats. J. Pharmacol. Exp. Ther. 112:158-175, 1954.

Woods, L.A. and Chernov, H.I.: A new morphine metabolite from cat urine. The Pharmacologist 8:206, 1966 (abstract).

Wright, C.I.: The enzymatic deacetylation of heroine and related morphine derivatives by blood serum. J. Pharmacol. 71:164-177, 1941.

Wright, C.I.: The deacetylation of heroin and related compounds by mammalian tissue. J. Pharmacol. 75:328-337, 1942.

Wright, C.I. and Barbour, F.A.: The respiratory effect of morphine, codeine and related substances IV. The effect of a-monoacetylmorphine, monoacetylidihydromorphine, diacetylmorphine (heroin) and diacetyl dihydromorphine on the respiratory activity of the rabbit. J. Pharmacol. 54:25-33, 1935.

Yeh, S.Y.: Isolation and identification of morphine ethereal sulfate (MES) normorphine (NM) and normorphine conjugate (NMC) as morphine (M) metabolites in man. Fed. Proc. 32:3094, 1973 (abstract).

Yeh, S.Y.: Urinary excretion of morphine and its metabolites in morphine dependent subjects. J. Pharmacol. Exp. Ther. 192:201-210, 1975.

Yeh, S.Y. and Woods, L.A.: Physiologic disposition of N-C^{14}-methylcodeine in the rat. J. Pharmacol. Exp. Ther. 166:86-95, 1969a.

Yeh, S.Y. and Woods, L.A.: The effect of tolerance and withdrawal on the *in vivo* metabolism of N-C^{14}-methyl-dihydromorphine in the rat. J. Pharmacol. Exp. Ther. 169:168-174, 1969b.

Yeh, S.Y. and Woods, L.A.: Maternal and fetal distribution of H^3-dihydromorphine in the tolerant and nontolerant rat. J. Pharmacol. Exp. Ther. 174:9-13, 1970a.

Yeh, S.Y. and Woods, L.A.: Isolation of morphine-3-glucuronide from urine and bile or rats injected with codeine. J. Pharmacol. Exp. Ther. 175:69-74, 1970b.

Yeh, S.Y., Chernov, H.I., and Woods, L.A.: Metabolism of morphine by cats. J. Pharm. Sci. 60:469-471, 1971.

Yoshimura, H., Ida, S., Oguri, K., and Tsukamoto, H.: Proc. 1st Sym. on Drug Metabolism and Action. Japan, Chiba, November, 1969a., p. 107.

Yoshimura, H., Oguri, K., and Tsukamoto, H.: Metabolism of drugs—LXII. Morphine and identification of morphine glucuronides in urine and bile of rabbits. Biochem. Pharmacol. 18:279-286, 1969b.

Zauder, H.L.: The effect of prolonged morphine administration on the *in vivo* and *in vitro* conjugation of morphine by rats. J. Pharmacol. 104:11-19. 1952.

Chapter 6

Barbiturates and Methaqualone

BARBITURATES

Barbital was introduced into medicine as the first hypnotic barbiturate over 70 years ago. Later, phenobarbital was synthesized and it is presently one of the most widely used agents in the management of convulsive and hyperactive conditions. Today, there are literally dozens of barbiturates available for clinical use, although only a few are widely prescribed for therapeutic purposes as hypnotics and anticonvulsants. The sedation and relaxation that result from barbiturate use are akin to the actions produced by intoxicating amounts of alcohol. However, barbiturate effects can vary qualitatively and quantitatively with the dose, the situation, the personality of the user, previous experience, etc. On the "street," the barbiturates ("goof balls" or "downs") most widely used are: secobarbital ("red devils"), amobarbital ("blue devils"), and pentobarbital ("yellow jackets"). The durations of action of secobarbital, amobarbital, and pentobarbital are considered to be short to intermediate (about 3-12 hours); these agents are preferred on the "street" to the shorter-acting barbiturates (e.g., hexobarbital) or longer-acting barbiturates (e.g., phenobarbital).

Barbiturates are extensively used and abused in the United States. For example, in 1972, over 4000 blood specimens analyzed at the Los Angeles County-University of Southern California Medical Center were reportedly barbiturate positive. The blood specimens were obtained from patients believed to have a drug-related illness (Lundberg, 1973). According to Bakewell and Wikler (1966), about 7% of psychiatric patients admitted to hospitals in the United States abused barbiturates or other sedatives. Certainly not all these individuals are associated with the criminal element who traffic in illicit drugs. Compulsive intake of these agents can result from their prolonged therapeutic use, as by persons who suffer from chronic insomnia or epilepsy and who, therefore, may regularly obtain barbiturates from legitimate sources. About 90% of suicide deaths involving drugs are attributable to barbiturates (California Public Health Statistical Report, 1967). Accidental deaths have occurred among opiate addicts who may use barbiturates in an attempt to intensify the effects of narcotics (by a mechanism that is not well understood). Accidental deaths have also been related to the simultaneous (and often inadvertent) ingestion of barbiturates with other CNS depressants, such as alcohol; synergistic CNS-depressant effects have been documented among several of these agents during periods of acute intoxication.

Barbituric acid is the chemical structure upon which the various barbiturate hypnotics are based (Fig. 1). The widely used barbiturates are 5,5-disubstituted derivatives of barbituric acid. Chemical modifications within the molecule can markedly alter the pharmacology of the compound, primarily by affecting the lipid solubility of the molecule. In general, the more lipid-soluble barbiturates tend to have a more rapid onset of action, are shorter acting, tend to be more rapidly metabolized, and may be reabsorbed extensively by the renal tubules. For example, highly lipid-soluble thiobarbiturates, in which the oxygen of C-2 is replaced by sulfur, are very short-acting drugs.

Absorption

Barbiturates are rarely injected parenterally by the compulsive user. This discussion centers primarily on the oral absorption of the barbiturate, since it is the route used most commonly.

Depending upon the side chain substitutions on the barbituric acid moiety, the resulting compounds may have different lipid solubilities. The highly lipid-soluble barbiturates are generally absorbed from the stomach quite rapidly, often more rapidly than alcohol; the less lipid-soluble barbiturates are absorbed relatively slowly and plasma concentrations of phenobarbital, for example, may rise for several hours after its oral administration.

When secobarbital was administered orally to nonfasted human subjects, 90% of the drug was absorbed within 1.5 hours (Clifford et al., 1974). Secobarbital was detected in blood for as long as 108 hours. Al-

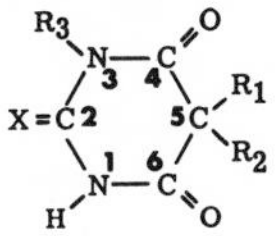

$$R_3 - N - C = O$$
$$X = C_2^{3} \quad {}^4C - R_1$$
$$\quad \quad {}^5C \stackrel{R_1}{R_2}$$
$$N - C = O$$
$$H$$

BARBITURATE	R_1	R_2	R_3	X
BARBITURIC ACID	H-	H-	H-	O=
THIOPENTAL	CH_3CH_2-	$CH_3CH_2CH_2CH-$ $\quad\quad\quad CH_3$	H-	S=
HEXOBARBITAL	CH_3-	⟨ ⟩-	CH_3-	O=
AMOBARBITAL*	CH_3CH_2-	$CH_3-CH-CH_2CH_2-$ $\quad\quad CH_3$	H-	O=
SECOBARBITAL*	$CH_2=CH-CH_2-$	$CH_3CH_2CH_2CH-$ $\quad\quad\quad CH_3$	H-	O=
PENTOBARBITAL*	CH_3CH_2-	$CH_3CH_2CH_2CH-$ $\quad\quad\quad CH_3$	H-	O=
MEPHOBARBITAL	CH_3CH_2-	⟨O⟩-	CH_3-	O=
PHENOBARBITAL*	CH_3CH_2-	⟨O⟩-	H-	O=
METHARBITAL	CH_3CH_2-	CH_3CH_2-	CH_3-	O=
BARBITAL	CH_3CH_2-	CH_3CH_2-	H-	O=

Fig. 1. Structures of selected barbiturates.
*These compounds are among the most abused barbiturates.

though food intake may slow the rate of barbiturate absorption from the gastrointestinal tract, evidently the total amount absorbed is not altered (Smith *et al.*, 1973).

The barbiturates are weak acids and are present primarily in the nonionized form at the acidic pH of the stomach. In this form, they more readily penetrate the gastric mucosa. Studies by Sjögren *et al.* (1965), however, indicate that in man the rate-limiting step in the oral absorption of some intermediate- and short-acting barbiturates is not their rate of passage through the gastrointestinal mucosa, but, their rate of de-aggregation and dissolution in the lumen.

According to Magnussen (1968), ethanol enhances absorption of the barbiturates possibly by increasing blood flow through the gastric mucosa. This interaction should be considered as part of an overall evaluation of the synergistic CNS depression observed after consumption of both barbiturates and alcohol.

In contrast to gastric absorption of barbiturates, intestinal absorption is reportedly much less dependent upon the chemical structure and lipid solubility of the compound (Kakemi et al., 1967, 1969). Experiments conducted in rats, in situ and in vitro, suggest that these drugs bind to protein at the surface of the intestinal mucosa, and that this binding is a limiting factor in the absorption of barbiturates. This absorption process apparently involves hydrophobic binding as well as possibly ionic and hydrogen binding. Formation of complexes between barbiturates and mucosal protein also has been implicated as a rate-limiting step in the buccal absorption of these drugs (Beckett and Moffatt, 1971.).

Distribution

The organs of metabolism (liver) and excretion (kidney) of barbiturates generally contain higher concentrations of these drugs than plasma or other tissues. The availability of numerous congeners of barbituric acid has resulted in extensive studies of the physicochemical factors that affect their concentrations in tissues. Three important factors are: lipid solubility, protein binding, and degree of ionization at physiologic pH (Sharpless, 1970).

Circulating barbiturates become bound to plasma albumin to varying degrees; in general, the more lipid-soluble barbiturates (such as hexobarbital) are bound to a greater extent than the poorly soluble ones (such as barbital). About 50% of the phenobarbital in plasma is said to be protein bound (Lous, 1954; Goldbaum and Smith, 1954; Waddell and Butler, 1957). Use of hemodialysis to remove toxic levels of barbiturates from the body becomes increasingly unsuccessful as these agents become increasingly bound to plasma proteins. Evidence has been obtained to suggest that, in rats, thiopental may be displaced from plasma proteins by high concentrations of nonsteroidal antiinflammatory agents, such as aspirin, phenylbutazone, and naproxen. This displacement can result in reinduction of thiopental's CNS depressant action (Chaplin et al., 1973). Similar interactions have been reported between barbiturates and other agents, including various sulfa drugs (Pagnini et al., 1971).

In addition to their binding to plasma proteins, the barbiturates also become avidly bound to tissue proteins so that, with the exception of body fat, tissue concentrations of these agents may be as high as or higher than their plasma concentrations. At equilibrium, the fat depots contain relatively high concentrations of the lipid-soluble (shorter-acting) barbiturates. The rates of penetration of barbiturates from the blood into the cerebrospinal fluid are considered to be largely dependent upon passive diffusion through a lipoid barrier (Kurz, 1964). Compared to plasma concentrations of barbiturates, concentrations in the cerebrospinal fluid and ocular fluid, which normally contain negligible amounts of protein, are quite low.

It is possible to alter the disposition of barbiturates by modifying the plasma pH. For example, when the alkalinity of the plasma is increased, more of the ionized form of the barbiturates appears in the plasma and less drug is available in a form that can penetrate into tissues. In this connection, Waddell and Butler (1957) observed that hyperventilation (which causes a respiratory alkalosis) or the administration of alkali (which produces a metabolic alkalosis) would result in a rise in total plasma concentration of phenobarbital and lessened hypnotic effect in experimental animals; these findings were related to lesser concentrations of the drug in brain tissue. Alkalosis also facilitates renal excretion of barbiturates by increasing the proportion of ionized to nonionized drug in the tubular urine and thereby reducing the amount of drug reabsorbed from the lumen.

Distribution of barbital, pentobarbital, and thiopental between the blood and pulmonary tissue of the dog has been largely explained on the basis of transport of the nonionic forms of these drugs across the pulmonary membrane (Effros et al., 1972). In vitro, distribution of these agents between red cells and plasma was such that cellular concentrations were greater than would be predicted simply from the transmembrane pH gradient.

The shorter-acting, highly lipid-soluble barbiturates readily penetrate the lipoid "blood-brain barrier"; the longer-acting agents penetrate more slowly such that over 15 minutes may be required to induce sleep in man after their intravenous administration. The penetration into brain by the lipid-soluble barbiturates is so rapid that in pharmacokinetic studies the brain has been considered as being in the same "compartment" as plasma (Lin et al., 1973). In the case of those barbiturates having low lipid solubility, brain was assigned to the "tissue compartment." In these studies, rate constants for the distribution of several barbiturates between the "plasma" compartment and "tissue" compartment were not positively correlated to the lipid solubilities of the drugs. These findings support the concept that in addition to lipid solubility, other factors (e.g., binding to plasma protein, transmembrane pH gradients, blood flow) are significant determinants of the tissue distribution of these drugs.

At equilibrium, barbiturates are rather uniformly distributed throughout brain tissue. Initially, however, those barbiturates that enter the brain most readily are found at highest concentrations in more highly perfused areas (cortex, geniculate bodies, and colliculi); those that gain access to the brain more slowly do not exhibit such regional differences in distribution (Sharpless, 1970).

In man and animals, brain and serum levels of phenobarbital have been reported to be similar at equilibrium (Buchtal and Svensmark, 1959). Conditions which affect the permeability of the blood-brain barrier, for example, meningitis, can alter the rate of entry of barbiturates to the brain, especially the entry rate of the longer-acting members of this class of drugs.

The duration of hypnotic action of the barbiturates can be attributed essentially to three processes: (1) redistribution, (2) metabolic elimination, and (3) renal excretion (Sharpless, 1970). In the broadest sense, these processes are all related somewhat to the lipid solubility. The less lipid-soluble barbiturates are largely excreted by the kidney as unchanged drug, and redistribution plays a relatively minor role in their disposition. The role of redistribution in terminating the actions of lipid-soluble barbiturates can be demonstrated by considering the case of thiopental (although it is not a barbiturate that is commonly abused). This barbiturate is almost completely metabolized in man. However, its rate of metabolism is reportedly too slow (10-15% per hour) to account for the very short duration of action of this compound (Brodie *et al.*, 1950). Rather, its brief action is related to its redistribution out of the CNS to other tissue compartments. Initially, after the administration of intravenous thiopental, the drug is taken up by tissues that are highly perfused, such as brain and certain visceral organs. Therefore, high concentrations of the drug are achieved in these tissues at early time periods. Later, the drug becomes redistributed to muscle and skin, and ultimately to fat. As these tissues take up the barbiturate, plasma concentration falls and the drug diffuses out of the brain to maintain equilibrium; the hypnotic action ceases. Thus, the duration of action of a single dose of this drug is determined not only by its rate of metabolic inactivation and renal excretion, but also by its redistribution out of the CNS into more, let us say, "inert" tissues. In this way, the duration of action of thiopental may cease when appreciable amounts of the drug are still present in the body; this is a potentially hazardous occurrence since upon repeated administration of a given dose of this drug cumulative CNS-depressant effects can result when the "inert" tissues become saturated and high levels of drug "spill" back into the circulation and subsequently penetrate to the brain. Indeed, this process of redistribution of barbiturates into the CNS can produce a characteristic barbiturate "hangover" for many hours after recovery from barbiturate anesthesia. The distribution of other barbiturates is in accord with these principles to varying degrees, depending upon their lipid solubilities.

Barbiturates readily cross the placental "barrier." Indeed, within a few minutes after administration of the shorter-acting barbiturates, the concentrations in fetal blood approach those in the maternal venous blood (Sharpless, 1970). In addition, phenobarbital levels in serum of the human umbilical blood have been reported to be approximately 95% of those in maternal serum (Eadie and Tyrer, 1973). When isolated human placenta was perfused with a dextran-saline solution to which various lipid-soluble drugs (including thiopental) and lipid-insoluble drugs (including barbital) were added, the drugs disappeared from the perfusion fluid into the placenta at different rates (Kurz and Fasching, 1968), the rates of disappearance increasing with increasing lipid solubility. Nevertheless, substances that were almost lipid-insoluble could pass (albeit more slowly) into the placenta from the perfusion fluid. Thus, the placental "barrier" exhibited characteristics of a porous membrane, as well as a lipoid membrane.

Pentobarbital, which is slightly soluble in lipid, and barbital, which is poorly soluble in lipid, were both detected in amniotic fluid after their intravenous injection to pregnant dogs (Carrier et al., 1969). Both drugs entered the amniotic fluid rapidly, despite a 50-fold difference in their oil-to-water partition coefficients. Indeed, compared to pentobarbital, a *greater* fraction of the administered dose of the less lipid-soluble barbital appeared in the amniotic fluid. Two possible explanations for these findings were: (1) that less barbital was distributed to maternal tissue than pentobarbital so that more barbital was available for distribution to the amniotic fluid; (2) that barbital was distributed in greater amounts in the amniotic fluid because of its greater water solubility compared to pentobarbital.

Barbiturates have been shown to penetrate the preimplantation blastocyst of the pregnant rabbit after being transferred into uterine secretions from the maternal circulation (Sieber and Fabro, 1971). Thiopental, for example, attained concentrations in the blastocyst that approximated those in the maternal plasma; metabolites of thiopental were also present in the blastocyst. Likewise, barbital penetrated to the blastocysts (primarily as unchanged drug). From these various observations, it should not be surprising that the abuse of these drugs during pregnancy can induce drug dependency in the newborn. Moreover, small amounts of barbiturates may also appear in human milk after the ingestion of large doses.

Metabolism

The pharmacologic actions of the barbiturates are largely limited by the processes of (1) redistribution; (2) renal excretion; and (3) metabolic transformation. In regard to the lattermost process, barbital appears to be an exception, being excreted quantitatively in the urine without appreciable change.* The biotransformation of barbiturates basically involves trans-

---

*Although barbital may be metabolized to some degree, metabolism is considered to be virtually negligible in the total disposition of the compound (Mark, 1963). Dealkylation of barbital has been reported to occur (Goldschmidt and Wehr, 1957); in the urine of rats, 5-ethylbarbituric acid was isolated to the extent of 2.5% of an administered dose of barbital. In man, N-methylation of barbital to metharbital has been a sporadic finding in the urine of barbital-treated subjects (Frey et al., 1959).

formation of lipid-soluble compounds into more polar metabolites that are usually (but not always) devoid of significant pharmacologic activity, and that are readily excreted via the kidney. The metabolites also may be secreted into bile and appear in the feces.

There are vast species differences in response to a given barbiturate, and a prime factor contributing to this variation is the rate and pattern of drug metabolism in different animal species (Burns, 1968).

Approximately 65-90% of a dose of barbital may be excreted in human urine in the unchanged form; for phenobarbital the values are 10-30%; pentobarbital and secobarbital, 0-3%; and amobarbital, 0-1% (Lous, 1966; Sharpless, 1970).† The lipid solubility of the barbiturates determines to some extent their rates of metabolism. However, from studies conducted *in vitro*, it seems that other factors are involved as well, at least insofar as the rates of metabolism of barbiturates by liver microsomal preparations were found not to be directly correlated with their oil-to-water partition coefficients (Jansson *et al.*, 1972).

A number of drugs that are chemically and pharmacologically dissimilar, but that are metabolized by the hepatic microsomal enzyme systems have been shown to inhibit the oxidation of barbiturates *in vivo* and thus to modify their duration of action (Rubin *et al.*, 1964b; Bousquet *et al.*, 1964; Butler *et al.*, 1965). The metabolism of these various agents may involve a common enzyme system and/or a common intermediate in the sequence of reactions leading to drug oxidation (Rubin *et al.*, 1964a).

It is well known that combinations of the opiate analgesics and barbiturates produce synergistic CNS depressant effects. The major basis for this synergism is probably associated with effects exerted within the CNS. It is also possible that at least a portion of the explanation resides in the observation that in rats certain barbiturates and opiates may be mutually inhibitory with respect to the metabolism of one another *in vivo* and *in vitro* (Rubin *et al.*, 1964a,b).

Some *endogenous* compounds may also modify barbiturate metabolism and action. In 1951, Lamson *et al.* observed that an i.v. injection of glucose administered to dogs awakening from hexobarbital-induced hypnosis resulted in a prolonged and deep hypnotic state. Indeed, various intermediary metabolites of glucose could also potentiate the effect

---

†Phenobarbital is frequently considered to be not "readily" metabolized. However, it may be rather *extensively* metabolized, though not *rapidly*; often the amount metabolized and the rate of metabolism are combined under the "umbrella" term, "readily metabolized." This terminology can be misleading. Another source of potential confusion may arise from the erroneous assumption that phenobarbital is metabolized only to *p*-hydroxyphenobarbital, an impression that perhaps arises from the numerous studies that emphasize that transformation in hepatic microsomal preparations.

of the barbiturates apparently by increasing their rate of penetration into brain. In the case of glucose itself, its prolongation of hexobarbital sleeping time is reportedly related more to a decreased microsomal metabolism of hexobarbital than to a centrally mediated mechanism (Peters and Strother, 1972). Evidence was obtained to indicate that glucose could decrease the activity of various components of the microsomal electron transport system of the liver. Also, it seems to interact with the hexobarbital oxidase at the active site and perhaps at a distant allosteric site.

The barbiturates are metabolized in the body primarily by enzyme systems present in the liver.* Conditions which impair hepatic function theoretically should modify barbiturate action. Indeed in experimental animals, liver damage has been shown to intensify barbiturate action (see Mark, 1963). In man, such studies have not been as conclusive, although the use of barbiturates in patients with hepatic impairment still merits a cautious approach. Shideman and his co-workers (1949) observed an unusually long duration of hypnotic action after a dose of thiopental in patients with hepatic dysfunction. Unfortunately, the prolonged action could not be directly attributed to the impairment of liver function. Similar comments apply to the studies of Dundee (1952). From their studies in man, Sessions and his associates (1954) concluded that the plasma disposition of pentobarbital was not significantly impaired by liver disease. Normally, the liver appears to have enough functional reserve so that the enzymes responsible for the metabolism of barbiturates can function adequately even in the presence of moderate hepatic impairment (Shideman *et al.*, 1947, 1953; Brodie *et al.*, 1959).

It is beyond the scope of this book to list or to describe all the known metabolites of the various barbiturates. Rather, we will review the general pathways that are involved and provide relevant examples for the commonly abused barbiturates.† Although the primary pathways of barbiturate metabolism are rather well defined, some minor metabolites and compounds formed from further metabolism of primary metabolites still remain largely unidentified. In some cases, the so-called "minor" metabolite fraction accounts for as much as 40% of an administered dose of a barbiturate (Freudenthal and Carroll, 1973).

One can consider essentially four metabolic routes of biotransformation of the barbiturates (Raventós, 1954): (1) oxidation or complete

---

*Thiobarbiturates may be metabolized to a lesser extent in other tissues, especially kidney and brain (Dorfman and Goldbaum, 1947; Gould and Shideman, 1952; Cooper and Brodie, 1955).

†The reader may wish to refer to the more extensive reviews of barbiturate metabolism by Mark, 1963; Williams and Parke, 1964; and Bush and Sanders, 1967.

removal of the substituent groups at the C-5 position; (2) N-dealkylation at N-3; (3) desulfuration of thiobarbiturates; and (4) cleavage of the barbituric acid ring between N-1 and C-6 (refer to Fig. 1).

Oxidation at the C-5 Position

Oxidation of groups at C-5 is the most important pathway for the metabolism of barbiturates. The reaction is mediated by the cytochrome P-450, NADPH-dependent system of the hepatic microsomes. Oxidation occurs preferentially at the penultimate (ω-1) carbon atom of an aliphatic side chain and, to a lesser extent, at the ultimate (ω) carbon. Primary alcohols are the initial products of ω-oxidation and these compounds may undergo a secondary oxidation to the corresponding carboxylic acids. The alcohols resulting from (ω-1)-oxidation of barbiturates may be oxidized secondarily to the corresponding ketones. In contrast to the initial oxidations, secondary oxidations are catalyzed by soluble, NAD-dependent enzymes of the liver. Penultimate oxidation can also occur when an alkyl chain is attached to a nitrogen atom in the barbiturate ring. Thus, 75% of a dose of N-*n*-butylbarbital (nBB) was converted to 3'-hydroxy-nBB, 3'-keto-nBB, or a conjugate of 3'-hydroxy-nBB in the rat (Vore *et al.*, 1974). Preliminary evidence also suggested that ω-oxidation and (ω-2) oxidation of the nBB had occurred. N-dealkylation to barbital was not detected.

When saturated or unsaturated ring structures are located at the C-5 position, they too may be oxidized to form more polar compounds, such as alcohols, ketones, phenols, or carboxylic acids, depending upon the nature of the substituent group. Ultimately, the products of C-5 oxidation may become conjugated, as for example with glucuronic acid, and appear in the urine in free or conjugated form. The conjugates do not appear to possess hypnotic activity.

N-Dealkylation

N-Substituted barbiturates may be converted to metabolites by removal of the N-alkyl group. In this instance, the metabolites usually retain pharmacologic (anticonvulsant and hypnotic) activity (Butler, 1952, 1953; Butler and Waddell, 1958). In man and in dog, metharbital and mephobarbital are converted almost entirely to barbital and phenobarbital, respectively (Butler *et al.*, 1952). The N-demethylation reaction occurs slowly, but the barbital and phenobarbital metabolites are themselves eliminated even more slowly so that they may accumulate during prolonged administration of the N-methylated parent drug, and their plasma concentrations may rise even higher than those of the parent drugs. The anti-

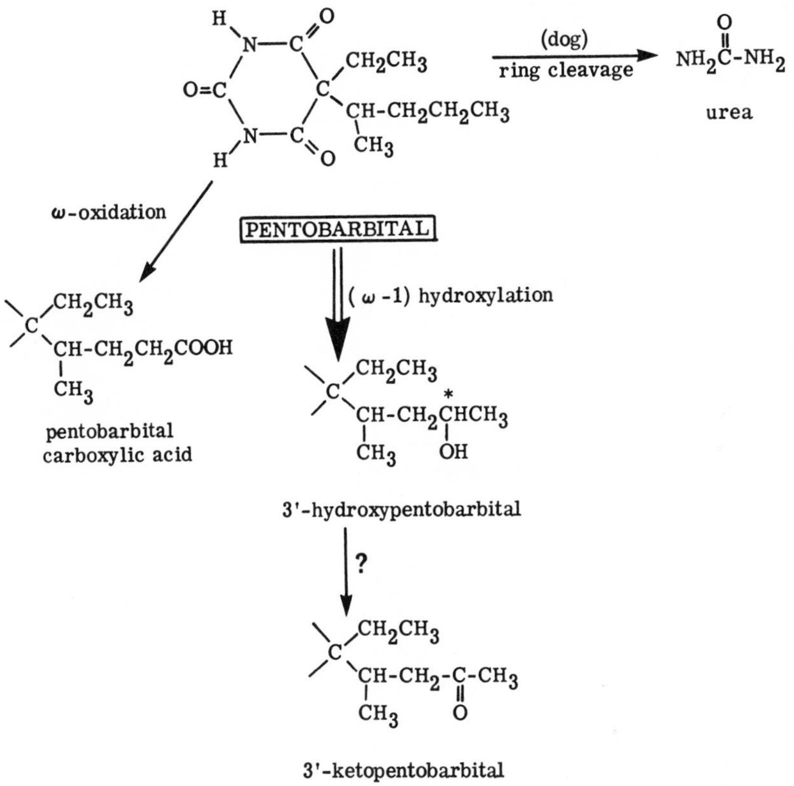

Fig. 2. Metabolism of pentobarbital. *New asymmetric center.

convulsant potency of mephobarbital is approximately one-half to one-third that of its demethylated metabolite (Swinyard *et al.*, 1954; Craig and Shideman, 1962, 1971).

N-Demethylation of barbiturates is catalyzed by enzyme systems localized in the microsomal fraction of the liver, that require NADPH and oxygen, and that are inhibited by carbon monoxide. As in other N-demethylation reactions, the products formed *in vitro* are the corresponding N-demethylated analogues and formaldehyde (see discussion of Flynn and Spector, 1974; McMahon, 1963; Okui and Kuroiwa, 1963). Both *in vivo* and *in vitro*, considerable differences occur in the rates of removal of the N-methyl groups of various barbiturates. For example, short-acting barbiturates, such as hexobarbital, are N-demethylated to a very slight extent compared to oxidation of their C-5 substituent groups.

Desulfuration

The sulfur atom of thiobarbiturates may be replaced by oxygen to yield the corresponding oxybarbiturates; for example, thiopental may be converted to pentobarbital. In man, this reaction is not considered to be a major route for elimination of thiobarbiturates.

Ring cleavage

Hydrolytic cleavage of the barbituric acid ring, although it may occur, is of minor pharmacologic importance *in vivo*. In animals, but not in man, evidence for a small amount of ring splitting has been obtained in the case of pentobarbital, amobarbital, and hexobarbital, among other barbiturates (Mark, 1963).

For completeness, we describe below the metabolism of several of the more commonly abused barbiturates.

Pentobarbital Metabolism (Fig. 2)

Pentobarbital is metabolically inactivated, primarily by penultimate (ω-1) hydroxylation of the C-5 [1-methylbutyl] side chain, giving rise to 3'-hydroxypentobarbital (Maynert and Dawson, 1952; Brodie *et al.*, 1953). This conversion results in the appearance of a new asymmetric center and four optically active isomers of 3'-hydroxypentobarbital.*

When ¹⁵N-labeled pentobarbital was administered orally to human volunteers, about 80% of the dose was accounted for in urine (Maynert, 1965a). About 40-50% of the dose was excreted as a mixture of diastereoisomeric alcohols over a period of 4-5 days. Two optically active metabolite fractions were isolated from the urine and were found to represent levorotatory (-) and dextrorotatory (+) 3'-hydroxypentobarbital at a ratio of 5.4 to 1. In contrast, dogs form 2.3 times more of the (+) al-

---

*We shall not attempt to provide a complete discussion of the stereochemistry of barbiturate metabolism. Different optical isomers of barbiturates can exert different pharmocologic actions (Freudenthal and Carrol, 1973; Christensen and Lee, 1973). There can also be differences among isomers with respect to anesthetic potency, tissue distribution, albumin binding, and metabolism (Furner *et al.*, 1969; Büch *et al.*, 1973; Maynert, 1965b).

It had been well known that certain minor molecular changes among the barbiturates altered the pharmacological activity of the respective derivatives, say, from hypnotic action toward convulsant activity. It had been assumed that geometrical changes in the barbiturate structure were necessary to produce such opposing effects. It has recently been reported that this phenomenon (change from anesthetic to convulsant activity) can occur within the same structure, differing only by steric configurations (Downes *et al.*, 1970).

cohol than the (-)alcohol. From studies involving rat liver enzyme preparations, it appears the rat is more like man, forming considerably more of the (-)alcohol than the (+)alcohol (Kuntzman *et al.*, 1967). Also, in rats the (-)alcohol fraction was reported to be further metabolized in liver preparations by a soluble enzyme in the presence of NAD. The metabolite formed is still unidentified; it may be 3'-ketopentobarbital. A carboxylic acid metabolite, formed by ω-oxidation of pentobarbital, has also been identified in the urine after giving pentobarbital to human subjects (Algeri and McBay, 1953; Frey *et al.*, 1959) or to dogs (Titus and Weiss, 1955). Also, in the dog, evidence of ring cleavage of pentobarbital was indicated by finding that about 2-3% of the dose was converted to urea.

About 35% of a dose of administered pentobarbital appears in human urine as compounds that have not yet been identified; Bush and Sanders (1967) suggest the possibility that glucuronide derivatives of the alcohols or of other metabolites containing a carboxyl group could account for much of this remainder.

In experimental animals, thiopental can be desulfurated to pentobarbital which is in turn further metabolized by oxidation of the C-5 side chain. Obviously, this desulfuration reaction is not a detoxication mechanism. In man, thiopental has not been noticeably desulfurated to pentobarbital (Furano and Greene, 1963).

Amobarbital Metabolism (Fig. 3)

The duration of action of amobarbital is largely dependent upon its rate of metabolic biotransformation (Dixit and Abraham, 1960; Hansch *et al.*, 1968). Amobarbital is metabolized primarily by penultimate oxidation to the 3'-hydroxy metabolite (Maynert, 1965a). The 3'-hydroxyamobarbital is reported to have about half the hypnotic potency in mice as amobarbital (Irrgang, 1965).

Essentially no unchanged amobarbital is excreted in human urine, even after large doses such as those associated with an overdosage of the drug (Mawer and Lee, 1968). Approximately 40-50% of a hypnotic dose of amobarbital is eliminated in human urine within 48 hours as 3'-hydroxyamobarbital (Balasubramaniam *et al.*, 1970). The remainder of the dose is presumably excreted in the feces, or in urine as unidentified conjugates. In this connection, Maynert (1965a) and Kamm and VanLoon (1966) did not detect glucoronide conjugates of 3'-hydroxyamobarbital in urine samples treated with β-glucuronidase. But since Butler (1956) reported the formation of a sulfate conjugate of p-hydroxyphenobarbital (Fig.4) from phenobarbital, it is possible that other nonglucuronide conjugates of 3'-hydroxyamobarbital may be present in human urine.

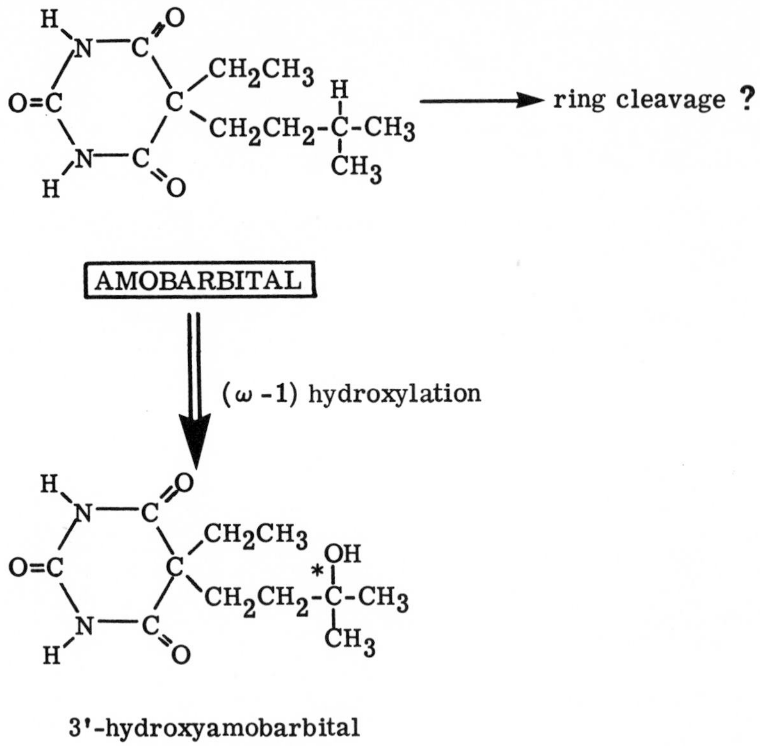

ring cleavage ?

AMOBARBITAL

(ω -1) hydroxylation

3'-hydroxyamobarbital

Fig. 3. Metabolism of amobarbital. *New asymmetric center.

Phenobarbital Metabolism (Fig. 4)

Butler *et al.* (1954) reported that in man only 11-23% of a dose of phenobarbital was excreted in the urine during the first day after administration. In fact, the drug and its metabolite, *p*-hydroxyphenobarbital, have been detected in human urine for up to 1 month after a single dose of 300 mg (Frey *et al.*, 1959).

In man, the major urinary metabolite of phenobarbital was reported to be *p*-hydroxyphenobarbital (Kutt *et al.*, 1964a,b). At low doses, phenobarbital was metabolized rather efficiently and no signs of toxicity appeared. In several subjects, as the dose of phenobarbital was increased, the amounts of excreted hydroxylated compound rose to a plateau at which time the blood levels of the unchanged drug began to rise and toxic signs began to appear. And yet, there were patients in whom no such plateau was observed, and in whom no excessive increases in blood levels of phenobarbital occurred.

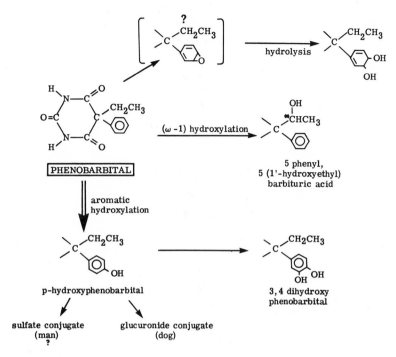

Fig. 4. Metabolism of phenobarbital. *New asymmetric center.

Parahydroxyphenobarbital is regarded as an inactive metabolite of phenobarbital (Butler, 1956). Prior to its urinary excretion, this metabolite can be conjugated to glucuronic acid in the dog, and possibly to sulfate in man.

After administering phenobarbital to rats, guinea pigs, and man, Harvey et al. (1972) identified 5-(1'-hydroxyethyl)-5-phenylbarbituric acid and 5-(3,4-dihydroxyphenyl)-5-ethylbarbituric acid as urinary metabolites. Also found was 5-(3,4-dihydroxy-1,5-cyclohexadien-1-yl)-5-ethylbarbituric acid. This lattermost compound may result from enzymatic epoxidation of phenobarbital to form an arene oxide intermediate, which subsequently opens in the presence of a microsomal epoxide hydrase to yield the dihydrodiol (Grover et al., 1971). It has been suggested that the barbiturates may bind to adenine-containing molecules and thus functionally deplete the cells of these important intracellular compounds (Voet and Rich, 1972). Since epoxide intermediates are frequently highly reactive molecular species, it is possible that these intermediates of barbiturate metabolism are partly responsible for certain barbiturate actions (Cookson et al., 1971; Harvey et al., 1972; Marquardt et al., 1972).

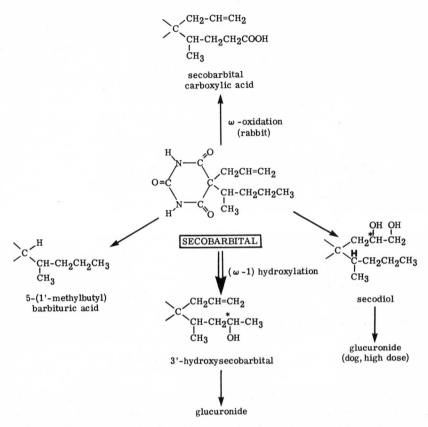

Fig. 5. Metabolism of secobarbital. *New asymmetric center.

Secobarbital Metabolism (Fig. 5)

At least three metabolites of secobarbital appear in human urine (Cochin and Daly, 1963; Waddell, 1965). Those that have been identified are: 5-(2',3'-dihydroxypropyl)-5-(1'-methylbutyl)barbituric acid (secodiol), and two stereoisomeric forms of 3'-hydroxysecobarbital. The 3'-hydroxysecobarbital reportedly had no hypnotic activity in mice at a dose as high as 180 mg/kg intravenously (Waddell, 1965). The three urinary metabolites accounted collectively for about 50% of the ingested dose of secobarbital. About 5% of the dose was excreted unchanged in the urine of the first 48 hours. Similar findings were reported in dogs. Another metabolite allegedly present sporadically and in minor amounts in the urines of man and dog was 5-(1'-methylbutyl)barbituric acid, formed by removal of the allyl group of secobarbital.

In an experimental model of secobarbital overdosage in man, a large i.v. dose (36 mg/kg) was injected intravenously into dogs and the disposition of the drug was studied (Muhlhauser *et al.*, 1974). The primary urinary metabolites were 3'-hydroxysecobarbital (37% of the dose) and secodiol (16%); under these experimental conditions the compounds were excreted free and as glucuronide conjugates (26%).

Rats and rabbits form primarily the 3'-hydroxysecobarbitals from secobarbital, both *in vivo* and *in vitro* (Niyogi, 1964; Tsukamoto *et al.*, 1963a). Secodiol is a minor metabolite in the rat, whereas in the rabbit a carboxylic acid metabolite of secobarbital is also excreted. Thiamylal, the 2-thio analogue of secobarbital, was converted in rabbits to several metabolites including secobarbital (1% of the dose), hydroxysecobarbital (0.01%), and carboxysecobarbital (0.1%) (Tsukamoto *et al.*, 1963b).

*Hexobarbital Metabolism**

Hexobarbital is metabolized in the C-5 cyclohexenyl group to 3'-hydroxyhexobarbital by the NADPH-dependent microsomal enzyme system of liver tissue. The hydroxylated compound may be converted to 3'-ketohexobarbital by an NAD- or NADP-dependent dehydrogenase localized in the soluble fraction of rabbit liver (Frey *et al.*, 1959; Toki *et al.*, 1963; Toki and Tsukamoto, 1964). The 1'-keto analogue is also formed from hexobarbital. Toki and Takenouchi (1965) have characterized the glucuronide of *a*-3'-hydroxyhexobarbital from the urine of rabbits given hexobarbital. This metabolite amounted to about 14% of the dose.

Both 3'-hydroxy- and 3'-ketohexobarbital may be N-demethylated in the microsomes (Bush *et al.*, 1953). Although hexobarbital may be N-demethylated directly, in most instances it is a negligible reaction; thus, when ketonorhexobarbital is found in the urine of animals given hexobarbital, it is believed to come from the demethylation of previously oxidized hexobarbital. The N-demethylation of hexobarbital has not been demonstrated in man (Mark, 1963).

Deininger (1955, 1956) injected mice with norhexobarbital and found that 3-5% of the dose was methylated to form hexobarbital. Thus, if N-demethylation does occur, it may be "masked" sometimes because of the reversibility of this reaction.

Finally, there is evidence that the barbituric acid ring and the cyclohexene ring of hexobarbital may be cleaved and that the products of these reactions are metabolized further.

*This barbiturate is rarely abused, but its biotransformation is described briefly because it is often used experimentally in studies of metabolism of barbiturates and other drugs. A complete review of the metabolism of hexobarbital has been written by Bush and Weller (1972).

Influence of metabolism on development of tolerance

As discussed in Chapter 10, the development of tolerance to the hypnotic effects of the barbiturates appears to involve both dispositional (peripheral) and adaptive (central) changes. The distribution of the barbiturates in tolerant versus nontolerant animals does not appear to be altered. Rather, the dispositional tolerance relates to the capacity of barbiturates to stimulate their own rates of metabolic inactivation by inducing the hepatic microsomal enzyme system. The induction of hepatic microsomal drug-metabolizing enzymes in man and experimental animals following treatment with barbiturates and other hypnotics has been extensively documented and reviewed (Burns, 1964; Conney, 1967; Remmer, 1959, 1969; Prescott, 1969 *inter alia*). At various times, the shorter-acting barbiturates have been reported not to induce the microsomal enzyme systems responsible for their own metabolism; however, induction has been shown to occur as long as these shorter-acting compounds are given in sufficient amount and at sufficiently short intervals to maintain adequate concentrations in the liver (Remmer, 1964). For this reason, studies designed to compare the congeners of a chemical series with respect to their intrinsic inductive potency, without comparing the disposition of the congeners to liver tissue may be misleading. From what we know about drugs in general, small molecular changes can result in rather remarkable differences in their physiologic disposition. Ideally, one would measure intrahepatic concentrations; on a more practical basis, plasma concentrations often suffice.

Most studies indicate that the enzyme inductive effect of barbiturates is related to an increase in the synthesis of an enzyme (cytochrome P-450) that is rate limiting in the sequence of reactions leading to drug oxidation. It has been reported, however, that in rats barbital can disproportionately influence the rates of drug metabolism and the activity of cytochrome P-450 (see Müller *et al.*, 1973). For example, aminopyrine N-demethylation could be enhanced 700% by treating 18-day-old rats with barbital, whereas the cytochrome P-450 activity was increased by only about 100%. Also, as the rats aged, an accompanying increase in rate of drug metabolism was proportionately greater than the accompanying increase in cytochrome P-450 activity. Under these conditions, it seems that the content of cytochrome P-450 in the liver microsomes was not necessarily the rate-limiting factor in drug biotransformation; similar findings have been reported at various times.

In addition to the occurrence of dispositional tolerance, a second mechanism of tolerance to barbiturates involves adaptive processes in the CNS. This mechanism is especially important in the case of the longer-acting barbiturates which are slowly metabolized by the microsomal enzyme system. For example, Ebert *et al.* (1964) provided evidence in rats that tolerance development to the hypnotic effects of barbital (as evidenced by a decrease in sleeping time after chronic administration of the barbiturate) was not associated with a significant acceleration of metabolism of barbital. During 24 hours after administration of barbital, 6% of the dose was metabolized in barbital-tolerant rats, as compared to 3% in the controls. This small difference could not account for the magnitude of tolerance. The only metabolite identified was 5-ethylbarbituric acid; at least two unidentified metabolites were present in the urine of both tolerant and control rats.

There is a tendency for users of longer-acting barbiturates to awaken from a state of acute intoxication at barbiturate plasma levels higher than those seen when nonhabituated individuals awaken (Lous, 1966). Moreover, Butler and his associates (1954) showed that repeated dosages of phenobarbital to human volunteers resulted in its accumulation at a time when the hypnotic effect was diminishing. The rate of metabolism of phenobarbital appeared to be identical in habitual and nonhabitual patients. These findings are indicative of a significant adaptive component to the development of tolerance to the hypnotic effect of barbiturates in man. Ebert *et al.* (1964) and Remmer (1969) observed similar findings in experimental animals. The enzyme inductive mechanism of tolerance seems to be more operative in the case of the short-acting barbiturates that are metabolized more rapidly and to a greater extent than the long-acting barbiturates.

Okamoto *et al.* (1975) rendered cats tolerant to the impairment of neurologic function produced by repeated pentobarbital administration. Both the dispositional and adaptive mechanisms of tolerance seemed to be operative. The dispositional mechanism occurred early and was virtually complete within a week. Thereafter, pentobarbital metabolism remained at a fairly constant level as long as the barbiturate dosage was continued. Despite this "plateau," it was still necessary to increase the pentobarbital dosage to retain maximal CNS depression over the next 5 weeks, when the study was terminated. This suggested the onset of an adaptive tolerance developing to pentobarbital actions and continuing until the study was terminated. Adaptive tolerance comprised less of the total tolerance to pentobarbital than dispositional tolerance. However, as pointed out, adaptive tolerance might have been more important *overall* because it seemed to progress gradually and linearly as long as the drug was given. Thus, the contribution to tolerance of the adaptive mechanism eventually might become more important than the dispositional mechanism over extended periods of continued drug exposure. Obviously, studies of barbiturate tolerance can be quite misleading if distinctions are not made between the tolerance mechanisms involved. A short-term experiment involving a decrease in sleeping time as an index of tolerance development would, according to these studies, reflect primarily changes in drug disposition. A well-developed adaptive tolerance would require more extended periods of treatment (say, more than 1 week). In studies involving barbiturate tolerance in experimental animals, extended dosage regimens are not routinely used.

We have alluded to studies wherein morphine tolerance was said to be transferred to mice by the injection of brain extracts prepared from morphine-tolerant rats or dogs (Chapter 10; Ungar and Cohen, 1966). Pentobarbital tolerance was not transferred. According to Turnbull and Stevenson (1968), the methodology used would be unlikely to produce barbiturate tolerance by a central (adaptive) mechanism; rather they submit that barbital tolerance is considered to be primarily an adaptive process occurring within the CNS). They reported reductions in hexobarbital sleeping time in mice which had been injected intraperitoneally 24 hours earlier with brain homogenates prepared from barbital-dependent rats. However, this apparent transfer of tolerance was shown to be due to the persistent presence of barbital in the injected brain homogenate, such that the drug could induce the microsomal enzyme systems in the recipient mice. parent transfer of tolerance was shown to be due to the persistent presence of barbital in the injected brain homogenate, such that the drug could induce the microsomal enzyme systems in the recipient mice.

It is widely recognized that there is a considerable degree of cross tolerance among various CNS depressant drugs particularly among barbiturates, general anesthetics, and alcohol (see review by Caldwell and Sever, 1974). Since barbiturates can stimulate hepatic enzymes responsible for the metabolic inactivation of many other drugs, cross tolerance between barbiturates and other drugs can at least be partially explained. The case with alcohol, on the other hand, is the subject of controversy since the degree of the participation of a microsomal system in alcohol oxidation has not been conclusively resolved (see Chapter 7 on Recreational Drugs of Abuse: Caffeine, Nicotine, Alcohol). Nevertheless, microsomal enzyme stimulation by barbiturates can modify the effects of many other drugs and chemicals that are metabolized by these enzyme systems. For example, barbiturates can affect the prothrombin time of patients receiving bishydroxycoumarin by increasing the rate of metabolic destruction of the latter drug. Metabolism of endogenous steroids that serve as substrates for the drug-metabolizing enzymes in the hepatic microsomes can also be affected by barbiturates; therefore, barbiturate administration can alter the actions of such steroids. In a group of barbiturate-dependent human subjects, Ballinger and his associates (1972) have reported that drug oxidation may increase markedly, and that hydroxylation of endogenous steroids that serve as substrates for the microsomal enzyme may be increased. Such drug-dependent patients might be tolerant to the effects of therapeutic agents which are metabolically inactivated in the liver, such that adjustments to higher doses might be required to maintain therapeutic levels in these individuals. Similarly, upon withdrawal of barbiturates, gradual loss of the enzyme inductive effect might require readjustment downward of the dosage of administered therapeutic agents in order to avoid accumulation to toxic levels. In their subjects, after withdrawal from barbiturates, the accelerated rate of microsomal enzyme activity returned to control levels. When rats are withdrawn from barbiturates, the accelerated metabolism may decrease below control levels before returning to normal.

It has been observed that barbiturate administration can be potentially hazardous to patients suffering from acute intermittent porphyria. The barbiturates can stimulate the activity of Δ-aminolevulinic acid (Δ-ALA) synthetase, an enzyme present in the mitochondria of hepatic parenchymal cells that catalyzes the rate-limiting step in the synthesis of porphyrins (Dean, 1953). By stimulating the formation of Δ-ALA synthetase, barbiturates may increase the production of porphyrins to hazardous levels in porphyric patients.

In studies of tolerance development to effects of barbiturates (and other drugs, for that matter), it is necessary to state clearly the pharmacologic effect that is under investigation. For example, York (1974) demonstrated that rats rendered tolerant to one effect of barbital (loss of the righting reflex) did not appear to be tolerant to another effect (activation of spontaneous motor activity). In animal studies of tolerance to barbiturates, the pharmacologic end point that is used most often is the loss of the hypnotic effect; the dose that is lethal does not always increase proportionately to the increased dose needed to maintain hypnosis (Gruber and Keyser, 1946). In man as well, abuse of barbiturates may result in development of tolerance to the hypnotic effects, such that doses 5-6 times the usual dose may be needed to satisfy the user. But, if the satiating dose is increased only moderately, a sudden acute intoxication may result (Isbell and White, 1953). Furthermore, barbiturate withdrawal symptoms may be particularly dangerous, including generalized convulsions, delirium, and death. In the case of abuse of the opiates, on the other hand, a marked tolerance has been shown to develop to both the euphoric and lethal actions, and the withdrawal syndrome is not usually as hazardous as barbiturate withdrawal (Fraser et al., 1957).

Caffeine can attenuate the hypnotic action of hexobarbital (Hach and Heim, 1971). This attenuation could be due to caffeine stimulation of hexobarbital metabolism and/or to stimulation of the CNS. Evidently, the stimulation of barbiturate metabolism by caffeine in rats is a relatively minor factor in comparison to interactions between these drugs at the level of the CNS (Aesbacher *et al.*, 1975).

In barbiturate-dependent individuals, Turnbull and Ballinger (1973) observed no evidence of an unusual metabolism or excretion of catecholamines and serotonin. Therefore, it seems that in man gross alterations in the disposition of these monoamines do not provide a neurochemical basis for barbiturate tolerance.

In a recent, preliminary report, Brezenoff and Mycek (1975) suggested that a cholinergic mechanism may be involved in the development of tolerance to the hypnotic effects of phenobarbital in rats. The development of tolerance to phenobarbital could be prevented either by depletion of brain acetylcholine using hemicholinium-3, or by treatment with the anticholinergic, atropine sulfate. Neither agent blocked a preexisting tolerance.

Excretion

Barbiturates are eliminated from the body primarily by renal excretion. Compared to adults, children seem to be able to eliminate phenobarbital more rapidly (Garrettson and Dayton, 1970), but neonates apparently eliminate it more slowly (Eadie and Tyrer, 1973).

In general, this class of drugs is excreted slowly in comparison to the rate of excretion of their polar metabolites. For example, after an oral dose of barbital, only 8% appeared in human urine over the first 12 hours, 20% in 24 hours, and 35-65% in 48 hours; traces of barbital were detected in urine for as long as 8-12 days after the dose (Sharpless *et al.*, 1970).

Numerous factors can influence the renal excretion of the barbiturates. First, the binding of barbiturates to plasma protein reduces the opportunity for barbiturate elimination via glomerular filtration. Of course, the barbiturates that are bound least, such as phenobarbital and barbital, would be least affected in this regard. Second, lipid-soluble barbiturates can be reabsorbed from renal tubules to a greater extent than lipid-insoluble ones. Third, when the pH of tubular urine is altered, the renal clearance of barbiturates can be modified due to altered proportions of ionized and nonionized forms of the drug in the renal tubular lumen. In this connection, Waddell and Butler (1957) have estimated that the rate of excretion of phenobarbital ($pK_a = 7.4$) might be tripled by the administration of sufficient amounts of sodium bicarbonate to alkalinize the urine. Indeed, enhanced clearance of barbiturates is the rationale for the use of alkali, in conjunction with diuretics, in treating barbiturate intoxication (see Lous, 1966). Clinical experiences and experimental studies in animals have shown that such increases in excretion result in shorter duration of barbiturate action. Finally, it is obvious that a disease or condition that compromises renal function may intensify barbiturate action such that severe CNS depression may be produced at normally tolerable doses.

Barbiturates also may be secreted into the bile. Within 6 hours after their intravenous injection into the rat, 28% of a dose of pentobarbital, and 18% of a dose of phenobarbital were found in the bile, mostly in the form of polar metabolites. These metabolites probably do not undergo an enterohepatic recirculation and therefore become eliminated in the feces.

Secretion of barbiturates into the bile appears to involve an active transport system that secretes many other organic acids (Lous, 1954; Maynert, 1965a; Klaassen, 1971). Thus, in studies of the biliary excretion of organic acids in intact animals, the use of barbiturates as anesthetic agents may complicate the interpretation of results because of the potential for an unintended interaction between the barbiturate and the investigational compound at the level of the biliary transport system.

METHAQUALONE

Among the groups of drugs that are abused at times are the nonbarbiturate sedatives. These drugs are frequently abused by persons who obtain them from physicians on prescription, and then continue their use whether or not drugs continue to be indicated. Within the past few years, one member of this group of drugs, methaqualone, has been widely abused by the younger members of the population, not for its sleep-inducing qualities but for its euphorigenic effects.

Methaqualone produces intoxicating effects similar to those of barbiturates and alcohol. Overdosage can result in death similar to that produced by the barbiturates. Tolerance develops to its euphorogenic effects, thus requiring larger doses by the subject.

Methaqualone was marketed in the early 1960's in the United States, but was available earlier in Japan. It is sold in the United States as Quaalude, Sopor, and Parest, and it is marketed in several other countries in combination with the antihistamine, diphenydramine, as Mandrax.

When introduced to the United States, methaqualone was touted as a nonbarbiturate, sedative-hypnotic, with a low abuse potential and only a rare instance of physical dependence. However, experiences in Japan had shown that methaqualone could be associated with compulsive drug-seeking behavior and with physical dependence. Methaqualone dependency was shown to represent about 43% of the total number of cases of drug addiction in psychiatric hospitals in Japan (Kato, 1969). In the United States, the use of methaqualone by the drug "culture" reached epidemic proportions in the early 1970's. The drug was placed under more strict control and is now a schedule II drug.

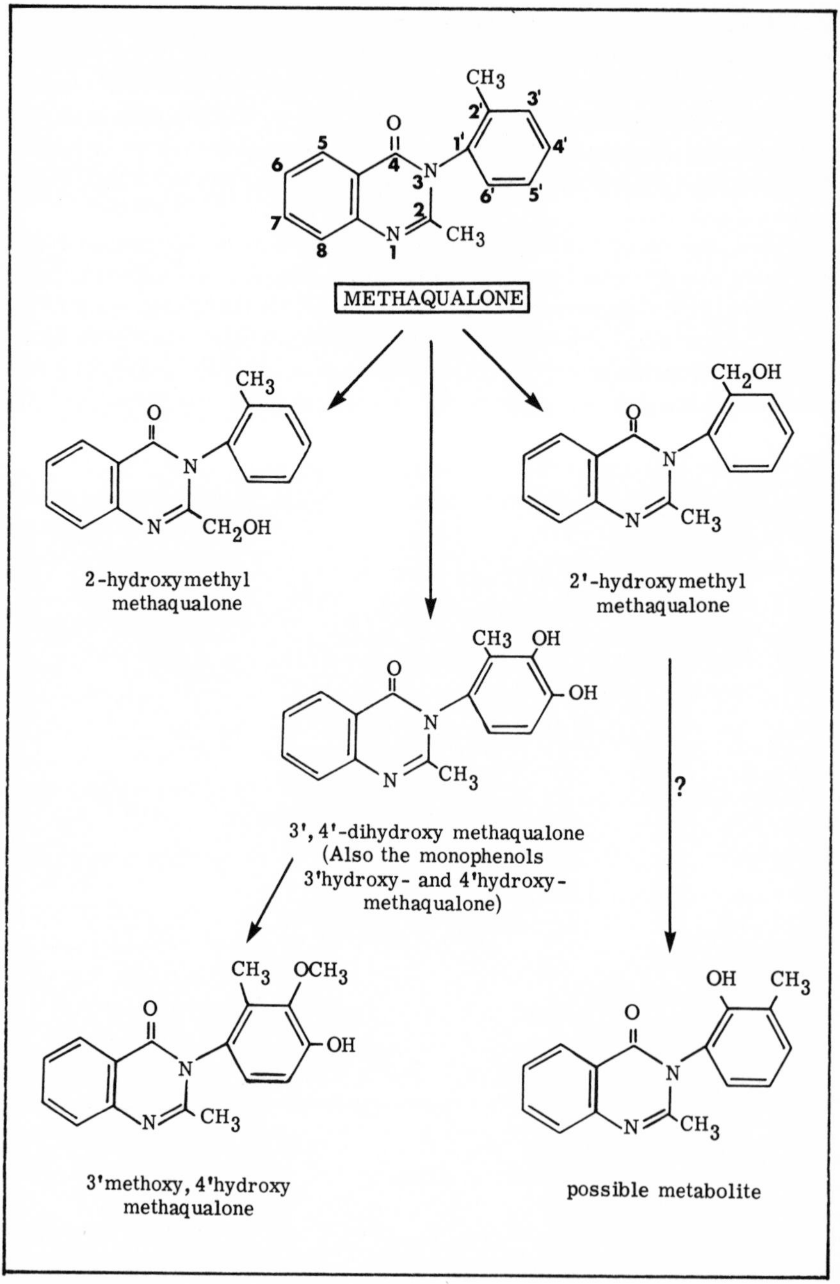

Fig. 6. Metabolism of methaqualone.

Methaqualone is a quinazolone derivative (Fig. 6). After oral administration to volunteers, 90-99% of a dose of methaqualone is absorbed within 2 hours (Morris *et al.*, 1972; Clifford *et al.*, 1974). *In vitro*, methaqualone becomes bound to plasma protein; 90% of the drug becomes protein bound at levels normally occurring with therapeutic use, and about 75% becomes bound at levels occurring with overdosages (Smart and Brown, 1970).

There are numerous studies of the disposition of methaqualone in animal species and in man. Morris *et al.* (1972) administered single oral doses (300 mg) of methaqualone to man and measured plasma concentrations for 8 hours. They calculated the half-life of the drug to be only 2.6 hours. However, they may have been estimating the half-life during the distribution phase of the drug. Alván *et al.* (1973) reported that the methaqualone half-life (estimated from the terminal phase of the plasma disposition curve) after a single oral dose of 300 mg to five subjects ranged from 20 to 41 hours (mean about 33 hours). In this study, they measured drug concentrations for up to 100 hours after drug administration. They found that methaqualone disappeared from plasma in a biphasic fashion and that measurements taken during the *distribution* phase would provide an estimate of an apparent half-life of about 4 hours. Clifford *et al.* (1974) performed a similar study in seven male subjects to whom 300 mg of methaqualone was administered, also in a single oral dose. They reported that the apparent $t_{1/2}$ that would be derived from the distribution phase would be about 1 hour; that for the terminal elimination phase would be about 16 hours.

Methaqualone is extensively metabolized *in vivo*; only small amounts of unchanged drug are found in urine after its administration to man or animals (Cohen *et al.*, 1962; Akagi *et al.*, 1963; Preuss *et al.*, 1966; Stillwell *et al.*, 1975). The biotransformation of methaqualone involves oxidation of the benzene ring and/or of the methyl groups in the 2- and 2'-positions of the molecule (Fig. 6). Most of the metabolites are monohydroxylated compounds; lesser amounts of several dihydroxylated compounds have also been detected. The majority of these compounds are excreted in urine as conjugates. In addition to these compounds, there is evidence that O-methoxylated metabolites of methaqualone are formed (Bonnichsen *et al.*, 1972; Ericsson *et al.*, 1973). In a recent, preliminary study, Stillwell *et al.* (1975) studied the metabolism of methaqualone in rats and men and isolated several metabolites in urine, identifying them by gas chromatography/mass spectroscopy. The majority of metabolites were conjugates. After enzymatic hydrolysis, they identified larger quantities of the mono- and dihydroxy compounds as well as dihydrodiols. They postulated that these lattermost compounds were formed via an epoxide-diol pathway with the epoxide serving as an intermediate.

Murata and Yamamoto (1970a,b,c) reported isolating 2-nitrobenzo-*o*-toluidine (NBT) in urine after giving methaqualone to rabbits. They then conducted studies to determine whether NBT could be formed from methaqualone in a rabbit liver 9000 *g* supernatant preparation in the presence of NADPH and oxygen. They found a product that was hydroxylated in the methyl group, and an *N*-oxide of methaqualone; however, no NBT was detected *in vitro*. They suggested that the *N*-oxide might be an intermediate in NBT formation *in vivo*. This prompted them to study the metabolism of methaqualone *N*-oxide in rabbits *in vivo* and *in vitro*. After administration of the *N*-oxide metabolite, NBT was present in rabbit urine. Other metabolites were methaqualone itself, and a monohydroxylated derivative of methaqualone. Likewise, NBT was produced after the incubation of methaqualone-*N*-oxide with fortified rabbit liver microsomes.

In summary, methaqualone is extensively metabolized in all animal species studied, and its metabolites are excreted in urine primarily as conjugates. The metabolites are primarily mono- and dihydroxylated compounds, although an *N*-oxide has also been isolated.

REFERENCES

Aesbacher, H -U., Atkinson, J., and Domahidy, B.: The effect of caffeine on barbiturate sleeping time and brain level. J. Pharmacol. Exp. Ther. *192*:635-641,1975.

Akagi, M., Oketani, Y., Takada, M., and Suga, T.: Studies on metabolism of 2-methyl-3-*o*-tolyl-4(3H)-quinazolinone II. Physiological disposition and metabolic fate of 2-methyl-3-*o*-tolyl-4(3H)-quinazolinone. Chem. Pharm. Bull. (Tokyo) *11*:321-323, 1963.

Algeri, E.J. and McBay, A.J.: The identification of pentobarbital by paper chromatography in medicolegal death. N. Engl. J. Med. *248*:423-424, 1953.

Alván, G., Lindgren, J -E., Bogentoft, C., and Ericsson, Ö.: Plasma kinetics of methaqualone in man after single oral doses. Eur. J. Clin. Pharmacol. *6*:187-190, 1973.

Bakewell, W.E. and Wikler, A.: Symposium: Nonnarcotic addiction. Incidence in a university hospital psychiatric ward. J.A.M.A. *196*:710-713, 1966.

Balasubramaniam, K., Lucas, S.B., Mawer, G.E., and Simons, P.J.: The kinetics of amylbarbitone metabolism in healthy men and women. Brit. J. Pharmacol. *39*:564-572, 1970.

Ballinger, B., Browning, M., O'Malley, K., and Stevenson, I.H.: Drug-metabolizing capacity in states of drug dependence and withdrawal. Brit. J. Pharmacol. *45*:638-643, 1972.

Beckett, A.H. and Moffatt, A.C.: The buccal absorption of some barbiturates. J. Pharm. Pharmacol. *23*:15-18, 1971.

Bonnichsen, R., Fri, C. -G., Negoita, C., and Ryhage, R.: Identification of methaqualone metabolites from urine extract by gas chromatography-mass spectrometry. Clin. Chim. Acta 40:309-318, 1972.

Bousquet, W.F., Rupe, B.D., and Miya, T.S.: Morphine inhibition of drug metabolism in the rat. Biochem. Pharmacol. 13:123-125, 1964.

Brezenoff, H.E. and Mycek, M.J.: Central cholinergic involvement in barbiturate tolerance. Fed. Proc. 34:3167, 1975 (abstract).

Brodie, B.B., Mark, L.C., Papper, E.M., Lief, P.A., Bernstein, E., and Rovenstine, E.A.: The fate of thiopental in man and a method for its estimation in biological material. J. Pharmacol. Exp. Ther. 98:85-96, 1950.

Brodie, B.B., Burns, J.J., Mark, L.C., Lief, P.A., Bernstein, E., and Papper, E.M.: The fate of pentobarbital in man and dog and a method for its estimation in biological material. J. Pharmacol. Exp. Ther. 109:26-34, 1953.

Brodie, B.B., Burns, J.J., and Weiner, M.: Metabolism of drugs in subjects with Laennec's cirrhosis. Med. Exp. 1:290-292, 1959.

Buchtal, F. and Svensmark, O.: Aspects of the pharmacology of dilantin and phenobarbital relevant to their dosages in the treatment of epilepsy. Epilepsia 1:373-384, 1959.

Büch, H.P., Schneider-Affeld, F., Rummer, W., and Knabe, J.: Stereochemical dependence of pharmacological activity in a series of optically active N-methylated barbiturates. Naunyn Schmiedebergs Arch. Pharmacol. 277:191-198, 1973.

Burns, J.J.: Implications of enzyme induction for drug therapy. Amer. J. Med. 37:327-331, 1964.

Burns, J.J.: Variation of drug metabolism in animals and the prediction of drug action in man. Ann. N.Y. Acad. Sci. 151:959-967, 1968.

Bush, M.T. and Sanders, E.: Metabolic fate of drugs: Barbiturates and closely related compounds. Ann. Rev. Pharmacol. 7:57-76, 1967.

Bush, M.T. and Weller, W.L.: Metabolic fate of hexobarbital. Drug Met. Rev. 1:249-290, 1972.

Bush, M.T., Butler, T.C., and Dickinson, H.L.: Metabolic fate of 5-(1-cyclohexen-1-yl)-1,5 dimethylbarbituric acid (hexobarbital, evipal) and of 5-(1-cyclohexen-1-yl)-5-methylbarbituric acid ("norevipal"). J. Pharmacol. Exp. Ther. 108:104-111, 1953.

Butler, T.C.: Quantitative studies of the metabolic fate of mephobarbital (N-methyl phenobarbital). J. Pharmacol. Exp. Ther. 106:235-245, 1952.

Butler, T.C.: Further studies of metabolic removal of alkyl groups from nitrogen in barbituric acid derivatives. Proc. Soc. Exp. Biol. 84:105-108, 1953.

Butler, T.C.: The metabolic hydroxylation of phenobarbital. J. Pharmacol. Exp. Ther. 116:326-336, 1956.

Butler, T.C. and Waddell, W.J.: N-Methylated derivatives of barbituric acid, hydantoin and oxazolidinedione used in treatment of epilepsy. J. Neurol. 8(suppl.):106-112, 1958.

Butler, T.C., Mahaffee, D., and Mahaffee, C.: The role of the liver in the metabolic disposition of mephobarbital. J. Pharmacol. Exp. Ther. 106:364-369, 1952.

Butler, T.C., Mahaffee, C., and Waddell, W.J.: Phenobarbital: Studies of elimination, accumulation, tolerance and dosage schedules. J. Pharmacol. Exp. Ther. 111:425-435, 1954.

Butler, T.C., Waddell, W.J., and Poole, D.T.: Demethylation of trimethadione and metharbital by rat liver microsomal enzymes: substrate concentration-yield relationships and competition between substrates. Biochem. Pharmacol. 14:937-942, 1965.

Caldwell, J. and Sever, P.S.: The biochemical pharmacology of abused drugs. II. Alcohol and barbiturates. Clin. Pharmacol. Ther. 16:737-749, 1974.

California Public Health Statistical Report: "Vital Statistics," p. 209. Bureau of Health Education, California State Department of Public Health, Berkeley, California, 1967.

Carrier, G., Hume, A.S., Douglas, B.H., and Wiser, W.L.: Disposition of barbiturates in maternal blood, fetal blood, and amniotic fluid. Amer. J. Obstet. Gynecol. 105:1069-1071, 1969.

Chaplin, M.E., Roszokowski, A.P., and Richards, R.K.: Displacement of thiopental from plasma proteins by nonsteroidal anti-inflammatory agents. Proc. Soc. Exp. Biol. Med. 143:667-671, 1973.

Christensen, H.D. and Lee, I.S.: Anesthetic potency and acute toxicity of optically active disubstituted barbituric acids. Toxicol. Appl. Pharmacol. 26:495-503, 1973.

Clifford, J.M., Cookson, J.H., and Wickham, P.: Absorption and clearance of secobarbital, heptabarbital, methaqualone, and ethinamate. Clin. Pharmacol. Ther. 16:376-389, 1974.

Cochin, J. and Daly, J.W.: The use of thin-layer chromatography for the analysis of drugs. Isolation and identification of barbiturates and nonbarbiturate hypnotics from urine, blood and tissues. J. Pharmacol. Exp. Ther. 139:154-159, 1963.

Cohen, Y., Font du Picard, Y., and Boissier, J.: Study of the distribution in a mouse of a carbon-14-labelled hypnotic, 2-methyl-3-o-tolyl(4H)-quinazolone. Arch. Int. Pharmacodyn. 136:271-282,1962.

Conney, A.H.: Pharmacological implications of enzyme induction. Pharmacol. Rev. 19:317-366, 1967.

Cookson, M.J., Sims, P., and Grover, P.L.: Mutagenicity of epoxides of polycyclic hydrocarbons correlates with carcinogenicity of parent hydrocarbons. Nature New Biol. 234:186-187, 1971.

Cooper, J.C. and Brodie, B.B.: The enzymatic metabolism of hexobarbital (EVIPAL). J. Pharmacol. Exp. Ther. 114:409-417, 1955.

Craig, C.R. and Shideman, F.E.: The role of phenobarbital in the anticonvulsant response to a single dose of mephobarbital. Pharmacologist 4:182, 1962.

Craig, C.R. and Shideman, F.E.: Metabolism and anticonvulsant properties of mephobarbital and phenobarbital in rats. J. Pharmacol. Exp. Ther. 176:35-41, 1971.

Dean, G.: Porphyria. Brit. Med. J. 2:1291-1301, 1953.

Deininger, R.: Papierchromatographischer Nachweis der Methylierung von nor-Evipan zu Evipan. Arch. Exp. Pathol. Pharmakol. 225:127-129, 1955.

Deininger, R.: Uber Wirkungsanderungen der Barbitursauren durch Beeinflussing der Methylierungsvorgange am Stickstoff in vivo. Arch. Exp. Pathol. Pharmakol. 227:316-327, 1956.

Dixit, B.N. and Abraham, D.J.: Barbiturates. Structural comparisons. I. Amobarbital, methylamobarbital, and butethal. J. Med. Chem. 12:330-332, 1960.

Dorfman, A. and Goldbaum, L.R.: Detoxification of barbiturates. J. Pharmacol. Exp. Ther. 90:330-337, 1947.

Downes, H., Perry, R.S., Osthend, R.E., and Karler, R.: A study of the excitatory effects of barbiturates. J. Pharmacol. Exp. Ther. 175:692-699, 1970.

Dundee, J.W.: Thiopentone narcosis in the presence of hepatic dysfunction. Brit. J. Anaesth. 24:81-100, 1952.

Eadie, M.J. and Tyrer, J.H.: Plasma levels of anticonvulsants. Aust. N.Z. J. Med. 3:290-303, 1973.

Ebert, A.G., Yim, G.K.W., and Miya, T.S.: Distribution and metabolism of barbital-^{14}C in tolerant and nontolerant rats. Biochem. Pharmacol. 13:1267-1274, 1964.

Effros, R.M., Corbeil, N., and Chinard, F.P.: Arterial pH and distribution of barbiturates between pulmonary tissue and blood. J. Appl. Physiol. 33:656-664, 1972.

Ericsson, Ö., Bogentoft, C., Lindberg, C., and Danielsson, B.: Methaqualone metabolites. Synthesis of eight phenolic monohydroxy derivatives of methaqualone. Acta Pharmacentica Suecica 10:257-262, 1973.

Flynn, E.J. and Spector, S.: Radioimmunoassay for hepatic N-demethylation of metharbital in vitro. J. Pharmacol. Exp. Ther. 189:550-556, 1974.

Fraser, H.F., Wikler, A., Isbell, H., and Johnson, H.K.: Partial equivalence of chronic alcohol and barbiturate intoxications. Quart. J. Stud. Alcohol 18:541-551, 1957.

Freudenthal, R.I. and Carroll, F.I.: Metabolism of certain commonly used barbiturates. Drug. Metab. Rev. 2:265-278, 1973.

Frey, H.H., Sudendey, F., and Krause, D.: Vergleichende Untersuchungen über Stoffwechsel, Ausscheidung und Nachweis von Schlafmitteln aus der Barbitursaure-Reihe. Arzneimittel Forsch. 9:294-297, 1959.

Furano, E.S. and Greene, N.M.: Metabolic breakdown of thiopental in man determined by gas chromatographic analysis of serum barbiturate levels. Anesthesiology 24:796-800, 1963.

Furner, R.L., McCarthy, J.S., Stitzel, R.E., and Anders, M.W.: Stereoselective metabolism of the enantiomers of hexobarbital. J. Pharmacol. Exp. Ther. 169:153-158, 1969.

Garrettson, L.K. and Dayton, P.G.: The disappearance of phenobarbital and diphenylhydantoin from serum of children. Clin. Pharmacol. Ther. 11:674-679, 1970.

Goldbaum, L. and Smith, P.K.: The interaction of barbiturates with serum albumin and its possible relation to their disposition and pharmacological actions. J. Pharmacol. Exp. Ther. 111:197-209, 1954.

Goldschmidt, S. and Wehr, R.: Über Barbiturate, III. Mitteilung. der Metabolismus von Veronal. Z. Physiol. Chem. 308:9-19, 1957.

Gould, T. and Shideman, F.E.: The in vitro metabolism of thiopental by a fortified, cell-free tissue preparation of the rat. J. Pharmacol. Exp. Ther. 104:427-439, 1952.

Grover, P.L., Sims, P., Huberman, E., Marquardt, H., Kuroki, T., and Heidelberger, C.: In vitro transformation of rodent cells by K-region derivatives of polycyclic hydrocarbons. Proc. Nat. Acad. Sci. U.S.A. 68:1098-1101, 1971.

Gruber, C.M. and Keyser, G.F.: A study on the development of tolerance and cross tolerance to barbiturates in experimental animals. J. Pharmacol. Exp. Ther. 86:186-196, 1946.

Hach, B. and Heim, F.: Vergleichende Untersuchungen über die zentralerrengende Wirkung von Coffeine und Chlorogensäure an weissen Mäussen. Arzneimittel Forsch. 21:23-25, 1971.

Hansch, C., Steward, A.R., Anderson, S.M., and Bentley, D.: The parabolic dependence of drug action upon lipophilic character as revealed by a study of hypnotics. J. Med. Chem. 11:1-11, 1968.

Harvey, D.J., Glazener, L., Stratton, C., Nowlin, J., Hill, R.M., and Horning, M.G.: Detection of a 5-(3,4-dihydroxy-1,5-cyclohexadien-1-yl-metabolite of phenobarbital and mephobarbital in rat, guinea pig and human. Res. Commun. Chem. Pathol. Pharmacol. 3:557-565, 1972.

Irrgang, K.: Zur Pharmakologie von 5-Aethyl-5-(3-hydroxyisoamyl)-barbitursäure, einem Stoffwechselprodukt der 5-Aethyl-5-isoamyl-barbitursäure. Arzneimittel Forsch. 15:688-691, 1965.

Isbell, H. and White, W.M.: Clinical characteristics of addictions. Amer. J. Med. 14:558-565, 1953.

Jansson, I., Orrenius, S., Ernster, L., and Schenkman, J.B.: A study on the interaction of a series of substituted barbituric acids with the hepatic microsomal monoxygenase. Arch. Biochem. Biophys. 151:391-400, 1972.

Kakemi, K., Arita, T., Hori, R., and Konishi, R.: Absorption and excretion of drugs. XXXII. Absorption of barbuturic derivatives from rat small intestine. Chem. Pharm. Bull. (Tokyo) 15:1883-1887, 1967.

Kakemi, K., Arita, T., Hori, R., Konishi, R., and Nishimura, K.: Absorption and excretion of drugs. XXXIII. The correlation between the absorption of barbituric acid derivatives from the rat small intestine and their binding to the mucosa. Chem. Pharm. Bull. (Tokyo) 17:248-254, 1969.

Kamm, J.J. and Van Loon, E.J.: Amobarbital metabolism in man. A gas chromatographic method for the estimation of hydroxyamobarbital in human urine. Clin. Chem. 12:789-796, 1966.

Kato, M.: An epidemiological analysis of the fluctuation of drug dependence in Japan. Int. J. Addict. 4:591-621, 1969.

Klaassen, C.D.: Biliary excretion of barbiturates. Brit. J. Pharmacol. 43:161-166, 1971.

Kuntzman, R., Ikeda, M., Jacobson, M., and Conney, A.H.: A sensitive method for the determination and isolation of pentobarbital-C14 metabolites and its application to in vitro studies. J. Pharmacol. Exp. Ther. 157:220-226, 1967.

Kurz, H.: The permeation of drugs across the so-called blood-brain-barrier at low temperature. Experientia 20:96-97, 1964.

Kurz, H. and Fasching, H.: The permeation of drugs across the placental barrier. Naunyn Schmiedeberg's Arch. Pharmacol. Exp. Pathol. 259:214, 1968.

Kutt, H., Winters, W., Kokenge, R., and McDowell, F.: Diphenylhydantoin metabolism, blood levels and toxicity. Arch. Neurol. 11:642-648, 1964a.

Kutt, H., Winters, W., Scherman, R., and McDowell, F.: Diphenylhydantoin and phenobarbital toxocity. The role of liver disease. Arch. Neurol. 11:649-656, 1964b.

Lamson, P.D., Greig, M.E., and Hobdy, D.J.: Modification of barbiturate anesthesia by glucose, intermediary metabolites and certain other substances. J. Pharmacol. Exp. Ther. 103:460-470, 1951.

Lin, Y.-J., Awazu, S., Hanano, M., and Nogami, H.: Pharmacokinetic aspects of elimination from plasma and distribution to brain and liver of barbiturates in rat. Chem. Pharm. Bull. (Tokyo) 21:2749-2756, 1973.

Lous, P.: Plasma levels and urinary excretion of three barbituric acids after oral administration to man. Acta Pharmacol. Toxicol. 10:147-165, 1954.

Lous, P.: Elimination of barbiturates. Int. Anesth. Clin. 4:341-350, 1966.

Lundberg, G.D.: Barbiturates: A great American problem. J.A.M.A. 224:1531, 1973.

Magnussen, M.P.: The effect of ethanol on the gastrointestinal absorption of drugs in the rat. Acta Pharmacol. Toxicol. 26:130-144, 1968.

Mark, L.C.: Metabolism of barbiturates in man. Clin. Pharmacol. Ther. 4:504-530, 1963.

Marquardt, H., Juroki, T., Huberman, E., Heidelberger, C., Grover, P.L., and Sims, P.: Malignant transformation of cells derived from mouse prostate by epoxides and other derivatives of polycyclic hydrocarbons. Cancer Res. 32:716-720, 1972.

Mawer, G.E. and Lee, H.A.: Value of forced diuresis in acute barbiturate poisoning. Brit. Med. J. 2:790-793, 1968.

Maynert, E.W.: The alcoholic metabolites of pentobarbital and amobarbital in man. J. Pharmacol. Exp. Ther. 150:118-121, 1965a.

Maynert, E.W.: On the specificity of penultimate oxidation: The fate of 5-ethyl-5-n-hexylbarbituric acid. J. Pharmacol. Exp. Ther. 150:476-483, 1965b.

Maynert, E.W. and Dawson, I.: Ethyl-(3-hydroxy-l-methylbutyl)-barbituric acids as metabolites of pentobarbital. J. Biol. Chem. 195:389-402, 1952.

Morris, R.N., Gunderson, M.S., Babcock, S.W., and Zaroslinski, J.F.: Plasma levels and absorption of methaqualone after oral administration to man. Clin. Pharmacol. Ther. 13:719-723, 1972.

Muhlhauser, R.O., Watkins, W.D., Murphy, R.C., and Chidsey, C.A.: Pharmacokinetic studies of the disposition of secobarbital in the dog. Drug Metab. Dispos. 2:513-520, 1974.

Müller, D., Forster, D., Dietze, H., Langenberg, R., and Klinger, W.: The influence of age and barbital treatment on the content of cytochrome P-450 and B5 and on the activity of glucose-7-phosphatase in microsomes of the rat liver and kidney. Biochem. Pharmacol. 22:905-910, 1973.

Murata, T. and Yamamoto, I.: Metabolic fate of 2-methyl-3-o-tolyl-4(3H)-quinazolinone. I. 2-nitrobenzo-o-toluidide as an urinary metabolite of 2-methyl-3-o-tolyl-4(3H)-quinazolinone in human. Chem. Pharm. Bull. (Tokyo) 18:133-137, 1970a.

Murata, T. and Yamamoto, I.: Metabolic fate of 2-methyl-3-o-tolyl-4(3H)-quinazolinone. II. Metabolism of 2-methyl-3-o-tolyl-4(3H)-quinazolinone by rabbit liver. Chem. Pharm. Bull. (Tokyo) 18:138-142, 1970b.

Murata, T. and Yamamoto, I.: Metabolic fate of 2-methyl-3-o-tolyl-4(3H)-quinazolinone. III. Metabolism of 2-methyl-3-o-tolyl-4(3H)-quinazolinone-N-oxide in vivo and in vitro. Chem. Pharmacol. Bull. (Tokyo) 18:143-146, 1970c.

McMahon, R.E.: The demethylation in vitro of N-methylbarbiturates and related compounds by mammalian liver microsomes. Biochem. Pharmacol. 12:1225-1228, 1963.

Niyogi, S.K.: Detection of secobarbital metabolite in the urine of the rat. Nature (London) 202:1225-1226, 1964.

Okamoto, M., Rosenberg, H., and Boisse, N.: Tolerance characteristics produced during the maximally tolerable chronic pentobarbital dosing in the cat. J. Pharmacol. Exp. Ther. 192:555-564, 1975.

Okui, S. and Kuroiwa, Y.: Studies on the metabolic N-demethylation. II. Barbiturates induced acceleration of N-methylbarbiturates metabolism. Chem. Pharm. Bull. (Tokyo) 11:163-167, 1963.

Pagnini, G., DiCarlo, R., DiCarlo, F., and Genazzani, E.: Enhancement of pentobarbital narcosis by drugs competing on the serum protein binding. Biochem. Pharmacol. 20:3247-3254, 1971.

Peters, M.A. and Strother, A.: A study of some possible mechanisms by which glucose inhibits drug metabolism in vivo and in vitro. J. Pharmacol. Exp. Ther. 180:151-157, 1972.

Prescott, L.F.: Pharmacokinetic drug interactions. Lancet 2:1239-1243, 1969.

Preuss, V.F.R., Hassler, H.M., and Kopf, R.: Zur Biotransformation des 2-methyl-3-o-tolyl-4(3H) chinazolinon (=methaqualone). Arzneimittel Forsch. 16:395-400, 1966.

Raventós, J.: The distribution in the body and metabolic fate of barbiturates. J. Pharm. Pharmacol. 6:217-235, 1954.

Remmer, H.: Der beschleunigte Abbau von Pharmaka in den Lebermikrosomen unter dem Einfluss von Luminal. Arch. Exp. Pathol. Pharmakol. 235:279-290, 1959.

Remmer, H.: Gewöhnung an Hexobarbital durch beschleunigten Abbau. Arch. Int. Pharmacodyn. 152:346-359, 1964.

Remmer, H.: "Tolerance to Barbiturates by Increased Breakdown," in Scientific Basis of Drug Dependence. Ed. Steinberg, H., London, J. & A. Churchill, Ltd., 1969, pp. 111-128.

Rubin, A., Tephly, T.R., and Mannering, G.J.: Kinetics of drug metabolism by hepatic microsomes. Biochem. Pharmacol. 13:1007-1016, 1964a.

Rubin, A., Tephly, T.R., and Mannering, G.J.: Inhibition of hexobarbital metabolism by ethylmorphine and codeine in the intact rat. Biochem. Pharmacol. 13:1053-1057, 1964b.

Sessions, J.T., Jr., Minkel, H.P., Bullard, J.C., and Ingelfinger, F.J.: The effect of bar-biturates in patients with liver disease. J. Clin. Invest. 33:1116-1127, 1954.

Sharpless, S.K.: Hypnotics and sedatives. In The Pharmacological Basis of Therapeutics, 4th ed. Eds. L.S. Goodman and A. Gilman, New York, Macmillan, 1970, pp. 121-134.

Shideman, F.E., Kelly, A.R., and Adams, B.J.: The role of the liver in the detoxication of thiopental (Pentothal) and two other thiobarbiturates. J. Pharmacol. Exp. Ther. 91:331-339, 1947.

Shideman, F.E., Kelley, A.R., Lee, L.E., Lowell, V.F., and Adams, B.J.: The role of the liver in the detoxication of thiopental (Pentothal) by man. Anesthesiology 10:421-427, 1949.

Shideman, F.E., Gould, T.C., Winters, W.D., Peterson, R.C., and Wilner, W.K.: The distribution and in vivo rate of metabolism of thiopental. J. Pharmacol. Exp. Ther. 107:368-378, 1953.

Sieber, S.M. and Fabro, S.: Identification of drugs in the preimplantation blastocyst and in the plasma, uterine secretion and urine of the pregnant rabbit. J. Pharmacol. Exp. Ther. 176:65-75, 1971.

Sjögren, J., Sölvell, L., and Karlsson, I.: Studies on the absorption rate of barbiturates in man. Acta Med. Scand. 178:553-559, 1965.

Smart, G.A. and Brown, S.S.: Preparative ultracentrifugation of small samples of plasma and the protein binding of methaqualone. Anal. Biochem. 35:518-523, 1970.

Smith, R.B., Dittert, L.W., Griffen, W.O., and Doluiso, J.T.: Pharmacokinetics of pentobarbitone after intravenous and oral administration. J. Pharmacokinet. Biopharmacol. 1:5-16, 1973.

Stevenson, I.H. and Turnbull, M.J.: Hepatic drug-metabolizing enzyme activity and duration of hexobarbitone anaesthesia in barbiturate-dependent and withdrawn rats. Biochem. Pharmacol. 17:2297-2305, 1968.

Stillwell, W.G., Gregory, P., and Horning, M.G.: GC-MS studies of the metabolism of methaqualone in man and the rat. Fed. Proc. 34:3330, 1975 (abstract).

Swinyard, E.A., Madsen, J.A., and Goodman, L.S.: The effect of SKF 525A on the anticonvulsant properties of antiepileptic drugs. J. Pharmacol. Exp. Ther. 111:54-63, 1954.

Titus, E. and Weiss, H.: The use of biologically prepared radioactive indicators in metabolic studies: Metabolism of pentobarbital. J. Biol. Chem. 214:807-820, 1955.

Toki, S. and Takenouchi, T.: Hexobarbital metabolism. Formation of a-l,5-dimethyl-5-(3-hydroxy-l-cyclo-hexen-l-yl)-barbituric acid glucuronide. Chem. Pharm. Bull. (Tokyo) 13:606-609, 1965.

Toki, K. and Tsukamoto, H.: Metabolism of drugs. XL. Enzymatic oxidation of methylhexabital. 3. Purification and properties of 3-hydroxy-methylhexabital dehydrogenase. J. Biochem. (Tokyo) 55:142-147, 1964.

Toki, K., Toki, S., and Tsukamoto, H.: Metabolism of drugs. 38. Enzymatic oxidation of methylhexabital. 2. Reversible oxidation of 3-hydroxy-methylhexabital. J. Biochem. (Tokyo) 53:43-49, 1963.

Tsukamoto, H., Yoshimura, H., and Ide, H.: Metabolism of drugs. 32. The metabolic fate of secobarbital, (5-allyl-5-(l-methylbutyl) barbituric acid. Chem. Pharm. Bull. (Tokyo) *11*:9-13, 1963a.

Tsukamoto, H., Yoshimura, H., Ide, H., and Mitsui, S.: Metabolism of drugs. XXXVI. The metabolic fate of thiamylal [5-allyl-5-(l-methylbutyl)-2-thiobarbituric acid]. Chem. Pharm. Bull. (Tokyo) *11*:427-430, 1963b.

Turnbull, M.J. and Ballinger, B.R.: Urinary excretion of monoamines and metabolites in patients dependent on and withdrawn from barbiturates. Psychopharmacologia *30*:103-108, 1973.

Turnbull, M.J. and Stevenson, I.H.: Tolerance experiments with barbitone-dependent rats. J. Pharm. Pharmacol. *20*:884-885, 1968.

Ungar, G. and Cohen, M.: Induction of morphine tolerance by material extracted from brain of tolerant animals. Int. J. Neuropharmacol. *5*:183-192, 1966.

Voet, D. and Rich, A.: Barbiturates and adenine derivatives. Molecular structure of a hydrogen-bonded complex. J. Amer. Chem. Soc. *94*:5888-5891, 1972.

Vore, M., Sweetman, B.J., and Bush, M.J.: The metabolism of l-*n*-butyl-5,5-diethylbarbituric acid (*N-n*-butyl-barbital) in the rat. J. Pharmacol. Exp. Ther. *190*:384-394, 1974.

Waddell, W.J.: The metabolic fate of 5-allyl-5-(l-methylbutyl)barbituric acid (secobarbital). J. Pharmacol. Exp. Ther. *149*:23-28, 1965.

Waddell, W.J. and Butler, T.C.: The distribution and excretion of phenobarbital. J. Clin. Invest. *36*:1217-1226, 1957.

Williams, R.T. and Parke, D.V.: The metabolic fate of drugs. Annu. Rev. Pharmacol. *4*:85-114, 1964.

York, J.L.: Tolerance to the stimulus properties of barbital. Fed. Proc. *33*:1906, 1974 (abstract).

Chapter 7

Recreational Drugs of Abuse: Caffeine, Nicotine, and Alcohol*

The drugs discussed in this chapter, caffeine, nicotine, and alcohol, differ somewhat from others in this monograph: the law does not forbid their use, and abstainers accept (or at least they tolerate) users in their midst without the social stigma associated with, say, the narcotic alkaloids. It has been said that drugs of abuse are those which are consumed solely for non-medical purposes with the intent of somehow modifying the sensorium and which may be detrimental to the individual and/or to society. Millions of people are psychologically and physically dependent upon alcohol; there can be no doubt that that agent should be included in this monograph; but one could argue, perhaps more emotionally than scientifically, that nicotine and caffeine do not deserve inclusion. For example, caffeine has been and still is used medically as a CNS stimulant. Furthermore, its consumption in beverages is not generally regarded as a threat to the consumer's health. Nevertheless, nicotine and caffeine are consumed ubiquitously for non-medical purposes by millions of people everyday—people who, to widely

*References for this chapter are separated into three sections on caffeine, nicotine, and alcohol, respectively.

varying degrees, appear to be psychologically and physically dependent upon these agents so that they may exhibit compulsive drug-seeking behavior, tolerance, and withdrawal symptoms (albeit mild). As with other abused drugs, the dependence involves the pharmacologic effects of these compounds (e.g., caffeine induced CNS stimulation) as well as more complex psychosocial factors. We believe that their inclusion here is a requisite for a complete survey of abused drugs.

CAFFEINE

Introduction

Caffeine is a xanthine alkaloid present in the seeds of the coffee plant, *Coffea arabica*, and in tea leaves (*Thea sinensis*). The intake of caffeine occurs most commonly when coffee and tea are consumed. Indeed, over a billion kilograms of coffee are consumed annually in the United States alone (one cup of coffee contains 100-150 mg of caffeine). Perhaps less appreciated is that significant amounts of caffeine (up to 50 mg per cup) are present in cocoa, obtained from the seeds of *Theobroma cacao*, and in "soft" drinks (up to 55 mg per 12 oz bottle) derived from the kola nut of the *Cola acuminata* tree. In addition, caffeine is present in many non-prescription medications, in many cases for reasons that are not always scientifically rational; of course it is also present in medications that are clearly utilized and advertised as stimulants.

There is little doubt that consumption of caffeine-containing beverages results in a CNS stimulant action, but individual manifestations of that stimulation may vary from no noticeable effects (e.g., sleep is unimpaired) to marked effects (e.g., insomnia). The great majority of consumers of caffeinated beverages do not appear to manifest overt evidence of ill health due to caffeine intake. Individuals with peptic ulcers may experience gastric upset after drinking coffee due to the stimulatory effects of caffeine on gastric secretion, as well as to the gastrointestinal irritating effects of the oils in coffee. Similarly, patients with certain cardiovascular diseases should be cautioned about the excessive intake of caffeinated beverages because caffeine may produce tachycardia and increase the blood pressure in some patients. Gross overconsumption would be expected to cause toxic symptoms such as restlessness and abnormal cardiac rate and rhythm.

The vast majority of coffee drinkers, hovering over the office coffee pot, probably benefits from the consumption of coffee; it does provide a relaxed sense of social acceptance and a mild central nervous system stimulation. Indeed, it can be argued that if judicious consumption of coffee were denied to a user, even one who has moderate hypertension, he might be more harmed in terms of emotional and physical discomforts than if he were not deprived of the beverage. In any case, coffee drinkers apparently are partially tolerant to some of the pharmacologic effects of caffeine (Goldstein, 1964; Colton *et al.*, 1968; Goldstein and Kaizer, 1969; Goldstein *et al.*, 1969). It appears that the tolerance is lowgrade on the basis that tolerant subjects can respond again when the dose of caffeine is increased only two- to fourfold (Eddy and Down, 1929; Strongin, 1933).

Tolerance does not appear to develop uniformly to all the effects of caffeine. For example, although heavy users may be less sensitive than light users to the nervousness and wakefulness caused by coffee, they are reportedly more aware of the stimulant and euphoriant actions. Abstainers become less content and more nervous and jittery when given caffeine, whereas users become more content and less nervous and jittery. In a placebo-controlled, double-blind study of performance and mood in coffee drinkers, caffeine had no measurable effect upon alertness and psychomotor coordination, although it did make the subjects *feel* more alert and physically active (Goldstein *et al.*, 1965b). Weiss and Laties (1962) have reviewed the enhancement of human performance by caffeine. Evidence is available to indicate that caffeine can counteract decrements in various functions caused by fatigue or sleep deprivation; however, arguments as to whether it enhances performance above control levels are often contradictory.

Dreisbach and Pfeiffer (1943) have described an increased incidence of headaches after withdrawing caffeine from users. In more recent studies, housewives who were habitual coffee users reported that if they were deprived of morning coffee, they would experience dysphoric symptoms which resembled a mild withdrawal syndrome, including irritability, lethargy, nervousness, restlessness, headache, and inefficiency (Goldstein and Kaizer, 1969). The validity of these user-solicited impressions was substantiated in a more objective study of these same women, using a placebo-controlled double-blind design (Goldstein *et al.*, 1969). The results suggested that coffee users appear to require caffeine in the morning as a "pick-me-up"; and when deprived of caffeinated coffee at breakfast, the users experienced dysphoric symptoms beginning approximately 12-16 hours after the last dose of caffeine. At this time period, over 90% of ingested caffeine should have been eliminated from the body, based upon an approximate 4-hour half-life of caffeine in man (Axelrod and Reichenthal, 1953).

Absorption

We have already mentioned that among caffeine consumers there are widely diverse levels of response to the CNS-stimulant actions. This diversity appears to be partly dependent upon individual differences in acquisition of tolerance to some but not all effects of caffeine. In addition, Goldstein and Kaizer (1969) have suggested that certain effects of caffeine may be due to its metabolites, and that individual differences in caffeine metabolism could lead to selective differences in the intensity of its pharmacologic effects. Of course, individual differences in absorption of caffeine from the gastrointestinal tract could further contribute to differences in individual responses. This might be expected because caffeine is a weakly basic alkaloid, a class of compounds that is generally considered to be absorbed slowly and erratically from the gastrointestinal tract. However, in a study of human volunteers who responded quite variably to caffeine, Goldstein et al. (1965a) reported that absorption of caffeine from the gastrointestinal tract was virtually complete in most subjects within 1 hour after ingestion and that differences in plasma levels among subjects were insufficient to account for the marked variations in response (wakefulness). The rapid and efficient absorption of caffeine from the gastrointestinal tract, reported by Goldstein and his associates, agreed well with the findings of Axelrod and Reichenthal (1953) in man and of Burg and Stein (1972) in mouse. It appears that caffeine is so weakly basic that it is sufficiently nonionized in acidic solutions so as to be absorbed to a significant degree even from the stomach; this appears to be the case in rat (Schanker et al., 1957) as well as in man (Chvasta and Cooke, 1971). In the latter study, at a gastric pH of 2.0, about 16% of ingested caffeine was absorbed from the stomach in 20 minutes; neutralization of the acidity of the stomach contents passing into the duodenum would further facilitate caffeine absorption from the intestinal tract.

Marks and Kelly (1973) addressed themselves to the question of whether, in man, caffeine was absorbed more rapidly from coffee than from tea. Animal experiments had indicated this to be the case; furthermore, in animals, caffeine in Coca Cola appeared to be more rapidly absorbed than from that in tea or coffee. In man, they found that the rise in plasma caffeine concentration was equally rapid (peak at 30 minutes) after tea or coffee, but was somewhat delayed (peak at 1-2 hours) after Coca Cola.

Distribution

Most available evidence indicates that caffeine is distributed mainly in total body water. In mice, however, Burg and Werner (1972) found that to be true only 1 hour after dosing with caffeine. Before and after that time period, the tissue: water ratio differed from one organ to another.

In man about 15% of circulating caffeine is bound to plasma protein (Axelrod and Reichenthal, 1953; Bertoli et al., 1968). In rabbits, passage of caffeine into the central nervous system after i.v. administration occurs rapidly (Hess *et al.*, 1968; Herz *et al.*, 1968). In mice and cats, certain central actions of caffeine (e.g., locomotor stimulation, convulsive activity, and EEG activation) correlated positively with penetration of the drug into the central nervous system. It appeared that these actions were due to the injected caffeine itself rather than to its metabolites. In dogs, concentrations of caffeine in plasma water approximated those in the cerebrospinal fluid, indicating virtually unhindered diffusion of the drug across the blood-brain barrier (Axelrod and Reichenthal, 1953). In contrast, there does appear to be a barrier which inhibits accumulation of caffeine in mouse brain and testes (Burg and Werner, 1972).

The half-life of caffeine in man is about 4 hours. Axelrod and Reichenthal (1953) found that significant amounts of caffeine can accumulate in the bodies of subjects consuming 8 cups of coffee over a 7-hour period, as would be expected from the half-life of the drug. Indeed, by the end of the day, they calculated that about 180 mg of caffeine was present in the body; that amount approximates the customary therapeutic dose of the drug. They observed no appreciable day-to-day accumulation of caffeine under these conditions. In contrast, Warren (1969) reported that it took 7 days for caffeine to disappear from the blood of habitual coffee drinkers. Once the subjects had cleared the caffeine, however, they eliminated a challenge dose within 24 hours. These findings led Warren to suggest that caffeine may be stored in tissues of habitual users and that the rate of caffeine metabolism may differ between users and abstainers.

Sieber and Fabro (1971) and Fabro and Sieber (1969) reported that 6 hours after an oral dose of ^{14}C-labeled caffeine to 6-day pregnant rabbits, an average of 23% of the administered label was excreted in the urine. About 8% of the total administered dose was excreted as unchanged caffeine, 12% as 1-methylxanthine, 2.5% as 1,3-dimethylxanthine plus 1,7-dimethylxanthine, and 1.7% as 1,3-dimethyluric acid (Fig. 1). Peak plasma radioactivity occurred 4 hours after dosing, although it had reached about 98% of this value at 2 hours; at 6 hours it was about 96% of the peak. At this time, ^{14}C activity was also present in endometrium, uterine secretion, and blastocyst. The highest level of radioactivity compared to maternal plasma was seen in uterine secretions (secretion to plasma ratio averaged 1.46). The ratio of radioactivity in the blastocyst to that in plasma was 0.85. Caffeine itself in both plasma and blastocyst was the major radioactive compound (more than 50% of the radioactivity). In the blastocyst, 1,3-dimethylxanthine, 1,7-dimethylxanthine, and 1,3-dimethyluric acid were also found; 1-methylxanthine, however, could be detected only in maternal plasma.

The findings that caffeine entered the preimplantation blastocyst were most interesting. Sieber and Fabro (1971) discuss these findings in relation to reports that caffeine may produce chromosomal breakages in cells of

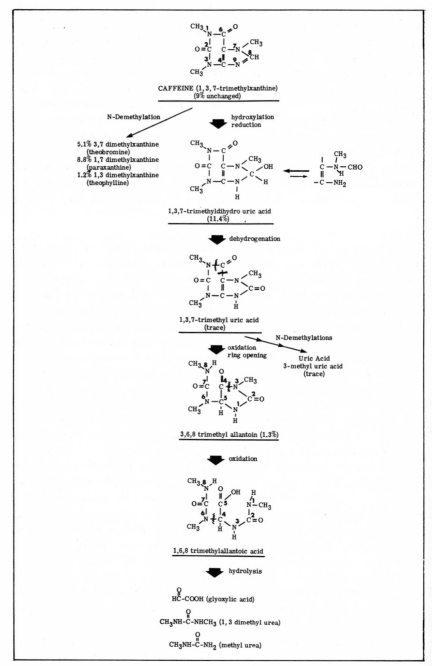

Fig. 1. Proposed routes of metabolism of caffeine in the rat. (from Rao *et al.*, 1973).

both plants and animals and may increase the incidences of congenital malformations in the offspring of mice. Caffeine possesses mutagenic properties although it has been estimated that the risk for humans is minimal. Goldstein and Warren (1962) showed that caffeine may be transferred from the mother to the 7-week-old human embryo.

Metabolism and Excretion

In man, most of ingested caffeine is metabolized; only about 1 to 10% is excreted unchanged in human urine. Indeed, this is true for several species that have been studied, including dog, rabbit, pig, rat, and man (Axelrod and Reichenthal, 1953; Burg and Stein, 1972). Basically, two reactions appear to be involved in the metabolism of caffeine: N-demethylation to various methyl-substituted xanthines and oxidation to various methyl-substituted uric acids (Fig. 1). More than 35% of orally ingested caffeine is excreted in human urine as 1-methyl uric acid and 1-methylxanthine. Also, 7-methylxanthine, 1,3-dimethylxanthine (theophylline), 3,7-dimethylxanthine (theobromine), 1,7-dimethylxanthine (paraxanthine), and 1,3-dimethyl uric acid have been found in human urine after ingestion of caffeine (Weissman et al., 1954; Cornish and Christman, 1957; Parke, 1968). The quantity of 1-methyl uric acid formed from caffeine in man is usually insufficient to warrant contraindicating caffeinated beverages to patients with gout; indeed, there is some doubt as to whether that metabolite is deposited at all in gouty tophi. Fortunately, caffeine does not appear to be totally N-demethylated in man to uric acid, a compound that might present a problem to the gouty patient.

In tissues, the major metabolite of caffeine was reported for mouse to be 1,7-dimethylxanthine (Burg and Werner, 1972). That metabolite also appears to be present in the erythrocytes of man 3 hours after an oral dose of 500 mg of caffeine (Warren, 1969).

The enzymes responsible for oxidation of caffeine are not known; caffeine itself does not appear to be a substrate for xanthine oxidase (Brodie et al., 1952). However, after the N-demethylation of caffeine to form 1-methylxanthine, oxidation to 1-methyluric acid might be catalyzed by xanthine oxidase since the 1-methylxanthine does appear to be a substrate for that enzyme. Apparently 3-, 7-, and 9-methylxanthine are not oxidized by xanthine oxidase to any measurable extent.

In mouse, microsomal preparations from liver and kidney failed to N-demethylate caffeine (Burg and Werner, 1972). Others have observed less than 4% N-demethylation of caffeine by mouse liver microsomes (Mazel and Henderson, 1965). Nevertheless, in vivo, caffeine is rapidly and extensively demethylated in the mouse.

As would be expected, marked differences exist among species with respect to the metabolism of caffeine. It has been reported that rat urine contained 15 possible metabolites of caffeine, some of which are shown in Fig. 1 (Khanna et al., 1972; Rao et al., 1973). These urinary compounds collectively constitute about 65% of an oral dose of caffeine.

In mouse, 64-90% of the total radioactivity from [^{3}H,^{14}C]-caffeine is excreted in urine (Burg and Stein, 1972). The major metabolites that were reported were 1,7-dimethylxanthine, 3-methylxanthine, 7-methylxanthine, and 1,3-dimethyl uric acid. Only 3-6% of the dose was recovered in urine as unchanged caffeine. About 3% of the radioactivity was found in feces; very little of this radioactivity was due to caffeine itself, or to its recognized methylated xanthine or uric acid metabolites.

Another 7% of the radioactivity was detected in the expired air as $^{14}CO_2$. Chronic administration of caffeine-1-N-$^{14}CH_3$ to mice did not alter the respiratory elimination of $^{14}CO_2$. This finding led Burg and Stein to conclude that the 1-methyldemethylase was probably not an inducible enzyme in mice under conditions of repeated caffeine intake. However, under basal (no drug) conditions, activity of 1-methyldemethylase in mice appears to be quite high; perhaps that enzyme was not inducible in that species simply because it was already at maximal activity under basal conditions. Indeed, the enzyme appears to be so active in mice that the animals excrete no detectable 1-methylxanthine and very little 1-methyl uric acid. In similar studies in rats, Cornish et al. (1970) reported that caffeine administration might stimulate microsomal N-demethylation.

It is probably more accurate to say that caffeine may stimulate or depress the activities of microsomal drug-metabolizing enzymes, depending upon species, dose, length of treatment, and enzyme studied (Mitoma et al., 1968, 1969; Cornish et al., 1970; Khanna et al., 1972; Khanna and Cornish, 1973). For example, doses of caffeine, coffee, and tea have been shown to stimulate certain hepatic microsomal O-demethylating and hydroxylating enzymes in the rat, but the level of cytochrome P-450 present in hepatic microsomes was unchanged (Lombrozo and Mitoma, 1970; Khanna and Cornish, 1973). Thus, as is the case with the 3-methylcholanthrene-type of enzyme inducers, caffeine may stimulate microsomal drug-metabolizing enzymes without concurrently elevating cytochrome P-450 levels. Based upon analyses of spectral difference data for that hemoprotein, Lombrozo and Mitoma (1970) have suggested that caffeine (like 3-methylcholanthrene) may produce a qualitative alteration in the nature of cytochrome P-450. Mitoma et al. (1968, 1969) showed that ethionine and actinomycin-D partially inhibited the stimulation of certain drug-metabolizing enzymes in rat liver microsomes caused by caffeine. They were, however, unable to show that caffeine would increase the incorporation of amino acids into microsomal protein.

Mitoma and his associates provided a rather interesting analysis of their data which suggests that the enzyme stimulatory effect of caffeine that they observed in rats may have relevance to man. Since the dosage of caffeine given to the rats was equivalent to that in 8 or 35 cups of coffee per day for a 70-kg man (depending upon the method used to calculate dosage equivalency), and since the half-life of caffeine in rats (5 hours) was similar to that in man, it does seem possible that moderate to heavy consumption of coffee or tea might induce the liver drug-metabolizing enzymes in man. Whether these effects of caffeine are important clinically, however, has not been established. At present, caffeine shares with many other compounds the capacity to influence these enzyme systems which are involved in the metabolism of steroids, foreign compounds, and drugs.

NICOTINE

Introduction

The literature dealing with nicotine absorption, distribution, fate, and other aspects of its physiologic disposition and pharmacology has been extensively reviewed (Larson *et al.*, 1961; McKennis, 1965; Schmiterlöw and Hansson, 1965; Hansson and Schmiterlöw, 1965; Larson and Silvette, 1968). These publications were an incalculable aid to the preparation of this section.

Approximately 600 billion cigarettes are smoked annually in the United States alone (Volle and Koelle, 1970). That number of cigarettes corresponds to 15 million miles of cigarette length (about 30 round trips to the moon)! The percentage of nicotine in cigarette tobacco is about 1.5% (present in the plant *Nicotiana tabacum* as the salt of organic acids). Heat liberates the nicotine, some of which is burned and some of which gains access to the respiratory tract. The smoke of the average cigarette yields approximately 6 to 8 mg; cigar smoke yields 15 to 40 mg nicotine.

A report from the United States Public Health Service (1964) Office of the Surgeon General, concluded that tobacco smoking was basically psychogenic, and that no dependence to nicotine or other tobacco constituents had been observed with any consistency. In agreement with the Surgeon General's report, the World Health Organization (1957) also stated that smoking should be labeled as habituation rather than addiction. The semantics involved in such discussions and the pros and cons of these matters appear in several publications (Goldfarb *et al.*, 1970; Eisinger, 1971; Russell, 1971; Frith, 1971; among others). Knapp *et al.* (1963) reported that heavy smokers went through mild withdrawal symptoms. Others have found no evidence of a characteristic and reproducible abstinence syndrome following nicotine withdrawal.

Russell (1971) makes a case to regard cigarette smoking as a true addiction in the sense that withdrawal, tolerance, and psychologic craving have been adequately demonstrated. He alludes to reports that the vital component of tobacco sought by most smokers is nicotine (Lucchesi et al., 1967). In the case of cigarette smoking, complex psychosocial and environmental factors undoubtedly play a role as a main motivating factor for smoking, in addition to a desire for certain physiologic effects produced by components of the cigarette smoke. It is difficult to determine which of the components in tobacco is responsible for its appeal. That nicotine is involved is further suggested by the studies of Clark (1969), who demonstrated that rats preferred to self-administer nicotine solutions as opposed to placebo solutions. Eisinger (1971) concluded that there appeared to be some relationship between nicotine intake and psychologic dependency (as opposed to physiologic dependency) to cigarette smoke, although it was not the most prominent dosage factor. He indicated that the best predictor of psychologic addiction was the number of cigarettes smoked per day. A study by Goldfarb and his associates (1970) indicated that smokers could perceive differences in nicotine content in cigarettes, but the physiologic effects did not necessarily correlate with perceived psychologic effects. Evidence was obtained to suggest that the smoking habit was somewhat independent of the physiologic effects of nicotine. According to Kuhn (1965), people who do not inhale cigarette smoke absorb little nicotine, and the pharmacologic effects of nicotine seem to be incidental to their compulsive smoking behavior. In contrast, other studies indicate that nicotine intake (by inference, nicotine effects) can regulate cigarette smoking (Kozlowski et al., 1975).

It is not clear whether people smoke to become aroused or to decrease arousal. Frith (1971) assumed that if some people smoked to become aroused, they should smoke mostly when they are at a low level of arousal; the converse would be true if people smoked to become relaxed. Based on data from a questionnaire given to smokers, in general the users smoked more in low arousal situations, implicating nicotine as a stimulant. But there were apparent differences between males and females and their reasons for smoking. Evidently, the male volunteers desired cigarettes more when they were bored and tired, whereas the females desired them more under stress conditions. These findings partially support those obtained in a similar study conducted by Horn (1969).

One can label tobacco smoking as habituation, addiction, dependency, or whatever—the semantics may be more of academic interest than anything else. It is now generally accepted that cigarette smoking is detrimental to health. It has been demonstrated as a specific cause of death in lung cancer and coronary heart disease. Furthermore, ex-smokers reportedly have lower mortality rates than smokers, although not as low as non-smokers. Although it does not seem appropriate in this publication to discuss such matters at length, we cannot resist the temptation to include a quotation which appeared recently in a full-page cigarette advertisement in a newspaper:

> ". . . Many people are against cigarettes. You've heard their arguments. And even though we're in the business of selling cigarettes, we're not going to advance arguments in favor of smoking. We simply want to discuss one irrefutable fact. A lot of people are still smoking cigarettes. In all likelihood, they'll continue to smoke cigarettes and nothing anybody has said or is likely to say is going to change their minds . . . ."

They are right; the fact *is* irrefutable.

Absorption

The abuse of nicotine occurs mainly when it is inhaled with tobacco smoke. Consequently, most of this section is devoted to the absorption of nicotine from the respiratory tract.[*] In a study of 4000 cigarette smokers, 78% of the males inhaled and 53% of the female smokers inhaled (Todd, 1969). Tobacco is also chewed as well as smoked, and it appears to be readily absorbed from the gastrointestinal tract (Gaede, 1941; Wolff and Giles, 1950) although less rapidly than after inhalation.

As one would predict from the physicochemical principles of the passage of drugs through membranes, the rate of absorption of the weak base nicotine from the gastrointestinal tract varies with pH. In an alkaline solution, nicotine exists mainly as the nonionized free base and its absorption is rapid; in an acidic solution, it exists primarily as the charged salt form and its absorption is markedly reduced. At any given pH (as long as the alkaloid is not *all* in the salt form), the size of the dose becomes a significant factor in the rate of nicotine absorption.

In animals and man, nicotine is rapidly absorbed from the respiratory tract. It has been estimated that a cigarette smoker absorbs 100-200 μg of nicotine every time he inhales a puff of smoke (Armitage *et al.*, 1974). Nicotine doses of this magnitude (1-2 μg/kg) have been shown to exert central effects in experimental animals (Armitage *et al.*, 1968). Failure to inhale tobacco smoke does not completely prevent the absorption of nicotine. Many early investigators had reported extensive (68 to 100%) absorption of pure nicotine vapors introduced into the mouth, but not inhaled into the respiratory tract. However, when cigarettes were smoked

---

[*] Interested readers may refer to the review by Larson *et al.* (1961) for a discussion of other routes of absorption of nicotine (such as the skin and various parts of the gastrointestinal tract).

without inhalation, absorption of only 10 to 20% of the total nicotine was reported (Biederbeck, 1908; Lehmann, 1909). Apparently, something in tobacco smoke interfered with the absorption of nicotine from the oral cavity. Wolff (1955), studying anesthetized dogs maintained with artificial respiration, introduced cigarette smoke into the pulmonary tract in such a way that the animals received dosages comparable to those experienced by the human smoker. In general, over 90% of the nicotine dosage disappeared from the lungs during a 60-minute smoking period. Absorption of nicotine in individuals who smoke cigarettes with and without inhaling reveal large variations in the percentages of nicotine absorbed from the mainstream smoke. However, one trend is clear: inhalation markedly increases absorption of nicotine. From 2 to 80% of nicotine may be absorbed from mainstream smoke without inhalation, compared to 60-95% absorbed with inhalation (Larson et al., 1961). As might be expected, more nicotine is absorbed with more prolonged and/or deeper inhalations.

In cigar smoking the amount of nicotine absorbed depends upon the alkalinity of the mainstream smoke and the length of the unsmoked cigar (Wenusch, 1935, 1940, 1942). Since the mainstream smoke of cigars is alkaline, it, therefore, contains more nicotine in the free base form. This free nicotine, condensing with water vapor in the mouth, is said to be absorbed almost quantitatively. Thus, although cigar smoke may not be inhaled, its alkalinity facilitates the absorption of nicotine in the mouth. With tobaccos having more acidic mainstream smoke (cigarettes), relatively small amounts of nicotine are absorbed in the oral cavity; with inhaltion this amount is increased markedly because the smoke particles have more time to settle out and agglomerate. These larger and heavier nicotine-containing particles allegedly cling more easily to membrane surfaces and facilitate the absorption of nicotine. According to these concepts, when cigarette smoke is not inhaled, little of the nicotine in the smoke is retained because the smoke remains in the mouth only a short time with little movement. Armitage and Turner (1970) studied the absorption of nicotine through the oral mucosa in anesthetized cats exposed to cigarette and cigar smoke periodically introduced into the mouth. The nicotine in cigar smoke (pH 8.5) was much more readily absorbed through the mucous membrane of the mouth than was the nicotine in cigarette smoke (pH 5.3). Extrapolating to man, the authors concluded that smokers who do not inhale may not obtain an effective dose of nicotine from acidic (cigarette) smoke but may obtain it from alkaline (cigar) smoke. Others have observed that nicotine absorption through the oral mucosa can be influenced by the particulate matter in the smoke and by pH (Schievelbein et al., 1973). That cigar smokers absorbed less nicotine than cigarette smokers who inhale was intimated from the observation that cigar smokers excreted less nicotine in the urine than did cigarette smokers (Kershbaum et al., 1967).

In summary, absorption of nicotine appears to depend upon the following factors: (1) length of time that the smoke is in contact with the mucous membranes; (2) pH of the body fluids with which the smoke comes in contact; (3) degree and depth of inhalation; (4) nicotine content of the tobacco that is being smoked; (5) moisture content of the tobacco smoked; (6) length of the butt; (7) alkalinity (cigar) or acidity (cigarette) of the tobacco smoked; (8) agglomeration of smoke particles (which appears to be more important in cigarette smoking); and (9) use of a holder or filter.

Distribution

In early studies of the absorption and distribution of nicotine in man, nicotine determinations were limited to measurements in the urine of smokers. However, when gas chromatographic measurements became available, investigations were undertaken to measure nicotine and its metabolites in body fluids and particularly in the blood of smokers (Schievelbein and Grundke, 1968; Issac and Rand, 1972). The findings in man are generally quite similar to those in experimental animals. The plasma decay curve is biphasic: an initial, rapid phase due to uptake of nicotine from blood into tissues is followed by a slower phase, probably representing metabolism and excretion of nicotine. The plasma half-life has been estimated at less than 30 minutes. Although plasma concentrations of nicotine were cumulative during a day of smoking, the rate of drug elimination was apparently high enough to prevent appreciable accumulation from one day to the next. (This is reminiscent of the distribution and accumulation characteristics of caffeine referred to earlier in this chapter.) In fact, when 8 hours had elapsed since smoking the last cigarette, the concentration of nicotine in plasma was in the same range as that found in nonsmokers.

Experiments conducted *in vitro* and *in vivo* have shown that nicotine is taken up to some extent by virtually all tissues, including erythrocytes, of man and animals. Werle *et al.* (1956) estimated that human blood from smokers and nonsmokers could bind nicotine equivalently (0.025 mg/ml). Early studies also indicated that nicotine was preferentially held by the corpuscular fraction of blood (Burstein, 1932; Guidetti, 1937). More recent studies indicate approximately equal distribution of nicotine in plasma and red blood cells (Tsujimoto *et al.*, 1955; Appelgren *et al.*, 1962). After injection of 0.3 mg/kg to dogs, nicotine was present in erythrocytes but not in plasma; after injection of 0.5 mg/kg, nicotine was divided about equally between blood cells and plasma; after 1 mg/kg, the drug predominated in plasma (Burstein, 1932). Experiments conducted both *in vitro* and *in vivo* indicated that nicotine in excess of 7.5 mg/gm of red cells would not be absorbed into red cells but would appear in plasma.

Depending upon a myriad of experimental conditions, one can find varying concentrations of nicotine in many tissues, including liver, lung, kidney, brain, muscle, ileum, heart, spleen, pancreas, plasma, and fetus. It is worth noting, however, that nicotine distribution in tissues does not necessarily parallel the vascularity of the individual organs.

The nonionized form of nicotine appears to penetrate cell membranes quite easily (Weiss, 1966, 1968) and in general its distribution is dependent upon three factors: (1) accessibility of nicotine to a particular tissue (i.e., blood flow); (2) the magnitude of the pH gradient between intra- and extracellular compartments; and (3) an extracellular pH sufficiently high that a portion of the nicotine would be present in the nonionized, free base form. Other factors appear to be involved as well. For example, Brown et al. (1969a,b, 1971, 1972) demonstrated that when isolated sympathetic ganglia of the rat were soaked in solutions containing nicotine, some nicotine accumulated inside the ganglion cells. Intracellular accumulation was enhanced when nicotine depolarized the ganglion cells. It was suggested that nicotine caused the intracellular pH to become lower than the extracellular pH, and it thus facilitated its own intracellular accumulation. In other studies in vitro, when the pH was increased from 7.2-7.4 to 8.2-8.4, a portion of nicotine uptake into rat atria (Bhagat, 1970) and monkey cerebral cortex (Alderdice and Weiss, 1974) seemed to be due to factors other than a simple diffusion. Also, the increasing accumulation of ^{14}C-nicotine into rat brain slices in response to an increase in pH was reportedly inhibited by iodoacetate and was attributed to an energy-dependent process. A number of investigators have observed extensive accumulation of nicotine in the salivary glands of several species of animals (Hansson and Schimterlöw, 1962; Tsujimoto, 1972). Studying the distribution of ^{14}C-labeled nicotine in the submaxillary gland of rat, Yamamoto et al. (1968) reported that decreasing the temperature in vitro decreased the apparent steady-state slice-to-medium concentration ratios; such a temperature dependency would be consistent with an active transport process. However, various metabolic inhibitors as well as preheating the slices had no effect on the transport process. Putney and Borzelleca (1971) provided calculations indicating that the temperature-dependent accumulation of nicotine in the submaxillary gland in vitro (observed by Yamamoto's group) was related to a temperature effect on the pK_a of nicotine.

Nicotine concentrations in several tissues (including brain) have been reported to be 3 to 8 times higher than the blood concentrations after the administration of nicotine (Tsujimoto et al., 1955; Hansson and Schmiterlöw, 1962). Appelgren and his associates (1962) obtained evidence of preferential distribution of nicotine in the CNS using the technique of whole body autoradiography of mice injected intravenously with [14]-C-labeled nicotine. Their findings were confirmed by Yamamoto and his colleagues (1967). Mansner (1970) reported that the cerebral hemispheres of the mouse contained 50% more nicotine than did the brain stem after nicotine was administered subcutaneously. In mice, peak concentrations of nicotine in the brain could be detected as early as 1 minute after its intravenous injection (Stalhandske, 1970b). These workers and others (Schmiterlöw et al., 1967) reported high concentrations of nicotine in the hippocampus. Such results are interesting in view of reports that the hippocampus has a very low threshhold for nicotine effects.

Small amounts of the nicotine metabolite, cotinine, have been found in brain; evidence suggests that it is formed in the liver and subsequently transported to the CNS. For example, maximal cotinine concentrations were observed first in the liver, later in the blood, and still later in the brain (Stalhandske, 1967). Moreover, the maximal concentrations of cotinine in blood were higher than those in brain. These and other studies indicate that cotinine transfer through the blood-brain barrier is slower and brain uptake is lower than for nicotine (Bowman et al., 1964; Turner, 1969).

In cats, as in other species, nicotine accumulates rapidly in brain (Turner, 1969). There were marked differences in the nicotine content in various regions of the cat brain. The cerebral hemispheres contained significantly more nicotine than hypothalamus and thalamus, while midbrain and cervical spinal cord contained the least amounts. These observations were consistent with autoradiographic evidence from the kitten brain (Schmiterlöw et al., 1967).

In cats about 5% of injected radioactivity appeared in gastric juice 2 hours after ^{14}C-labeled nicotine administration; the major portion of the radioactivity was due to nicotine and its metabolite, cotinine (Turner, 1969). Likewise, substantial amounts of cotinine were found in the stomach of mice after its parenteral injection (Bowman et al., 1964). It is reasonable to assume that most of this nicotine and cotinine in gastric juice was reabsorbed as they passed down the gastrointestinal tract and encountered pH changes favorable to facilitate their absorption. Although the appearance of cotinine and nicotine in the gastric juice after parenteral administration of nicotine could be due to their secretion into the stomach, the large concentrations of these compounds present in the salivary glands suggest an alternate route to the stomach via swallowed saliva.

Nicotine disappears rapidly from the circulation due both to widespread distribution into tissues as well as to rapid metabolism (Tsujimoto et al., 1955; Hug, 1970). When 100 μg/kg of nicotine were injected intravenously into rats, there was a rapid biphasic disappearance of the nicotine from plasma such that 102 and 12 μg/ml were the concentrations at 2 and 60 minutes, respectively. The adrenals, liver, and certain brain areas maintained a three- to fivefold concentration gradient over plasma. Even in lung, heart, intestinal walls, spleen, thymus, and skeletal muscle, nicotine concentrations were about twice those in plasma; and in kidney the concentrations were from 6 to 15 times greater. Nicotine uptake by fatty tissue was slow and concentrations of nicotine therein did not exceed plasma concentrations.

Okumura (1937) reported that the distribution of nicotine between blood and tissues in rabbits was altered after repeated subcutaneous injections of nicotine. Gradually more nicotine appeared in blood and less in different organ tissues, especially the CNS. In contrast, when dogs were repeatedly injected with nicotine, the concentrations of nicotine increased not only in blood, but also in tissues, especially in the CNS. The net effect in dogs was that the tissue-to-blood partition coefficient was not decreased as it was in rabbits, but was increased. It was proposed that rabbits may develop tolerance to nicotine effects because with repeated exposure, proportionately more of the drug appeared in the blood, and less in the CNS. Accordingly, the dog would not develop tolerance to repeated doses of nicotine, but instead would become more sensitive to the central effects of the drug because of its increased distribution into the CNS. It has since been shown, however, that the dog also may develop tolerance to certain central effects of nicotine.

In a study of blood levels of nicotine in dogs that were anesthetized and exposed to a machine to simulate the pattern of cigarette smoking, about 50% of the dose was abstracted into the respiratory tract (Issac and Rand, 1969).* Blood nicotine concentrations determined during four successive puffs of smoke reached a peak after each puff, but the concentrations fell rapidly between puffs so that there was only slight accumulation over a 3-minute period of smoking. In fact, blood levels of nicotine were detected for only about 2 minutes when nicotine was injected intravenously to dogs at a dose of 28 μg/kg (the dose estimated to be abstracted in the lungs of a human smoker over a period of 10 minutes when inhaling). The intensity and duration of the effects of both smoke and injected nicotine on heart rate and blood pressure corresponded to the blood levels of nicotine.

There is some question as to whether the cardiovascular responses to nicotine are due to central and/or peripheral effects of the drug. That the effects of smoking or injected nicotine on blood pressure and heart rate correlated with the blood levels of nicotine with respect to both intensity and duration, suggested that nicotine circulating outside the CNS caused these responses. However, depression of the knee jerk produced in these dogs persisted for some time after nicotine could no longer be detected in blood, a finding to be expected if the depression is due to a central effect of nicotine in the spinal cord. Inhibition of the knee reflex has also been

---

*In general, 80-100% of the nicotine in tobacco smoke is abstracted after inhalation into the lungs of human smokers, and only 10-50% is abstracted without inhalation (Mitchell, 1962).

reported in human smokers (Clark and Rand, 1968; Domino and von Baumbargen, 1969).

It was observed that 3-day-old and adult mice could tolerate high doses of nicotine (Stalhandske et al., 1969; Stalhandske and Slanina, 1970b, 1972). In contrast, 12-day-old mice were highly sensitive to the toxic effects of nicotine. It was suggested that after 12 days of age, the subsequent decrease in sensitivity to nicotine might have been due to an enhanced enzymic detoxication by the liver. However, other factors must be involved because the 3-day-old mice tolerated doses of nicotine as high as the adults despite a much *lower* capacity to metabolize it. Because the CNS can take up nicotine and because that tissue is prominently involved in the overall pharmacology of nicotine (Silvette et al., 1962), it was proposed that the different sensitivities to lethal effects of nicotine in mice of different ages were likely due in part to age-related differences in distribution of the drug in the CNS. This hypothesis was tested experimentally. Mice, at ages 3, 12, and 35 days, were injected intraperitoneally with lethal doses of ^{14}C-labeled nicotine, and the concentrations of nicotine in the brain and blood were determined at death. As mice aged from 12 to 35 days, the average lethal nicotine concentration in the brain increased and the nicotine metabolizing capacity of the liver increased; however, these changes were offset by an increasing accumulation of nicotine in the brains of 35-day-old mice. The *net* result was an increase in the LD_{50} (from 2.7 to 11.5 mg/kg).

As the mice aged from 3 to 12 days old, the average lethal nicotine concentration decreased in the brain, and there was an increased capacity to accumulate nicotine in that tissue. However, the capacity of the liver to detoxify nicotine increased with age. The *net* effect of these changes was that the LD_{50} decreased from 11.2 to 2.7 mg/kg.

The electrical activity observed in mouse brain is said to begin when dendrites first invade the molecular layer of the cerebral cortex at about 6 days of age; on the sixteenth or seventeenth day of life, this electrical activity becomes identical with that seen in adult mice. Moreover, auto-radiographic studies revealed age-related changes in the distribution of nicotine within the brain. At 3 days of age, the cerebral cortex was almost devoid of nicotine, but at 12 days its nicotine concentration had increased considerably. Likewise, Schmiterlöw et al. (1967) showed by microauto-radiography that nicotine had a specific affinity to neurons in the cerebral cortex. The implication was that the increased accumulation of nicotine in the cortex reflected the functional development of neuronal components.

Changes in drug accumulation with increasing age are very difficult to evaluate because several physiologic, anatomic, and biochemical components are developing concomitantly. One explanation for these changes, for example, could be increasing vascularization of the CNS with increasing age. However, Schmiterlöw et al. (1967), presented evidence that nicotine localization in *cat* brain was *not* governed solely by blood supply. The increased myelinization that occurs with age could be another cause for the increased accumulation of the lipid-soluble nicotine in brain. However, autoradiographic studies showed that nicotine penetrated white matter more slowly than gray matter and evidently membranes of the lamellar myelin sheath presented a *barrier* to the penetration of nicotine (Schmiterlöw *et al.*, 1965; Schoolar *et al.*, 1960; Roth and Barlow, 1961).

There appear to be sex and strain differences among rats with respect to the accumulation of nicotine in brain and their sensitivity to its behavioral effects (Rosecrans and Schechter, 1972). Male and female Sprague-Dawley and Fisher rats were given several doses of nicotine subcutaneously. Brain levels of nicotine were determined and behavioral responses to the drug were measured. Females of both strains accumulated more nicotine in brain than similarly treated males, and were more sensitive to its behavioral effects. However, the complexities of demonstrating significant correlations between levels of nicotine in brain and behavioral responses to the drug are emphasized by the fact that the Fisher rats appeared more sensitive to the behavioral effects of nicotine although the brain drug levels were generally lower in this strain.

Nicotine is known to exert pharmacologic effects on a number of different tissues, including adrenal medulla, pituitary, and sympathetic and parasympathetic ganglia. It has been found that nicotine accumulates in these tissues and in pancreatic islets of mice, parafollicular cells in the thyroid of mice, and ultimobranchial gland of chicks (Slanina and Tjälve, 1973). Since biogenic amines have been shown to be operative in these various endocrine cell systems (Pearse, 1969) and since nicotine accumulated in these cells, it has been suggested that nicotine shares common transport and/or storage mechanisms with biogenic amines in these cells, and that it can thereby interfere with their functions. In support of this hypothesis are several studies showing various effects of nicotine on biogenic amines *in vivo* and *in vitro* (Pepeu, 1965; Armitage and Hall, 1967; Bhagat *et al.*, 1967; Goodman and Weiss, 1972; Volle and Koelle, 1970; Thompson, 1968; Thompson *et al.*, 1969). Nicotine, atropine, and some local anesthetics have been shown to accumulate in pancreatic islets, parafollicular cells of the thyroid, pituitary, and adrenal medulla. The ability of these cells to accumulate such drugs, all of which may influence adrenergic or cholinergic mechanisms, was considered as indicative that all these drugs could affect the release and/or storage of the hormones produced by these different cell systems by influencing intracellular biogenic amines. Finally, it has been said that nicotine causes a release of the adrenergic transmitter at the sympathetic nerve terminals of blood vessels, which in turn causes a contraction of the vessel wall. This action of nicotine is allegedly dependent upon an intact norepinephrine uptake mechanism into the neuron (Su and Bevan, 1970). This, in turn, implies that nicotine also may be transported to the inside of the neuron by that mechanism. Bevan and Su (1972) provided evidence that nicotine was indeed concentrated in the nerve-containing layer of the rabbit aortic strip, probably within the neuron. Moreover, uptake of nicotine was prevented by drugs that blocked the norepinephrine uptake mechanism and the subsequent release of the transmitter by nicotine. Similarly, nicotine has been reported to be taken up by neurons of other tissues, including the CNS (Schmiterlöw and Hansson, 1965), the superior cervical ganglion (Appelgren et al., 1963; Brown et al., 1969a,b), and rat atria (Bhagat, 1970).

In animals and man, the placenta is permeable to nicotine. In 1935, Sontag and Wallace detected increases in the fetal heart beat when pregnant women smoked cigarettes. Nicotine, cotinine, and other metabolites rapidly pass into the fetus when ^{14}C-labeled nicotine is administered intravenously to pregnant mice (Tjälve et al., 1968) and pregnant rat (Mosier and Jansons, 1972). The observed higher concentrations of nicotine in fetal plasma compared to maternal plasma suggest that the net flow of nicotine is in the direction of the fetus. Nicotine and its metabolites have also been found in amniotic fluid.

In a study of 6-day pregnant rabbits, ^{3}H-nicotine was injected intravenously (Fabro and Sieber, 1969; Sieber and Fabro, 1971). Significant levels of radioactivity were found in plasma, endometrium, uterine secretions, and blastocysts 1 hour after dosing. Similar levels of radioactivity were detected in endometrium and plasma. But, in uterine secretions of the pregnant rabbits, the tritium activity was 10 times greater than that in plasma. In contrast, tritium activity in the uterine secretions of nonpregnant rabbits was only slightly higher than that of plasma. Apparently, the mechanisms by which drugs appear in uterine secretions are influenced by pregnancy. In the preimplantation blastocyst, the concentration of nicotine was four times greater than that in plasma. Relatively small amounts of the nicotine metabolite desmethylcotinine were produced in the mother and also were found in the blastocyst.

It is difficult to assess the pharmacologic and/or toxicologic importance of the transfer of nicotine and its metabolites into the blastocyst and fetus. However, reports are available to indicate that commonly used drugs may be harmful to the conceptus before implantation (Adams et al., 1961; Lutwak-Mann and Hay, 1962; Chang, 1964; Schardein et al., 1965). For example, exposure to nicotine during early pregnancy can cause a decreased number of implantations in rats. Moreover, women who smoke during pregnancy are reported to have a higher abortion rate than nonsmokers, and their babies are more likely to be premature and/or of relatively low birth weight (Peterson et al., 1965).

Suzuki and associates (1974) reported that when nicotine was administered to the pregnant rhesus monkey, marked cardiovascular disturbances occurred in both mother and fetus and led to fetal asphyxia. These effects might have been due to nicotine-induced disturbances in uterine perfusion, to direct effects of transmitted nicotine upon the fetus, or to a combination of both. They found high concentrations of nicotine in several tissues of the fetus. In addition, the concentration of nicotine in the fetal circulation rapidly surpassed the maternal level, reaching a maximum in 16 minutes and retaining high concentrations for over 2 hours following the injection. Moreover, the disappearance of nicotine from the fetal circulation was slower than that from the maternal circulation. It was concluded that the cardiovascular disturbances, acidosis, and hypoxia observed in the monkey fetus following administration of nicotine to the mother were due to direct effects of the nicotine transferred from mother to fetus as well as to indirect effects of the drug (diminished perfusion of the fetus).

Metabolism

General

Only about 10% of absorbed nicotine is excreted unchanged, the remainder being metabolized rapidly primarily by the liver. It is generally accepted that neither nicotine nor its metabolic products are retained in the body to any great degree or for extended periods. For example, Wolff *et al.* (1949), studying subjects who smoked 20 cigarettes in 7 hours, reported a rapid detoxication of nicotine and estimated that 80-90% of the absorbed nicotine had been metabolized during the smoking period.

It is of historical interest that as early as 1876, Lautenbach provided indirect evidence for the detoxication of nicotine by the liver. Nicotine injected subcuteneously or into a systemic vein of a dog was fatal, whereas its injection into the mesenteric or splenic vein produced only mild poisoning with prompt recovery. In the latter case, of course, the drug passed through the liver before entering the general circulation. Haag and his associates (1945), studying the toxicity of nicotine in mice in which liver damage had been produced by carbon tetrachloride, noted that the mice with damaged livers tolerated repeated nicotine administrations poorly as compared to control animals. Similarly, when the livers of guinea pigs were damaged by phosphorus poisoning, its "detoxifying power" was found to drop about 70% (Werle and Uschold, 1948).

Miller and Larson (1953) reported that liver tissue metabolized nicotine more rapidly than other tissues; indeed this finding is common to many studies. Tsujimoto (1957) demonstrated nicotine was oxidized by liver

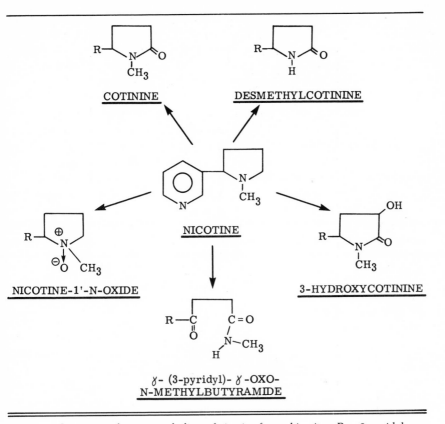

Fig. 2. Structures of some metabolites of nicotine formed *in vitro*. R = 3-pyridyl.

homogenates of various species. Later nicotine was found to be metabolized by an O_2/NADPH-dependent 9000 g supernatant fraction of rabbit liver homogenates (Hucker, 1958; Hucker and Gillette, 1959; Hucker *et al.*, 1959, 1960; Stalhandske, 1970a). Neither microsomes nor the 78,000 g supernate alone would oxidize the alkaloid, but activity was restored upon re-combining these components. The role of the supernate was to maintain NADP in the reduced form while the nicotine was oxidized in the microsomes. Liver enzymes can catalyze the oxidation of nicotine to cotinine, desmethylcotinine, nicotine 1'-N-oxide, hydroxycotinine, and γ-(3-pyridyl)- γ -oxo-N-methylbutyramide (Fig. 2).

Other tissues mentioned as sites of metabolic detoxication of nicotine include lung*, kidney, and brain (see Larson *et al.*, 1961). Cardiac muscle

*In dogs, however, it has been reported that the lung is not a significant detoxifying organ for nicotine (Biebl *et al.*, 1932).

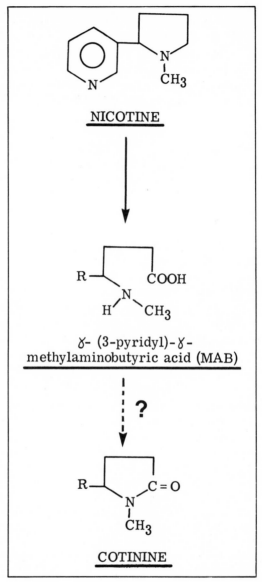

Fig. 3. Formation of cotinine from nicotine by lactamization of MAB. R = 3-pyridyl.

(Ganz et al., 1951; Geiling, 1951), skeltal muscle, spleen, mucous surfaces of the small intestine, adrenals, skin, and blood usually fail to metabolize nicotine in most species studied. The extrahepatic metabolism of nicotine differs somewhat with the experimental designs used, so that the tissues that can metabolize nicotine do not always exhibit a consistent ranking from one species to another, or from one study to another. Werle and Müller (1941) pointed out that studies of the metabolism of nicotine conducted *in vitro* should be done with organs removed from the sacrificed animals as soon as possible because the detoxication capacity rapidly decreases at death. Undoubtedly, this contributes substantially to reported variations in the metabolism of nicotine *in vitro*. Nonenzymatic reactions may also account for some apparent biotransformations of nicotine (Wada *et al.*, 1959).

Cotinine

Chromatographic evidence obtained from urine suggested that certain metabolites of nicotine in dog and man were similar; i.e., cotinine, hydroxycotinine, and desmethylcotinine were excreted in urine of both species (Bowman *et al.*, 1959a,b; McKennis *et al.*, 1959). It can now be confidently concluded that cotinine is the major metabolite formed by man and other mammalian species *in vivo* and *in vitro*. About 10% of an orally administered dose of nicotine has been identified in human urine as cotinine. Although cotinine is present in cigarette smoke, the amount appearing in urine directly from the smoke appears to be small.

Another major metabolic product of nicotine appears to be γ-(3-pyridyl)-γ-methylaminobutyric acid (MAB) (Fig. 3) (McKennis *et al.*, 1957, 1958; McKennis, 1960, 1965). *In vitro*, a spontaneous lactamization of MAB may occur to form cotinine, so that at body pH and temperature, MAB might be a precursor to cotinine *in vivo* (Fig. 3). However, formation of cotinine from nicotine has been observed under conditions unlikely to involve lactamization of MAB (Bowman *et al.*, 1959a,b; Hucker and Gillette, 1959; Hucker *et al.*, 1959).

Hucker and his associates (1960), addressing themselves to the mechanism of conversion of nicotine to cotinine, proposed that nicotine was initially oxidized to 5'-hydroxynicotine by an NADPH-dependent oxidase present in rabbit liver microsomes. The alcohol could then be presumed to be oxidized to cotinine by a soluble enzyme, akin to aldehyde oxidase (Fig. 4). Hill *et al.* (1972) suggested that in fact aldehyde oxidase was the enzyme responsible for production of cotinine from nicotine. Recently, Murphy (1973) provided evidence for the formation of the nicotine-$\Delta^{1'(5')}$-iminium ion when nicotine was oxidized in the presence of rabbit liver microsomal enzymes and NADPH (Fig. 5). The formation of this ion was apparently catalyzed by an enzyme system having characteristics of a mixed function oxidase. It was proposed that the nicotine-$\Delta^{1'(5')}$-iminium ion was formed by loss of water from the initial oxidation product 5'-hydroxynicotine. The importance of the formation of this iminium ion intermediate remains to be determined. If 5'-hydroxynicotine were rapidly equilibrating with intermediates (for example, the iminium ion), then the oxygen of cotinine would be derived mainly from water, rather than from

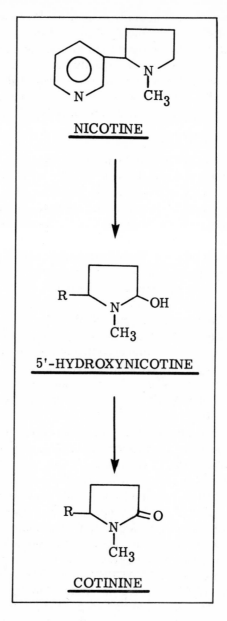

Fig. 4. Formation of cotinine from nicotine by oxidation of 5'-hydroxynicotine. R = 3-pyridyl.

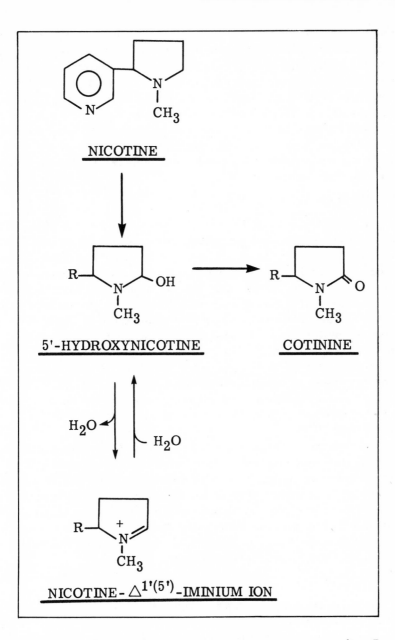

Fig. 5. Formation of cotinine from nicotine via an iminium ion intermediate. R = 3-pyridyl.

molecular oxygen. When the production of cotinine from nicotine was studied *in vitro* in an atmosphere of $^{18}O_2$, the mass spectrum of cotinine indicated no incorporation of ^{18}O. These findings suggest that an exchange of the oxygen of 5'-hydroxynicotine occurred prior to its conversion to cotinine. In other words, there was support of a postulate of an iminium ion intermediate in the formation of cotinine from nicotine.

Cotinine can be further metabolized in animals and man. One metabolite has been tentatively assigned the structure 3-hydroxycotinine (McKennis *et al.*, 1963a; Dagne and Castagnoli, 1971). Desmethylcotinine is also formed from cotinine.

Demethylation

In early studies involving the injection of *randomly* labeled nicotine into animals, investigators were frequently unable to detect $^{14}CO_2$ in the expired air probably due to the low specific activity of the compound. Based on these findings, Larson and Haag (1943) concluded that no evidence existed to indicate that the detoxication of nicotine involved demethylation of the molecule. However, when N-$^{14}CH_3$-nicotine was later synthesized and injected into rats, approximately 10% of the N-methyl group administered was converted to $^{14}CO_2$ and appeared in the expired air. The finding that desmethylcotinine was isolated from urine after the administration of nicotine to dogs clearly established N-demethylation as a significant route of nicotine metabolism (McKennis *et al.*, 1959, 1962; Hansson and Schmiterlöw, 1962). Recently, the demethylation of nicotine to nornicotine and to desmethylcotinine has been demonstrated in the pig (Harke *et al.*, 1974).

Other studies (Papadopoulos and Kinzios, 1963) indicated that at least two processes were involved in the metabolism of nicotine by rabbit liver homogenates: an oxidative process yielding cotinine primarily, and a demethylation process resulting in formation of the demethylated products of nicotine and cotinine, nornicotine and desmethylcotinine, respectively. Formation of nornicotine from nicotine cannot be considered as a detoxication reaction for nicotine, at least not in all species studied (Hucker and Larson, 1958; Larson and Haag, 1943).

N-Oxide Formation

In recent experiments conducted *in vitro* and *in vivo*, nicotine was shown to be converted to nicotine-1'-N-oxide (Papadopoulos, 1964a,b,; Booth and Boyland, 1970, 1971; Beckett *et al.*, 1971a), in contrast to earlier studies where it was not found (Werle *et al.*, 1950). Two isomers of nicotine-1'-N-oxide have been resolved from human urine: one isomer has the pyridyl group *cis* to the methyl group at the quaternary nitrogen atom;

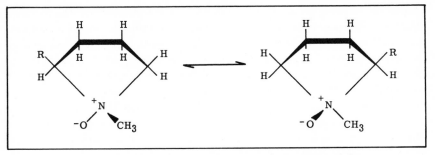

Fig. 6. Two isomers of nicotine-1'-N-oxide. R = 3-pyridyl.

the other has the pyridyl group *cis* to the oxygen atom at the quaternary nitrogen (Booth and Boyland, 1970; Fig. 6). The liver is the most active tissue in converting nicotine not only to cotinine, but also to both isomers of nicotine-1'-N-oxide. The kidney and lung were also able to form these three metabolites but in lesser quantities.

The factors responsible for the carcinogenic effect of cigarette smoking on the human lung have been studied extensively. Several carcinogenic compounds have been identified in tobacco smoke. It has been proposed that N-oxides may be able to act as general biologic oxygenating agents so that their formation could interfer with essential systems involved in basic cell metabolism (see Booth and Boyland, 1971). The demonstration that nicotine-1'-N-oxide is a nicotine metabolite is particularly interesting in view of the similarity in structure between it and certain carcinogenic purine N-oxides. Since nicotine is converted to cotinine *in vitro* by lung tissue of numerous species including man, and to both isomers of nicotine-1'-N-oxide by the guinea pig lung (Hansson *et al.*, 1964), it is, therefore, reasonable to assume that these metabolites may be formed from nicotine *in vivo* in the lungs of cigarette smokers, where they may be carcinogenic and/or that they could be transported to the lungs after formation in the liver. In terms of *acute* toxicity, it has been stated that the formation of nicotine-1'-N-oxide and cotinine from nicotine represent detoxication mechanisms (McKennis, 1960; Truhaut *et al.*, 1964; Bizard *et al.*, 1956; Bowman *et al.*, 1964). This may not be true over extended periods of exposure to nicotine.

Recently, the smoking of tobacco has become associated with the induction of urinary tract tumors. Indeed, the nicotine metabolites cotinine and nicotine-1'-N-oxide have been implicated. Gorrod and his associates (1974) demonstrated that the ratio of cotinine to nicotine-1'-N-oxide present in the urine was significantly higher in male smokers with cancer of the urinary bladder than in male smokers who were healthy; this change seemed to be independent of urinary pH, urine volume, or daily cigarette consumption. The authors suggested that a shift may have occurred in diseased patients in certain oxidative pathways of nicotine metabolism. If such a shift were shown to occur in patients with cancer of the bladder, it still would remain to be proven whether the shift was causally related to mechanisms of tumor formation or, not of merely a consequence of the disease or its treatment. In any case, the findings are interesting in view of findings by Beckett and his associates (1971a,b) that male smokers could be divided into two groups with respect to cotinine excretion. One group excreted over 20% of a nicotine dose as cotinine, the other less than 5%, suggesting that one group formed more cotinine than the other. Gorrod and co-workers suggest the possibility that the first group might be more at risk for the development of cancer of the urinary bladder than the second group. However, correlation does not prove cause and effect. If these findings are substantiated, excretion of these nicotine metabolites might be used to predict the susceptibility of individuals to this neoplastic disease.

Reduction of N-Oxide

Booth and Boyland (1971) demonstrated the anaerobic enzymic reduction of nicotine-1'-N-oxide to nicotine by guinea pig liver preparations. Among various tissues, liver tissue was most active in this respect (Dajani et al., 1972). Of the extrahepatic tissues, the small intestine exhibited the most activity, having 40 to 65% of the liver activity; kidney, heart, lung, and spleen had only 5 to 10% of the hepatic activity; blood and brain had no significant reducing capacity. Reduction of nicotine-1'-N-oxide was also observed when it was incubated anaerobically with suspensions of rat intestinal content. (It is well known that bacteria of the gut can reduce various N-oxides.) In man, circulating nicotine-1'-N-oxide does not appear to be appreciably metabolized (Beckett et al., 1970; Jenner et al., 1973). When administered intravenously, the N-oxide was recovered quantitatively in the urine; neither nicotine nor cotinine were detected. On the other hand, when nicotine-1'-N-oxide was administered orally, the N-oxide, nicotine, and cotinine were found in the urine. It was proposed that the N-oxide was reduced to nicotine by reductases in the gut and that the nicotine was absorbed and partly metabolized to cotinine by the liver. Support for this hypothesis was provided by the observation that rectal administration of a solution of nicotine-1'-N-oxide resulted in negligible absorption of the unchanged compound, and yet substantial amounts of nicotine and cotinine appeared in the urine.

Formation of 3-Pyridylacetic Acid

Werle and Meyer (1950), using liver slices incubated with nicotine, had claimed that methylamine was produced from nicotine. Others were unable to confirm these findings (Schievelbein and Werle, 1957; Owen and Larson, 1958). In 1960, McKennis and his associates tentatively identified γ-(3-pyridyl)- γ -oxo-N-methylbutyramide as a metabolite of cotinine in dogs. This metabolite could provide through enzymatic hydrolysis a source of methylamine, and subsequently of CO_2 and 3-pyridylacetic acid (Fig. 7). Evidence for the metabolism of nicotine to 3-pyridylacetic acid was obtained by McKennis and his associates (1961). As summarized in Fig. 8, several routes for formation of 3-pyridylacetic acid from nicotine have been proposed (Werle *et al.*, 1950; McKennis *et al.*, 1964a,b; McKennis, 1960, 1965; De Clercq and Truhaut, 1962; Meacham *et al.*, 1972).

N-Methylation

Although 80 to 90% of the radioactivity from administered nicotine-^{14}C was excreted in dog urine, only 10% of that radioactivity was present as unchanged nicotine (McKennis *et al.*, 1963b). Approximately 30% of the urinary radioactivity was composed of derivatives of nicotine in which the pyrrolidine ring had undergone fragmentation or oxidative changes (McKennis, 1965).* Chromatography of dog urine revealed two radioactive components (accounting for approximately 16% of urinary radioactivity), each with properties consistent with quaternary ammonium compounds. It, therefore, appeared that nicotine might be N-methylated in dogs. The properties of one of these compounds were consistent with those of the nicotine isomethonium ion; the other, the cotinine methonium ion (Fig. 8). The latter was also present in human urine after oral administration of cotinine. Since both cotinine and nicotine can be metabolized to various pyridino compounds and since such compounds are known to undergo N-methylation, it seems likely that many metabolites of nicotine could arise from these reactions. Axelrod (1962) reported that nornicotine could also be methylated to nicotine by a purified enzyme preparation from rabbit lung.

Age Dependency

As has been found for many drugs metabolized by the hepatic micro-somes, the metabolism of nicotine is rather limited in newborn and fetal animals as compared with adults (Stalhandske *et al.*, 1969; Suzuki *et al.*, 1974; Tjälve *et al.*, 1968). Cotinine is the major metabolite of nicotine in fetal, newborn, and young mice. After the third week of life, however, other metabolites are formed, probably as a result of the development of other enzyme systems involved in nicotine metabolism. After birth, the ability of the liver to metabolize nicotine increases, approaching the adult level at about 4 weeks of age. After the first 3 days of birth, there does

---

*In this connection, radioactive urea has been reported to be one of the products of the metabolism of nicotine-methyl-^{14}C in the rat (McKennis *et al.*, 1962).

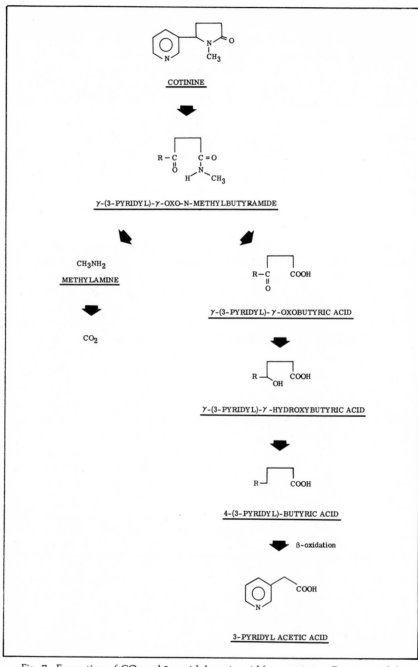

Fig. 7. Formation of CO_2 and 3-pyridyl acetic acid from cotinine. R = 3-pyridyl.

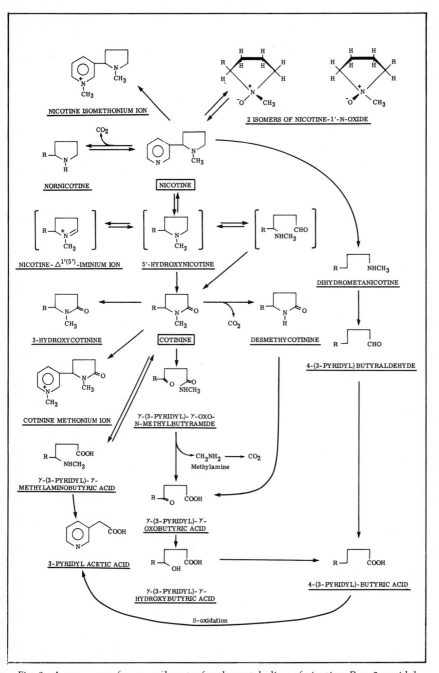

Fig. 8. A summary of proposed routes for the metabolism of nicotine. R = 3-pyridyl.

appear to be a positive relationship between the rate of metabolism of nicotine *in vitro* and its lethal toxicity in young mice, as discussed previously. In addition, the K_m value for cotinine formation from nicotine decreases during the first month after birth, implying in a simplistic sense that over this time period there occurs an increase in enzyme "affinity" for the drug substrate.

Tolerance

Over the years, the nature of tolerance to nicotine and tobacco smoking has received considerable attention (see Beckett *et al.*, 1971b). While it is tempting to suggest that tolerance was related to the induction of hepatic microsomal enzymes and subsequent enhanced metabolic detoxication of nicotine, various reports indicated that induction was rather an unpredictable consequence of repeated nicotine administration. Indeed, reports of inhibition appear in the literature as frequently as reports of induction. As an indication of induction, in dog, rabbit, rat, and man, chronic exposure to nicotine has resulted in a decreased percentage of the drug excreted unchanged in urine (Finnegan *et al.*, 1947; Werlé and Uschold, 1948; Werle *et al.*, 1956). However, most studies in animals and man suggest that the metabolism of nicotine upon repeated administration may only be increased to a limited extent at best, may not be affected at all, or indeed it may be decreased (Takeuchi *et al.*, 1954; Werle and Müller, 1941). Nicotine treatment has had a dual effect on its own hepatic metabolism: stimulation in one condition and inhibition in another (Stalhandske and Slanina, 1970a). Beckett and his associates (1971a,b) studied the effect of smoking on nicotine metabolism *in vivo* in man. Their results were no less complex than those obtained in animal experimentation. In general there was a poor correlation between the urinary recoveries of nicotine and cotinine and the approximate number of cigarettes smoked daily by the volunteers. Moreover, typical urinary excretion patterns of male and female smokers and nonsmokers showed no significant differences in the time taken to eliminate half the nicotine dose. In short, although smoking may cause alterations in nicotine metabolism, one must be extremely cautious in generalizing that the induction of hepatic microsomal enzymes (hence the stimulated metabolism of nicotine) results in the development of tolerance to certain effects of nicotine by smokers. Chapter 10 of this book reviews others studies of tolerance to nicotine effects.

Metabolic Interactions between Nicotine and Other Drugs

In recent years, one area of pharmacology that has received particular attention is the modification of the metabolism of drugs by concurrent or previous exposure to other drugs or chemicals. Studies of the effect of smoking on the activity of drug-metabolizing enzymes have been conducted (Pantuck *et al.*, 1972; Welch *et al.*, 1968, 1969). However, going a step further to examine the effect of the *nicotine* present in the tobacco smoke on drug metabolism is quite difficult. One major obstacle is that components of tobacco smoke other than nicotine (e.g., 3,4-benzpyrene and various polycyclic hydrocarbons) produce effects on drug metabolism that could be attributed erroneously to nicotine.

Ruddon and Cohen (1970) observed increased activities of several enzymes of rat liver following the acute and chronic administration of nicotine. However, the increases in enzyme activity after acute nicotine administration were observed only when convulsive doses of the alkaloid were administered. Therefore, the "stress" produced by large doses of nicotine might have been responsible for the elevations of the enzyme activities noted (there is ample evidence that certain experimentally induced stresses can directly or indirectly increase the activities of various liver microsomal enzymes). In their chronic studies, nicotine was administered in the drinking water so that the dose was given more evenly over 24-hour periods. Rather modest elevations (in the order of 25 to 50%) occurred in activities of certain drug-metabolizing enzyme systems. The increased activity could not be maintained when the average daily dose dropped below 4.4 mg/kg. To compare their studies to those in man, they alluded to estimates by Larson *et al.* (1961) that a pack-a-day cigarette smoker absorbed about 1 mg/kg/day of nicotine. A two-pack-a-day smoker should then absorb about 2 mg/kg/day, so that their dose of 5 to 6 mg/kg/day in a rat did not seem to be unreasonable in their opinion. In any case, in comparison to the polycyclic hydrocarbons and the 3,4-benzpyrene inducers present in tobacco smoke, nicotine was a relatively weak inducer at best.

It has been shown that phenobarbital, an inducer of the microsomal drug-metabolizing enzymes, can stimulate the metabolism of nicotine-N-$^{14}CH_3$. *In vitro*, an increased conversion of nicotine to cotinine and an increased formation of $^{14}CO_2$ were observed, the latter suggesting that phenobarbital induced the N-demethylation reactions involved in nicotine metabolism (McKennis *et al.*, 1962; Stahlhandske, 1970b). Cotinine breakdown *in vivo* was also stimulated by phenobarbital pretreatment. These findings would explain the observation that the urine of phenobarbitalized animals contained lower concentrations of *both* nicotine and cotinine, but higher concentrations of other nicotine metabolites, some of which were shown to be metabolites of cotinine. Other apparently paradoxical findings might also be explained by these studies. Beckett and Triggs (1967) administered nicotine to volunteers and found less unchanged nicotine in the urine of smokers than in the urine of nonsmokers. The data suggested that the smokers had metabolized more nicotine than nonsmokers, but they were unable to detect an increase in cotinine excretion. From the foregoing animal studies, it is possible that the rate of cotinine metabolism may have been simultaneously increased with an increase in nicotine metabolism.

Phenobarbital pretreatment of mice did not decrease the brain concentrations of nicotine when the latter was administered intravenously; it did do so when nicotine was administered intraperitoneally (Stalhandske, 1967). These findings were compatible with a very rapid passage of nicotine into the brain and a high affinity of nicotine for that tissue. Furthermore, phenobarbital pretreatment increased the intraperitoneal LD_{50} of nicotine two- to threefold but did not change the intravenous LD_{50} value. Such findings are relevant to the controversy of whether nicotine death is primarily provoked by a central or a peripheral action.

From the foregoing, it should be evident that the metabolism of nicotine by mammalian tissues has been investigated extensively; but relatively little is known about the molecular interactions of this compound with other constituents of living cells. Wei-Chiang and Van Vunakis (1974) recently isolated a nicotine analogue of nicotinamide adenine dinucleotide (DPN or NAD) from an incubation mixture containing nicotine, NAD, and pig brain NADase. The structure of the compound was identical with NAD itself except that the nicotinamide moiety of NAD had been replaced by nicotine. The nicotine-NAD could not substitute for NAD in the horse liver alcohol dehydrogenase reaction. Indeed, it inhibited this dehydrogenase rather effectively. Similar results were obtained for a nicotine-NADP, with respect to specific NADP dehydrogenases. One cannot help but be curious about the role of these NAD and NADP analogues in the pharmacologic effects produced by nicotine.

Excretion

In mammals, the urine is the main route of excretion of nicotine and its metabolites. As far as the mechanism of urinary excretion of nicotine is concerned, Ozawa (1930) reported that the drug was eliminated by the toad from both glomeruli and tubules; the site of nicotine excretion in the mammalian kidney is unknown.

Finnegan *et al.* (1947) showed that the percent of administered nicotine that was excreted unchanged in the urine of dogs increased with increasing nicotine dosage. Urinary excretion of nicotine in the dog was virtually complete within 16 hours after administration. In rabbits, Yamamoto and his associates (1954) reported an average of 7.7% of injected nicotine was excreted in the urine in 24 hours; only trace amounts were excreted over a second 24-hour period. In rats, almost all the radioactivity from a dose of ^{14}C-labeled nicotine is excreted in urine, 8 to 25% of the radioactivity being due to unchanged nicotine (Ganz *et al.*, 1951; Geiling, 1951).

In man, nicotine appears in the urine within about 1.5 hours after smoking a cigar or cigarette. At about 2 hours, its excretion generally begins to decline. Although the excretion of nicotine in urine is usually complete within 15 to 24 hours after smoking one cigarette, Lickint and Lukesch (1956) demonstrated that the urine of individuals who smoked 10 cigarettes over a 2-hour period contained nicotine up to 48 hours later. In early studies, Bodnar and his associates (1935) found 1.31 mg of nicotine in urine after subjects had inhaled smoke from 10 cigarettes; after the same number of cigarettes was smoked without inhalation, no nicotine was found in the urine. Corcoran and his associates (1939) reported that the amounts of nicotine excreted in the urine of smokers varied from 1 to 10 mg every 24 hours. It is rather interesting that individuals who do not smoke but who are exposed to tobacco smoke in enclosed areas may also excrete nicotine in their urine (about 5% of the amount found in smokers' urines) (Horning *et al.*, 1973). This observation was in accord with findings that nonsmokers had low concentrations of a compound in their plasma which was indistinguishable from nicotine by gas-liquid chromatography (Issac and Rand, 1972).

The amount of nicotine excreted unchanged by man varies somewhat with the pH of the urine, 2-4% being excreted unchanged when the urine is maintained at pH 7-7.5, and 10-13% when urinary pH is 5-5.5 (Haag and Larson, 1942). These findings agree with theoretical prediction: at basic pH the nonionized form of nicotine would predominate and be more readily reabsorbed from the urinary tract than would the ionic form of nicotine. Once reabsorbed, the nicotine would become reexposed to metabolic processes within the body. The converse would be expected at an acidic urinary pH. Borzelleca (1961), by measuring the blood pressure and respiration in dogs given nicotine, provided evidence that more nicotine was reabsorbed when the urine was alkaline than when it was acidic. Harke and Fleischmann (1973) reported that the urinary excretion of unchanged nicotine by cigarette smokers was increased with both increasing urinary volume and decreasing urinary pH whereas the urinary excretion of cotinine did not appear to be dependent upon these factors. Others, however, have reported that cotinine excretion in man was dependent upon urinary flow rate and pH (Beckett *et al.*, 1972).

Nicotine-1'-*N*-oxide is also present in urine of smokers (Booth and Boyland, 1970; Beckett *et al.*, 1971a). The amount excreted in 24 hours was approximately half that of the cotinine excreted, so that N-oxidation appears to be an important route of metabolism of nicotine in man. Urinary excretion of nicotine-1'-*N*-oxide was reported to be independent of urinary pH and volume, as expected for a highly polar, water-soluble compound.

Small amounts of nicotine are eliminated in feces. Ganz *et al.* (1951) reported that 3 hours following intravenous injection of radioactive nicotine into mice, 1.2% of the total radioactivity was excreted in bile and appeared in feces; at 6 hours, 2.2% was found in feces. Nicotine is also eliminated in the bile of dogs (Hermann *et al.*, 1930) and rats (Ryrfeldt and Hansson, 1971).

Other routes of elimination of nicotine have been studied over the years. Studies by Larson (1952) suggested that the elimination of absorbed nicotine via expired air cannot be considered significant due to the poor volatility of nicotine from dilute solutions. In contrast, nicotine can be excreted in human sweat (see Larson *et al.*, 1961) and human milk. Hatcher and Crosby (1928) conducted a study on a woman 8 days postpartum. She had been smoking 20 to 25 cigarettes daily for 6 days prior to the study; on the seventh day, after smoking seven cigarettes in a 2-hour period, small amounts of nicotine were found in extracts of her milk. Bisdom (1937), on the other hand, claimed to find nicotine extensively excreted in the milk of a nursing mother who smoked an average of 60 cigarettes daily; enough of the drug was in her milk so that nicotine intoxication could be induced in the nursling. Perlman and his associates (Perlman and Dannenberg, 1942; Perlman *et al.*, 1942) reported the presence of nicotine in the milk of smoking mothers at less than one-tenth the concentration present in urine.

ALCOHOL

Introduction

The consumption of alcohol (ethyl alcohol) dates back to the Middle Ages when it was used as a therapeutic agent for various maladies. The name "whiskey" in Gaelic means "water of life." Like other drugs discussed in this chapter, alcohol is consumed throughout the world daily by millions of people. The vast majority of users do not become dependent upon alcohol, and the drug has surely gained some degree of social acceptance (although Prohibition attests to its stormy history in that respect). Nevertheless, an estimated 5 to 10 million people in the United States alone are dependent upon alcohol, and alcoholism is generally regarded as the most prevalent form of drug abuse, presenting a sociomedical problem of major proportion.

In preparing this section of the monograph, we were once again fortunate to have available some excellent reviews regarding the pharmacodynamics of ethanol. Of particular help to us were reviews by Lieber (1968), Wallgren (1970), Carter and Isselbacher (1971), Kalant (1971), Hawkins and Kalant (1972), and Myerson (1973).

Absorption[*]

Alcohol can be absorbed along the whole length of the gastrointestinal tract; it has been estimated that 20% of absorption occurs in the stomach

---

[*]Although alcohol can be absorbed through the lungs (by inhaling its vapors) and from other sites of administration, these sites are rarely involved in the abuse patterns of alcohol consumption and, hence, are not considered here.

and 80% in the intestines (Pawan, 1972; Linn and Kriesberg, 1973). Generally, absorption from the GI tract is so rapid that within 15 minutes after drinking alcohol over half the dose is absorbed. Although the absorption of alcohol from the human stomach is a passive process, it can be modified by several factors, including the concentration of ingested alcohol, the beverage being consumed, the amount of alcohol ingested, gastric emptying, and the simultaneous intake of food (Hogben et al., 1957; Davenport, 1967; and Cook and Birchall, 1969). Furthermore, the absorption of alcohol from the stomach can be influenced indirectly by high concentrations of alcohol which can induce spasm of the pylorus (Ritchie, 1970).

In contrast to its gastric absorption, alcohol absorption from the small intestine appears to be unrelated to the presence of food or to alcohol concentration (Ritchie, 1970). Gastric emptying time (and consequently the time to onset of a rapid intestinal absorption) is probably a prime factor contributing to the variable rates of absorption of ingested alcohol among individuals.

Despite the rapid and virtually complete absorption of alcohol from the upper GI tract, significant amounts of alcohol are found in the proximal jejunum and ileum after drinking alcohol. Studies by Halsted et al. (1973) suggested that the alcohol found in the lower tract resulted from its passage from the vascular space into the gut lumen, rather than from transit along the intestinal tract. In any case, sufficient amounts of alcohol are probably retained in both upper and lower intestine during frequent and prolonged drinking to contribute significantly to the intestinal dysfunction frequently occurring among alcoholics.

Distribution

After oral administration of alcohol in man, peak concentrations are obtained in blood generally within 1-3 hours. Normally, the concentrations of alcohol then begin to decline and the drug is cleared from the body within 8-12 hours after administration (Haggard et al., 1941).

Absorbed alcohol becomes distributed in the total body water and it gains ready access into brain tissue. The drug is found in similar concentrations in the water of blood, urine, saliva, and alveolar air. (Jacobsen, 1952; Dubowski, 1963; Ritchie, 1970; Pawan and Grice, 1968). In fact, alcohol has been used to measure the total body water in man (Pawan and Hoult, 1963; Pawan, 1965). In addition, its distribution properties have other utility. For example, the predicted ratio of the concentration of alcohol in blood versus vitreous humor would be 0.79 based upon the ratio of water content of the two fluids. Felby and Olsen (1969) reported that ratio to be 0.73 in human cadavers; the low value probably reflects some postmortem hemoconcentration. Such findings may be useful in forensic medicine when blood samples cannot be obtained from cadavers for analysis of alcohol content.

Alcohol can readily traverse the placental "barrier" (Idänpään-Heikkilä et al., 1971, 1972; Fritchie et al., 1972; Ho et al., 1972; Dilts, 1970; Waltman and Iniquez, 1972). Recently, Akesson (1974) studied the distribution of ^{14}C-ethanol and its radioactive metabolites in pregnant mice. One minute after intravenous injection of labeled alcohol, high concentrations of radioactivity were found in most maternal tissues, except in fat where the water content was low, and in the fetus where the placental barrier delayed the passage of alcohol for about 10 minutes. In maternal organs, high concentrations of metabolites of alcohol were found in liver, pancreas, heart, and bone marrow. This distribution may be clinically significant since all these organs may be functionally and/or biochemically affected by chronic alcohol consumption. For example, alcoholic myocardiopathy may be the result of disturbances of cardiac metabolism in alcoholics (such as decreases in uptake of free fatty acids and increases in uptake of triglycerides). In the fetus, high concentrations of radioactive metabolites were found in the liver and bones, the latter being especially interesting since skeletal defects have been reported to occur in malformed offspring among alcoholic women (Jones and Smith, 1973a,b).

Metabolism of Alcohol

General

Approximately 10% of a dose of ethanol is eliminated unchanged from the body via the urine, sweat, and expired air; the remainder is metabolized, principally in the liver (Thompson, 1956). The metabolism of ethanol results in its oxidation to acetaldehyde, acetate, and ultimately to CO_2 and H_2O via the Krebs cycle (Fig. 9). A large fraction of the carbon of ethanol becomes incorporated into hepatic lipids. Minute amounts of alcohol are also converted to the corresponding glucuronide and sulfate conjugates.

Several enzymatic systems can catalyze the oxidation of alcohol to acetaldehyde in the body. However, the proportionate contribution of any single enzyme system to the overall metabolism of alcohol is a subject of controversy and debate. At least three enzymatic systems appear to be capable of catalyzing the oxidation of ethanol to acetaldehyde: (1) a soluble, NAD-dependent alcohol dehydrogenase (ADH); (2) an NADPH-dependent microsomal ethanol-oxidizing system (MEOS); and (3) a peroxidative system involving catalase and H_2O_2. Recent papers by Lieber et al. (1975) and by Thurman et al. (1975) present extensive reviews of the various pathways proposed for ethanol oxidation by the liver.

Acetaldehyde, produced by the oxidation of alcohol, is further metabolized to acetate in the presence of an NAD-dependent mitochondrial

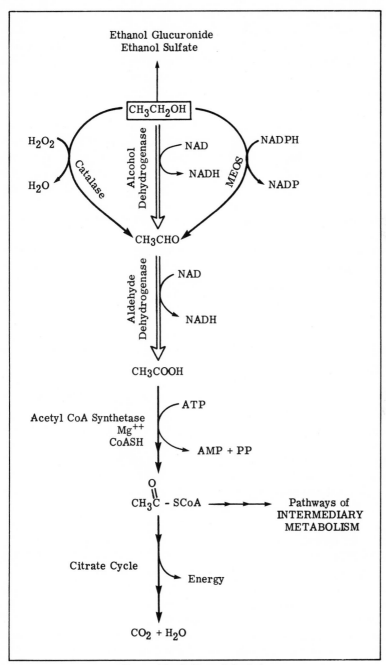

Fig. 9. Metabolism of alcohol.

enzyme, acetaldehyde dehydrogenase (AcDH). This enzyme is present in ox liver (Racker, 1949), human liver (Kraemer and Deitrich, 1968), rat kidney (Büttner, 1965), and bovine, rat, and monkey brain (Erwin and Deitrich, 1966). Acetaldehyde has been demonstrated in both the blood and alveolar air after alcohol consumption, but the concentrations in the body are generally quite low due to its rapid oxidation in the presence of AcDH (except after the administration of disulfiram which inhibits AcDH, apparently by competing with NAD for the active site(s) of that enzyme).

Few studies of acetaldehyde disposition have been conducted after the long-term administration of high doses of alcohol to alcoholics. Majchrowicz and Mendelson (1970) studied the blood concentrations of acetaldehyde and ethanol in chronic alcoholics before, during, and after a 10- to 15-day period of experimentally induced intoxication. Evidence was obtained to indicate that acetaldehyde can be readily eliminated even under these high-dose, prolonged treatment conditions.

Others have reported that acetaldehyde concentrations in the blood are higher in alcoholics compared to nonalcoholics (Korsten et al., 1974). Some of the discrepancies between studies probably reflects differences in study design (e.g., dose, frequency of administration) and differences in patient population (e.g., with respect to extent of liver damage).

Acetaldehyde, among other aldehydes, is postulated to be largely responsible for the so-called alcohol "hangover." Various studies indicate that acetaldehyde can contribute to other toxic effects accompanying alcohol intake. Although precise mechanisms are unknown, those under consideration invoke indirect and direct effects of acetaldehyde. Some indirect effects may be related to: (1) the NADH generated by the oxidation of acetaldehyde such that pathologic effects are mediated through an NAD/NADH imbalance; (2) increased release by acetaldehyde of catecholamines or other biogenic amines; and (3) coupling of acetaldehyde with endogenous amines, particularly dopamine (see Chapter 10).

It has been shown that acetaldehyde dehydrogenase activity in liver tissue can be stimulated in mice pretreated for several days with phenobarbital, but not in mice pretreated with alcohol (Redmond and Cohen, 1971). Theoretically, this stimulation could result in lower steady-state levels of the pharmacologically active acetaldehyde in alcoholics who might be using barbiturates regularly. Thus, it was proposed that lowered acetaldehyde levels could contribute to the cross tolerance that barbiturate users often exhibit toward alcohol.

In regard to the acetate formed from acetaldehyde oxidation, it too appears to be readily eliminated. For example, in organ slices from the rat, acetate was oxidized four times and six times more rapidly in the liver and kidney, respectively, than was ethanol (Von Wartburg and Eppenberger,

1961). Likewise, Freundt (1973), studying the pharmacokinetics of acetate and its elimination from the blood and cerebrospinal fluid of dogs and rabbits, provided evidence to suggest no rate-limiting significance attributable to acetate.

Alcohol Metabolism by Alcohol Dehydrogenase (ADH)

The enzyme ADH catalyzes the reaction:

$$CH_3CH_2OH + NAD^+ \longleftrightarrow CH_3CHO + NADH + H^+$$

Much of the earlier work showing that hepatic ADH is primarily responsible for the oxidation of the major portion of alcohol to acetaldehyde has been extended, reevaluated, and/or reviewed in recent years (Mannering *et al.*, 1963; Lieber and DeCarli, 1970a,b,c,; Kalant *et al.*, 1971; Videla *et al.*, 1973). ADH is a zinc-containing, NAD-dependent enzyme that exhibits optimal activity at pH 10.4. The existence of various forms of ADH was indicated when, in 1965, an atypical ADH was found in human liver. This variant exhibited a higher activity *in vitro* than did the normal enzyme (Von Wartburg *et al.*, 1965). Although the existence of a highly active form of ADH might have helped to explain the individual differences that occur in response to alcohol, subsequent studies revealed no significant differences in the rate of disappearance of alcohol from the blood of carriers of the normal versus the atypical enzyme (Von Wartburg and Papenberg, 1966; Edwards and Evans, 1967). At least seven isoenzymes of ADH have been reported to occur in human liver (Schenker and Von Wartburg, 1970). Moreover, a preliminary study by Hempel *et al.* (1975) indicates that in rats the ADH present in a carcinogen-induced hepatoma differs somewhat from the ADH found in normal liver tissue. For example, ethanol was a poor substrate for the hepatoma ADH ($K_m = 220$ mM) compared to the ADH found in normal liver tissue ($K_m = 0.3$ mM).

Human liver ADH exhibits substrate affinity not only toward ethanol but also toward methanol and ethylene glycol; these are clinically significant observations for the treatment of methanol and ethylene glycol poisoning. Ethanol can competitively inhibit the ADH-catalyzed oxidation of methanol to formaldehyde, and of ethylene glycol to glycol aldehyde. It is believed that these aldehyde intermediates are important in contributing to the toxic effects of these alcohols (Röe, 1955).

According to Krebs and Perkins (1970), appreciable quantities of ethanol are formed by bacteria in the gut. This alcohol is removed from the portal blood probably by the ADH system in liver tissue.

In recent years, the availability of sensitive and specific analytical techniques has made it possible to demonstrate the endogenous production of trace amounts of methanol in man (Eriksen and Kulkarni, 1963). It is conceivable, therefore, that the metabolism of *endogenous* methanol might be competitively inhibited by ethanol during chronic ethanol ingestion, with a resultant accumulation of methanol. In addition, the trace amounts of methanol present in many alcoholic beverages may accumulate during chronic ingestion of alcoholic beverages and contribute significantly to the toxic effects of the beverages. Majchrowicz and Mendelson (1971) studied the blood methanol levels in alcoholics consuming bourbon (which contained small amounts of methanol) or grain alcohol (which contained no methanol). Methanol was found to accumulate in the blood in *all* the subjects studied during chronic intake of either beverage and the blood levels of methanol were only slightly higher in bourbon drinkers compared to grain alcohol drinkers. These findings suggest that a major fraction of the accumulated methanol was derived from endogenous sources. It is not known if the methanol-forming enzyme system described by Axelrod and Daly (1965), which converts *S*-adenosylmethionine to methanol and *S*-adenosylhomocysteine, is capable of producing the quantities of methanol found in the blood in this methanol accumulation study. Regardless of the source of the methanol, the findings suggested that the methanol accumulated as a result of competitive inhibition of ADH by ethanol. The authors speculated that the degree of intoxication observed during chronic alcohol ingestion and/or the alcohol withdrawal syndrome could be related to the accumulation of methanol in blood.

In addition to its presence in liver tissue, ADH is also present in kidney, gastrointestinal mucosa, and lung tissue (Larsen, 1963). In recent years, ADH activity has also been reported to occur in rat brain (Raskin and Sokoloff, 1968, 1970). Thus, although it is generally agreed that the liver is the principal site of alcohol metabolism, extrahepatic tissues can also metabolize alcohol (Bartlett and Barnet, 1949; Larsen, 1959; Forsander *et al.*, 1960; Lieber, 1967). The extrahepatic metabolism of alcohol may be quite small, or at times it may represent as much as 20-25% of the.dose.

Compared to other molecular conversions discussed in this book, alcohol is metabolized via relatively simple pathways; however, the consequences of its metabolism are quite complex. Alcohol is quickly and almost completely oxidized to acetate which (via acetyl CoA) becomes involved in many basic metabolic processes essential to normal cell function. The radiocarbon of ethanol-^{14}C can be traced to a variety of metabolites of which acetyl CoA serves as a precursor (e.g., fatty acids and cholesterol). It is not surprising, therefore, that alcohol can exert far-reaching effects on the user of this drug. Moreover, the oxidation of alcohol by ADH results in the simultaneous generation of NADH from NAD. The reduced nucleotide may contribute significantly to some of the metabolic effects of ethanol, including alcoholic hypoglycemia, hyperuricemia, hypertriglyceridemia, and acidosis secondary to hyperlactacidemia.* The generation of NADH in liver can also interfere with the metabolism of other substances, such as galactose, norepinephrine, and serotonin.

The effect of alcohol metabolism on uric acid metabolism illustrates how the relatively simple biotransformation of alcohol can have profound consequences on intermediary metabolism. The increased generation of NADH accompanying ethanol oxidation can increase the conversion of pyruvate to lactate; lactate can then decrease the renal tubular transport of uric acid, resulting in hyperuricemia and a concomitant decrease in urinary excretion of uric acid. Thus, the metabolism of alcohol can contribute to the onset of a disorder often occurring among alcoholics, namely, gouty arthritis (Newcombe, 1972).

Recent statistics indicate that in urban areas of the United States, cirrhosis of the liver is a leading cause of death in young and middle-aged individuals, and that cirrhosis occurs in two-thirds of chronic alcoholics. While earlier studies tended to attribute much of the hepatotoxic effects of alcoholism to associated nutritional deficiencies, cirrhotic changes can also be attributed to direct effects of alcohol or its metabolites on the hepatocyte, as well as to alterations in intermediary metabolism produced by the oxidation of alcohol.

In general, a poor correlation exists between hepatic ADH activity *in vitro* and the rates of ethanol metabolism in a given species *in vivo* (Lieber, 1967). This is probably due to many factors, such as pH, blood flow, metabolism by other hepatic enzyme systems that can oxidize alcohol, and extrahepatic metabolism of alcohol. A prime factor is probably the variable rate of mitochondrial regeneration of NAD. There is evidence that the ADH reaction is the rate-limiting step in the overall metabolism of alcohol and that *in vivo* the rate of the ADH reaction is normally governed by the rate of re-oxidation of NADH (Theorell and Chance, 1951). Thus, although many studies indicate a faster metabolism of alcohol and a more rapid clearance from the body with chronic consumption, the precise mechanisms by which these changes occur are not known.

Modification of Alcohol Metabolism via the ADH Pathway

Some heterocyclic compounds, such as pyrazole, have been used as inhibitors of ADH, both *in vitro* and *in vivo*. Various studies wherein alcohol metabolism was inhibited by pyrazole and alcohol intoxication was intensified indicate that the intoxicating effects of alcohol are due to alcohol itself (Goldberg and Rydberg, 1969; Goldberg *et al.*, 1972; Blum *et al.*,

---

*The reader may wish to refer to several reviews for detailed discussions and excellent compilations of studies of the metabolic effects of alcohol consumption (Lieber, 1968; Kalant *et al.*, 1971; Newcombe, 1972).

1971; Rydberg and Neri, 1972; LeBlanc and Kalant, 1973). However, such studies must be interpreted cautiously because pyrazole can also act directly on the CNS to intensify alcohol effects.

The metabolic rate of alcohol in the body is approximately 100 mg/kg of body weight/hour; thus, the "average" individual can metabolize approximately two-thirds of a "shot" of 80 proof whiskey per hour. However, since ADH becomes saturated at blood concentrations of alcohol usually exceeding 16 mg%, the rate of metabolism of alcohol by ADH becomes constant beyond these levels and *theoretically* little can be done clinically to accelerate the rate of ethanol metabolism via this enzymatic mechanism.

Fructose has been reported by some workers to stimulate the rate of metabolism of alcohol in man and to hasten the return to sobriety (Patel *et al.*, 1969; Lowenstein *et al.*, 1970); others report that fructose produces a slight decrease in, or has no significant effects on alcohol metabolism, and that it produces no faster return to sobriety (Camps and Robinson, 1968; see also review by Lieber, 1968). In a review of ethanol disposition in man, Pawan (1972) described a series of studies of the effects of various factors on alcohol disposition in man. In his experience, physical exercise, vitamin supplements, caffeine, black coffee, marked dietary alterations, and starvation all failed to stimulate alcohol metabolism. The only factor that did stimulate alcohol metabolism (15-30%) was fructose.

Although triiodothyronine has also been reported to enhance the rate of disappearance of ethanol from the blood of alcoholics and to hasten the return to sobriety (Goldberg *et al.*, 1960); other studies have failed to show such effects (Kalant *et al.*, 1962; Rawat and Schambye, 1967).

There has been some question about the adaptability of the ADH system after chronic alcohol administration. Some reports show that alcohol can increase the activity of ADH; others report no such effect (Myerson, 1973; Hawkins and Kalant, 1972). More uniform are the results showing that upon prolonged alcohol intake, particularly of large doses, there is ultimately a *decrease* of ADH activity, probably coincident with the onset of a more generalized hepatic dysfunction. In man, short-term ethanol ingestion may increase the rate of ethanol metabolism (Mendelson *et al.*, 1965), but eventually as liver disease develops and progresses, alcohol oxidation decreases (Figueroa and Klotz, 1962; Pietz *et al.*, 1960). On the other hand, some workers have found no impairment of alcohol clearance in alcoholics with hepatic cirrhosis (Asada and Galambos, 1963; Lieberman, 1963). The matter of adaptation of the ADH system with chronic alcohol consumption remains unsettled; surely, some of the discrepancies between various studies relate to the degree to which liver disease has progressed, and to other aspects of experimental design (dose of ethanol, route and frequency of administration, duration of exposure, species, composition of the diet, etc.).

The Metabolism of Alcohol by Catalase

Keilin and Hartree (1936, 1945) first showed that catalase, in the presence of a hydrogen peroxide (H_2O_2) generating system, could catalyze the oxidation of ethanol via the following reaction:

$$CH_3CH_2OH + H_2O_2 \rightleftharpoons CH_3CHO + 2H_2O$$

Most studies show that this reaction can take place under appropriate conditions *in vitro*, but a significant role for this system in ethanol metabolism *in vivo* has not been consistently demonstrated. The H_2O_2 required in the catalase peroxidative system may be produced as the result of the action of certain microsomal enzymes (such as NADPH oxidase and cytochrome P-450). In their review of ethanol metabolism, Lieber and his associates (1975) were led to conclude that catalase was unlikely to contribute substantially to the ADH-independent oxidation of ethanol; Thurman *et al.* (1975) have presented an opposing view.

The reader is referred to the next section for a further discussion of catalase and alcohol metabolism. A peroxidative system involving catalase is so closely tied to a discussion of oxidation of alcohol by other liver microsomal enzymes that we felt it would be more meaningful to combine the review of the peroxidative and microsomal systems.

The Metabolism of Alcohol by the Microsomal Ethanol Oxidizing System (MEOS)

Lieber and DeCarli (1968a,b, 1969, 1970a,b) provided evidence for the presence in hepatic microsomes of an enzyme system that could catalyze the oxidation of alcohol according to:

$$CH_3CH_2OH + NADPH + H^+ + O_2 \xrightarrow{\hspace{1cm}} CH_3CHO + NADP^+ + 2H_2O$$
$$\text{MEOS}$$

This system appears to be similar in some respects to the mixed function oxidase system responsible for drug hydroxylations (the drug metabolizing enzyme system or DMES). For example, each system requires NADPH and oxygen, and is inhibited by carbon monoxide. Furthermore, alcohol can induce changes in the absorption spectra of microsomal hemoproteins similar to the changes induced by other drugs that undergo microsomal metabolism. Also, the activities of both the DMES and of the MEOS have been reported to be enhanced by chronic pretreatment with either phenobarbital or alcohol. Evidence has been obtained to indicate that alcohol can interfere with the metabolism of a variety of drugs *in vivo* and *in vitro* (Rubin *et al.*, 1970; Misra *et al.*, 1970). While this could mean that alcohol is metabolized by the same or similar enzyme systems in hepatic microsomes as those which metabolize various drugs, it is also possible, as suggested by the studies of Imai and Sato (1967), that nonspecific interactions can take place between alcohol and microsomal hemoproteins, resulting in conformational changes in the hemoproteins that impair their ability to catalyze drug hydroxylation reactions.

Studies Favoring a Role for a MEOS in Alcohol Oxidation

The MEOS activity has been distinguished from ADH by its localization in microsomes (rather than soluble fraction), by its pH optimum (7.2 versus 10.4 for ADH), and by its NADPH cofactor requirement (rather than NAD). Indeed, an impressive array of evidence has accumulated to suggest that the MEOS may play a significant role in alcohol metabolism, and that neither catalase nor ADH is an essential component of its activity. For example, various inhibitors, such as pyrazole, produce differential effects on catalase, ADH, and the MEOS (Lieber and DeCarli, 1969, 1970a,b,c; Lieber *et al.*, 1975). However, the differential effects of various inhibitors on the MEOS and catalase activities, under the conditions in which they are normally measured, do not necessarily prove that MEOS is distinct from a catalase system because MEOS activity was found to be indistinguishable, in both the presence and absence of inhibitors, from that of the catalase system functioning at a low rate of H_2O_2 generation (Lin *et al.*, 1972; Thurman *et al.*, 1972, 1975). Recent evidence supporting the view that the MEOS is distinctly separate from ADH or catalase activity comes from the studies of Mezey *et al.* (1972, 1973), who showed that a cytochrome P-450-rich component of the microsomes that was free of ADH and contained only minimal amounts of catalase was capable of catalyzing the oxidation of alcohol. The exact mechanism by which this cytochrome P-450-rich MEOS fraction catalyzes the oxidation of alcohol remains unknown, and its contribution to the overall metabolism of alcohol *in vivo* remains unsettled.

In rats fed for 24 days with diets containing ethanol, Lieber and DeCarli (1970a) found a higher rate of alcohol clearance from the blood together with a higher MEOS activity, compared to control rats fed isocaloric diets without alcohol. ADH and catalase activities were unchanged by either diet. Moreover, the more rapid clearance of alcohol *in vivo* was found even when the rats were treated with the ADH inhibitor, pyrazole.

Roach and Creaven (1969) studied the disappearance of alcohol from blood after acute i.v. administration of various doses of alcohol to mice. Their kinetic data suggested that at high concentrations of alcohol (i.e., when sufficient alcohol was present to saturate the ADH system) another pathway emerged for the metabolic elimination of alcohol. Preliminary results indicated that the MEOS was such a pathway. Thus, in cases of chronic intake of high doses of alcohol, changes could occur in alcohol metabolism such that MEOS could assume a significant role in the metabolism of alcohol.

Studies Opposing a Role for MEOS in Alcohol Oxidation

It has been estimated that 70-80% of absorbed alcohol is metabolized by ADH, the remaining 20-30% being metabolized by the MEOS. But these estimates of the involvement of the MEOS have not been universally accepted by all researchers in this field. In fact, over the years, quite different interpretations of the data regarding the importance and significance of the MEOS have been published (see review by Thurman *et al.*, 1975). Lieber and DeCarli (1970a) suggested that there might be insufficient amounts of ADH under usual circumstances to account for the metabolism of alcohol *in vivo*. On the other hand, Papenberg *et al.* (1970) concluded from their studies (*in vitro* and using the isolated perfused rat liver) that ADH activity was sufficient to account for the expected oxidation of alcohol seen in the whole animal. In addition, Hawkins and Kalant (1972), in their review of the role of the MEOS *in vivo*, concluded that most evidence failed to indicate a significant role for the MEOS in alcohol metabolism after either acute or chronic administration of alcohol. Tephly and his associates (1969) studied the oxidation of alcohol in rat, particularly with respect to the significance of the MEOS *in vivo*. They observed that treating rats for 3 days with phenobarbital, the microsomal enzyme inducer, had no effect on the metabolism of ethanol-1-^{14}C to ^{14}CO$_2$ *in vivo*. In contrast, phenobarbital stimulated the DMES activity threefold. Likewise, administration of the microsomal enzyme inhibitor SKF-525A did not affect the oxidation *in vivo* of ethanol-1-^{14}C, although it did inhibit the DMES. One might have predicted that if a microsomal mixed function oxidase system were operative in metabolizing alcohol *in vivo*, it would have been inhibited by SK&F-525A and stimulated by phenobarbital. Based on the lack of effects of these agents, it was concluded that the MEOS did not appear to play a significant role in alcohol oxidation *in vivo*. Similar findings have been reported by other investigators (Khanna and Kalant, 1970; Klaassen, 1970; Mezey, 1971; Khanna *et al.*, 1971, 1972). Furthermore, administration of CCl$_4$ to rats, at a dose that drastically reduced the MEOS activity, had no effect on: (a) ADH activity; (b) metabolism of ethanol by liver slices; or (c) disappearance of ethanol from the blood or the whole body.

Cytochrome P-450 has been shown to exhibit significant peroxidative activity (Hrycay and O'Brien, 1971), and it is conceivable that the cytochrome P-450-rich fraction that promoted the oxidation of ethanol (Mezey *et al.*, 1972, 1973) did so simply via a peroxidative mechanism. In this connection, substitution of an NADPH-generating system of the MEOS by a H$_2$O$_2$-generating system resulted in comparable oxidation of ethanol by the microsomes (Roach et al., 1969; Isselbacher and Carter, 1970). In fact, the Michaelis constants for ethanol oxidation with either the NADPH- or H_2O_2-generating system were reported to be the same.

Vatsis and Schulman (1973), from their studies of a strain of mouse having a uniquely labile catalase, concluded that alcohol oxidation was not related to a separate MEOS, but rather was due to contaminating amounts of catalase in microsomal preparations. They also noted that investigators frequently have been unable to demonstrate alcohol oxidation in microsomes devoid of catalase activity. On the other hand, substantial oxidation of alcohol has been reported to occur in liver microsomal preparations containing little or no catalase or ADH activity (Teschke et al., 1972, 1973, 1975; Mezey et al., 1972, 1973). The question has been raised of whether the sensitivity of the catalase assay was high enough in certain laboratories, or whether catalase had, in fact, been eliminated from the experimental preparations used (Thurman et al., 1975).

In a recent preliminary report, induction of MEOS activity after chronic ethanol administration to rats was not attributed to an adaptive increase in a catalase-H_2O_2 system (Teschke et al., 1975). When rats were pair fed with nutritionally adequate liquid diets containing ethanol or isocaloric dextrinmaltose, ethanol significantly increased MEOS activity with either ethanol or butanol as substrates, even after removal of catalase by chromatography. This finding is of particular significance because butanol is not readily metabolized by the catalase system so, evidently, the catalase had indeed been removed in the chromatography step. The MEOS stimulation was associated with an increased activity of NADPH-cytochrome c reductase, cytochrome P-450, NADH-cytochrome b_5 reductase, and cytochrome b_5 (each reported to be a component of the microsomal electron transport chain). Hasumura et al. (1975) likewise reported that the oxidation of ethanol to acetaldehyde by rat liver microsomes was not directly correlated to changes in activity of the NADPH oxidase/catalase/H_2O_2 system caused by different treatments, but did seem to be at least partially related to changes in activity of form I of cytochrome P-450 (the form of the hemoprotein having the highest affinity to cyanide).

Similarities between MEOS and DMES

As already mentioned, the MEOS is similar in many respects to the hepatic microsomal drug-metabolizing enzyme system (DMES). These observations might explain, at least in part, certain clinical phenomena: (a) the increased susceptibility of intoxicated individuals to the sedative effect of certain CNS depressants; (b) the oft-observed tolerance of nondrinking alcoholics to effects of other drugs such as barbiturates and tranquilizers. It is known that one drug can mutually inhibit the metabolism of another when each is metabolized by enzyme systems that share common intermediates (Rubin et al., 1964a,b). In the presence of high levels of alcohol, the MEOS could become saturated; addition into this system of drugs (such as barbiturates) that were metabolized by an enzyme system (DMES) that shared common intermediates could delay their metabolism and prolong their effects. In this connection, studies in rat show that an acute dose of alcohol can inhibit hydroxylation of barbiturates in vivo (Coldwell et al., 1973). Similarly, in man the clearance of pentobarbital and meprobamate from the blood can be slowed in the presence of alcohol (Rubin et al., 1970). Ethanol has been shown to inhibit the metabolism of a variety of drugs (Rubin and Lieber, 1968; Rubin et al., 1970; Ariyoshi et al., 1970). Such metabolic interactions do not, of course, preclude CNS interactions, wherein one drug modulates receptor expression for the other drug. In fact, this is probably the predominant basis for synergism between alcohol and barbiturates when both are consumed simultaneously.

It has been observed that nonintoxicated alcoholics often become cross tolerant to the effects of many other drugs. Alcohol has been shown to interact with the hepatic endoplasmic reticulum, stimulating the activity of NADPH-dependent enzyme systems therein. These systems are capable of catalyzing not only the oxidation of alcohol (via the MEOS) but the oxidation of a variety of chemically and pharmacologically unrelated drugs (via the DMES). The net result of the latter (DMES) stimulation would be a decrease in responsiveness to effects of those drugs which were metabolically inactivated (Rubin and Lieber, 1968, 1971). In a series of studies by Kater et al. (1968a,b; 1969a,b,c), the rate of metabolism of alcohol was shown to be more than twice as rapid in alcoholic patients who had recently been drinking as compared to abstinent control subjects. They administered three drugs (tolbutamide, warfarin, and diphenylhydantoin), each known to be metabolized by hepatic microsomal enzymes, to a group of alcoholics with prolonged and heavy intake of alcohol and to a group of abstinent controls. The half-life of each drug in the blood of the alcoholic subjects was significantly shorter than in the abstinent controls. Kater and his associates postulated that the accelerated drug disappearance caused by alcohol may be clinically significant. Thus, a diabetic patient whose blood sugar is controlled by tolbutamide therapy might be more difficult to treat if he were to consume alcohol regularly. Likewise, an epileptic, well controlled on diphenylhydantoin therapy, might experience seizures if he were to ingest alcohol regularly.

Klaassen (1969) observed that administration of phenobarbital, chlordane, and 3-methylcholanthrene to rats induced DMES and increased the clearance of alcohol from blood. These findings support the view that microsomal enzyme systems are important in the elimination of alcohol and that these systems bear some resemblances to the DMES. But conflicting results continue to appear in the literature. Mezey and Tobon (1971) and Kostelnik and Iber (1973) reported poor correlation between ethanol clearance from blood and MEOS activity after withdrawal of alcohol from alcoholics. Also, Kalant et al. (1970) reported that chronic administration of alcohol failed to affect the metabolism of pentobarbital in vivo or in vitro via the DMES.

The effect of phenobarbital administration on the rate of ethanol disappearance from blood and on the activities of the ethanol-oxidizing systems was studied in chronic alcoholic patients by Mezey and Robles (1973). The mean rate of ethanol disappearance from blood increased significantly from 15.7 to 20.1 mg/100/ ml/hour after phenobarbital administration. This increase in the rate of alcohol disappearance was not accompanied by any significant stimulation of the activities of either ADH or the MEOS (confirmed by liver biopsy specimens).

Further evidence against a similarity between MEOS and DMES comes from studies wherein microsomes were "solubilized" and reconstituted under conditions which retained their DMES activity but which lost the MEOS activity (Vatsis and Schulman, 1973). Furthermore, although alcohol is reported to bind to hepatic microsomal hemoproteins as do drug substrates, the spectral changes produced by alcohol binding suggest that alcohol is bound to the lipophilic membrane near the hemoprotein cytochrome P-450, rather than to the hemoprotein itself as is observed with certain drug substrates (Imai and Sato, 1967).

Studies of morphologic changes in the smooth endoplasmic reticulum (SER) of liver produced after alcohol treatment do not seem to be any less conflicting than other studies concerning alcohol metabolism. Chronic alcohol consumption has been associated with proliferation of the hepatic smooth endoplasmic reticulum (SER). It was suggested that this proliferation and the increased activity of the MEOS and DMES might be related to metabolic tolerance to alcohol, as well as to cross tolerance between alcohol and other drugs (Rubin et al., 1968; Misra et al., 1970). However, Porta et al. (1969, 1970) noted SER proliferation only after 2 weeks of ethanol feeding, but not after 4 and 16 weeks of treatment, times when ethanol tolerance was still present, of course. Perhaps more important was their observation that SER proliferation occurred even when the ethanol in the diet was replaced by isocaloric amounts of fat.

Ishii et al. (1973) studied biochemical changes in SER membranes before and after administration of alcohol. They observed an increased cytochrome P-450 content and an enhanced activity of the MEOS in microsomes derived from the SER after alcohol treatment, but catalase activity was not increased.

This matter of similarity and dissimilarity between the MEOS and DMES systems appears to be somewhat critical to an understanding of interactions between alcohol and other drugs. From the foregoing, it should be distressingly clear that the effects of alcohol on the hepatic microsomes are complex and poorly understood. Perhaps this is no better emphasized than by a study by Ariyoshi and Takabatake (1970) wherein not only did alcohol intake by rats stimulate the DMES activity, as reflected by increased V_{max} values, but also altered the K_m value for certain of these enzyme systems. The authors proposed that ethanol caused both qualitative and quantitative changes in the SER which secondarily changed DMES activities.

Excretion of Alcohol

Alcohol is eliminated slowly from the body, compared to its rapid rate of absorption from the GI tract. Therefore, drug accumulation and resultant inebriation can occur after relatively short periods of only moderate consumption of alcoholic beverages.

Up to 95% of a low dose of ethanol is oxidized in the body to CO_2 which is then eliminated via the expired air. Lesser amounts of alcohol (about 2%) are eliminated unchanged via this route. After *excessive* consumption of alcohol, the amount that is eliminated unchanged in the breath can approach 10% of the dose.

In man, an additional portion of alcohol (up to 5-10% depending upon the dose) may be excreted unchanged in urine. In some species, the glucuronide or sulfate conjugate of alcohol may be excreted. Indeed, some alcohol has also been shown to be eliminated in sweat, tears, bile, and saliva. These are not surprising observations since, as described above, the drug tends to "follow" the total body water.

It is well known that, in general, a certain range of blood concentrations of alcohol will normally be associated with a certain level of inebriation. For medico-legal purposes, it is often important to determine the degree to which an individual is intoxicated with alcohol and, for that purpose, blood concentrations of drug can be measured directly. However, it is easier to measure urinary concentrations of alcohol and, from those values, to infer blood concentrations based upon the knowledge that the urine concentrations are normally about 1.3 times those in blood. It is even easier to determine the concentration of alcohol in the expired breath and to estimate the blood concentration based upon information that, in general, it is normally about 2000 times greater than the breath concentration.

Of course, such assessments make some assumptions that may not always be valid. For example, we have already alluded to studies wherein it was established that chronic drinkers may develop tolerance to the CNS-depressant effects of alcohol so that, at a given blood level, a heavy user may not be as intoxicated as the intermittent "social drinker." Also, if alcohol were consumed shortly before a breath test for alcohol were started, the results of that test may be erroneously high simply due to the residual alcohol remaining in the mouth, stomach, and pulmonary tract.

Alcohol Tolerance*

The absorption, distribution, and excretion of alcohol do not appear grossly or consistently different between tolerant and nontolerant animals. In contrast, many studies show that the rate of alcohol *metabolism* increases upon chronic dosing, by mechanisms that are not resolved. It was recently reported that in rats treated chronically with alcohol an enhanced rate of metabolism of alcohol occurred *in vivo* and *in vitro* (Israel *et al.*, 1975). The stimulated metabolism was attributed to an increased activity of liver (Na^+ and K^+)-ATPase, which in turn, increased the utilization of ATP and thus enhanced the rate of mitochondrial reoxidation of reducing equivalents.

It has been reported that alcohol disappears from the blood of drinkers faster than from the blood of nondrinkers (Kater *et al.*, 1969a,b,c,; Conney, 1967; Lieber and DeCarli, 1968b; Rubin *et al.*, 1968). When alcoholics abstain for a few weeks, the rate of disappearance of alcohol returns toward that observed in nondrinking controls. Shah and associates (1972) found no correlation between ADH activity and the rate of ethanol disappearance from blood. Based upon studies involving human liver biopsy specimens, they postulated that, in general, the activities of the microsomal enzymes increased with prolonged drinking and that this increased activity would gradually disappear with abstinence. They further postulated that alcohol, at *modest* levels of consumption, binds to ADH such that sufficient amounts of free alcohol are not present to stimulate the microsomal enzyme systems. However, with chronic consumption of high doses of alcohol, ADH binding sites could become saturated, and abundant amounts of unbound alcohol could then become available to stimulate the microsomal systems (viz., DMES and MEOS). Accordingly, the rate of whole body ethanol metabolism among heavy drinkers would be a function of *both* ADH and MEOS activities, and would depend upon the availability of cofactors for these systems. Thus, it would be surprising to find a positive correlation between ADH levels (or any *one* of these factors for that matter)

---

*For the sake of completeness, some material in Chapter 10 on tolerance is repeated here in condensed form. For a more complete discussion, the reader is referred to Chapter 10.

and alcohol metabolism rates *in vivo*. In fact, in their studies of alcoholics, the rate of disappearance of alcohol from blood decreased during 10 weeks of abstinence, but liver ADH *increased* over this same time period.

Although the activities of the hepatic ADH, AcDH and peroxidative enzyme systems in man and experimental animals have at various times been reported to be increased with chronic ethanol administration, tolerance to alcohol is not *always* accompanied by increased activities of these enzymatic systems (Lieber and DeCarli, 1970a,b; Tobon and Mezey, 1971; Videla *et al.*, 1973). Changes in microsomal enzyme activity have been invoked to explain tolerance to alcohol and cross tolerance between alcohol and some other drugs (Lieber *et al.*, 1975). It appears that tolerance to alcohol sometimes may be due to an accelerated metabolism of the drug as well as to desensitization of receptor processes within the CNS.

In general, alcohol metabolism in brain tissue has not been considered to be particularly important. In 1968, Raskin and Sokoloff demonstrated ADH-like activity in brain tissue. Although no concrete evidence is available to indicate a significant role for this enzyme with respect to the central effects of alcohol, its activity has been shown to increase adaptively during chronic alcohol ingestion (Raskin and Sokoloff, 1970). Indeed, the onset and magnitude of this increase were reportedly similar to the acquisition and extent of behavioral tolerance to ethanol observed in rats (LeBlanc *et al.*, 1969).

At the present time, it seems generally fashionable to implicate changes in brain monoamines as a neurochemical basis for drug tolerance and dependence. Few attempts have been made to relate tolerance to and dependence on ethanol with direct measurements of central monoamine metabolism. Experiments of Griffiths *et al.* (1973), measuring brain biogenic amines before and after alcohol withdrawal, suggested an involvement of brain monoamines in alcohol dependence and withdrawal.

Dopamine and its corresponding aldehyde can condense in the body to form small amounts of an alkaloid tetrahydropapaveroline (THP). Interestingly, this compound is an essential intermediate in the biosynthesis of the opiate alkaloids in the opium poppy. Based upon the structural resemblance between morphine and THP, and the concept that alcohol intake may stimulate THP formation, Davis *et al.* (1970a,b,c) proposed that tolerance and dependence to alcohol and morphine might be related. In fact, they reported that cross tolerance not only could develop between morphine and alcohol, but also that THP could be metabolized to opium alkaloids in rats. Moreover, *in vitro*, alcohol could augment the formation of alkaloids from dopamine. Despite the criticisms of this hypothetical association between opiate and alcohol dependency (Seevers, 1970; Goldstein and Judson, 1971), a recent preliminary study in rats indicates that a biochemical event (the alteration of cerebral calcium) may underlie certain actions of both the opiates and alcohol (Ross and Cardenas, 1975). Reviews of this area of research have been provided by Caldwell and Sever (1974) and by Rahwan (1974).

Conclusions

Liver ADH normally plays a major role in the metabolism of alcohol *in vivo;* that fact should not be overshadowed simply because of the multitude of recent reports about non ADH-related pathways. It is interesting that the mechanisms involved in the non ADH-related biotransformation of alcohol are still subjects of controversy and equivocation, despite the simple chemical structure of the compound and its seemingly simple oxidative bioconversion. That ethanol may be metabolized by a microsomal sub-fraction of the liver cell is widely accepted. Whether the mechanism of that biotransformation depends upon a unique MEOS or a catalase/H_2O_2/NADPH oxidase system in the microsomes is unresolved. Equally disputed is the significance of a role for microsomal oxidation in the *in vivo* metabolism of alcohol, especially in individuals who use alcohol chronically, either alone or combined with other drugs. The complexity of these issues is evident from two recent publications that, in essence, present opposing views of the role of MEOS and catalase in ethanol metabolism (Lieber *et al.*, 1975; Thurman *et al.*, 1975).

Several dispositional factors contribute significantly to the variable responses produced in man by alcohol. Although alcohol can be absorbed from the GI tract quickly and extensively, its rate of absorption can be highly variable depending on such factors as the volume and nature of the beverage consumed, the presence or absence of food in the gut, and gastric emptying. In addition, because alcohol is so extensively metabolized, variations in individual rates of metabolism can contribute substantially to variations in drug effects among individuals, and in the same individuals exposed to alcohol at different times.

Caffeine References

Axelrod, J. and Reichenthal, J.: The fate of caffeine in man and a method for its estimation in biological material. J. Pharmacol. Exp. Ther. *107*:519-523, 1953.
Bertoli, M.A., Dragoni, G., and Rodari, A.: Tissue distribution of labeled caffeine in mice. Med. Nucl. Radiobiol. Lat. *11*:231, 1968.

Brodie, B.B., Axelrod, J., and Reichenthal, J.: Metabolism of theophylline in man. J. Biol. Chem. *194*:215-222, 1952.

Burg, A.W. and Stein, M.E.: Urinary excretion of caffeine and its metabolites in the mouse. Biochem. Pharmacol. *21*:909-922, 1972.

Burg, A.W. and Werner, E.: Tissue distribution of caffeine and its metabolites in the mouse. Biochem. Pharmacol. *21*:923-936, 1972.

Chvasta, T.E. and Cooke, A.R.: Emptying and absorption of caffeine from the human stomach. Gastroenterology *61*:838-843, 1971.

Colton, T., Gosslin, R.E., and Smith, R.P.: The tolerance of coffee drinkers to caffeine. Clin. Pharmacol. Ther. *9*:31-39, 1968.

Cornish, H.H. and Christman, A.A.: A study of the metabolism of theobromine, theophylline and caffeine in man. J. Biol. Chem. *228*:315-323, 1957.

Cornish, H.H., Wilson, C.E., and Abar, E.L.: Effect of foreign compounds on liver microsomal enzymes. Amer. Indust. Hyg. Ass. J. *31*:605-608, 1970.

Dreisbach, R.H. and Pfeiffer, C.C.: Caffeine withdrawal headache. J. Lab. Clin. Med. *28*:1212-1218, 1943.

Eddy, N.B. and Down, A.W.: Tolerance and cross-tolerance in the human subject to the diuretic effect of caffeine, theobromine and theophylline. J. Pharmacol. Exp. Ther. *33*:167-174, 1929.

Fabro, S. and Sieber, S.M.: Caffeine and nicotine penetrate the preimplantation blastocyst. Nature (London). *223*:410-411, 1969.

Goldstein, A.: Wakefulness caused by caffeine. Arch. Exp. Pathol. Pharmakol. *248*:269-278, 1964.

Goldstein, A. and Kaizer, S.: Psychotropic effects of caffeine in man. III. A questionnaire survey of coffee drinking and its effect in a group of housewives. Clin. Pharmacol. Ther. *10*:477-488, 1969.

Goldstein, A. and Warren, R.: Passage of caffeine into human gonadal and fetal tissue. Biochem. Pharmacol. *11*:166-167, 1962.

Goldstein, A., Warren, R., and Kaizer, S.: Psychotropic effects of caffeine in man. I. Individual differences in sensitivity to caffeine-induced wakefulness. J. Pharmacol. Exp. Ther. *149*:156-159, 1965a.

Goldstein, A., Kaizer, S., and Warren, R.: Psychotropic effects of caffeine in man. II. Alertness, psychomotor coordination and mood. J. Pharmacol. Exp. Ther. *150*:146-151, 1965b.

Goldstein, A., Kaizer, S., and Whitby, O.: Psychotropic effects of caffeine in man. IV. Quantitative and qualitative differences associated with habituation to coffee. Clin. Pharmacol. Ther. *10*:489-497, 1969.

Herz, A., Neteler, B., and Teschemacher, H.J.: Vergleichende Untersuchungen über zentrale Wirkungen von Xanthindervaten in Hinblick auf deren Stoffenechsel und Verteilung im Organismus. Arch. Pharmakol. Exp. Pathol. *261*:486-502, 1968.

Hess, R., Teschemacher, H.J., and Herz, A.: Über die Permeation von Xanthinderivaten in Gehirn und Liquor in Abhängigkeit von Lipoidlöslichkeit, Gewebsbindung und Stoffwechsel. Arch. Pharmacol. Exp. Pathol. *261*:469-485, 1968.

Hogben, C.A.M., Tucco, D.J., Brodie, B.B., and Schanker, L.S.: On the mechanism of intestinal absorption of drugs. J. Pharmacol. Exp. Ther. *125*:275-282, 1958.

Khanna, K.L. and Cornish, H.H.: The effect of daily ingestion of caffeine on the microsomal enzymes of rat liver. Fd. Cosmet. Toxicol. *11*:11-17, 1973.

Khanna, K.L., Rao, G.S., and Cornish, H.H.: Metabolism of caffeine-^{3}H in the rat. Toxicol. Appl. Pharmacol. *23*:720-730, 1972.

Lombrozo, L. and Mitoma, C.: Effect of caffeine on hepatic microsomal cytochrome P-450. Biochem. Pharmacol. *19*:2317-2323, 1970.

Marks, V. and Kelly, J.F.: Absorption of caffeine from tea, coffee and Coca Cola. Lancet 1:827, 1973.

Mazel, P. and Henderson, J.F.: On the relationship between lipid solubility and microsomal metabolism of drugs. Biochem. Pharmacol. 14:92-94, 1965.

Mitoma, C., Sovich, T.J., and Neubauer, S.E.: The effect of caffeine on drug metabolism. Life Sci. 7:145-151, 1968.

Mitoma, C., Lombrozo, L., LeValley, S.E., and Dehn, F.: Nature of the effect of caffeine on the drug-metabolizing enzymes. Arch. Biochem. Biophys. 134:434-441, 1969.

Parke, D.V.: The Biochemistry of Foreign Compounds. London, Pergamon Press Ltd., 1968, p. 152.

Rao, G.S., Khanna, K.L., and Cornish, H.H.: Identification of two new metabolites of caffeine in the rat urine. Experientia 29:953-955, 1973.

Schanker, L.S., Shore, P.A., Brodie, B.B., and Hogben, C.A.M.: Absorption of drugs from the stomach. I. The rat. J. Pharmacol. Exp. Ther. 120:528-539, 1957.

Sieber, S.M. and Fabro, F.: Identification of drugs in the preimplantation blastocyst and in the plasma, uterine secretion and urine of the pregnant rabbit. J. Pharmacol. Exp. Ther. 176:65-75, 1971.

Strongin, E.I.: A study of the development of tolerance for caffeinated beverages. J. Exp. Physiol. 16:725-744, 1933.

Warren, R.N.: Metabolism of xanthine alkaloids in man. J. Chromatog. 40:468-469, 1969.

Weiss, B. and Laties, V.G.: Enhancement of human performance by caffeine and the amphetamines. Pharmacol. Rev. 14:1-36, 1962.

Weissman, B., Bromberg, P.A., and Gutman, A.B.: Chromatographic investigation of purines in normal human urine. Proc. Soc. Exp. Biol. Med. 87:257-260, 1954.

Nicotine References

Adams, C.E., Hay, M.F., and Lutwak-Mann, C.: The action of various agents upon the rabbit embryo. J. Embryol. Exp. Morphol. 9:468-491, 1961.

Alderdice, M.T. and Weiss, G.B.: On C-14 nicotine distribution and movements in slices from monkey cerebral cortex. Arch. Int. Pharmacodyn. 209 (1):162-171, 1974.

Appelgren, L.E., Hansson, E., and Schmiterlöw, C.G.: The accumulation and metabolism of ^{14}C labelled nicotine in the brain of mice and cats. Acta. Physiol. Scand. 56:249-257, 1962.

Appelgren, L.E., Hansson, E., and Schmiterlöw, C.G.: Localization of radioactivity in the superior cervical ganglion of cats following injection of ^{14}C-labelled nicotine. Acta. Physiol. Scand. 59:330-336, 1963.

Armitage, A.K. and Hall, H.G.: The effects of nicotine on the electrocorticogram and spontaneous release of acetylcholine from the cerebral cortex of the cat. J. Physiol. (London) 191:115-116, 1967.

Armitage, A.K. and Turner, D.M.: Absorption of nicotine in cigarette and cigar smoke through the oral mucosa. Nature (London) 226:1231-1232, 1970.

Armitage, A.K., Hall, G.H., and Morrison, C.F.: Pharmacological basis for the tobacco smoking habit. Nature (London) 217:331-334, 1968.

Armitage, A.K., Dollery, C.T., George, C.F., Houseman, T.H., Lewis, P.J., and Turner, D.M.: Absorption and metabolism of nicotine by man during cigarette smoking. Brit. J. Clin. Pharmacol. 1:180P-181P, 1974.

Axelrod, J.: The enzymatic N-methylation of serotonin and other amines. J. Pharmacol. 138:28-33, 1962.

Beckett, A.H. and Triggs, E.J.: Enzyme induction in man caused by smoking. Nature (London) *216*:587, 1967.

Beckett, A.H., Gorrod, J.W., and Jenner, P.: Absorption of (-)-nicotine-1'-N-oxide in man and its reduction in the gastrointestinal tract. J. Pharm. Pharmacol. *22*:722-723, 1970.

Beckett, A.H., Gorrod, J.W., and Jenner, P.: The analysis of nicotine-1'-N-oxide in urine, in the presence of nicotine and cotinine, and its application to the study of *in vivo* nicotine metabolism in man. J. Pharm. Pharmacol. *23*:55S-61S, 1971a.

Beckett, A.H., Gorrod, J.W., and Jenner, P.: The effect of smoking on nicotine metabolism *in vivo* in man. J. Pharm. Pharmacol. *23*:62S-67S, 1971b.

Beckett, A.H., Gorrod, J.W., and Jenner, P.: A possible relation between pKa_1 and lipid solubility and the amounts excreted in urine of some tobacco alkaloids given to man. J. Pharm. Pharmacol. *24*:115-120, 1972.

Bevan, J.A. and Su, C.: Uptake of nicotine by the sympathetic nerve terminals in the blood vessel. J. Pharmacol. Exp. Ther. *182*:419-426, 1972.

Bhagat, B.: Influence of various drugs on accumulation of ^{3}H-nicotine in isolated rat atria. Eur. J. Pharmacol. *10*:11-18, 1970.

Bhagat, B., Kramer, S.Z., and Seifter, J.: The effects of nicotine and other drugs on the release of injected ^{3}H-norepinephrine and on endogenous norepinephrine levels in the rat brain. Eur. J. Pharmacol. *2*:234-235, 1967.

Biebl, M., Essex, H.E., and Mann, F.C.: The role of the liver in the destruction or inactivation of nicotine. Amer. J. Physiol. *100*:167-172, 1932.

Biederbeck, J.: Neue Untersuchungen uber die Absorption von Nikotin und Ammoniak aus Luftmischungen und dem Zigarettenrauch. Inaugural Dissertation Wurzburg, F. Staudenraus, 1908, 24 pp.

Bisdom, C.J.W.: Alcohol—en nicotine—vergiftiging bij zuigelingen. Mschr. Kindergeneesk *6*:332-341, 1937.

Bizard, G., Vanlerenberghe, J., and Lespagnol, C.: Activite comparee de la nicotine et de son N-oxyde. Therapie *11*:1109-1113, 1956.

Bodnar, J., Nagy, V.L., and Dickmann, A.: Uber die Nicotinaufnahme des Organismus bein Rauchen und das Schicksal des aufgenommenen Nicotins. Biochem. Z. *276*:317-322, 1935.

Booth, J. and Boyland, E.: The metabolism of nicotine into two optically-active stereoisomers of nicotine-1'-oxide by animal tissues *in vitro* and by cigarette smokers. Biochem. Pharmacol. *19*:733-742, 1970.

Booth, J. and Boyland, E.: Enzymic oxidation of (-)-nicotine by guinea-pig tissues *in vitro*. Biochem. Pharmacol. *20*:407-415, 1971.

Borzelleca, J.F.: Die Resorption von Nicotin aus der Harnblase des Hundes. Arch. Int. Pharmacodyn. *133*:444-451, 1961.

Bowman, E.R., Turnbull, L.B., and McKennis, H., Jr.: Oxidation of cotinine *in vivo*. Fed. Proc. *18*:371, 1959a.

Bowman, E.R., Turnbull, L.B., and McKennis, H., Jr.: Metabolism of nicotine in the human and excretion of pyridine compounds by smokers. J. Pharmacol. Exp. Ther. *127*:92-95, 1959b.

Bowman, E.R., Hansson, E., Turnbull, L.B., McKennis, H., Jr., and Schmiterlöw, C.G.: Disposition and fate of (-)-cotinine-^{3}H in the mouse. J. Pharmacol. Exp. Ther. *143*:301-308, 1964.

Brown, D.A. and Halliwell, J.V.: Intracellular pH in rat isolated superior cervical ganglia in relation to nicotine-depolarization and nicotine-uptake. Brit. J. Pharmacol. *45*:349-359, 1972.

Brown, D.A., Hoffmann, P.C., and Roth, L.J.: ³H-nicotine in cat superior cervical and nodose ganglia after close-atrial injection *in vivo*. Brit. J. Pharmacol. *35*:406-417, 1969a.

Brown, D.A., Halliwell, J.V., and Scholfield, C.N.: Nicotine uptake by isolated rat ganglia. Brit. J. Pharmacol. *37*:510-511, 1969b.

Brown, D.A., Halliwell, J.V., and Scholfield, C.N.: Uptake of nicotine and extracellular space indicators by isolated rat ganglia in relation to receptor activation. Brit. J. Pharmacol. *42*:100-113, 1971.

Burstein, A.I.: Adsorption von Nicotin durch die Formelemente des Blutes. Arbeitsphysiologie *6*:105-110, 1932.

Chang, M.C.: Effects of certain antifertility agents on the development of rabbit ova. Fert. Steril. *15*:97-106, 1964.

Clark, M.S.: Self administered nicotine solutions preferred to placebo by the rat. Brit. J. Pharmacol. *35*:367, 1969.

Clark, M.S.G. and Rand, M.J.: Effect of tobacco smoke on the knee-jerk reflex in man. Eur. J. Pharmacol. *3*:294-302, 1968.

Corcoran, A.C., Helmer, O.M., and Page, I.H.: The determination of nicotine in urine. J. Biol. Chem. *129*:89-97, 1939.

Dagne, E. and Castagnoli, N., Jr.: The structure of hydroxycotinine, a nicotine metabolite. Abstr. Papers, Amer. Chem. Soc. No. 162, Medi 58, 1971.

Dajani, R.M., Gorrod, J.W., and Beckett, A.H.: Hepatic and extrahepatic reduction of nicotine 1'-N-oxide in rats. Biochem. J. *130*:88, 1972.

De Clerq, M. and Truhaut, R.: Sur les mecanismus d'action de la nicotine. Effet de la nicotine et de ses metabolites sur la biosynthese du DPN. Bull. Soc. Chim. Biol. *44*:227-234, 1962.

Domino, E.F. and von Baumbargen, A.M.: Tobacco cigarette smoking and patellar reflex depression. Clin. Pharmacol. Ther. *10*:72-79,1969.

Eisinger, R.A.: Nicotine and addiction to cigarettes. Brit. J. Addict. *66*:150-156, 1971.

Fabro, S. and Sieber, S.M.: Caffeine and nicotine penetrate the pre-implantation blastocyst. Nature (London) *223*:410-411, 1969.

Finnegan, J.K., Larson, P.S., and Haag, H.B.: Studies on the fate of nicotine in the body. V. Observations on relation of nicotine dosage to per cent excreted in urine, rate of excretion and rate of detoxication. J. Pharmacol. Exp. Ther. *91*:357-361, 1947.

Frith, C.D.: Smoking behavior and its relation to the smoker's immediate experience. Brit. J. Soc. Clin. Psychol. *10*:73-78, 1971.

Gaede, D.: Uber die Nikotinaufnahme aus Kautaback. Arch. Exp. Pathol. *197*:72-77, 1941.

Ganz, A., Kelsey, F.E., and Geiling, E.M.K.: Excretion and tissue distribution studies on radioactive nicotine. J. Pharmacol. Exp. Ther. *103*:209-214, 1951.

Geiling, E.M.K.: Biosynthesis and pharmacology of radioactive digitalis and other medicinally important drugs. Med. Ann. District of Columbia *20*:197-201, 242, 1951.

Goldfarb, T.L., Jarwik, M.E., and Glick, S.D.: Cigarette nicotine content as a determinant of human smoking behavior. Psychopharmacologia *17*:89-93, 1970.

Goodman, F.R. and Weiss, G.B.: Effects of nicotine on uptake and metabolism of ions and serotonin in slices obtained from different brain areas. San Francisco, 1972, p. 85. Abstracts circulated at Fifth Int. Congr. Pharmacol., July 23-28, 1972.

Gorrod, J.W., Jenner, P., Keysell, G.R., and Mikhael, B.R.: Oxidative metabolism of nicotine by cigarette smokers with cancer of the urinary bladder. J. Nat. Cancer Inst. *52*:1421-1424, 1974.

Guidetti, E.: Comportamento della nicotina nel sangue. Minerva Med. *2*:302-306, 1937.

Haag, H.B. and Larson, P.S.: Studies on the fate of nicotine in the body. I. The effect of pH on the urinary excretion of nicotine by tobacco smokers. J. Pharmacol. Exp. Ther. 76:235-239, 1942.

Haag, H.B., Larson, P.S., and Finnegan, J.K.: Studies on factors influencing the toxicity of nicotine. The effects of water and food deprivation; disturbed liver function and rate of administration. J. Pharmacol. Exp. Ther. 85:356-362, 1945.

Hansson, E. and Schmiterlöw, C.G.: Physiological disposition and fate of C-14-labelled nicotine in mice and rats. J. Pharmacol. Exp. Ther. 137:91-102, 1962.

Hansson, E. and Schmiterlöw, C.G.: Metabolism of nicotine in various tissues in tobacco alkaloids and related compounds. Ed., U.S. Von Euler, Oxford, Pergamon Press, 1965, pp. 87-97.

Hansson, E., Hoffman, P.C., and Schmiterlöw, C.G.: Metabolism of nicotine in mouse tissue slices. Acta Physiol. Scand. 61:380-392, 1964.

Harke, V.H.P. and Fleischmann, B.: Untersuchungen uber die Ausscheidung von Nikotin und Cotinin beim Zigarettenraucher. Arzneimittel Forsch. 23:1822-1824, 1973. (English abstract).

Harke, H.-P., Schuller, D., Frahm, B., and Mauch, A.: Demethylation of nicotine and cotinine in pigs. Res. Commun. Chem. Pathol. Pharmacol. 9:595-599, 1974.

Hatcher, R.A. and Crosby, H.: The elimination of nicotine in the milk. J. Pharmacol. Exp. Ther. 32:1-6, 1928.

Hermann, H., Caujolle, F., and Jourdan, F.: Sur 1-elimination de quelques alcaloids et genalcaloides par les voies biliaires. C.R. Acad. Sci. 190:78-79, 1930.

Hill, D.L., Laster, W.R., Jr., and Struck, R.F.: Enzymatic metabolism of cyclophosphamide and nicotine and production of a toxic cyclophosphamide metabolite. Cancer Res. 32:658-665, 1972.

Horn, D.: Use of Tobacco, United States Department of Health, Education and Welfare. National Clearing House for Smoking and Health, 1969.

Horning, E.C., Horning, M.G., Carroll, D.I., Stillwell, R.N., and Dzidic, I.: Nicotine in smokers, non-smokers and room air. Life Sci. 13:1331-1346, 1973.

Hucker, H.B.: Metabolism of nicotine in vitro. J. Pharmacol. Exp. Ther. 122:33A-34A, 1958.

Hucker, H.B. and Gilette, J.R.: In vitro metabolism of nicotine to cotinine. Fed. Proc. 18:404, 1959.

Hucker, H.B. and Larson, P.S.: Studies on the metabolism of nornicotine in the dog. J. Pharmacol. Exp. Ther. 123:259-262, 1958.

Hucker, H.B., Gillette, J.R., and Brodie, B.B.: Cotinine: An oxidation product of nicotine formed by rabbit liver. Nature (London) 183:47, 1959.

Hucker, H.B., Gillette, J.R., and Brodie, B.B.: Enzymatic pathway for the formation of cotinine, a major metabolite of nicotine in rabbit liver. J. Pharmacol. Exp. Ther. 129:94-100, 1960.

Hug, C.C., Jr.: Distribution of nicotine in the rat. Pharmacologist 12:220, 1970.

Isaac, P.F., and Rand, M.J.: Blood levels of nicotine and physiological effects after inhalation of tobacco smoke. Eur. J. Pharmacol. 8:269-283, 1969.

Isaac, P.F. and Rand, M.J.: Cigarette smoking and plasma levels of nicotine. Nature (London) 236:308-310, 1972.

Jenner, P., Gorrod, J.W., and Backett, A.H.: The absorption of nicotine-1'-N-oxide and its reduction in the gastrointestinal tract in man. Xenobiotica 3:341-349, 1973.

Kershbaum, A., Bellett, S., Hirabayashi, M., Feinberg, N.J., and Eilberg, R.: Effect of cigarette, cigar, and pipe smoking on nicotine excretion. Arch. Intern. Med. 120:311-314, 1967.

Knapp, H.P., Bliss, C.M., and Wells, H.: Addictive aspects in heavy cigarette smoking.

Amer. J. Psychiat. *119*:966-972, 1963.

Kozlowski, L.T., Jarvik, M.E., and Gritz, E.R.: Nicotine regulation and cigarette smoking. Clin. Pharmacol. Ther. *17*:93-97, 1975.

Kuhn, H.: Tobacco alkaloids and their pyrolysis products in the smoke. In Tobacco Alkaloids and Related Compounds. Ed., Von Euler, Oxford, Pergamon Press, 1965.

Larson, P.S.: Metabolism of nicotine and nature of tobacco smoke irritants. Indust. Eng. Chem. *44*:279-283, 1952.

Larson, P.S. and Haag, H.B.: Studies on the fate of nicotine in the body. III. On the pharmacology of some methylated and demethylated derivatives of nicotine. J. Pharmacol. Exp. Ther. 77:343-349, 1943.

Larson, P.S. and Silvette, H.: Tobacco Alkaloids and Related Compounds. Ed. U.S. von Euler, Oxford, Pergamon Press, 1965, pp. 119-120.

Larson, P.S. and Silvette, H.: Tobacco: Experimental and Clinical Studies, Supplement I. Williams & Wilkins, Baltimore, 1968.

Larson, P.S., Haag, H.B., and Silvette, H.: Tobacco: Experimental and Clinical Studies. Baltimore, Williams & Wilkins Co., 1961, pp. 26.

Lautenbach, B.F.: On a new function of the liver. Phila. Med. Times 7:387-394, 1876-77.

Lehmann, K.B.: Chemische und toxikologische Studien uber Tabak, Tabakrauch und das Tabakrauchen. Arch. Hyg. (Munich) *68*:319-420, 1909.

Lickint, F. and Lukesch, H.: Ein Beitrag zur Ermittlung der Nicotinausscheidung in dem Harn nach Tabakgenuss. Pharmazie *11*:39-42, 1956.

Lucchesi, B.R., Schuster, C.R., and Empley, G.S.: The role of nicotine as a determinant of cigarette smoking frequency in man with observations of certain cardiovascular effects associated with the tobacco alkaloid. Clin. Pharmacol. Ther. *8*:787-796, 1967.

Lutwak-Mann, C. and Hay, M.F.: Effect on the early embryo of agents administered to the mother. Brit. Med. J. *2*:944-946, 1962.

Mansner, R.: Correlation of some central effects of nicotine to its concentration in mouse brain. Scand. J. Clin. Lab. Invest. *25*:(Suppl. 113) 94, 1970.

McKennis, H., Jr.: Tobacco Alkaloids and Related Compounds. Ed. U.S. von Euler, Oxford, Pergamon Press, 1965, pp. 53-75.

McKennis, H., Jr.: Excretion and metabolism of nicotine. Ann. N.Y. Acad. Sci. *90*:36-42, 1960.

McKennis, H., Jr., Turnbull, L., and Bowman, E.R.: γ-(3-Pyridyl)-γ-methylaminobutyric acid as a urinary metabolite of nicotine. J. Amer. Chem. Soc. *79*:6342-6343, 1957.

McKennis, H., Jr.; Turnbull, L.B., and Bowman, E.R.: Metabolism of nicotine to (+)-γ-(3-pyridyl)-γ-methylaminobutyric acid. J. Amer. Chem. Soc. *80*:6597-6600, 1958.

McKennis, H., Jr., Turnbull, L.B., Bowman, E.R., and Wada, E.: Demethylation of cotinine *in vivo*. J. Amer. Chem. Soc. *81*:3951-3954, 1959.

McKennis, H., Jr., Bowman, E.R., and Turnbull, L.B.: The isolation and structure of a ketoamide formed in the metabolism of nicotine. J. Amer. Chem. Soc. *82*:3974-3976, 1960.

McKennis, H., Jr., Bowman, E.R., and Turnbull, L.B.: Mammalian degradation of (-)-nicotine to 3-pyridyacetic acid and other compounds. Proc. Soc. Exp. Biol. Med. *107*:145-148, 1961.

McKennis, H., Jr., Turnbull, L.B., Schwartz, L., Tamaki, E., and Bowman, R.: Demethylation in the metabolism of (-)-nicotine. J. Biol. Chem. *237*:541-546, 1962.

McKennis, H., Jr., Turnbull, L.B., Bowman, E.R., and Tamaki, E.: The synthesis of hydroxycotinine and studies on its structure. J. Org. Chem. *28*:383-387, 1963a.

McKennis, H., Jr., Turnbull, L.B., and Bowman, E.R.: N-Methylation of nicotine and cotinine *in vivo*. J. Biol. Chem. *238*:719-723, 1963b.

McKennis, H., Jr., Schwartz, S.L., Turnbull, L.B., Tomaki, E., and Bowman, E.R.: The metabolic formation of γ-(3-pyridyl)-γ hydroxybutyric acid and its possible intermediary role in the mammalian metabolism of nicotine. J. Biol. Chem. *239*:3981-3989, 1964a.

McKennis, H., Jr., Schwartz, S.L., and Bowman, E.R.: Alternate routes in the metabolic degradation of the pyrrolidine ring of nicotine. J. Biol. Chem. *239*:3990-3996, 1964b.

Meacham, R.H., Jr., Bowman, E.P., and McKennis, H., Jr.: Additional routes in the metabolism of nicotine to 3-pyridylactate. The metabolism of dihydrometanicotine. J. Biol. Chem. *247*:902-908, 1972.

Miller, A.W., Jr., and Larson, P.S.: Observations on the metabolism of nicotine by tissue slices. J. Pharmacol. Exp. Ther. *109*:218-222, 1953.

Mitchell, R.I.: Controlled measurement of smoke-particle retension in the respiratory tract. Amer. Rev. Resp. Dis. *85*:526-533, 1962.

Mosier, H.D., Jr. and Jansons, R.A.: Distribution and fate of nicotine in the rat fetus. Teratology *6*:303-311, 1972.

Murphy, P.: Enzymatic oxidation of nicotine to nicotine-$\Delta^{1'(5')}$ iminium ion. J. Biol. Chem. *248*:2796-2800, 1973.

Okumura, Y.: Untersuchung uber die Ursache der Nicotingewohnung. I-III. Jikken Yakubutsugaku Zassi *13*:277-307, 1937.

Owen, F.B. and Larson, P.S.: Studies on the fate of nicotine in the animal body. VIII. Observations on the number and chemical nature of nicotine metabolites in the dog and cat. Arch. Int. Pharmacodyn. *115*:402-407, 1958.

Ozawa, S.: The seat of elimination of drugs in the kidney. Jap. J. Med. Sci. Pharmacol. *4*:92-94, 1930.

Pantuck, E.J., Kuntzman, R., and Conney, A.H.: Decreased concentration of phenacetin in plasma of cigarette smokers. Science *175*:1248-1250, 1972.

Papadopoulos, N.M.: Nicotine-1'-oxide: A metabolite of nicotine in animal tissues. Arch. Biochem. Biophys. *106*:182-185, 1964a.

Papadopoulos, N.M.: Formation of nornicotine and other metabolites from nicotine *in vitro* and *in vivo*. Can. J. Biochem. *42*:435-442, 1964b.

Papadopoulos, N.M. and Kintzios, J.A.: Formation of metabolites from nicotine by a rabbit liver preparation. J. Pharmacol. Exp. Ther. *140*:269-277, 1963.

Pearse, A.G.E.: The cytochemistry and ultrastructure of polypeptide hormone-producing cells of the APUD series and the embryologic, physiologic and pathologic implications of the concept. J. Histochem. Cytochem. *17*:303-313, 1969.

Pepeu, G.: Nicotina e acetilcolina cerebrale. Arch. Ital. Sci. Farmacol. *15*:93-94, 1965.

Perlman, H.H. and Dannenberg, A.M.: Nicotine: Excretion in breast milk and urine from cigaret smoking; its effect on nursling. A.M.A. Meeting, Atlantic City, June 8-12, 1942. Pediat. Sect., p. 84.

Perlman, H.H., Dannenberg, A.M., and Sokoloff, N.: The excretion of nicotine in breast milk and urine from cigaret smoking. Its effect on lactation and the nursling. J.A.M.A. *120*:1003-1009, 1942.

Peterson, W.F., Morese, K.N., and Kaltreider, D.F.: Smoking and prematurity. A preliminary report based on study of 7740 Caucasians. Obstet. Gynecol. *26*:775-779, 1965.

Putney, J.W., Jr., and Borzelleca, J.F.: On the mechanisms of ^{14}C-nicotine distribution in rat submaxillary gland *in vitro*. J. Pharmacol. Exp. Ther. *178*:180-191, 1971.

Rosecrans, J.A. and Schechter, M.D.: Brain area nicotine levels in male and female rats of two strains. Arch. Int. Pharmacodyn. Ther. 196:46-54, 1972.

Roth, I.J. and Barlow, C.F.: Drugs in the brain. Science 134:22-31, 1961.

Ruddon, R.W. and Cohen, A.M.: Alteration of enzyme activity in rat liver following the acute and chronic administration of nicotine. Toxic Appl. Pharmacol. 16:613-625, 1970.

Russell, M.A.H.: Cigarette smoking: Natural history of a dependence disorder. Brit. J. Med. Psychol. 44:1-16, 1971.

Ryrfeldt, A.M. and Hansson, E.: Biliary excretion of quaternary ammonium compounds and tertiary amines in the rat. Acta Pharmacol. Toxicol. 30:59-68, 1971.

Schardein, J.L., Woosley, E.T., Hamilton, L.E., and Kaump, D.H.: Effects of aspirin and phenylbutazone on the rabbit blastocyst. J. Reprod. Fert. 10:129-132, 1965.

Schievelbein, H. and Grundke, K.: Gaschromatographische Methode zur Bestinmung von Nikotin in Blut and Geweben. Z. Analyt. Chem. 237:1, 1968.

Schievelbein, H. and Werle, E.: Zur Frage der Entstehung von Methylamin beim Abbau des Nikotins durch Leber und zum Abbau von Methylamin durch Leber. Arzneimittel Forsch. 7:117-119, 1957.

Schievelbein, H., Eberhardt, R., and Loschenkohl, K.: Absorption of nicotine through the oral mucosa. I. Measurement of nicotine concentration in the blood after application of nicotine and total particulate matter. Agents and Actions 3:254-258, 1973.

Schmiterlöw, C.G. and Hansson, E.: Tobacco Alkaloids and Related Compounds. Ed. U.S. von Euler, Oxford, Pergamon Press, 1965, pp. 75-87.

Schmiterlöw, C.G., Hansson, E., Andersson, G., Appelgren, L.E., and Hoffman, P.C.: Distribution of nicotine in the central nervous system. Ann. N.Y. Acad. Sci., 142:2-14, 1967.

Schmiterlöw, C.G., Hansson, E., Appelgren, L.E., and Hoffman, P.C.: Physiological disposition and biotransformation of ^{14}C-labeled nicotine. In Isotopes in Experimental Pharmacology. Ed. L.J. Roth, Chicago, The University Press, 1965, pp. 75-89.

Schoolar, J.C., Barlow, C.F., and Roth, J.J.: The penetration of carbon-14 urea into cerebrospinal fluid and various areas of the cat brain. J. Neuropathol. Exp. Neurol. 19:216-227, 1960.

Sieber, S.M. and Fabro, S.: Identification of drugs in the preimplantation blastocyst and in the plasma, uterine secretion and urine of the pregnant rabbit. J. Pharmacol. Exp. Ther. 176:65-75, 1971.

Silvette, H., Hoff, E.C., Larson, P.S., and Haag, H.B.: The actions of nicotine on central nervous system functions. Pharmacol. Rev. 14:137-173, 1962.

Slanina, P. and Tjälve, H.: Accumulation of nicotine in pancreatic islets and calcitonin-producing cells in mice and chicks demonstrated by micro- and whole-body autoradiography. J. Endocrinol. 58:21-30, 1973.

Sontag, L.W. and Wallace, R.F.: The effect of cigaret smoking during pregnancy upon the fetal heart rate. Amer. J. Obstet. 29:77-83, 1935.

Stalhandske, T.: Factors affecting the uptake, elimination and toxicity of nicotine in the mouse. Acta Pharmacol. Toxicol. 25(Suppl. 4):41, 1967.

Stalhandske, T.: The metabolism of nicotine and cotinine by a mouse liver preparation. Acta Physiol. Scand. 78:236-248, 1970a.

Stalhandske, T.: Effects of increased liver metabolism of nicotine on its uptake, elimination and toxicity in mice. Acta Physiol. Scand. 80:222-234, 1970b.

Stalhandske, T. and Slanina, P.: Effect of nicotine treatment on the metabolism of nicotine in the mouse liver in vitro. Acta Pharmacol. Toxicol. 28:75-80, 1970a.

Stalhandske, T. and Slanina, P.: Lethal brain concentrations of nicotine in mice of different ages. Acta Pharmacol. Toxicol. *28*:233-240, 1970b.

Stalhandske, T. and Slanina, P.: Age dependent changes in nicotine distribution in the brain of the mouse. Acta Pharmacol. Toxicol. *31*:341-352, 1972.

Stalhandske, T., Slanina, P., Tjälve, H., Hansson, E., and Schmiterlöw, C.G.: Metabolism *in vitro* of ¹⁴C-nicotine in livers of foetal, newborn and young mice. Acta Pharmacol. Toxicol. *27*:363-380, 1969.

Su, C. and Bevan, J.A.: Blockade of nicotine-induced norepinephrine release by cocaine, phenoxybenzamine and desipramine. J. Pharmacol. Exp. Ther. *175*:533-540, 1970.

Suzuki, K., Horiguchi, T., Comas-Urrutia, A.C., Mueller-Heubach, E., Morishima, H., and Adamsons, K.: Placental transfer and distribution of nicotine in the pregnant rhesus monkey. Amer. J. Obstet. Gynecol. *119*:253-262, 1974.

Takeuchi, M., Kurogochi, Y., and Yamaoka, M.: Experiments on the repeated injection of nicotine into albino rats. Folia Pharmacol. Jap. *50*:66-69, 1954.

Thompson, J.H.: The effect of nicotine on intestinal serotonin levels. Eur. J. Pharmacol. *2*:329-332, 1968.

Thompson, J.H., Spezia, Ch. A. and Angulo, M.: The release of intestinal serotonin in rats by nicotine. J.A.M.A. *207*:1883-1886, 1969.

Tjälvĕ, J., Hansson, E., and Schmiterlöw, C.G.: Passage of ¹⁴C nicotine and its metabolites into mice foetuses and placentae. Acta Pharmacol. Toxicol. *26*:539-555, 1968.

Todd, G.F. (ed.) Statistics of Smoking in the United Kingdom. London, Tobacco Research Council, 1969.

Truhaut, R., De Clerq, M., and Loisillier, F.: Sur les toxicites aigue et chronique de la cotinine, et sur son effet cancerigene chez le rat. Pathol. Biol. *12*:39-42, 1964.

Tsujimoto, A.: Studies on nicotine metabolism. II. Nicotine oxidation by animal tissues. Fol. Pharm. Japon. *53*:553-565, 1957.

Tsujimoto, A., Tsujimura, Y., Yoshimoto, S., and Komura, I.: Nicotine distribution in dog and rabbit. Fol. Pharm. Japon *51*:26, 1955.

Tsujimoto, A., Kojima, S., Ikeda, M., and Toshihiro, D.: Excretion of nicotine and its metabolites in dog and monkey saliva. Toxicol. Appl. Pharmacol. *22*:365-374, 1972.

Turner, D.M.: The metabolism of (14C) nicotine in the cat. Biochem. J. *115*:889-896, 1969.

United States Public Health Service, Smoking and Health. Washington, D.C. Publication No. 1103, 1964.

Volle, R.L. and Koelle, G.B.: Ganglionic Stimulating and Blocking Agents. In The Pharmacological Basis of Therapeutics Fourth Edition. Ed. L.S. Goodman and A. Gilman, New York City, Macmillan, 1970, pp. 585-600.

Wada, E., Kisaki, T., and Saito, K.: Autoxidation of nicotine. Arch. Biochem. *79*:124-130, 1959.

Wei-Chiang, S. and Van Vunakis, H.: Nicotine and its metabolites. IV. Formation of the nicotine analogue of DPN by pig brain DPNASE. Res. Commun. Chem. Pathol. Pharmacol. *9*:405-412, 1974.

Weiss, G.B.: The effect of pH on nicotine-induced contracture and Ca⁴⁵ movements in sartorius muscle. J. Pharmacol. Exp. Ther. *154*:605-612, 1966.

Weiss, G.B.: Dependence of nicotine-C¹⁴ distribution and movements upon pH in frog sartorius muscle. J. Pharmacol. Exp. Ther. *160*:135-147, 1968.

Welch, R.M., Harrison, Y.E., Conney, A.H., Poppers, P.J., and Finster, M.: Cigarette smoking: Stimulatory effect on metabolism of 3,4-benzpyrene by enzymes in human placenta. Science *160*:541-542, 1968.

Welch, R.M., Harrison, Y.E., Gommi, B.W., Poppers, P.J., Finster, M., and Conney,

A.H.: Stimulatory effect of cigarette smoking on the hydroxylation of 3,4-benzpyrene and the N-demethylation of 3-methyl-4-monomethylaminoazobenzene by enzymes in human placenta. Clin. Pharmacol. Ther. *10*:100-109, 1969.

Wenusch, A.: Beitrag zur Kenntnis der Tabaksorten. Z. Untersuch. Lebensm. 1935, pp. 506-510.

Wenusch, A.: Uber die nikotinaufnahme beim Tabakrauchen. Med. Klin. *36*:1159-1161, 1940.

Wenusch, A.: Uber die absoluten Mengen des beim Rauchen aufgenommen Nikotins. Chem. Ztg. *66*:254-255, 1942.

Werle, E. and Koebke, K.: Uber den Abbau von Nikotin und Nikotyrin durch Lebergewebe. Justus Liebigs Ann. Chem. *562*:60-66, 1949.

Werle, E. and Meyer, A.: Uber den Abbau von Tabakalkaloiden durch tierische Gewebe. Biochem. Z. *321*:221-235, 1950.

Werle, E. and Müller, R.: Uber den Abbau von Nicotin durch tierisches Gewebe. II. Biochem. Z. *308*:355-358, 1941.

Werle, E. and Uschold, E.: Uber fermentative Nicotinentgiftung durch tierisches Gewebe. Biochem. Z. *318*:531-537, 1948.

Werle, E., Koebke, K., and Meyer, A.: Uber den Abbau des Nicotins durch tierisches Gewebe. Biochem. Z. *320*:189-198, 1950.

Werle, E., Schievelbein, H., and Spieth, D.: Zur Pharmakologie des Nikotins und zur Entgiftung des Nikotins durch den tierischen Organismus. Arzneimittel Forsch. *6*:322-330, 1956.

Wolff, W.A.: The fate of cigarette smoke in the dog lung: Nicotine fraction. J. Pharmacol. Exp. Ther. *113*:55, 1955.

Wolff, W.A. and Giles, W.E.: Studies on tobacco chewing. Fed. Proc. *9*:248, 1950.

Wolff, W.A., Hawkins, M.A., and Giles, W.E.: Nicotine in blood in relation to smoking. J. Pharmacol. Exp. Ther. *95*:145-148, 1949.

World Health Organization Expert Committee on Addiction-Producing Drugs. Seventh Report of an Expert Committee. World Health Organization Tech. Rep. Ser. *116*:3-15, 1957.

Yamamoto, I., Takeuchi, M., and Tsujimoto, A.: Microdetermination of nicotine in rabbit urine by CNBr reaction. (In Japanese). Fol. Pharm. Jap. *50*:70-75, 1954.

Yamamoto, I., Inoki, R., Tamari, Y., and Iwatsubo, K.: Effect of reserpine on brain levels of ^{14}C-nicotine in relation to nicotine induced convulsions. Arch. Int. Pharmacodyn. *166*:102-109, 1967.

Yamamoto, I., Inoki, R., and Iwatsubo, K.: Penetration of nicotine-^{14}C into several rat tissues *in vivo* and *in vitro*. Toxicol. Appl. Pharmacol. *12*:560-567, 1968.

Alcohol References

Akesson, C.: Autoradiographic studies on the distribution of ^{14}C-2-ethanol and its nonvolatile metabolites in the pregnant mouse. Arch. Int. Pharmacodyn. *209*:296-304, 1974.

Ariyoshi, T., Takabatake, E. and Remmer, H.: Drug metabolism in ethanol induced fatty liver. Life Sci. *9*:361-369, 1970.

Asada, M. and Galambos, J.T.: Liver disease, hepatic alcohol dehydrogenase activity, and alcohol metabolism in the human. Gastroenterology *45*:67-72, 1963.

Axelrod, J. and Daly, J.: Pituitary gland: Enzymic formation of methanol from S-adenosylmethionine. Science 150:892-893, 1965.

Bartlett, G.R. and Barnet, H.N.: Some observations on alcohol metabolism with radioactive ethyl alcohol. Quart. J. Stud. Alcohol 10:381-397, 1949.

Blum, K., Geller, I., and Wallace, J.E.: Interaction effects of ethanol and pyrazole in laboratory rodents. Brit. J. Pharmacol. 43:67-73, 1971.

Büttner, H.: Aldehyd-und Alkoholdehydrogenase-Aktivität in Leber und Niere der Ratte. Biochem. Z. 341:300-314, 1965.

Caldwell, J. and Sever, P.S.: The biochemical pharmacology of abused drugs. II. Alcohol and barbiturates. Clin. Pharmacol. Ther. 16:737-749, 1974.

Camps, F.E. and Robinson, A.E.: Influence of fructose on blood alcohol levels in social drinkers. Med. Sci. Law 8:161-167, 1968.

Carter, E.A. and Isselbacher, K.J.: The role of microsomes in the hepatic metabolism of ethanol. Ann. N.Y. Acad. Sci. 179:282-294, 1971.

Coldwell, B.B., Paul, C.J., and Thomas, B.H.: Phenobarbital metabolism in ethanol-intoxicated rats. Can. J. Physiol. Pharmacol. 51:458-463, 1973.

Conney, A.H.: Pharmacological implications of microsomal enzyme induction. Pharmacol. Rev. 19:317-366, 1967.

Cooke, A.R. and Birchall, A.: Absorption of ethanol from the stomach. Gastroenterology 57:269-272, 1969.

Davenport, H.W.: Ethanol damage to canine oxyntic glandular mucosa. Proc. Soc. Exp. Biol. Med. 126:657-662, 1967.

Davis, V.E. and Walsh, M.J.: Alcohol amines and alkaloids: A possible biochemical basis for alcohol addiction. Science 167:1005-1007, 1970a.

Davis, V.E. and Walsh, M.J.: Morphine and ethanol physical dependence: A critique of a hypothesis. Science 170:1114-1115, 1970b.

Davis, V.E., Walsh, M.J., and Yamanaka, Y.: Augmentation of alkaloid formation from dopamine by alcohol and acetaldehyde in vitro. J. Pharmacol. Exp. Ther. 174:401-412, 1970c.

Dilts, P.V.: Placental transfer of ethanol. Amer. J. Obstet. Gynecol. 107:1195-1198, 1970.

Dubowski, K.M.: Alcohol and Traffic Safety. Washington, D.C., U.S. Government Printing Office, 1963, p. 97.

Edwards, J.A. and Evans, D.A.P.: Ethanol metabolism in subjects possessing typical and atypical liver alcohol dehydrogenase. Clin. Pharmacol. Ther. 8:824-829, 1967.

Eriksen, S.P. and Kulkarni, A.B.: Methanol in normal human breath. Science 141:639-640, 1963.

Erwin, V.G. and Deitrich, R.A.: Brain aldehyde dehydrogenase, its localization, purification and properties. J. Biol. Chem. 241:3533-3539, 1966.

Felby, S. and Olsen, J.: Comparative studies of postmortem ethyl alcohol in vitreous humor, blood, and muscle. J. Forensic Sci. 14:93-101, 1969.

Figueroa, R.B. and Klotz, A.P.: Alterations of liver alcohol dehydrogenase and other hepatic enzymes in alcoholic cirrhosis. Gastroenterology 43:10-12, 1962.

Forsander, O.A., Raiha, N., and Suomalainen, H.: Oxydation des Athylalkohols in isolierter Leber und isoliertem Hinterkorper der Ratte. Z. Physiol. Chem. 318:1-5, 1960.

Freundt, K.J.: On the pharmacokinetics of the ethanol metabolite acetate: Elimination from the blood and cerebrospinal fluid. Arzeimittel Forsch. 23:949-951, 1973.

Fritchie, G.E., Ho, B.T., McIsaac, W.M., and Idänpään-Heikkilä, J.E.: Biological aspects of alcohol. Houston, University of Texas Press, 1972, pp. 285-292.

Goldberg, L. and Rydberg, U.: Inhibition of ethanol metabolism *in vivo* by administration of pyrazole. Biochem. Pharmacol. *18*:1462-1479, 1969.

Goldberg, L., Hollstedt, C., Neri, A., and Rydberg, U.: Synergistic action of pyrazole on ethanol incoordination: Differential, metabolic and CNS effects. J. Pharm. Pharmacol. *24*:593-601, 1972.

Goldberg, M., Hehir, R., and Hurowitz, M.: Intravenous triiodothyronine in acute alcoholic intoxication. N. Engl. J. Med. *263*:1336-1339, 1960.

Goldstein, A. and Judson, B.A.: Alcohol dependence and opiate dependence: Lack of relationship in mice. Science *171*:290-292, 1971.

Griffiths, P.J., Littleton, J.M., and Ortiz, A.: Evidence of a role for brain monoamines in ethanol dependence. Brit. J. Pharmacol. *48*:354P, 1973.

Haggard, H.W., Greenberg, L.A., and Carroll, R.P.: Studies in the absorption, distribution and elimination of alcohol. VIII. The diuresis from alcohol and its influence on the elimination of alcohol in the urine. J. Pharmacol. Exp. Ther. *71*:348-357, 1941.

Halsted, C.H., Robles, E.A., and Mezey, E.: Distribution of ethanol in the human gastrointestinal tract. Amer. J. Clin. Nutr. *26*:831-834, 1973.

Hasumura, Y., Teschke, R., and Lieber, C.S.: Hepatic microsomal ethanol-oxidizing system (MEOS): Dissociation from reduced nicotinamide adenine dinucleotide phosphate oxidase and possible role of form I of cytochrome P-450. J. Pharmacol. Exp. Ther. *194*:469-474, 1975.

Hawkins, R.D. and Kalant, H.: The metabolism of ethanol and its metabolic effects. Pharmacol. Rev. *24*:67-157, 1972.

Hempel, J., Cederbaum, A., Pietruszko, R., and Rubin, E.: New alcohol dehydrogenase from rat hepatoma. Fed. Proc. *34*:676, 1975 (abstract).

Ho, B.T., Fritchie, G.E., Idänpään-Heikkilä, J.E., and McIssac, W.M.: Placental transfer and tissue distribution of ethanol-1-^{14}C. A radioautographic study in monkeys and hamsters. Quart. J. Stud. Alcohol. *33*:485-493, 1972.

Hogben, C., Adrian, M., Schanker, L.S., Tocco, D.J., and Brodie, B.B.: Absorption of drugs from the stomach. II. The human. J. Pharmacol. Exp. Ther. *120*:540-545, 1958.

Hrycay, E.G. and O'Brien, P.J.: Cytochrome P-450 as a microcomal peroxidase utilizing a lipid peroxide substrate. Arch. Biochem. Biophys. *147*:14-27, 1971.

Idänpään-Heikkilä, J.E., Fritchie, G.E., Ho, B.T., and McIsaac, W.M.: Placental transfer of C-14 ethanol. Amer. J. Obstet. Gynecol. *110*:426-428, 1971.

Idänpään-Heikkilä, J., Jouppila, P., Akerblom, H.K., Isoaho, R., Kauppila, E., and Koivisto, M.: Elimination and metabolic effects of ethanol in mother, fetus, and newborn infant. Amer. J. Obstet. Gynecol. *112*:387-393, 1972.

Imai, Y. and Sato, R.: Studies on the substrate interactions with P-450 in drug hydroxylation by liver microsomes. J. Biochem. *62*:239-249, 1967.

Ishii, H., Joly, J., and Lieber, C.S.: Effect of ethanol on the amount and enzyme activities of hepatic rough and smooth microsomal membranes. Biochim. Biophys. Acta *291*:411-420, 1973.

Israel, Y., Videla, L., Fernandez-Videla, V., and Bernstein, J.: Effects of chronic ethanol treatment and thyroxine administration on ethanol metabolism and liver oxidative capacity. J. Pharmacol. Exp. Ther. *192*:565-574, 1975.

Isselbacher, K.J. and Carter, E.A.: Ethanol oxidation by liver microsomes: evidence against a separate and distinct enzyme system. Biochem. Biophys. Res. Commun. *39*:530-537, 1970.

Jacobsen, E.: The metabolism of ethyl alcohol. Pharmacol. Rev. *4*:107-135, 1952.

Jones, K.L. and Smith, D.W.: Recognition of the fetal alcohol syndrome in early infancy. Lancet 2:999-1001, 1973a.

Jones, K.L., Smith, D.W., Ulleland, C.N., and Streissguth, A.P.: Pattern of malformation in offspring of chronic alcoholic mothers. Lancet 1:1267-1271, 1973b.

Kalant, H.: The Biology of Alcoholism. New York, Plenum Press, 1971, pp. 1-62.

Kalant, H., Sereny, G., and Charlebois, R.: Evaluation of triiodothyronine in the treatment of acute alcoholic intoxication. N. Engl. J. Med. 267:1-6, 1962.

Kalant, H., Khanna, J.M., and Marshman, J.: Effect of chronic intake of ethanol on pentobarbital metabolism. J. Pharmacol. Exp. Ther. 175:318-324, 1970.

Kalant, H., Leblanc, A., and Gibbins, R.: Tolerance to, and dependence on, some nonopiate psychotropic drugs. Pharmacol. Rev. 23:135-191, 1971.

Kater, R.M., Iber, F.L., and Carulli, N.: Differences in ethanol metabolism in alcoholic and nonalcoholic subjects. Amer. J. Clin. Nutr. 21:532-533, 1968a (abstract).

Kater, R.M.H., Zieve, P.D., Tobon, F., Roggin, G.M., and Iber, F.L.: Heavy drinking accelerates drugs' breakdown in liver. J.A.M.A. 206:1709, 1968b.

Kater, R.M.H., Carulli, N., and Iber, F.L.: Differences in the rate of ethanol metabolism in recently drinking alcoholic and nondrinking subjects. Amer. J. Clin. Nutr. 22:1608-1617, 1969a.

Kater, R.M.H., Tobon, F., and Iber, F.L.: Increased rate of tolbutamide metabolism in an alcoholic patient. J.A.M.A. 207:363-365, 1969b.

Kater, R.M.H., Roggin, G., Tobon, F., Zieve, P., and Iber, F.L.: Increased rate of clearance of drugs from the circulation of alcoholics. Amer. J. Med. Sci. 258:35-39, 1969c.

Keilin, D. and Hartree, E.F.: Coupled oxidation of alcohol. Proc. Roy. Soc. Ser. B Biol. Sci. 119:141-159, 1936.

Keilin, D. and Hartree, E.F.: Properties of catalase. Catalysis of coupled oxidation of alcohols. Biochem. J. 39:293-301, 1945.

Khanna, J.M. and Kalant, H.: Effect of inhibitors and inducers of drug metabolism on in vivo ethanol metabolism. Biochem. Pharmacol. 19:2033-2041, 1970.

Khanna, J.M., Kalant, H., and Lin, G.: Effect of carbon tetrachloride treatment on ethanol metabolism. Biochem. Pharmacol. 20:3269-3279, 1971.

Khanna, J.M., Kalant, H., and Lin, G.: Significance in vivo of the increase in microsomal ethanol-oxidizing system after chronic administration of ethanol, phenobarbital and chlorcyclizine. Biochem. Pharmacol. 21:2215-2226, 1972.

Klaassen, C.D.: Ethanol metabolism in rats after microsomal metabolizing enzyme induction. Proc. Soc. Exp. Biol. Med. 132:1099-1102, 1969.

Korsten, M., Matsuzaki, S., Feinman, L., and Lieber, C.S.: High blood acetaldehyde levels after ethanol administration. Difference between alcoholic and nonalcoholic subjects. New Eng. J. Med. 292:386-389, 1974.

Kostelnik, M.E. and Iber, F.L.: Correlation of alcohol and tolbutamide blood clearance rates with microsomal alcohol-metabolizing enzyme activity. Amer. J. Clin. Nutr. 26:161-164, 1973.

Kraemer, R.J. and Deitrich, R.A.: Isolation and characterization of human liver aldehyde dehydrogenase. J. Biol. Cham. 243:6402-6408, 1968.

Krebs, H.A. and Perkins, J.R.: The physiological role of liver alcohol dehydrogenase. Biochem. J. 118:635-644, 1970.

Larsen, J.A.: Extrahepatic metabolism of ethanol in man. Nature (London) 184:1236, 1959.

Larsen, J.A.: Elimination of ethanol as a measure of the hepatic blood flow in the cat. II. The significance of the extrahepatic elimination of ethanol. Acta Physiol. Scand. 57:209-223, 1963.

LeBlanc, A.E., and Kalant, H.: Central nervous system interaction of pyrazole and ethanol in the rat. Can. J. Physiol. Pharmacol. 51:612-615, 1973.

LeBlanc, A.E., Kalant, H., Gibbins, R.J., and Berman, N.D.: Acquisition and loss of tolerance to ethanol by the rat. J. Pharmacol. Exp. Ther. 186:244-250, 1969.

Lieber, C.S.: Metabolic derangement induced by alcohol. Annu. Rev. Med. 18:35-54, 1967.

Lieber, C.S.: Metabolic effects produced by alcohol in the liver and other tissues. Adv. Intern Med. 14:151-199, 1968.

Lieber, C.S. and DeCarli, L.M.: Hepatic microsomes: A new site for ethanol oxidation. J. Clin. Invest. 47:62a, 1968a.

Lieber, C.S. and DeCarli, L.M.: Ethanol oxidation by hepatic microsomes: Adaptive increase after ethanol feeding. Science 162:917-918, 1968b.

Lieber, C.S. and DeCarli, L.M.: Microsomal ethanol oxidizing activity. Its role *in vivo*. Clin. Res. 27:306, 1969.

Lieber, C. and DeCarli, L.: Hepatic microsomal ethanol-oxidizing system. *In vitro* characteristics and adaptive properties *in vivo*. J. Biol. Chem. 245:2505-2512, 1970a.

Lieber, C.S. and DeCarli, L.M.: Effect of drug administration on the activity of the hepatic microsomal ethanol oxidizing system. Life Sci. 9:267-276, 1970b.

Lieber, C.S. and DeCarli, L.M.: Reduced nicotinamide-adenine dinucleotide phosphate oxidase:activity enhanced by ethanol consumption. Science 170:78-80, 1970c.

Lieber, C.S. and DeCarli, L.M.: Paradoxical effects of barbiturates on ethanol metabolism. Gastroenterology 60:177, 1971.

Lieber, C.S., Teschke, R., Hasumura, Y., and DeCarli, L.M.: Differences in hepatic and metabolic changes after acute and chronic alcohol consumption. Fed. Proc. 34:2060 2073, 1975.

Lieberman, F.L.: The effect of liver disease on the rate of ethanol metabolism in man Gastroenterology 44:261-266, 1963.

Lin, G., Kalant, H., and Khanna, J.M.: Catalase involvement in microsomal ethanol oxidizing system. Biochem. Pharmacol. 21:3305-3308, 1972.

Linn, J.E. and Kriesberg, R.A.: Alcoholism. South. Med. J. 66:1415-1420, 1973.

Lowenstein, L.M., Simone, R., Boulter, P., and Nathan, P.: Effect of fructose on alcohol concentrations in the blood of man. J.A.M.A. 213:1899-1901, 1970.

Majchrowicz, E. and Mendelson, J.H.: Blood concentrations of acetaldehyde and ethanol in chronic alcoholics. Science 168:1100-1102, 1970.

Majchrowicz, E. and Mendelson, J.H.: Blood methanol concentrations during experimentally induced ethanol intoxication in alcoholics. J. Pharmacol. Exp. Ther 179:293-300, 1971.

Mannering, G.J., Tephly, T.R. and Parks, R.E., Jr.: Metabolism of methanol. Univ Minn. Med. Bull. 34:190-192, 1963.

Mendelson, J.H., Stein, S., and Mello, N.K.: Effects of experimentally induced intoxication on metabolism of ethanol-1-C^{14} in alcoholic subjects. Metabolism 14:1255-1266, 1965.

Mezey, E.: Effect of phenobarbital administration on ethanol oxidizing enzymes and on the rates of ethanol degradation. Biochem. Pharmacol. 20:508-510, 1971.

Mezey, E. and Robles, E.A.: Effect of phenobarbital administration on ethanol metabolism and on ethanol metabolizing enzymes in man. Gastroenterology 64:170 1973.

Mezey, E. and Tobon, F.: Rates of ethanol clearance and activities of the ethanol oxidizing enzymes in chronic alcoholic patients. Gastroenterology 61:707, 1971.

Mezey, E., Potter, J.J., and Reed, W.D.: Ethanol oxidation by components of the microsomal enzyme systems. Clin. Res. 20:461, 1972.

Mezey, E., Potter, J.J., and Reed, W.D.: Ethanol oxidation by a component of liver microsomes rich in cytochrome P-450. J. Biol. Chem. *248*:1183-1187, 1973.

Misra, P.S., Lefevre, A., Rubin, E., and Lieber, C.S.: Effect of ethanol ingestion on ethanol, meprobomate and pentobarbital metabolism. Gastroenterology *58*:308, 1970.

Myerson, R.M.: Metabolic aspects of alcohol and their biological significance. Med. Clin. North Amer. *57*:925-940, 1973.

Newcombe, D.S.: Ethanol metabolism and uric acid. Metabolism *21*:1193-1203, 1972.

Papenberg, J., von Wartburg, J.P., and Aebi, H.: Metabolism of ethanol and fructose in the perfused rat liver. Enzym. Biol. Clin. *11*:237-250, 1970.

Patel, A.R., Paton, A.M., Rowan, T., Lawson, D.H., and Linton, A.L.: Clinical studies on the effect of laevulose on the rate of metabolism of ethyl alcohol. Scott. Med. J. *14*:268-271, 1969.

Pawan, G.L.S.: The determination of total body-water in man by non-isotopic methods: A comparative study. Biochem. J. *96*:15P-16P, 1965.

Pawan, G.L.: Metabolism of alcohol (ethanol) in man. Proc. Nutr. Soc. *31*:38-89, 1972.

Pawan, G.L.S. and Grice, K.: Distribution of alcohol in urine and sweat after drinking. Lancet *2*:1016, 1968.

Pawan, G.L.S. and Hoult, W.H.: The determination of total body water in man by ethanol dilution. Biochem. J. *87*:6P-7P, 1963.

Pietz, D.G., Rosenak, B.D., and Harger, R.N.: Alcohol metabolism in hepatic dysfunction. Amer. J. Gastroenterol. *34*:140-151, 1960.

Porta, E.A., Sugioka, G., and Hartroft, W.S.: Quantitative morphologic changes in hepatocytic mitochondria and smooth endoplasmic reticulum of rats in acute and chronic alcoholism. Amer. J. Pathol. *55*:A55, 1969.

Porta, E.A., Koch, O.R., and Hartroft, W.S.: Recent advances in molecular pathology: A review of the effects of alcohol on the liver. Exp. Mol. Pathol. *12*:104-133, 1970.

Racker, E.: Aldehyde dehydrogenase, a diphosphopyridine nucleotide-linked enzyme. J. Biol. Chem. *177*:883-892, 1949.

Rahwan, R.: Speculations on the biochemical pharmacology of ethanol. Life Sci. *15*:617-633, 1974.

Raskin, N.H. and Sokoloff, L.: Brain alcohol dehydrogenase. Science *162*:131-132, 1968.

Raskin, N.H. and Sokoloff, L.: Adaptation of alcohol dehydrogenase activity in brain to chronic ethanol ingestion. Neurology *20*:391-392, 1970.

Rawat, A.K. and Schambye, P.: The influence of *l*-thyroxine on the metabolism of ethanol in rat liver. Acta Pharmacol. Toxicol. *25* (Suppl. 4):45, 1967.

Redmond, G. and Cohen, G.: Induction of liver acetaldehyde dehydrogenase: Possible role in ethanol tolerance after exposure to barbiturate. Science *171*:387-389, 1971.

Ritchie, J.M.: The Aliphatic Alcohols, in The Pharmacological Basis of Therapeutics, 4th ed. Eds. Goodman, L.S. and Gilman, A., New York, MacMillan, 1970, pp. 135-150.

Roach, M.K. and Creaven, P.J.: Ethanol blood levels following acute i.v. administration in mice. Experientia *25*:508-509, 1969.

Roach, M.K., Reese, S.N. Jr., and Creaven, P.J.: Ethanol oxidation in the microsomal fraction of rat liver. Biochem. Biophys. Res. Commun. *36*:596-602, 1969.

Röe, O.: The metabolism and toxicity of methanol. Pharmacol. Rev. *7*:399-412, 1955.

Ross, D.H. and Cardenas, H.L.: Opiates and alcohol: Evidence for a common biochemical action. Fed. Proc. *34*:779, 1975 (abstract).

Rubin, A., Tephly, T.R. and Mannering, G.J.: Kinetics of drug metabolism by hepatic microsomes. Biochem. Pharmacol. *13*:1007-1016, 1964a.

Rubin, A., Tephly, T.R., and Mannering, G.J.: Inhibition of hexobarbital metabolism by ethylmorphine and codeine in the intact rat. Biochem. Pharmacol. *13*:1053-1057, 1964b.

Rubin, E. and Lieber, C.S.: Hepatic microsomal enzymes in man and rat: Induction and inhibition by ethanol. Science 162:690, 1968.

Rubin, E. and Lieber, C.S.: Alcohol, alcoholism, and drugs. Science 172:1097-1102, 1971.

Rubin, E., Hutterer, F., and Lieber, C.S.: Ethanol increases hepatic smooth endoplasmic reticulum and drug metabolizing enzymes. Science 159:1469-1470, 1968.

Rubin, E., Gang, H., Misra, P.S., and Lieber, C.S.: Inhibition of drug metabolism by acute ethanol intoxication. Amer. J. Med. 49:801-806, 1970.

Rydberg, U. and Neri, A.: 4-Methylpyrazole as an inhibitor of ethanol metabolism Differential, metabolic and central nervous effects. Acta Pharmacol. Toxicol 31:431-432, 1972.

Schenker, T.M. and Von Wartburg, J.P.: Heterogeneity and polymorphism of human liver alcohol dehydrogenase. Experientia 26:687, 1970.

Seevers, M. H.: Morphine and ethanol physical dependence: A critique of a hypothesis Science 170:1113-1114, 1970.

Shah, M.N., Clancy, B.A., and Iber, F.L.: Comparison of blood clearance of ethanol and tolbutamide and the activity of hepatic ethanol-oxidizing and drug-metabolizing enzymes in chronic alcoholic subjects. Amer. J. Clin. Nutr. 25:135-139, 1972.

Tephly, T.R., Tinelli, F., and Watkins, W.D.: Alcohol metabolism: Role of microsomal oxidation in vivo. Science 166:627-628, 1969.

Teschke, R., Hasumura, Y., Joly, J.-G., Ishii, H., and Lieber, C.S.: Microsomal ethanol oxidizing system (MEOS): Purification and properties of a rat liver system free of catalase and alcohol dehydrogenase. Biochem. Biophys. Res. Commun. 49:1187 1193, 1972.

Teschke, R., Joly, J.-G., Hasumura, Y., and Lieber, C.S.: Hepatic microsomal ethanol oxidizing system (MEOS): Preparation of a catalase and alcohol dehydrogenase (ADH) free system. Gastroenterology 64:169, 1973.

Teschke, R., Hasumura, Y., and Lieber, C.S.: Hepatic microsomal alcohol oxidizing system (MAOS): Adaptive increase in activity following chronic ethanol consumption by a catalase independent mechanism. Fed. Proc. 34:719, 1975 (abstract).

Theorell, H. and Chance, R.: Studies on liver alcohol dehydrogenase. II. The kinetics of the compound of horse liver alcohol dehydrogenase and reduced diphosphopyridine nucleotide. Acta Chem. Scand. 5:1127-1144, 1951.

Thompson, G.N.: Alcoholism. Springfield, Ill., Charles C. Thomas Publisher, 1956.

Thurman, R.G., Ley, G.H., and Scholz, R.: Hepatic microsomal ethanol oxidation Hydrogen peroxide formation and the role of catalase. Eur. J. Biochem. 25:420-430 1972.

Thurman, R.G., McKenna, W.R., Brentzel, H.J., Jr., and Hesse, S.: Significant path ways of hepatic ethanol metabolism. Fed. Proc. 34:2075-2081, 1975.

Tobon, F. and Mezey, E.: Effects of ethanol administration on hepatic ethanol and drug metabolizing enzymes and on rates of ethanol degradation. J. Lab. Clin. Med 77:110-121, 1971.

Vatsis, K.P. and Schulman, M.P.: Absence of ethanol metabolism in 'acatalatic microsomes that oxidize drugs. Biochem. Biophys. Res. Commun. 52:588-594, 1973

Videla, L., Bernstein, J., and Israel, Y.: Metabolic alterations produced in the liver by chronic ethanol administration. Biochem. J. 134:507-514, 1973.

Von Wartburg, J.P. and Eppenberger, H.M.: Vergleichende Untersuchungen über den oxydatwen Abbau von 1-C^{14}-Athanol und 1-C^{14}-Azetat in Leber und Niere Helvet. Physiol. Pharmacol. Acta 19:303-322, 1961.

Von Wartburg, J.P. and Papenberg, J.: Alcohol dehydrogenase in ethanol metabolism Psychosomat. Med. 28:405-413, 1966.

Von Wartburg, J.P., Papenberg, J., and Aebi, H.: An atypical human alcohol dehydrogenase. Can. J. Biochem. *43*:889-898, 1965.

Wallgren, H.: International Encyclopedia of Pharmacology and Therapeutics. Oxford, Pergamon Press, 1970, pp. 161-188.

Waltman, R. and Iniquez, E.S.: Placental transfer of ethanol and its elimination at term. Obstet. Gynecol. *40*:180-185, 1972.

Chapter 8

The Cannabinoids

Marihuana and hashish are among the most widely used drugs known to man. They are derived from the hemp plant, *Cannabis sativa*. The use of this plant for medicinal purposes was first described in 2737 B.C. by the Chinese Emperor, Shen Nung, and medical applications for extracts of cannabis were recognized in the *United States Pharmacopoeia* as late as 1937. Its nonmedical use is also well known. Recognition of the increasingly widespread use of cannabis preparations has generated much controversial debate in political and social circles, as well as in the scientific community. Possible harmful effects of marihuana and the possibility of its legalization and acceptance as a recreational substance (such as alcohol, coffee, tea, and cigarettes) are being debated.

Cannabis sativa is most widely used in the United States in the form of either marihuana, the dried flowering tops of the plant, or as hashish, the resin derived from the flowering tops. *Cannabis sativa* exists in various forms (Doorenbos *et al.*, 1971), but is usually dioecious, i.e., male and female plants grow separately, with both producing flowers. It had been thought that only the female plant produced pharmacologically active con-

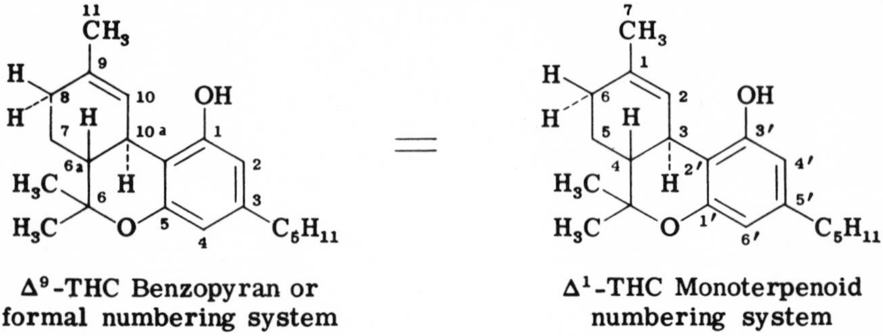

Δ^9-THC Benzopyran or formal numbering system

Δ^1-THC Monoterpenoid numbering system

Fig. 1. Nomenclature and numbering system for the tetrahydrocannabinols

stituents and, therefore, only the female plant was officially recognized as a source of cannabis preparations for medicinal purposes. Recent studies have demonstrated that the flowering tops of both male and female plants contain similar quantities of tetrahydrocannabinols, the psychoactive constituents, (Ohlsson *et al.*, 1971; Fetterman *et al.*, 1971) and that cannabinoid-containing extracts from both sexes are pharmacologically equipotent (Valle *et al.*, 1968).

Cannabis contains a multitude of chemical constituents, the cannabinoids* receiving the most attention. More than 20 cannabinoids have been isolated from the plant and their chemical structures elucidated (Shani and Mechoulam, 1970; Mechoulam, 1970). Some confusion exists as to the chemical nomenclature of the tetrahydrocannabinols since two numbering systems have been used by various workers (Fig. 1). One system treats the cannabinoids as substituted dibenzopyrans, and the other system treats them as substituted terpenes. Consequently, one of the cannabinoids can be referred to as either Δ^9-THC or Δ^1-THC, each describing the identical chemical structure. The dibenzopyran numbering system will be used throughout this chapter. The chemical structures of some cannabinoids are presented in Fig. 2.

There are two genotypes of *Cannabis sativa*; one is low in THC and high in cannabidiol content, and the other is low in cannabidiol and high in THC content. The former genotype is used for rope and fiber production, while the latter (high THC content) is used for its euphoriant effects (Ohlsson *et al.*, 1971; Fetterman *et al.*, 1971). Even within a specific genotype, the THC content of different portions of the plant varies con-

*Mechoulam (1970) uses the term cannabinoids to include the C_{21} compounds typical of and present in *Cannabis sativa*, their carboxylic acids, analogs, and transformation products.

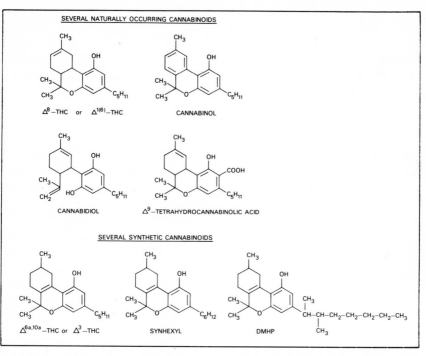

Fig. 2. Structures of some naturally occurring and synthetic cannabinoids.

siderably. This variation is primarily due to genetic factors, although environmental factors such as climate, light, and soil are also important.

The classical works of Adams et al. (1940, 1942) and Todd (1942) speculated that the active constituent of marihuana was a mixture of isomers of tetrahydrocannabinols. It was not until 1964 that Mechoulam and co-workers synthesized and characterized Δ^9-THC and subsequently demonstrated that it was the major pharmacologically active constituent of marihuana and hashish (Gaoni and Mechoulam, 1964; Mechoulam and Gaoni, 1967; Mechoulam et al., 1970). Additional pharmacologic studies in animals (Grunfeld and Edery, 1969) and man (Isbell, 1967; Hollister et al., 1968; Waskow et al., 1970) have substantiated this finding. The Δ^8 isomer (Fig. 2) is also biologically active (Mechoulam, 1970; Hollister and Gillespie, 1973; Karniol and Carlini, 1973); however, this compound represents less than 10% of the total THC content of marihuana (Hively et al., 1966).

In fresh samples of cannabis, 95% of the THC present is in the form of its acid, a pharmacologically inactive compound. In fact, cannabinolic acids (Fig. 2) are the major cannabinoids in nature, and they are slowly converted to the decarboxylated compounds upon storage. More specifically, Δ^9-THC-acid forms the active Δ^9-THC as the plant ages (Waller, 1971).

The chemistry of the cannabinoids and their structure-activity relationships have been extensively reviewed by Mechoulam (1970). Maximal activity occurs when the double bond is in the Δ^9 or Δ^8 positions; $\Delta^{6a,10a}$-THC (Fig. 2) is relatively inactive (Mechoulam et al., 1970) until its pentyl side chain is replaced by a hexyl group (to form synhexyl, Hollister et al., 1968, Fig. 2). Substituting a dimethylheptyl side chain in the $\Delta^{6a,10a}$ analog of THC results in a further increase in pharmacologic activity. The resulting compound, DMHP or EA1476 (Fig. 2), was shown to be a potent hypothermic and hypotensive agent in dogs (Boyd and Meritt, 1965; Hardman et al., 1971). In addition, studies in man also demonstrated its marked cardiovascular effects, i.e., tachycardia and postural hypotension (Sim and Tucker, 1963; Sidell et al., 1973; Lemberger et al., 1974).

The results of many studies of the pharmacologic effects of marihuana which appeared in the literature through the mid-1960's must be evaluated cautiously. Research into the pharmacology of cannabis had been severely hampered by the lack of standardization, and especially by the marked variation in potency of the marihuana preparations studied. This was largely the result of the poor state of knowledge of the chemistry of the cannabinoids and the lack of reference standards with which to compare the THC content of preparations. Researchers used marihuana of unknown origin, and in many cases clinical studies were carried out with "alleged" marihuana which had been confiscated by local law enforcement agencies. The quality of marihuana research has been markedly affected by the development of programs for large-scale synthesis of Δ^9-THC and cultivation of standardized, chemically assayed Cannabis sativa. The availability of these materials has been a major factor in increasing the quality of research conducted in this field.

Since no sensitive means to analyze the tetrahydrocannabinols were available before 1965, meaningful studies of the absorption, distribution, and metabolism of these compounds in animals or humans were lacking. The need for radioactive Δ^9-THC was obvious, and Miras (1965) successfully isolated ^{14}C-Δ^9-THC from Cannabis plants grown in a $^{14}CO_2$ environment. Later, radiolabeled Δ^9-THC was chemically synthesized (Burstein and Mechoulam, 1968; Agurell et al., 1969; Timmons et al., 1969; Nilsson et al., 1969) and became available for metabolic studies.

ABSORPTION

As stated above, results from much of the earlier research in the marihuana field must be interpreted cautiously due to the lack of pure, chemically defined materials. There are two additional considerations which are important regarding the contemporary research being conducted *in vivo*: (1) the vehicle in which the Δ⁹-THC dosage is prepared, and (2) the route of administration. The vehicle problem is one which is inherent to Δ⁹-THC, since it is lipophilic and insoluble in the vehicles usually used for studies *in vivo* (i.e., 0.9% saline and water). Therefore, suitable solvents must be added to water to solubilize Δ⁹-THC and its analogues prior to their oral or parenteral administration. Some techniques include: (a) binding or suspending the Δ⁹-THC in an albumin solution and diluting the solution or suspension with saline, (b) solubilizing the drug in a surfactant such as Tween-80 (Polysorbate-80), Triton-X, or polyvinyl-pyrolidine (PVP). Attempts have also been made to dissolve the drug in solvents such as polyethylene glycol, propylene glycol, sesame oil, DMSO, or ethanol and to administer the resulting mixture directly.

The role of the vehicle in which Δ⁹-THC is administered has been extensively studied in man by Perez-Reyes *et al.* (1973c). The drug was formulated in capsules containing ³H- Δ⁹-THC (37 mg), either dissolved in sesame oil or ethanol, or emulsified in 5.5% sodium glycocholate (a bile salt). The volunteers reported an intense and unpleasant psychologic "high" when sodium glycocholate and sesame oil were used as the vehicles, whereas the "high" from Δ⁹-THC dissolved in ethanol was described as moderate and very pleasant. The "high" reported after Δ⁹-THC in sodium glycocholate appeared 15-30 minutes after administration compared to an onset within 1 hour when sesame oil or ethanol was the vehicle. Plasma levels of total radioactivity were considerably higher and of longer duration after the sesame oil and sodium glycocholate vehicles than after the ethanol vehicle, and appeared to parallel the psychologic high.

In addition to the difficulty in comparing results between laboratories due to the different vehicles for Δ⁹-THC, use of various routes of administration has also added to the controversy. Most studies involving metabolism and disposition use small animals such as rats or mice and for the sake of convenience drugs are usually administered by the intraperitoneal or subcutaneous route. It is now clear from autoradiographic studies that Δ⁹-THC is not completely absorbed from the injection site after either intraperitoneal or subcutaneous injection (McIsaac *et al.*, 1971; Ho *et al.*, 1971; Kennedy and Waddell, 1972; Idänpään-Heikkilä *et al.*, 1971). Thus it appears that for acute experiments in animals the intravenous route should provide the most consistent results.

Isbell *et al.*, (1967) compared effects of Δ⁹-THC in man after giving the drug via the pulmonary and oral routes. They estimated the potency of Δ⁹-THC to be 2.6 to 3 times greater after smoking than after oral ingestion and suggested that more efficient absorption could be a possible explanation. Indeed, the initial plasma levels of radioactivity were found to be greater after smoking marihuana cigarettes containing ^{14}C- Δ^9-THC than after oral administration of equivalent amounts of ^{14}C- Δ^9-THC (Lemberger et al. 1972a).

DISTRIBUTION

Before radiolabeled Δ^9-THC became available, studies on the disposition of this drug were not feasible unless very large doses were administered. This was because no sensitive methods existed for detecting Δ^9-THC in tissues or biologic fluids after pharmacologic doses. After administering a large dose (100 mg/kg) of Δ^9-THC orally to rats, Forney and co-workers (King and Forney, 1967; Forney and Kiplinger, 1971) were able to measure Δ^9-THC by gas-liquid chromatography in blood, brain, liver, lung, and spleen after 3 hours. The levels in these tissues declined during a 12-hour period after administration. However, in the epididymal fat pads Δ^9-THC was just becoming measurable at this time, suggesting that Δ^9-THC was redistributed to adipose tissue.

The first studies using radioactive Δ^9-THC were by Miras and co-workers (1965; Joachimoglu et al., 1967). They obtained ^{14}C- Δ^9-THC of low specific activity (3.7 μCi/gm) so that sufficient sensitivity was not attained. However, they were able to conclude that in rats given ^{14}C- Δ^9-THC, less than 0.5% of an intraperitoneally administered dose of radioactivity was present in the brain and about 5% in the liver after 90 minutes. The rats excreted the radioactivity slowly in urine over several days, totally in the form of metabolites of Δ^9-THC. Agurell et al. (1969, 1970) intravenously administered ^{3}H- Δ^9-THC of high specific activity (140 μCi/mg) in the form of an emulsion. In rats, only 50% of the administered dose was eliminated during the first week, suggesting that the remainder was bound to tissues. Subsequently, they studied the distribution of radioactivity in rabbits. At 2 hours, the highest levels of radioactivity were present in urine and bile, the major excretory fluids. Among the tissues studied at 2 hours, the kidney contained the highest level of radioactivity followed by lung and liver (the lung had about twice that of liver). Radioactivity was also present at significant levels in the adrenals, spleen and ileum. Brain and spinal cord had the lowest levels of radioactivity among the tissues examined. This is of particular interest since this drug exerts its effects predominantly on the CNS and therefore appears to be extremely potent in its effect on neural tissue. At 72 hours the levels of radioactivity present in adipose tissue had increased from the 2-hour level while all other tissues had considerably less radioactivity than at the earlier time. These results are consistent with the aforementioned concept that Δ^9-THC is lipophilic and redistributed from blood and other tissues into adipose tissue. In rats, Klausner and Dingell (1971) studied the tissue distribution of intravenously administered ^{14}C- Δ^9-THC prepared in a solution of 30% propylene glycol and 70% rat serum. The rats were killed after 15 minutes and the diethyl ether-extractable radioactivity measured (this procedure should extract all the Δ^9-THC and part of the radioactivity present as metabolites). Their findings confirmed that lung contained quite high concentrations of radioactivity and that brain contained the least. In addition to determining total radioactivity, they measured the Δ^9-THC concentration in tissue at various times and found the highest concentration of unchanged drug (70.3 $\mu g/gm$) in lung at 15 minutes, declining to less than 3.3 $\mu g/gm$ by 2 hours. The Δ^9-THC concentration in fat at 15 minutes (2.3 $\mu g/gm$) more than doubled by 2 hours. Whole body autoradiographic studies after Δ^9-THC administration revealed a pattern of distribution of radioactivity similar to that reported using more conventional techniques (Agurell et al., 1969, 1970; Klausner and Dingell, 1971; Freudenthal et al., 1972; Kennedy and Waddell, 1972; Ryrfeldt et al., 1973).

Kreuz and Axelrod (1973) chronically administered ^3H- Δ^9-THC to rats for 30 days. They reported that the drug and its metabolites accumulated in fat and in the brain upon repeated administration. Dewey et al. (1973) also reported accumulation of radioactivity in brains of pigeons after subacute administration of ^3H- Δ^9-THC. This might be of some clinical relevance, since in man this drug is taken repeatedly and may accumulate in lipoid tissues and brain after prolonged usage.

Ho et al. (1970) studied the distribution in rats of inhaled ^3H- Δ^9-THC (administered in marihuana smoke). The results obtained were similar to those reported after administering the drug intravenously. The radioactivity persisted in brain for at least 7 days, most being in the form of metabolites.

In mice, Christensen et al. (1971) compared brain and liver levels of radioactivity and Δ^9-THC after the intravenous or intracerebral injection of ^{14}C- Δ^9-THC. At 10 minutes after the intravenous dose, about 1% of the radiolabel was present in the brain, of which about one-third was in the form of THC metabolites. In contrast, after the intracerebral injection of Δ^9-THC, the major portion (90%) of radioactivity was present as Δ^9-THC after 10 minutes, suggesting that brain tissues are unable to metabolize Δ^9-THC.

McIsaac et al. (1971) administered H^3- Δ^9-THC intravenously to squirrel monkeys and examined the regional distribution of radioactivity in brain. The animals were sacrificed at various times; half the brain was examined for the localization of radioactivity using autoradiographic techniques, whereas total radioactivity and unchanged Δ^9-THC were determined in the other hemisphere by solvent extraction and chromatography.

In general, most of the radioactivity was localized in the gray matter after 15 minutes. The radioactivity appeared to be uniformly distributed in all cortical regions, cerebellar cortex, caudate, pons, thalamus, hippocampus, and medulla; considerably less radioactivity was in the hypothalamus. They estimated that about 80% of the radioactivity was present as unchanged Δ^9-THC at this time. Similar results were reported from autoradiographic studies in rat and mouse (Kennedy and Waddell, 1972; Shannon and Fried, 1972). In contrast, Layman and Milton (1971) were unable to demonstrate a selective distribution of radioactivity in any area of the brain of rats given ^{3}H- Δ^9-THC intraperitoneally; all areas contained about equal concentrations of radioactivity. Their most interesting finding was the low, but measurable level of radioactivity present in brain 1 month after a single dose of the radioactive compound!

The binding of Δ^9-THC and its metabolites has been studied in brain at the subcellular level (Colburn et al., 1974; Dewey et al., 1974). After intravenous or intracerebral administration of radiolabeled Δ^9-THC to rats or dogs, the drug and its metabolites localized in the synaptosomal (pinched off nerve endings) and myelin fractions. In vitro, Δ^9-THC partitions between synaptosomal membranes and a buffer solution and is actively taken up by the synaptosomal membranes (Seeman et al., 1972). Since synaptosomes are thought to be important in brain function, this binding of Δ^9-THC may be of major significance in elucidating its site and mechanism of action.

The widespread usage of marihuana among young people and women of childbearing age emphasizes the need for teratologic studies of Δ^9-THC and the importance of studies of its distribution in pregnant animals. Teratogenic effects appear to be associated with injection of marihuana extracts (Persaud and Ellington, 1967, 1968; Geber, 1969), but no such effects were seen after relatively large doses of pure synthetic Δ^9-THC (Borgen and Davis, 1971; Pace et al., 1971). However, after very large doses (200-300 mg/kg i.p.) to pregnant mice, Mantilla-Platta et al. (1973) reported a significant increase in deaths in utero, a reduction of fetal body weight, and birth of offspring with cleft palate. Idänpään-Heikkilä et al. (1969) injected ^{3}H- Δ^9-THC into pregnant hamsters either intraperitoneally or subcutaneously. After 15 or 30 minutes, the levels of placental radioactivity were two to three times those present in the fetus. After ^{14}C- Δ^9-THC administration to pregnant mice, radioactivity accumulated in the fetus (Harbison and Mantilla-Plata, 1972, 1975), and the quantity of radioactivity in the fetus was found to be affected by factors which modify the metabolism of Δ^9-THC. In contrast, Pace et al. (1971) reported that maternal cotyledons of rat placenta could effectively prevent the passage of most radioactivity into the fetus after Δ^9-THC administration, resulting in only very low levels of radioactivity in the fetus. The differences in results of these studies may be explained by differences in species and/or routes of administration.

After administration of ^{14}C- Δ^9-THC to lactating female rats, radioactivity was excreted into the milk and found in the organs of the suckling infants (Jakubovic et al., 1973). Extrapolation of these data to humans is unwise due to the large doses (53 mg/kg) given to rats; however, the injudicious use of marihuana by nursing mothers could be potentially hazardous to the developing neonate.

PLASMA CONCENTRATIONS

Studies conducted in vitro indicate that at least two-thirds of the Δ^9-THC in plasma is bound to the lipoproteins; the remainder of the drug is believed to be bound to albumin (Wahlquist et al., 1970; Dingell et al., 1971; Klausner et al., 1975). Despite this binding of Δ^9-THC to plasma proteins, the drug is readily distributed into tissues; evidently the binding in plasma, though extensive, is readily reversible and/or weak. It should be noted that Klausner and coworkers (1975) observed marked differences in the plasma binding of Δ^9-THC when the drug was administered to intact rats compared to its direct addition to rat plasma; it is likely that this difference is at least partially related to the formation of metabolites of Δ^9-THC in vivo. For example, one metabolite of Δ^9-THC, 11-OH- Δ^9-THC, is extensively bound (90-94%) to plasma proteins, but primarily to albumin and the a-lipoprotein fractions (Widman et al., 1971, 1973).

In vivo, the concentrations of Δ^9-THC and its metabolites in blood have been studied in many species, including man. In rabbit, Agurell et al. (1970) found that after intravenous administration, ^3H- Δ^9-THC rapidly disappeared from plasma and after 30 minutes only 3-4% of the radioactivity was present as unchanged drug. The radioactivity declined in a biphasic fashion with the half-life at the terminal end of the curve being about 2 hours. In the rat, Klausner and Dingell (1971) also found a biphasic plasma decay curve; the half-life of the drug was about ten times longer than in the rabbit. In man, Lemberger et al. (1970a, 1971a) investigated the plasma concentrations of intravenously administered ^{14}C- Δ^9-THC. In volunteers, who claimed no previous exposure to cannabis, Δ^9-THC disappeared from plasma rapidly during the first few hours; thereafter, the Δ^9-THC concentrations fell more slowly (half-life of 56 hours). It is likely that the initial, rapid phase is due to distribution of the Δ^9-THC from the intravascular compartment to the tissue compartment, as well as to metabolism of the compound. Total radioactivity and ether-extractable radioactivity (containing metabolites) also showed biphasic plasma decay curves. When this study was repeated in chronic marihuana smokers (i.e., subjects who smoked marihuana daily for at least 1 year prior to the experiment), a biphasic plasma decay curve was seen again. However, the half-life of the drug was only 27 hours. There were no group differences in the apparent volumes of distribution of Δ^9-THC. Both groups of subjects appeared to be similar in all respects, except for the fact that one group smoked marihuana chronically. It appears that a constituent of the marihuana cigarette (such as Δ^9-THC itself, another cannabinoid, or a polycyclic hydrocarbon absorbed during the smoking process) may induce enzymes that catalyze the disappearance of Δ^9-THC. Evidence in support of this hypothesis is that the rate of metabolism of Δ^9-THC by rat lung is increased by pretreating the rats with a polycyclic hydrocarbon (Nakazawa and Costa, 1971). In man, Δ^9-THC disappears from plasma similarly after inhalation and after intravenous administration (Lemberger et al., 1972a; Galanter et al., 1972; Agurell et al., 1973). Δ^9-THC and its metabolites were detectable in human plasma for at least 3 days. This persistence of drug and its metabolites in the body is reminiscent of the animal studies alluded to earlier in which drug concentrations in the body were also prolonged. It appears that Δ^9-THC and its metabolites are stored in human tissues as well. This finding is of considerable interest because animal studies indicate that the highest concentrations of Δ^9-THC and its metabolites are present in lung tissue and because in man inhalation is the usual route of administration.

After oral administration of ^{14}C- Δ^9-THC (dissolved in ethanol), man absorbed 90-95% of the dose from the gastrointestinal tract (Lemberger et al., 1971b; Weiss et al., 1972). Plasma levels increased slowly, reached a peak at 3 hours, and then gradually declined (Lemberger et al., 1971b,c). The peak psychologic effects also occurred at about 3 hours (Lemberger et al., 1971c, 1972a). Plasma levels of radioactivity after oral or inhaled ^{14}C-Δ^9-THC correlated well with the pharmacologic effects (Lemberger et al., 1971b,c, 1972a; Galanter et al., 1972; Weiss et al., 1972; Agurell et al., 1975). Of considerable interest is that the onset, intensity, and duration of psychologic effects appeared to correlate positively with the rise, peak, and decreasing levels of metabolites rather than with the levels of Δ^9-THC itself (Lemberger et al., 1972a). This is discussed below in greater detail.

In 1971, Agurell et al. synthesized ^{3}H-11-OH- Δ^8-THC and studied its metabolic disposition in rabbits after intravenous administration (Nilsson et al., 1973). These investigators found that 11-OH- Δ^8-THC was initially removed from the blood rapidly. After 10 minutes, there was a reappearance of the unchanged drug in the circulation and it reached its peak plasma concentration at 60 minutes. They reported a positive correlation between the blood levels of 11-OH- Δ^8-THC and its overt pharmacologic effects.

After administration to rabbits, radiolabelled 11-OH- Δ^8-THC was metabolized rapidly and the radioactivity was excreted predominantly in urine. Only a small percent of the total urinary radioactivity was due to the presence of parent drug; the remainder appeared to have properties of a carboxylic acid (Nilsson et al., 1973). Similar results were obtained in man by Lemberger et al. (1972b) who administered ^{3}H-11-OH- Δ^9-THC intravenously to infrequent marihuana users and demonstrated that the unchanged drug disappeared from plasma in a biphasic fashion with a half-life of 22 hours. In man, the pharmacokinetics of 11-OH- Δ^9-THC were similar to those seen after Δ^9-THC administration. 11-OH- Δ^9-THC was excreted in both urine and feces to approximately the same extent as Δ^9-THC, i.e., 22% excreted in urine and 50% in feces. The metabolites present in urine and feces after 11-OH- Δ^9-THC administration were found to be both qualitatively and quantitatively the same as those seen after Δ^9-THC administration (Lemberger et al., 1972b). Recently, Wall et al. (1975) obtained similar results after the administration of 11-OH- Δ^9-THC and also concluded that after intravenous administration, Δ^9THC and 11-OH- Δ^9-THC followed similar pathways.

METABOLISM

Pyrolytic Transformations of Cannabinoids

Since inhalation is the most widely used route of administration of marihuana, several laboratories have investigated the effect of combustion and smoking on the constituents of cannabis. In some cases the results are equivocal because the techniques, temperatures of combustion, and other conditions varied between laboratories. These problems are, however, difficult to resolve since each group is critical of the conditions of others and each states that their study best simulates the smoking of marihuana by actual users.

Claussen and Korte (1968) reported that during the smoking process, the carboxylic acids (see Fig. 2) of the cannabinoids present in marihuana are decarboxylated to free cannabinols, most notably to tetrahydrocannabinol and cannabidiol. Manno et al. (1970), using a smoking machine, analyzed the constituents of marihuana smoke and calculated that if each inhalation of smoke were retained in the alveoli and bronchial tree for 30 seconds, about half the Δ^9-THC originally present in the cigarette would be absorbed. They found less than 0.1% of cannabinoids in the butt (or "roach" as it is called by experienced marihuana smokers). They also found no evidence for isomerization of Δ^9-THC to Δ^8-THC. Mikes and Waser (1971), using artificially smoked cigarettes impregnated with synthetic Δ^9-THC, also found no evidence for isomerization of Δ^9-THC or for the

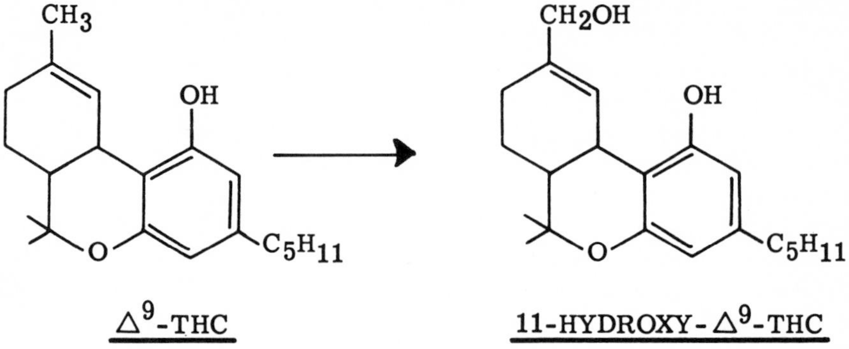

Fig. 3. Metabolic conversion of Δ⁹-THC to 11-OH-Δ⁹-THC.

formation of any pyrolysis products. However, in their study, cigarette butts were found to contain about 22% of the originally added Δ⁹-THC after the completion of the smoking process. Truitt (1971) and co-workers have also reported similar results and concluded that about 50% of the total dose of Δ⁹-THC is delivered to the smoker only when the butt is completely consumed. Coutselinis and Miras (1970), using a similar experimental design, studied the effect of the smoking process on Δ⁹-THC. They found Δ⁹-THC to be more labile when it was the only cannabinoid present. This is of interest since Galanter *et al.* (1973) noted that an authentic marihuana cigarette containing a known amount of Δ⁹-THC appeared to be more psychoactive in man than was a placebo cigarette to which an identical quantity of synthetic Δ⁹-THC had been added. One obvious explanation for the increased activity of crude marihuana when compared to synthetic Δ⁹-THC is that some material present in marihuana potentiates the effects of Δ⁹-THC. Indeed, evidence by Paton and Pertwee (1971) suggests that cannabidiol may play such a role. They found that cannabidiol potentiated pentobarbital sleep time, apparently by exerting an inhibitory effect on the liver microsomal system responsible for the metabolic inactivation of the barbiturate. If cannabidiol inhibited the metabolism of Δ⁹-THC, then crude marihuana would have a "built-in" synergist. This issue is discussed in greater detail below (inhibition of Δ⁹-THC metabolism).

Agurell and Leander (1971) recently reported that only 14-29% of the cannabinoids added to cigarettes are transferred to the respiratory system via mainstream smoke. They calculated that the experienced cannabis smoker, using deep inhalations, absorbed more than 80% of the cannabinoids presented to the lungs in the mainstream smoke. Their studies also demonstrated that, except for decarboxylation of the cannabinolic

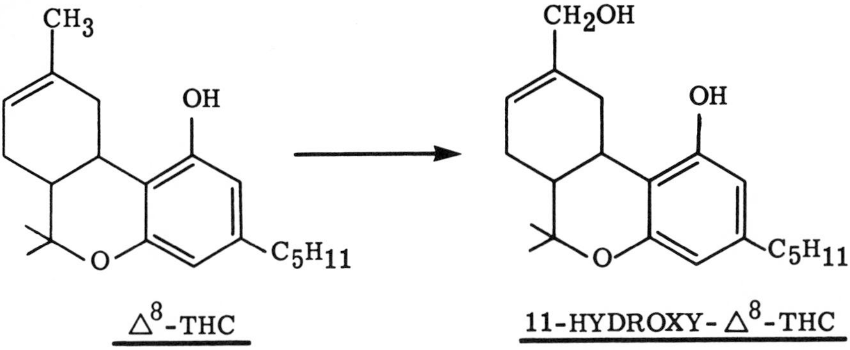

Fig. 4. Metabolic conversion of Δ⁸-THC to 11-OH-Δ⁸-THC.

acids, the smoking process produced only negligible changes in the cannabinoids in marihuana.

Metabolism of Cannabinoids *in Vitro*

As is usually the case in areas of great scientific interest, many laboratories in different parts of the world have simultaneously studied the metabolic fate of tetrahydrocannabinols in liver microsomal enzyme preparations. Early reports in the literature described the structural identification of one of the major metabolites of Δ^9-THC formed *in vitro*. When radiolabeled Δ^9-THC was incubated with the 10,000 g liver supernate (containing the microsomal enzymes) obtained from rats and rabbits, a polar metabolite was identified as 11-hydroxy- Δ^9-THC (Fig. 3) (Nilsson *et al.*, 1970; Wall *et al.*, 1970). This metabolite represented approximately 40% of the substrate initially present. Simultaneously, others described the hydroxylation of Δ^8-THC to 11-OH- Δ^8-THC (Fig. 4) (Foltz *et al.*, 1970; Burstein *et al.*, 1970; Ben-Zvi *et al.*, 1970). These various investigators reported that in preliminary behavioral studies in mice and rats, 11-OH- Δ^9-THC and its Δ^8 analog were as potent or more potent pharmacologically than their respective parent compounds. Christensen *et al.* (1971) reported that 11-OH- Δ^9-THC had pharmacologic activity approximately 2-15 times that of Δ^9-THC, depending upon its route of administration; the intracerebral route produced greater effects than the intravenous route.

In addition to the formation of an 11-hydroxylated metabolite of Δ^9-THC, 8,11-dihydroxy- Δ^9-THC has been isolated and identified and represents approximately 30% of the original Δ^9-THC added to the incubation flask (Wall *et al.*, 1970; Wall, 1971). A minor metabolite was 8 β-

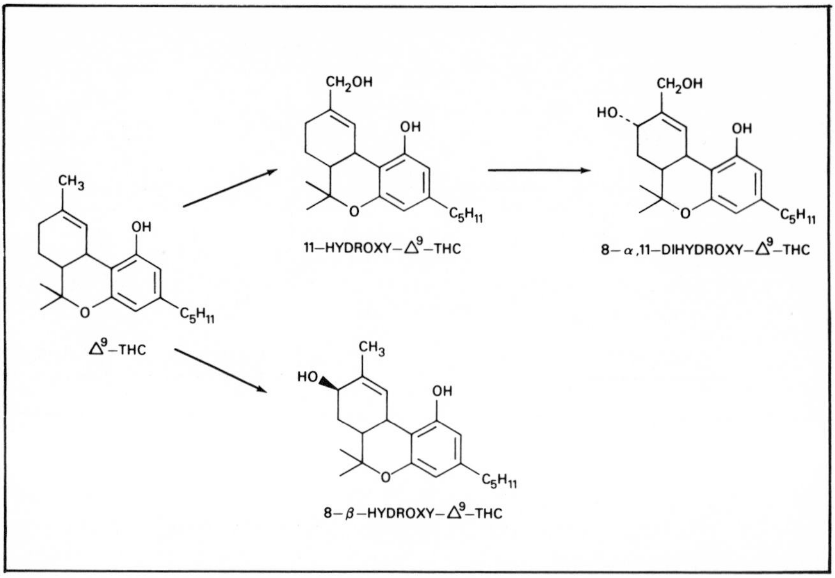

Fig. 5. Metabolic pathways for Δ⁹-THC *in vitro*.

hydroxy- Δ⁹-THC. The dihydroxy compound was inactive even when very large doses were studied (Christensen *et al.*, 1971), whereas the 8 β-hydroxy compound did exhibit pharmacologic activity (Wall *et al.*, 1970; Edery *et al.*, 1971; Wall, 1971) (Fig. 5). When Δ⁹-THC was incubated with a 10,000 g supernate prepared from human liver obtained at autopsy, both the 11-OH- Δ⁹-THC and 8,11-dihydroxy- Δ⁹-THC were formed (Christensen *et al.*, 1971). When Δ⁹-THC was incubated with a mouse liver microsomal preparation, 8 α-hydroxy- Δ⁹-THC was isolated in addition to 11-OH- Δ⁹-THC (Ryrfeldt *et al.*, 1973; Ben-Zvi *et al.*, 1974; Jones *et al.*, 1974).

Utilizing Δ⁸-THC as a substrate for the liver microsomal system, Wall (1971) not only confirmed the formation of 11-OH- Δ⁸-THC as the major metabolite, but also identified 7 α,11-dihydroxy- Δ⁸-THC and 7 β,11-di-hydroxy- Δ⁸-THC as additional metabolites (Fig. 6). The hydroxylation of the methyl groups at C-11 and C-8 positions of Δ⁹-THC and at the C-11 and C-7 positions of Δ⁸-THC is not surprising because these positions are allylic to the double bond; a similar metabolic conversion is seen with the barbiturate hexobarbital whose metabolism by hepatic drug-metabolizing enzymes has been studied extensively.

Maynard *et al.* (1971) have recently reported hydroxylation at the 1'-and 3'-positions on the side chain of Δ⁸-THC (Fig. 6) using a dog liver

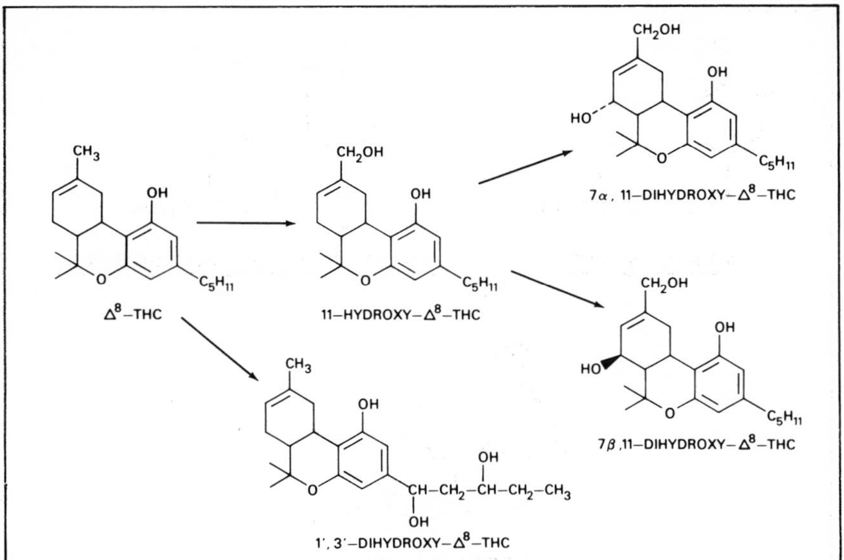

Fig. 6. Metabolic conversions for Δ⁸-THC *in vitro*.

10,000 g supernatant fraction in the presence of NADPH and oxygen. These appear, however, to be only minor metabolites of Δ⁸-THC. Using a squirrel monkey liver preparation to which Δ⁹-THC was added as the substrate, Gurny et al. (1972) identified 8-keto- Δ⁹-THC and 9,10-epoxyhexahydrocannabinol as metabolites (Fig. 7). When Δ⁸-THC was the substrate, 7-keto- Δ⁸-THC was isolated (Fig. 7). Mechoulam et al. (1972) synthesized these compounds and tested them in monkeys for behavioral effects. The epoxy compound produced typical cannabis effects, whereas 8-keto- Δ⁹-THC was inactive at doses up to 5 mg/kg i.v. In contrast, 7-keto- Δ⁸-THC produced ataxia and stupor at a dose of 1 mg/kg.

Recently, Agurell et al. (in press) demonstrated that isolated perfused dog lung produced metabolites of Δ⁹-THC which were extensively hydroxylated in the side chain. Among these metabolites were 3′-hydroxy-Δ⁹-THC and 4′-hydroxy- Δ⁹-THC. Of special interest was the finding that these compounds were more potent than Δ⁹-THC when tested for pharmacologic effects after i.v. administration to rhesus monkeys. These metabolites were not produced to any appreciable extent by dog liver 10,000g preparations.

Nakazawa and Costa (1971), using microsomes prepared from rat lung, demonstrated that Δ⁹-THC was metabolized to two unidentified products that had not previously been found in studies involving liver

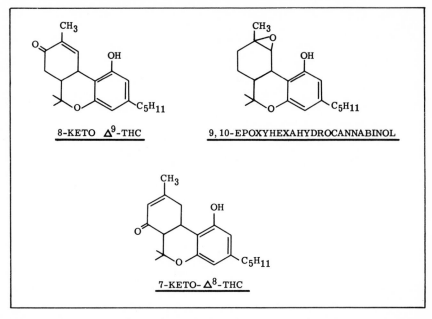

Fig. 7. Several metabolic products of Δ⁹ and Δ⁸-THC involving ketone and epoxide formation.

microsomes. These compounds appear to be more polar than Δ^9-THC but less polar that 11-OH- Δ^9-THC. The pulmonary biotransformation of Δ^9-THC was enhanced by pretreating the rats with 3-methylcholanthrene, an inducer of drug-metabolizing enzymes localized in the microsomal fraction of lung tissue (Gilman and Conney, 1963). In addition, the 3-methylcholanthrene enhanced the behavioral effects of Δ^9-THC, suggesting that the two aforementioned metabolites might be active compounds. In any event, the major route of marihuana administration in humans is inhalation, and the fact that lung tissue can metabolize Δ^9-THC is quite interesting.

A new *in vitro* metabolite of Δ^9-THC has recently been isolated and identified as 11-oxo- Δ^9-THC, the aldehyde formed by oxidation of 11-OH-Δ^9-THC (Fig. 8) (Ben Zvi and Burstein, 1974). Cannabinol is a pharmacologically inactive constituent of marihuana. It is hydroxylated at the C-11 methyl group, and the resultant 11-hydroxycannabinol (Fig. 9) is its major metabolite (Widman et al., 1971; Wall, 1971). Two minor metabolites of cannabinol have been tentatively identified as the hydroxylated products of both cannabinol and 11-hydroxycannabinol; the hydroxylation allegedly occurs at the 2'-position of the pentyl side chain (Wall, 1971).

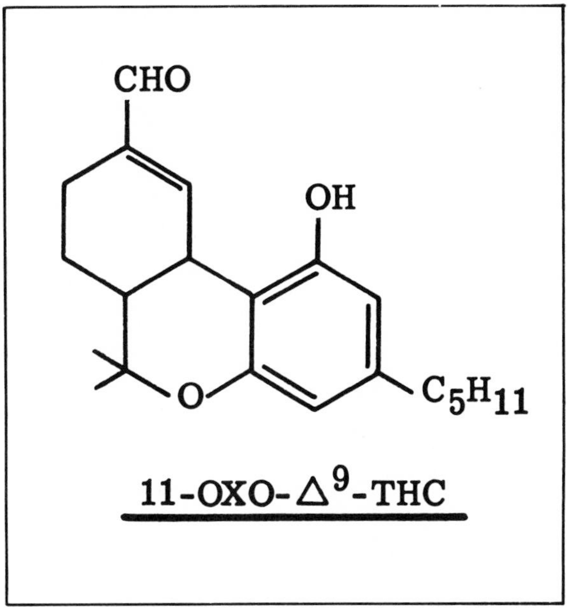

CHO

OH

C_5H_{11}

11-OXO-Δ^9-THC

Fig. 8. Structure of 11-oxo-Δ^9-THC, an aldehyde intermediate of Δ^9-THC.

Nilsson *et al.* (1971, 1973) studied the metabolism of cannabidiol by a rat liver microsomal enzyme system and identified two metabolites: 11-hydroxycannabidiol (the major metabolite) and a product hydroxylated at the 3'-position of the pentyl side chain (Fig. 10). It is unknown whether these hydroxylated metabolites of cannabidiol are pharmacologically active.

In summary metabolic studies with tetrahydrocannabinols and other cannabinoids have been carried out using livers obtained from rabbit, dog, mouse, rat, guinea pig, and human; in all these species the same or similar hydroxylated compounds appear to be formed from cannabinoids.

Metabolism of Tetrahydrocannabinols *in Vivo*

Metabolic studies *in vivo* confirm certain of the findings *in vitro*. 11-Hydroxylation appears to be an important route of metabolism for Δ^8-THC and Δ^9-THC *in vivo* for mice (Christensen *et al.*, 1971), rabbits (Burstein *et al.*, 1970; Ben-Zvi *et al.*, 1970), and rats (Foltz *et al.*, 1970). In mice, Christensen *et al.* (1971) found 11-OH-Δ^9-THC present within 30 seconds after the intravenous injection of Δ^9-THC. At 3 minutes, both the

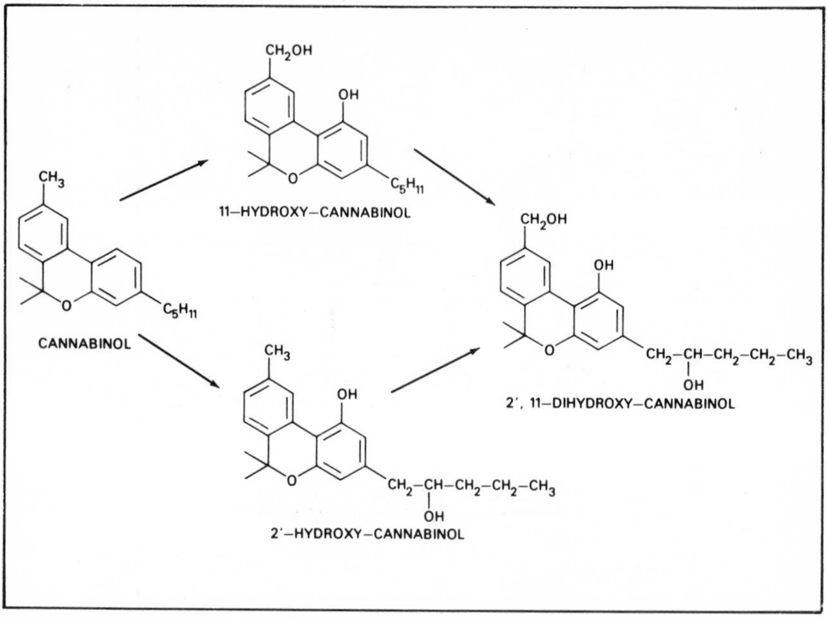

Fig. 9. Metabolic pathways for cannabinol *in vitro*.

11-hydroxy and 8,11-dihydroxy metabolites were present in blood. In man, 11-OH- Δ^9-THC is formed rapidly, appearing in plasma within 10 minutes after intravenous administration of Δ^9-THC (Lemberger et al., 1970a).

In addition to 11-OH- Δ^9-THC, an 11-carboxy metabolite of Δ^9-THC and 8 α- and 8 β-hydroxy- Δ^9-THC have also been identified in plasma (Wall et al., 1972, 1975). In man, 11-OH- Δ^9-THC and 8,11-dihydroxy- Δ^9-THC are excreted primarily in the feces (Lemberger et al., 1971b; Wall et al., 1975). The 11-hydroxymetabolite represents about 22% of the total radioactivity recovered in feces, 8,11-dihydroxy- Δ^9-THC represents slightly less. Also present in feces are unidentified radioactive compounds having characteristics of more polar compounds, and perhaps they are conjugates of Δ^9-THC metabolites. In urine, only a small quantity (about 3%) of the total radioactivity recovered was present as 11-OH- Δ^9-THC (Lemberger et al., 1970a; Woodhouse, 1972).

After administering Δ^9-THC to rabbits, Agurell et al. (1970) found radioactive compounds in urine that exhibited acidic characteristics and that were not hydrolyzed by β-glucuronidase. In man, about 20-30% of the radioactivity of an administered dose of ^{14}C- Δ^9-THC appeared in the

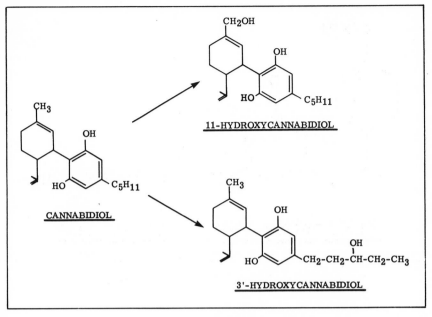

Fig. 10. Metabolic conversion of cannabidiol *in vitro*.

urine, all in the form of metabolites (Lemberger *et al.*, 1970a, 1971a,b). About 90% of the urinary compounds contributing to the radioactivity had acidic properties (i.e., they were extractable into ethyl acetate at pH 3 but not at pH 7). Possibly these polar acidic metabolites present in human urine are identical with those found in rabbit urine by Agurell and associates. In contrast to urine, human feces did not contain any acidic compounds (Lemberger *et al.*, 1971b).

Recently, Burstein *et al.* (1972) isolated an acidic metabolite from rabbit urine and tentatively identified it as 11-carboxy-2'-hydroxy- Δ^9-THC (Fig. 11). They postulated that the other acidic metabolites of Δ^9-THC might be amides or esters of this compound. Cochromatography of this rabbit metabolite with material obtained from human urine suggested that man also formed 11-carboxy-2'-hydroxy- Δ^9-THC. In addition to this acidic metabolite, others including 11-carboxy- Δ^9-THC (Wall *et al.*, 1973) and a dicarboxylic compound (11-carboxy-3'-carboxy- Δ^9-THC) (Nordquest *et al.*, 1974) have been identified.

Recently, a new minor metabolite of Δ^8-THC, 1-methoxy-11-hydroxy- Δ^8-THC (Fig. 12) has been reported to be formed in rats (Estevez *et al.*,

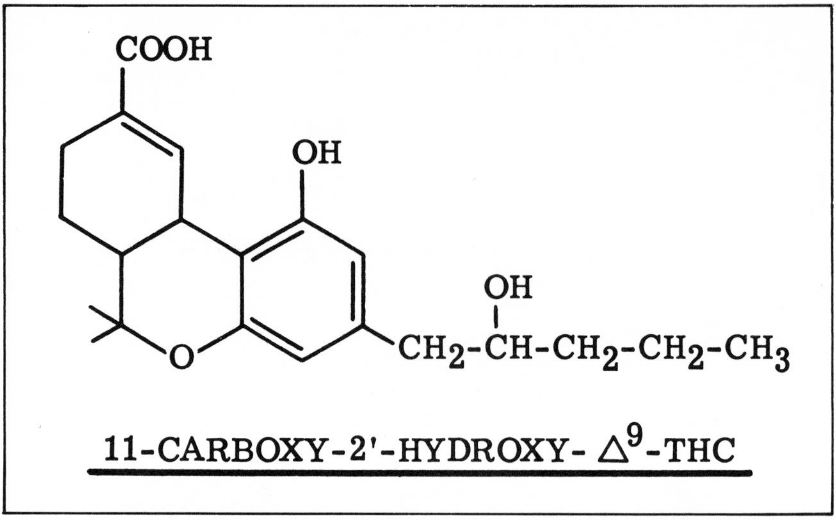

COOH

OH

OH

$CH_2-CH-CH_2-CH_2-CH_3$

11-CARBOXY-2'-HYDROXY- Δ^9-THC

Fig. 11. Structure of a carboxylic acid derivative of Δ^9-THC.

1973). This compound has not been found previously; confirmation of its formation would be important in considering a pharmacologic role for this metabolite.

Factors Affecting Δ^9-THC Metabolism

The knowledge that Δ^9-THC is a substrate for the hepatic microsomal enzyme system has prompted numerous investigators to study the effects of other drugs known to affect these enzymes in the metabolism of Δ^9-THC *in vitro* and *in vivo*.

Stimulation of Δ^9-THC Metabolism. From the studies of Conney and Burns (1959, 1962, 1963) and of Remmer (1958a,b, 1962), we know that pretreating animals or man (Burns and Conney, 1965) with a variety of diverse chemicals can stimulate the metabolism of other chemicals taken concurrently. Several investigators have attempted to stimulate the metabolism of Δ^9-THC by pretreating animals with the prototype enzyme inducer phenobarbital. Wall *et al.* (1970) and Nilsson *et al.* (1970), in their *in vitro* studies, routinely used phenobarbital-pretreated animals to study the metabolism of Δ^9-THC. Livers from animals not pretreated with phenobarbital provided similar results with respect to the kind and number

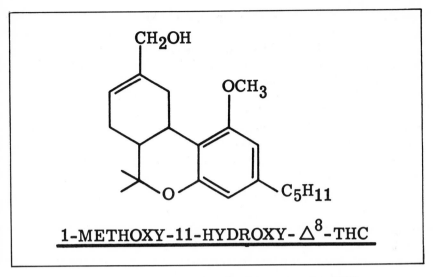

Fig. 12. Structure of a methoxylated derivative of Δ 8-THC.

of metabolites formed, but they yielded lesser amounts of the metabolites (Wall, 1971).

Pretreating mice with phenobarbital reduced the mortality induced by Δ⁹-THC, presumably by increasing Δ⁹-THC metabolism to pharmacologically inactive compounds (Mantilla-Plata and Harbison, 1971). Fujimoto (1972) demonstrated that phenobarbital pretreatment of mice modified the effects of Δ⁹-THC on hexobarbital sleep time. Although the data were consistent with those expected after induction of liver enzymes by phenobarbital, the data suggested that the interaction was in fact at the level of the CNS, and he emphasized the need to delineate between interactions occurring at the CNS and liver in assessing the interaction *in vivo* of Δ⁹-THC with other drugs. In contrast to all these findings, Gill *et al.* (1973) found no effect in rats of phenobarbital pretreatment on the metabolism *in vitro* of Δ⁹-THC.

Kupfer and co-workers (Burstein and Kupfer, 1971; Kupfer *et al.*, 1973) studied the microsomal metabolism of Δ⁹-THC in rats pretreated with DDT, a potent inducer of hepatic microsomal enzymes. Liver microsomes obtained from the DDT-treated rats metabolized ·Δ⁹-THC faster than control rats, and more of the hydroxylated metabolites were formed. We have already cited studies wherein lung microsomes prepared from rats pretreated with the enzyme inducer, 3-methylcholanthrene, were shown to metabolize Δ^9-THC faster than lung microsomes prepared from control animals (Nakazawa and Costa, 1971). In man, chronic cannabis users appear to metabolize Δ^9-THC more rapidly than nonusers (Lemberger *et al.*, 1971a). Whether this is due to Δ^9-THC or some other component of marihuana smoke increasing the metabolism of Δ^9-THC is unknown. Welch *et al.* (1969) have shown that placental tissue from women who smoke tobacco chronically can metabolize more 3,4-benzpyrene *in vitro* than placental tissue from nonsmokers. It remains to be determined if a common constituent of marihuana and tobacco smoke (e.g., polycyclic hydrocarbons) is responsible for the stimulated metabolism of Δ^9-THC and benzpyrene in humans.

In animals, attempts have been made to determine whether subacute administration of Δ^9-THC induces its own metabolism. The reports are conflicting. Ho *et al.* (1973) reported that subacute administration of Δ^9-THC to rats resulted in greater metabolism of Δ^9-THC by liver homogenates, but not by lung homogenates. Others have been unable to repeat these findings with Δ^9-THC (McMillan *et al.*, 1973; Schou *et al.*, 1972). However, in pigs, Schou has shown that although Δ^9-THC did not stimulate its own metabolism, marihuana extract did stimulate the metabolism of Δ^9-THC *in vivo*. Sofia (1973) suggested that chronic Δ^9-THC treatment may have stimulated the hepatic microsomal enzymes responsible for metabolizing zoxazolamine and hexobarbital since it decreased the duration of sleep time caused by these drugs. Moreover, administration of marihuana extract or marihuana smoke to rats and hamsters can induce benzpyrene hydroxylase (also known as aryl hydrocarbon hydroxylase) in lung, but induces it only a negligible extent in liver (Okamoto *et al.*, 1972; Marcotte and Witschi, 1972).

Inhibition of Δ^9-THC Metabolism. Theoretically, any drug which is metabolized by the liver microsomal enzyme system that metabolizes Δ^9-THC is also capable of inhibiting the metabolism of Δ^9-THC by acting as an alternate substrate (Rubin *et al.*, 1964a,b). Δ^9-THC binds to cytochrome P-450 of hepatic microsomes producing a type I spectral shift, similar to that produced by hexobarbital (Cohen *et al.*, 1971; Kupfer *et al.*, 1972). Δ^9-THC also has a high affinity for cytochrome P-450 and, therefore, should be a potent inhibitor of other type I microsomal oxidations. In fact, Δ^9-THC inhibits the oxidation of aminopyrine and hexobarbital (Dewey *et al.*, 1970; Dingell *et al.*, 1971, 1973).

Several interactions have been noted to occur between marihuana or Δ^9-THC and other drugs administered to animals. Sleeping times after hexobarbital (Garriot *et al.*, 1967) and pentobarbital administration (Kubena and Barry, 1970; Gill *et al.*, 1970) have been reported to be prolonged following pretreatment of animals with Δ^9-THC. Since Δ^9-THC is itself a CNS depressant, one explanation for this finding is that there is an additive or potentiating effect between Δ^9-THC and the barbiturates. Another possible explanation is that Δ^9-THC potentiates the effects of barbiturates by inhibiting their metabolism. The latter view is supported (though not to the exclusion of the former view) by studies which clearly show that Δ^9-THC can inhibit the metabolism of hexobarbital *in vitro* (Cohen *et al.*, 1971; Dingell *et al.*, 1971). Rating *et al.* (1972) measured the concentration of hexobarbital in blood and cerebral tissue after administering it to rats pretreated with Δ^8-THC. They found no significant difference in the hexobarbital concentration in brain or blood between pretreated and untreated control rats, suggesting the metabolism played no important role. Kubena and Barry (1970) reported a potentiating effect in rats between Δ^9-THC and the sleep time induced by barbital, a barbiturate that is supposedly *not* metabolized to any significant extent by hepatic microsomal enzymes. It appears likely, therefore, that both a direct CNS depressant effect and inhibition of the liver microsomes may be involved in the Δ^9-THC potentiation of barbiturate sleeping times. Paradoxically, pretreating rats with Δ^9-THC before the administration of amphetamine or methamphetamine potentiates both the magnitude and duration of the stimulated spontaneous motor activity elicited by the amphetamines (Garriot *et al.*, 1967; Kubena and Barry, 1970; Phillips *et al.*, 1971). This potentiation increases with increasing doses of Δ^9-THC. Drugs which inhibit the metabolism of amphetamines will potentiate their pharmacologic effects (Consolo *et al.*, 1967; Sulser *et al.*, 1966; Lemberger *et al.*, 1970b). In the case of inhibitors which possess CNS depressant activity in their own right (e.g., chlorpromazine), the net effect will depend upon the dosage administered (Sulser and Dingell, 1968). Thus, when small doses of chlorpromazine were used with amphetamine, the net effect was stimulation. However, when amphetamine was given with larger doses of chlorpromazine, a CNS depression occurred and the amphetamine effect was masked. The mechanism of Δ^9-THC potentiation of amphetamine effects is unknown. However, an inhibitory effect on amphetamine metabolism seems likely. To make matters even more complex, Pirch *et al.* (1973) reported that marihuana extract *antagonized* amphetamine locomotor stimulation. Furthermore, Howes (1973) reported a differential effect of Δ^9-THC on amphetamine lethality in aggregated mice (an increase or decrease depending upon the dose). Studies in man by Evans *et al.* (1974) and Dalton *et al.* (1974) showed that marihuana smoking produced only an additive effect on the pharmacologic effects of secobarbital or amphetamine.

SKF-525A, the prototype inhibitor of the hepatic microsomal enzyme system (Axelrod, 1954a; Cooper *et al.*, 1954), is a potent inhibitor of the metabolism of Δ⁹-THC *in vitro* (Dingell *et al.*, 1971, 1973) and *in vivo* (Gill and Jones, 1972; Estevez *et al*, 1973). Pretreatment with this compound has been found to potentiate the toxicity and mortality in mice due to Δ⁹-THC (Mantilla-Plata and Harbison, 1971) and to delay the onset of behavioral effects of Δ⁹-THC in rats (Peterson *et al.*, 1971). This effect of SKF-525A on toxicity and lethality of Δ⁹-THC suggests that Δ⁹-THC itself is pharmacologically active; in contrast, this effect of SKF-525A on behavioral actions of Δ⁹-THC suggests that a metabolite (or metabolites) is (are) responsible for the behavioral effects of Δ⁹-THC. This matter of an active metabolite of Δ⁹-THC is discussed further in a subsequent section of this chapter.

The interaction between a single dose of Δ⁹-THC and ethanol has been examined in animals (Phillips *et al.*, 1971; Dewey *et al.*, 1971) and in man (Manno *et al.*, 1971). The combination of these drugs resulted in a potentiation of their depressant effects. Chronic usage of ethanol is known to stimulate the liver microsomal enzymes which metabolize drugs, whereas inhibitory effects have been seen after acute alcohol administration (Rubin and Lieber, 1971). No direct evidence exists to suggest that Δ⁹-THC and ethanol inhibit each other's metabolism and/or that they interact at the level of the CNS.

Recent evidence has demonstrated that although Δ⁹-THC is the psychoactive principle of marihuana, the other cannabinoids are not without effect. Cannabidiol, for example, produces no pharmacologic effects in animals (Edery *et al.*, 1971; Christensen *et al.*, 1971) or in man (Hollister, 1973; Perez-Reyes *et al.*, 1973a) when administered alone at doses up to 100 mg orally or 30 mg intravenously. However, when administered with pentobarbital, it potentiates the sleep time by inhibiting the metabolism of this barbiturate (Paton and Pertwee, 1972). Indeed, Jones and Pertwee (1972) found that cannabidiol inhibited the metabolism of Δ⁹-THC *in vitro*, suggesting that cannabidiol could affect the action of Δ⁹-THC *in vivo*. As a matter of fact, the pharmacologic effects of Δ⁹-THC in animals have been modified by pretreatment with cannabidiol (Karniol and Carlini, 1973; Borgen and Davis, 1974). Recently, Siemens *et al.* (1975) showed that cannabidiol affected the distribution of Δ⁹-THC, causing more to be localized in lung tissue. They concluded that this was unrelated to inhibition of metabolism since pretreatment with SKF-525A did not produce this effect.

Sex Differences in Δ⁹-*THC Metabolism.* A sex difference is seen in rats with respect to the metabolism of drugs by the microsomal enzymes (Quinn *et al.*, 1958; Kuntzman *et al.*, 1964). In most laboratory strains, male rats metabolize drugs and steroids more rapidly than females, and the administration of testosterone to females (or estrogen to males) can abolish this difference. Burstein and Kupfer (1971) reported that liver microsomes obtained from male rats metabolize Δ^9-THC at a faster rate than those from females. In addition, the hypothermic and behavioral responses of rats, to whom marihuana extract distillate and synthetic Δ^9-THC were administered, indicated that a sex difference existed; both effects were more pronounced in the female than in the male rat (Cohen et al., 1971; Borgen et al., 1973).

BIOCHEMICAL CORRELATES OF CLINICAL FINDINGS

Tolerance versus Reverse Tolerance

The availability of large supplies of synthetic Δ^9-THC has facilitated animal investigations designed to answer the question whether or not tolerance develops to the effects of marihuana. In animals, several studies have reported the development of tolerance to some effects of Δ^9-THC (Silva et al., 1968; McMillan et al., 1970; Frankenheim et al., 1971; Kosersky et al., 1974). It is not known whether this tolerance is dispositional (e.g., induction of enzymes resulting in a faster disappearance of the drug and, hence, lower blood and brain levels, as has been postulated for the barbiturates) or if it is cellular tolerance similar to that postulated to occur with opiate derivatives (Jaffe, 1970) (see Chapter 10). Metabolic studies revealed no differences in the absorption, disposition, or metabolism of Δ^9-THC in tolerant versus nontolerant pigeons (McMillan et al., 1973; Dewey et al., 1973). In these studies, the doses of Δ^9-THC used were high (up to 10 mg/kg/day) compared to doses used in man where Δ^9-THC is active at doses as low as 3-6 μg/kg (Kiplinger et al., 1971; Evans et al., 1973). Therefore, the animal models might not represent what occurs in man. In addition, tolerance may develop for only some of the multiple effects of Δ^9-THC, while other effects might be unaltered with repeated drug administration (Hollister and Tinklenberg, 1973; Renault et al., 1974).

Phillips et al. (1971) reported an increased sensitivity to Δ^9-THC stimulatory effects after its repeated administration to rats. Similarly, many marihuana users claim that they do not achieve a "high" the first time they use this drug. The first scientific study to demonstrate this was reported by Weil et al. (1968). They found chronic users of marihuana achieved a "high" after a 2-gm dose of marihuana, whereas about 90% of naive subjects (nonusers of marihuana) did not respond to the same dose of marihuana. This effect has been referred to as "reverse" tolerance, and it appears to be a complex phenomenon to say the least. Similar findings were reported by some (Meyer et al., 1971; Lemberger et al., 1971a), but not by others. For example, Perez-Reyes et al. (1974) reported that marihuana, as currently used by young Americans, produces neither tolerance nor reverse tolerance. A well-controlled prospective clinical study is needed to resolve this controversy.

The finding that chronic users of marihuana metabolize Δ^9-THC faster than nonusers (Lemberger *et al.*, 1971a) suggests that with chronic marihuana usage, hepatic microsomal enzyme systems are induced. "Reverse" tolerance might be explained, therefore, if a metabolite of Δ^9-THC were, in fact, active. Conversely, tolerance might be explained if metabolism of Δ^9-THC were a deactivation process. Other important factors to be considered in explaining "reverse" tolerance are (1) an alteration in receptor sensitivity for Δ^9-THC; (2) a familiarity through learning (and consequently a heightened response to the effects of Δ^9-THC); and (3) cumulative effects occurring after repeated administration of Δ^9-THC due to its marked lipid solubility and resultant tissue storage.

Spontaneous Recurrence ("Flash Back")

There have been many reports of spontaneous recurrences or a "flash back" phenomenon after the ingestion of lysergic acid diethylamide (LSD). These effects have been described as occurring as long as 6 months to 1 year after the drug's administration, and it appears unlikely that they are related to the actual presence of drug in the subjects. Keeler *et al.* (1968) reported four cases of spontaneous recurrence of the effects of marihuana. In three of the four cases, the individuals had smoked considerably large quantities of marihuana within brief time intervals and experienced a marihuana-type "high" for up to several weeks later. It is possible that with the acute administration of relatively large doses, the material accumulates in and is later released from its tissue stores. By this redistribution, prolonged effects could occur. In contrast to the experience with LSD, there had been no reported incidents of "flash backs" occurring from marihuana after prolonged marihuana-free intervals until the report of Kolansky and Moore (1972). Since many marihuana users also partake in the use of other drugs, there is a possibility that recurrence represents an interaction between marihuana and another drug or that marihuana may trigger a flashback to a previous LSD experience (Favazza and Domino, 1969). In addition, it is well known that marihuana and hashish are adulterated with other pharmacologically active compounds (Canadian Commission, 1970; Kok *et al.*, 1971; Morris, 1970; Fisher and Brinkman, 1973) so that one must be cautious in attributing recurrent effects specifically to the Δ^9-THC component of marihuana. Likewise, it is important to be cautious in attributing fatalities to marihuana until sufficiently sensitive methods are available to determine the presence or absence of other potentially toxic substances in biologic fluids obtained from subjects whose deaths were associated with marihuana usage.

PHARMACOLOGIC ACTIVITY— Δ^9-THC VERSUS AN ACTIVE METABOLITE

Before the elucidation of the metabolites of Δ^9-THC, many investigators assumed that Δ^9-THC was the active component of marihuana. However, Grunfeld and Edery (1969), based upon their findings that Δ^9-THC was much more active in animals after intraperitoneal administration than subcutaneous administration, suggested that a metabolite of Δ^9-THC might be responsible for its effects. Indeed, this suggestion is consistent with the hypothesis that Δ^9-THC is enzymatically converted to more active metabolites when passing through the liver. With the knowledge of the metabolic products of Δ^9-THC and the isolation of 11-OH- Δ^9-THC and 11-OH- Δ^8-THC in sufficient quantities for animal testing, it was shown that, in fact, these hydroxylated compounds were as potent, or more potent, in a variety of animal test systems than were the corresponding Δ^8- and Δ^9-THC (Foltz et al., 1970; Truitt, 1970; Nilsson et al., 1970; Burstein et al., 1970; Ben-Zvi et al., 1970; Wall et al., 1970; Christensen et al., 1971; Brady and Carbone, 1973; Gill, 1975; Byck and Ritchie, 1973).

In chronic cannabis smokers, there is indirect evidence that after oral administration or inhalation, metabolites of Δ^9-THC are responsible for its activity (Lemberger et al., 1971b,c, 1972a; Weiss et al., 1972; Galanter et al., 1972). Oral administration of Δ^9-THC at an active dose (20 to 30 mg), in conjunction with ^{14}C-labeled compound, made possible the correlation of plasma levels of Δ^9-THC with its pharmacologic effects. The plasma levels of Δ^9-THC were relatively low in comparison to the quantity of its metabolic products present in plasma at the time of peak psychologic effect. The amount of unchanged Δ^9-THC in plasma was of the same magnitude as that found initially after an intravenous dose of 0.5 mg of Δ^9-THC. When such an i.v. dose was given, the pharmacologic effects observed were minimal compared to the oral route, even though similar plasma levels of unchanged Δ^9-THC were achieved. This would be consistent with the hypothesis that a metabolite of Δ^9-THC is in part responsible for its pharmacologic activity. After inhalation of ^{14}C- Δ^9-THC, concentrations of unchanged Δ^9-THC are high initially, but it is the plasma levels of metabolites which show a temporal correlation with the psychologic effects (Lemberger et al., 1972a; Galanter et al., 1972). Similar conclusions have been drawn by Agurell et al. (1975) who used a GC-MS technique for analyzing blood levels of cannabinoids. Additional indirect evidence supporting this hypothesis comes from the studies of McMillan and co-workers (1973) who administered radiolabeled Δ^9-THC to pigeons intramuscularly. They observed the animals' behavior and, at various times after administration of the drug, determined plasma levels of total radioactivity and unchanged Δ^9-THC. They found that plasma concentrations of unchanged

Δ^9-THC reached a peak before the peak behavioral effects, whereas plasma concentrations of Δ^9-THC metabolites coincided with the peak behavioral effects. In addition, plasma levels of Δ^9-THC were extremely low 24 hours after drug administration, although the animals were still markedly affected. At this time the levels of metabolites were still high.

Although plasma levels of 11-OH- Δ^9-THC after Δ^9-THC administration were low relative to other metabolites (Lemberger *et al.*, 1970a; Perez-Reyes *et al.*, 1973c), plasma levels do not necessarily reflect the levels of drug in brain. 11-OH- Δ^9-THC blood levels are about one-eighth the levels in brain, whereas blood levels of Δ^9-THC are higher than those in brain (Gill and Lawrence, 1974). Ryrfeldt *et al.* (1973) also reported a greater tendency for the 11-hydroxy metabolite of Δ^9-THC to distribute into brain and other tissues. This has been substantiated by Perez-Reyes *et al.* (1975) who found in mice that 11-OH- Δ^9-THC penetrates the brain four times faster after intravenous injection than does Δ^9-THC. Recent studies by Lemberger and co-workers (1972b, 1973) provide direct evidence that 11-OH- Δ^9-THC may play an important role in the actions of Δ^9-THC in man. After intravenous administration of 11-OH- Δ^9-THC (1 mg total dose) or Δ^9-THC, they found a marked increase in subjective symptoms, a pronounced psychologic "high," and marked tachycardia. The effects from 11-OH- Δ^9-THC were rapid in onset and of greater intensity than after the same dose of Δ^9-THC. Their findings that the metabolic fate of 11-OH- Δ^9-THC was both quantitatively and qualitatively similar to that seen after the administration of Δ^9-THC suggest that after administration of marihuana or hashish, the Δ^9-THC is rapidly converted in man to 11-OH- Δ^9-THC which is responsible in part for the psychopharmacologic effect. Hollister (1974), using a similar method of administration, also studied the activity of 11-OH- Δ^9-THC in man and found it to be more potent than Δ^9-THC.

Perez-Reyes *et al.* (1972) also found 11-OH- Δ^9-THC to be active in subjects given the drug by slow infusion (1 mg per 5 minutes); however, they did not detect any major difference in activity between Δ^9-THC and its 11-OH metabolite. Perhaps the different techniques in rate of administration are responsible for these differences seen between these and the above-mentioned studies.

The activities of other cannabinoids have been studied in man (Perez-Reyes *et al.*, 1973a,b; Hollister, 1973). Cannabidiol was found to be inactive and 8 β-OH- Δ^9-THC had only a fraction of the activity of Δ^9-THC. In general, they found cannabinol to be essentially inactive, unless very large doses were administered.

Animal studies designed to stimulate or inhibit the metabolism of Δ^9-THC have attempted to resolve the question about an active metabolite. Sofia and Barry (1970) studied the influence of SKF-525A on the potentiating effects of Δ^9-THC on barbital sleeping time in mice. They found that SKF-525A enhanced the effect of Δ^9-THC on barbital sleeping time in mice and concluded that Δ^9-THC itself and not a metabolite was responsible for its depressant effects since the conversion to a metabolite had theoretically been inhibited. However, Truitt (1971) has found that 11-OH- Δ^9-THC, can also potentiate barbital sleeping time. Other studies suggesting that Δ^9-THC is indeed the active material have been performed. In mice, SKF-525A increased the toxicity of Δ^9-THC, whereas pretreatment with phenobarbital decreased its toxic effect (Mantilla-Plata and Harbison, 1971). In addition, Kaymakcalan and Deneau (1971) found that the analgesic effect of Δ^9-THC was enhanced in hepatectomized rats, indicating to them that Δ^9-THC itself was the active drug. These findings can be explained or clarified if one assumes that both the parent compound (Δ^9-THC) and its metabolite, 11-hydroxy- Δ^9-THC, are active compounds, whether equipotent or not. A parallelism can be drawn from amphetamine metabolism, where it has been shown that this drug and its metabolite p-hydroxyamphetamine are both potent sympathomimetic amines (Axelrod, 1954b). If both Δ^9-THC and 11-OH- Δ^9-THC are active and, as is known, 11-OH- Δ^9-THC is also converted by hepatic microsomal enzymes to 8,11-dihydroxy- Δ^9-THC (an inactive metabolite), then the effect of inhibitors (i.e., SKF-525A) of the microsomal enzymes or of stimulators (i.e., phenobarbital) would be exerted at both enzymatic steps. Thus, all the effects interpreted as preventing the conversion of Δ^9-THC to 11-OH- Δ^9-THC would also prevent the metabolism of 11-OH- Δ^9-THC to the dihydroxy compound. Accordingly, if the second enzymatic conversion were more sensitive to the effects of inhibitors or stimulators than the first, then the 11-OH- Δ^9-THC might accumulate in the case of the inhibitor studies, or be metabolized faster in the case of the stimulator studies. This could account for the increased or decreased effects from inhibitors or stimulators, respectively. The recent studies of Gill and Jones (1972) appear to support this contention, at least with respect to studies using SKF-525A. These investigators administered ^{3}H- Δ^9-THC of high specific activity intravenously to mice and correlated the brain levels of both Δ^9-THC and 11-OH- Δ^9-THC with the degree of catalepsy produced. Prior treatment of the mice with SKF-525A resulted in only slight inhibition of the hydroxylation of Δ^9-THC but marked inhibition of the metabolism of 11-OH- Δ^9-THC (the overall result was a threefold increase in brain concentrations of 11-OH- Δ^9-THC). Estevez et al. (1973) have reported similar findings in rats. These results are consistent with the hypothesis that a metabolite of Δ^9-THC is responsible for its behavioral effects.

   Since Δ^9-THC is metabolized by lung tissue as well as by liver tissue, the possibility exists that Δ^9-THC is converted to active metabolites in the

Table I. Excretion of Radioactivity after Administration
of Radiolabeled Δ^9-Tetrahydrocannabinol in Several Species

Species	Route	Dose recovered (%)	Time period (days)	Radioactivity excreted (%) In urine	Radioactivity excreted (%) In feces	Ref.
Rat	i.v.	50	10	10	40	Agurell et al. (1969)
Rabbit	i.v.	60	3	45	15	Agurell et al. (1970)
Mouse	i.p.	90	5	10	80	Mantilla-Plata and Harbison (1971)
Rhesus monkey	p.o.	70	14	24	46	Forrest et al. (1972)
Squirrel moneky	p.o.	90	14	3	87	Forrest et al. (1972)
Man nonuser	i.v.	67	7	22	45	Lemberger et al. (1971a)
chronic user	i.v.	71	7	31	40	Lemberger et al. (1971a)

lung. The complex problem of whether Δ^9-THC itself is the active pharmacologic agent or if indeed it is acting *via* a metabolite remains to be elucidated, although much evidence now suggests that 11-OH- Δ^9-THC plays a major role in the effects of Δ^9-THC.

EXCRETION

Δ^9-THC is extensively metabolized by many species and its metabolites are excreted in urine and feces. In rat, after ^{3}H- Δ^9-THC administration, about 50% of the injected dose of radioactivity was recovered in excreta within 10 days; 7 to 12% in urine and about 40% in feces (Agurell *et al.*, 1969; Klausner and Dingell, 1971). Turk *et al.* (1973) and Widman *et al.* (1974) studied the excretion of radioactivity in bile duct cannulated rats after the intravenous administration of ^{3}H- Δ^9-THC. They found 60 to 70% of the radioactivity in the bile, indicating that radioactivity in feces was derived from biliary excretion of Δ^9-THC and its metabolites.

In rabbit, Agurell *et al.* (1970) recovered 60% of the administered dose in 3 days; about 45% in urine and 15% in feces. Mantilla-Plata and Harbison (1971) have shown that after intraperitoneal injection of ^{14}C- Δ^9-THC to pregnant mice, 90% of the dose of radioactivity was recovered in 5 days; 10% was in urine and 80% was in feces (Table I).

Forest *et al.* (1972) have studied the excretion of ^{3}H- Δ^9-THC in both rhesus and squirrel monkeys after oral administration. In squirrel monkey, only 3% of the radioactivity was excreted in urine and about 87% excreted in feces (60% within the first day, suggesting poor oral absorption) (Table I). In rhesus monkey, 22 to 26% of the administered radioactivity was excreted in urine and about 46% in feces. Rhesus monkey may be a good animal model for studying Δ^9-THC elimination since it most closely resembles man in this respect (see below).

After intravenous administration of ^{14}C- Δ^9-THC to human marihuana abstainers, 67% of the administered dose of radioactivity was excreted in 1 week: 22% in urine and 45% in feces (Lemberger *et al.*, 1971a). In chronic marihuana smokers, 71% of the total dose was recovered in the excreta, but compared to nonusers, a significantly greater proportion of radioactivity was excreted in urine (Table I). *

Miras and Coutselinis (1970) studied the disposition of ^{14}C- Δ^9-THC in chronic hashish smokers (smoking duration of 20-30 years) who had indwelling biliary cannulas. After inhaling 100 mg of ^{14}C- Δ^9-THC, the subjects excreted unchanged Δ^9-THC and several polar metabolites into the bile. The presence of Δ^9-THC in bile and its absence in feces indicate that in man there is an enterohepatic circulation for Δ^9-THC or that it is metabolized by bacterial flora.

In all species studied, the rate of excretion of radioactive metabolites of Δ^9-THC was greatest during the initial collection periods and tapered off with successive time intervals. The rate of disappearance of the drug in different species appears to correlate well with the plasma half-lives; for example, in rabbits the half-life of the drug is short and it is rapidly metabolized and excreted, whereas in man the half-life of Δ^9-THC is long and it is excreted more slowly. The excretion of Δ^9-THC in several species is compared in Table I.

---

*After oral administration to marihuana smokers of either ^{14}C- Δ^9-THC (dissolved in ethanol) (Lemberger *et al.*, 1972a) or of ^{3}H- Δ^9-THC dissolved in ethanol, sesame oil, or emulsified in sodium glycocholate (Perez-Reyes *et al.*, 1973c), a similar pattern of excretion of radioactivity was found.

CONCLUDING REMARKS

Despite the long history of cannabis usage in man, Δ^9-THC is unique in that its pharmacology has been examined in humans almost simultaneously with animal studies. Within the past few years there has been rapid progress made in elucidating the pharmacology of this interesting group of compounds.

From pharmacologic studies of Δ^9-THC and its analogues, it appears that this group of compounds merits further investigation as possible therapeutic agents (Lemberger, 1972c; Grinspoon, 1972; Pars, 1973). It is interesting that the tetrahydrocannabinols appear to have many actions that would be welcomed by clinicians. To date, potential therapeutic effects have been found in the treatment of asthma (Tashkin *et al.*, 1973; Vachon *et al.*, 1973), glaucoma (Heppler *et al.*, 1972; Heppler and Frank, 1971), and depression related to terminal cancer (Regelson *et al.*, 1975).

REFERENCES

Adams, R.: Marihuana. Harvey Lectures *37*:168-197, 1941-1942.

Adams, R., Pease, D.C., and Clark, J.H.: Isolation of cannabinol, cannabidiol and quebranchitol from red oil of Minnesota wild hemp. J. Amer. Chem. Soc. *62*:2194-2196, 1940.

Agurell, S. and Leander, K.: Stability, transfer and absorption of cannabinoid constituents of cannabis (hashish) during smoking. Acta Pharmacentica Suecica *8*:391-402, 1971.

Agurell, S., Nilsson, I.M., Ohlsson, A., and Sandberg, F.: Elimination of tritium-labelled cannabinols in the rat with special reference to the development of tests for the identification of cannibis users. Biochem. Pharmacol. *18*:1195-1201, 1969.

Agurell, S., Nilsson, I.M., Ohlsson, A., and Sandberg, F.: On the metabolism of tritium-labelled Δ^{-1}-tetrahydrocannabinol in the rabbit. Biochem. Pharmacol. *19*:1333-1339, 1970.

Agurell, S., Nilsson, I.M., Nilsson, J.L.G., Ohlsson, A., Widman, M., and Leander, K.: Metabolism of 7-hydroxy- $\Delta^{1(6)}$-THC and CBN. Acta. Pharmacentica Suecica *8*:698, 1971.

Agurell, S., Gustafsson, B., Holmstedt, B., Leander, K., Lindgren, J-E., Nilsson, I., Sandberg, F., and Asberg, M.: Quantitation of Δ-1-tetrahydrocannabinol in plasma from cannabis smokers. J. Pharm. Pharmacol. *25*:554-558, 1973.

Agurell, S., Levander, S., Binder, M., Bader-Bartfai, A., Gustafsson, B., Leander, K., Lindgren, J-E., Ohlsson, A., and Tobisson, B.: Pharmacokinetics of Δ-^{8}-tetrahydrocannabinol (Δ-^{6}-tetrahydrocannabinol) in man after smoking—relations to physiological and psychological effects. In International Conference on the Pharmacology of Cannabis. Eds. Szara, S. and Braude, M.C., New York, Raven Press, 1976.

Axelrod, J.: An enzyme for the deamination of sympathomimetic amines. Properties and distribution. J. Pharmacol. Exp. Ther. *110*:2, 1954a.

Axelrod, J.: Studies on sympathomimetic amines. II. The biotransformation and physiological disposition of D-amphetamine D-*p*-hydroxyamphetamine and D-methamphetamine. J. Pharmacol. Exp. Ther. *110*:315-326, 1954b.

Ben-Zvi, Z. and Burstein, S.: 7-Oxo- Δ¹-tetrahydrocannabinol: A novel metabolite of Δ¹-tetrahydrocannabinol. Res. Commun. Chem. Pathol. Pharmacol. *8*:223-229, 1974.

Ben-Zvi, Z., Mechoulam, R., and Burstein, S.: Identification through synthesis of an active Δ¹⁽⁶⁾-tetrahydrocannabinol metabolite. J. Amer. Chem. Soc. *92*:3468-3469, 1970.

Ben-Zvi, Z., Burstein, S., and Zikopoulos, J.: Metabolism of Δ¹-tetrahydrocannabinol by mouse hepatic microsomes: Identification of 6*a*-hydroxytetrahydrocannabinol. J. Pharmacol. Sci. *63*:1173-1174, 1974.

Borgen, L.A. and Davis, W.M.: Effects of synthetic Δ⁹-tetrahydrocannabinol on pregnancy and offspring in the rat. Toxicol. Appl. Pharmacol. *20*:480-486, 1971.

Borgen, L.A. and Davis, W.M.: Cannabidiol interaction with Δ⁹-tetrahydrocannabinol. Res. Commun. Chem. Pathol. Pharmacol. *7*:663-670, 1974.

Borgen, L.A., Lott, G.C., and Davis, W.M.: Cannabis-induced hypothermia: A dose-effect comparison of crude marihuana extract and synthetic Δ⁹-tetrahydrocannabinol in male and female rats. Res. Commun. Chem. Pathol. Pharmacol. *5*:621-626, 1973.

Boyd, E.S. and Meritt, D.A.: Effects of a tetrahydrocannabinol derivative on some motor systems in the cat. Arch. Int. Pharmacodyn. *153*:1, 1965.

Brady, R.O. and Carbone, E.: Comparison of the effects of Δ⁹-tetrahydrocannabinol, 11-hydroxy- Δ⁹-tetrahydrocannabinol, and ethanol on the electrophysiological activity of the giant axon of the squid. Neuropharmacology *12*:601-605, 1973.

Burns, J.J. and Conney, A.H.: Enzymatic stimulation and inhibition in the metabolism of drugs. Proc. Roy. Soc. Med. *58*:955-960, 1965.

Burstein, S. and Kupfer, D.: Hydroxylation of trans- Δ¹-tetrahydrocannabinol by hepatic microsomal oxygenase. Ann. N.Y. Acad. Sci. *191*:61-66, 1971.

Burstein, S. and Mechoulam, R.: Stereo-specifically labeled Δ¹⁽⁶⁾-tetrahydrocannabinol. J. Amer. Chem. Soc. *90*:2420, 2421, 1968.

Burstein, S.H., Menezes, F., and Williamson, E.: Metabolism of Δ¹⁽⁶⁾-tetrahydrocannabinol, an active marihuana constituent. Nature (London) *225*:87-88, 1970.

Burstein, S., Rosenfeld, J., and Wittstruck, T.: Isolation and characterization of two major urinary metabolites 1f- Δ¹-tetrahydrocannabinol. Science *176*:422-423, 1972.

Byck, R. and Ritchie, J.M.: Δ⁹-Tetrahydrocannabinol: Effects on mammalian non-myelinated nerve fibers. Science *180*:84-85, 1973.

Canadian Commission of Inquiry, Interim Report of the non-medical use of drugs. Ottawa, Canada, Queen's Printer, 1970, pp. 74, 107.

Christensen, H.D., Freudenthal, R.D., Gidley, J.D., Rosenfeld, R., Boegli, G., Testino, L., Brine, D.R., Pitt, G.G., and Wall, M.E.: Activity of Δ⁸ and Δ⁹-tetrahydrocannabinol and related compounds in the mouse. Science *172*:165-167, 1971.

Claussen, U. and Korte, F.: Uber das verhalten von Hanf und von Δ⁹-6a, 10a-*trans*-tetrahydrocannabinol beim rauchen. Liebigs Ann. Chem. *713*:162-165, 1968.

Cohen, G.M., Petersen, G.J., and Mannering, G.J.: Interactions of Δ⁹-tetrahydrocannabinol with the hepatic microsomal drug metabolizing system. Life Sci. *10*:1207-1215, 1971.

Colburn, R.W., Ng, L.K.Y., Lemberger, L., and Kopin, I.J.: Subcellular distribution of Δ⁹-tetrahydrocannabinol in rat brain. Biochem. Pharmacol. *23*:873-877, 1974.

Conney, A.H. and Burns, J.J.: Stimulatory effect of foreign compounds on ascorbic acid biosynthesis and on drug metabolizing enzymes. Nature (London) 184:363, 1959.

Conney, A.H. and Burns, J.J.: Factors influencing drug metabolism. Adv. Pharmacol. 1:31-58, 1962.

Conney, A.H. and Burns, J.J.: Induced synthesis of oxidative enzymes in liver microsomes by polycyclic hydrocarbons and drugs. Advan. Enzyme Regulat. 1:189-214, 1963.

Consolo, S., Dolfini, E., Garrattini, S., and Valzelli, L.: Desipramine and amphetamine metabolism. J. Pharm. Pharmacol. 19:253-256, 1967.

Cooper, J.R., Axelrod, J., and Brodie, B.B.: Inhibitory effects of β-diethylaminoethyl diphenylpropylacetate on a variety of drug metabolic pathways in vitro. J. Pharmacol. Exp. Ther. 112:55, 1954.

Coutselinis, A.S. and Miras, C.J.: The effects of the smoking process on cannabinols. United Nations Secretariat—Scientific Research on Cannabis, No. 23, 1970.

Dalton, W.S., Martz, R., Rodda, B.E., Lemberger, L., and Forney, R.B.: Clinical effects of marihuana secobarbital combination. Pharmacologist 16:281, 1974.

Dewey, W.L., Harris, L.S., Howes, J.F., Kennedy, S., and Anderson, R.N.: In Committee on Problems of Drug Dependence, Nat. Res. Counc. Publ. Nat. Acad. Sci., Washington, D.C., 1970, pp. 6818-6826.

Dewey, W.L., Harris, L.S., Dennis, B., Fisher, S., Kessaris, J., Kersons, L., and Watson, J.: Some acute and chronic interactions between Δ⁹-THC and ethanol and between Δ⁹-THC and morphine in mice. Pharmacologist 13:296, 1971.

Dewey, W.L., McMillan, D.E., Harris, L.S., and Turk, R.F.: Distribution of radioactivity in brain of tolerant and nontolerant pigeons treated with ³H- Δ⁹-tetrahydrocannabinol. Biochem. Pharmacol. 22:399-405, 1973.

Dewey, W.L., Martin, B.R., Harris, L.S., and Beckner, J.S.: Disposition of ³H- Δ⁹-tetrahydrocannabinol in brain of pregnant dogs and their fetuses. Pharmacologist 16:260, 1974.

Dingell, J.V., Wilcox, H.G., and Klausner, H.A.: Biochemical interactions of Δ⁹-tetrahydrocannabinol. Pharmacologist 13:296, 1971.

Dingell, J.V., Miller, K.W., Heath, E.C., and Klausner, H.A.: The intracellular localization of Δ⁹-tetrahydrocannabinol in liver and its effects on drug metabolism in vitro. Biochem. Pharmacol. 22:949-958, 1973.

Doorenbos, N.J., Fetterman, P.S., Quimby, M.W., and Turner, C.E.: Cultivation, extraction, and analysis of Cannabis sativa. L. Ann. N.Y. Acad. Sci. 191:3-14, 1971.

Edery, H., Grunfeld, Y., Ben-Zvi, Z., and Mechoulam, R.: Structural requirements for cannabinoid activity. Ann. N.Y. Acad. Sci. 191:40-53, 1971.

Estevez, V.S., Englert, L.F., and Ho, B.T.: A new methylated metabolite of (-)-11-hydroxy- Δ⁸-tetrahydrocannabinol in rats. Res. Commun. Chem. Pathol. Pharmacol. 6:821-827, 1973.

Evans, M.A., Martz, R., Brown, D.J., Rodda, B.E., Kiplinger, G.F., Lemberger, L., and Forney, R.B.: Impairment of performance with low doses of marihuana. Clin. Pharmacol. Ther. 14:936-940, 1973.

Evans, M.A., Martz, R., Lemberger, L., Rodda, B.E., and Forney, R.B.: Clinical effects of marihuana dextroamphetamine combination. Pharmacologist 16:281, 1974.

Favazza, A. and Domino, E.: Recurrent LSD experience (flashbacks) triggered by marijuana. Univ. Mich. Med. Center J., Dec., 1969, pp. 214-216.

Fetterman, P.S., Keith, E.S., Waller, C.W., Guerrero, O., Doorenbos, N.J., and Quimby, M.W.: Mississippi-grown Cannabis Sativa L.: A preliminary observation on the chemical definition of phenotype and variations in THC content versus age, sex, and plant part. J. Pharmaceut. Sci. 60:1246-1249, 1971.

Fisher, G. and Brinkman, H.R.: Multiple drug use of marihuana users. Dis. Nerv. Syst. *34*:40-43, 1973.

Foltz, R.L., Fentiman, A.F., Leighty, E.G., Walter, J.L., Drewes, H.R., Schwartz, W.E., Page, T.F., and Truitt, E.B.: Metabolite of (-)-*trans*- Δ⁸-tetrahydrocannabinol: Identification and synthesis. Science *168*:844-845, 1970.

Forney, R.B. and Kiplinger, G.F.: Toxicology and pharmacology of marihuana. Ann. N.Y. Acad. Sci. *191*:74-82, 1971.

Forrest, I.S., Green, D.E., Otis, L.S., and Wursch, M.S.: Excretion of ³H- Δ⁹-tetrahydrocannabinol (THC) in rhesus and squirrel monkeys. Fed. Proc. *31*:506, 1972.

Frankenheim, J., McMillan, D., and Harris, L.: Effects of 1- Δ⁹- and 1- Δ⁸-*trans*-tetrahydrocannabinol on schedule-controlled behavior of the pigeon. J. Pharmacol. Exp. Ther. *178*:241, 1971.

Freudenthal, R.I., Martin, J., and Wall, M.E.: Distribution of Δ⁹-tetrahydrocannabinol in the mouse. Brit. J. Pharmacol. *44*:244-249, 1972.

Fujimoto, J.M.: Modification of the effects of Δ⁹-tetrahydrocannabinol by phenobarbital pretreatment in mice. Toxicol. Appl. Pharmacol. *23*:623-634, 1972.

Galanter, M., Wyatt, R.J., Lemberger, L., Weingartner, H., Vaughan, T.B., and Roth, W.T.: Effects on humans of Δ⁹-tetrahydrocannabinol administered by smoking. Science *176*:934-936, 1972.

Galanter, M., Weingartner, H., Vaughan, T.B., Roth, W.T., and Wyatt, R.J.: Δ⁹-Transtetrahydrocannabinol and natural marihuana. Arch. Gen. Psychiat. *28*:278-281, 1973.

Gaoni, Y. and Mechoulam, R.: Isolation, structure and partial synthesis of active constituent of hashish. J. Amer. Chem. Soc. *86*:1646-1647, 1964.

Garriott, J.C., King, L.J., Forney, R.B., and Hughes, F.W.: Effects of some tetrahydrocannabinols on hexobarbital sleeping time and amphetamine induced hyperactivity in mice. Life Sci. *6*:2119-2128, 1967.

Geber, W.F.: Effect of marihuana extract on fetal hamsters and rabbits. Toxicol. Appl. Pharmacol. *14*:276, 1969.

Gill, E.W.: The physicochemical mode of action of THC on cell membranes. International Conference on the Pharmacology of Cannabis. Eds., Szara, S. and Braude, M.C., New York, Raven Press, 1975.

Gill, E.W. and Jones, G.: Brain levels of Δ⁹-tetrahydrocannabinol and its metabolites in mice—correlation with behaviour, and the effect of the metabolic inhibitors SKF 525A and piperonyl butoxide. Biochem. Pharmacol. *21*:2237-2248, 1972.

Gill, E.W. and Lawrence, D.K.: Blood and brain level of Δ⁹-tetrahydrocannabinol in mice—the effect of 7-hydroxy- Δ¹-tetrahydrocannabinol. Biochem. Pharmacol. *23*:1140-1143, 1974.

Gill, E.W., Paton, W.D.M., and Pertwee, R.G.: Preliminary experiments on the chemistry and pharmacology of cannabis. Nature (London) *228*:134-6, 1970.

Gill, E.W., Jones, G., and Lawrence, D.K.: Contribution of the metabolite 7-hydroxy-Δ¹-tetrahydrocannabinol towards the pharmacological activity of Δ¹-tetrahydrocannabinol in mice. Biochem. Pharmacol. *22*:175-184, 1973.

Gilman, A.G. and Conney, A.H.: The induction of aminoazo dye *N*-demethylase in nonhepatic tissues by 3-methylcholanthrene. Biochem. Pharmacol. *12*:591-593, 1963.

Grinspoon, L.: The therapeutic potential of cannabis. Drug Ther. *2*:53-63, 1972.

Grunfeld, Y., and Edery, H.: Psychopharmacological activity of the active constituents of hashish and some related cannabinoids. Psychopharmacologia *14*:200, 1969.

Gurny, O., Maynard, D.E., Pitcher, R.G., and Kierstead, R.W.: Metabolism of (-) Δ⁹- and (-) Δ⁸-tetrahydrocannabinol by monkey liver. J. Amer. Chem. Soc. *94*:7928-7929, 1972.

Harbison, R.D. and Mantilla-Plata, B.: Prenatal toxicity, maternal distribution and placental transfer of tetrahydrocannabinol. J. Pharmacol. Exp. Ther. *180*:446-453, 1972.

Harbison, R.D. and Mantilla-Plata, B.: Influence of alteration of THC metabolism on THC-induced teratogenesis. In International Conference on the Pharmacology of Cannabis. Eds., Szara, S. and Braude, M.C., New York, Raven Press, 1975.

Hardman, H.F., Domino, E.F., and Seevers, M.H.: General pharmacological actions of some synthetic tetrahydrocannabinol derivatives. Pharmacol. Rev. *23*:295-315, 1971.

Hepler, R.S. and Frank, I.R.: Marihuana smoking and intraocular pressure. J.A.M.A. *217*:1392, 1971.

Hepler, R.S., Frank, I.M., and Ungerleider, J.T.: Pupillary constriction after marihuana smoking. Amer. J. Opthal. *74*:1185-1190, 1972.

Hively, R.L., Mosher, W.A., and Hoffman, F.W.: Isolation of Δ⁶-*trans*-tetrahydrocannabinol from marihuana. J. Amer. Chem. Soc. *88*:1832-1836, 1966.

Ho, B.T., Fritchie, G.E., Kralik, P.M., Englert, L.F., McIsaac, W.M., and Idanpaan-Heikkila, J.: Distribution of tritiated 1- Δ⁹-tetrahydrocannabinol in rat tissues after inhalation. J. Pharm. Pharmacol. *22*:538-539, 1970.

Ho, B.T., Taylor, D., Englert, L.F., and McIsaac, W.M.: Brain Research, *31*:233-236, 1971. Neurochemical effects of L- Δ⁹-tetrahydrocannabinol in rats following repeated inhalation. Brain Res. *31*:233-236, 1971.

Ho, B.T., Estevez, V.S., and Englert, L.F.: Effect of repeated administration on the metabolism of (-)- Δ⁹-tetrahydrocannabinols in rats. Res. Commun. Chem. Pathol. Pharmacol. *5*:215-218, 1973.

Hollister, L.E.: Cannabidiol and cannabinol in man. Experientia *29*:825-826, 1973.

Hollister, L.E.: Structure-activity relationships of cannabis constituents in man. Clin. Pharmacol. Therap. *15*:208-209, 1974.

Hollister, L.E. and Gillespie, H.K.: Delta ⁸-and delta ⁹-tetrahydrocannabinol comparison in man by oral and intravenous administration. Clin. Pharmacol. Ther. *14*:353-357, 1973.

Hollister, L.E. and Tinklenberg, J.R.: Subchronic oral doses of marihuana extract. Psychopharmacologia *29*:247-252, 1973.

Hollister, L.E., Richards, R.K., and Gillespie, H.K.: Comparison of tetrahydrocannabinol and synhexyl in man. Clin. Pharmacol. Ther. *9*:783-791, 1968.

Howes, J.F.: The effect of Δ⁹-tetrahydrocannabinol on amphetamine-induced lethality in aggregated mice. Res. Commun. Chem. Pathol. Pharmacol. *6*:895-900, 1973.

Idänpään-Heikkilä, J., Fritchie, G.E., Englert, L.F., Ho, B.T., and McIsaac, W.M.: Placental transfer of tritiated-1- Δ⁹-tetrahydrocannabinol. N. Engl. J. Med. *281*:330, 1969.

Idänpään-Heikkilä, J.E., McIsaac, W.M., and Ho, B.T.: Unpublished observations, 1971.

Isbell, H., Gorodetsky, G.W., Jasinski, D., Claussen, U., Spulak, F., and Korte, F. Effects of (-) delta-9-transtetrahydrocannabinol in man. Psychopharmacologia, *11*:184-188, 1967.

Jaffe, J.H.: In, The Pharmacological Basis of Therapeutics. Eds. Goodman, L.S. and Gilman, A., New York, Macmillan, 1970, p. 279.

Jakubovic, A., Hattori, T., and McGeer, P.L.: Radioactivity in suckled rats after giving 14-C-tetrahydrocannabinol to the mother. Eur. J. Pharmacol. *22*:221-223, 1973.

Joachimoglu, G., Kiburis, J., and Miras, C.: United Nations Document ST/SOA/Ser.S/15, 1967.

Jones, G. and Pertwee, R.G.: A metabolic interaction *in vivo* between cannabidiol and

Δ¹-tetrahydrocannabinol. Brit. J. Pharmacol. 45:375-377, 1972.

Jones, G., Widman, M., and Agurell, S.: Monohydroxylated metabolites of Δ¹-tetra-hydrocannabinol in mouse brain. Acta Pharmacentica Suecica 11:283-294, 1974.

Karniol, I.G. and Carlini, E.A.: Pharmacological interaction between cannabidiol and Δ⁹-tetrahydrocannabinol. Psychopharmacologia 33:53-70, 1973.

Kaymakcalan, S. and Deneau, G.A.: Some pharmacological effects of synthetic Δ⁹-tetrahydrocannabinol (THC). Pharmacologist 13:247, 1971.

Keeler, M.H., Keifler, C.B., and Liptzin, M.B.: Spontaneous recurrence of marihuana effect. Amer. J. Psychiat. 125:140-142, 1968.

Kennedy, J.S. and Waddell, W.J.: Whole body autoradiography of the pregnant mouse after administration of 14-C- Δ -9-THC Toxicol. Appl. Pharmacol. 22:252, 1972.

King, L.J. and Forney, R.B.: The absorption and excretion of the marihuana constituents, cannabinol and tetrahydrocannabinol. Fed. Proc. 26:540, 1967.

Kiplinger, G.F., Manno, J.E., Rodda, B.E., and Forney, R.B.: Dose-response analysis of the effects of tetrahydrocannabinol in man. Clin. Pharmacol. Ther. 12:650-657, 1971.

Klausner, H.A. and Dingell, J.V.: The metabolism and excretion of Δ⁹-tetrahydrocannabinol in the rat. Life Sci. 10:49-59, 1971.

Klausner, H.A., Wilcox, H.G., and Dingell, J.V.: The use of zonal ultracentrifugation in the investigation of the binding of Δ⁹-tetrahydrocannabinol by plasma proteins. Drug Metab. Disp., 3:314-319, 1975.

Kok, J.C.F., Fromberg, E., Geerlings, P.J., Van Der Helm, H.J., Kamp, P.E., Van Der Slooten, E.P.J., and Willems, M.A.M.: Analysis of illicit drugs. Lancet 1:1065, 1971.

Kolansky, H. and Moore, W.T.: Toxic effects of chronic marihuana use. J.A.M.A. 222:35-41, 1972.

Kosersky, D.S., McMillan, D.E. and Harris, D.L.: Δ⁹-Tetrahydrocannabinol and 11-hydroxy- Δ⁹-tetrahydrocannabinol: Behavioral effects and tolerance development. J. Pharmacol. Exp. Ther. 189:61-65, 1974.

Kreuz, D.S. and Axelrod, J.: Delta-9-tetrahydrocannabinol: localization in body fat. Science 179:391-393, 1973.

Kubena, R.K. and Barry, H.: Interactions of Δ¹-tetrahydrocannabinol with barbiturates and methamphetamine. J. Pharmacol. Exp. Ther. 173:94-100, 1970.

Kuntzman, R., Jacobson, M., Schneidman, K., and Conney, A.H.: Similarities between oxidative drug-metabolizing enzymes and steroid hydroxylases in liver microsomes. Pharmacol. Exp. Ther. 146:280, 1964.

Kupfer, D., Jansson, I., and Orrenius, S.: Spectral interactions of marihuana constituents (cannabinoids) with rat liver microsomal monooxygenase system. Chem. Biol. Interactions 5:201-206, 1972.

Kupfer, D., Levin, E., and Burstein, S.H.: Studies on the effects of Δ¹-tetrahydrocannabinol (Δ¹-THC) and DDT on the hepatic microsomal metabolism of Δ¹-THC and other compounds in the rat. Chem. Biol. Interactions 6:59-66, 1973.

Layman, J.M. and Milton, A.S.: Distribution of tritium labelled Δ⁹-tetrahydrocannabinol in the rat brain following intraperitoneal administration. Brit. J. Pharmacol. 42:308-310, 1971.

Lemberger, L.: The metabolism of the tetrahydrocannabinols. Advan. Pharmacol. Chemother. 10:221-255, 1972c.

Lemberger, L., Silberstein, S.D., Axelrod, J., and Kopin, I.J.: Marihuana: Studies on the disposition and metabolism of delta-9-tetrahydrocannabinol in man. Science 170:1320-1322, 1970a.

Lemberger, L., Sernatinger, E., and Kuntzman, R.: Effect of desmethylimipramine, iprindole, and dl-erythro-a-(3,4-dichlorophenyl)-B-(t-butyl amino) propanol HCl on the metabolism of amphetamine. Biochem. Pharmacol. *19*:3021-3028, 1970b.

Lemberger, L., Tamarkin, N.R., Axelrod, J., and Kopin, I.J.: Delta-9-tetrahydrocannabinol: Metabolism and disposition in long-term marihuana smokers. Science *173*:72-74, 1971a.

Lemberger, L., Axelrod, J., and Kopin, I.J.: Metabolism and disposition of tetrahydrocannabinols in naive subjects and chronic marihuana users. Ann. N.Y. Acad. Sci. *191*:142-154, 1971b.

Lemberger, L., Axelrod, J., and Kopin, I.J.: Metabolism and disposition of Δ⁹-tetrahydrocannabinol in man. Pharmacol. Rev. *23*:371-380, 1971c.

Lemberger, L., Weiss, J.L., Watanabe, A.M., Galanter, I.M., Wyatt, R.J., and Cardon, P.V.: Delta-9-tetrahydrocannabinol. Temporal correlation of the psychologic effects and blood levels after various routes of administration. N. Engl. J. Med. *286*:685-688, 1972a.

Lemberger, L., Crabtree, R.E., and Rowe, H.M.: 11-Hydroxy- Δ⁹-tetrahydrocannabinol: Pharmacology, disposition, and metabolism of a major metabolite of marihuana in man. Science *177*:62-64, 1972b.

Lemberger, L., Martz, R., Rodda, B., Forney, R., and Rowe, H.: Comparative pharmacology of Δ⁹-tetrahydrocannabinol and its metabolite, 11-OH- Δ⁹-tetrahydrocannabinol. J. Clin. Invest. *52*:2411-2417, 1973.

Lemberger, L., McMahon, R., Archer, R., Matsumoto, K., and Rowe, H.: Pharmacologic effects and physiologic disposition of delta-6a,10a-dimethyl heptyl tetrahydrocannabinol (DMHP) in man. Clin. Pharmacol. Ther. *15*:380-386, 1974.

Manno, J.E., Kiplinger, G.F., Haine, S.E., Bennett, I.F., and Forney, R.B.: Comparative effects of smoking marihuana or placebo on human motor and mental performance. Clin. Pharmacol. Ther. *11*:808-815, 1970.

Manno, J.E., Kiplinger, G.F., Scholz, N., Forney, R.B., and Haine, S.E.: The influence of alcohol and marihuana on motor and mental performance. Clin. Pharmacol. Ther. *12*:202, 1971.

Mantilla-Plata, B. and Harbison, R.D.: Phenobarbital and SKF-525A effect on Δ⁹-tetrahydrocannabinol (THC) toxicity and distribution in mice. Pharmacologist *13*:297, 1971.

Mantilla-Plata, B., Clewe, G.L., and Harbison, R.D.: Teratogenic and mutagenic studies of Δ⁹-tetrahydrocannabinol in mice. Fed. Proc. *32*:746A, 1973.

Marcotte, J. and Witschi, H.P.: Induction of pulmonary aryl hydrocarbon hydroxylase by marihuana. Res. Commun. Chem. Pathol. Pharmacol. *4*:561-568, 1972.

Maynard, D.E., Gurny, O., Pitcher, R.G., and Kierstead, R.W.: (-)- Δ⁸-Tetrahydrocannabinol: Two novel *in vitro* metabolites. Experientia *27*:1154-1155, 1971.

McIsaac, W.M., Fritchie, G.E., Idenpaan Heikkila, J.E., Ho, B.T., and Englert, L.F.: Distribution of marihuana in monkey brain and concomitant behavioral effects. Nature (London) *230*:593-594, 1971.

McMillan, E.E., Harris, L.S., Frankenheim, J.M., and Kennedy, J.S.: 1- Δ⁹-Trans-tetrahydrocannabinol in pigeons; tolerance to the behavioral effects. Science *169*:501, 1970.

McMillan, D.E., Dewey, W.L., Turk, R.F., Harris, L.S., and McNeil, J.H.: Blood levels of ³H- Δ⁹-tetrahydrocannabinol and its metabolites in tolerant and nontolerant pigeons. Biochem. Pharmacol. *22*:383-397, 1973.

Mechoulam, A. and Gaoni, Y.: The absolute configuration of delta-1-tetrahydrocannabinol., the major active constituent of hashish. Tetrahedron Lett. *12*:1109-1111, 1967.

Mechoulam, R.: Marihuana chemistry. Science *168*:1159-1166, 1970.

Mechoulam, R., Shani, A., Edery, H., and Grunfeld, Y.: The chemical basis of hashish activity. Science *169*:611, 1970.

Mechoulam, R., Varconi, H., Ben-Zvi, Z., Edery, H., and Grunfeld, Y.: Synthesis and biological activity of five tetrahydrocannabinol metabolites. J. Amer. Chem. Soc. *94*:7930-7931, 1972.

Meyer, R.E., Pillard, R.C., Shapiro, L.M., and Mirin, S.M.: Administration of marihuana to heavy and casual marihuana users. Amer. J. Psychiat. *128*:198-204, 1971.

Mikes, F. and Waser, P.G.: Marihuana components: Effects of smoking on Δ⁹-tetrahydrocannabinol and cannabidiol. Science *172*:1158-1160, 1971.

Miras, C.J.: Some aspects of cannabis action. In Hashish: Its Chemistry and Pharmacology (Ciba foundation study group No. 21). Eds. Wolstenholme, G.E.W. and Knight, J., Boston, Mass., Little, Brown, 1965, pp. 37-47.

Miras, C.J. and Coutselinis, A.S.: The distribution of tetrahydrocannabinol-¹⁴C in humans. United Nations Secretariat—Scientific Research on Cannabis No. 24, 1970.

Morris, S.D.: Testimony given before U.S. Senate Special Subcommittee on Alcoholism and Narcotics: Committee on Labor and Public Welfare. "Drug Abuse and Alcoholism in the Armed Services," Dec. 2, 1970.

Nakazawa, K. and Costa, E.: Metabolism of Δ⁹-tetrahydrocannabinol by lung and liver homogenates of rats treated with methylcholanthrene. Nature (London) *234*:48-49, 1971.

Nilsson, J.L.G., Nilsson, I.M., and Agurell, S.: Synthesis of ³H- and ¹⁴C-labeled tetrahydrocannabinols. Acta. Chem. Scand. *23*:2209-2211, 1969.

Nilsson, I.M., Agurell, S., Nilsson, J.L.G., Ohlsson, A., Sandberg, F., and Wahlqvist, M.: Δ¹-Tetrahydrocannabinol: Structure of a major metabolite. Science *168*:1228, 1970.

Nilsson, I.M., Agurell, S., Leander, K., Nilsson, J.L.G., and Widman, M.: Cannabidiol: Structure of three metabolites formed in rat liver. Acta Pharmaceutica Suecica *8*:701, 1971.

Nilsson, I., Agurell, S., Nilsson, J.L.G., Widman, M., and Leander, K.: Two cannabidiol metabolites formed by rat liver. J. Pharm. Pharmacol. *25*:486-487, 1973.

Nordqvist, M., Agurell, S., Binder, M., and Nilsson, I.M.: Structure of an acidic metabolite of Δ¹-tetrahydrocannabinol isolated from rabbit urine. J. Pharm. Pharmacol. *26*:471-473, 1974.

Ohlsson, A., Abou-Chaar, C.I., Agurell, S., Nilsson, I.M., Olofsson, K., and Sandberg, F.: Cannabinoid constituents of male and female *Cannabis sativa*. Bull. Narcotics *23*:29-32, 1971.

Okamoto, T., Chan, P-C., and So, B.T.: Effect of tobacco, marijuana and benzo(a)pyrene on aryl hydrocarbon hydroxylase in hamster lung. Life Sci. *11*:733-741, 1972.

Pace, H.B., Davis, W.M., and Borgen, L.A.: Teratogenesis and marihuana. Ann. N.Y. Acad. Sci. *191*:123-131, 1971.

Pars, H.G.: The other side of marihuana research. Anesthesiology *38*:519-520, 1973.

Paton, W.D.M. and Pertwee, R.G.: The general pharmacology of cannabis. Acta Pharmaceutica Seucica *8*:691, 1971.

Paton, W.D.M. and Pertwee, R.G.: Effect of cannabis and certain of its constituents on pentobarbitone sleeping time and phenazone metabolism. Brit. J. Pharmacol. *44*:250-261, 1972.

Perez-Reyes, M., Lipton, M.A., Timmons, M.C., Wall, M.E., Brine, D.R., and Davis,

K.H.: Pharmacology of orally administered Δ⁹-tetrahydrocannabinol. Clin. Pharmacol. Ther. *14*:48-55, 1973c.

Perez-Reyes, M., Timmons, M.C., Lipton, M.A., Davis, K.H., and Wall, M.E.: Intravenous injection in man of Δ ⁹-tetrahydrocannabinol and 11-OH- Δ⁹-tetrahydrocannabinol. Science *177*:633-634, 1972.

Perez-Reyes, M., Timmons, M.C., Davis, K.H., and Wall, E.M.: A comparison of the pharmacological activity in man of intravenously administered Δ⁹-tetrahydrocannabinol, cannabinol, and cannabidiol. Experientia *29*:1368-1369, 1973a.

Perez-Reyes, M., Timmons, M.C., Lipton, M.A., Christensen, H.D., Davis, K.H., and Wall, M.E.: A comparison of the pharmacological activity of Δ⁹-tetrahydrocannabinol and its monohydroxylated metabolites in man. Experientia *29*:1009-1010, 1973b.

Perez-Reyes, M., Timmons, M.C., and Wall, M.E.: Long-term use of marihuana and the development of tolerance or sensitivity to Δ ⁹-tetrahydrocannabinol. Arch. Gen. Psychiat. *31*:89-91, 1974.

Perez-Reyes, M., Wagner, D., Brine, D., Christensen, H.D., and Wall, M.E.: The rate of plasma disappearance of tetrahydrocannabinols in humans and their rate of penetration to the brain of mice. International Conference on the Pharmacology of Cannabis. Eds. Szara, S. and Braude, M.C., New York, Raven Press, 1975.

Persaud, I. and Ellington, A.: Cannabis in early pregnancy. Lancet *2*:1306, 1967.

Persaud, I. and Ellington, A.: Teratogenic activity of cannabis resin. Lancet *2*:406-407, 1968.

Peterson, D.W., Cohen, G.M., and Sparber, S.B.: The delay of the behavioral effects of Δ⁹-tetrahydrocannabinol in rats by 2-diethylaminoethyl 2,2-diphenylvalerate HCl (SKF 525-A). Life Sci. *10*:1381-1386, 1971.

Phillips, R.N., Brown, D.J., and Forney, R.B.: Enhancement of depressant properties of alcohol or barbiturates in combination with aqueous suspended delta-9-tetrahydrocannabinol in rats. J. Forensic Sci., April, 1971.

Pirch, J.H., Cohn, R.A., Osterholm, K.C., and Barratt, E.S.: Antagonism of amphetamine locomotor stimulation in rats by single doses of marihuana extract administered orally. Neuropharmacology *12*:485-493, 1973.

Quinn, G.P., Axelrod, J., and Brodie, B.B.: Species, strain, and sex differences in the metabolism of hexobarbitone, aminopyrine, antipyrine, and aniline. Biochem. Pharmacol. *1*:152, 1958.

Rating, D., Broermann, I., Honecker, H., Kluwe, S., and Coper, H.: Effect of subchronic treatment with (-)- Δ⁸-*trans*-tetrahydrocannabinol (Δ⁸-THC) on food intake, body temperature, hexobarbital sleeping time, and hexobarbital elimination in rats. Psychopharmacologia *27*:349-357, 1972.

Regelson, W., Butler, J.R., Schulz, J., Kirk, T., Peek, L., and Green, M.L.: Δ⁹-THC as an effective antidepressant and appetite stimulating agent in advanced cancer patients. International Conference on the Pharmacology of Cannabis, Eds. Szara, S., and Braude, M.C., New York, Raven Press, 1975.

Remmer, H.: Action of adrenal cortex on the degradation of drugs in liver microsomes. Naturwissenscahfen *45*:522-523, 1958a.

Remmer, H.: Die Verstarkung der Abbaugeschwindig keit von Evipan durch Glykocorticoide. Arch. Exp. Pathol. Pharmakol. Naunyn-Schmiedebergs *233*:184-191, 1958b.

Remmer, H.: Drugs as activators of drug enzymes. Proc. First Int. Pharmacol. Mtg. *6*:235-249, 1962.

Renault, P.F., Schuster, C.R., Freedman, D.X., Sikic, B., de Mello, D.N., and Halaris, A.: Marihuana smoke to humans. Arch. Gen Psychiat. *31*:95-102, 1974.

Rubin, A., Tephly, T.R., and Mannering, G.J.: Kinetics of drug metabolism by hepatic microsomes. Biochem. Pharmacol. 13:1007-1016, 1964a.

Rubin, A., Tephly, T.R., and Mannering, G.J.: Inhibition of hexobarbital metabolism by ethylmorphine and codeine in the rat. Biochem. Pharmacol. 13:1053-1057, 1964b.

Rubin, E. and Lieber, C.S.: Alcoholism, alcohol, and drugs. Science 172:1097-1102, 1971.

Ryrfeldt, A., Ramsay, C.H., Nilsson, I.M., Widman, M., and Agurell, S.: Whole-body autoradiography of Δ¹-tetrahydrocannabinol and Δ¹(6)-tetrahydrocannabinol in mouse. Acta. Pharmaceutica Suecica 10:13-28, 1973.

Schou, J., Worm, K., Andersen, J.M., Nielsen, E., and Steentoft, A.: Studies on the metabolism and disposition of delta-9-tetrahydrocannabinol (delta-9-THC) in Danish pigs before and after prolonged intravenous administration of delta-9-THC. Fifth International Cong. Pharmacol. (abst. of papers), July 23-28, 1972. San Francisco.

Seeman, P., Chau-Wong, M., and Moyyen, S.: The membrane binding of morphine, diphenyl-hydantoin, and tetrahydrocannabinol. Can. J. Physiol. Pharmacol. 50:1193-1200, 1972.

Shani, A. and Mechoulam, R.: A new type of cannabinoid. Synthesis of Cannabielsoic Acid A by a Novel Photooxidative cyclisation. Chem. Commun. p. 273, 1970.

Shannon, M.E. and Fried, P.A.: The macro- and microdistribution and polymorphic electroencephalographic effects of Δ⁹-tetrahydrocannabinol in the rat. Psychopharmacologia 27:141-156, 1972.

Sidell, F.R., Pless, J.E., Neitlich, H., Sussman, P., Copelan, H.W., and Sim, V.M.: Dimethylheptyl-delta-6a,10a-tetrahydrocannabinol: Effects after parenteral administration to man. Proc. Soc. Exp. Biol. Med. 142:867-873, 1973.

Siemens, A.J., Kalant, H., and deNie, J.C.: Metabolic interactions between Δ¹-Tetrahydrocannabinol and other cannabinoids. In Pharmacology of Marihuana. Ed. M.C. Braude and S. Szara. New York, Raven Press, 1975.

Silva, M.T.A., Carlini, E.A., Claussen, U., and Korte, F.: Lack of cross-tolerance in rats among (-) Δ⁹-*trans*-tetrahydrocannabinol (Δ⁹-THC), cannabis extract, mescaline and lysergic acid diethylamide (LSD-25). Psychopharmacologia 13:322-340, 1968.

Sim, V.M. and Tucker, La M.A.: Summary report on EA1476 and EA2233, Clearinghouse for Federal Scientific and Technical Information, AD 342332:1-65, 1963.

Sofia, R.D.: Interactions of chronic and acute Δ¹-tetrahydrocannabinol pretreatment with zoxazolamine and barbiturates. Res. Commun. Chem. Pathol. Pharmacol. 5:91-98, 1973.

Sofia, R.D. and Barry, H.: Depressant effect of Δ¹-tetrahydrocannabinol enhanced by inhibition of its metabolism. Eur. J. Pharmacol. 13:134-137, 1970.

Sulser, F. and Dingell, J.V.: The potentiation and blockade of the central action of amphetamine by cloropromazine. Biochem. Pharmacol. 17:634-636, 1968.

Sulser, F., Owens, M.L., and Dingell, J.V.: On the mechanism of amphetamine potentiation by desipramine (DMI). Life Sci. 5:2005-2010, 1966.

Tashkin, D.P., Shapiro, B.J., and Frank, I.M.: Acute pulmonary physiological effects of smoked marijuana and oral Δ⁹-tetrahydrocannabinol in healthy young men. N. Engl. J. Med. 289:336-341, 1973.

Timmons, M.L., Pitt, C.G., and Wall, M.E.: Deuteration and tritiation of delta-8 and delta-9-tetrahydrocannabinol use of trifluoroacetic acid as a convenient labelling reagent. Tetrahedron Lett. 36:3129-3132, 1969.

Todd, A.R.: The chemistry of hashish. Sci. J. Roy. Coll. Sci. 12:37, 1942.

Truitt, E.B., Jr.: Pharmacological activity in a metabolite of 1-*trans*- Δ⁸-tetrahydrocannabinol. Fed. Proc. 29:619, 1970.

Truitt, E.B.: Biological disposition of tetrahydrocannabinols. Pharmacol. Rev. 23:273-278, 1971.

Turk, R.F., Dewey, W.L., and Harris, L.S.: Excretion of trans- Δ⁹-tetrahydrocannabinol and its metabolites in intact and bile duct-cannulated rats. J. Pharm. Sci. 62:737-740, 1973.

Vachon, L., Fitzgerald, M.X., Solliday, N.H., Gould, I.A., and Gaensler, E.A.: Single-dose effect of marihuana smoke. N. Engl. J. Med. 288:985-989, 1973.

Valle, J.R., Lapa, A.J., and Barros, G.G.: Pharmacological activity of cannabis according to sex of plant. J. Pharm. Pharmacol. 20:798, 1968.

Wahlqvist, M., Nilsson, I.M., Sandberg, F., Agurell, S., and Granstand, B.: Binding of Δ¹-tetrahydrocannabinol to human plasma proteins. Biochem. Pharmacol. 19:2579-2584, 1970.

Wall, M.E.: The in vitro and in vivo metabolism of tetrahydrocannabinol (THC). Ann. N.Y. Acad. Sci. 191:23-39, 1971.

Wall, M.E., Brine, D.R., Brine, G.A., Pitt, C.G., Freudenthal, R.I., and Christensen, H.D.: Isolation, structure, and biological activity of several metabolites of Δ⁹-tetrahydrocannabinol. J. Amer. Chem. Soc. 92:3466-3467, 1970.

Wall, M.E., Brine, D.R., and Pitt, C.G.: Synthesis of 11-hydroxy- Δ⁹-tetrahydrocannabinol and other physiologically active metabolites of Δ⁸- and Δ⁹-tetrahydrocannabinol. J. Amer. Chem. Soc. 94:8578-8581, 1972.

Wall, M.E., Brine, D.R., and Perez-Reyes, M.: Abs. 33rd Int. Congress of Pharmaceutical Sci., Stockholm. p. 258, 1973.

Wall, M.E., Brine, D.R., and Perez-Reyes, M.: Metabolism of Cannabinoids in man. Int. Conference on the Pharmacol. of Cannabis. Eds. Szara, S. and Braude, M.C., New York, Raven Press, 1975.

Waller, C.W.: Chemistry of marihuana. Pharmacol. Rev. 23:265-271, 1971.

Waskow, I.E., Olsson, J.E., Salzman, C., and Katz, M.M.: Psychological effects of tetrahydrocannabinol. Arch. Gen. Psychiat. 22:87, 1970.

Weil, A.T., Zinberg, N.E., and Nelsen, J.M.: Clinical and psychological effects of marihuana in man. Science 162:1234-1242, 1968.

Weiss, J.L., Watanabe, A.M., Lemberger, L., Tamarkin, N.R., and Cardon, P.V.: Cardiovascular effects of delta-9-tetrahydrocannabinol in man. Clin. Pharmacol. Ther. 13:671-684, 1972.

Welch, R.M., Harrison, Y.E., Gommi, B.W., Poppers, P.J., Finster, M., and Conney, A.H.: Stimulatory effect of cigarette smoking on the hydroxylation of 3,4-benzpyrene and the N-demethylation of 3-methyl-4-monomethyl amino azo benzene by enzymes in human placenta. Clin. Pharmacol. Ther. 10:100-109, 1969.

Widman, M., Nilsson, I.M., and Nilsson, J.L.G.: Metabolism of cannabis. IX. Cannabinol: Structure of a major metabolite formed in rat liver. Life Sci. 10:157-162, 1971.

Widman, M., Nilsson, I.M., Nilsson, J.L.G., Agurell, S., Borg, H., and Granstrand, B.: Plasma protein binding of 7-hydroxy- Δ¹-tetrahydrocannabinol: An active Δ¹-tetrahydrocannabinol metabolite. J. Pharm. Pharmacol. 25:453-457, 1973.

Widman, M., Nordqvist, M., Agurell, S., Lindgren, J-E., and Sandberg, F.: Billiary excretion of Δ¹-tetrahydrocannabinol and its metabolites in the rat. Biochem. Pharmacol. 23:1163-1172, 1974.

Woodhouse, E.J.: Confirmation of the presence of 11-hydroxy- Δ⁹-tetrahydrocannabinol in the urine of marihuana smokers. Amer. J. Pub. Health 62:1394-1396, 1972.

Chapter 9

Cocaine and Miscellaneous Drugs of Abuse

COCAINE

Cocaine is the principle active alkaloid found in the leaves of the coca plant, *Erythroxylon coca*. This plant is indigenous to South America and grows as a shrub on the slopes of the Andes Mountains, where it has been used for centuries by the Indians of Bolivia and Peru. Originally, the natives chewed the leaves for religious purposes and it was known as "the divine plant of the Incas" (Del Pozo, 1967). Later, the coca leaf was used for other purposes; for example, mine workers in Peru and Bolivia chew coca leaves as a CNS stimulant to achieve a feeling of well-being and to increase their physical strength, endurance, and stamina. To facilitate the extraction of the cocaine as the leaf is being chewed, some lime (alkali) is added to the leaf!

Cocaine was isolated from coca leaves in 1850 and accounts for about 1% of the leaf's content. Sigmund Freud, who personally used cocaine, was impressed with its medical attributes and in 1885 wrote a treatise, "On the General Effects of Cocaine," in which he recommended that cocaine could be utilized for the treatment of morphine withdrawal and dependence. Later, the problem of psychologic dependence (habituation) associated with

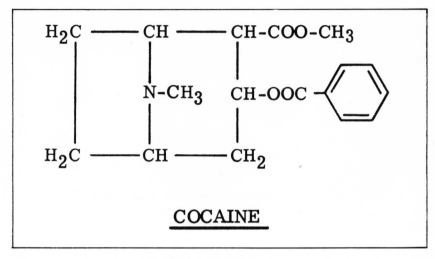

Fig. 1. Structure of cocaine.

cocaine usage became known (it has been suggested that Freud became a therapeutic nihilist as a result of his unfortunate experiences with cocaine). In the 1880's, cocaine was shown to possess potent local anesthetic properties; it was, and still is, used for this medical purpose, particularly in the field of ophthalmology. Cocaine was once a constituent of the soft drink Coca-Cola, which was prepared from extracts of coca leaf; however, in 1906 a new formulation was developed in which coca extract was used as a flavoring, but only after the cocaine was removed (Canadian Commission, 1973).

The illicit use of cocaine is not as extensive as with other drugs; however, its use is definitely on the increase. Since cocaine is very expensive and difficult to obtain on the illicit market, it is considered a "status" drug among drug users. This has earned cocaine the nickname "the big K" (the "king"); it is also referred to as "coke" or "snow" (because it exists as a very light-weight, white, crystalline powder). Chemically, cocaine is benzoylmethylecgonine (Fig. 1). Although cocaine does not resemble the opiates chemically or pharmacologically, it is classified as a narcotic and is controlled by the same regulations.

Cocaine is a CNS stimulant, producing effects similar to those described earlier for the amphetamines (Chapter 2). After intravenous injection, cocaine produces a euphoric "rush" like amphetamine, and after chronic administration of large doses it can produce a similar toxic psychosis which is associated with feelings of super strength, delusions of grandeur, twitching, and convulsions. In addition to CNS stimulation, cocaine produces irregular breathing and other effects related to its action on the sympathetic nervous system (SNS), including anorexia, mydriasis, and hypertension as a result of vasoconstrictor actions. The stimulation of the SNS by cocaine is mediated by inhibition of the uptake of norepinephrine at the nerve ending, thus potentiating the pharmacologic effects of that neurohormone (Tainter and Chang, 1927; Bacq, 1936, Whitby et al., 1960; Hertting et al., 1961).

Absorption

Cocaine is readily absorbed from mucous membranes of the mouth and nose (despite the fact that local vasoconstrictor effect somewhat impedes its absorption). As a drug of abuse, cocaine is administered either intravenously or, more commonly, by inhalation into the nostrils as a snuff, a practice known as "snorting." This technique was previously discussed for the harmala derivative cohoba (Chapter 4). When snuffed, cocaine has been postulated to have a direct action on the CNS as a result of the direct communication of the nasal vessels with the cranial cavity (Holmstedt and Lindgren, 1967). Unfortunately, due to the potent vasoconstrictor properties of cocaine and the resultant tissue hypoxia, individuals who snuff the drug are prone to develop gangrene and/or perforation of the nasal septum. In contrast to its rapid absorption from mucous membranes, cocaine is not absorbed (or is only poorly absorbed) after oral administration. This is a result of its rapid destruction in the stomach to inactive compounds. Woods et al., (1951) injected cocaine into dogs by various routes of administration and measured its plasma concentrations. After intravenous administration (10 mg/kg), plasma levels decreased in a biphasic manner, the initial rapid decrease represents tissue distribution, whereas the β phase represents metabolism and excretion of the drug. Cocaine disappeared with a half-life of about 3 hours. After subcutaneous administration (15 mg/kg) of cocaine, plasma concentration peaked at 45 minutes and remained relatively constant for 5-6 hours. The authors concluded that this represented a "state of relative equilibrium between the absorption of cocaine from the subcutaneous depot and detoxication mechanisms." Plasma concentrations of cocaine were considerably lower after direct intubation of the drug into the stomach, suggesting either poor absorption or degradation of the compound in the gastrointestinal tract. Others have reported similar findings (Campbell and Adriani, 1958; Steinhaus, 1952).

In dogs, Campbell and Adriani (1958) studied the absorption of cocaine from a variety of sites, including topical, subcutaneous, and several mucosal surfaces. They found that the absorption of cocaine from mucosal membranes differed with the area of application. Instillation of cocaine into the trachea yielded higher peak blood levels than did application into the pharynx. It is thought that after tracheal instillation the drug was more rapidly absorbed because it entered the alveoli. Indeed, after inhalation of cocaine by nebulization, the drug was rapidly absorbed. When an aqueous solution of cocaine was applied topically to the skin of dogs, no drug was absorbed. In contrast, if the skin was first abraded and the cocaine applied either in a water-soluble ointment base or in an aqueous solution, the drug was rapidly absorbed; peak blood levels occurred in 6-10 minutes and approximated those seen after subcutaneous infiltration.

In rabbits, Woods *et al.* (1951) found measurable plasma concentrations of cocaine after subcutaneous injection (30 mg/kg); however, the values were much lower than those found in dog at comparable doses, suggesting that rabbit metabolizes cocaine to a greater extent than dog.

Tissue Distribution

Thirty minutes after the intravenous injection of cocaine (20 mg/kg) to dogs, the drug was present at high concentrations in spleen (47 μg/ml), kidney (40 μg/ml), cerebral cortex (30 μg/ml), followed in order of decreasing concentration by pancreas, omental fat, liver, cardiac muscle, skeletal muscle, and plasma (5.5 μg/ml) (Woods *et al.*, 1951). The high concentrations of cocaine found in tissues is predictable, since the drug is an amine, and amines generally have a high affinity for tissues. The presence of large concentrations of cocaine in brain tissue is interesting, since other drugs of abuse generally do not become distributed in brain to such an extent. The localization of cocaine in brain was utilized to study certain permeability characteristics of the blood-brain barrier (Strait and Aird, 1938; Strait *et al.*, 1941; Angel and Lafferty, 1969; Sherman, 1970). Cocaine and certain of its metabolites have also been identified in cerebrospinal fluid (Strait and Aird, 1938; Hawks *et al.*, 1975). Norcocaine, a minor cocaine metabolite, has been found in monkey brain after cocaine administration; the cocaine:norcocaine ratio was 5.5 and 3.3 at 10 and 30 minutes, respectively (Hawks *et al.*, 1975).

Misra *et al.* (1974) investigated the tissue distribution in rats of ^{3}H-ecgonine (see Fig. 3), a metabolite of cocaine. In the rat, ecgonine crossed the blood-brain barrier, but only to a small extent, 0.7 μg/gm being present in brain 15 minutes after intravenous administration (10 mg/kg). Ecgonine was concentrated mainly in the kidney, with lower concentrations in liver, lung, cardiac muscle, and spleen. Ecgonine concentrations in plasma were higher than in all other tissues except kidney. This probably reflects the rapid renal excretion of this cocaine metabolite.

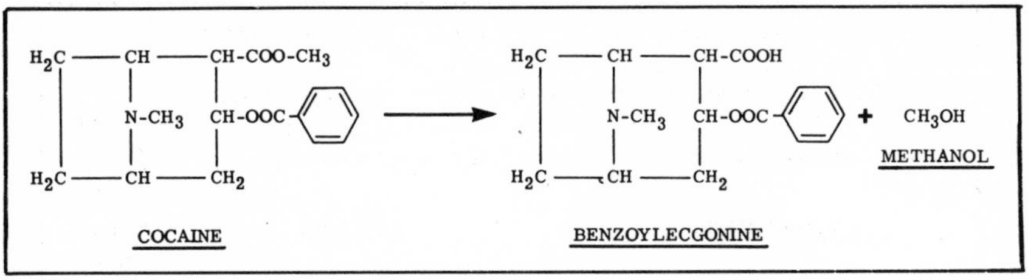

Fig. 2. Deesterification of cocaine to benzoylecgonine.

Metabolism *in Vitro*

Glick and co-workers (Glick and Glaubach, 1941; Glick *et al.*, 1942) demonstrated that cocaine could be hydrolyzed by rabbit serum. The enzymatic activity was attributed to tropinesterase (atropinesterase). Using electrophoretic techniques, they found the activity primarily in the α- and β- globulins, with no activity present in the albumin fraction. Blaschko *et al.* (1946) confirmed the hydrolysis of cocaine in rabbit serum, but concluded that it was not related to the presence of tropinesterase because serum from rabbits deficient in this enzyme also hydrolyzed cocaine. Similar results were reported by Ammon and Savelsberg (1949) who also postulated that cocaine was metabolized to benzoylecgonine and methanol (Fig. 2). Glick and Glaubach (1941) were unable to demonstrate hydrolysis of cocaine by serum or plasma from other mammalian species, including man. Similarly, Blaschko *et al.* (1955) found that cocaine was not hydrolyzed by human plasma or horse serum. These investigators, studying the metabolism of α-cocaine, an isomer of cocaine, found it to be extensively metabolized by rabbit and horse serum, as well as by human plasma. The hydrolysis of α-cocaine was inhibited by eserine. This hydrolysis, coupled with the observation that ox serum that was deficient in pseudocholinesterase activity failed to hydrolyze α-cocaine, suggested that the enzyme responsible for α-cocaine hydrolysis was pseudocholinesterase.

Heim and Haas (1950), studying the ability of different guinea pig tissues to hydrolyze cocaine to benzoylecgonine, found the liver to have greater activity than kidney, brain, or muscle tissue. Iwatsubo (1965) was unable to detect significant hydrolysis of cocaine by "solubilized" microsomes (deoxycholate-treated) which were incubated in buffer without cofactors; however, this preparation was capable of hydrolyzing other esters, including aspirin, phenylacetate, and tributyrin. In contrast, rat liver microsomes fortified with an NADPH-generating system did metabolize

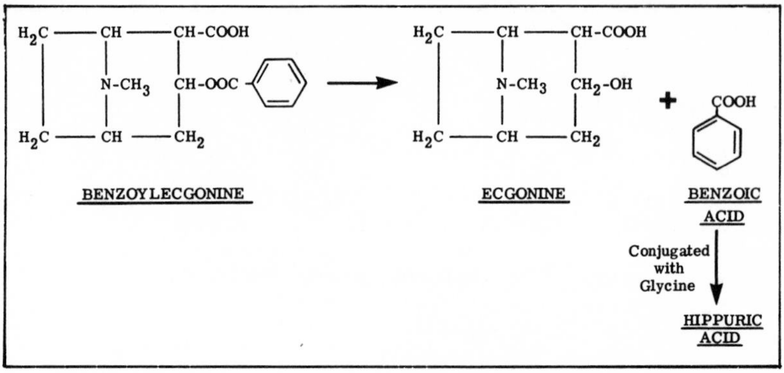

Fig. 3. Metabolism of benzoylecgonine to ecgonine and benzoic acid.

cocaine by de-esterification and N-demethylation to form benzoylecgonine, ecgonine, and norcocaine (Axelrod and Cochin, 1957; Ramos-Aliaga and Chiriboga, 1970; Leighty and Fentiman, 1974).

Metabolism *in Vivo*

After cocaine administration to man and a variety of animal species, its metabolic products are excreted in urine; relatively little unchanged cocaine is excreted (Williams, 1959a).

Langecker and Lewit (1938) investigated the toxicity of cocaine in rabbits, guinea pigs, and cats. They observed that cocaine was relatively nontoxic to rabbits and suggested that this species rapidly metabolized cocaine by hydrolysis of the two ester groups to form inactive metabolites, benzoylecgonine, and ecgonine. Indeed, they found that benzoylecgonine and ecgonine were less toxic than cocaine and postulated that hydrolysis of cocaine represented a detoxication mechanism.

Since significant quantities of ecgonine were not found in the urine of animals treated with cocaine, whereas large quantities of benzoylecgonine were found, it can be assumed that initially, cocaine is hydrolyzed at the methyl group to form methanol and benzoylecgonine (Wiechowski, 1901; Fish and Wilson, 1969). The latter compound is subsequently metabolized to ecgonine and benzoic acid (Fig. 3) (Sanchez, 1957; Ortiz, 1966; Valanju *et al.*, 1973). The benzoic acid may then be conjugated with glycine and excreted as hippuric acid (Ringer, 1911). All these metabolites are devoid of cocaine's pharmacologic activities (Hawks *et al.*, 1975).

The presence of ecgonine in urine of cocaine-treated animals, as well as its presence in urine from coca chewers, indicated that it may be an end

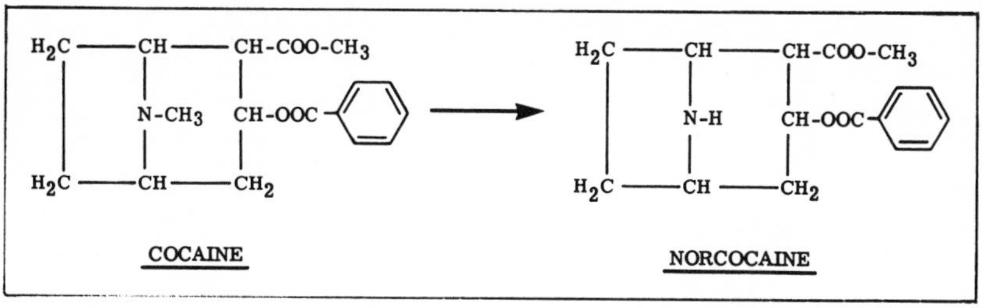

Fig. 4. N-demethylation of cocaine to norcocaine.

product of cocaine metabolism (Montesinos, 1965). In support of this view are results of a recent study in which over 99% of a dose of ecgonine given to rats was recovered unchanged in the excreta (Misra *et al.*, 1974).

After administration of N-$^{14}CH_3$-cocaine to mice, Werner (1967) found $^{14}CO_2$ present in expired air. This finding implies that norcocaine (Fig. 4) is formed *in vivo* from cocaine. Although Leighty and Fentiman (1974) were unable to detect any norcocaine in the urine of rats treated with cocaine, Hawks *et al.* (1975) did identify norcocaine in monkey brain, plasma, and cerebrospinal fluid after cocaine administration. Unlike the other cocaine metabolites identified to date, norcocaine is biologically active, being equipotent to cocaine in its ability to inhibit the uptake of norepinephrine by rat brain synaptosomes (Hawks *et al.*, 1975).

Excretion

Results of early studies concerning excretion of cocaine were not in good agreement with each other. Investigators reported recovering from 0 to about 90% of an administered dose as unchanged cocaine in urine (Wiechowski, 1901; Rifatwachdani, 1913; Tatum and Seevers, 1929; McIntyre, 1936; Langeker and Lewit, 1938; Woods *et al.*, 1951; Fish and Wilson, 1969). Several factors may be responsible for this large range, including (1) species used; (2) route of administration; and (3) urinary pH.

In rabbits, less than 1% of an administered dose of cocaine was recovered in urine as parent drug (Wiechowski, 1901; Tatum and Seevers, 1929; Woods *et al.*, 1951). In contrast, the recovery of unchanged cocaine in dog urine ranged from 1 to 12% of the administered dose (Wiechowski, 1901; Woods *et al.*, 1951). In man, McIntyre (1936) reported that after peritonsilar injection of cocaine, about 54% of the dose was excreted in the urine unchanged, whereas others reported finding 1-21% of the dose in urine in unchanged form when cocaine was administered by intramuscular or submucosal injection or by mouth (chewing coca leaves).

Fish and Wilson (1969) administered cocaine intramuscularly to subjects whose urinary pH was modified by the administration of ammonium chloride or sodium bicarbonate. When the urine was at pH 5.3, 8.7% of cocaine was excreted unchanged. When the urine was at pH 7.4, only 0.4% cocaine was excreted unchanged. When they studied the effect of urinary pH on benzoylecgonine excretion, opposite effects were seen (50% of the dose was excreted at pH 7.4 and 35% at pH 5.3). When one sums the excretion of unchanged cocaine and its metabolite benzoylecgonine, about 40-50% of the administered dose of cocaine is accounted for in urine.

Although cocaine is commonly used by drug addicts, it has not been detected routinely in urine screening procedures because of lack of adequate sensitivity methodology. Recently, a new technique, termed "spin immuno-assay," was perfected for detecting benzoylecgonine in urine. Using this assay, Valanju et al. (1973) identified benzoylecgonine in 15% of 1000 randomly selected urine samples submitted from drug abuse treatment programs in New York City. In less than 1% of these urine samples was cocaine present in detectable quantities. Ecgonine was also found in some urines; however, it was never present in the absence of benzoylecgonine. In contrast, benzoylecgonine was often present in the absence of ecgonine.

PHENCYCLIDINE

Phencyclidine is a phenylmethylamine derivative that is abused (Fig. 5). Although sold as a veterinary tranquilizer under the trade name Sernylan, phencyclidine is commonly known simply as PCP, or "angel dust." Phencyclidine was evaluated clinically as a sedative, analgesic, and general anesthetic (Greifenstein et al., 1958), but was discarded as a possible therapeutic agent for use in man when it was shown to have psychotomimetic and hallucinogenic properties at moderate to high doses.

The pharmacologic effects of phencyclidine have been studied in animals (Chen et al., 1959) and man (Domino, 1964, 1972). Clinically, phencyclidine can produce intense derealization, depersonalization, and thought disorders, and it is often difficult to distinguish its effects from the early symptoms of acute schizophrenia (Luby et al., 1959; Cohen, 1971). In addition to its psychotomimetic effects, other CNS effects of phencyclidine include euphoria at moderate doses and CNS depression (including cataleptoid effects) at large doses which may progress to coma. Paradoxically, at very high doses phencyclidine can produce CNS excitation, agitation, and possibly convulsions. PCP also produces sympathomimetic effects including hypertension and tachycardia. These effects might be expected since phencyclidine structurally resembles the sympathomimetic amines (Fig. 5).

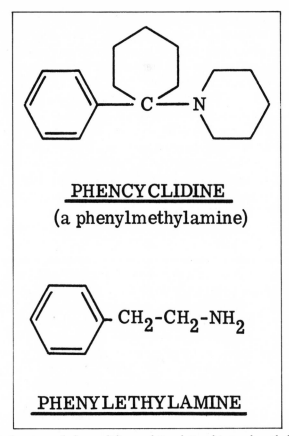

PHENCYCLIDINE
(a phenylmethylamine)

$CH_2-CH_2-NH_2$

PHENYLETHYLAMINE

Fig. 5. Structure of phencyclidine and its relationship to phenethylamine.

On the "street," PCP may be sold to the unaware user as an adulterant in other drugs, or as a substitute for other drugs of abuse, including Δ^9-THC and mescaline. In fact, in a study of 26 confiscated Δ^9-THC samples, 18 samples were actually PCP, and none were Δ^9-THC (Canadian Commission, 1973).

Unfortunately, very little information dealing with the physiologic disposition of phencyclidine has been reported in the scientific literature. The drug has been administered either orally or by the intravenous route; it is well absorbed after oral administration and has a rapid onset of action. The effects may last from minutes to hours, the duration of action being dependent upon the dosage administered (Domino, 1972).

Phencyclidine is primarily excreted in the urine in the form of its metabolites (Canadian Commission, 1973). There are allegedly several hydroxylated metabolites (the hydroxylation occurring in the piperidine ring), and these compounds are reported to possess greater convulsant activity than phencyclidine itself (Domino, 1972). Studies of the metabolism of ^{14}C-PCP in man reveal that it is rapidly converted to a monohydroxy derivative which is excreted in the urine (Ober et al., 1963).

Species differences exist in the metabolism of phencyclidine. For example, the amount of dihydroxylated metabolite varies from 0% in the cat to as much as 75% in the rat. Low levels of this metabolite are excreted in human urine. The quantity of the monohydroxylated metabolite of PCP found in urine is small in rat and cat (5-14%); however, larger quantities are excreted in man (about 68%) (Hucker, 1970).

KHAT

Khat is a stimulant drug used in a similar fashion to coca. Khat is the name given to the leaves obtained from the shrub *Cathala edulis*. Its synonyms are kat, chat, or quat. It has been used by the natives of East Africa (Kenya, Ethiopa, Abyssinia, and Somaliland) and inhabitants of the eastern portion of the Arabian peninsula. The abuse of khat is associated with attempts to overcome fatigue; thus its abuse pattern is akin to that for coca leaves by natives of Peru and Bolivia, or for coffee (caffeine) by Americans. The sweet, astringent, licorice-tasting leaves are either chewed or ingested in the form of a tea.

Khat contains a mixture of the alkaloids cathine, cathidine, and cathinine. Cathine, the major psychoactive principle, was shown to be identical to pseudonorephedrine, a drug that is structurally similar to the phenalkylamines such as norephedrine (phenylpropanolamine), amphetamine, and ephedrine (Holmstedt and Linnarson, 1972; Schultes, 1969) (Fig. 6). In fact, it is a stereoisomer of norephedrine, one of the most widely used nasal decongestants in prescription and over-the-counter drug combinations. In addition to pseudonorephedrine and other amphetamine-like alkaloids, the plant contains tannins that are responsible for the astringent properties of khat. It is said that the plant would be more toxic to its users if the tannins did not impede the absorption of the psychoactive principle.

Although little is known about the physiologic disposition of pseudonorephedrine, it seems reasonable to assume that it would be handled like norephedrine, the major metabolite of ephedrine (Williams, 1959b; also see Chapter 2). After the administration to man of a single 50-mg dose of norephedrine, Heimlich et al. (1961) reported that more than 95% of the administered dose was excreted as unchanged drug in the urine

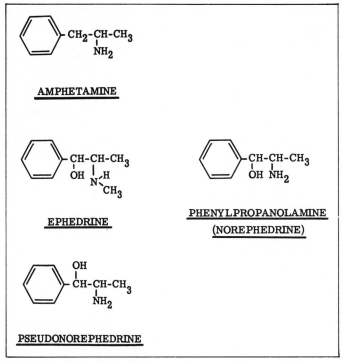

Fig. 6. Structure of pseudonorephedrine and its resemblance to other sympathomimetic amines.

in 24 hours. The half-life of norephedrine in man was calculated to be 3.9 hours. Thus the drug is rapidly and almost completely excreted within 24 hours; very little, if any, of the drug is metabolized.

FLY AGARIC

Fly agaric, the common name given to the mushroom *Amanita muscaria*, grows wild in various regions of Northern Europe and Asia. This mushroom is used by Eastern Siberian tribesmen for its euphorigenic CNS effects and for its stimulant actions producing increased physical activity (Wasson, 1967). The mushrooms are eaten in their natural state or soaked in water for several days and the resultant solution is drunk as a tea. Wasson (1967) has postulated that fly agaric may be the mysterious plant

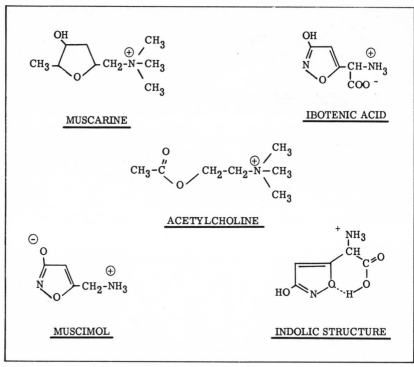

Fig. 7. Structure of muscarine and related alkaloids found in fly agaric; their resemblance to acetylcholine and the indoles.

"soma" reported to be used 3000 years ago as a "divine" inebriant by the Aryians and described in early Hindu writings and Sanskrit hymns.

After ingestion of small amounts of the fly agaric mushroom, the individual may experience dizziness, nausea, somnolence, euphoria, colored visions, and hallucinations (auditory and visual). Higher doses may produce severe intoxication with vivid hallucinations, twitching, agitation, and death (Waser, 1967).

Fly agaric contains a mixture of alkaloids, including muscarine (Fig. 7), a parasympathomimetic agent that has been studied extensively (Eugster, 1967; Eugster and Waser, 1954). Muscarine structurally resembles acetylcholine, the natural transmitter released at the parasympathetic nerve ending. However, muscarine cannot be responsible for the psychotomimetic effects of fly agaric since it (a) is present in too low concentrations in the plant, (b) has weak CNS activity after oral administration, and (c) probably does not cross the blood-brain barrier (it is a quaternary ammonium compound).

Other substances present in small quantities in fly agaric include acetylcholine, choline, and possibly bufotenine. If this lattermost compound (previously discussed in Chapter 4) is present in this mushroom, its occurrence is in such small quantities that it cannot contribute significantly to the CNS effects of fly agaric (Eugster, 1967).

Several years ago, two highly active compounds, muscimol and ibotenic acid (Fig. 7), were isolated from *Amanita muscaria* (Müller and Eugster, 1965; Eugster *et al.*, 1965; Good *et al.*, 1965). Ibotenic acid is an amino acid and muscimol is its decarboxylated product. Ibotenic acid can be drawn to resemble the psychotomimetic indole compounds (Fig. 7) and it has been proposed that it may be acting like these psychotomimetic compounds (Waser and Bersin, 1969).

Waser (1967), after ingesting moderate doses (10-15 mg) of muscimol, reported CNS effects similar to those observed after eating small quantities of the dried fly agaric mushrooms. Even when ingested at doses of 75 mg, ibotenic acid was less active than muscimol; it did, however, produce some CNS actions. These studies suggest that muscimol is the primary active principle of fly agaric responsible for the CNS effects.

Little is known about the metabolism of muscimol. However, it is known that the compound is excreted in the urine in its unchanged form or as an active metabolite. This fact is supported by reports that among Siberian tribesmen, the urine of fly agaric users can be ingested by other persons who then experience the hallucinogenic effects associated with the drug (or mushroom). Indeed, this process can be repeated three or four times in succession without any noticeable loss of the inebriating effects of fly agaric (Wasson, 1967).

IBOGAINE

Ibogaine is the major active alkaloid found in the roots and beans of *Tabernonthe iboga*. The plant grows as a shrub in Africa, where the roots and beans (Congolese ordeal bean; Iboga bean) are chewed by the natives for their CNS stimulant properties. In addition, the drug is widely used for religious ceremonies in secret cults. It has been used recently in the United States as a psychotomimetic mind-altering drug, and it has been included as a Schedule I dangerous drug by the United States Drug Enforcement Agency. In addition to its psychotomimetic effects, ibogaine can produce many unpleasant side effects, including visual hallucinations, epileptic seizures, and coma.

Structurally, ibogaine (Fig. 8) is an indolic compound which has a

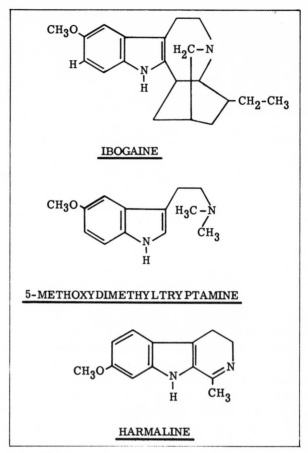

Fig. 8. Structure of ibogaine and its resemblance to harmaline and 5-methoxy-DMT.

tryptamine skeleton resembling methoxydimethyltryptamine; it therefore resembles the Harmala alkaloids, harmine and harmaline (Fig. 8). To date, few reports exist regarding the physiologic disposition of ibogaine. Dhahir (1971) found that the drug was present at high concentrations in liver and kidney after administration to rats. The disappearance rate of ibogaine from the whole rat was about 4% of the administered dose per hour. No ibogaine was detectable in the rat 12 hours after its administration. About 5% of the administered dose of ibogaine was excreted in rat urine as unchanged drug. An unidentified metabolite of ibogaine, which represented 15% of the injected dose, was also present in urine (Dhahir, 1971).

BETEL NUT

Betel nut (also known as areca nut) is the dried seed which grows on the palm tree, *Areca catechu*. The nut is a component of a mixture of materials known as betel and is used by East Indian natives for its euphorogenic properties. Betel is a mixture of the leaves of the pepper plant (*Piper betel*), lime (calcium oxide), and the betel nut. The method for making this preparation consists of smearing fresh pepper leaves with lime, then wrapping this around slices of the betel nut. The whole concoction is then placed in the mouth and chewed as a masticatory. The betel nut in this mixture imparts a red color to the saliva, urine, and feces and stains the teeth. The major alkaloid of the betel nut is arecoline (Fig. 9). It is a partially hydrogenated nicotinic acid derivative.

Arecoline has been used therapeutically in humans in China as a vermifuge; however, its use elsewhere is limited to veterinary practice.

In addition to its euphorigenic effect, arecoline produces many symptoms related to effects on the parasympathetic nervous system, including sweating, salivation, miosis, and other effects similar to pilocarpine. At excessive doses it is very toxic and produces convulsions and coma.

As previously discussed for coca chewing, it appears that the lime present in the betel mixture facilitates the absorption of arecoline from the preparation. Arecoline, being a basic drug, can more readily be absorbed at an alkaline pH (when it is present in its un-ionized form). Although nothing has been reported on the metabolism of arecoline, one could assume it would probably be deesterified in the body to form arecaidine, a relatively inert compound (Fig. 9). It is also possible that the compound is N-demethylated.

VOLATILE SOLVENTS

The abuse of volatile solvents by inhalation is an increasing sociomedical problem. In some countries, for example, Hawaii and Japan, this form of drug abuse has supplanted other agents. These solvents comprise a heterogeneous group, all sharing the physical properties of being volatile and capable of inhalation.

The major difficulty in controlling this form of abuse is the ready availability of these products in commercial establishments and their ability to be purchased without fear of legal repercussions. In addition, they are inexpensive. Thus, very little deterrent exists to prevent the abuse of these agents. The commerical agents considered in this section include glues (e.g., model airplane glue), gasoline, industrial solvents, paints, lacquers, varnishes, paint thinners, paint removers, lighter fluids, dry cleaning fluids,

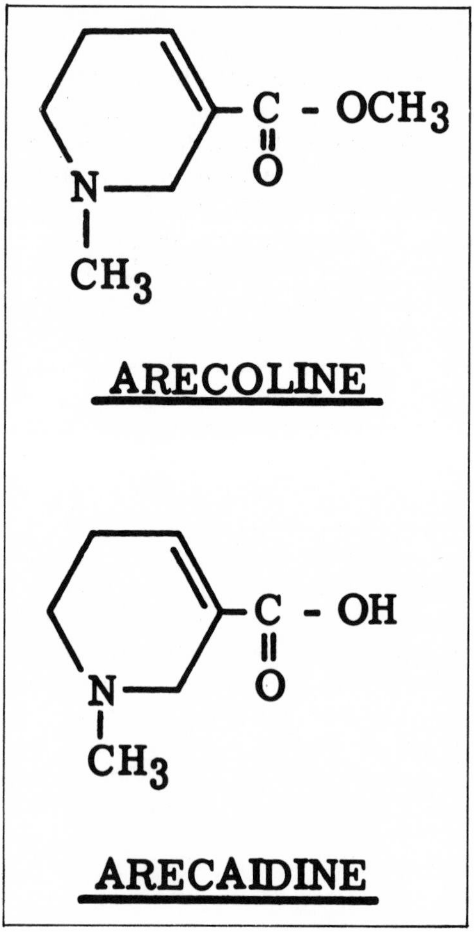

Fig. 9. Structure of arecoline and a postulated metabolite.

nail polish removers, as well as those aerosols containing propellants (deodorants, household fresheners, insecticides, and hair sprays). The active chemical constituents of these commercial preparations also represent a heterogeneous group, including (a) inorganic and aliphatic compounds such as nitrous oxide, acetone, ethyl acetate, ether, hexane, petroleum ether, naphtha, and chlorinated compounds (e.g., chloroform, carbon tetrachloride, perchlorethylene, trichlorethylene), and (b) aromatic and cyclic compounds such as benzene, toluene, xylene, and cyclohexane.

In addition, in recent years the freons [e.g., CCl_2F_2 (freon 12 or dichlorodi-fluromethane) and CCl_3F (freon 11 or trichlorofluoromethane)], have been added to a variety of commerical products as propellants, thus enabling the sale of many products as aerosols that have much consumer appeal (as well as appeal to the misguided drug abuser).

The abuse of volatile solvents is not a new problem. The medically used general anesthetics have been abused for many years as euphoriants. Much has been written about nitrous oxide (laughing gas) "jags," ether "frolics," and chloroform parties. Today, the abuse of volatile solvents is primarily a problem associated with youngsters (preteens and adolescents) who use these chemicals for their soporific, euphoric, or psychotomimetic effects. Their use by adults is rare.

In addition to their direct actions on the cerebrum, the inhalation of these agents in large quantities produces a hypoxic state which may also be responsible for the delirium produced. Although subjects inhale these drugs for their euphoriant effects, the agents may also produce direct toxic effects. Fatal reactions have been reported, including suffocation after inhaling freon (secondary to the production of a frozen epiglottis and larynx); bone marrow depression and cardiac arrhythmias after glue sniffing (benzene); cerebral edema after inhaling various solvents (Press and Done, 1967; Bass, 1970; Powers, 1965; Winek *et al.*, 1967).

Absorption and Distribution

This heterogeneous group of compounds all share the same physical property—extreme volatility at or near room temperature. Their route of administration is by inhalation which is accomplished by (a) directly sniffing the fumes from the container; (b) placing the material on a handkerchief and then holding this over one's nose (here the material is very readily evaporated due to contact with the warm skin); (c) placing the material in a paper or plastic bag and inhaling the vapors; or (d) spraying the material directly into the oral-pharyngeal cavity (as in the case of the aerosol preparations). In any case, after inhalation, absorption of the chemical is rapid since it can directly enter the alveolar sac where the drug equilibrates with the blood perfusing the lungs. The drug then rapidly diffuses across the alveolar membrane and capillary wall into the bloodstream. In this manner, high concentrations of drug can be achieved in the blood (and brain) within a short period of time. The rapidity of effect depends upon the partial pressure of the gas and its solubility in the blood. Since much information is known about the general anesthetics, they will be used as examples because the same principles also apply to the abused volatile solvents.

Ether, chloroform, and nitrous oxide are used both medically and as drugs of abuse. The rapidity of onset of their effect depends on their solubility in blood (the aqueous phase). Ether is very soluble in blood, having a blood:gas partition coefficient of 12.1 at body temperature (i.e., the ratio of ether concentration in blood to ether concentration in a gas phase when the two are in equilibrium). Chloroform behaves similarly, with a blood:gas partition coefficient of 9.4. In contrast, nitrous oxide is rather insoluble in blood (blood:gas partition coefficient of 0.47).

The tissue distribution of these volatile agents depends on regional blood flow as well as other factors, including the partial pressure of the gas in arterial blood and tissues and the solubility of the gas in the tissues. In general, the gaseous anesthetic agents distribute to all tissues (except fat) to about the same extent, with a tissue to blood ratio of about 1. However, the tissue to blood ratio, when fat is the tissue, is much higher, varying with the specific drug, e.g., chloroform has a fat:blood ratio of 26, those for nitrous oxide and ether are 3 and 5, respectively (Wollman and Dripps, 1970). The volatile gases produce their rapid effects in part as a result of the large blood supply to the brain (25% of the cardiac output).

Metabolism and Excretion

In general, after being absorbed, volatile solvents are usually excreted unchanged, being metabolized only to a small extent at best. The body converts them to more polar, water-soluble substances that are more readily excreted. The metabolism of these volatile chemicals will be briefly summarized. For a more extensive review, the reader is directed to Williams' classic textbook on detoxication mechanisms (1959c).

That aromatic and cyclic volatile solvents are metabolized to more polar compounds was recognized in the mid and late 1800's. With time, much has been learned about mechanisms, etc. Parke and Williams (1950, 1953) found that after the oral administration of benzene (0.5 gm/kg) to rabbits, about 45% of the administered dose was excreted unchanged in the expired air. The percentage excreted unchanged in expired air was dose dependent, more being excreted in the unchanged form with larger doses of benzene. An additional 1 to 2% of the dose was completely oxidized to CO_2 and eliminated in the expired air. Another 25, 2, and 5% of the administered dose was metabolized to phenol, catechol, and quinol, respectively (Fig. 10). These three phenolic derivatives were then excreted in urine, primarily as ethereal sulfate conjugates. A few minor metabolites of benzene were also present in urine. Less than 0.5% of administered benzene was excreted in feces in rabbits. Teisinger and Soucek (1952) reported that in man about 46% of an inhaled dose of benzene is retained in the body tissues for longer than 5 hours. With time, about 10-40% is excreted in urine as phenols and about 12% is expired as free benzene.

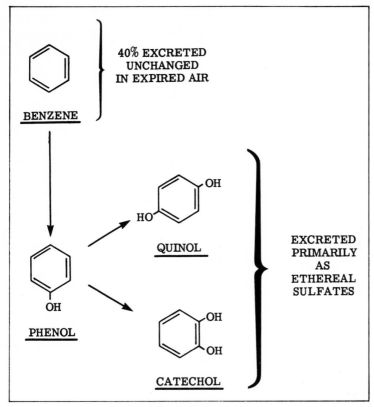

Fig. 10. Metabolism of benzene.

The physiologic disposition of toluene is markedly different than that of benzene. In man and animals, about 80% of an injected or inhaled dose of toluene is oxidized in the body to benzoic acid which is subsequently conjugated with glycine and excreted in urine as hippuric acid (Fig. 11). The remaining 20% is excreted unchanged in expired air via the lungs.

Xylene is a mixture of isomers of dimethylbenzene with the methyl groups in varying positions with respect to each other. In general, the xylenes are primarily oxidized on one of the methyl groups to toluic acids (Fig. 11), which are then excreted in the urine as glycine conjugates. This accounts for 80-90% of a dose. In addition, p-xylene is hydroxylated to a phenol (2,5-dimethylphenol) which accounts for from 2 to 4% of the administered dose (Williams, 1959c).

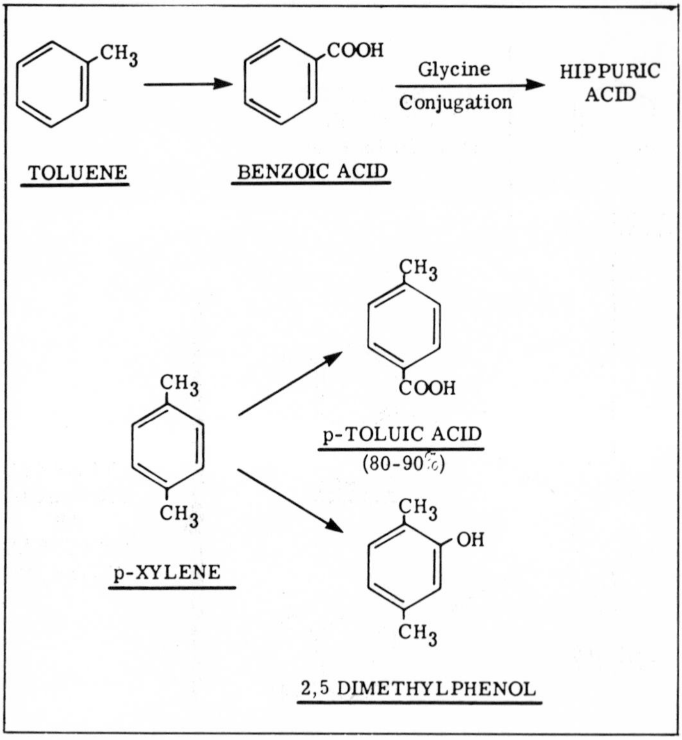

Fig. 11. Metabolism of toluene and p-xylene.

Another volatile chemical is cyclohexane. Elliot *et al.* (1959) reported that rabbits excreted a considerable percentage (29-50%) of this agent via expired air in its unchanged form. In addition, about 10% of the dose was excreted by this route as CO_2. The major metabolite of cyclohexane, the glucuronide of cyclohexanol, accounts for about 40% of the administered dose and is excreted in urine. In addition to the monohydroxylated compound, the 1,2-dihydroxy compound (1,2-cyclohexanediol) is also excreted as a glucuronide, accounting for about 6% of the dose (Fig. 12).

The abused volatile substances containing aliphatic components may be either metabolized to more polar substances or excreted unchanged. Acetone, a normal product of lipid metabolism, is usually metabolized and channeled into one or two carbon pathways such as acetate. However, when acetone is produced in larger quantities, as in diabetic acidosis, or

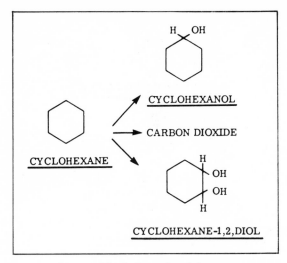

Fig. 12. Metabolism of cyclohexane.

when inhaled as a drug of abuse, it is excreted primarily as the unchanged compound in the breath and to a lesser extent in the urine.

Ether, one of the first of the abused volatile solvents, is excreted primarily in expired air. Over 90% of the drug is handled in this manner (Haggard, 1924). In addition, a small percentage (1-2%) is excreted in urine and sweat, and traces are excreted by percutaneous diffusion through intact skin (Stoelting and Eger, 1969).

The volatile chlorinated hydrocarbons are also abused. After chloroform ($CHCl_3$) administration, it is excreted in expired air almost completely unchanged. A small percent (about 5%) is metabolized by dehalogenation (Van Dyke et al., 1964). After carbon tetrachloride (CCl_4) administration, it is eliminated predominantly by the lungs as unchanged drug and to a small extent as CO_2 (McCollister et al. 1951). A small percent of a dose of this chemical is excreted in urine. After inhalation, trichlorethylene is excreted unchanged in expired air (about 44% of the administered dose). The remainder of the dose is extensively metabolized in the body to form trichlorethanol and trichloracetic acid (Fig. 13) (Butler, 1949). It has been postulated that trichlorethylene is slowly metabolized to chloral hydrate, a hypnotic used therapeutically (the combination of chloral hydrate and alcohol is referred to as knockout drops or a "Mickey Finn"). Chloral hydrate is further metabolized to trichlorethanol and trichloracetic acid.

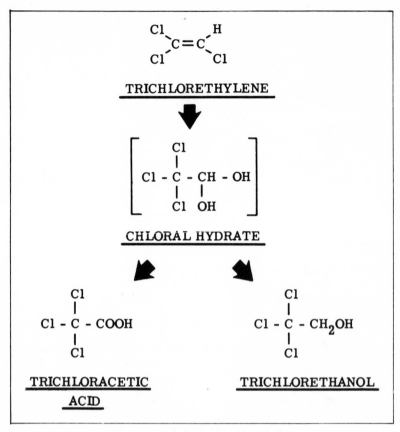

Fig. 13. Metabolism of trichlorethylene.

REFERENCES

Ammon, I. and Savelsberg, W.: Die enzymatische Spaltung von Atropin, Cocain und chemisch verwandten Estern. Hoppe Seyler's Z. Physiol. Chem. *284*;135-156, 1949.

Angel, C. and Lafferty, C.R.: The effect of pretreatment with anesthetic agents on cocaine accumulation in rat brain. Ala. J. Med. Sci. *6*:311-314, 1969.

Axelrod, J. and Cochin, J.: The inhibitory action of nalorphine on the enzymatic *N*-demethylation of narcotic drugs. J. Pharmacol. Exp. Ther. *121*:107-112, 1957.

Bacq, Z.M.: Action des amines sur la membrane nicitante et modifications de cette action par la cocaine et l'enervation. Mem. Acad. Med. Belg. *25*:6-61, 1936.

Bass, M.: Sudden sniffing death. J.A.M.A. *212*:2075, 1970.

Blaschko, H., Chou, T.C., and Wajda, I.: The affinity of atropine-like esters for esterases. Brit. J. Pharmacol. 2:108-115, 1946.

Blaschko, H., Himms, J.M., and Stromblad, B.C.R.: The enzymic hydrolysis of cocaine and alpha-cocaine. Brit. J. Pharmacol. 10:442-444, 1955.

Butler, T.C.: Reduction and oxidation of chloral hydrate by isolated tissues *in vitro*. J. Pharmacol. Exp. Ther. 95:360-362, 1949.

Campbell, D. and Adriani, J.: Absorption of local anesthetics. J.A.M.A. 168:873-877, 1958.

Canadian Commission. Final Report of the Commission of Inquiry into the nonmedical use of drugs. Information Canada, Ottawa, 1973.

Chen, G., Ensor, C.R., Russell, D., and Bohner, B.: The pharmacology of 1-(1-phenyl-cyclohexyl)piperidine HCl. J. Pharmacol. Exp. Ther. 127:241-250, 1959.

Cohen, S.: The psychotomimetic agents. Prog. in Drug Res. 15:85, 1971.

Del Pozo, E.C.: Empiricism and magic in Aztec pharmacology. In Ethnopharmacologic Search for Psychoactive Drugs. Ed. D.H. Efron, Washington D.C., Publ. Health Ser. Publ. No. 1645, 1967, pp. 59-76.

Dhahir, H.I.: A comparative study on the toxicity of ibogaine and serotonin. Dissertation Abstr. Intern. B. 32, No. 4, 2311-2312, 1971.

Domino, E.F.: Neurobiology of phencyclidine (Sernyl), a drug with an unusual spectrum of pharmacological activity. Int. Rev. Biol. 6:303-347, 1964.

Domino, E.F.: Pharmacology of madness—the hallucinogens. In Drug Abuse. Proceedings of the International Conference. Ed. Zarafonetis, C.J.D., Lea & Febiger, Philadelphia 1972, pp. 307-320.

Elliott, T.H., Parke, D.V., and Williams, R.T.: Studies in detoxication. Biochem. J. 72:193-200, 1959.

Eugster, C.H.: Isolation, structure and syntheses of central-active compounds from *Amanita muscaria* (L. ex. Fr.) hooker. In Ethnopharmacologic Search for Psychoactive Drugs. Ed. D.H. Efron, Pub. Health Ser. Publ. No. 1645, Washington D.C., 1967, pp. 416-418.

Eugster, C.H., Muller, G.F.R., and Good, R.: Wirks toffe aus *Amanita muscaria*:Ibolensaeure und Muscazon. Tetrahedron Lett. 1813-1815, 1965.

Eugster, C.H. and Waser, P.G.: Zur Kenntnis des Muscarins. Experientia 10:298-300, 1954.

Fish, F. and Wilson, W.D.C.: Excretion of cocaine and its metabolites in man. J. Pharm. Pharmacol. 21:135S-138S, 1969.

Glick, D. and Glaubach, S.: The occurrence and distribution of atropinesterase, and the specificity of tropinesterases. J. Gen. Physiol. 25:197-205, 1941.

Glick, D., Glaubach, S., and Moore, D.H.: Azolesterase activities of electrophoretically separated proteins of serum. J. Biol. Chem. 144:525-528, 1942.

Good, R., Muller, G.F.R., and Eugster, C.H.: Pramuscimol und Muscazon aus *Amanita muscaria*. Helv. Chim. Acta. 48:927-930, 1965.

Greifenstein, F.E., DeVault, M., Yoshitake, J., and Gajewski, J.E.: A study of a l-aryl cyclohexylamine for anesthesia. Anesth. Analgesia 37:283-294, 1958.

Haggard, H.W.: Absorption, distribution, and elimination of ethyl ether. J. Biol. Chem. 59:737-802, 1924.

Hawks, R.L., Kopin, I.J., Colburn, R.W., and Thoa, N.B.: Norcocaine: A pharmacologically active metabolite of cocaine found in brain. Life Sci. 15:2189-2195, 1975.

Heim, F. and Haas, A.: Uber den fermentativen Abbau von Pantokain Novakain und Kokain durch Extrakte aus Meerschweinchenleber, -niere, -gehirn und -muskulatur. Arch. Exper. Pathol. Pharmakol. 211:458-461, 1950.

Heimlich, K.R., MacDonnell, D.R., Flanagan, T.L., and O'Brien, P.D.: Evaluation of a sustained release form of phenylpropanolamine hydrochloride by urinary excretion studies. J. Pharm. Sci. *50*:232-237, 1961.

Hertting, G., Axelrod, J., Whitby, L.G.: Effect of drugs on the uptake and metabolism of ³H-norepinephrine. J. Pharmacol. Exp. Ther. *134*:146, 1961.

Holmstedt, B. and Lindgren, J.-E.: Chemical constituents and pharmacology of South American snuffs. In Ethnopharmacologic Search for Psychoactive Drugs. Ed. D.H. Efron, Pub. Health Ser. Publ. No. 1645, Washington D.C., 1967, pp. 339-373.

Holmstedt, B. and Linnarson, A.: Chemistry and means of determination of hallucinogens and marihuana. In Drug Abuse. Proceedings of the International Conference. Ed. Zarafonetis, C.J.D., Lea & Febinger, Philadelphia, 1972, pp. 291-305.

Hucker, H.B.: Species differences in drug metabolism. Ann. Rev. Pharmacol. *10*:99-118, 1970.

Iwatsubo, K.: Studies on the classification of the enzymes hydrolyzing ester-form drugs in liver microsomes. Jap. J. Pharmacol. *15*:244-256, 1965.

Langecker, H. and Lewit, K.: Uber die Entgiftung von Cocain und Percain sowie von Atropin im Organismus. Arch. Exp. Pathol. Pharmacol. *190*:492-499, 1938.

Leighty, E.G. and Fentiman, A.F.: Metabolism of cocaine to norcocaine and benzoyl ecgonine by an *in vitro* microsomal enzyme system. Res. Commun. Chem. Pathol. Pharmacol. *8*:65-74, 1974.

Luby, E.D., Cohen, B.D., Rosenbaum, G., Gottlieb, J.S., and Kelley, R.: Study of a new schizophrenomimetic drug—Sernyl. Arch. Neurol. Psychiat. *81*:363-369, 1959.

McCollister, D.D., Beamer, W.H., Atchison, G.J., and Spencer, H.C.: The absorption, distribution and elimination of radioactive carbon tetrachloride by monkeys upon exposure to low vapor concentrations. J. Pharmacol. Exp. Ther. *102*:112-124, 1951.

McIntyre, A.R.: Renal excretion of cocaine in a case of acute cocaine poisoning. J. Pharmacol. Exp. Ther. *57*:133, 1936.

Misra, A.L., Vadlamani, N.L., Bloch, R., Nayak, P.K., and Mule, S.J.: Physiologic disposition and metabolism of (³H) ecgonine (cocaine metabolite) in the rat. Res. Commun. Chem. Pathol. Pharmacol. *8*:55-63, 1974.

Montesinos, A.F.: Metabolism of cocaine. Bull. Narcotics *17*:11-15, 1965.

Müller, G.F.R. and Eugster, C.H.: Muscimol, ein pharmakodynamisch Wirksamer Stoff aus *Amanita muscaria*. Helv. Chim. Acta *48*:910-926, 1965.

Ober, R.E., Gwynn, G.W., Chang, T., McCarthy, D.A., and Glazko, A.J.: Metabolism of l-(l-phenylcycolhexyl)-piperidine (Sernyl). Fed. Proc. *22*:639, 1963.

Ortiz, R.V.: Distribution and metabolism of cocaine in the rat An. Fac. Quim. Farm., Univ. Chile *18*:15-19, 1966.

Parke, D.V. and Williams, R.T.: Studies in detoxication. Biochem. J. *46*:236-243, 1950.

Parke, D.V. and Williams, R.T.: Studies in detoxication. Biochem. J. *55*:337-340, 1953.

Powers, D.: Aplastic anemia secondary to glue sniffing. N. Engl. J. Med. *273*:700, 1965.

Press, H.E. and Done, A.K.: Solvent sniffing. Physiologic effects and community control measures for intoxication from intentional inhalation of organic solvents. Pediatrics *39*:451-611, 1967.

Ramos-Aliaga, R. and Chiriboga, J.: Enzymic N-demethylation of cocaine and nutritional status. Arch. Latinoamer. Nutr. *20*:415-428, 1970.

Rifatwachdani, S.: Fate of cocaine and ecgonine in the organisms. Biochem. Z. *54*:83-91, 1913.

Ringer, A.I.: On the maximum production of hippuric acid in animals with consideration of the origin of glycocoll in the animal body. J. Biol. Chem. *10*:327-338, 1911.

Sanchez, C.A.: Chromatographic analysis of ecgonine in the urine of subjects habitually chewing coca leaves. An. Fac. Farm. Bioquim., Univ. of S. Marcos 8:82-86, 1957.

Schultes, R.E.: The plant kingdom and hallucinogens. Part I, Bull. Narcot. XXI: 3-16, 1969; Part II, Bull Narcot. XXI: 15-27, 1969.

Sherman, G.P.: A possible determinant of drug action—the blood-brain barrier. Amer. J. Pharmacol. 142:127-133, 1970.

Steinhaus, J.E.: Comparative study of experimental toxicity of local anesthetic agents. Anesthesiology 13:577-586, 1952.

Stoelting, R.K. and Eger, E.I.: Percutaneous loss of nitrous oxide, cyclopropane, ether and halothane in man. Anesthesiology 30:278-289, 1969.

Strait, L.A. and Aird, R.B.: Detection of cocaine-HCl in cerebrospinal fluid by spectroscopic analysis. Physiol. Rev. 53:213, 1938.

Strait, L.A., Aird, R.B. and Weiss, S.: Method for rapid isolation and spectrographic measurement of cocaine from brain tissue. J. pharmacol. Exp. Ther. 73:363-374,

Tainter, M.L. and Chang, D.K.: The antagonism of the pressor action of tyramine by cocaine. J. Pharmacol. Exp. Ther. 30:193-207, 1927.

Tatum, A. and Seevers, M.: Experimental cocaine addiction. J. Pharmacol. 36:401-410, 1929.

Teisinger, J. and Soucek, B.: Significance of metabolism of toxic gases for their absorption and elimination by man. Časop. lék. česk. 91:1372-1375, 1952.

Valanju, N.N., Baden, M.M., Valanju, S.N., Mulligan, D., and Verma, S.K.: Detection of biotransformed cocaine in urine from drug abusers. J. Chromatogr. 81:170-173, 1973.

Van Dyke, R.A., Chenoweth, M.B., and Van Poznak, A.: Metabolism of volatile anesthetics. Biochem. Pharmacol. 13:1239-1247, 1964.

Waser, P.G.: The pharmacology of Amanita muscaria. In Ethnopharmacologic Search for Psychoactive Drugs. Ed. D.H. Efron, Pub. Health Ser. Publ. No. 1645, Washington, D.C., 1967, pp. 419-439.

Waser, P.G. and Bersin, P.: Turnover of monoamines in brain under the influence of muscimol and ibotenic acid, two psychoactive principles of Amanita muscaria. In Psychotomimetic Drugs. Ed. D.H. Efron, New York, Raven Press, pp. 155-162.

Wasson, R.G.: Fly agaric and man. In Ethnopharmacologic Search for Psychoactive Drugs. Ed. D.H. Efron, Pub. Health Ser. Publ. No. 1645, Washington, D.C., 1967, pp. 405-414.

Werner, V.G.: Untersuchungen zum Stoffwichsel von Tropan-Alkaloiden, Hoppe-Seyler's Z. Physiol. Chem. 348:1151-1157, 1967.

Whitby, L.G., Hertting, G., and Axelrod, J.: The effect of cocaine on the disposition of noradrenaline labelled with tritium. Nature (London) 187:604, 1960.

Wiechowski, W.: Decomposition of cocaine and atropine in the animal organism. Arch. Exp. Pathol. Pharmacol. 46:155-162, 1901.

Williams, R.T. Detoxication mechanisms. New York, J. Wiley & Sons, 1959a, pp. 556-557.

Ibid., 1959b, pp. 137.

Williams, R.T.: op. cit., 1959c. pp. 23-237.

Winek, C.L., Collom, W.D., and Wecht, C.H.: Fatal benzene exposure by glue sniffing. Lancet 1:683, 1967.

Wollman, H. and Dripps, R.D.: Uptake, distribution, elimination, and administration of inhalational anesthetics. In the Pharmacological Basis of Therapeutics, 4th ed. Eds., L.S. Goodman and A. Gilman, New York, Macmillan, 1970, pp. 60-70.

Woods, L.A., McMahon, F.G., and Seevers, M.H.: Distribution and metabolism of cocaine in the dog and rabbit. J. Pharmacol. Exp. Thera. 101:200-204, 1951.

Chapter 10

Tolerance

DEFINITIONS (AND PERSONAL PHILOSOPHIES)

Drug tolerance may be described as a state of decreased responsiveness to any pharmacologic effect of a drug as a consequence of prior exposure to that drug so that more drug must be administered to produce an effect equivalent to that produced after the original dose. Although tolerance develops to the effects of many abused drugs, it is not *always* observed. Thus, many who use cocaine and marihuana report that they continue to obtain the same degree of satisfaction after continued use, without increasing the dosage beyond that used originally. We have been intrigued by studies relating the phenomenon of tolerance to complex molecular or biochemical events; our presentation reflects this interest.* In the broadest sense, tolerance to the central effects of a drug may occur: (a) by an

*The interested reader may wish to refer to the many excellent reviews of this subject including: Cochin, 1970a,b, 1971, 1972; Murphree, 1962; Domino, 1962; Shideman, 1961; Toman, 1963; Burns and Shore, 1961; Bousquet, 1962; Remmer, 1962a,b, 1972; Conney, 1969a,b; Burns and Conney, 1964; Dole, 1970; Clouet, 1968, 1971; Eddy *et al.*, 1965; Way and Adler, 1960; Reynolds and Randall, 1957; Goldstein *et al.*, 1968; Kalant *et al.*, 1971; Singh, 1972; Singer, 1971; Truitt, 1971; Nahas, 1973.

alteration in physiologic disposition of the drug; and/or (b) by adaptation of cells in the CNS. In the former case, we include factors which would reduce the concentration of active drug at receptor sites in the CNS: decreased absorption, reduced uptake and distribution to the CNS (for example, increased binding of drug to plasma proteins resulting in less drug being available for transport into the CNS), accelerated metabolic conversion to inactive or less active metabolites and accelerated excretion. Cellular adaptation, however, is considerably more complex. Superficially and in the teleological sense, adaptation may be considered to represent an attempt by cells in the CNS to maintain homeostasis of their internal and external milieu which is optimal for cell survival. But, how do cells "adapt" to drug effects? What are the biochemical correlates of adaptation?

The numerous studies of mechanisms of tolerance, though providing considerable insight, leave these basic questions essentially unanswered for many abused drugs. Surely there is no scarcity of sound, titillating, and controversial hypotheses, each with their equally zealous and capable proponents and detractors. The inherent biochemical and anatomic complexity of the CNS contributes, in no small part, to the often contradictory findings between laboratories, as each fraction of the whole is examined individually. But, in addition to this unavoidable problem, investigators apparently do not always attempt to control certain controllable variables so as to minimize conflicting results between different laboratories. The reasons for this include sincere belief in the "superiority" of one's own experimental design, habit, personal preference, convenience, or even, in some cases, downright obstinacy and reluctance to share the "golden grail" of discovery. For example, it has been shown that the development of tolerance to opiates is dependent, among other factors, upon species, dosage frequency and route of administration, and the specific pharmacologic response that is measured to assess tolerance. Thus, Ferguson and Mitchell (1969) have reported that the degree of tolerance to the analgesic effects of morphine in man was proportional to the severity of induced pain. In fact, LeBlanc et al. (1973) in their studies of tolerance noted that performance of a task while under the influence of ethanol, opiates, barbiturates, or amphetamines could modify the development of tolerance. They have designated this phenomenon as "behavioral augmentation of tolerance." Still, individual investigators pursue a myriad of experimental designs seemingly ignoring earlier findings from other laboratories, and at the same time, they wonder at the contradictory results obtained between laboratories, often conjuring provocative and unnecessary explanations. These same researchers meet periodically to discuss their findings and then return to their respective laboratories and their own individual approaches, apparently without concern for the subtle differences in experimental design that can and will lead to profound differences in results. Interestingly, similar comments were offered by Domino (1962) in his review of CNS depressants published over a decade ago. Of course, such comments are not restricted to studies of tolerance mechanisms; indeed, they span the spectrum of investigations involving many other disciplines of science.

In a recent review of opiate receptors, Goldstein (1974) pointed out some valid reasons for the relatively slow advances in studies of opiate receptors. These include the frequent inappropriateness of techniques for purification of proteins which are largely water-soluble; the complications inherent in studying binding of drugs to membrane receptors imbedded in a lipid matrix; and the possible dissociation of drug and receptor during laboratory work-up due to the typical reversibility of drug-receptor binding.

Perhaps workshops, designed to introduce some systematization and homogeneity into experimental design, might facilitate obtaining answers to mechanisms of tolerance, although surely not all participants would agree with all selected policies. We note with interest the numerous papers which end with statements such as "our findings in mice should be extended to other species which develop tolerance to this drug in order to determine their relevance to the underlying mechanisms of tolerance." Yet this extension to other species is rarely done by the same investigators, and when it is done by others, they rarely use an experimental design *identical* to that used originally even when such identity is experimentally practical. Also, more consideration should be given to the role of *discrete* areas of brain likely to be involved in adaptive tolerance to drugs. It seems unlikely that the whole brain, an anatomically and biochemically heterogeneous tissue, is closely involved in the neural basis of tolerance to the opiates. In rats, administration of the narcotic antagonist, nalorphine, into the anterior hypothalamus has been shown to block development of tolerance to hypothermic and analgesic effects of morphine (Lomax and Kirkpatrick, 1967). Likewise, ablation of certain nuclei of the hypothalamus can suppress morphine dependence and modify tolerance to morphine (Kerr and Pozuelo, 1971a,b, 1972). Catecholamine synthesis has been reported to be modified in the hypothalamus and striatum of tolerant rats (Clouet and Ratner, 1970). Analgesia has been observed after electrical stimulation of periaqueductal and periventricular structures of rat, cat, rhesus monkey, and man. This analgesia resembles the analgesia produced by narcotic analgesics in several respects, including tolerance, cross tolerance, and antagonism by naloxone (Akil et al., 1972; Mayer and Hayes, 1974; Pert and Yaksh, 1974). Despite these clues and the availability of biochemical and biophysical techniques which permit study of minute quantities of factors localized in heretofore inaccessible brain areas, some investigators continue to include whole brain in tolerance studies.

The definition of tolerance provided above applies to only a specific drug action and not necessarily to all its actions. If tolerance to central effects of a drug represents a single fundamental change induced by the drug on the CNS, then tolerance should develop similarly to all the central effects produced by a specific dose of the drug. Experimental findings do not bear out this prediction. Not only may tolerance develop to one effect but not another, but also there are differences in the rates of acquisition of and loss of tolerance to different effects of the same drug. Such findings are often overlooked in our eagerness to assign a single biochemical modification to a single underlying cause of tolerance.

However, one should not be overly critical of multiple approaches to the same problem because, after all, the myriad of experimental designs used by different investigators is not without some advantage, not the least of which is the hope that someone will discover the "right" design. In fact, for all we know, the animal model most suitable for extrapolation to man in studies of drugs of abuse and their mechanisms of action may, indeed, be the decerebrate dog. Having expressed some of our general philosophies, we shall now discuss the postulated mechanisms of tolerance to specific pharmacologic agents.

TOLERANCE TO EFFECTS OF MORPHINE AND MORPHINE SURROGATES

Dispositional Tolerance

During the past 20 years, the hypothesis that tolerance to the central depressant effects (i.e., analgesia, sedation, hypothermia, respiratory depression) of morphine was related to an alteration in its physiologic disposition has received considerable attention. The vast preponderance of evidence indicates that this mechanism does not contribute significantly to attenuation of opiate effects upon repeated administration. Thus, altered absorption, distribution, metabolism, and excretion do not appear essential to development of opiate tolerance, and at equivalent brain concentrations opiates exert lesser central effects in animals having had prior exposure than in naive control animals (Cochin, 1970a,b; Murphree, 1962; Clouet, 1968, 1971; Dole, 1970; Clouet and Ratner, 1964; Reynolds and Randall, 1957; Goodman and Gilman, 1970; Mulé and Woods, 1962). Indeed, many studies show that intracellular and subcellular distribution of free opiates in anatomic subdivisions of brains of tolerant animals is not consistently or sufficiently altered to indicate a causal relationship between tolerance development and an altered microdistribution in brain (Clouet, 1968; Mulé et al., 1967; Kaneto and Mellett, 1960). Sometimes, in fact, just the opposite findings have been observed. In the case of the narcotic levorphanol, for example, Richter and Goldstein (1970) have demonstrated the presence of two to five times *more* free levorphanol in ultrafiltrates of brain from levorphanol-tolerant mice than from nontolerant mice—more than enough levorphanol to produce pharmacologic effects in nontolerant animals. These results support those of the many earlier studies wherein opiate tolerance was attributed to cellular subsensitivity rather than altered disposition.

Nevertheless, some recent findings appear to be in contrast to the majority of studies separating opiate tolerance from opiate pharmacodynamics. Cheney *et al.* (1970) have reported that locomotor activity in mice is stimulated by morphine and that tolerance develops rapidly to this stimulation; "brain" tolerance also develops, but at a slower rate. The early phase of tolerance, but not the later phase, corresponded to a faster conjugation and excretion of the opiate. Cochin (1970a), on the other hand, has observed neither the opiate-induced locomotor stimulation in mice, nor has he observed tolerance to develop as quickly as reported by Cheney. However, he has emphasized the potential importance of Cheney's findings suggestive of a dispositional tolerance, that is if they can be replicated in other laboratories. In this regard, Shuster (1971) has suggested that it "would make sense in studying tolerance mechanisms to study only those brain proteins that are rapidly labeled *in vivo*" because narcotic tolerance can be induced experimentally within 1 day or less, implicating proteins having rapid turnover rates as fundamental to production of tolerance. We believe that such studies may be misleading if there are truly rapid and slow onset types of tolerance having different biochemical determinants.

Recently Roe *et al.* (1973) and Börner and Abbott (1973) have observed, in limited numbers of subjects, substantial increases in amounts of codeine, (the methylated metabolite of morphine) excreted in the urine of morphine/heroin-tolerant patients and addicts compared to nontolerant subjects. The authors suggest that this increased quantity of codeine in urine is a specific metabolic alteration in opiate tolerant subjects and that it may be a useful marker for detecting addicted individuals. It is also possible, since codeine is less pharmacologically active than morphine, that increased codeine formation in chronic opiate users could contribute significantly to the development of tolerance to morphine—a concept previously regarded as untenable. However, in addition to the small numbers of subjects participating in their studies, the relevancy of their findings to underlying mechanisms of tolerance is questionable because: (1) although the increase in urinary codeine in tolerant versus nontolerant subjects was considerable (about 10- to 20-fold), the total amount of codeine excreted in tolerant subjects (10-12%) was still small relative to the total dose of morphine administered; and (2) the nontolerant (control) patients received what we consider to be inordinately large doses of morphine (50 mg orally to nontolerant subjects and 180 or 195 mg intravenously over a 30-minute period to two cardiac surgery patients), whereas the doses given to the addicts were not reported. It is possible that with these large dosages, alternate pathways of metabolism may become increasingly more important and not really represent the actual situation.

Although altered disposition of opiates may contribute to tolerance in certain experimental conditions, most evidence favors an adaptive mechanism, for which explanations are still being sought.

Theories Explaining Adaptive Tolerance

Immune Mechanisms

We have already mentioned that there may be, under certain conditions, a slow and fast development of tolerance with apparently different underlying mechanisms. As if it were not enough to try to explain these two types of tolerance, there also appears to be a single-dose tolerance to opiates which is not present 24 hours after an initial dose, but appears later and becomes more pronounced the longer the delay between the initial ("sensitizing") and "challenging" doses (Cochin and Kornetsky, 1964; Cochin and Mushlin, 1970; Kornetsky and Bain, 1968). If single-dose tolerance is a reality, the mechanism is probably different from that accounting for tolerance after repeated doses of opiate. These findings and others are suggestive of an immune mechanism of tolerance (DeCato and Adler, 1973; Berkowitz and Spector, 1972; Ringle and Herndon, 1972; Wainer et al., 1973; Cochin, 1971, 1972). Recently it was suggested that single-dose tolerance may be a behavioral phenomenon, reflecting prior experience of the animal with the test procedure, rather than a pharmacologic tolerance due to the opiate *per se* (Gebhart and Mitchell, 1971; Kayan and Mitchell, 1972a,b). These workers were unable to demonstrate that tolerance to morphine became more pronounced as the time interval between the two doses of morphine was lengthened. However, an immune mechanism of tolerance cannot be excluded, especially in light of knowledge that under appropriate conditions, (1) narcotic tolerance can take several weeks to develop fully and can persist for many months, (2) factors from serum and tissues of tolerant animals can be passively transferred to nontolerant animals and can influence opiate action in that recipient, (3) inhibitors of protein synthesis decrease tolerance, and (4) proteins or antibodies have been demonstrated in sera of mice actively immunized with the morphine immunogen, 3-carboxymethyl morphine coupled to bovine serum albumin. These antibodies can bind morphine with concomitant reduction in analgesic (mouse writhing test) activity. It was considered unlikely that this decrease in pharmacologic activity was due to a dissociation of morphine from the antigen, which would then allow free morphine to produce the tolerance. Dihydromorphine also could be bound to these antibodies and morphine could displace it; however, neither serotonin nor the narcotic antagonist naloxone could displace morphine, indicating some degree of specificity of the binding process for opiate agonists. *In vivo*, the serum half-life of dihydromorphine was shown to be prolonged in immunized mice presumably owing to the narcotic being present in its bound form for extended periods. Of interest is that proteins with strong affinities for opiates have been found in sera of heroin addicts (Ryan *et al.*, 1971, 1972). On the other hand, Weksler *et al.* (1973) observed that serum from addicts did not bind more morphine than normal serum (despite increases in certain immunoglobulins among the addicts).

The transfer of narcotic tolerance by serum from morphine-treated rats and rabbits to mice has been reported by Cochin and Kornetsky (1968) although these authors have indicated the inconsistency of their findings. In contrast, others have demonstrated that factors in serum from tolerant men and dogs potentiated, instead of attenuated, morphine analgesia in mice (Kiplinger and Clift, 1964). The repeated and nonsterile injection of contaminated "street" opiates further supports the attractive possibility that opiates might increase antibody production. Nevertheless, dramatic differences in findings from rat and rabbit versus dog and man suggest that such tolerance transfer factors in serum, if they are real, are either too different among various species and/or are too unstable to permit replication of results in different laboratories. An interesting finding is that when offspring of chronically morphinized female rats were challenged with morphine at 8 weeks of age and tested on the hot plate for their analgesia response, they were significantly less sensitive ("tolerant") to the drug than offspring from untreated rats (Cochin, 1972). Such persistent effects in second generation animals must, as Cochin states, "reflect profound cellular changes."

Transfer of Tolerance by Factors in Brain

Among the most provocative, and controversial, findings of recent years have been the reports of transfer of morphine tolerance by intraperitoneal injection of brain homogenates from tolerant animals to nontolerant animals. These findings originated from the laboratory of Ungar and his co-workers. Initially, they reported the transfer of analgetic (tail pinch) tolerance from morphine tolerant rats and dogs to nontolerant mice, and characterized the transfer factor as a dialyzable peptide or low molecular weight protein (Ungar and Cohen, 1966). Injection of the dialysate of brain homogenate from morphine-tolerant animals also conferred cross tolerance to the opiate meperidine but not to pentobarbital, indicative of specificity toward narcotic drugs. Similarly, Tulanay *et al.*

(1970) transferred analgetic tolerance (heat stimulus) from tolerant to nontolerant rats. However, the small changes in reaction times in their study, though statistically significant, may have been due to factors other than drug, viz., prior experience of the animals on the hot plate. That this is possible is suggested by studies indicating that hot plate responses can be influenced by modifications in the testing procedure and apparatus (Kayan and Mitchell, 1972a,b; Gebhart and Mitchell, 1971).

Many laboratories have tried unsuccessfully to reproduce Ungar's original findings. Tirri (1967) could not transfer analgetic (tail pinch) or hypothermic tolerance from tolerant mice to nontolerant mice. Smits and Takemori (1968) were unsuccessful in attempts to transfer analgesic tolerance (heat stimulus) from rat to mouse and Tilson *et al.* (1972) were unable to transfer analgetic tolerance (electric foot shock) from tolerant to nontolerant rats. In one of their publications, Ungar and Galvan (1969) noted that workers attempting tolerance transfer without success had not accurately replicated the experimental design of their original publication. They again demonstrated the transfer of tolerance, this time by injecting partially purified extracts of brain homogenates and using other criteria for determining tolerance besides analgesia (which included morphine-hypothermia and lethality). Recognizing the importance of confirming the findings of Ungar and his associates, Goldstein *et al.* (1971) attempted to replicate these studies. Exerting meticulous care to duplicate Ungar's experimental designs, these workers in an admirable cooperative attempt, shared Ungar's laboratory for several days and even exchanged experimental animals between their respective laboratories to determine whether genetic influences might have contributed to contradictory findings. The reported findings of Goldstein and co-workers were all negative or equivocal. Indeed, for some experiments the same data were apparently interpreted differently by the two groups such that Goldstein stated, "because we were unable to agree with Dr. Ungar on the interpretation of the results, they are not included here but will presumably be published independently by him." Despite the unsuccessful attempts of these two groups to describe conditions for reliable transfer of tolerance, they are to be congratulated for their willingness to pursue the problem in a spirit of mutual respect and apparent concern for those subtle parameters of experimental design which might contribute to interlaboratory differences.

The interpretation of data relating to transfer of tolerance appears to present problems even to their proponents. For example, Ungar and Galvan (1969) conceded that the same analgesia data, interpreted on the basis of increases in graded reaction times rather than quantally, would lead to conclusions that no transfer of tolerance occurred in the former case, and that transfer of tolerance did occur in the latter case. They also recognized inexplicable differences in potencies of identically prepared brain extracts and the differential suitability of various tests to show the transfer of tolerance.

The foregoing studies, indicating that under certain conditions systemic injections of brain extracts from tolerant animals may confer tolerance to nontolerant animals, are particularly interesting in light of hypotheses relating tolerance to a compensatory increase in the synthesis of brain proteins, peptides, or neurohormones. In his excellent review of mechanisms of tolerance, Cochin (1970b) discusses several contemporary theories invoking compensatory biochemical mechanisms to explain tolerance. The hypotheses are consistent with modern drug-receptor theory and simultaneously attempt to explain both tolerance and physical dependence. A feature common to all of the theories is that chronic opiate administration affects the synthesis and/or activity of an endogenous, centrally acting substance (perhaps a neurohumor or proteinaceous receptor enzyme). For example, Collier (1965) has hypothesized that repeated administration of opiates induces the synthesis of "silent receptor" proteins in the CNS which serve to prevent access of the drugs to active receptors whose occupation is essential for pharmacologic activity. If this were the case, and if these "silent receptor" proteins were transferable from animal to animal, then it remains to be explained why the transfer was demonstrable only under certain, apparently ill-defined experimental conditions, and from dog and rat to mouse, but not from mouse to mouse. Also we must optimistically accept that the transfer factor has a sufficiently small molecular weight and stability to be absorbed intact from an intraperitoneal site of administration and be distributed unchanged to discrete loci in the CNS presumably involved in neural adaptation.

Numerous studies have implied that *de novo* synthesis of protein is involved in the genesis of tolerance (Cohen *et al.*, 1965; Cox and Osman, 1970; Loh *et al.*, 1969), although the precise mechanisms involved are difficult to explain at the present state of our knowledge. The persistence of tolerance long after free morphine is detectable in the CNS suggests that a change has occurred in a chemical constituent which is basic to normal cell function and which has a relatively slow turnover rate; clearly brain proteins would qualify as candidates (Cochin and Kornetsky, 1964; Clouet, 1971). In this connection, Misra *et al.* (1971a) have reported that up to 3 weeks after only a single injection of radioactively labeled morphine, consistently higher concentrations of radioactivity were present in rat cerebral cortex than could be accounted for solely on the basis of free morphine. These authors suggested that morphine, or a metabolite thereof, was bound firmly and persistently in the central nervous system and that cumulative deposition of a "conjugate" may be fundamental to the cellular adaptation of opiate tolerance.

More recent studies have provided significant advances in the search for an explanation for opiate action. A component of nervous tissue can selectively bind opiate drugs. This binding is highly stereospecific for opiate enantiomers and appears to be related to the relative pharmacologic potencies of the opiates studied. It is proposed that the components of tissue that bind the opiates so selectively may represent specific opiate receptors in the CNS (Pert and Snyder, 1973; Wong and Horng, 1973; Goldstein, 1974). Investigations are continuing to determine the role of stereospecific binding of opiates in analgesia, tolerance, and physical dependence.

Castles and his associates (1972) have demonstrated by autoradiographic techniques that newly formed RNA in brains of tolerant rats did not disappear as rapidly as RNA from brains of nontolerant rats, the most marked difference being visualized in the hippocampus. These authors postulated that RNA could serve as a silent receptor for morphine, a particularly interesting view in light of studies describing opiate binding by rat brain RNA. This same group has observed gradual decreases in the template activity of brain chromatin isolated from morphine-tolerant rats compared to nontolerant controls; these data are consistent with the possibility that RNA transcription (and/or protein synthesis) and tolerance development to opiates are closely interdependent phenomena (Castles *et al.*, 1973). Datta and Antopol (1973) have reported dose-dependent *decreases* in brain RNA synthesis upon chronic administration of morphine to mice. It is difficult to know from any of these findings alone whether or not the changes in RNA are specific responses of the CNS to chronic administration of opiates, which might support a postulate relating altered RNA synthesis to basic mechanisms underlying opiate tolerance. In the study by Datta and Antopol, for example, the indication was that the decrease in RNA synthesis was not specific for brain RNA, since they also reported a decrease in *hepatic* RNA synthesis.

Matsuda (1970) has reported that both caffeine and a phenothiazine derivative (TPN-12), neither of which have an affinity for the opiate analgesic receptor, enhance morphine analgesia and attenuate development of morphine tolerance in the rat and monkey. He has speculated that the three agents (caffeine, TPN-12, and morphine) may share a common affinity for a nonanalgesic receptor site (Collier's "silent receptor"?). Thus, caffeine and TPN-12 would compete with morphine for this site and more morphine would become available to the analgesic receptor. These speculations imply that caffeine and TPN-12 would suppress an established tolerance to morphine; this was indeed observed.

Drugs which induce specific biochemical "lesions" in the protein synthetic pathway have also been shown to influence tolerance development. For example, actinomycin-D which inhibits DNA-dependent RNA synthesis, hence, *de novo* protein synthesis, reduced or prevented tolerance development (Cox *et al.*, 1968). It has also been demonstrated that actinomycin-D, at doses which did not affect the *resting* levels of RNA synthesis, but did oppose an increase in the synthesis of RNA, reduced the rate of development of morphine tolerance (Cohen *et al.*, 1965). Thus, the suppression of synthesis of new RNA (hence, by inference, the synthesis of new proteins or peptides) suppressed morphine tolerance. Furthermore, when given to animals already tolerant to morphine, actinomycin-D did not lessen the tolerance (Dole, 1970). Other drugs which inhibit protein synthesis directly or indirectly (cycloheximide, puromycin, cyclophosphamide, 6-mercaptopurine, 5-fluorouracil, and 8-azaguanine) reduced to varying degrees the development of tolerance to the central depressant effects of morphine in rats and mice (Cox and Osman, 1969; Feinberg and Cochin, 1972; Spoerlin and Scrafini, 1967; Smith *et al.*, 1966). One could criticize these studies utilizing "inhibitors of protein synthesis" as tools to elaborate the mechanism(s) of tolerance because the inhibitors themselves possess pharmacologic activities other than blockade of protein synthesis (Shuster, 1971). For example, actinomycin-D increases brain permeability to morphine so that what appears to be suppressed tolerance by actinomycin-D could simply be due to more morphine gaining access to the CNS (Cochin, 1970a,b; Loh *et al.*, 1969). Also actinomycin-D was shown to inhibit the development of acute tolerance to morphine at a time when urinary nitrogen was unaffected; i.e., presumbaly when protein synthesis was not suppressed (Cox *et al.*, 1968). On the other hand, cycloheximide has been shown to inhibit protein synthesis and prevent tolerance development under conditions whereby its own overt pharmacologic and/or toxicologic effects were not observable, and at doses which had no effects on brain uptake of morphine (Loh *et al.*, 1969). Also, all the aforementioned agents, which inhibit different steps in the protein synthetic pathway, suppressed the development of opiate tolerance under a variety of experimental conditions; it seems likely, therefore, that the inhibition of protein synthesis contributed significantly to the suppression of tolerance.

Tantalizing as they may be, the hypotheses relating tolerance to synthesis of new protein have been refuted by several laboratories. Certain protein synthesis inhibitors, namely, ethionine and chloramphenicol, fail to suppress the development of morphine tolerance. However, relatively high concentrations of chloramphenicol are required to inhibit protein synthesis in rat brain (Cox and Osman, 1970; Dole, 1970). As far as ethionine is concerned, it is a relatively specific inhibitor of protein synthesis (blocking methionine incorporation) and until we know more about the specific protein structure involved in tolerance development (if any are involved) we will be unable to know the relevancy of this lack of effect of ethionine on tolerance.

If tolerance did considerably change the levels of major proteins in the CNS, the changes should be detectable by comparing the protein contents of brains from normal and tolerant animals. Accordingly, Hahn and Goldstein (1971) solubilized proteins from whole brains of tolerant and nontolerant mice and examined them for their amounts and electrophoretic patterns. They observed no significant quantitative or qualitative differences in the major protein bands studied, and concluded that any change in the amount of a morphine "receptor" or other proteins associated with tolerance probably involved only a small fraction of total brain protein in discrete brain areas. Other studies have indicated that protein synthesis in rat brain was unchanged (Castles et al., 1972) or reduced (Clouet and Neidle, 1970) during the development of opiate tolerance.

Finally, it has already been mentioned that cycloheximide could inhibit the development of tolerance to certain depressant effects of morphine. However, recently Karbowski (1973) reported that cycloheximide did not inhibit tolerance to the *stimulant* effect of morphine on mouse locomotor activity.

Brain Neurotransmitters

Over the years, several putative neurotransmitters, including acetylcholine, epinephrine, norepinephrine, dopamine, and serotonin have been implicated in morphine's analgesic and possibly addictive properties. Although changes in concentrations of brain neurotransmitters and their precursors have been studied in relation to morphine administration, the changes have not been sufficiently dramatic, consistent, or temporally in phase with the development of tolerance to indicate unequivocally that they initiate the tolerance. The possible relationships between neurotransmitters and tolerance have been thoroughly reviewed (Reynolds and Randall, 1957; Way et al., 1968; Way and Shen, 1971; Way, 1972; Dole, 1970; Eidelberg and Schwartz, 1970; Kerr and Pozuelo, 1971a,b). At a recent symposium entitled "The Opiate Narcotics: Neurochemical Mechanisms in Analgesia and Dependence," there were discussions of endogenous constituents of brain that appear to act as agonists at morphine receptor sites, and that appear to be distributed in brain similar to the distribution observed for stereospecific morphine receptors (Hughes et al., 1975; Terenius and Wahlström, 1975; Pasternak et al., 1975; Kosterlitz and Hughes, 1975; among others).* The substance or substances, termed enkephalin and

*Articles from this symposium appear in Life Sciences *16*(12), 1753-1906, 1975 and *17*(1), 1-96, 1975.

morphine-like factor (MLF), exhibit properties of low molecular weight peptides (MW   2000). Several groups of investigators are presently studying these endogenous ligands for the opiate receptor; it is theorized that enkephalin may be an endogenous neurotransmitter or a modulator of neurotransmitters at the opiate receptor. This is an interesting theory; at this time the evidence is preliminary and one does not yet know what significance, if any, these substances may have in opiate tolerance and dependence.

Serotonin. New methods for measuring the neurotransmitters in brain have improved in recent years, the previous studies of opiate effects on the steady-state concentrations of biogenic amines have become extended to include studies of *turnover* of these amines, and some hypotheses which had been previously "disproven" have been reexamined. For example, considerable interest has been rekindled recently in the relationship between tolerance and turnover of brain serotonin, a compound implicated in mechanisms of sleep, thermoregulation, behavior, and pain, all functions which can be affected by morphine (Gregory, 1961; Way *et al.*, 1968; Way, 1972). Also, molecular models of serotonin and morphine reveal some degree of complementarity, and the two compounds have been known to interact with respect to their effects on the nervous system (Way, 1972).

Until recently, several laboratories had reported that steady-state concentrations of brain serotonin were unchanged after chronic morphinization, but any possible relationships between tolerance and the *turnover* of serotonin were largely unexplored. This possibility, coupled with the aforementioned concepts relating enzyme adaptation to tolerance, suggested to Way and his associates that an enzyme involved in serotonin synthesis might be involved in the development of tolerance to morphine. These investigators blocked the rate of metabolism of serotonin to 5-hydroxyindole acetic acid (5-HIAA) by administering the monoamine oxidase inhibitor pargyline to mice. Then, based on the assumption that brain serotonin was converted solely to 5-HIAA (Neff *et al.*, 1967), they calculated the rate of synthesis (turnover) of serotonin. They observed that serotonin turnover was significantly higher in morphine-tolerant animals than in nontolerant animals or animals receiving a single dose of morphine. Similar findings were reported by Haubrich and Blake (1969) using a different procedure to measure serotonin turnover. Regional studies of serotonin turnover in discrete brain areas after pargyline treatment indicated that the higher serotonin levels observed had occurred predominantly in the hypothalamus and brain stem of tolerant mice (I.Ho *et al.*, 1972a). Furthermore, suppression of morphine tolerance occurred in rats and mice when serotonin synthesis was suppressed by administering the tryptophan hydroxylase inhibitor, *p*-chlorophenylalanine (PCPA).

Tryptophan hydroxylase is the rate-limiting enzyme in the synthesis of serotonin. PCPA was thought to have little or no effect on the synthesis of brain catecholamines (Way *et al.*, 1968; Shen *et al.*, 1970; Ho *et al.*, 1972a).

When the attenuation of morphine analgetic tolerance by PCPA was studied in two strains of rats, one strain having a more functional serotonergic system than the other, this attenuation was more pronounced in the strain having the more functional serotonergic system (Rech and Tilson, 1973). This finding further supports the hypothesis that brain serotonin plays a vital role in the development of tolerance. Moreover, when the serotonin concentration was depleted in mouse brain by intracerebrally administered 5,6-dihydroxytryptamine, which specifically destroys brain serotonergic nerve endings, tolerance development to morphine was inhibited (Ho *et al.*, 1973). Additional evidence for a role for serotonin in the development of opiate tolerance is that after administering either cyclic AMP or the natural serotonin precursor, tryptophan (which has been reported to be capable of increasing serotonin turnover in brain) the development of tolerance to morphine has been accelerated in mice (Ho *et al.*, 1972a,b).

Other findings also support the postulate of a relationship, though not necessarily causal, between opiate tolerance and increased serotonin synthesis (Maruyama *et al.*, 1971; Loh *et al.*, 1969; Way, 1972). When rats were treated with morphine, an association was observed between development of tolerance and an increase in activity of tryptophan hydroxylase (presumably reflecting an increase in serotonin synthesis) in the midbrain and synaptosomes (pinched off nerve endings) of the septal areas (Azmitia *et al.*, 1970; Knapp and Mandell, 1972). In contrast, Schechter *et al.* (1972) detected neither an increase in activity of this enzyme in the whole brain of morphine-tolerant mice, nor a change in steady-state concentration of serotonin after pargyline administration. They also attempted to repeat Way's studies of the *in vivo* synthesis of serotonin in mice and found no evidence of changes in serotonin turnover associated with the development of tolerance to morphine. They agreed with the findings in rats of Algeri and Costa (1971) that there appears to be no demonstrable relation between serotonin turnover and the development of morphine tolerance. They mentioned that the increases in tryptophan hydroxylase activity in the midbrain of tolerant rats, reported by Azmitia and co-workers (1970), were difficult to interpret because a greater increase in enzyme activity was found in saline-injected versus untreated rats than in morphine-injected versus saline-injected rats.

Cheney and his co-workers have also challenged the serotonin synthesis/tolerance development relationship (Cheney *et al.*, 1970, 1971; Cheney and Goldstein, 1971; Cheney and Costa, 1972). Using a direct method to measure serotonin synthesis which involved administering a pulse dose of ^{3}H-tryptophan (a precursor of serotonin), they followed the incorporation of tritium into serotonin. They reported that no change occurred in turnover of brain serotonin during the development of analgetic tolerance (hot plate) to morphine, and that despite a 30% reduction in brain serotonin induced by PCPA, it had no effect on tolerance development. Furthermore, Marshall and Grahame-Smith (1971), using still another method to measure serotonin turnover, were unable to confirm an increased turnover in brains of mice rendered tolerant to morphine.

If serotonin turnover were fundamental to the overall expression of tolerance, then a relationship should be demonstrable between serotonin turnover and tolerance to an effect of morphine other than analgesia. Unfortunately, Warwick et al. (1973) and Oka et al. (1972) have reported that tolerance to the hypothermic effect of morphine in rats did not appear to involve the serotonergic system.

Florez and associates (1973) observed that *acute* tolerance to morphine in the respiratory center of decerebrate cats was not blocked by PCPA (indeed, PCPA *facilitated* tolerance development), was only partially inhibited by pargyline, was not modified by reserpine, and was delayed by a-methyltyrosine. Although their results are not totally consistent with the hypothesis relating development of morphine tolerance to serotonin turnover, they must be assessed cautiously considering both the surgical intervention in the experimental animal model used in these experiments and the acute nature of the tolerance studied. The controversy of a relation between serotonin turnover and morphine tolerance continues, and only future experimentation can provide conclusive evidence.

Catecholamines. Earlier reports in the literature had indicated close, though not completely understood, interrelationships among brain cyclic AMP, biogenic amine synthesis, and CNS function. These interrelationships, coupled with the known morphine-induced alteration of biogenic amines, suggested to Naito and Kuriyama (1973) that perhaps morphine tolerance was mediated by changes in cyclic AMP metabolism. Accordingly, they measured the effect of morphine administration on the activity of adenyl cyclase, which catalyzes the synthesis of cyclic AMP. They reported that adenyl cyclase activity was significantly higher in the cerebral cortex of morphine-tolerant mice than in the cortex of nontolerant mice, or mice given a single dose of morphine. Whether this elevation is related to secondary effects of cyclic AMP on biogenic amine synthesis and/or to the genesis of tolerance remains to be determined.

That brain catecholamine turnover may be related to the development of tolerance was suggested by studies in mice and rats wherein chronic morphinization produced an increase in the incorporation of radiocarbon from ^{14}C-tyrosine into brain catecholamines. At the same time, the total concentration of catecholamine decreased (Smith *et al.*, 1970; Clouet and Ratner, 1970). Smith observed that in mice, tolerance developed to the increased catecholamine synthesis and that this effect was blocked by the opiate antagonist, naloxone. Clouet and Ratner did not observe this tolerance in rats, and Smith suggested that they may have used a dose of morphine which produced maximal synthesis of catecholamines. Apparently, however, the increase in catecholamine synthesis is not specific to the opiates, since others have reported similar increases in alcohol-dependent animals. Indeed, many workers have shown that several agents used as tools to modify the central adrenergic, serotonergic, and cholinergic activities also modify the effects of opiates, although again such effects often are inconsistent and nonspecific. As regards catecholamine uptake, no alterations were observed in the uptake of norepinephrine by brain slices or synaptosomes from mice rendered tolerant to morphine versus nontolerant mice, suggesting that this uptake process is not involved in the development of opiate tolerance (Carmichael and Israel, 1973).

A role for the biogenic amine, dopamine, in tolerance development has also been studied (Clouet and Ratner, 1970; Takagi and Nakama, 1966; Gunne *et al.*, 1969). It has been suggested that acute administration of opiates may block dopaminergic systems and, thus, produce analgesia (VanderWende and Spoerlein, 1972, 1973). From this concept, chronic opiate administration would produce tolerance via a simple homeostatic adjustment to dopaminergic blockade, i.e., by increasing dopamine turnover and/or modifying the neuronal dopaminergic receptor. Indeed, it has been observed that administration of dopaminergic agonists suppresses morphine analgesic activity, whereas dopaminergic antagonists potentiate it. Furthermore, chronic morphine administration has been reported to increase the turnover of dopamine. Tetrabenazine, which is reported to deplete both dopamine and norepinephrine more than it depletes serotonin, suppressed the development of opiate tolerance in mice. That this effect was related to dopamine depletion and not to depletion of other amines was indicated by the reversal of the suppression of tolerance by administering the dopamine precursor, dopa. Dopa returned dopamine levels to normal and left norepinephrine levels in brain still lowered significantly (VanderWende and Spoerlein, 1972; Takagi and Kuriki, 1969). Unfortunately, however, it has been reported that dopa can also deplete the brain stores of serotonin (Ng *et al.*, 1970). The interdependency among brain amines makes it most difficult to attribute an effect to one amine based upon modifications of its concentrations. Also, evidence has indicated that depletion of brain dopamine and norepinephrine by 6-OH-dopamine, an agent which is thought to specifically destroy sympathetic nerve endings, did *not* affect the initiation of tolerance to morphine in rats (Bhargava *et al.*, 1973) or mice (Friedler *et al.*, 1972).

It has been reported that serotonin complexes with dopamine, and the suggestion was made that in this way serotonin modulates dopamine activity (VanderWende and Johnson, 1970). The authors believe that this concept may be pertinent to the findings of Way and his associates wherein serotonin synthesis increased with the development of tolerance. The increased serotonin synthesis could be secondary to primary effects of the narcotic on stimulating dopamine synthesis. If serotonin modulated dopamine, it would be expected that as dopamine levels increased, serotonin levels would increase in a compensatory manner to maintain homeostasis. We fail to see how one can discriminate between primary and secondary effects at the present time. With the available data, it is equally feasible that the serotonin-dopamine complex represents a mechanism whereby dopamine modulates serotonin activity, that increased serotonin synthesis is the primary change occurring during tolerance development, and that the increased dopamine synthesis occurs secondarily to the rise in serotonin synthesis. The main point worth reemphasizing is that the interdependency of brain amines must be considered when attributing a change in one amine to a pharmacologic event. Perhaps the contradictory nature of much of the findings concerning neurotransmitters and opiate tolerance relates to optimistic assumptions of independency among these amines.

Miscellaneous

Iwata *et al.* (1970) demonstrated in rats that plasma copper levels rose with analgetic (tail clip) tolerance to morphine. The copper chelator, diethyldithiocarbamate (DDC) both prevented the rise in plasma copper and suppressed the tolerance. No measurable effect of DDC was observed on brain norepinephrine or dopamine. Unfortunately, DDC also potentiated analgesia after a single dose of morphine so that based on these findings the elevated plasma copper after chronic morphinization need not be fundamentally involved in mediating tolerance—a concept difficult to accept at the present state of knowledge. The study has a failing observed in many other studies in that it tacitly assumes that the modifying agent (DDC) has only one specific effect under the conditions of the experiment (i.e., copper chelation) which may or may not be true.

Conclusions

How can we collate all these findings to develop a rational concept explaining opiate tolerance? Many basic biochemical mechanisms of brain tissue, including phospholipid metabolism (Mulé, 1967), synthesis and metabolism of neurotransmitters (Verri *et al.*, 1968; Ziegler *et al.*, 1972; Beleslin and Polak, 1965; Way, 1972), protein and nucleic acid metabolism (Clouet, 1971), monoamine oxidase (Catravas *et al.*, 1973) and adenyl cyclase reactions (Naito and Kuriyama, 1973), indeed, even the citric acid cycle (Sherman and Mitchell, 1973) are modified during development of tolerance to opiates. Thus, the opiates produce profound and ubiquitous biochemical alterations in brain. Such alterations remind us of the renowned "chicken and the egg" story; frankly, we don't know which came first.

At the very least, for a biochemical change to be designated as a biochemical correlate of opiate tolerance, it should be: (1) temporally related to the acquisition and loss of tolerance, (2) demonstrably related to tolerance in several species which exhibit tolerance to these drugs; (3) demonstrably related to tolerance to several pharmacologic effects of the drug; (4) produced by similar drugs to which cross tolerance is known. Even then, the extrapolation, *a priori*, from biochemical correlate of tolerance to biochemical *determinant* of tolerance may be injudicious, especially without having definitive information about the precise nature of the pharmacologic receptors involved in opiate action.

Previously mentioned studies dealing with adaptive mechanisms of opiate tolerance pose many unresolved questions. It is interesting to note how some previously discarded hypotheses are now being reevaluated as more sophisticated methodology, as well as the experiences of many capable investigators, are applied to studies of the complex biochemical phenomena fundamental to opiate tolerance. We wonder, somewhat apprehensively, how many other cellular functions, enzyme systems, neurotransmitters, and pharmacologic test systems may be responsive to chronic opiate administration, and how such responsiveness may relate to the initiation of opiate tolerance. At the present time it is not possible to integrate the findings relating to the complex mechanisms of opiate tolerance.

TOLERANCE TO EFFECTS OF BARBITURATES

Tolerance to the effects of barbiturates is not much better understood than tolerance to the effects of opiates. This area of research has been reviewed in recent years by Kalant, Leblanc, and Gibbins (1971) and a relatively brief discussion of more recent work will be presented here.

Dispositional Tolerance

Decreased absorption, enhanced excretion, or altered distribution of barbiturates upon chronic administration do not appear to be crucial for the development of tolerance to the effects of barbiturates. However, it is well established that, in contrast to the opiates, repeated administration of barbiturates accelerates their oxidation to metabolites that are less pharmacologically active than the administered drug (Burns and Shore, 1961; Remmer, 1962a,b, 1972; Burns and Conney, 1964; Conney, 1969a,b). Furthermore, the acquisition and loss of barbiturate tolerance under appropriate experimental conditions have been shown to correspond to the accelerated oxidation and to parallel a stimulation of the activity of the hepatic microsomal enzyme systems catalyzing the metabolism of barbiturates (and other drugs). Henceforth, the drug-induced stimulation of this enzyme system will be referred to as enzyme induction.* As predicted, the apparent relationship between enzyme induction and the initiation of barbiturate tolerance also helps to explain cross tolerance among different barbiturates. Because this microsomal enzyme system is rather nonspecific in its spectrum of potential substrates, one barbiturate may stimulate the metabolic inactivation ("detoxication") of a second barbiturate and, thus, reduce the magnitude and duration of its pharmacologic activity.

The induction seems to depend upon many factors, including the lipid solubility of the drug, the dose and frequency of administration, and the duration of drug action. Consequently, the shorter-acting barbiturates may require several daily injections to activate the microsomal enzyme system, whereas the longer-acting barbiturates need be injected only once or twice. In either instance, after 3 to 4 days, the microsomal enzyme activity rises to a new steady-state plateau level which persists until the end of the treatment, and returns to normal after several days to weeks, depending upon experimental conditions.

Enzyme induction by barbiturates appears to be due partly to an increase in the synthesis of cytochrome P-450, which is believed by many

---

*It is beyond the scope of this chapter to review at length the numerous studies of enzyme induction by over 200 drugs and chemicals, although this subject has been discussed in Chapter 1. There are pharmacologic and physiologic consequences of enzyme induction beyond its implication in barbiturate tolerance. These include: (1) metabolic interactions of more than one drug administered in combination, i.e., one drug may stimulate the metabolism of another; and (2) drug interactions with endogenous chemicals, since the microsomal enzyme system can catalyze the metabolism of certain endogenous compounds such as steroids. The interested reader may refer to many publications including those by Burns and Conney, 1964; Conney, 1967, 1969a,b; Zeidenberg et al., 1967; LaDu et al., 1971; Remmer, 1962a,b, 1972; Fujita et al., 1973; and Estabrook et al., 1973.

investigators to be the rate-limiting terminal oxidase in the microsomal drug-metabolizing enzyme system (Fujita *et al.*, 1973). However, barbiturates exert other effects on hepatic physiology that appear to contribute to their increased metabolism. For example, Ohnhaus and his colleagues (1971) reported that pretreating rats for 4 days with phenobarbital caused a 12- to 15-fold decrease in the plasma half-life of several drugs metabolized by the microsomal drug-metabolizing enzyme system, but only a three- to fourfold increase in the activity of this enzyme system measured *in vitro*. Their studies indicated that phenobarbital, in addition to increasing microsomal enzyme activity, could also cause a progressive increase in hepatic blood flow over the 4-day course of treatment (33 to 75% above control values). The time course of enzyme induction appeared to follow the change in hepatic blood flow, and they suggested that the increased flow contributed substantially to differences observed between *in vitro* and *in vivo* alterations in rates of drug oxidations after pretreatment with phenobarbital. Thus, it would appear that drug metabolism can be increased by barbiturates not only by increased enzyme cytochrome P-450 synthesis, but also by increased hepatic blood flow. Increased blood flow and enlarged liver occurring during the barbiturate regimen may be viewed as an adaptation to the enhanced metabolic needs of the tissue because of the "demands" of the inductive process. For example, Remmer (1972) has estimated a 30% increase in energy consumption by the liver to "provide" for the enhanced synthesis of enzymes during induction. The phenomenon of enzyme induction can in turn be considered simply as an adaptation of hepatic parenchymal cells exposed to foreign chemicals. Thus, stimulated metabolism accelerates the conversion of lipid-soluble foreign compounds (e.g., barbiturates) to more water-soluble metabolites and, in this way, facilitates their urinary excretion.

Phenobarbital administration has also been shown to stimulate bile flow and increase the biliary transport maximum for certain dyes, such as sulfobromophthalein. Such effects contributed substantially to enhancing the clearance of these dyes from plasma (Klaassen and Plaa, 1968). Other agents which depend upon the biliary route for elimination would be expected to be similarly affected. Other evidence also suggests that enzyme induction by barbiturates appears to involve more factors than an increase in cytochrome P-450 synthesis. As discussed in Chapter 1, a *qualitative* difference in cytochrome P-450 with barbiturate induction is also indicated, in addition to the more well-known quantitative difference.

Parli *et al.* (1972) have questioned the applicability of induction studies with barbiturates in experimental animals that are given unusually high doses when compared with man and under rigidly controlled conditions. In their studies, a marked enzyme induction by dichlorophenobarbital was observed in rats and dogs but not in man. In addition, Dayton and Perel (1971) have suggested that induction may have limited clinical significance. On the other hand, there are numerous studies indicating that barbiturates and many other drugs do induce the metabolism of a number of drugs (including other barbiturates and hypnotics) in man with the result that their pharmacologic effects are modified in accord with the pharmacologic activity of the metabolites formed. We also know that, in contrast to the development of tolerance to the opiates, with barbiturate tolerance there is an upper limit to the dose to which man can become tolerant, presumably related, at least in part, to some maximal rate of metabolic detoxication that an individual can attain. It has also been reported that the increase in hydroxylation of barbiturates upon their repeated administration to man is coincident with an increase in cytochrome P-450 in human liver. Most investigators agree that the magnitude and duration of action of hexobarbital, pentobarbital, amobarbital, and other intermediate or short-acting barbiturates are determined mainly by the rate at which these drugs are metabolized by the drug-metabolizing enzyme systems in the hepatic microsomes, and that enzyme induction by these drugs can contribute significantly to the development of tolerance to their effects. Moreover, as we have already mentioned, the low order of substrate specificity of the inducible microsomal enzyme system may contribute substantially to cross tolerance among different barbiturates and to metabolic interactions between barbiturates and other drugs. From their studies in rats chronically treated with hexobarbital or pentobarbital, Stevenson and Turnbull (1971) concluded that tolerance to these barbiturates was entirely due to enzyme induction. They were unable to demonstrate tolerance to the effects of the long-acting, poorly metabolized drug barbital. Their results may have been influenced by the method used to assess tolerance, i.e., sleeping time after direct injection of barbiturate into the lateral cerebral ventricles. In most instances, tolerance to both the short- and long-acting barbiturates can be demonstrated in both man and experimental animals.

Adaptive Tolerance

Whereas dispositional tolerance may be acceptable to explain, at least partly, the development of tolerance to the effects of shorter-acting' barbiturates, it does not appear to fully explain tolerance to the longer-acting barbital which is metabolized to only a small degree, say less than 10% in *both* tolerant and nontolerant animals. This is not to say that barbital is not capable of stimulating microsomal enzyme activity; indeed, it does stimulate this activity and accordingly may accelerate the metabolism of other barbiturates and drugs. It appears, however, that barbital is a poor substrate for the enzyme system in question. That CNS adaptation is involved in tolerance to the hypnotic effects of barbiturates is further indicated by (1) the longer time required to produce sleep in animals tolerant to pentobarbital as compared to nontolerant animals—presumably due to a CNS subsensitivity; and (2) the higher plasma barbiturate levels found when tolerant animals regain their righting reflex compared to those found in nontolerant animals (Singh, 1972). Frey and Kampmann (1965), studying tolerance to the anticonvulsant effects of phenobarbital in mice, concluded that this tolerance was produced by an initial central adaptation and a subsequent superimposed accelerated enzymic oxidation of the drug.

The specific enzyme systems, proteins, or neurotransmitters or as yet unidentified substances that may be involved in the adaptive tolerance to barbiturates are unknown. The effects of barbiturates on brain neurotransmitters are either too trivial to represent primary changes in tolerance, are too inconsistently demonstrated, or are not specific for tolerance to barbiturate effects. Also, barbiturates, like opiates, can modify several biochemical systems in brain that are basic to cell function. For example, active transport of sodium and potassium ions across cell membranes is decreased by barbiturates due to their inhibition of the activity of the sodium-potassium-stimulated ATPase. Since ion transport is essential for maintenance of the normal resting potential across the cell membrane, inhibition of transport might be expected to decrease the responsivity of cells. But is this a change fundamental to the production of barbiturate tolerance? This question can also apply to the effects of barbiturates on suppressing the oxidative metabolism of brain tissue, and/or on modifying neurotransmitter synthesis or function—are these causes or manifestations of tolerance? Indeed, the observations that such diverse drugs as barbiturates, alcohol, amphetamines, and various hallucinogens can all affect oxygen uptake in brain, or alter brain ATP concentrations, for example, suggest that these metabolic changes are indirect consequences of the primary actions of these drugs.

Conclusions

Some biochemical mechanisms underlying dispositional tolerance to barbiturates have been elucidated over the past 15 years. An increase in the metabolic breakdown of barbiturates by stimulation of their own rates of metabolism appears to support and even cause tolerance to effects of the shorter-acting barbiturates under special conditions. But, adaptation due to decreased responsiveness of the CNS receptors may play a much greater role in the development of tolerance particularly to the effects of the longer acting, less metabolized barbiturates. The basis of this cellular tolerance to barbiturates is, as in the case of the opiates, essentially unknown.

TOLERANCE TO EFFECTS OF ETHYL ALCOHOL

Certain observations about chronic alcohol ingestion are widely accepted: (1) alcoholics often exhibit cross tolerance to the effects of many drugs and, therefore, they frequently require unusually high doses of barbiturates, (for example, to induce sedation); and (2) in order to maintain the desired state of inebriation, alcoholics must frequently increase their dosage of ethanol. At the same time, the alcoholic is frequently unable to maintain a given blood level of ethanol.

Dispositional Tolerance

Chronic ingestion of alcohol has been reported to stimulate alcohol metabolism, resulting in a faster alcohol clearance from the body (refer to Lieber et al., 1975 and to alcohol section of Chapter 7, "Recreational Drugs of Abuse"). The metabolism of ethanol results in its stepwise oxidation to acetaldehyde, then acetate, and ultimately to CO_2 and H_2O via the Krebs cycle. Several enzymatic systems catalyze alcohol oxidation in the body, but the proportionate contribution of any single system to the overall metabolism of ethanol, especially after chronic administration, is a controversial subject. We shall consider essentially three enzymatic systems which catalyze the oxidation of ethanol: (1) a soluble NAD-dependent alcohol dehydrogenase (ADH)/acetaldehyde dehydrogenase (AcDH) system; (2) a NADPH-dependent microsomal ethanol-oxidizing system (MEOS); and (3) a peroxidative catalase system dependent upon the generation of hydrogen peroxide from NADPH and oxygen perhaps via a hepatic microsomal NADPH oxidase.

ADH

Much of the earlier work showing that hepatic ADH is primarily responsible for the oxidation of the major portion of alcohol to acetaldehyde has been extended, reevaluated, and reviewed in recent years (Mannering et al., 1963; Kalant et al., 1971; Videla et al., 1973; Lieber and DeCarli, 1970; Lieber et al., 1975; Thurman et al., 1975). AcDH catalyzes the oxidation of acetaldehyde to acetate (Redmond and Cohen, 1971). The activity of the hepatic ADH/AcDH system in man and experimental animals has at various times been reported to be elevated upon chronic ethanol administration; but, conflicting results have been reported (Misra et al., 1971b). If any generalization is possible, it would be that tolerance to alcohol is not *always* accompanied by increased activity in the hepatic ADH/AcDH system—in other words, it does not appear that metabolic tolerance to alcohol is singularly based upon stimulation of the activity of this enzyme system (Lieber and DeCarli, 1970; Tobon and Mezey, 1971). More recent studies of the effects of chronic alcohol intake on *brain* ADH are most interesting. The activity of ADH has been reported to be increased in the brain of alcohol tolerant rats. The enzyme stimulation was temporally in phase with the acquisition of behavioral tolerance, and the degree of enzyme stimulation paralleled the magnitude of tolerance. In contrast, brain AcDH and liver AcDH activities were unchanged by chronic alcohol administration (Raskin and Sokoloff, 1970).

Videla *et al.* (1973) have been interested in the possible rate-limiting step in hepatic alcohol metabolism. According to these investigators, the rate limitation depends upon cofactor regeneration, viz., the rate of mitochondrial reoxidation of NADH to NAD. Accordingly, they demonstrated that certain uncouplers of oxidative phosphorylation could markedly increase the rate of alcohol metabolism both *in vitro* and *in vivo*, in nontolerant rats. But, these agents did not increase the rate of alcohol metabolism in alcohol-tolerant rats. Alcohol metabolism in tolerant rats was already stimulated (in the absence of uncouplers) but without any significant concomitant increases in the activities of ADH or catalase. Also, the magnitude of stimulated metabolism in tolerant rats could not be entirely accounted for by the modest increases they observed in the peroxidative metabolism of alcohol. They suggested that, in tolerant rats, the increased rate of alcohol oxidation was no longer limited by the ability of mitochondria to reoxidize NADH, as it is in nontolerant animals. Of course, this implies that chronic ethanol administration stimulates ethanol metabolism by uncoupling oxidative phosphorylation which in turn increases the regeneration of NAD from NADH. Although their data indicated a faster mitochondrial oxygen consumption *in situ* after chronic ethanol ingestion (suggestive of uncoupling), only a minor uncoupling by ethanol occurred *in vitro*, depending upon the criteria used to assess uncoupling. Indeed, there have been many reports of uncoupling of mitochondrial oxidative phosphorylation by chronic alcohol administration, but there have been equal numbers of reports in which uncoupling was not demonstrable.

The MEOS Controversy

Recently Lieber and DeCarli (1970) demonstrated the existence of a microsomal ethanol-oxidizing system (MEOS) whose activity was adaptively increased after chronic alcohol administration, and under conditions which did not increase the activity of either ADH or catalase. This adaptive response in MEOS activity paralleled an increase in ethanol disappearance from blood, even when ADH activity was inhibited. Furthermore, when catalase activity was abolished by cyanide or aminotriazole, MEOS activity was only minimally inhibited. Such findings are, of course, indicative that the MEOS is completely independent of catalase or ADH activity, and is involved in the accelerated metabolism of alcohol that can occur upon its repeated administration (Lieber *et al.*, 1975).

Lieber and DeCarli (1970) have estimated that *in vivo* perhaps two-thirds of alcohol is metabolized by ADH, the remaining one-third being metabolized by the MEOS. This estimate has been questioned by other researchers in the field. For example, in some studies reviewed by Thurman *et al.* (1975) there is the suggestion that the hepatic microsomal metabolism of ethanol is dependent upon a catalase H_2O_2 system rather than a unique MEOS (see Chapter 7).

As discussed below, there appear to be certain similarities between the microsomal enzyme systems that can catalyze the metabolism of drugs (DMES) and ethanol (MEOS). Thus, it is not surprising that ethanol can induce both the DMES and the MEOS (Lieber *et al.*, 1975). Furthermore, it seems reasonable to propose that alcoholics may become cross-tolerant to the effects of some drugs at least partly because alcohol stimulates the metabolic elimination of these compounds. In a recent study, alcoholic volunteers (who had abstained from alcohol) and nonalcoholic volunteers were given alcohol for 1 month. In both groups, plasma clearances of alcohol, meprobamate and pentobarbital were significantly increased after the alcohol ingestion. Similar findings occurred in rats and were attributed to the induction of hepatic microsomal drug-metabolizing enzyme systems by chronic alcohol administration (Misra *et al.*, 1971).

Conversely, the cross tolerance to *alcohol* that is often seen in *bar-biturate* users may be related to general stimulatory effects of barbiturates on these microsomal systems (Lieber and DeCarli, 1975). Certainly, other explanations are possible. For example, Redmond and Cohen (1971) observed that the repeated administration of phenobarbital to mice increased liver AcDH activity but not the activity of ADH. Theoretically, this would decrease the steady-state tissue concentrations of the pharmacologically active acetaldehyde and contribute to decreased pharmacologic effects of alcohol among barbiturate users.

The concept of metabolic cross tolerance between alcohol and drugs has been disputed actively (Devenyi and Wilson, 1971; Hatfield *et al.*, 1972; see also alcohol section of Chapter 7). In fact, some researchers report *increases* in plasma concentrations of various drugs in ethanol-tolerant animals, ruling out, in their opinion, enzyme induction as a mechanism of cross tolerance. The discrepancies that are often found surely relate, at least in part, to the times chosen for the measurement of drug levels, as well as to species, dose, etc. The times chosen for measuring drug levels may provide contrasting results, because alcohol can either inhibit drug metabolism or can stimulate it, depending on whether it is present or absent in the tissue preparations or biological fluid being analyzed.

The matter of a functional role of a MEOS in drug metabolism is a subject of considerable dispute. For example, Khanna *et al.* (1972), conducting studies in rats, showed that: (1) phenobarbital administration induced the MEOS without effecting alcohol metabolism *in vitro* or *in vivo*; and (2) repeated alcohol administration increased alcohol clearance from blood and increased the rate of alcohol metabolism, but did not alter MEOS activity in rats fed high protein-low fat diets. Other findings have led to conclusions that changes in MEOS activity bear no relation whatever to the metabolic tolerance to alcohol and/or to the cross tolerance between alcohol and other drugs. For example, Vatsis and Schulman (1973), from their studies of a strain of mouse having a uniquely labile catalase, concluded that alcohol oxidation was unrelated to drug oxidation or to a separate MEOS. In support of their conclusions the authors cited studies wherein microsomes could be solubilized and reconstituted under conditions which retained drug-hydroxylating activity, but which resulted in loss of ability to catalyze the oxidation of alcohol. They believe that proposing the existence of a unique MEOS independent of microsomal catalase is unwarranted since, in their experiments, catalase appeared to account for the activity attributed to the MEOS. They also noted that investigators frequently have been unable to demonstrate alcohol oxidation in microsomes devoid of catalase activity. More recently, however, other workers have been able to demonstrate substantial oxidation of alcohol by liver microsomal preparations containing little or no catalase activity (Mezey *et al.*, 1973; Teschke *et al.*, 1972; Lieber *et al.*, 1975), although there has been a question raised as to the methods used to determine catalase activity and/or to remove catalase from the tissue preparations (Thurman *et al.*, 1975).

Lieber and DeCarli (1970) have emphasized that the MEOS in both man and rat bears several notable similarities to the DMES: (1) both systems are inhibited by carbon monoxide (implicating a vital role for cytochrome P-450) and are dependent upon the presence of oxygen and NADPH; (2) female rats have lower MEOS and DMES activities than male rats and both enzyme systems are more adaptive in female rats than in males; and (3) both systems frequently have been reported to be inducible by repeated alcohol or drug administration coincident with proliferation in hepatic smooth endoplasmic reticulum. Thus, clearances from blood of both alcohol and certain drugs can increase in parallel to increases in the activities of the MEOS, and certain enzymes in the DMES, e.g., aniline hydroxylase and cytochrome P-450 (Rubin and Lieber, 1971). Unfortunately, many of the above-mentioned findings have been disputed. For example, in male Sprague-Dawley rats, Klaassen (1969) observed that phenobarbital, chlordane, and 3-methylcholanthrene, agents which induce the DMES, failed to increase the clearance of alcohol from blood. That alcohol and other drugs serve as substrates for different microsomal enzyme systems is suggested by other findings; for example, the MEOS is reportedly relatively insensitive to the established DMES-inhibitor, SKF-525A, even at concentrations as high as 10^{-3} M.

Chronic administration of alcohol or the prototype barbiturate inducer, phenobarbital, is reported to produce similar effects on the microsomes under specialized experimental conditions: (1) in male rats, both agents can increase microsomal protein; (2) both agents may stimulate the DMES; (3) both may stimulate cholesterol biosynthesis; and (4) both may induce microsomal hemoprotein cytochrome P-450. The hemoprotein induced by alcohol has some characteristics similar to the hemoprotein induced by phenobarbital. However, studies of alcohol binding to alcohol-induced hemoprotein reveal that the induced hemoprotein exhibits spectral changes similar to those seen with microsomal hemoproteins isolated from animals previously treated with the polycyclic hydrocarbon type of inducers (Rubin et al., 1971). It is known that these hydrocarbon inducers stimulate drug metabolism and affect cytochrome P-450 in a manner different from the barbiturates (Alvares et al., 1967, 1968; Parli and Mannering, 1970). Furthermore, although alcohol is reported to bind to hepatic microsomal hemoproteins as do drug substrates, spectral changes produced by alcohol binding suggest it is bound to the lipophilic membrane near the hemoprotein cytochrome P-450, rather than to the hemoprotein itself as is observed with many drug substrates (Imai and Sato, 1967).

Studies in rat and man indicate that, like many so-called inducers, alcohol can *inhibit* drug metabolism as well as *stimulate* it (Mallov and Baesl, 1972). These are particularly interesting findings in view of the large numbers of alcoholics, and considering the vast numbers of nonalcoholic drugs they consume. Thus, the well-known synergism between various CNS depressants and alcohol and the well-known *causes célèbres* among movie stars that have arisen therefrom may be partly related to inhibition of drug metabolism by alcohol, as well as to the more widely recognized interactions at CNS receptors. In contrast, the frequently observed cross tolerance between alcohol and other drugs may be related to stimulation by one drug of the metabolism of another. In any case, it can be anticipated that alcohol intake, like barbiturate intake, can alter the magnitude and duration of action of many drugs which are readily metabolized and taken before, simultaneously, or after alcohol.*

Adaptive Tolerance

At equivalent concentrations of blood or brain alcohol, an alcoholic appears less inebriated than a nonalcoholic, indicating adaptive tolerance. Davis and Walsh (1970) have postulated that the alcohol metabolite, acetaldehyde, might cause an aberrant metabolism of dopamine in brain, such that morphine-like alkaloids are formed in the CNS which then may serve as a basis for tolerance and addicting liability of alcohol. Seevers (1970) and Goldstein and Judson (1971) have called attention to certain disparities between this rather unconventional hypothesis and certain pharmacological observations, not the least of which is that no specific mutual cross tolerance or cross dependence has been demonstrated between morphine-like drugs and the alcohol/barbiturate class of drugs. In a recent preliminary report by Ross and Cardenas (1975), another type of association was shown between opiate and alcohol actions. Acute administration of either morphine or alcohol to rats depleted cerebral calcium. Naloxone antagonized the depletion caused by both drugs, but did not antagonize it when a similar depletion was produced by reserpine or pentobarbital. Moreover, tolerance and cross tolerance developed to depletion of cerebral calcium by morphine and alcohol, and this tolerance was blocked by cycloheximide. If confirmed, these findings would support the view that a common biochemical event may underlie certain actions of opiates and alcohol, chemicals that are miles apart by physicochemical criteria and that, superficially at least, are miles apart from a pharmacologic viewpoint.

That cross tolerance between alcohol and barbiturates may be related to CNS adaptation rather than metabolic interactions has been suggested by Hatfield et al. (1972). In their studies, the expression of tolerance to alcohol was different between male and female rats. Their findings suggest that in rats a sex-related decrease in CNS sensitivity, rather than an altered metabolic rate, underlies cross tolerance between drugs and alcohol. In this regard, Remmer (1962b) has reported that repeated treatment of female rats with alcohol decreased the sleeping time after hexobarbital, but without a concomitant increase in the rate of metabolism of hexobarbital *in vitro*. Such findings suggest that ethanol modified hexobarbital distribution and/or modified the sensitivity of the CNS to the barbiturate. Finally, LeBlanc et al. (1969) have reported that in rats tolerant to alcohol-induced impairment of motor performance, tolerance could not be attributed to

---

*In this discussion we are, of course, not considering the presence of hepatic disease which could also affect drug metabolism in the alcoholic.

stimulation of alcohol metabolism, to alterations of alcohol levels in blood, and/or to decreased entry of alcohol into the CNS. These investigators proposed that chronic alcohol administration in some way decreased the sensitivity of the CNS to the effects of alcohol.

A review by Kalant (1962) carefully outlines the multitude of effects that alcohol can exert on the CNS, such as modifying oxygen uptake, amino acid metabolism, concentrations of γ-aminobutyric acid (a putative neurotransmitter thought to mediate transfer of inhibitory impulses at synapses between communicating nerve cells), and concentrations of several hormone systems linked closely to CNS function via hypothalmic centers. We shall not belabor the "chicken and the egg" allegory again, except to restate that the mechanisms of adaptive tolerance to alcohol are no less complex than those for opiates and barbiturates. It is only a matter of conjecture which, if any, of these vital biochemical systems modified by alcohol initiate the adaptive tolerance in the alcoholic.

TOLERANCE TO EFFECTS OF MARIHUANA

Among the drugs considered in this book, perhaps marihuana best serves to illustrate differences in the expression of tolerance depending upon the drug effect or the species being studied. For example, it has been shown rather consistently that tolerance develops to marihuana-induced impairment of simple behavioral responses (food reinforcement and avoidance) in several species, including rat, mouse, pig, rhesus monkey, chicken, and dog. Also, tolerance to various physiologic effects of marihuana, including suppression of spontaneous motor activity, analgesia (as measured by the hot plate method), and hypothermia, have been demonstrated in various species (Abel et al., 1972, 1973; Nahas, 1973; McMillan et al., 1973). In contrast, Ham and Noordwijk (1973) were unable to demonstrate tolerance in mice and Siamese hamsters to the aggressive-suppressant effects of Δ^9-tetrahydrocannabinol (Δ^9-THC), the major active principle of marihuana. Similarly, in chimpanzees, Ferraro and Grilly (1971) did not observe tolerance to Δ^9-THC-induced impairment of a match-to-sample task. McMillan et al. (1971) stressed that, as with other abused drugs, tolerance does not develop to all the effects of marihuana in a given species. For example, although tolerance was reported to develop to certain behavioral effects of Δ^9-THC in dog, no tolerance was observed to occur to its sedative or anorectic effects. There are also reports of an "acute tolerance" developing to hypothermic and locomotor excitatory response of Δ^9-THC in rats after only one or two doses (Davis et al., 1972; Lomax, 1971).

There is still considerable controversy as to whether or not man develops tolerance to any behavioral impairment induced by marihuana. Nahas (1973) has stated in his discussion about tolerance to the euphoriant effects of marihuana: ". . . rapid tolerance to psychoactive drugs is most likely to develop in the average human being, especially if he is an adolescent with a labile personality and an uncertain future, or if he belongs to the underprivileged groups . . ." Aside from the cynical inference that the average human being is a culturally deprived adolescent who is mentally unstable and unsure of what lies ahead, the further implication of the statement is that certain psychosocial factors increase the likelihood of developing a rapid tolerance to marihuana. We agree with Nahas that these factors may lead the habitual marihuana smoker to *increase his dose*. But, increasing dosage does not necessarily mean that the smoker is tolerant to the drug effects. Either the *drug intake* causes tolerance to develop or it does not; increasing the dosage for reasons other than maintaining the pharmacologic effects of the drug ought not to be casually attributed to a tolerance potential of the drug itself.

As regards marihuana-induced psychologic effects (viz., euphoria) in man there may also develop a so-called *"reverse* tolerance" (an abysmal misnomer); that is, the habitual user requires less dosage to achieve the desired degree of psychological gratification (Weil *et al.*, 1968; Lemberger *et al.*, 1970; Hollister and Tinklenberg, 1973; McMillan *et al.*, 1971; Nahas, 1973).

Dispositional Tolerance

One explanation proposed for tolerance to marihuana is that certain of its effects (including impairment of certain physiologic and simple behavioral functions) are mainly due to its content of Δ^9-THC, whereas other effects (for example, induction of euphoria) might be due mainly to the formation of hydroxylated metabolites of Δ^9-THC *in vivo*. When administered intravenously to healthy human volunteers, Δ^9-THC is completely metabolized (Lemberger *et al.*, 1970). Indeed, it has been shown by Lemberger *et al.* (1971, 1972) that long-term marihuana smokers clear Δ^9-THC faster from plasma than naive subjects. There may well be, then, an increased formation of one or more pharmacologically active Δ^9-THC metabolites whose formation may contribute at least in part to the alleged phenomenon of "reverse tolerance." Mechoulam (1970) has suggested that 11-hydroxy- Δ^9-THC or another metabolite may be a possible candidate. In rats several investigators observed a significant induction by chronic Δ^9-THC administration of the hepatic microsomal drug-metabolizing enzyme system, and an associated increase in formation of two pharmacologically active cannabinols, 11-hydroxy- Δ^9-THC and 8,11-dihydroxy- Δ^9-THC

(B.T. Ho *et al.*, 1973a). According to this concept then, Δ⁹-THC might stimulate its own metabolism to hydroxylated metabolites upon long-term exposure to the drug. Thus, the effects attributable to Δ⁹-THC would become diminished (tolerance) and the effects due to the metabolites would become increasingly evident ("reverse tolerance"). Other investigators have not observed this inductive phenomenon in pigs (Schou *et al.*, 1972).

An alternative explanation for the alleged reverse tolerance to the euphorogenic properties of marihuana in man is that it is a phenomenon by which the naive smoker learns, by experience, to perceive the euphoria in a more discriminating fashion once he has gained some insight into what to expect (so-called learning sensitization). The experienced user also learns to improve his smoking technique. And, of course, a relaxed atmosphere and social acceptance within the smoker's peer group are likely to contribute to the sense of well-being attributed to marihuana itself (Jones and Stone, 1970; Truitt, 1971; Hollister, 1971). Indeed, simply the long (3-day) half-life of Δ⁹-THC and its metabolites in naive smokers (Lemberger *et al.*, 1970) would imply accumulation of the drug *in vivo* with habitual usage, which accumulation could account for the increased effects after habitual use. Unfortunately, the phenomenon of reverse tolerance which is supposed to occur in man (Weil *et al.*, 1968) has not been studied experimentally in a systematic way and may relate only to those environmental and learning factors mentioned above. In addition, reverse tolerance is not *always* observed in marihuana users and could not be demonstrated in pigeons (McMillan *et al.*, 1971).

It has been shown that Δ⁹-THC can *inhibit* the activity of drug-hydroxylating enzymes in hepatic microsomes (Cohen *et al.*, 1971; Ham *et al.*, 1972). This inhibition could result in accumulation *in vivo* of Δ⁹-THC and *decreased* formation of its metabolites. Inhibition of Δ⁹-THC biotransformation might then cause an apparent tolerance to develop with respect to those effects caused by the metabolites, and a "reverse tolerance" to the effects attributable to the parent drug. In man, "reverse tolerance" to the euphorigenic effects of Δ⁹-THC might then be explained by increasing amounts of Δ⁹-THC if it were the active euphoriant. It has also been shown that inhibition of Δ⁹-THC metabolism by SKF-525A resulted in an increase in certain depressant effects of the drug (Sofia and Barry, 1970). It is not unusual to observe opposite effects of drugs on the microsomal drug-metabolizing enzyme system, depending upon whether the drug is present or absent in the microsomal preparation at the time of assay. Often when the drug is present, enzyme inhibition is observed; when the drug is absent, induction is frequently reported. The long half-life of Δ⁹-THC, about 1 week in the rat (Agurell *et al.*, 1969) and about 3 days in man, (Lemberger *et al.*, 1970), suggests that Δ⁹-THC may well be present in liver tissue in sufficient quantities upon repeated administration so that the net effect observed on microsomal hydroxylases could be inhibition. However, tolerance to chronic consumption of marihuana occurs at a time when hydroxylating enzyme activity is *stimulated*, not inhibited (Truitt, 1970; B.T. Ho *et al.*, 1973a). Also, Campo (1973) has shown in rats that chronic oral administration of Δ^9-THC stimulated its own rate of metabolism by liver tissue. Indeed, in man also, Δ^9-THC is cleared faster and metabolites appear more rapidly in chronic marihuana users (Lemberger *et al.*, 1970, 1971). Consequently, for the habitual user, it seems more credible that if the liver enzymes play any role in tolerance and/or reverse tolerance, it would be related to enzyme induction rather than inhibition.

It has been reported that tolerance to the hypotensive effects of orally administered Δ^9-THC in the spontaneously hypertensive rat (SHR) develops rapidly relative to tolerance to the centrally mediated anorectic effects; it has been suggested by Nahas *et al.* (1972, 1973a) that hypotensive tolerance is related to loss of a peripheral hypotensive effect of Δ^9-THC developed over a 5-day treatment period. This interval is comparable to that observed for development of the immune response in rats. This observation, coupled with the known extensive binding of Δ^9-THC to plasma lipoprotein, led the authors to suggest that the loss of the hypotensive effect of Δ^9-THC upon repeated administration to SHR may be related to initiation of antibody formation in response to a protein-bound Δ^9-THC haptene. Drug molecules as small as Δ^9-THC may evoke immune responses, as mentioned earlier in the section of this chapter dealing with possible mechanisms of opiate tolerance. These authors demonstrated that the immunosuppressant, azathioprine (Imuran), at doses which produced no overt pharmacologic effects, markedly suppressed the development of hypotensive tolerance to Δ^9-THC in the SHR (Nahas *et al.*, 1973b). This interesting finding requires additional study to ensure that it is not related to unspecific effects of azathioprine.

Findings of other investigators are discordant with Nahas' results. Δ^9-THC, administered intraperitoneally at doses similar to those used orally by Nahas, did not produce tolerance to the hypotensive effects in the spontaneously hypertensive rat (Lewis *et al.*, 1975). Also, Birmingham *et al.* (1972) observed a fall in blood pressure after administering Δ^9-THC to SHR and rats with hypertension secondary to adrenal hyperplasia. But, the fall was progressive over a several-day treatment period; that is, no tolerance was observed. It may well be that experimental subtleties such as the drug vehicle or route of administration contribute significantly to the contrasting findings. Various surfactants, solvents, oils, and suspending agents can and do influence the rate of Δ^9-THC absorption, as well as produce their own pharmacologic effects (Truitt, 1971). We allude to our earlier statements regarding the difficulties in comparing data by different investigators when there are subtle differences in methods used at different laboratories.

As might be expected, cross tolerance and reciprocal cross tolerance have been demonstrated among several pharmacologically active tetrahydrocannabinols, such as Δ^9-THC and Δ^8-THC (active principles found in marihuana), Δ^6,^{10}-dimethylheptyltetrahydrocannabinol (DMHP) and 3-(n-hexyl)- Δ^{6a},^{10a}-THC (synhexyl). Most curious is the inference of cross tolerance between morphine and Δ^9-THC (McMillan *et al.*, 1970, 1971). Morphine analgesia was quantified by its inhibition of the tail flick response of mice exposed to a heat stimulus. A single dose of Δ^9-THC (10 mg/kg) did not affect responses in this pharmacologic test procedure, nor did it alter the inhibitory ("analgesic") effects of morphine. But pretreating mice with this dose of Δ^9-THC once daily for 7 days preceding the injection of morphine (but not on the day of morphine injection) lessened the inhibition of the tail flick response produced by morphine almost as much as did a 7-day pretreatment with morphine itself. In contrast to these findings, studies of scheduled-controlled behavior in pigeons failed to demonstrate a reciprocal cross tolerance between Δ^9-THC and morphine. Also, in pigeons, the narcotic antagonist, naloxone, attenuated morphine tolerance, but had little effect on tolerance to Δ^9-THC. These studies are interesting in view of reports that some U.S. troops in Viet Nam smoked opiate-suffused marihuana (smack grass), and that substantial amounts of the opiate survive the combustion process (Myers *et al.*, 1972).

Adaptive Tolerance

Ho *et al.* (1973a,b) have suggested that behavioral tolerance to Δ^9-THC, demonstrated to occur in various animal experiments, may be due to a decrease in CNS sensitivity to unchanged Δ^9-THC; whereas, *reverse* tolerance to the psychologic effects, which allegedly develops in man, may be due, at least in part, to an increase in the rate of formation of an active hydroxylated metabolite. Thus, an adaptive tolerance to marihuana has not been excluded from consideration. However, it is a possibility that requires considerably more study. As is the case for drugs discussed earlier in this chapter, Δ^9-THC modifies some very basic biochemical systems in rat brain, such as increasing catecholamine turnover (Maitre *et al.*, 1970), and serotonin concentrations (Sofia *et al.*, 1971). Nor is Δ^9-THC to be outdone by the opiates, barbiturates, or alcohol with respect to conflicting data relevant to its induced changes in the CNS. Ho *et al.* (1973b), in their studies of the activities of several enzymes involved in catecholamine synthesis in rat brain, reported that serotonin synthesis was *not* increased by chronic administration of Δ^9-THC.

Further evidence for participation of adaptive phenomena in marihuana tolerance comes from studies by McMillan *et al.* (1973). They reported that pigeons, tolerant to certain behavioral effects of intramuscularly administered Δ^9-THC, absorb, metabolize, and excrete Δ^9-THC in a manner similar to nontolerant pigeons. Also, concentrations of Δ^9-THC and its metabolites are at least as high in the blood of tolerant birds as they are in nontolerant birds, evidence favoring an adaptive mechanism of tolerance. Unfortunately, the concentrations of Δ^9-THC and its metabolites that are measured in blood may not accurately reflect their respective concentrations in brain, as the authors noted; also their analytical techniques did not permit definitive separations and identifications of *individual* Δ^9-THC metabolites. Their data also supported the contention of formation of a pharmacologically active metabolite of Δ^9-THC *in vivo*. When tritiated Δ^9-THC was injected intramuscularly into naive pigeons, the concentration of radioactivity in blood was maximal within 15 minutes, but the behavioral effects induced by the drug never appeared until at least 45 minutes after injection and usually later. Also, the concentrations of radioactivity in several brain areas were equivalent after administration of a single challenge dose of tritiated Δ^9-THC to nontolerant pigeons, or to pigeons rendered tolerant to Δ^9-THC (Dewey *et al.*, 1973). When the tritiated drug was administered repeatedly over a 2-week period, radioactivity accumulated in brain coincident with the development of tolerance. These data indicate that it is unlikely that tolerance develops because of diminished entry of *total* cannabinoid into brain—although individual cannabinoid metabolites in brain could differ qualitatively and/or quantitatively in tolerant versus nontolerant birds. Nevertheless, their results strongly support a postulate of an adaptive mechanism of tolerance to Δ^9-THC, rather than a dispositional mechanism under their experimental conditions.

Most studies suggest that marihuana possesses both excitatory and depressant actions. It has been hypothesized that when tolerance develops to the depressant action, the underlying excitatory action becomes manifest (Masur *et al.*, 1971). The hypothesis gains credibility from a study by Alvez and Carlini (1973) who observed in rats that a single dose of *Cannabis* extract reduced muricidal behavior (presumably a CNS depressant action), but multiple doses increased muricidal behavior (presumably a CNS stimulant action). On the other hand, Ueki *et al.* (1972), administering Δ^9-THC to a strain of rats that was more prone to spontaneous muricidal behavior, reported that the drug induced muricidal behavior even after the *first* dose.

TOLERANCE TO THE EFFECTS OF
PSYCHOTOMIMETICS

Among the psychotomimetic agents to be considered in this section will be the amphetamines, lysergic acid diethylamide (LSD), mescaline, and derivatives of these commonly known prototypes. These agents are discussed together not only because of their pharmacologic similarities as psychotomimetics, but also because they have often been studied together and frequently exhibit varying degrees of tolerance, cross tolerance, and reciprocal cross tolerance with respect to various autonomic and subjective effects in both man and experimental animals. These similarities may at first seem to simplify any discussion of tolerance to one specific psycho-tomimetic drug, because any conclusions might apply to another (which we do with some confidence in the case of opiates). As we shall see, this would be most unwise.

LSD/Mescaline

Appel and Freedman (1968) observed that LSD, bromolysergic acid (BOL), psilocybin, mescaline, and amphetamine all disrupt bar-pressing behavior in rats on a fixed ratio schedule of milk reinforcement. Each agent, administered repeatedly, produced tolerance, and with the exception of amphetamine, cross tolerance developed to this behavioral disruption. Cross tolerance between amphetamine and LSD was not demonstrable. On the basis that these findings mirrored observations in man with respect to relative potencies, tolerance potential, and cross tolerance potential, the fixed ratio schedule appeared to be a suitable model for studying at least certain properties of these drugs in experimental animals—not a minor experimental advance in this most difficult area of research.

Although earlier studies had demonstrated that reciprocal cross tolerance developed in man between LSD and mescaline, mechanistic studies in infrahuman species were lacking. Accordingly, Winter (1971) undertook a study of the development of tolerance to LSD and cross tolerance to mescaline in rats responding on a fixed ratio schedule of positive reinforcement. After producing tolerance to LSD effects in their behavioral system, Winter observed a cross tolerance to mescaline. Determination of the total amount and concentration of LSD in brain and liver revealed no significant qualitative, quantitative, or temporal dif-ferences between rats receiving LSD for the first time versus those pretreated with either drug. These data clearly indicated an adaptive mechanism of tolerance to LSD, rather than tolerance by a dispositional mechanism. Moreover, the cross tolerance of LSD to mescaline suggested that the drugs shared some common characteristic(s) in their interactions with certain CNS receptors. Indeed, it has been reported that these two agents produce similar changes in blood and brain amines (Giarman and Freidman, 1965).

Silva and Carlini (1968), using rope climbing and bar pressing behavioral methods in rats, observed reciprocal cross tolerance between LSD and mescaline, but not between these agents and Δ⁹-THC. Indeed, in human subjects as well, tolerance to LSD did not exhibit a cross tolerance to Δ⁹-THC (Isbell et al., 1967). Thus, even though these three drugs are reported to induce some similar psychogenic effects in man, these data suggest that Δ⁹-THC may act through mechanisms different from the other two agents.

Tryptamine, which is present in the brain of several species, has been shown to share many pharmacologic properties with LSD and LSD-type psychotomimetics. It has even been suggested that LSD exerts its pharmacologic effects by acting as an agonist at tryptaminergic receptors in the CNS, and that certain disorders in perception and thinking may be a consequence of abnormal utilization of tryptamine in situ. Martin and Eades (1972) undertook an investigation to provide evidence that tryptamine and LSD share a common mode of action, using the phenomenon of tolerance and cross tolerance between the two agents as the index of similarity. Infusions of LSD and tryptamine in the spinal dog increased heart rate, respiratory rate, and pupillary diameter, facilitated the flexor reflex, and evoked the stepping reflex. When LSD was administered daily, tolerance developed to these effects of LSD and cross tolerance had likewise developed to these effects of tryptamine.

Also, in addition to producing similar spectra of pharmacologic actions in the dog and man, both LSD and tryptamine exhibit a similar susceptibility to certain antagonists (Martin and Eades, 1970). These observations supported the hypothesis that tryptamine and LSD have a common mode of action and that LSD exerts some of its pharmacologic effects by acting as an agonist at tryptamine receptors.

Tolerance and cross tolerance to certain psychotomimetic drugs appear to depend upon many factors including route and order of administration. Tilson and Sparber (1971) rendered rats tolerant to the behavioral-disruptive effects of mescaline either infused directly into the ventricles of the brain or injected intraperitoneally. When rats were tolerant to intraperitoneally administered mescaline, they were not tolerant to intraventricularly administered mescaline, and vice versa. In a subsequent study using similar methods, these same investigators observed that when rats were tolerant to intraventricularly administered dextroamphetamine, they were not cross-tolerant to intraventricularly administered mescaline. However, when the drug order was reversed (that is, amphetamine challenge to mescaline tolerant rats), cross tolerance did develop. When both drugs were administered intraperitoneally, cross tolerance did not develop regardless of the order of drug presentation (Sparber and Tilson, 1972). The authors discussed these puzzling findings in relation to the possible differential effects of these drugs on the firing of neurons in midbrain raphe nuclei, which harbors cells that have been implicated in the actions of these and other psychotomimetics. Finally, they observed that tolerance to intraventricularly administered amphetamine did not confer tolerance to that same drug administered intraperitoneally. These findings emphasize the potential hazards of conducting studies of tolerance mechanisms whereby the drug is administered directly into the CNS because clearly the expression of tolerance (hence, presumably the mechanism of tolerance) to certain behavioral effects of centrally administered drugs may differ rather significantly from the mechanism of tolerance observed when the drugs are administered peripherally.

Knoll and Vizzi (1970) determined that certain substitutions in the *para*-position of methamphetamine conferred LSD-like activity to the molecule. Accordingly, they synthesized the *para*-bromo derivative of methamphetamine and found it to possess about one-tenth the LSD activity in experimental animals. Perhaps more importantly, a marked and prolonged tolerance developed in rat and rabbit to several of its pharmacologic effects, and cross tolerance developed between it and LSD. The low order of psychotomimetic activity of this compound in animals superimposed upon its profound capacity to induce self-tolerance and cross tolerance to LSD lead the authors to propose that it may have therapeutic potential. Thus, treatment of an LSD user with this agent would be expected initially to produce minimal psychogenic effects, which would disappear upon repeated administration. The patient would then presumably be "protected" against effects of abusive psychotomimetic agents of the LSD variety, and, perhaps, even protected against endogenous psychotomimetic agents, the existence of which has been proposed to play some role in human psychosis.

Amphetamine

The overt psychological effects produced after morphine and methamphetamine administration are quite different, as even the novice in pharmacology would recognize. Nevertheless, these agents, apparently miles apart in their pharmacologic activities, do share some common properties including: (1) antinociceptive activity (hot plate in mouse); (2) induction of tolerance to that activity; and (3) alteration of that activity by drugs known to cause changes in putative neurotransmitters in the CNS. In fact, amphetamine and morphine have been used experimentally as an analgesic combination since they are reported to be synergistic (Forrest *et al.*, 1973).

Recently Pleuvry (1971) demonstrated that these agents exhibit a reciprocal cross-tolerance with respect to antinociceptive activity in mouse. While it is tempting to speculate that the cross tolerance implies that the two agents act on some common complex physiologic or biochemical mechanism, these rather unexpected findings are probably best interpreted cautiously in view of the multitude of overt dissimilarities in pharmacologic activities between these agents.

In studies in rats, it was concluded that amphetamine injections did not induce tolerance to hyperactivity over a 2-week treatment period (Lewander, 1971; Lu *et al.*, 1972). In contrast, it was observed that when rats were treated orally with amphetamine for a 9-month period, locomotor activity was stimulated during the first 3 months of treatment, but during the last 6 months locomotor activity in the drug group was similar to that of the control group (Herman *et al.*, 1971). The "chicken and the egg" allegory notwithstanding, estimations by Herman and his associates of norepinephrine and serotonin levels in nine discrete areas of brain after the 9 months of amphetamine treatment revealed no changes in serotonin concentration, but did reveal significant decreases in norepinephrine levels in the pons. Other investigators studying the effects of amphetamine on catecholamines in the CNS have not completely confirmed these results. While it may be that tolerance to amphetamine is associated with changes in adrenergic or cholinergic mechanisms in some areas of the brain, it is not presently possible to precisely pinpoint the discrete areas of the brain involved and/or which individual amines are involved.

Weiner (1972) has thoroughly reviewed several theories proposed to explain tolerance to the effects of amphetamines and a summary of part of his discussion is appropriate here. According to the false transmitter hypothesis, β-hydroxylated phenylethylamines may be taken up and retained in storage vesicles of adrenergic neurons, thus, displacing the neurotransmitter, norepinephrine. When the nerve is stimulated, the less active hydroxylated phenylethylamine would be released instead of norepinephrine, thus, producing a lesser response than is expected (hence, the name "false transmitter" hypothesis). More specific evidence, accumulated from studies in rats, suggests that amphetamine tolerance may relate to gradual neuronal accumulation and release of the β-phenylethylamine, *p*-hydroxynorephedrine. According to Lewander (1971), three types of pharmacologic effects of amphetamine are distinguishable according to our present knowledge: (1) peripheral effects, such as hyperthermia, to which tolerance develops and which are attenuated or abolished by p-hydroxynorephedrine pretreatment; (2) some allegedly central effects, such as anorexia, to which tolerance also develops and which are not diminished by the presence of p-hydroxynorephedrine in central and peripheral noradrenergic neurons; (3) central effects such as increased locomotor activity and stereotyped behavior, to which tolerance does not develop and which are not affected by the presence of p-hydroxynorephedrine in central and peripheral adrenergic neurons. According to this classification, tolerance to the various pharmacologic effects of amphetamine is likely to be caused by different mechanisms. From his study of amphetamine tolerance in rats, Lewander concluded that p-hydroxynorephedrine might be involved in tolerance to the *peripheral* but probably not the central effects of amphetamine. However, more research is needed in other species, including man, to support this hypothesis.

Another hypothesis to explain amphetamine tolerance, stated rather simply, is that the adrenergic neuron is depleted of its neurotransmitter, norepinephrine. This depletion is accomplished by chronic use of amphetamine when first the amphetamine displaces the neurotransmitter from intraneuronal storage sites, and second, when it inhibits tyrosine hydroxylase and, thus, blocks the resynthesis of the neurotransmitter.

Other hypotheses that have been proposed to explain the development of amphetamine tolerance invoke general concepts that are discussed earlier in this chapter and include: compensatory biochemical adjustments to maintain a disrupted homeostasis in the CNS; and induction of enzymes or receptors which are closely involved in the drug's action. There is no evidence to support theories of altered metabolism, brain uptake, distribution, or excretion of amphetamine as possible mechanisms for development of tolerance to its effects (Ellison *et al.*, 1971). In the words of Weiner (1972): "The exact mechanism by which tolerance develops to amphetamine is unknown . . . From the foregoing remarks one might conclude that the complex effects of amphetamine on behavior are well matched by its equally complex biochemical effects on amine-containing neurons."

TOLERANCE TO EFFECTS OF NICOTINE AND CAFFEINE

The widespread use and social acceptance of nicotine in cigarette smoke and of caffeine in coffee makes us often forget that these agents are also drugs with important psychologic effects. One may, in fact, be critical of us for including them in a discussion of drugs of abuse. However, we believe that, in fact, they do fall into this category and, thus, at least a brief discussion of some recent findings about these agents is warranted for the sake of completing our survey.

Nicotine

Cardiovascular and vasoconstrictor effects of nicotine result from stimulation of the sympatho-adrenal axis, and subsequent release of catecholamines from these sites. Consequently, when rats are treated with nicotine, the urinary excretion of catecholamines is elevated—an effect to which tolerance develops after about 1 week of daily treatment. Possible mechanisms proposed for this tolerance are (1) induction of enzymes responsible for the metabolic inactivation of nicotine; (2) depletion of catecholamine stores in nerve terminals and in the adrenal medulla so that less catecholamines are available for release; (3) increases in reuptake and/or enzymatic processes responsible for catecholamine inactivation. These possibilities were examined in 1971 by Westfall and Brase. Using hexobarbital and zoxazolamine sleeping times as indices of induction of the drug-metabolizing enzyme activity, these investigators observed no induction (that is, no shortening of the sleeping time) in rats following subcutaneous injection of nicotine (1.0 mg/kg) daily for up to 14 days. There was also no indication of induced nicotine oxidase activity *in vitro*. These results argued against a metabolic tolerance to nicotine based upon enzyme induction. Earlier studies wherein induction of liver microsomal enzymes was demonstrated by nicotine administration were rightfully criticized for the outlandish doses that were used (5-40 mg/kg). Other reports of induction following cigarette smoking are not too helpful owing to the presence of many other classical enzyme inducers present in the smoke, such as the polycyclic hydrocarbon benzpyrene.

Westfall and Brase (1971) also studied the possibility that chronic nicotine administration might interfere with mechanisms which store, release, or inactivate catecholamines. Confirming and extending some earlier findings, they could detect no alterations of tissue concentrations of catecholamines during chronic nicotine administration, and no alterations in cardiac uptake or turnover of tritiated norepinephrine in nicotine-treated animals. However, the enzymes monoamine oxidase (MAO) and catechol-O-methyltransferase (COMT) were both significantly elevated. These enzymes respectively catalyze the metabolic inactivation of tissue and circulating catecholamines. Consideration of the temporal relationship between the increased enzyme activities and the time course of acquisition and loss of tolerance implicated COMT induction as a mechanism of tolerance to chronic nicotine administration in rats. More specifically, according to their conclusions, nicotine stimulates release of catecholamines so that their levels are initially elevated in plasma and urine. The elevated levels of catecholamines in plasma cause a compensatory stimulation of COMT which metabolizes the catecholamines and lowers their levels in plasma and urine despite continued nicotine administration (tolerance).

Tolerance to the CNS effects of nicotine in man is suggested by loss of unpleasant effects, such as vomiting and sweating, frequently experienced by the novice smoker. Moreover, in several species of experimental animals, tolerance has been shown to develop to various behavioral and physiologic effects of nicotine (Schechter and Rosecrans, 1972). When nicotine was repeatedly injected subcutaneously into rats at doses of 0.8 mg/kg, a biphasic response was observed with respect to motor activity (Morrison and Stephenson, 1972). Motor activity was depressed initially and subsequently was stimulated. According to the investigators, there were opposite central effects of the drug upon repeated administration; tolerance developed to the depressant effect but not to the stimulant effect. The mechanism of tolerance to the central effects of nicotine is unknown. However, their results did indicate that tolerance to the central depressant effect was not related to an enhanced metabolism of catecholamines via COMT induction.

Caffeine

Colton and his colleagues (1967) have suggested that there are more contradictions in the literature with respect to caffeine than for any other pharmacologic agent. While this may be true, a tolerance to two actions of caffeine has been demonstrated in man, namely, diuresis and stimulation of parotid gland secretion. Tolerance to various CNS effects of caffeine has not been convincingly demonstrated in man; there is evidence that the sleep disturbing properties of this alkaloid are clearly more marked among nonusers than among habitual users of coffee. Moreover, it has been shown that coffee drinkers are less apt to exhibit nervousness or wakefulness than abstainers (Goldstein et al., 1965, 1969; Goldstein and Kaizer, 1969). In a study involving normal medical students, Colton and his associates (1967) attempted to confirm the existence of tolerance to caffeine. They observed that in normal medical students a small dose of caffeine (150 mg) added to decaffeinated coffee produced no consistent change in resting pulse rates of those who habitually consumed caffeinated beverages, but did reduce the rate significantly among those who do not drink coffee. They proposed that a heightened vagal tone appears to be responsible for the bradycardia, and that this enhanced tone becomes masked by direct excitatory actions on the heart after high doses of caffeine. In their opinion, though the measurement was a simple one, the results were unambiguous; coffee drinkers were significantly less sensitive than non-coffee drinkers to the pulse-reducing actions of caffeine.

Often there are contradictory observations on pulse rate responses to doses of caffeine in man. Dose is almost certainly one of the more important considerations. Second, the interval between the injection of caffeine and the time of observation as well as the ages of the subjects used in these studies might explain some of the conflicting impressions in the clinical literature. Another undoubtedly crucial variable is the development of tolerance to caffeine. It is possible that the conflicting literature reflects a failure on the part of the investigators to separate in their selection of patients or volunteers those who are nonconsumers of coffee, moderate consumers, and heavy consumers. From the available studies, tolerance to caffeine does not appear to reflect differences in absorption, metabolism, or excretion of the drug although the question deserves more study. Plasma levels of the alkaloid were not significantly different 1, 2, and 3 hours after oral ingestion of 300 mg of caffeine in either habitual coffee drinkers or abstainers. Although a considerable amount of caffeine accumulates in the body of moderately heavy coffee drinkers during the day, there is no evidence for day-to-day accumulation of drug. These findings suggest that tolerance to the effects of caffeine in man is adaptive in nature. In any case, tolerance to caffeine in man appears to be of a low order of magnitude. This is suggested by the demonstration that the tolerant individual responds when the dose is raised only two- to fourfold. Furthermore, habitual coffee drinkers have experienced distressing signs and symptoms including extra-systoles when their daily consumption of caffeinated beverages was approximately doubled.

CONCLUSION

We hope that the studies described in this chapter provide the reader with an overview of the progress being made in the field of tolerance and mechanisms of tolerance. Clearly, for certain drugs, dispositional tolerance plays a significant role; for others a less understood and considerably more complex mechanism of adaptive tolerance is indicated. We believe, as stated earlier in this chapter, that among the difficulties in interpreting the findings of many studies is the multitude of experimental designs used to study the phenomenon of tolerance. However, the inherent complexity of the CNS and the interdependencies of various putative neurotransmitters surely contribute to our lack of understanding of the biochemical determinants of adaptive tolerance.

REFERENCES

Abel, E., McMillan, D., and Harris, L.: Tolerance to the behavioral and hypothermic effects of 1-9-tetrahydrocannabinol in neonatal chicks. Experientia 28:1188-1189, 1972.

Abel, E.L., McMillan, D.E., and Harris, L.S.: Tolerance to the hypothermic effects of Δ⁹-tetrahydrocannabinol as a function of age in the chicken. Brit. J. Pharmacol. 47:452-456, 1973.

Agurell, S., Nilsson, I.M., Ohlson, A., and Sandberg, F.: Elimination of tritium-labelled cannabinols in the rat with special reference to the development of tests for the identification of Cannabis users. Biochem. Pharmacol. 18:1195-1201, 1969.

Akil, H., Mayer, D.J., and Liebeskind, J.C.: Comparaison chez le rat entre l'analgésie induite par stimulation de la substance grise péri-aqueducale et l'analgésie morphinique. C.R. Acad. Sci. 274:3603-3605, 1972.

Algeri, S. and Costa, E.: Physical dependence on morphine fails to increase serotonin turnover rate in rat brain. Biochem. Pharmacol. 20:877-884, 1971.

Alvares, A.P., Schilling, G., Levin, W., and Kuntzman, R.: Studies on the induction of CO-binding pigments in liver microsomes by phenobarbital and 3-methyl-cholanthrene. Biochem. Biophys. Res. Commun. 29:521-526, 1967.

Alvares, A.P., Schilling, G., Levin, W., and Kuntzman, R.: Alteration of the microsomal hemoprotein by 3-methylcholanthrene: Effects of ethionine and actinomycin D.J. Pharmacol. Exp. Ther. 163:417-424, 1968.

Alves, C.N. and Carlini, E.A.: Effects of acute and chronic administration of Cannabis sativa extract on the mouse-killing behavior of rats. Life Sci. 13:75-85, 1973.

Appel, J.B. and Freedman, D.X.: Tolerance and cross-tolerance among psychotomimetic drugs, Psychopharmacologia 13:267-274, 1968.

Azmitia, E.C., Jr., Hess, P., and Reis, D.: Tryptophane hydroxylase changes in midbrain of the rat after chronic morphine administration. Life Sci. 9:633-637, 1970.

Beleslin, D. and Polak, R.L.: Depression by morphine and chloralose of acetylcholine from the cat's brain. J. Physiol. (London) 177:411-419, 1965.

Berkowitz, B. and Spector, S.: Evidence for active immunity to morphine in mice. Science 178:1290-1292, 1972.

Bhargava, H.N., Afifi, A.H., and Way, E.L.: Effect of chemical sympathectomy on morphine antinociception and tolerance in rats. Fed. Proc. 32:687, 1973.

Birmingham, M.K., Oliver, J.T., Possanza, G.J., Lanlois, Y., and Stewart, P.B.: Reduction in blood pressure of hypertensive rats by marihuana extract and tetrahydrocannabinol. Fed. Proc. 31:986, 1972.

Börner, U. and Abbott, S.: New observations in the metabolism of morphine. The formation of codeine from morphine in man. Experientia 29:180-181, 1973.

Bousquet, W.F.: Pharmacology and biochemistry of drug metabolism. J. Pharm. Sci. 51:297-309, 1962.

Burns, J.J. and Conney, A.H.: Therapeutic implications of drug metabolism. Sem. Hematol. 1:375-400, 1964.

Burns, J.J. and Shore, P.A.: Biochemical effects of drugs. Ann. Rev. Pharmacol. 1:79-104, 1961.

Campo, R.A.: Development of tolerance in pigeons to behavioral effects of a new benzopyran derivative. J. Pharmacol. Exp. Ther. 184:521-527, 1973.

Carmichael, F.J. and Israel, Y.: In vitro inhibitory effects of narcotic analgesics and other psychotropic drugs on the active uptake of norepinephrine in mouse brain tissue. J. Pharmacol. Exp. Ther. 186:253-260, 1973.

Castles, T.R., Campbell, S., Gouge, R., and Lee, C.C.: Nucleic acid synthesis in brains from rats tolerant to morphine analgesia. J. Pharmacol. Exp. Ther. *181*:399-406, 1972.

Castles, T.R., Bristow, R.L., and Hodgson, J.R.: Chromatin template activity during morphine-induced analgesia and the development of analgesic tolerance. Fed. Proc. *32*:587, 1973.

Catravas, G.N., Cohan, S.I., McHale, C.G., and Abbott, J.R.: Morphine-induced changes in the activity of enzymes in specific brain areas of the tolerant rat. Fed. Proc. *32*:687, 1973.

Cheney, D.L. and Costa, E.: Narcotic tolerance and dependence and serotonin turnover. Science *178*:647, 1972.

Cheney, D. and Goldstein, A.: The effect of *p*-chlorophenylalanine on opiate-induced running, analgesia, tolerance and physical dependence in mice. J. Pharmacol. Exp. Ther. *177*:309-315, 1971.

Cheney, D.L., Goldstein, A., and Sheehan, P.: Rate of development and reversibility of brain tolerance and physical dependence in mice treated with opiates. Fed. Proc. *29*:685, 1970.

Cheney, D., Goldstein, A., Algeri, S., and Costa, E.: Narcotic tolerance and dependence: Lack of relationship with serotonin turnover in the brain. Science *171*:1169-1170, 1971.

Clouet, D.H.: Biochemical responses to narcotic drugs in the nervous system and in other tissues. Int. Rev. Neurobiol. *11*:99-128, 1968.

Clouet, D.H. (Ed.): Narcotic Drugs: Biochemical Pharmacology. New York, Plenum Press, 1971.

Clouet, D.H. and Neidle, A.: The effect of morphine on the transport and metabolism of intracisternally-injected leucine in the rat. J. Neurochem. *17*:1069-1074, 1970.

Clouet, D.H. and Ratner, M.: The effect of altering liver microsomal N-demethylase activity on the development of tolerance to morphine in rats. Biochem. Pharmacol. *144*:362-372, 1964.

Clouet, D.H. and Ratner, M.: Catecholamine biosynthesis in brains of rats treated with morphine. Science *168*:854-856, 1970.

Cochin, J.: Biochemical aspects of tolerance. Seevers Symposium, Univ. Mich. Med. Center J. *36*:209-248, 1970a.

Cochin, J.: Possible mechanisms in the development of tolerance. Fed. Proc. *29*:19-27, 1970b.

Cochin, J.: Role of possible immune mechanisms in the development of tolerance. Narcotic Drugs: Biochemical Pharmacology. Ed. D.H. Clouet, New York, Plenum Press, 1971, pp. 432-448.

Cochin, J.: Some aspects of tolerance to the narcotic analgesics. Drug Addiction. Experimental Pharmacology. Eds. Singh, J.M., Miller, L., and Lal, H., New York, Futura Publishing Company, 1972, pp. 365-375.

Cochin, J. and Kornetsky, C.: Development of tolerance to morphine in the rat after single and multiple injections. J. Pharmacol. Exp. Ther. *145*:1-10, 1964.

Cochin, J. and Kornetsky, C.: Factors in blood of morphine tolerant animals that attenuate or enhance effects of morphine in non-tolerant animals. The Addictive State. Ed. Wickler, A., Baltimore, Williams & Wilkins, 1968, 268-279.

Cochin, J. and Mushlin, B.E.: The role of dose-interval in the development of tolerance to morphine. Fed. Proc. *29*:685, 1970.

Cohen, G.M., Peterson, D.W., and Mannering, G.J.: Interactions of Δ⁹-tetrahydro-cannabinol with the hepatic microsomal drug metabolizing system. Life Sci. Part I *10*:1207-1215, 1971.

Cohen, M., Keats, A.S., Krivoy, W., and Ungar, G.: Effect of actinomycin-D on morphine tolerance. Proc. Soc. Exp. Biol. Med. *119*:381-384, 1965.

Collier, H.O.J.: A general theory of the genesis of drug dependence by induction of receptors. Nature (London) *205*:181-182, 1965.

Colton, T., Gosselin, R.E., and Smith, R.P.: The tolerance of coffee drinkers to caffeine. Clin. Pharmacol. Ther. *9*:31-39, 1967.

Conney, A.H.: Pharmacological implications of microsomal enzyme induction. Pharmacol. Rev. *19*:317-366, 1967.

Conney, A.H.: Drug metabolism and therapeutics. Sem. Med. Beth Israel Hosp., Boston *280*:653-660, 1969a.

Conney, A.H.: Microsomal enzyme induction by drugs. Pharmacol. Phys. *3*:1-6, 1969b.

Cox, B.M. and Osman, O.H.: The role of protein synthesis inhibition in the prevention of morphine tolerance. Proc. Brit. Pharmacol. Soc. *35*:373-374p, 1969.

Cox, B.M. and Osman, O.H.: Inhibition of the development of tolerance to morphine in rats by drugs which inhibit ribonucleic acid or protein synthesis. Brit. J. Pharmacol. *38*:157-170, 1970.

Cox, B.M., Ginsburg, M., and Osman, O.H.: Acute tolerance to narcotic analgesic drugs in rats. Brit. J. Pharmacol. Chemother. *33*:245-246, 1968.

Datta, R.K. and Antopol, W.: Inhibitory effect of chronic administration of morphine on RNA polymerase activities of mouse liver and brain nuclei. Toxicol. Appl. Pharmacol. *25*:71-76, 1973.

Davis, V.E. and Walsh, M.J.: Alcohol, amines and alkaloids: A possible biochemical basis for alcohol addiction. Science *167*:1005-1007, 1970.

Davis, W., Moreton, J., King, W., and Pace, H.: Marihuana on locomotor activity: Biphasic effect and tolerance development. Res. Commun. Chem. Pathol. Pharmacol. *3*:29-35, 1972.

Dayton, P.G. and Perel, J.M.: Physiological and physiocochemical bases of drug interactions in man. Ann. N.Y. Acad. Sci. *179*:67-87, 1971.

DeCato, L., Jr. and Adler, F.L.: Neutralization of morphine activity by antibody. Res. Commun. Chem. Pathol. Pharmacol. *5*:775-788, 1973.

Devenyi, P. and Wilson, M.: Barbiturate abuse and addiction and their relationship to alcohol and alcoholism. Can. Med. Ass. J. *104*:215-218, 1971.

Dewey, W.L., McMillan, D.E., Harris, L.S., and Turk, R.F.: Distribution of radioactivity in brain of tolerant and nontolerant pigeons treated with ^{3}H- Δ^9-tetrahydrocannabinol. Biochem. Pharmacol. *22*:399-405, 1973.

Dole, V.P.: Biochemistry of addiction. Annu. Rev. Biochem. *39*:821-840, 1970.

Domino, E.F.: Sites of action of some central nervous system depressants. Ann. Rev. Pharmacol. *2*:215-250, 1962.

Eddy, N.B., Halbach, H., Isbell, H., and Seevers, M.H.: Drug dependence: Its significance and characteristics. Bull. World Health Organization *32*:721-733, 1965.

Eidelberg, E. and Schwartz, A.: Possible mechanisms of action of morphine on brain. Nature (London) *225*:1152-1153, 1970.

Ellison, T., Okun, R., Silverman, A., and Siegel, M.: Metabolic fate of amphetamine in the cat during development of tolerance. Arch. Int. Pharmacodyn. Ther. *190*:135-149, 1971.

Estabrook, R.W., Gillette, J.R., and Leibman, K.C. (Eds.): A report of the second international symposium on microsomes and drug oxidations. *In* Drug Metabolism and Disposition. Baltimore, Williams & Wilkins Co., Vol. 1, Jan/Feb, 1973.

Feinberg, M.P. and Cochin, J.: Inhibition of development of tolerance to morphine by cycloheximide. Biochem. Pharmacol. *21*:3082-3085, 1972.

Ferguson, R.K. and Mitchell, C.L.: Pain as a factor in the development of tolerance to morphine analgesia in man. Clin. Pharmacol. Ther. *10*:372-382, 1969.

Ferraro, D. and Grilly, D.: Lack of tolerance to Δ⁹-tetrahydrocannabinol in chimpanzees. Science *179*:490-492, 1973.

Florez, J., Delgado, G., and Armijo, J.A.: Brain amines and development of acute tolerance to and dependence on morphine in the respiratory center of decerebrate cats. Neuropharmacology *12*:355-362, 1973.

Forrest, W.H., Jr., Brown, C.R., Mahler, D.L., Katz, J., Schroff, P., Defalque, R., Brown, B., and James, K.: The evaluation of morphine and dexamphetamine combinations for analgesia. Clin. Pharmacol. Ther. *14*:132, 1973.

Frey, H.H. and Kampmann, E.: Tolerance to anticonvulsant drugs. Acta Pharmacol. Toxicol. *22*:159-171, 1965.

Friedler, G., Bhargava, H., Quock, R., and Way, E.: The effect of 6-hydroxydopamine on morphine tolerance and physical dependence. J. Pharmacol. Exp. Ther. *183*:49-55, 1972.

Fujita, T., Shoeman, D.W., and Mannering, G.J.: Differences in P-450 cytochromes from livers of rats treated with phenobarbital and with 3-methylcholanthrene. J. Biol. Chem. *248*:2192-2201, 1973.

Gebhart, G. and Mitchell, C.: Further studies on the development of tolerance to the analgesic effect of morphine: The role played by the cylinder in the hot plate testing procedure. Arch. Int. Pharmacodyn. Ther. *191*:96-103, 1971.

Giarman, N.J. and Freidman, D.X.: Biochemical aspects of the action of psychotomimetic drugs. Pharmacol. Rev. *17*:1-25, 1965.

Goldstein, A.: Mini Review—Opiate Receptors. Life Sci. *14*:615-623, 1974.

Goldstein, A. and Judson, B.A.: Alcohol dependence and opiate dependence: lack of relationship in mice. Science *172*:290-292, 1971.

Goldstein, A. and Kaizer, S.: Psychotropic effects of caffeine in man. III. A questionnaire survey of coffee drinking and its effects in a group of housewives. Clin. Pharmacol. Ther. *10*:477-488, 1969.

Goldstein, A., Warren, R., and Kaizer, S.: Psychotropic effects of caffeine in man. I. Individual differences in sensitivity to caffeine-induced wakefulness. J. Pharmacol. Exp. Ther. *149*:156-159, 1965.

Goldstein, A., Aronow, L., and Kalman, S.M.: Principles of Drug Action. New York, Harper and Row, 1968.

Goldstein, A., Kaizer, S., and Whitby, O.: Psychotropic effects of caffeine in man. IV. Quantitative and qualitative differences associated with habituation to coffee. Clin. Pharmacol. Ther. *10*:489-497, 1969.

Goldstein, A., Sheehan, P., and Goldstein, J.: Unsuccessful attempts to transfer morphine tolerance and passive avoidance by brain extracts. Nature (London) *233*:126-129, 1971.

Goodman, L.S. and Gilman, A. (Eds.): The Pharmacological Basis of Therapeutics, 4th Ed. New York, Macmillan, 1970.

Gregory, I.: Alcoholism and drug addiction. Minn. Med. *44*:445-453, 1961.

Gunne, L.M., Jonsson, J., and Fuxe, K.: Effects of morphine intoxication on brain catecholamine neurons. Eur. J. Pharm. *5*:338-342, 1969.

Hahn, D.L. and Goldstein, A.: Amounts and turnover rates of brain proteins in morphine-tolerant mice. J. Neurochem. *18*:1887-1893, 1971.

Ham, M. ten, and Noordwijk, Van J.: Lack of tolerance to the effect of two tetrahydrocannabinols on aggressiveness. Psychopharmacologia *29*:171-176, 1973.

Ham, M. ten, Tokelaar, E.M., and Koomen, J.M.: Influence of two tetrahydrocannabinols on the activity of biotransformation enzymes. Paper presented to the 30th

Congress of the International Council on Alcohol and Drug Dependence, Amsterdam, 1972.

Hatfield, G., Miya, T., and Bousquet, W.: Ethanol tolerance and ethanol drug interactions in the rat. Toxicol. Appl. Pharmacol. 23:459-469, 1972.

Haubrich, D.R. and Blake, D.E.: Effect of acute and chronic administration of morphine on the metabolism of brain serotonin in rats. Fed. Proc. 28:793, 1969.

Herman, Z.S., Trzeciak, H., Chrusciel, T.L., Kmieciak-Kolada, K., Drybanski, A., and Sokola, A.: The influence of prolonged amphetamine treatment and amphetamine withdrawal on brain biogenic amine content and behavior in the rat. Psychopharmacologia 21:74-81, 1971.

Ho, B.T., Estevez, V.S., and Englert, L.F.: Effect of repeated administration on the metabolism of (-)- Δ^9-tetrahydrocannabinols in rats. Res. Commun. Chem. Pathol. Pharmacol. 5:215-218, 1973a.

Ho, B.T., Taylor, D., and Englert, L.F.: The effect of repeated administration of (-)- Δ^9-tetrahydrocannabinol on the biosynthesis of brain amines. Res. Commun. Chem. Pathol. Pharmacol. 5:851-854, 1973b.

Ho, I., Loh, H., and Way, E.: Effect of cyclic AMP on morphine analgesia tolerance and physical dependence. Nature (London) 238:397-398, 1972a.

Ho, I., Lu, S., Stolman, S., Loh, H., and Way, E.: Influence of p-chlorophenylalanine on morphine tolerance and physical dependence and regional brain serotonin turnover studies in morphine tolerant-dependent mice. J. Pharmacol. Exp. Ther. 182:155-165, 1972b.

Ho, I., Loh, H., and Way, E.: Influence of 5,6-dihydroxytryptamine on morphine tolerance and physical dependence. Eur. J. Pharmacol. 21:331-336, 1973.

Hollister, L.E.: Marihuana in man: 3 years later. Science 172:21-29, 1971.

Hollister, L.E. and Tinklenberg, J.R.: Subchronic oral doses of marihuana extract. Psychopharmacologia 29:247-252, 1973.

Hughes, J., Smith, T., Morgan, B., and Fothergill, L.: Purification and properties of enkephalin—The possible ligand for the morphine receptor. Life Sciences 16(12):1753-1758, 1975.

Imai, Y. and Sato, R.: Studies on the substrate interactions with P-450 in drug hydroxylation by liver microsomes. J. Biochem. (Tokyo) 62:239-249, 1967.

Isbell, H., Gorodetzsky, C.W., Jasinsky, D., Claussen, U., Spulak, F.V. and Korte, F.: Effects of (-)- Δ^9-tetrahydrocannabinol in man. Psychopharmacologia 11:184-188, 1967.

Iwata, H., Watanabe, K., and Matsui, Y.: Plasma copper levels and their significance in morphine analgesia and tolerance. Eur. J. Pharmacol. 11:298-302, 1970.

Jones, R.T. and Stone, G.C.: Psychological studies of marihuana and alcohol in man. Psychopharmacologia 18:108-117, 1970.

Kalant, H.: Some recent physiological and biochemical investigations on alcohol and alcoholism—a review. Quart. J. Stud. Alcohol 23:52-93, 1962.

Kalant, H., Leblanc, A., and Gibbins, R.: Tolerance to, and dependence on, some non-opiate psychotropic drugs. Pharmacol. Rev. 23:135-191, 1971.

Kaneto, H. and Mellett, L.B.: The intracellular binding of N-methyl-C^{14}-morphine in brain tissue of rat. Pharmacologist 2:98, 1960.

Karbowski, M.J.: Lack of effects of cycloheximide on tolerance development to a stimulatory effect of morphine on mice. Fed. Proc. 32:687, 1973.

Kayan, S. and Mitchell, C.: Studies on tolerance development to morphine: Effect of the dose-interval on the development of single dose tolerance. Arch. Int. Pharmacodyn. Ther. 199:407-414, 1972a.

Kayan, S. and Mitchell, C.: The role of the dose-interval on the development of tolerance to morphine. Arch. Int. Pharmacodyn. Ther. *198*:238-241, 1972b.

Kerr, F.W.L. and Pozuelo, J.: Suppression of physical dependence and induction of hypersensitivity to morphine by stereotoxic hypothalamic lesions in addicted rats. Proc. Mayo Clin. *46*:653-665, 1971a.

Kerr, F.W.L. and Pozuelo, J.: Suppression or reduction of morphine dependence in rats by discrete stereotoxic lesions in the hypothalamus. Fed. Proc. *30*:375, 1971b.

Kerr, F.W.L. and Pozuelo, J.: Suppression of physical dependence and induction of hypersensitivity to morphine by stereotoxic hypothalamic lesions in addicted rats and a new theory of addiction. Drug Addiction: Experimental Pharmacology. Eds. Singh, J.M., Miller, L., and Lal, H., New York, Futura Publishing Company, 1972, p. 343-364.

Khanna, J.M., Kalant, H. and Lin, G.: Significance *in vivo* of the increase in microsomal ethanol-oxidizing system after chronic administration of ethanol, phenobarbital and chorcyclizine. Biochem. Pharmacol. *21*:2215-2226, 1972.

Kiplinger, G.F. and Clift, J.W.: Pharmacological properties of morphine-potentiating serum obtained from morphine tolerant dogs and men. J. Pharmacol. Exp. Ther. *146*:139-146, 1964.

Klaassen, C.D.: Ethanol metabolism in rats after microsomal metabolizing enzyme induction. Proc. Soc. Exp. Biol. Med. *132*:1099-1102, 1969.

Klaassen, C.D. and Plaa, G.L.: Studies on the mechanism of phenobarbital-enhanced sulfobromophthalein disappearance. J. Pharmacol. Exp. Ther. *161*:361-366, 1968.

Knapp, S. and Mandell, A.J.: Narcotic Drugs: Effects on the serotonin biosynthetic systems of the brain. Science *177*:1209-1211, 1972.

Knoll, J. and Vizzi, E.S.: Cross-tolerance between *para*-bromo-methamphetamine and LSD-25. Pharmacology *4*:278-286, 1970.

Kornetsky, C. and Bain, G.: Morphine: Single-dose tolerance. Science *162*:1011-1012, 1968.

Kosterlitz, H.W. and Hughes, J.: Some thoughts on the significance of enkephalin, the endogenous ligand. Life Sciences *17*(1):91-96, 1975.

LaDu, B.N., Mandel, H.G., and Way, E.L. (Eds.): Fundamentals of Drug Metabolism and Drug Disposition. Baltimore, Williams & Wilkins, 1971.

LeBlanc, A.E., Kalant, H., Gibbons, R.J., and Berman, H.D.: Acquisition and loss of tolerance to ethanol by the rat. J. Pharmacol. Exp. Ther. *168*:244-250, 1969.

LeBlanc, A.E., Gibbons, R.J., and Kalant, H.: Behavioral augmentation of tolerance to ethanol in the rat. Psychopharmacologia *30*:117-122, 1973.

Lemberger, L., Silberstein, S., Axelrod, J., and Kopin, I.: Marihuana: Studies on the disposition and metabolism of delta-9-tetrahydrocannabinol in man. Science *170*:1320-1322, 1970.

Lemberger, L., Tamarken, N.R., Axelrod, J., and Kopin, I.J.: Delta-9-tetrahydrocannabinol: Metabolism and disposition in long-term marihuana smokers. Science *173*:72-74, 1971.

Lemberger, L., Weiss, J.L., Watanabe, A.M., Gallanter, I.M., Wyatt, R.J., and Cardon, P.V.: Delta-9-tetrahydrocannabinol: Temporal correlation of the psychologic effects and blood levels after various routes of administration. N. Engl. J. Med. *286*:685-688, 1972.

Lewander, T.: A mechanism for the development of tolerance to amphetamine in rats. Psychopharmacologia *21*:17-31, 1971.

Lewis, S.C., Forney, R.B., and Brown, D.J.: Absence of tolerance to the hypotensive effects of Δ⁹-tetrahydrocannabinol in hypertensive rats. Tox. Appl. Pharmacol. 29(1):78, 1974 (abstract).

Lieber, C., and DeCarli, L.: Hepatic microsomal ethanol-oxidizing system. *In vitro* characteristics and adaptive properties *in vivo*. J. Biol. Chem. 245:2505-2512, 1970.

Lieber, C.S., Teschke, R., Hasumura, Y., and DeCarli, L.M.: Differences in hepatic and metabolic changes after acute and chronic alcohol consumption. Fed. Proc. 34:2060-2074, 1975.

Loh, H., Shen, F., and Way, E.: Inhibition of morphine tolerance and physical dependence development and brain serotonin synthesis by cycloheximide. Biochem. Pharmacol. 18:2711-2721, 1969.

Lomax, P.: Acute tolerance to the hypothermic effect of marihuana in the rat. Res. Commun. Chem. Pathol. Pharmacol. 2:159-167, 1971.

Lomax, P. and Kirkpatrick, W.E.: The effect of N-allylmorphine on the development of acute tolerance to the analgesic and hypothermic effects of morphine in the rat. Med. Pharmacol. Exp. 16:165-170, 1967.

Lu, T- C., Ho, B.T., and McIsaac, W.M.: Effects of repeated administration of DL-amphetamine and methamphetamine on tolerance to hyperactivity. Experientia 28:1461, 1972.

Maitre, L., Stachelin, M., and Bein, H.J.: Effect of an extract of *Cannabis* and of some cannabinols on catecholamine metabolism in rat brain and heart. Agents and Actions 1:136-143, 1970.

Mallov, S., and Baesl, T.J.: Effect of ethanol on rats of elimination and metabolism of zoxazolamine, hexobarbital and warfarin sodium in the rat. Biochem. Pharmacol. 21:1667-1678, 1972.

Mannering, G.J., Tephly, T.R., and Parks, R.E., Jr.: Metabolism of methanol. Univ. Minn. Med. Bull. 34:190-192, 1963.

Marshall, I., and Grahame-Smith, D.G.: Evidence against a role of brain 5-hydroxytryptamine in the development of physical dependence upon morphine in mice. J. Pharmacol. Exp. Ther. 179:634-641, 1971.

Martin, W.R. and Eades, C.G.: The action of tryptamine on the dog spinal cord and its relationship to the agonistic actions of LSD-like psychotogens. Psychopharmacologia 17:242-257, 1970.

Martin, W.R., and Eades, C.G.: Cross tolerance to tryptamine in the LSD tolerant dog. Psychopharmacologia 27:93-98, 1972.

Maruyama, Y., Hayashi, G., Smits, S., and Takemori, A.: Studies on the relationship between 5-hydroxytryptamine turnover in brain and tolerance and physical dependence in mice. J. Pharmacol. Exp. Ther. 178:20-29, 1971.

Masur, J., Martz, R.M.W., and Carlini, E.: Effects of acute and chronic administration of *Cannabis sativa* and (-)-delta-9-transtetrahydrocannabinol on the behavior of rats in an open field arena. Psychopharmacologia 19:388-397, 1971.

Matsuda, K.: Experimental studies on the effective procedure to inhibit the development of tolerance to and dependence on morphine. Arzneimettel Forsch. (Drug Res.) 20:1596-1604, 1970.

Mayer, D., and Hayes, R.: Narcotic and Stimulation-Produced Analgesia. Fed. Proc. 33:502, 1974 (abstract No. 1644).

McMillan, D.E., Harris, L.S., Frankenheim, J.M., and Kennedy, J.S.: 1- Δ⁹-Tetrahydrocannabinol in pigeons: Tolerance to the behavioral effects. Science 169:501-503, 970.

McMillan, D.E., Dewey, W.L., and Harris, L.S.: Characteristics of tetrahydrocannabinol tolerance. Ann. N.Y. Acad. Sci. *191*:83-99, 1971.

McMillan, D.E., Dewey, W.L., Turk, R.F., Harris, L.S., and McNeil, J.H., Jr.: Blood levels of ³H- Δ⁹-tetrahydrocannabinol and its metabolites in tolerant and non-tolerant pigeons. Biochem. Pharmacol. *22*:383-397, 1973.

Mechoulam, R.: Marihuana chemistry. Science *108*:1159-1166, 1970.

Mezey, E., Potter, J.J., and Reed, W.D.: Ethanol oxidation by a component of liver microsomes rich in cytochrome P-450. J. Biol. Chem. *248*:1183-1187, 1973.

Misra, A.L., Mitchell, C.L., and Woods, L.A.: Persistence of morphine in central nervous system of rats after a single injection and its bearing on tolerance. Nature (London) *232*:48-50, 1971a.

Misra, P., Lefeure, A., Ishii, H., Rubin, E., and Lieber, C.: Increase of ethanol, meprobamate, and pentobarbital metabolism after chronic ethanol administration in man and in rats. Amer. J. Med. *51*:346-351, 1971b.

Morrison, C.F. and Stephenson, J.A.: The occurrence of tolerance to a central depressant effect of nicotine. Brit. J. Pharmacol. *45*:151-156, 1972.

Mulé, S.J.: Morphine and the incorporation of P_i^{32} into brain phospholipids of non-tolerant, tolerant, and abstinent guinea pigs. J. Pharmacol. Exp. Ther. *156*:92-100, 1967.

Mulé, S.J. and Woods, L.A.: Distribution of N-¹⁴C-methyl labelled morphine. I. In central nervous system of nontolerant and tolerant dogs. J. Pharmacol. Exp. Ther. *136*:232-241, 1962.

Mulé, S.J., Redman, C.M., and Flesher, J.W.: Intracellular disposition of H³-morphine in the brain and liver of nontolerant and tolerant guinea pigs. J. Pharmacol. Exp. Ther. *157*:459-471, 1967.

Murphree, H.B.: Clinical pharmacology of potent analgesics. Clin. Pharmacol. Ther. *3*:473-504, 1962.

Myers, S.A., Craves, F.B., Caldwell, D.F., and Loh, H.F.: Inhalation induced tolerance and physical dependence: The hazard of opiate suffused marihuana. Milit. Med. *137*:431-433, 1972.

Nahas, G.G.: Marihuana-Deceptive Weed. New York, Raven Press Publishers, 1973.

Nahas, G., Schwartz, I., Palacek, J., and Zagury, D.: Tolérance au Δ⁹-tetrahydrocannabinol chez le rat hypertendu. C.R. Acad. Sci. *275*:1931-1932, 1972.

Nahas, G.G., Schwartz, I.W., Adamec, J., and Manger, W.M.: Tolerance to delta-9-tetrahydrocannabinol in the spontaneously hypertensive rat. Proc. Soc. Exp. Biol. Med. *142*:58-60, 1973a.

Nahas, G. Schwartz, I., Palacek, J. and Zagury, D.: Effêt d'un inhibiteur de la réponse immunogène sur le developpement de la tolérance au delta 9 tétrahydrocannabinol. C.R. Acad. Sci. *276*:667-668, 1973b.

Naito, K. and Kuriyama, K.: Effect of morphine administration on adenyl cyclase and 3', 5'-cyclic nucleotide phosphodiesterase activities in the brain. Japan J. Pharmacol. *23*:274-276, 1973.

Neff, N.H., Tozer, T.N., and Brodie, B.B.: Application of steady-state kinetics to studies of the transfer of 5-hydroxyindoleacetic acid from brain to plasma. J. Pharmacol. Exp. Ther. *158*:214-218, 1967.

Newman, L., Lutz, M., Gould, M., and Domino, E.: Δ⁹-Tetrahydrocannabinol and ethyl alcohol: Evidence for cross-tolerance in the rat. Science *175*:1022-1023, 1972.

Ng, L.K.Y., Chase, T.N., Colburn, R.W., and Kopin, I.J.: L-Dopa-induced release of cerebral monoamines. Science *170*:77-78, 1970.

Ohnhaus, E.E., Thorgeirsson, S.S., Davies, D.S., and Breckinridge, A.: Changes in liver blood flow during enzyme induction. Biochem. Pharmacol. *20*:2561-2570, 1971.

Oka, T., Nozaki, M., and Hosoya, E.: Effects of p-chlorophenylalanine and cholinergic antagonists on body temperature changes induced by the administration of morphine to nontolerant and morphine-tolerant rats. J. Pharmacol. Exp. Ther. 180:136-143, 1972.

Parli, C.J. and Mannering, G.J.: Induction of drug metabolism. IV. Relative abilities of polycyclic hydrocarbons to increase levels of microsomal 3-methyl-4-methylaminoazobenzene N-demethylase activity and cytochrome P-450. Mol. Pharmacol. 6:178-183, 1970.

Parli, C.J., Peck, F.B., Jr., and Lee, N.: In vivo metabolism studies on 5-(3,4-dichlorophenyl)-5-ethyl-barbituric acid (dichlorophenobarbital). Life Sci. 11:623-630, 1972.

Pasternak, G.W., Goodman, R., and Snyder, S.H.: An endogenous morphine-like factor in mammalian brain. Life Sciences 16(12):1765-1769, 1975.

Pert, A., and Yaksh, T.: Sites of morphine induced analgesia in the primate brain: Relation to pain pathways. Brain Res. 80:135-140, 1974.

Pert, C.B. and Snyder, S.H.: Opiate receptor: Demonstration in nervous tissue. Science 179:1011-1014, 1973.

Pleuvry, B.J.: Cross tolerance between methylamphetamine and morphine in the mouse. J. Pharm. Pharmacol. 23:969-970, 1971.

Raskin, N. and Sokoloff, L.: Adaptation of alcohol dehydrogenase activity in brain to chronic ethanol ingestion. Neurology (Minneapolis) 20:391-392, 1970.

Rech, R.H. and Tilson, H.A.: Effects of p-chlorophenylalanine (p-CPA) on morphine analgesia and development of tolerance and dependence in two strains of rats. Pharmacologist 15:202, 1973.

Redmond, G. and Cohen, G.: Induction of liver acetaldehyde dehydrogenase: Possible role in ethanol tolerance after exposure to barbiturate. Science 171:387-389, 1971.

Remmer, H.: Drugs as activators of drug enzymes. Proc. First Intern. Pharmacol. Mtg. 6:235-256, 1962a.

Remmer, H.: Drug tolerance. Ciba Foundation Symposium on Enzymes and Drug Action. Boston, Little Brown and Co, 1962b, pp. 276-300.

Remmer, H.: Enzymatic mechanisms of drug tolerance. Drug Addiction: Experimental Pharmacology. Eds. Singh, J.M., Miller, L., and Lal, H., New York, Futura Publishing Company, 1972, pp. 377-391.

Reynolds, A.K. and Randall, L.O.: Morphine and allied drugs. Toronto, University of Toronto Press, 1957.

Richter, J. and Goldstein, A.: Tolerance to opioid narcotics, II. Cellular tolerance to levorphanol in mouse brain. Proc. Nat. Acad. Sci. 66:944-951, 1970.

Ringle, D.A. and Herndon, B.L.: In vitro morphine binding by sera from morphine-treated rabbits. J. Immunol. 109:174-175, 1972.

Roe, R., Börner, U., Abbott, S., Scott, R., and Becker, C.: Altered morphine metabolism in man: An indicator of the duration of addiction. Clin. Res. 21:472, 1973.

Ross, D.H. and Cardenas, H.L.: Opiates and alcohol: evidence for a common biochemical action. Fed. Proc. 34:3171, 1975 (abstract).

Rubin, E. and Lieber, C.S.: Alcoholism, alcohol and drugs. Science 172:1097-1102, 1971.

Rubin, E., Lieber, C.S., Alvares, P., Levin, W., and Kuntzman, R.: Ethanol binding to hepatic microsomes—its increase by ethanol consumption. Biochem. Pharmacol. 20:229-231, 1971.

Ryan, J.J., Parker, C.W., and Williams, R.C.: Gamma-globulin binding of morphine in heroine addicts. J. Lab. Clin. Med. 80:155-164, 1972.

Ryan, J.J., Parker, C.W., and Williams, R.C.: Serum binding of morphine in heroine addicts. Clin. Res. 19:182, 1971.

Schechter, M.D. and Rosecrans, J.A.: Behavioral tolerance to an effect of nicotine in the rat. Arch. Int. Pharmacodyn. 195:52-56, 1972.

Schechter, P., Lovenberg, W., and Sjoerdsma, A.: Dissociation of morphine tolerance and dependence from brain serotonin synthesis rate in mice. Biochem. Pharmacol. 21:751-753, 1972.

Schou, J., Worm, K., Morkholdt A.J., Nielsen, E., and Steentoft, A.: Studies on the metabolism and disposition of delta-9-tetrahydrocannabinol (delta-9-THC) in Danish pigs before and after prolonged intravenous administration of delta-9-THC. Fifth Int. Cong. Pharmacol. San Francisco, Calif. 1972, abstract 1226.

Seevers, M.: Morphine and ethanol physical dependence: A critique of a hypothesis. Science 170:1113-1115, 1970.

Shen, F., Loh, H., and Way, E.: Brain serotonin turnover in morphine tolerant and dependent mice. J. Pharmacol. Exp. Ther. 175:427-434, 1970.

Sherman, A.D. and Mitchell, C.L.: Influence of naloxone and tolerance on citric acid cycle response to morphine and pain. Neuropharmacology 12:363-366, 1973.

Shideman, F.E.: Clinical pharmacology of hypnotics and sedatives. Clin. Pharmacol. Ther. 3:313-344, 1961.

Shuster, L.: Tolerance and physical dependence. Narcotic Drugs: Biochemical pharmacology, Ed. Clouet, D.H., New York, Plenum Press, 1971, pp. 408-423.

Silva, M.T.A. and Carlini, E.A.: Lack of cross-tolerance in rats among (-)- Δ⁹-trans-tetrahydrocannabinol (Δ⁹-THC) Cannabis extract, mescaline and lysergic acid diethylamide (LSD 25). Psychopharmacologia 13:310-332. 1968.

Singer, A.J. (Ed.): Marihuana: Chemistry, pharmacology, and pattern of social use. Ann. N.Y. Acad. Sci. 191:1-269, 1971.

Singh, H.: Factors affecting the development of tolerance to pentobarbital and thiopental. Drug Addiction: Experimental pharmacology, (Eds.) Singh, J.M., Miller, L., and Lal, H., New York, Futura Publishing Co., 1972, pp. 235-246.

Smith, A., Karmin, M., and Garitt, J.: Blocking effect of puromycin, ethanol, and chloroform on the development of tolerance to an opiate. Biochem. Pharm. 15:1877-1879, 1966.

Smith, C., Villarreal, J., Bednarczyk, J., and Sheldon, M.: Tolerance to morphine-induced increases in (¹⁴C) catecholamine synthesis in mouse brain. Science 170:1106-1108, 1970.

Smits, S.E. and Takemori, A.E.: Lack of transfer of morphine tolerance by administration of rat cerebral homogenates. Proc. Soc. Exp. Biol. Med. 127:1167-1171, 1968.

Sofia, R.D. and Barry, H.: Depressant effect of delta-1-tetrahydrocannabinol enhanced by inhibition of its metabolism. Eur. J. Pharmacol. 13:134-137, 1970.

Sofia, R.D., Dixit, B.N., and Barry, H.: The effect of Δ⁹-tetrahydrocannabinol on serotonin metabolism in the rat brain. Life Sci. 10:425-436, 1971.

Sparber, S.B. and Tilson, H.A.: Tolerance and cross-tolerance to mescaline and amphetamine as a function of central and peripheral administration. Psychopharmacologia 23:220-230, 1972.

Spoerlin, M.T. and Scrafini, J.: Effects of time and 8-azaguanine on the development of morphine tolerance. Life Sci. 6:1549-1564, 1967.

Stevenson, I.H., and Turnbull, M.J.: Methods for investigating barbiturate tolerance. Brit. J. Pharmacol. 41:422, 1971.

Takagi, H. and Kuriki, H.: Suppressive effect of tetrabenazine on the development of tolerance to morphine and its reversal by DOPA. Int. J. Neuropharm. 8:195-196, 1969.

Takagi, H. and Nakama, M.: Effect of morphine and nalorphine on the content of dopamine in mouse brain. Jap. J. Pharmacol. *16*:483-484, 1966.

Terenius, L. and Wahlström, A.: Morphine-like ligand for opiate receptors in human CSF. Life Sciences *16*(12):1759-1764, 1975.

Teschke, R., Hasumura, Y., Joly, J.G., Ishii, H., and Lieber, C.S.: Microsomal ethanol-oxidizing system (MEOS): Purification and properties of a rat liver system free of catalase and alcohol dehydrogenase. Biochem. Biophys. Res. Commun. *49*:1187-1193, 1972.

Thurman, R.G., McKenna, W.R., Brentzel, H.J., Jr., and Hesse, S.: Significant pathways of hepatic ethanol metabolism. Fed. Proc. *34*:2075-2081, 1975.

Tilson, H.A. and Sparber, S.B.: Differences in tolerance to mescaline produced by peripheral and direct central administration. Psychopharmacologia *19*:313-323, 1971.

Tilson, H., Stolman, S., and Rech, R.: Attempts to transfer tolerance in rats treated chronically with morphine. Res. Commun. Chem. Pathol. Pharmacol. *4*:581-586, 1972.

Tirri, R.: Transfer of induced tolerance to morphine and promazine by brain homogenate. Experientia *23*:278, 1967.

Tobon, F. and Mezey, E.: Effects of ethanol administration on hepatic ethanol and drug metabolizing enzymes and on rates of ethanol degradation, J. Lab. Clin. Med. *77*:110-121, 1971.

Toman, J.E.P.: Some aspects of central nervous pharmacology. Annu. Rev. Pharmacol. *3*:153-184, 1963.

Truitt, E.B., Jr.: Pharmacological activity in a metabolite of 1-*trans*-Δ^8-tetrahydrocannabinol. Fed. Proc. *29*:619, 1970.

Truitt, E.: Biological disposition of tetrahydrocannabinols. Pharmacol. Rev. *23*:273-278, 1971.

Tulunay, F.C., Kiran, B.K., and Kaymakcalan, S.: Transfer of morphine tolerance in rats by brain extracts. J. Pharm. Pharmacol. *22*:871-872, 1970.

Ueki, S., Fujiwara, M., and Ogawa, N.: Mouse-killing behavior induced by Δ^9-tetrahydrocannabinol in the rat. Abstracts to the Fifth Int. Cong. Pharmacol. #1427, San Francisco, Calif., 1972.

Ungar, G. and Cohen, M.: Induction of moprhine tolerance by material extracted from brain of tolerant animals. Int. J. Neuropharmacol. *5*:183-192, 1966.

Ungar, G. and Galvan, L.: Conditions of transfer of morphine tolerance by brain extracts. Proc. Soc. Exp. Biol. Med. *130*:287-291, 1969.

VanderWende, C. and Johnson, J.C.: Interaction of serotonin with the catecholamines. I. Inhibition of dopamine and norepinephrine oxidation. Biochem. Pharmacol. *19*:1991-2000, 1970.

VanderWende, C.V. and Spoerlein, M.: Antagonism by dopa of morphine analgesia. A hypothesis for morphine tolerance. Res. Commun. Chem. Pathol. Pharmacol. *3*:37-45, 1972.

VanderWende, C. and Spoerlein, M.T.: Role of dopaminergic receptors in morphine analgesia and tolerance. Res. Commun. Chem. Pathol. Pharmacol. *5*:35-43, 1973.

Vatsis, K.P. and Schulman, M.P.: Absence of ethanol metabolism in acatalatic microsomes that oxidize drugs. Biochem. Biophys. Res. Commun. *52*:588-594, 1973.

Verri, R.A., Graeff, F.G., and Corrado, A.P.: Effect of reserpine and alpha-methyl-tyrosine on morphine analgesia. Int. J. Neuropharmacol. *7*:283-292, 1968.

Videla, L., Bernstein, J., and Israel, Y.: Metabolic alterations produced in the liver by chronic ethanol administration. Biochem. J. *134*:507-514, 1973.

Wainer, B.H., Fitch, F.W., Rothberg, R.M., and Schuster, C.R.: *In vitro* morphine antagonism by antibodies. Nature (London) *241*:537-538, 1973.

Warwick, R.O., Blake, D.E., Miya, T.S., and Bousquet, W.F.: Serotonin involvement in thermoregulation following administration of morphine to nontolerant and morphine-tolerant rats. Res. Commun. Chem. Pathol. Pharmacol. *6*:19-32, 1973.

Way, E.: Role of serotonin in morphine effects. Fed. Proc. *31*:113-120, 1972.

Way, E.L., and Adler, T.K.: The pharmacologic implications of the fate of morphine and its surrogates. Pharmacol. Rev. *12*:383-446, 1960.

Way, E.L. and Shen, F.H.: Catecholamines and 5-hydroxytryptamine. Narcotic Drugs: Biochemical pharmacology. Ed. Clouet, D.H., New York, Plenum Press, 1971, pp. 229-253.

Way, E.L., Loh, H.H., and Shen, F.: Morphine tolerance, physical dependence, and synthesis of brain 5-hydroxytryptamine. Science *162*:1290-1309, 1968.

Weil, A.T., Zenberg, N.E., and Nelson, J.M.: Clinical and psychological effects of marihuana in man. Science *16*:1234-1242, 1968.

Weiner, N.: Pharmacology of central nervous system stimulants *In* Drug Abuse: Proc. of Intnl. Conf., Ed. Zarafonetis, C.J.D., Philadelphia, Lea and Febiger, 1972, pp. 243-251.

Weksler, M.E., Cherubin, C., Kilcoyne, M., Koppel, G., and Yoel, M.: Absence of morphine-binding activity in serum from heroine addicts. Clin. Exp. Immunol. *13*:613-617, 1973.

Westfall, T.C. and Brase, D.A.: Studies on the mechanism of tolerance to nicotine-induced elevations of urinary catecholamines. Biochem. Pharmacol. *20*:1627-1635, 1971.

Winter, J.C.: Tolerance to a behavioral effect of lysergic acid diethylamide and cross-tolerance to mescaline in the rat: Absence of a metabolic component. J. Pharmacol. Exp. Ther. *178*:625-630, 1971.

Wong, D.T. and Horng, J.S.: Stereospecific interaction of opiate narcotics in binding of ³H-dihydromorphine to membranes of rat brain. Life Sci. *13*:1543-1556, 1973.

Zeidenberg, P., Orrenius, S., and Ernster, L.: Increase in levels of glucuronylating enzymes and associated rise in activities of mitochondrial oxidative enzymes upon phenobarbital administration in the rat. J. Cell Biol. *32*:528-531, 1967.

Ziegler, H., Del Basso, P., and Longo, V.G.: Influence of 6-hydroxydopamine and alpha-methyl-*p*-tyrosine on the effects of some centrally acting agents. Physiol. Behav. *8*:391-396, 1972.

Subject Index